THE GOSPEL
ACCORDING TO JOHN

VOLUME 29A

THE ANCHOR BIBLE is a fresh approach to the world's greatest classic. Its object is to make the Bible accessible to the modern reader; its method is to arrive at the meaning of biblical literature through exact translation and extended exposition, and to reconstruct the ancient setting of the biblical story, as well as the circumstances of its transcription and the characteristics of its transcribers.

THE ANCHOR BIBLE is a project of international and interfaith scope. Protestant, Catholic, and Jewish scholars from many countries contribute individual volumes. The project is not sponsored by any ecclesiastical organization and is not intended to reflect any particular theological doctrine. Prepared under our joint supervision, THE ANCHOR BIBLE is an effort to make available all the significant historical and linguistic knowledge which bears on the interpretation of the biblical record.

THE ANCHOR BIBLE is aimed at the general reader with no special formal thinking in biblical studies; yet, it is written with the most exacting standards of scholarship, reflecting the highest technical accomplishment.

This project marks the beginning of a new era of co-operation among scholars in biblical research, thus forming a common body of knowledge to be shared by all.

William Foxwell Albright
David Noel Freedman
GENERAL EDITORS

THE ANCHOR BIBLE

THE GOSPEL
ACCORDING TO
JOHN

(xiii–xxi)

INTRODUCTION, TRANSLATION, AND NOTES

BY

RAYMOND E. BROWN, S.S.

Doubleday & Company, Inc.
Garden City, New York

NIHIL OBSTAT
Myles M. Bourke, S.S.L., S.T.D.
Censor Deputatus

IMPRIMATUR
Joseph P. O'Brien, S.T.D.

January 27, 1970
New York

ISBN: 0-385-03761-9
Library of Congress Catalog Card Number 66–12209
Copyright © 1970 by Doubleday & Company, Inc.
All Rights Reserved
Printed in the United States of America
First Edition
Twenty-third Printing
1985

*This completed commentary is dedicated
to my father
in his seventieth year*

*A small gesture of gratitude
for a lifetime of generosity*

PREFACE

The original plan of the Anchor Bible series was to complete the work on the Johannine Gospel and Epistles within two volumes. However, the expansion of the series to include the Apocrypha made other adjustments possible, and the editors have graciously approved a third volume for the Johannine writings. Volumes 29 and 29A (the present volume) treat the Fourth Gospel; volume 30 will be devoted to the Epistles of John. The present writer is particularly pleased to have a full volume devoted to chapters xiii–xxi of the Gospel; for while these chapters are shorter than chapters i–xii, the Passion and Resurrection accounts contained in them require detailed comparison with the Synoptic Gospels. The indexes in the present volume cover both Gospel volumes. Because there are many references to verses in the first half of the Gospel, an appendix (VI) has been included for the convenience of the reader, giving the English translation of chapters i–xii, as it was printed section by section in volume 29.

Volume 29 was published in 1966, and so an interval of four years has passed before the completion of the commentary. In part the interval was taken up by another project to which there was a previous commitment, namely, the editorship of *The Jerome Biblical Commentary* (Englewood Cliffs, N.J.: Prentice-Hall, 1968). But the span of time has also been necessitated by the amount of work required for the present volume. The writer is grateful to the the editors for their exceptional patience in not pressing to have the book appear before it was ready. Recalling the list of scholars who died before finishing work on the Fourth Gospel (Bernard, Hoskyns, Lightfoot, Sanders, Van den Bussche—not to mention the original author), he deems himself fortunate to see his 1,400-page commentary at last in print.

The present volume takes into account literature on the second part of the Gospel (chs. xiii–xxi) up to the middle of 1969; but in the interval since volume 29 was published, there have appeared important contributions pertinent to the Introduction and to the first part of the Gospel. We mention first E. Malatesta's magnificent bibliography, *St. John's Gospel, 1920–65* (Analecta biblica 32; Rome: Pontifical Biblical Institute, 1967). By combining this with the material on John in B. Metzger's *Index to Periodical Literature on Christ and the Gospels* (New Testament Tools and Studies 6; Leiden: Brill, 1966), one has a virtually complete coverage of all that has been written on the subject. In vol. 29, pp. xxviii–xxxii, we discussed and rejected the theory that the Fourth Gospel was composed by combining three or more already written and self-subsisting sources. The only one of these putative pre-Gospel sources to which we attributed some plausibility was a Signs Source (pp. xxxi, 195); and now such a source has been elaborately reconstructed and defended by R. T. Fortna, *The Gospel of Signs* (Cambridge University Press, 1970). The anti-synagogue motif in the Gospel (vol. 29, pp. LXX–LXXV) has been studied in profundity by J. L. Martyn, *History and Theology in the Fourth Gospel* (New York: Harper, 1968). Johannine eschatology (vol. 29, pp. CXV–CXXI) has been the subject of investigation by a pupil of O. Cullmann, namely, P. Ricca, *Die Eschatologie des Vierten Evangeliums* (Zürich: Gotthelf, 1966). The textual tradition of the Gospel (vol. 29, pp. CXXXI–CXXXII) has been analyzed in great detail by R. Kieffer, *Au delà des recensions* (Uppsala: Almquist, 1968), who has developed a theory of textual relationships based on a minute study of John vi 52–71. H. Leroy, *Rätsel und Missverständnis* (Bonner Biblische Beiträge 30; Bonn: Hanstein, 1968), has examined form-critically the Johannine phenomenon of misunderstanding (vol. 29, p. CXXXV). A very important contribution has been made by W. A. Meeks, *The Prophet-King* (SNT XIV; 1967), who has studied the Johannine Jesus in the light of the Moses traditions in Jewish and Samaritan thought. The Moses theme was mentioned frequently in vol. 29 (pp. LX, 49–50, 86, 235, 322, etc.), but Meeks has increased the evidence and given a lucid explanation of chapter vii. F.-M. Braun has added to his impressive work *Jean le Théologien* (vol. 29, General Selected Bibliography) still a third volume, entitled *Sa théologie: Le mystère de Jésus-Christ* (Paris: Gabalda, 1966).

The list of recent studies of individual passages in John i–xii would be too long, but two monographs deserve special attention: A. Feuillet, *Le prologue du quatrième évangile* (Paris: Desclée de Brouwer, 1968), and O. Kiefer, *Die Hirtenrede* (on John x; Stuttgart: Katholisches Bibelwerk, 1967). Among the general commentaries on the Gospel that have appeared since 1966 we may mention: H. van den Bussche, *Jean* (Bruges: Desclée de Brouwer, 1967); J. Marsh, *Saint John* (Pelican Commentaries: Harmondsworth: Penguin, 1968); J. N. Sanders and B. A. Mastin, *The Gospel According to St. John* (Harper's Commentaries; New York: Harper, 1968). *Facile princeps* is the first part of R. Schnackenburg's impressive commentary in the Herders theologischer Kommentar series; the German of this (Introduction; chs. i–iv) appeared in 1965 when our volume 29 was in press, and an English translation in 1968 (New York: Herder & Herder).

In concluding these prefatory remarks, the writer must acknowledge his indebtedness to many who assisted him. Michael Kinney and Judith Dollenmayer, as well as their predecessor Susan Burchardt Watt, along with the staff at Doubleday, were helpful in every way. David Noel Freedman turned to this volume, as to its predecessor, his careful editorial eye and gave many fruitful suggestions. Once again John Kselman generously devoted much time to checking typescript, and this is a better work for his help. Lawrence Plutko took on himself the tedious task of checking thousands of Scripture references, and many students at St. Mary's Seminary, Baltimore, helped in proofreading. To these and to all who gave him ideas the writer expresses his gratitude.

CONTENTS

PRINCIPAL ABBREVIATIONS

1. BIBLICAL AND APOCRYPHAL WORKS

Besides the standard abbreviations of books of the Bible used in the series:

Deuterocanonical Books of the OT:

Tob	Tobit
Judith	Judith
I & II Macc	I & II Maccabees
Sir	Sirach or Ecclesiasticus
Wis	Wisdom of Solomon
Bar	Baruch

Apocryphal Books related to the OT:

Jub	Jubilees
En	Enoch or Henoch
II Bar	II Baruch
I & II Esd	I & II Esdras
Ps Sol	Psalms of Solomon

2. PUBLICATIONS

AASOR	Annual of the American Schools of Oriental Research
APCh	*Apocrypha and Pseudepigrapha of the Old Testament in English* by R. H. Charles (2 vols.; Oxford: Clarendon, 1913)
BA	Biblical Archaeologist
BAG	W. Bauer (as translated by W. F. Arndt and F. W. Gingrich), *A Greek-English Lexicon of the New Testament* (University of Chicago, 1957)
BASOR	Bulletin of the American Schools of Oriental Research
BCCT	*The Bible in Current Catholic Thought,* ed. J. L. McKenzie, in honor of M. Gruenthaner (New York: Herder & Herder, 1962)

BDF   F. Blass and A. Debrunner (as translated by R. W. Funk), *A Greek Grammar of the New Testament and Other Early Christian Literature* (University of Chicago, 1961). References to sections

BibOr   Bibbia e Oriente

BiLeb   Bibel und Leben

BiRes   Biblical Research

BiTod   The Bible Today

BNTE   *The Background of the New Testament and Its Eschatology*, eds. W. D. Davies and D. Daube, in honor of C. H. Dodd (Cambridge, 1956)

BS   Bibliotheca Sacra (Dallas)

BVC   Bible et Vie Chrétienne

BZ   Biblische Zeitschrift

BZAW   Beihefte zur Zeitschrift für die alttestamentliche Wissenschaft

CBQ   Catholic Biblical Quarterly

CD   Cairo Genizah Document of the Damascus Covenanters (the Zadokite Documents)

ChQR   Church Quarterly Review

CINTI   *Current Issues in New Testament Interpretation*, eds. W. Klassen and G. F. Snyder, in honor of O. A. Piper (New York: Harper, 1962)

ColctMech   Collectanea Mechliniensia

ConcTM   Concordia Theological Monthly

CSCO   Corpus Scriptorum Christianorum Orientalium (Louvain)

CSEL   Corpus Scriptorum Ecclesiasticorum Latinorum (Vienna)

DB   H. Denzinger and C. Bannwart, *Enchiridion Symbolorum*, rev. by A. Schönmetzer, 32nd ed. (Freiburg: Herder, 1963). References to sections

DBS   Dictionnaire de la Bible—Supplément

ECW   *Early Christian Worship* by Oscar Cullmann (see General Selected Bibliography, vol. 29)

EstBíb   Estudios Bíblicos

ET   Expository Times

ETL   Ephemerides Theologicae Lovanienses

ÉvJean   *L'Évangile de Jean* by M.-E. Boismard *et al.* (Recherches Bibliques, III: Louvain: Desclée de Brouwer, 1958)

EvTh   Evangelische Theologie

EWJ   *The Eucharistic Words of Jesus* by J. Jeremias (rev. ed.; New York: Scribner, 1966)

GCS   Die Griechischen Christlichen Schriftsteller (Berlin)

GeistLeb   Geist und Leben

HPG   *The Holy Places of the Gospels* by C. Kopp (New York: Herder & Herder, 1963)

HST   *The History of the Synoptic Tradition* by R. Bultmann
(New York: Harper, 1963)

HTR   Harvard Theological Review

IBNTG   *An Idiom-Book of New Testament Greek* by C. F. D. Moule
(2nd ed.; Cambridge, 1963)

IMEL   *In Memoriam Ernst Lohmeyer,* ed. W. Schmauch (Stuttgart:
Evangelisches Verlagswerk, 1951)

Interp   Interpretation

JBL   Journal of Biblical Literature

JeanThéol   *Jean le Théologien* by F.-M. Braun (see General Selected
Bibliography, vol. 29)

JG   *Johannine Grammar* by E. A. Abbott (London: Black,
1906). References to sections

JohSt   *Johannine Studies* by A. Feuillet (New York: Alba, 1964)

JTS   Journal of Theological Studies

LFAE   *Light from the Ancient East* by A. Deissmann (rev. ed.;
New York: Doran, 1927)

MTGS   J. H. Moulton, *A Grammar of New Testament Greek;* III,
Syntax, by N. Turner (Edinburgh: Clark, 1962)

MüTZ   Münchener theologische Zeitschrift

NovT   Novum Testamentum

NRT   Nouvelle Revue Théologique

NTA   New Testament Abstracts

NTAuf   *Neutestamentliche Aufsätze,* eds. J. Blinzler, O. Kuss, and F.
Mussner, in honor of J. Schmid (Regensburg: Pustet,
1963)

NTE   *New Testament Essays* by Raymond E. Brown (Milwaukee:
Bruce, 1965; reprinted New York: Doubleday Image,
1968)

NTEM   *New Testament Essays in Memory of T. W. Manson,* ed.
A. J. B. Higgins (Manchester University, 1959)

NTPat   *Neotestamentica et Patristica,* in honor of O. Cullmann
(SNT VI, 1962)

NTS   New Testament Studies

1QH   Qumran Hymns of Thanksgiving

1QM   Qumran War Scroll

1QpHab   Qumran Pesher on Habakkuk

1QS   Qumran Manual of Discipline

OTQ   *Old Testament Quotations in the Gospel of John* by E. D.
Freed (SNT XI, 1965)

PEQ   Palestine Exploration Quarterly

PG   Patrologia Graeca-Latina (Migne)

PL   Patrologia Latina (Migne)

RB   Revue Biblique

RecLC   *Recueil Lucien Cerfaux* (3 vols.; Gembloux, 1954–62)
RExp   Review and Expositor
RHPR   Revue d'Histoire et de Philosophie Religieuses
RivBib   Rivista Biblica (Brescia)
RSO   Rivista degli Studi Orientali
RSPT   Revue des Sciences Philosophiques et Théologiques
RSR   Recherches de Science Religieuse
RThom   Revue Thomiste
SacPag   *Sacra Pagina*, eds. J. Coppens, A. Descamps, and E. Massaux (Louvain, 1959)
SBT   Studies in Biblical Theology (London: SCM)
SC   Sources Chrétiennes (Paris: Cerf)
ScEccl   Sciences Ecclésiastiques (Montreal)
ScotJT   Scottish Journal of Theology
SeinSend   Sein und Sendung
SFG   *Studies in the Fourth Gospel*, ed. F. L. Cross (London: Mowbray, 1957)
SMRFJC   *The Significance of the Message of the Resurrection for Faith in Jesus Christ*, ed. C. F. D. Moule (SBT, No. 8, 2nd series; London: SCM, 1968)
SNT   Supplements to Novum Testamentum (Leiden: Brill)
ST   Studia Theologica (Oslo)
StB   H. L. Strack and P. Billerbeck, *Kommentar zum Neuen Testament aus Talmud und Midrasch* (6 vols.; Munich: Beck, 1922–61)
StEv   *Studia Evangelica* (Papers from the Oxford International Congresses of NT Studies, published at Berlin, Akademie-Verlag)
TalBab   The Babylonian Talmud, English edition by I. Epstein (London: Soncino, 1961)
TalJer   The Jerusalem Talmud
TD   Theology Digest
TGl   Theologie und Glaube
TLZ   Theologische Literaturzeitung
TNTS   *Twelve New Testament Studies* by John A. T. Robinson (SBT, No. 34; London: SCM, 1962)
TWNT   *Theologisches Wörterbuch zum Neuen Testament*, ed. G. Kittel (Stuttgart: Kohlhammer, 1933–)
TWNTE   Same work translated into English by G. W. Bromiley (Grand Rapids: Eerdmans, 1964–)
TZ   Theologische Zeitschrift
VD   Verbum Domini
VT   Vetus Testamentum
ZAW   Zeitschrift für die alttestamentliche Wissenschaft
ZDPV   Zeitschrift des Deutschen Palästina-Vereins

ZGB	M. Zerwick, *Graecitas Biblica* (4th ed.; Rome: Pontifical Biblical Institute, 1960). References are to sections; these are the same in the English translation of the 4th ed. by J. Smith (Rome, 1963)
ZKT	Zeitschrift für katholische Theologie
ZNW	Zeitschrift für die neutestamentliche Wissenschaft und die Kunde der älteren Kirche
ZTK	Zeitschrift für Theologie und Kirche

3. VERSIONS

KJ	The Authorized Version of 1611, or the King James Bible
LXX	The Septuagint
MT	Masoretic Text
NEB	The New English Bible (New Testament, 1961)
RSV	The Revised Standard Version, 1946, 1952
SB	La Sainte Bible—"Bible de Jérusalem"—traduite en français (Paris: Cerf). D. Mollat, *L'Evangile de saint Jean* (2nd ed., 1960)
Vulg.	The Vulgate

4. OTHER ABBREVIATIONS

NT	New Testament
OT	Old Testament
Aram.	Aramaic
Boh.	Bohairic (Coptic)
Eth.	Ethiopic
Gr.	Greek
Heb.	Hebrew
OL	Old Latin
OS	Old Syriac (OS^{cur}; OS^{sin} denote the Curetonian and Sinaiticus mss. respectively)
Sah.	Sahidic (Coptic)
App.	Appendixes in the back of the volume
P	Papyrus
par.	parallel verse(s)
vol. 29	Volume 29 of The Anchor Bible: *The Gospel According to John, i–xii* by Raymond E. Brown

*   Asterisk after a manuscript indicates the original hand of the copyist, as distinct from later correctors

[ ]   Brackets in the translation indicate a textually dubious word or passage

When in the NOTES or COMMENT a bibliographical reference is given in an abbreviated form—for example, the author's name accompanied by a page number or *art. cit.* —full bibliographical information can be found in the nearest sectional bibliography or in the General Selected Bibliography (vol. 29, pp. CXLV–CXLVI).

III. THE BOOK OF GLORY

"The hour" of Jesus wherein he is lifted up to his Father and glorified so that he may give the Spirit to those who believe in him and thus beget them as children of God.

"But all those who did accept him
he empowered to become God's children."

In vol. 29, pp. cxxxviii–cxxxix, we explained the rationale for dividing the body of the Fourth Gospel into "The Book of Signs" (i 19 – xii 50) and "The Book of Glory" (xiii 1 – xx 31). There are notable differences between the Books. First, during the public ministry, as described in the Book of Signs, Jesus' words and deeds were addressed to a wide audience, provoking a crisis of faith—some believed and some refused to believe. The Book of Glory, however, is addressed to the restricted audience of those who believed. Second, the signs of the first Book anticipated what Jesus would do for men once he was glorified. The second Book describes the glorification, i.e., "the hour" of passion, crucifixion, resurrection, and ascension wherein Jesus is lifted up to the Father to enjoy again the glory that he had with the Father before the world existed (xvii 5). These differences are apparent in the first verse of the Book of Glory: "Jesus was aware that *the hour had come* for him to pass from this world to the Father. Having loved *his own* who were in the world, he now showed his love for them to the very end" (xiii 1).

The career of the Johannine Jesus has been compared to the arc of a pendulum, swinging from on high to a low point and then rising to the heights again. Certainly one can verify this in the hymn that we call the Prologue. It begins in heaven: "The Word was in God's presence" (i 1); then comes the crisis of the ministry: "He was in the world . . . yet the world did not recognize him" (i 10) and "We have seen his glory, the glory of an only Son coming from the Father" (i 14); finally the view is lifted once more to heaven: "It is God the only Son, ever at the Father's side" (i 18). The same pendulum arc is found in the Gospel proper. The Son is the one who has come down from heaven (iii 13), but he is rejected by many who prefer darkness to the light (iii 19); and his career reaches its nadir when he is rejected by his own people: "Even though Jesus had performed so many of his signs before them, they refused to believe in him" (xii 37). The Book of Signs described this first half of the arc of the pendulum, namely, the downswing; the Book of Glory is the description of the upswing. The "lifting up" of the Son of Man which will draw all men to him (predicted in xii 32) begins on the cross where Jesus is physically lifted up from the earth. For other men crucifixion would have been an abasement; but because Jesus lays down his life with power to take it up again (x 18), there is a triumphant element in the Johannine concept of crucifixion. It is a death that achieves glorification, and the crucified Jesus is proclaimed as king in the principal languages of the world (xix 19–20). The elevation of Jesus continues in the resurrection which is interpreted as part of the ascension of Jesus to the Father (xx 17). Yet John does not close the Gospel narrative once the pendulum has finished its upward swing and Jesus is with the Father. If Jesus is God's Son, he is a Son dedicated to enlarging God's family and to having other men share in the love of God even as he shares in it. And so the first action of the glorified Jesus is to give the disciples a Holy Spirit (xx 22) that begets them from above (iii 3, 5), so that God becomes their Father and Jesus their brother (xx 17).

We have said that the "lifting up" begins with the crucifixion and ends with the resurrection and ascension. Why then do we include in the Book of Glory chs. xiii–xvii which describe Jesus' Last Supper with his disciples and the long Last Discourse? In the Book of Signs we saw the phenomenon whereby Jesus' discourses, coming after the signs, served to interpret the signs. In the Book of Glory the Last Supper and the Discourse that precede the action of glorification serve to interpret that action. The footwashing in xiii dramatically acts out the significance of Jesus' death—it is a death that cleanses the disciples and gives them a heritage with him. The majestic Last Discourse reassures the disciples that Jesus' death is not the end. It is his going away to the Father; but over and over again Jesus promises that he will return (in resurrection, in indwelling, in the Paraclete, in the parousia), and his return will be marked by peace and joy. His return will enable the disciples to dwell in union with him (xv 1–17), a union similar to his own union with the Father (xvii 21).

The solemnity of Johannine thought and style is clearly in evidence in the Book of Glory, and certainly this presentation of Jesus in his last hours is one of the most beautiful compositions in the religious literature of mankind. The Johannine redactor will state that no book or books can adequately capture Jesus of Nazareth (xxi 25), but the Book of Glory worthily lives up to the claim that it enshrines the witness borne to Jesus by that disciple whom he especially loved and who was closest to his heart (xix 35, xxi 24, xiii 23, 25).

We shall treat the Book of Glory as consisting of three parts and a conclusion:

> PART ONE: THE LAST SUPPER (xiii–xvii);
> PART TWO: THE PASSION NARRATIVE (xviii–xix);
> PART THREE: THE RISEN JESUS (xx 1–29);
> CONCLUSION (xx 30–31).

Detailed outlines will be given with each part.

THE BOOK OF GLORY

Part One: The Last Supper

OUTLINE

PART ONE: THE LAST SUPPER
(chs. XIII–XVII)

A. xiii 1–30:   THE MEAL. (§§46–47)

        (1–20) The footwashing. (§46)

                1: Introduction to the Book of Glory.

                2–11: The footwashing, interpreted as a symbol of Jesus' death, with a secondary reference to Baptism.

                        2–3: Introduction.

                        4–5: Footwashing.

                        6–10a: Interpretation by dialogue.

                        10b–11: Reference to Judas.

                12–20: Another interpretation of the footwashing, as an example of humble service.

                        12–15, 17: Interpretation by discourse.

                        16 and 20: Isolated sayings with Matthean parallels.

                        18–19: Reference to Judas.

        (21–30) Prediction of the betrayal. (§47)

B. xiii 31 –
    xvii 26:   THE LAST DISCOURSE. (§§48–59)

        (xiii 31 – xiv 31) *Division 1:* The departure of Jesus and the future of the disciples. (§§49–52)

            xiii 31–38: *Introduction:* Theme of Jesus' departure and his commandment of love. Peter's denial. (§49)

            xiv 1–14: *Unit 1:* Jesus is the way to the Father for those who believe in him. (§50)

                      1–4: Jesus' departure and return.

                      5: Transitional question.

                      6–11: Jesus as the way.

                      12–14: Power of belief in Jesus (transition to what follows).

                15–24: *Unit 2:* The Paraclete, Jesus, and the Father will come to those who love Jesus. (§51)

                      15–17: The coming of the Paraclete (but not to the world).

                      18–21: The coming (back) of Jesus.

                      22: Transitional question.

                      23–24: The coming of the Father (with Jesus).

25–31: *Unit 3:* Jesus' final thoughts before departure.
(§52)
    25–26: Sending the Paraclete to teach.
    27ab: The parting gift of peace.
    27c–29: Jesus' departure.
    30–31: Struggle with the Prince of the
    World.

(xv–xvi) *Division 2:* The life of the disciples and their encounter
with the world after Jesus shall have departed. (§§53–
56)

xv   1–17: *Subdivision 1:* The vine and the branches.
(§53)
    1–6: The *mashal.*
    7–17: Paraenetic development on love.
        7–10: Remaining in Jesus and his
        love.
        11: Transitional reference to joy.
        12–17: The commandment of love
        for one another.

xv 18 –
xvi 4a: *Subdivision 2:* The world's hatred for Jesus
and his disciples. (§54)
    xv 18–21: The world hates and persecutes
    the disciples.
    22–25: The guilt of the world.
    26–27: The witness of the Paraclete.
    xvi 1–4a: The persecution of the disciples.

xvi 4b–33: *Subdivision 3:* Duplicate of Division 1.
(§§55–56)
    4b–15: *Unit 1:* Jesus' departure and the
    coming of the Paraclete. (§55)
        4b: Transitional.
        5–7: Jesus' departure and the dis-
        ciples' sadness.
        8–11: The Paraclete against the
        world.
        12–15: The Paraclete as guide of
        the disciples.
    16–33: *Unit 2:* Jesus' return will bring the
    disciples joy and understanding.
    (§56)
        16–23a: The disciples will see
        Jesus again and rejoice.
        23b–33: They will have requests
        granted and understand Jesus
        plainly.

(xvii) *Division 3:* The concluding prayer of Jesus. (§§57–59)

 1–8: *Unit 1:* Jesus, having completed his work, prays for glory. (§57)

  1–5: Jesus asks for glory.

  6–8: Jesus' work of revelation among the disciples.

 9–19: *Unit 2:* Jesus prays for those whom the Father has given him. (§58)

  9–16: The disciples and the world.

  17–19: The consecration of the disciples and of Jesus.

 20–26: *Unit 3:* Jesus prays for those who believe through the disciples' word. (§59)

  20–23: The oneness of those who believe in Jesus.

  24–26: Jesus' wish that the believers be with him.

46. THE MEAL:
—THE FOOTWASHING
(xiii 1–20)

XIII 1 It was just before the Passover feast, and Jesus was aware that the hour had come for him to pass from this world to the Father. Having loved his own who were in this world, he now showed his love for them to the very end.

2 The devil had already induced Judas, son of Simon, the Iscariot, to betray Jesus. And so during supper, 3 fully aware that the Father had handed over all things to him, and that he had come forth from God and was going to God, 4 Jesus rose from the table and took off his robe. He picked up a towel and tied it around himself. 5 Then he poured water into a pitcher and began to wash his disciples' feet and to dry them with the towel he had around him.

6 So he came to Simon Peter who said to him, "Are you going to wash my feet, Lord?" 7 Jesus answered, "You may not realize now what I am doing, but afterwards you will understand." 8 Peter replied, "You shall not wash my feet—ever!" "If I do not wash you," Jesus answered, "you will have no heritage with me." 9 "Lord," Simon Peter said to him, "then not only my feet, but my hands and face as well." 10 Jesus told him, "The man who has bathed has no need to wash [except for his feet]; he is clean all over. And now you men are clean, though not all of you." (11 The reason he said, "Not all of you are clean," was that he knew his betrayer.)

12 After he had washed their feet, Jesus put on his robe and returned to his place. Then he said to them,

"Do you understand what I have done for you?
13 You address me as 'Teacher' and 'Lord,'
   and rightly so, for that is what I am.
14 Now, if I washed your feet,

3: *was going;* 4: *rose, took off;* 5: *poured;* 6: *came, said;* 8: *replied;* 9: *said;* 10: *told.*
In the historical present tense.

even though I am Lord and Teacher,
you too must wash one another's feet.

15 For it was an example that I gave you:
you are to do exactly as I have done for you.

16 Let me firmly assure you,
no servant is more important than his master;
no messenger is more important than the one who sent him.

17 Now, once you understand this,
happy are you if you put it into practice.

18 What I say does not refer to all of you:
I know the kind of men I chose.
But the purpose is to have the Scripture fulfilled:
'He who feeds on bread with me
has raised his heel against me.'

19 I tell you this now, even before it happens,
so that, when it does happen, you may believe
that I AM.

20 Let me firmly assure you,
whoever welcomes anyone I shall send
welcomes me;
and whoever welcomes me
welcomes Him who sent me."

NOTES

xiii 1. *It was just before the Passover feast.* This is a free translation. Literally there is a prepositional phrase followed by two participles and a main verb: "Before the Passover feast, Jesus, being aware . . . , having loved . . . , now showed his love." Bultmann, p. 352, following W. Bauer and some of the Greek Fathers, argues that the chronological phrase must modify the first participle (=Jesus was aware before Passover), because one cannot affix a date to Jesus' love. Jeremias, EWJ, p. 80, who thinks that the Last Supper was a Passover meal, agrees because he does not want this phrase to be used to date the Last Supper in a pre-Passover period. However, Grossouw, p. 128, thinks that grammatically the phrase should be constructed with the main verb and that what is dated before Passover is not a state of love but a concrete expression of love, i.e., Jesus' death (including the footwashing as symbolic of that death). Perhaps we should not try to be too exact, since the phrase probably modifies both the knowledge and the act of love. It is inserted to give a theological, as well as a chronological, setting to Jesus' whole passion and not just to the meal. John has been building up to this with previous references to the coming Passover in xi 55 and especially in xii 1 ("six days before Passover"—for the activities of the intervening days see xii 12, 36). The evening of this meal and the next day, on which Jesus will die, constitute Passover Eve; see COMMENT.

to pass. Metalambanein is used in v 24 and in I John iii 14 for passing from death to life. Venerable Bede saw here a play on the name of the feast of Passover (Nestorius also; see C. A. Phillips and J. R. Harris, ET 38 [1926–27], 233), and some modern scholars have followed him. But there is no indication in LXX usage or in Josephus that this verb was associated with the idea of "pass over." Rather xiii 1 seems simply to be a recasting of the words of Jesus in xvi 28: "Now I am leaving the world and I am going back to the Father."

from this world. The "world," often in the sense of the realm of evil, will appear frequently in these last chapters; see vol. 29, pp. 508–10. The world has its own whom it loves (xv 19) just as Jesus has his own whom he loves. Here, however, the contrast between the world and the Father is not so much the contrast between evil and good as the contrast between what is below and what is above (iii 31).

Having loved. The participle is a complexive aorist covering the public ministry.

who were in this world. This anticipates xvii 15: "I am not asking you to take them out of the world."

showed his love. Literally "loved"; the aorist indicates a definite act. This verse is discussed by C. Spicq, RB 65 (1958), 360–62.

to the very end. The phrase *eis telos* has a twofold meaning: "utterly, completely" and "to the end of life," i.e., to the death. Voluntary death is presented as the supreme expression of love in xv 13. The related verb *telein* appears on Jesus' lips at the moment of death: "It is finished" (xix 30). In vol. 29, pp. 485, 491–93, we have seen similarities between the Johannine account of the end of the public ministry and the last part of Deuteronomy. We may now recall Deut xxxi 24: "When Moses had finished writing all the words of this Law in a book, even to the very end [LXX: *eis telos*]. . . ."

2. *already.* Mark xiv 10–11 and par. portray Judas' betrayal of Jesus to the chief priests as having taken place before the Last Supper. John may be in agreement, although this verse need mean no more than that Judas had come to the planning stage.

induced Judas. There are two readings: (a) The devil had already put (*ballein*) into the heart that Judas should betray him. (b) The devil had already put into the heart of Judas that he should betray him. Bultmann, p. 353[4], suggests that (b) was original and that it was changed by the scribes to the more ambiguous (a) because it seemed to contradict vs. 27. However, (a) is better attested (P[66], Vaticanus, Sinaiticus) and should be preferred as the more difficult reading; (b) probably represents a scribal attempt at clarification. But if we do accept (a), whose heart is involved? Barrett, p. 365, thinks that it is the devil's own heart (=the devil made up his mind); yet the fact that the verb is in the active voice is a difficulty. Others suggest that Judas' heart is meant: the devil had put into (Judas') heart that Judas should betray Jesus. The construction is awkward, but W. Bauer thinks that the mention of Judas' name was left until the end of the sentence for dramatic effect. There is little real import in the difference between the two interpretations of (a).

Judas, son of Simon, the Iscariot. The mss. are divided as to whether "Iscariot" modifies Judas or Simon; we have taken the former possibility, following P[66], Vaticanus, and Sinaiticus. See NOTE on vi 71.

to betray Jesus. Literally "to hand him over"; see NOTE on vi 64.

during supper. This phrase actually comes before the rest of vs. 2 in a construction of two consecutive genitive absolutes: "And the supper being in progress, the devil having put it . . . , ³ Jesus fully aware. . . ." There is strong attestation for an alternative reading: "when the supper was over"; however, vs. 26 indicates that there are still plates of food on the table. John does not use the article before "supper" and the article might have been expected if he were referring to the Passover meal. The Synoptists do not refer to the meal as a supper, but Paul speaks of the eucharistic commemorative meal as "the Lord's supper" in I Cor xi 20. John gives no information about the site where the meal was eaten. Presumably it was in Jerusalem because of xviii 1. Nothing is said of an upper room (Mark xiv 14–15).

3. *handed over.* Literally "given into his hands"; the same expression is found in iii 35.

had come forth from God and was going to God. Ignatius, *Magnesians* vii 2, seems to echo this: ". . . Jesus Christ who came forth from the one Father, the one with whom he is and the one to whom he has returned." See second NOTE on v 19.

4. *took off.* Literally "laid [down]"; this is the same verb (*tithenai*) used in x 11, 15, 17, 18 for the laying down of life. A deliberate parallel is not out of the question since the corresponding action of *taking up* (both the robe and life) is also expressed by one verb (*lambanein*) in xiii 12 and x 17, 18. All of this serves to relate the footwashing to the death of the Lord.

robe. We would have expected the singular *himation* since the outer robe is obviously meant; but John has the plural "clothes" both here and in vs. 12.

tied it around. Jesus girds himself like a servant (Luke xii 37, xvii 8).

5. *a pitcher.* Literally "the pitcher"; the article shows that the vessel is a normal utensil for the meal. Jeremias, EWJ, p. 100⁵, sees the use of the article as one of the numerous Semitisms in these verses. Outside of this passage the word *niptēr* occurs only in a Cyprian inscription from Roman times; but since *niptein* means "to wash," it is a vessel for washing (the *-tēr* suffix is agential or instrumental). In the ancient Near East washing was not normally done in a basin of standing water but by pouring water over the parts of the body (II Kings iii 11).

disciples'. Who were at the Last Supper? At least ten people were necessary for a Passover meal. Mark xiv 17 and Matt xxvi 20 mention the Twelve (Luke xxii 14, "the apostles"). Jeremias, EWJ, p. 46, points out that this would not necessarily exclude the presence of the women who had followed Jesus from Galilee (Mark xv 40–41). John does not mention the Twelve, but a comparison of xiii 18 ("men I chose") with vi 70 ("Did I not choose the Twelve of you myself?") makes it plausible that the evangelist was thinking of the Twelve. Those mentioned by name in the Johannine account of the meal are in the Synoptic lists of the Twelve: Judas Iscariot, Peter, Thomas, Philip, another Judas (Lucan lists), and even the Beloved Disciple if he is John of Zebedee (vol. 29, p. xcvii).

feet. The disciples seem to have been on couches, reclining on their left sides. Each would use his left arm to support his head and his right arm to reach the dishes that were on a table which was placed in the center of the couches (see NOTE on vs. 23). Jesus would have come around the outside of the couches to wash the disciples' feet which were stretched out behind them. Reclining was not the normal position at meals in a home but was customary at Passover (Jeremias, EWJ, pp. 48–49).

6. *came to Simon Peter.* That Peter was first (Augustine) is less likely than that he was last (Origen). The evidence is insufficient; but after his discussion with Peter, Jesus says, "And now you men are clean." Also see NOTE on vs. 23.

my feet. The unusual position of the possessive in the Greek may indicate emphasis: *"my feet"*; so Bernard, but BDF, §473[1] disagrees.

7. *now.* Missing in OS[sin] and some OL copies; P[66] shows confusion.

afterwards. Literally "after these things [*tauta*]." In itself the phrase is vague (see NOTE on ii 12), but the meaning is probably the same as in xii 16: "At first the disciples did not understand *these things;* but *when Jesus had been glorified,* then they recalled that it was precisely *these things* that had been written about him and *these things* they had done to him."

8. *ever.* The *ou mē* has the force of an oath here (Jeremias, EWJ, pp. 209–10).

you will have. Literally a present tense; its use as a future is considered an Aramaism by P. Joüon, RSR 17 (1927), 214.

9. *Simon Peter.* The textual witnesses vary on the form of the name; perhaps the name is a scribal clarification of an original "he."

face. Literally "head."

10. *bathed.* Up to now the conversation has dealt with "washing" (*niptein*); here the theme of "bathing" (*louein*) is introduced. The former verb tends to be used for washing a part of the body; the latter, for the whole body. *Niptein* was used in ix 7, 11 where it is probable that the blind man washed only his eyes or face.

to wash [except for his feet]. M.-E. Boismard, RB 60 (1953), 353–56, favors the shortest possible text, omitting all these words, as did the Greek minuscule ms. 579, Tertullian, and some OL witnesses. It is more common to question only the bracketed words, the omission of which is supported by Codex Sinaiticus, some Vulg. witnesses, and important Church Fathers. In fact, the Latin Fathers betray no knowledge of the bracketed phrase before Ambrose's time in the late 4th century when that reading came into the West from the East (see Haring, *art. cit.*). A peculiar expansion is found in Codex Bezae and some OL witnesses: "to wash the head but only the feet."

you men are clean, though not all of you. T. H. Weir, ET 24 (1912–13), 476, suggests the possibility of a double meaning in the underlying Semitic, reflecting the ambiguity of Heb. *kōl* and Aram. *gemîr*, meaning "all, whole, entire." The disciples could have understood Jesus to mean that they had been clean but not entirely (their feet were dusty), while he really meant that not all of them were clean, for one was a sinner.

11. (*The reason . . .*). For this verse Codex Bezae reads simply: "For he knew his betrayer."

betrayer. Literally "the one who was handing him over," a present participle suggesting that the betrayal was already in process (see first NOTE on vs. 2). However, Jeremias, EWJ, p. 179[2], thinks of it as an Aramaism, namely, a present used with a future meaning.

12. *returned to his place.* Literally "reclined again."

Do you understand. This could be interpreted as an imperative: "Understand what I have done for you." We have put what follows in poetic format (vol. 29, p. CXXXIII), but it is not certain that all the verses between 12 and 20 are in solemn discourse style. SB puts only 16, 19, and 20 in poetic format.

13. *'Teacher' and 'Lord'*. Both titles (*rab, mār*) were given to rabbis by their disciples (StB, II, 558). The order in which the two titles are mentioned may reflect the development of the disciples' understanding, for "Teacher" is more common in the earlier chapters of the Gospel and "Lord" in the later chapters.

14. *if I . . . you too*. This type of argument, *a minori ad maius*, was frequently used by the rabbis (Barrett, p. 369).

Lord and Teacher. It may be significant that Jesus changes the order of the titles, for here it is a question of what he is in reality. On the other hand, the change in order may simply be a variation for the sake of style.

16. *servant* and *master*. Or "slave" and "lord." In the basic parabolic comparison *kyrios* is used in the sense of owner or master, but there is probably a play on *kyrios* as "Lord," used in the preceding verses.

messenger. The word *apostolos* has the meaning of emissary in the basic parabolic comparison, but it is not impossible that John is thinking of the disciples as "apostles," i.e., those sent to preach the resurrection. See NOTE on ii 2.

17. *once*. Literally "if," with a reference to present reality (BDF, §372^{1a}): they now understand; in the future they will put it into practice.

happy. The Gr. *makarios* is often translated "blessed," but this leads to confusion; for two sets of words (and ideas) should be kept distinct, one that we may call "participial," the other "adjectival":

Passive participle: Heb. *bārūk*, Gr. *eulogētos*, Lat. *benedictus*, Eng. *blessed*.

Adjective: Heb. *'ašrē*, Gr. *makarios*, Lat. *beatus*, Eng. *happy* (or as an adjective "blessed" but there is no way to keep this distinct from the participle).

In its proper sense as a passive participle *bārūk* is used only of God. "Blessed be the Lord" (Ps xxviii 6) means: let the Lord be blessed by men; let Him be adored and worshiped. When this participle is extended to men, it invokes on them the benevolence of God and other men. Thus, a "blessing" is an invocation asking that it come about that one is blessed or praised or granted favors. On the other hand, the adjectival set of words represented by *'ašrē* are not part of a wish and do not invoke a blessing. Rather they recognize an existing state of happiness or good fortune. In the OT the adjectival words are used only of men, although in the NT *makarios* is used twice of God (I Tim i 11, vi 15). The recognition of the good fortune of men is often implicitly from God's point of view; occasionally the happiness is a future joy that will be received in judgment, but toward which one is well on the way and of which one has incipient possession. Consequently, a macarism or beatitude is properly an approving proclamation of fact, involving an evaluative judgment. In the NT the macarism reflects the judgment that an eschatological state has been made possible by the heralding of the Kingdom. Matthew and Luke have many of Jesus' macarisms; John has only two (here and xx 29); Revelation has seven.

18. *I chose*. Apparently the idea is that Jesus chose Judas even though he knew the kind of man Judas was, and thus the Johannine Jesus made no mistake. Barrett, p. 370, points out another grammatical possibility: Jesus knew whom he had really chosen and he did not choose Judas. However, compare vi 70: "Did I not choose the Twelve of you myself? And yet one of you is a devil." (Remember that vi 70 is related to the eucharistic passage in vi 51–58, a passage that may once have stood in the context of the Last Supper; see vol. 29, p. 287.)

the purpose is. Literally a *hina* subordinate clause, this construction has also been interpreted as a third person imperative: "Let the Scripture be fulfilled"

(BDF, §387³). John's usual understanding, however, is in terms of purpose: the event occurs in order to fulfill the OT (see NOTE on xii 38).

the Scripture. Mark has seventeen citations of the OT in his Passion Narrative; John has nine; this is one of the four they have in common. Neither Matthew nor Luke cite it. (See Dodd, *Tradition*, pp. 31–33.) The rabbis understood this passage in Ps xli 10(9) to refer to Ahithophel's conspiracy with Absalom against David (II Sam xv 12).

fulfilled. The use of the aorist passive of *plēroun* to refer to the fulfillment of sacred words previously uttered is common in Matthew (twelve times) and in John (eight times); it is used only once in Mark (xiv 49, for xv 28 may not be genuine) and in Luke (xxiv 44; cf. iv 21, xxi 22). This type of fulfillment formula is not found at Qumran (J. A. Fitzmyer, NTS 7 [1960–61], 303). In most Gospel instances of the formula the reference is to a fulfillment of the OT, namely, "What was said by the Lord," or "What was said through the prophet," or simply "the Scripture." Yet we note that Matt ii 22 records the fulfillment of an unidentifiable prophetic text, while John xviii 9 and 32 refer to the fulfillment of Jesus' own words. In Matthew the evangelist points out the fulfillment (yet cf. xxvi 56), and the fulfillment texts in Matthew are scattered throughout the Gospel. In three of the Johannine instances (here, xv 25, and xvii 12), as in the single instances in Mark and in Luke, it is Jesus himself who notes the fulfillment. The Johannine fulfillment texts are all in the context of "the hour," i.e., of the passion—this is true even of xii 38, the sole fulfillment text in the Book of Signs. See J. O'Rourke, "John's Fulfillment Texts," ScEccl 19 (1967), 433–43; C. F. D Moule, "Fulfilment-Words in the New Testament: Use and Abuse," NTS 14 (1967–68), 293–320.

feeds on bread with me. The overwhelming evidence of the textual witnesses favors this reading. By exception, Codex Vaticanus has "my bread," but this may represent a scribal harmonization with the psalm passage ("my bread" in both LXX and MT of Ps xli 10[9]—if, as customarily, the suffix in Heb. *laḥmī* is understood as a genitive; actually, it could be read as a dative, "with me"). On the other hand, "with me" in John may be a scribal echo of Mark xiv 18. John's form of the citation differs from the psalm in LXX in the use of "feeding on" (*trōgein*) instead of "eating" (*esthiein*) and in the use of the singular noun for "bread" (so also MT) instead of the plural. Both MT and LXX read "magnified" instead of John's "raised."

raised his heel against me. To show the bottom of one's foot to someone in the Near East is a mark of contempt; see E. F. Bishop, ET 70 (1958–59), 331–32. Such action was especially grave on the part of a friend who had shared one's table. Because the meal is dominated by the struggle between Jesus and the devil (xiii 2, 27), some would see here a reminiscence of Gen iii 15: "You shall bruise [LXX: "watch"] his heel"; but this seems far-fetched.

19. *I tell you this . . . before it happens.* The same theme appears in xiv 29, xvi 4; also Matt xxiv 25. It is an echo of the OT : "Before it came to pass, I announced it to you" (Isa xlviii 5).

now. Literally "from now" (*ap' arti*); yet the meaning seems to be simply "at this time"; in xiv 29 an unambiguous *nyn* is used. However, BDF, §12³, thinks that it means "surely" (=*amēn*) and compares it with the usage in Matt xxvi 29, 64.

you may believe. There is better evidence for the aorist subjunctive (indicating a single action: the coming to full faith) than for the present (indicating a continued belief). The passion, death, resurrection, and ascension, conceived as a whole, will lead the disciples to an act of complete faith in Jesus.

that I AM. Some would supply an implicit predicate, "the Messiah," because of the rabbinical understanding of Ps xli mentioned above. However, the connection of the psalm with the Davidic Messiah is not hinted at by John, and we should probably interpret this as an absolute *egō eimi* (vol. 29, p. 533) on the analogy of other passages like John viii 58 where there is nothing to suggest "Messiah" as predicate.

COMMENT: GENERAL

The Date and Nature of the Last Supper

According to the Synoptics (Mark xiv 12 and par.) Jesus ate a *Passover* meal with his disciples on the night before he died; Jeremias, EWJ, pp. 41 ff., has shown this in great detail. The OT legislation (Lev xxiii 5) prescribed the eating of the Passover meal on the evening that concluded the 14th of Nisan and began the 15th of Nisan (in the lunar calendar the beginning of a new day was reckoned from sunset). Thus, for the Synoptic Gospels the evening on which the Last Supper was eaten, together with the next morning and afternoon on which Jesus was crucified, constituted the 15th of Nisan, the feast of Passover. As for the day of the week, Mark xv 42 specifies that the afternoon of the crucifixion preceded the Sabbath; thus the 15th of Nisan ran from sundown on Thursday to sundown on Friday.

John gives a different picture. The Last Supper is set in the period *before* Passover (NOTE on vs. 1), and the condemnation and crucifixion of Jesus are clearly dated to Passover Eve, the 14th of Nisan (xviii 28, xix 14). Only after Jesus' body was in the tomb did sunset mark the opening of the feast when the Passover meal could be eaten. Despite the difference of calendric dates, John xix 31 agrees with Mark that the day of the week involved was Thursday evening/Friday.

Which version is correct? Was the most significant day in Jesus' life the 15th of Nisan (Passover) or the 14th of Nisan (Passover Eve)? Correspondingly was the Last Supper the Passover meal or not? This is perhaps the most disputed calendric question in the NT and one that we cannot hope to solve in the brief discussion below. As a preliminary we mention a recent theory that has been proposed on the basis of the solar calendar known to have been used by the Qumran Essenes. In this calendar Passover, the 15th of Nisan, always fell on a Tuesday evening/ Wednesday. Accordingly there has been an attempt to show that Jesus ate the Last Supper on a Tuesday evening, that he was arrested the same night, that the various trials took place in the next few days, and that finally he was put to death on Friday, the official 14th of Nisan. This theory has been strongly defended by A. Jaubert, *The Date of the Last Supper* (Staten Island, N.Y.: Alba, 1965; see also NTS 7 [1960–61], 1–30) and by E. Ruckstuhl, *Chronology of the Last Supper* (New York: Desclée, 1965). However, along with Benoit, Gächter, Jeremias, and Blinzler, the present writer does not find sufficient biblical evidence for such an elaborate reconstruction and regards it as highly unlikely that Jesus, who was not an Essene, would have followed an Essene calendar (for the acceptance of a calendar was a religious question). See R. E. Brown, "The Date of the Last Supper," BiTod 11 (1964), 727–33; also in NTE, pp. 160–67 or 207–17.

Jeremias, EWJ, pp. 75–79, who follows the Synoptic chronology, has made a heroic attempt to show that all the individual actions that the Gospels report on Friday (trials, flogging, carrying a cross, men coming in from the fields, crucifixion, purchasing spices, opening a tomb, and burial) could have taken place on Passover without violation of the Jewish Law. However, so much activity on a feast remains a difficulty; and it seems more plausible to accept John's chronology whereby such activity was taking place on an ordinary day, not a holyday. The real reason for Jeremias' position is his conviction that the Last Supper was a Passover meal. That there are Passover characteristics in the meal, even in John, is undeniable; see also P. Benoit, "The Holy Eucharist," *Scripture* 8 (1956), 97–108. Yet this fact does not settle the chronological question. Did Jesus anticipate the Passover meal because he knew of Judas' plot to betray him to death before Passover? Was Jesus following some calendar other than the official one, so that for him Thursday evening was the 15th of Nisan, while it was the 14th on the official calendar? (A difference between a Galilean and a Jerusalem reckoning of days has been suggested by Lagrange; a difference between a Pharisee and a Sadducee reckoning has been suggested by Billerbeck. Yet the supporting evidence is very weak.)

We suggest then that, for unknown reasons, on Thursday evening, the 14th of Nisan by the official calendar, the day before Passover, Jesus ate with his disciples a meal that had Passover characteristics. The Synoptists or their tradition, influenced by these Passover characteristics, too quickly made the assumption that the day was actually Passover; John, on the other hand, preserved the correct chronological information. Of course, both the Synoptic and the Johannine traditions were interested in the theological possibilities stemming from the Passover context in which Jesus died. If the fourth evangelist does not identify the day itself as Passover, he still has Jesus condemned to death at noon on Passover Eve (xix 14), the very hour at which the priests began to slaughter the paschal lambs in the temple area. The references to the hyssop in xix 29 and to the unbroken bones in xix 36 may be other Passover allusions. (For the relation of John's dating of Passover to the later Quartodeciman struggle in the Church, see K. A. Strand, JBL 84 [1965], 251–58.)

Comparison of the Johannine and Synoptic Accounts of the Meal

John's account of the Last Supper differs from the Synoptic account in more than chronology. By way of omission John lacks the story of the preparation for the meal (Mark xiv 12–16 and par.) and the eucharistic words of Jesus over the bread and the wine (Mark xiv 23–25 and par.— yet see vol. 29, p. 287). By way of additional material John reports a footwashing (xiii 1–20) and a long Last Discourse (xiii 31–xvii 26), neither of which is found in the Synoptic Gospels.

Nevertheless there are some interesting details about what happened *at the meal* that the two traditions have in common:

DETAILS COMMON TO JOHN AND TO ALL THREE SYNOPTIC GOSPELS:

1. A warning about betrayal (by Judas): John xiii 18–19, 21–30; occurring before the Eucharist in Mark xiv 17–21, Matt xxvi 20–25; occurring after the Eucharist in Luke xxii 22–23. The theme that the betrayer is one who has eaten with Jesus occurs in different ways in Mark xiv 18 and John xiii 18. The statement "One of you will betray me" is found in Mark, Matthew, and John. The reference to dipping food in a dish is found in Mark xiv 20, Matt xxvi 23, and John xiii 26–27; but the Johannine account is more dramatic. On the other hand, the puzzled reaction about whom Jesus means is more dramatic in Mark xiv 19 and par. than in John xiii 22.

2. A prediction of Peter's denial: made during the meal in John xiii 38 and Luke xxii 31–34; made after leaving the supper room on the way to the Mount of Olives in Mark xiv 29–31 and Matt xxvi 33.

3. A reference to the fruit of the vine: John xv 1–6; Mark xiv 25 and par. The treatment is quite different.

4. A covenant theme is implicit in John's references to a (new) commandment (xiii 34, xv 12, 17—see p. 614 below) and explicit in the Synoptic description of the blood of the (new) covenant in Mark xiv 24 and par.

DETAILS COMMON TO JOHN AND TO MARK/MATTHEW:

5. A prediction of the scattering of the disciples: during the supper in John xvi 32; after leaving the supper room in Mark xiv 27, Matt xxvi 31.

DETAILS COMMON TO JOHN AND TO LUKE:

6. A lesson to the disciples on humility: John xiii 12–17; Luke xxii 24–27. The wording is very different, but Luke xxii 27 describes something resembling what Jesus does in John's account of the footwashing (p. 568 below).

7. A reference to the future of the disciples in the Father's kingdom or house: John xiv 2–3; Luke xxii 30. Again the wording is very different.

The closest similarities are in 1, 2, and 5; and even in these instances there are significant differences between John and the Synoptics. Although there are interesting peculiarities shared by John and Luke, John is not so close to Luke in the Last Supper account as will be the case in the passion account. Thus, John does not seem to be dependent on the Synoptic accounts of the meal but to have independent tradition.

The Meaning of the Footwashing

Prima facie it would seem that there could be no difficulty about the meaning of the scene with which John opens the account of the Last Supper. Verses 14–17 state explicitly that what Jesus did in washing the feet of his disciples was an example of self-sacrificing humility to be imitated by them. A few small Christian sects have understood this imitation in a literal way and have made footwashing a mandatory practice; other groups have made it a laudatory custom, for example, as part of the Holy Thursday liturgy or, in the case of Benedictine monasticism, as part of the hospitality due to guests. But the majority of Christians from the very beginning seem to have felt that what Jesus was commanding in 14–17 was an imitation of the spirit of the footwashing. And so even where footwashing has been a part of the liturgy, it has generally been understood as a sacramental rather than as a sacrament, understood, that is, as a sacred rite of lesser importance.

Many commentators on John are satisfied with the symbolism of humility suggested by the narrative itself and see no other meaning. In antiquity such was the view of Chrysostom and of Theodore of Mopsuestia; in modern times such has been the view of Lagrange, Bernard, Fiebig, and Van den Bussche, to mention a few. J. Michl, *art. cit.*, has vigorously defended this position. Yet there are difficulties. Verses 6–10 indicate that what Jesus has done in the footwashing is essential if the disciples are to gain a heritage with him (vs. 8) and apparently this action cleanses them of sin (10). Something more than an example of humility seems to be involved. Moreover, there is a lack of harmony in the narrative: vs. 7 states that understanding will come only afterwards, i.e., seemingly, after the resurrection (see NOTE); but vss. 12 and 17 imply that understanding is possible now, as it should have been if only an example of humility were involved.

These difficulties have led scholars to seek another symbolism in the footwashing besides that of humility. This would not be strange, since John has several instances of twofold symbolism, for example, of the bread of life. Origen related the footwashing to the preparation to preach the Gospel. Bultmann sees in vss. 6–11 a parabolic action symbolizing the purification of the disciples through the word of Jesus (xv 3). Schwank, "Exemplum," builds the example of humility into a symbol of union through love and sees deep ecclesiological implications in it. Hoskyns and

Richter think of the footwashing as a symbol of the death of Jesus. Other scholars have explored the sacramental possibilities of the symbolism. The use of water naturally suggests Baptism and we shall discuss below the patristic support for a baptismal interpretation of the footwashing. Some modern writers (Goguel, Macgregor) have seen a reference to the Eucharist, because in John the footwashing (an act of love) replaces the action of Jesus over the bread and the wine (an action that also involves love for one another—see I Cor xi 20–22). Cullmann has revived the theory of Loisy and W. Bauer that the footwashing refers both to Baptism and to the Eucharist. Led by Augustine, Latin writers from the 4th century on and modern Roman Catholic authors have seen a reference to Penance in vs. 10: ". . . has no need to wash *except for his feet*," for Penance cleanses sins committed after the baptismal washing (see Grelot, *art. cit.*). Lohmeyer has even seen the footwashing as a type of apostolic ordination (see NOTE on vs. 16).

We cannot discuss all these theories. Of the sacramental suggestions only a reference to Baptism can possibly meet the criteria we have suggested for Johannine sacramentalism (vol. 29, pp. cxi–cxiv). For instance, a reference to the Eucharist lacks the external criterion of early and widespread recognition in antiquity (Hugh of St. Victor in the Middle Ages is one of the earliest proponents); nor is there an internal indication that the author intended a reference to the Eucharist since there is no mention of bread, wine, eating, or drinking. We shall discuss a reference to Baptism below, but in so doing we are by no means implying that at the footwashing Jesus baptized his disciples. Nor do we necessarily suggest that Jesus intended the footwashing as a symbol for Baptism; we are discussing only the author's intentions. Elsewhere in John sacramental symbolism has been on a secondary level, reinterpreting deeds or words of Jesus that had a primary meaning more pertinent to the ministry itself. Therefore, if the footwashing is a symbol for Baptism, it may first have been a symbol for Jesus' death; and we must discuss this possibility as well.

The Unity of the Scene

Closely related to the problem of one or more symbolic meanings for the footwashing is the problem of whether vss. 1–20 constitute an original unit. If the only meaning of the footwashing is as an example of humility, then the scene may represent a not unusual Johannine combination of action (1–11) and subsequent interpretation by discourse (12–20). Hirsch and Lohmeyer are among those who hold for unity, and this position has recently been defended by Weiser, *art. cit.* But if 6–11 constitute another interpretation of the footwashing, then it is unlikely that both interpretations, one by dialogue (6–11) and one by discourse (12–20), were always part of the scene. Another argument against unity is the conflicting indication mentioned above about whether the footwashing will be understood only in the future (7) or can be already understood (12, 17). Those who hold that the scene is composite offer explanations according to the various theories of the composition of the Gospel (vol. 29, pp. xxv ff.). Let us see how Bultmann and Boismard apply their theories to this scene (cf. vol. 29, pp. 67–71).

Bultmann, pp. 351–54, thinks that the story of the footwashing represents a special written source that underwent editing. In this source vss. 4–5 were originally joined to 12–20, while 7–11 were added later by the evangelist. In the introductory verses (1–3) in which there is a certain amount of repetition, only part of vs. 1 and the whole of vs. 3 were original; the rest of vs. 1 was an introduction to the prayer of ch. xvii, and vs. 2 was a redactional gloss. For a critique of this treatment of 1–3 see Grossouw, *art. cit.*

Boismard, *art. cit.*, thinks that we are not dealing with the secondary editing of an original account but with two complete accounts that have been combined. "Moralizing" and "Sacramental" are the titles he gives the two accounts according to whether the footwashing was interpreted as a symbol of humility or of Baptism. Each account had an introduction, a description of the footwashing, and an interpretation; each was followed by a prediction of the betrayal.

	Moralizing Account	Sacramental Account
Introduction	1–2	3
Footwashing	4–5	4–5
Interpretation	12–15, 17	6–10(11)
Betrayal Prediction	18–19	21–30

(Verses 16 and 20 are treated as redactional.)

In Boismard's estimation the "moralizing" interpretation of the footwashing was the more original; in this he agrees with Bultmann, Merx, Wellhausen, W. Bauer, and many others, while Spitta and Richter treat the ("sacramental") interpretation in 6–10 as the more original.

Personally we find Boismard's reconstruction of two accounts too rigorously systematic. For instance, vss. 21–30 seem to be traditional Last Supper material with parallels in the Synoptic tradition; to include it as an integral part of one account *of the footwashing* seems artificial, especially since there is no convincing reason to relate it to the "sacramental" account. Grossouw, *art. cit.*, has persuasively criticized the attempt to find the introductions to two accounts in vss. 1–3. We grant that there is a duplication between vss. 1 and 3; but if 1 constitutes an introduction distinct from 3, we may more plausibly consider it as an introduction to the whole Book of Glory. The supreme act of love to which 1 alludes is, as the reference to "the hour" indicates, the act of the passion, death, resurrection, and ascension. (Verse 1 is not so closely related to 12–20 as Boismard holds, for these verses are concerned with an example of humility and do not specifically mention love.) Verse 1 shares the theme of "his own" with the Prologue to the Gospel; and just as the Prologue is the introduction to the whole Gospel and to the Book of Signs in particular, the redactor may have added this verse to recall the Prologue and to introduce the Book of Glory. In this case, vss. 2–3 would constitute the real introduction to the footwashing.

The only point in Boismard's theory for which there is impressive evidence is the suggestion of duplicate *interpretations* of the footwashing. The following modification of Boismard's theory brings out the parallelism of 6–11 and 12–20 as two interpretations:

6–11		*12–20*
7	*understanding* the footwashing	12
8	importance of what Jesus has done: it gives heritage or is an example to be imitated	15
10a	salvific effect on disciples: it is itself cleansing or makes those happy who imitate its spirit	17
10b	it does not affect all the disciples	18a
11	the exception is the betrayer	18b–19

(We have bracketed the last two lines in order to acknowledge the possibility of the thesis advanced in Richter's book, p. 309, that 10b–11 were not original but were introduced as an editorial imitation of 18–19.) If two complete interpretations of the footwashing now stand side by side in the Johannine scene, which one belongs to the early edition of the Gospel? (This is not necessarily the same as the question of which is the oldest; we suggested in vol. 29, p. XXXVII, that at times the redactor added to the Gospel genuinely ancient material.) Format alone would suggest that the first interpretation (6–11) is more original. We have seen that, when in the course of editing or redacting another unit of Johannine material has been added to the Gospel, there was a tendency to tack this onto the end of a section rather than to break up the already existing unit (cf. iii 31–36, vi 51–58, xii 44–50; also xv–xvi below). In the instance under discussion 6–11 is much more closely tied to the action of the footwashing than is 12–20 which could easily have been appended. The dialogue in 6–10 has no other possible reference than to the footwashing, while some of the sayings in 12–20 are general and appropriate to other moments of Jesus' career. That 12–20 is to some extent a collection of miscellaneous material is recognized by Boismard and others who treat 16 and 20 as redactional additions because they are closely parallel to sayings in Matt x (see pp. 569, 572 below). Richter, *art. cit.,* has done a very interesting study of the relationship of 12–20 to sayings in chs. xv–xvi. (We may compare xiii 16 with xv 15, 20 on the theme of the servant and master; xiii 18 with xv 16 on the theme of Jesus' choosing the disciples. If John xiii 16, 20 are related to Matt x, so is John xv 18–xvi 2 [p. 694 below].) Now we shall suggest (below pp. 586–87) that chs. xv–xvi were not part of the Last Discourse in the first edition of the Gospel, and so the parallelism with them may indicate that xiii 12–20 was not the first explanation of the footwashing. In the same line of reasoning the verb *trōgein* in 18 may relate xiii 12–20 to the *secondary* interpretation of the bread of life in vi 51–58, the only other place in John where *trōgein* occurs (four times).

The reason why Boismard thinks that vss. 12–17 represent an earlier interpretation of the footwashing than 6–10 is in part because he explains 6–10 sacramentally. In general we have seen that the sacramental references in John represent a secondary layer of symbolism. Actually we suggest that the reference to Baptism in 6–10 is a secondary allusion, similar to the secondary allusion to the Eucharist in vi 35–50 (see vol. 29, p. 274), and that the primary reference in 6–10 is to the footwashing as a prophetic action symbolic of Jesus' passion and death (so Hoskyns, p. 437; Richter, *art. cit.*). In demeaning himself to wash his disciples' feet Jesus is acting out beforehand his humiliation in death, even as Mary acted out beforehand the anointing of his body for burial (xii 1–8). The footwashing is an action of service for others, symbolic of the service he will render in laying down his life for others (see NOTE on vs. 4); that is why Jesus can claim that the footwashing is necessary if the disciples are to share in his heritage (8) and that it will render the disciples clean (10). Naturally the disciples would not understand this symbolism until after "the hour" was over (7). Such an understanding of 6–10 as primarily christological and only secondarily sacramental is one more reason for considering these verses as more original than 12–20, for certainly the christological emphasis would be closer to the purpose of the Gospel (xx 31) than the moral emphasis.

We may summarize our approach to 1–20 as follows:

vs. 1 is an introduction to the Book of Glory.

vss. 2–11 are a unit consisting of an introduction, the account of the footwashing and an interpretation. The footwashing is presented as a prophetic action symbolizing Jesus' death in humiliation for the salvation of others. A secondary baptismal symbolism has also been woven into the text. Verses 2–10a appeared in an early edition of the Gospel; vss. 10b–11 may be an addition matching 18–19, inserted at the time that 12–20 were appended.

vss. 12–20 contain another interpretation of the footwashing current in Johannine circles whereby it was looked on as a moral example of humility to be imitated by others. To this interpretation miscellaneous material (16, 20) has been added. This section was appended to 2–10a probably at the same time that xv–xvi were appended to xiv in the formation of the Last Discourse.

COMMENT: DETAILED

Verse 1: Introduction to the Book of Glory

"The hour" that is the subject of the Book of Glory (p. 541 above) will see Jesus' death; this verse makes clear that in the Johannine conception Jesus approached his death as an act of love for those who believed in him (see NOTE on "to the very end"). It also makes clear that his death was a victory because it was a return to his Father. (Functionally John xiii 1 has some similarity to Luke ix 51: "When the days were reaching fulfillment for him to be taken up, he set his face to go to Jerusalem." In Luke this marks the terminus of the Galilean ministry and the beginning of the movement toward the death that will take Jesus up to heaven; and it is followed by Jesus' long discourses with his disciples on the road to Jerusalem.) These two ideas of love for the disciples he is leaving behind and of return to the Father intertwine to form the leitmotif of the Book of Glory. From the opening verse John stresses Jesus' awareness of all that would happen to him, a theme repeated in vs. 3 and in xviii 4, xix 28. This agrees with what Jesus said in x 18: no one could take his life from him until he would lay it down of his own accord. For the possibility that xiii 1 once followed x 42, see vol. 29, p. 414.

Verses 2–3: Introduction to the Footwashing

If we interpret the footwashing as a prophetic action symbolic of Jesus' death, by introducing Jesus' death vs. 1 also introduces the footwashing; but a more immediate preparation for the footwashing is supplied by 2–3. The betrayal is mentioned in 2 precisely so that the reader will connect the footwashing and the death of Jesus. Jesus undertook this action symbolic of his death only after the forces had been set in motion that would lead to crucifixion. There is a certain duplication between vss. 2 and 27 in describing the control that the devil achieved over Judas: 2 says that the devil put it into the heart (see NOTE) that Judas should betray Jesus, while 27 says that Satan entered into Judas. In having two references to Judas, one at the beginning of the meal and one later, John is not untraditional; cf. Mark xiv 10–11 before the meal, and Mark xiv 17–21 during the meal. But is there any progression in the two Johannine references as there is in Mark? One may argue that vs. 2 refers to the planning stage, while in 27 Satan actually takes control over Judas and the betrayal is quickly consummated. Boismard, however, thinks that the two verses are duplicates and assigns them respectively to his two different accounts. We cannot decide, but we would point out that in speaking of "Satan" rather than of "the devil," vs. 27 may be using older vocabulary (NOTE on vi 70). Luke xxii 3, "Then Satan entered into Judas," is closer to 27 in wording but closer to 2 in setting (before the meal). See vol. 29, p. 453, for the relative value of the two Johannine explanations of Judas' disloyalty: victim of avarice and tool of Satan.

Verse 3 mentions that the Father had handed over all things to Jesus. Since this was mentioned also during the ministry (iii 35, vi 39, x 29), we cannot think that here it is a special power due to Jesus because he has already been glorified in "the hour." Boismard uses this verse to argue for the baptismal signification of the footwashing; he recalls Matt xxviii 18–19: "All authority in heaven and earth has been given to me . . . baptize them in the name of the Father. . . ." However, in John the handing over of all things to Jesus is not so much a question of universal authority as of salvific mission. The footwashing as an action symbolic of Jesus' death is performed because he knows that he has the power to save others and the power to lay down his own life for this purpose.

Verse 3 also states that Jesus acted the way he did because he knew that he had come forth from God and was going to God. This is another hint that the footwashing is related to Jesus' death. "That he had come forth from God" may have been mentioned to emphasize that it was *God's Son* who was to subject himself to death and thus to give more poignancy to the element of humiliation visible in the footwashing and in the death that it symbolizes. The emphasis on Jesus' knowledge in vs. 3 reminds us of the similar emphasis in vs. 1. If we are correct in theorizing that vs. 1 was composed by the redactor as an introduction for the Book of Glory, he may have borrowed from vs. 3 (just as he borrowed from the Prologue and from xv 13).

Verses 4–5: The Footwashing

Since feet shod only in sandals tend to get dusty on unpaved roads, it was customary hospitality to provide water for a guest to wash his own feet. But as the Midrash Mekilta on Exod xxi 2 tells us, the washing of a master's feet could not be required of a Jewish slave. As a sign of devotion, however, occasionally disciples would render this service to their teacher or rabbi; and Jesus seems to allude to this custom in vss. 13–14. Thus, in the footwashing Jesus humiliates himself and takes on the form of a servant. It is almost as if he is acting out the words of Luke xii 37: "Happy are those servants whom the master finds awake when he comes. . . . He will tie a cloth around himself and have them sit at table, and he will come and serve them." It is possible that, besides being seen as an act of humble devotion, the footwashing would have been understood as a traditional act of love. Schwank, "Exemplum," points to chapter xx of *Joseph and Asenath*, an Alexandrian Jewish work probably composed between 100 B.C. and A.D. 100. When Asenath, Joseph's bride-to-be, offers to wash his feet, Joseph protests that a servant girl could do it; but Asenath exclaims devotedly: "Your feet are my feet . . . another shall not wash your feet" (xx 1–5).

There was nothing in the ritual for the Passover meal that can be compared to the footwashing. Footwashing was done when one entered the house, not during the course of a meal. The Passover ritual prescribed a washing of the hands after the second cup, but there is no evidence that Jesus' action was a variant upon that custom.

Verses 6–11: Interpretation of the Footwashing (a Dialogue)

The key to the symbolism of the footwashing lies in the conversation between Jesus and Peter. It is difficult to be certain whether in voicing his objection Peter is a spokesman for the other disciples (as in vi 68) or is acting impetuously on his own (as in xviii 10, xxi 7). Although the conversation has its symbolic overtones, there is nothing implausible in the basic implication, namely, that Peter was embarrassed at his master's gesture. The first of the overtones appears in vs. 7. Jesus is doing more than giving a lesson in humility that the disciples could easily understand; what is involved has theological implications that can be understood only after "the hour" is over (cf. ii 22, xii 16). Michl, p. 706, argues that vs. 7 means simply that Peter will see the full depth of Jesus' humility and love, exhibited in the footwashing, after he has seen the death of Jesus. However, to be exact, 7 speaks of the later understanding of the footwashing itself, not of the spirit of the footwashing.

Verse 8 has another overtone of deeper meaning: the footwashing is so important that without it a disciple loses his heritage with Jesus. Michl would tell us that Jesus is talking about the importance of love here; but once again the text does not refer to the necessity of the spirit exhibited in the footwashing but to the necessity of the washing itself. Moreover, Jesus does not say to Peter, "If you do not allow yourself to be washed" (a phrasing that would give primacy to Peter's participation) but "If *I* do not wash you"—a salvific action of Jesus is involved, not simply an example to be imitated. Contrast vs. 17 which puts the burden of action on the disciples if the footwashing is to have its effect.

The word "heritage" in vs. 8 is significant. The Greek expression *echein meros* can mean simply "to share with; be a partner with," and this seems to be the sense understood by Michl. But *meros* means more than fellowship; for *meros* (also *meris*) is used in LXX to translate Heb. *ḥēleq*, the word that describes the God-given heritage of Israel. (See P. Dreyfus, "Le thème de l'héritage dans l'Ancien Testament," RSPT 42 [1958], 3–49.) Each of the tribes except Levi was to have its "share" in the Promised Land, and this was its heritage from God (Num xviii 20; Deut xii 12, xiv 27). When the hopes of Israel turned to an afterlife, the "share" or "heritage" of God's people was pictured in heavenly terms. The eschatological use of *meros* for eternal reward is found elsewhere in the

Johannine writings (Rev xx 6, xxi 8, xxii 19). This interpretation of *meros* in vs. 8 is reinforced by the fact that Jesus speaks of a heritage "with me." The theme of the union of the disciples with Jesus in heaven appears in the Last Discourse (xiv 3, xvii 24). By way of distant similarity, it is interesting that in the Lucan account of the Last Supper the question of the disciples' position in the future kingdom was raised: "You may eat and drink at my table in the kingdom" (Luke xxii 30). We remember also Luke xxiii 43: "This day you will be *with me* in Paradise."

Therefore, it is clear that the footwashing is something that makes it possible for the disciples to have eternal life with Jesus. Such emphasis is intelligible if we understand the footwashing as a symbol for Jesus' salvific death. Grossouw, p. 131, compares Peter's rebellion at the footwashing to Peter's negative reaction at the first prediction of the suffering of the Son of Man (Mark viii 31–33). We may have here John's way of stressing the necessity of accepting the scandal of the cross. As an argument for a secondary baptismal symbolism for the footwashing, we may note that the idea of inheritance (*klēronomia*, not *meros*) is mentioned in the NT in a baptismal context (I Pet i 3–4; Titus iii 7).

The narrative continues in vs. 9 with a typical Johannine misunderstanding (vol. 29, p. cxxxv), but it is interesting to see how the author combines this literary technique with an element of Peter's characteristic impetuosity. Peter has gone to the opposite extreme: if the footwashing brings heritage with Jesus, then the more washing, the better. This misunderstanding causes Jesus to indicate that the salvific factor is not the physical washing itself but what it symbolizes (vs. 10a). Leaving aside for the moment the bracketed phrase in 10a, we must discuss the meaning of Jesus' statement, "The man who has bathed has no need to wash; he is clean all over." If the "bathed" (see NOTE) refers to the footwashing, then Jesus is telling Peter that he has missed the point in thinking that the number or extent of the washings will increase his heritage with Jesus. Only the footwashing is important because that symbolizes Jesus' death. Many authors think that Jesus was anxious to prevent the disciples from interpreting his action as a mandate for ritual washings of the type found in Judaism, and so they see here a type of polemic against the repeated washings demanded by the Pharisees (W. Bauer, Lohmeyer—see Mark vii 1–5), or against Essene washings (Schlatter), or against washings among the disciples of John the Baptist (Baldensperger, Dodd, Schnackenburg).

The use of the verb "to bathe" for the footwashing is the principal evidence for a (secondary) baptismal interpretation of the footwashing. The verb "to bathe," *louein,* and its cognates are standard NT vocabulary for Baptism. In Acts xxii 16 Ananias says to Saul: "Rise and be baptized and wash away [*apolouein*] your sins, calling on his name." Titus iii 5 proclaims: "He saved us . . . by the bath [*loutron*] of regeneration and renewal in the Holy Spirit." See also I Cor vi 11; Eph v 26; Heb x 22; and the variant in Rev i 5. Richter, *art. cit.,* p. 17, and *op. cit.,* pp. 296–98, argues against a baptismal reference by maintaining that in Johannine thought Baptism is not described in terms of cleansing; rather it is the blood of Jesus that cleanses (I John i 7; Rev vii 14). However, cleansing by Baptism and by Jesus' blood are not mutually exclusive (cf. Heb ix 22 with x 22; Titus ii 14 with iii 5). The fact that John does not explicitly mention the cleansing aspect of Baptism does not necessarily mean that this aspect was unknown to the Johannine community. Indeed, cleansing from sin was so much a part of the Jewish expectation of the eschatological washing (vol. 29, p. 51) that it could scarcely have been absent from any Christian understanding of Baptism.

What external support exists for the baptismal interpretation of the footwashing? Haring, *art. cit.*, documents the strong patristic adherence to a baptismal reference, especially in the West; but Richter, *op. cit.*, 1–36, argues that we must evaluate this adherence carefully. Most of the Latin Fathers who see a reference to Baptism in "The man who has bathed has no need to wash [except for his feet]" do so because they distinguish between the *bathing* (a Baptism of the disciples that had taken place earlier, for example, by John the Baptist) and the *footwashing* (a forgiveness of subsequent sin). An interpretation of the footwashing itself as a symbol of baptismal cleansing is found among the earlier Fathers only in Tertullian, Cyprian, Aphraates, and Cyril of Alexandria; and even this evidence is not unambiguous. For instance, Tertullian, *Treatise on Baptism* xii 3; SC 35:83, clearly thinks of the bathing in John xiii 10a as a previous Baptism and thus implicitly would not interpret the footwashing baptismally. Yet in the same work, ix 4; SC 35:79, Tertullian cites among the NT types of Baptism the fact that Christ "administered water to his pupils"—most probably a reference to the Teacher's (xiii 14) washing the feet of his disciples (although a reference to iv 14 cannot be ruled out). Thus, there is some early external support for the footwashing as a symbol of Baptism, but it is minimal.

In discussing the patristic evidence, we found the suggestion that the bathing in xiii 10a is not the same as the footwashing. Such a view is espoused by some modern scholars as well. Jeremias, EWJ, p. 49, thinks that Jesus was referring to the ritual bath demanded before Passover by the laws of levitical purity (Num xix 19). Others like Fridrichsen, *art. cit.*, think that the bathing refers to some type of spiritual action, for example, cleansing by the word of Jesus (xv 3) and that this makes unnecessary all washings, even the footwashing. Grossouw, *art. cit.*, points out that we are not told that Peter's feet were washed; yet he is declared clean with the others. However, such an interpretation seems to reduce the conversation about the footwashing in 6–8 to nonsense: if the footwashing (as an action symbolic of Jesus' death) is not the bath that cleanses, why does Jesus insist that without it Peter can have no heritage with him?

The inclusion of the phrase "except for the feet" in some textual witnesses to vs. 10a is probably related to this problem. The most plausible explanation is that a scribe, faced with the statement, "The man who has bathed has no need to wash," and not recognizing that the bath was the footwashing, thought that he had to insert an exceptive phrase to show that Jesus did not mean to exclude the footwashing when he said there was no need to wash. In so doing he unwittingly provided later theologians with an even richer sacramental doctrine, for the phrase could be interpreted as a reference to the necessity of Penance after the bath of Baptism. W. Knox, *art. cit.,* takes the phrase "except for the feet" as genuine (belonging to the Gospel but not to the oldest tradition) and suggests that John is allowing a washing for Christians who are basically clean but have fallen into sins that do not rob them of their baptismal purity (unlike Judas who is not really clean). Knox recalls the distinction in I John v 16 between sins not unto death and sins unto death. While such a theory is in line with the later interpretation that the phrase refers to Penance, we think that the scribal addition of the phrase is more easily postulated than the scribal omission.

The simplest explanation of the footwashing, then, remains that Jesus performed this servile task to prophesy symbolically that he was about to be humiliated in death. Peter's questioning, provoked by the action, enabled Jesus to explain the salvific necessity of his death: it would bring men their heritage with him and it would cleanse them of sin. The question may have occurred to the reader whether such a highly symbolical action was really performed by Jesus, especially since we have no Synoptic corroboration. Barrett, p. 363, like D. F. Strauss before him, has suggested that the footwashing is an imaginative, fictional illustration of the saying recorded in Luke's account (xxii 27) of the Last Supper: "For which is the greater, the one who sits at table or the one who serves? Is it not the one who sits at table? But I am among you as one who serves." Nevertheless, it may be pointed out that elsewhere in the Gospel we have seen that the genius of the evangelist lies more in eliciting the theological significance of what has come to him from the tradition than in inventing illustrations. And if two different interpretations of the footwashing arose in Johannine circles, the tradition of the footwashing must have been old. While such a prophetic action may seem implausible to modern eyes, one could point to much more bizarre actions by Jeremiah and Ezekiel predicting the fall of Jerusalem. That Jesus did indulge in prophetic action is part of the Synoptic tradition too, as we see in the story of the cursing of the fig tree.

Verse 10b and vs. 11 make clear that Judas had not been changed by the footwashing. Peter had protested to Jesus but had quickly accepted the footwashing when Jesus pointed out its salvific purpose. But Judas' heart (vs. 2) was already filled with evil intent, and he had not opened himself up to the love that Jesus was extending toward him. Many commentators have suggested that 10b–11 are editorial and not, like 2–10a, part of the original narrative.

Verses 12–20: Interpretation of the Footwashing (a Discourse)

The second interpretation of the footwashing is that Jesus has acted out for his disciples an example which they must be prepared to imitate. The rabbi has done for the disciples an act of service that occasionally generous disciples might do for a rabbi; the disciples must be willing to do similar acts of service for one another. That the practice was taken seriously is attested in I Tim v 10 where one of the qualifications for a woman to be enrolled as a widow is that she have shown hospitality and have "washed the feet of the saints." J. A. T. Robinson, p. 145, has pointed out similarities with the scene in Mark x 32–45. There, after Jesus had foretold his death, James and John asked to share his glory. Jesus insisted that they must first share his fate and be baptized with his baptism; and he stated that the great must be as the servant, and that his own service consisted in giving his life. Thus there are elements of both interpretations of the footwashing in the Marcan scene. It is interesting that Luke xxii 24–26, the parallel to Mark x 42–45, is part of the Last Supper scene. (We called attention above to Luke xxii 27 as similar in theme to the footwashing and to Luke xxii 28–29 as similar to the theme of heritage in John xiii 8.) Luke's form of the passage is not so clearly oriented to Jesus' death as is Mark's, but it is related to the betrayal of Jesus. Perhaps Luke xxii 24–29 represents a mixture of Synoptic tradition and a truncated echo of a tradition similar to that found in John.

Even taken simply as an example of humility, the footwashing does not lose its association with the death of Jesus; the general context would indicate this. Therefore xv 12–13, with its command to carry love to the point of laying down one's life for others, is an excellent commentary on what Jesus means in xiii 15 when he says: "You are to do exactly as I have done for you."

We must pause briefly to consider vs. 16. Although it is related to the theme of 12–15, probably it was not originally part of the interpretation of the footwashing. We may compare it to parallels in the Synoptic tradition:

John xiii 16: "No servant is more important than his master;
no messenger [*apostolos*] is more important than the one who sent him."

Matt x 24–25: "No disciple is greater than his teacher;
[no servant is greater than his master;]
it is sufficient for the disciple to be like his teacher,
for the servant to be like his master."

Luke vi 40: "No disciple is greater than his teacher;
but everyone when he is fully taught will be like his teacher."

Obviously John is closer to Matthew. (The bracketed line in Matthew is missing in the OL and OS^sin. Was there a scribal omission to harmonize with Luke, or a scribal addition to form a quatrain in which the second line would be like the fourth?) While John does not have Matthew's disciple/teacher comparison, the question of teacher comes up in vs. 13; indeed 13 mentions "Teacher" and "Lord" [*kyrios*=master], the two roles that appear in the Matthean passage. Verse 16 contains the only use of *apostolos* (messenger) in John, while the only use of *apostolos* in Matthew occurs in the context of the comparison we have been considering (Matt x 2; also *apostellein* in x 5, 16, 40). On the basis of these similarities Sparks, *art. cit.*, has argued that the fourth evangelist knew Matthew's Gospel. In a more nuanced study, Dodd, *art. cit.*, shows that if John was really copying Matthew, there is no logical explanation for the omissions, since the disciple/teacher comparison would have been most useful in relation to the footwashing and vs. 13. Rather the original saying of Jesus probably circulated in variant forms, and these were reported independently by the different evangelists. Nevertheless, we should note that John has several parallels to the material in Matt x:

John xii 25	=Matt x 39	(see vol. 29, pp. 473–74)
John xii 26	=Matt x 38	(see vol. 29, p. 475)
John xii 44	=Matt x 40	(see vol. 29, pp. 490–91)
John xiii 16	=Matt x 24–25	
John xiii 20	=Matt x 40	(see below)
John xv 18–xvi 4a	=Matt x 17–25	(see p. 694 below)

Both Gospels are drawing on a common collection of material which each uses in its own way.

Verse 17 is the last direct reference to the footwashing, the explanation of which began in vs. 12. The two verses agree in their stress that the disciples can now understand the footwashing as an example of humility (contrast vs. 7). The Johannine beatitude in 17 (see NOTE) may be compared in theme to the beatitudes found in Luke xi 28: "Happy are those who hear the word of God and keep it" (see John xii 47), and in Matt xxiv 46: "When the master comes, happy is that servant whom he finds putting his instructions into practice." See also Matt vii 24. In vs. 17 the "this" (plural *tauta*) is probably a general reference to the footwashing and its lesson. However, if there was once an institution of the Eucharist in John's account of the Last Supper (perhaps preserved in part as vi 51–58—vol. 29, p. 287), then the *tauta* and *poiein* ("put into practice, do") of vs. 17 might be compared to Luke's eucharistic command: "Do this [*touto poieite*] in commemoration of me" (xxii 19).

Both interpretations of the footwashing, 6–10 and 12–17, end with a reference to the one exception among the disciples who has not been touched by what Jesus has done. (However, besides serving as a conclusion to the footwashing scene, vss. 18–19 also serve as a transition to 21–30, the next section which will treat more directly of Judas' betrayal. Richter, *op. cit.*, pp. 308–9, argues strongly that the connection between 18–19 and 17 is not original, that 18–19 at one time followed 10a, and that its replacement to the present site was the occasion for the editorial insertion of 10b–11). In both vss. 11 and 18 John makes clear that Jesus was perfectly aware that Judas had turned against him irrevocably. Yet in 18 we are told why Jesus accepted this betrayal: Scripture had to be fulfilled. The same explanation was offered in xii 38 ff. for the refusal of the Jewish people to accept Jesus.

The recourse to Ps xli 10(9) may have been traditional on the part of the early Christians, for it is cited implicitly in Mark xiv 18: "I assure you, one of you will betray me, *one who is eating [esthiein] with me.*" (That Mark was aware of a scriptural background for what was happening can be deduced from xiv 21: "The Son of Man goes his way *as it is written of him.*") Mark's implicit citation echoes the LXX form of the psalm; John's explicit citation is closer to MT than to LXX (see NOTE on "feeds on bread with me"). We would agree with Dodd, *Tradition,* pp. 36–37 (against Freed, OTQ, p. 92), that John's use of the psalm is independent of Mark's. In particular, we note John's use of the verb *trōgein* ("feed on"), also used in vi 51–58. Is this another indication that vi 51–58 once stood in the same context as xiii 12–20? If one were to accept the short form of the Lucan institution of the Eucharist, the saying "This is my body" would be followed immediately by "The hand of him who betrays me is with me on the table" (Luke xxii 19a and 21). See also the close traditional association of betrayal and the Eucharist in I Cor xi 23. It would not be illogical then to associate John's reference to betrayal, "He who feeds on bread with me has raised his heel against me," with a eucharistic section such as vi 51: "The bread that I shall give is my own flesh." In any case, xiii 18 is the only passage in the Johannine account of the Last Supper that mentions that bread has been eaten.

In the psalm the next verse continues: "But you, O Lord, be gracious to me and *raise me up.*" The next verse in John speaks of coming to believe in Jesus as the one who says, "I AM"; and such a belief is possible only after the crucifixion and resurrection: "When you *lift up* the Son of Man, then you will realize that I AM" (viii 28—on "lift up" see vol. 29, p. 146). The foretelling of the betrayal by Judas, which is the action that initiates the process of death and resurrection, will help to bring the disciples to believe in the Jesus who has been lifted up to his Father. In the theme of prediction in 19, John is very close to the claims of God voiced in Ezek xxiv 24: "When this comes about, then you will know that I am the Lord," and in Isa xliii 10: "You are my witnesses and my servant whom *I chose* that *you may . . . believe* and understand *that I AM [egō eimi]*."

In this sequence dealing with Judas, vs. 20 seems strangely out of place. Richter, *art. cit.,* p. 26, imaginatively suggests that Judas' betrayal may have tended to make people suspicious of the apostles sent out by Jesus, and so vs. 20 was designed to gain acceptance for the apostles. Attempts to relate vs. 20 to the general context of the footwashing are also forced; for example, the suggestion that the theme of loving service runs throughout. A more plausible thesis is that 20 which has a parallel in Matt x 40 once was more closely related to 16 which has a parallel in Matt x 24–25, and that when 16 was brought into its present context so was 20. If this is true, 16 was fitted closely into the sequence about the footwashing, while 20 was loosely tacked on to the end. We note that both 16 and 20 begin with "Let me firmly assure you" (Amen, amen), and both deal with sending. The Matthean parallel for 20 is as follows:

John xiii 20: "Whoever welcomes anyone I shall send welcomes me;
        and whoever welcomes me welcomes Him who sent [*pempein*] me."
Matt x 40:   "Whoever receives you receives me;
        and whoever receives me receives Him who sent [*apostellein*] me."

Dodd, *art. cit.*, is right in insisting that the same *logion* is involved but that it is independently reported in the two Gospels; there seem to be other variants and combinations in Mark ix 37 (=Luke ix 48) and Luke x 16.

[The Bibliography for this section is included in the Bibliography at the end of §47.]

47. THE MEAL:
—PREDICTION OF THE BETRAYAL
(xiii 21–30)

XIII 21 After these words Jesus was deeply troubled. "Let me firmly assure you," he declared, "one of you will betray me." 22 The disciples looked at one another, puzzled as to whom he could mean. 23 One of them, the disciple whom Jesus loved, was at the table close beside Jesus; 24 so Simon Peter signaled him to ask Jesus whom he meant. 25 [From his position] he leaned back against Jesus' chest and said to him, "Lord, who is it?" 26 Jesus answered, "It is the one to whom I give this morsel of food which I am going to dip in the dish." And he dipped the morsel [and took it] and gave it to Judas, son of Simon the Iscariot. 27 At that moment, after the morsel of food, Satan entered into him. So Jesus told him, "Be quick, and do what you are going to do." (28 Of course, none of those at table understood why he said this to him; 29 for some had the idea that, since Judas held the money box, Jesus was telling him to buy what was needed for the feast or to give something to the poor.) 30 And so, as soon as he took the morsel, Judas went out. It was night.

24: *signaled;* 25: *said;* 26: *answered,* [*took*], *gave;* 27: *told.* In the historical present tense.

NOTES

xiii 21. *After these words.* This may be simply an editorial connective. There is nothing in what follows that is necessarily related to the footwashing or its interpretation(s).

deeply troubled. Tarassein; see NOTE on xi 33.

declared. Literally "he testified and said"; MTGS, p. 156, points to this parataxis (in John more usually, "answered and said") as a Semitism. There are several possible Semitisms in this section: a pronoun resuming a relative in 26 (ZGB, §201); also the clause "and took it" in 26—see NOTE. Wilcox, *art. cit.,* discusses the Semitisms at length.

23. *disciple whom Jesus loved.* The Beloved Disciple appears in six passages, all in the Book of Glory; see vol. 29, pp. XCIII ff.

at the table close beside Jesus. Literally "was reclining on Jesus' bosom."

How does John envisage the position of those reclining (NOTE on "feet" in 5) at the Last Supper? F. Prat, RSR 15 (1925), 512–22, has studied table arrangements and places of honor among the Jewish contemporaries of Jesus. He suggests that the table disposition at this supper was that of the Roman *triclinium*, that is, three couches in a squared-off horseshoe pattern, arranged around a central table. If the Twelve were present with Jesus, there may have been five disciples on each of the two side couches, and two disciples with Jesus in the middle (place of honor) on the top couch or *lectus medius*. Although we might expect the place of second honor to have been on Jesus' right (cf. Ps cx 1), Prat, p. 519, asserts that in such an arrangement it was on Jesus' left. Now from the Gospel evidence it is clear that the Beloved Disciple is pictured on Jesus' right, so that when he tilted his head back, it was at Jesus' chest. (In view of the thesis that the Beloved Disciple was John, we may recall Mark x 37 where James and *John* ask to sit at Jesus' right and left in his glory.) Perhaps Judas is to be pictured on Jesus' left, for Jesus can hand him a morsel of food. As treasurer (xii 6) he may have warranted a (or even *the*) place of honor among the disciples. If vs. 24 is read to mean that Peter signaled to the Beloved Disciple without speaking to him (see below), then Peter may have been at a distance from Jesus; and this would be in harmony with Peter's not asking the question himself. Since he was visible to the Beloved Disciple, he is probably to be pictured on the couch on the right, perhaps at the far end if he was the last to have his feet washed (NOTE on vs. 6). Curiously Prat puts Peter on Jesus' left and has him lean over Jesus' body to whisper to the Beloved Disciple! There have been elaborate attempts to assign places to the other disciples, but this is sheer imagination—even the above reconstruction is highly speculative.

24. *Peter signaled.* Literally "nodded." K. G. Kuhn, "The Lord's Supper and the Communal Meal at Qumran," in *The Scrolls and the New Testament*, ed. K. Stendahl (New York: Harper, 1957), p. 69, points out that at the Essene and Qumran meals (Josephus *War* II.viii.5;※132; and 1QS vi 10) one could speak only in due order. On this analogy he concludes that the Beloved Disciple must have been in a higher place than Peter and have had the right to speak before Peter. However, the action of Peter may be understood more simply if he was at a distance and did not want to shout aloud such a question. Thinking that the Fourth Gospel is dependent on and modifying the Synoptic account where the disciples in general pose the question about whom Jesus meant, Loisy, p. 395, maintains that John has "individualized" the scene by making Peter alone ask the question. But if this is all the product of inventive imagination, why was the evangelist not content to have the Beloved Disciple ask the question, rather than complicating the picture by introducing Peter as well? It is less a strain on credulity to think that the evangelist was dealing with a reminiscence enshrined in the tradition that came to him.

to ask Jesus whom he meant. There are many textual variants, but basically the readings can be classified into two: (a) "to ask who it was about whom he was speaking," supported by P66, Bezae, Alexandrinus, the Coptic and Syriac; (b) "and said to him, 'Tell who it is about whom he is speaking,'" supported by Vaticanus, the Latin, and Origen. The second reading supposes that Peter was near enough to the Beloved Disciple to speak to him (then why signal?) and that the Beloved Disciple knew and could tell Peter about whom Jesus was speaking (why then did the Disciple ask Jesus?). The second reading almost certainly represents a scribal misunderstanding. Boismard, RB 60 (1953), 357–59, has analyzed all the variants. He suggests that the original read simply: "Simon Peter signaled him" (so Chrysostom). Scribes expanded this in two different ways by adding either (a) "to ask about whom he was speaking" or (b) "and said to him, 'Tell who it is.'" For Boismard the extant mss. readings represent combinations of these earlier expansions.

25. [*From his position*]. The adverb *houtōs* is literally "just as he was" or "accordingly" (after Peter's signal) or "without more ado"—see NOTE on "sat down" in iv 6. It is omitted in important witnesses.

leaned back. There is some ms. evidence for a stronger form of the same verbal root, meaning "fell back."

26. *morsel of food. Psōmion* has been used in Greek Christianity for the eucharistic host, and so some scholars suggest that Jesus was giving the Eucharist to Judas. Loisy and W. Bauer use I Cor xi 29, which speaks of the condemnation of those who eat the body of the Lord without discerning, to explain why Satan entered Judas after he ate the (eucharistic) morsel. But would the writer expect his readers to understand that the morsel was the Eucharist when he has not described the institution? That would be feasible only in the dubious hypothesis that he was observing the *disciplina arcani* by hiding the institution from outsiders who might read the Gospel.

dipped the morsel. The same action is described in Mark xiv 20 and Matt xxvi 23, but the vocabulary is different; and John's account seems to be independent. The Marcan and Matthean reference to the dipping into the dish precedes the description of the institution of the Eucharist, but the Lucan reference to the traitor (xxii 21–23—Luke does not mention the dipping) follows the institution.

[*and took it*]. Omitted in a strong combination of witnesses, this may be a scribal harmonization with a similar phrase in the Synoptic account of the institution of the Eucharist ("having taken" in Matt xxvi 26–27). Yet ZGB, §367, points to it as a possible example of the redundant coordinate verb construction frequent in Semitic usage.

Simon the Iscariot. So read the strongest witnesses here; contrast xiii 2.

27. *Satan entered into him.* The same vocabulary for the "entering in" of evil spirits is found in Mark v 12 and Luke viii 30. This is the only time "Satan" occurs in John.

So Jesus told him. The implication is that Jesus knew that Judas had made up his mind; for Jesus' knowledge of men's hearts see ii 23–25.

Be quick. This translates an adverb in the comparative. Either the comparative has the weakened sense of a simple positive or it is elative ("as quickly as possible"): BDF, §244[1].

what you are going to do. Literally "what you do"; there is probably a conative inflection in the present tense used here (MTGS, p. 63). This command resembles the words spoken by Jesus to Judas in Gethsemane according to a variant of Matt xxvi 50: "Friend, do [or let it be done] what you have come for." See W. Eltester, NTPat, pp. 70–91.

28. *none of those at table understood.* In light of vs. 26 perhaps the Beloved Disciple and Peter are to be excepted. In the Synoptic accounts the disciples are not told specifically who the betrayer is, beyond the general description that he is one of those who dip food from the same dish used by Jesus. (The information in Matt xxvi 25 that Jesus answered affirmatively when Judas asked, "Is it I?" is surely secondary; in any case Matthew does not indicate that others

overheard.) That the disciples did not know that Jesus meant Judas is confirmed by their seeming unawareness of Judas' purpose when he approached Jesus in the garden.

29. *the money box.* See NOTE on xii 6.

buy what was needed for the feast. Some scholars, e.g., Loisy, have used this to prove that the Johannine Last Supper on Thursday evening was not the Passover meal, for what was needed for the Passover festival had not yet been purchased (contrast Mark xiv 12–16); and so presumably the Passover meal was to be eaten on Friday evening. But then why would Judas be sent out to make the purchases on Thursday *night* when all day Friday remained for shopping? Jeremias, EWJ, p. 53, argues that this statement fits best with Synoptic chronology whereby Thursday evening and Friday constituted Passover. He suggests that the shops would have been open on Thursday evening, even though Passover had begun; but they would not be open on Friday (the feast day) nor on the Sabbath. Therefore it was thought that Judas was being sent to make purchases before the shops closed for the "weekend holiday."

to give something to the poor. Jeremias, EWJ, p. 54, points out that it was customary to give to the poor on Passover night.

30. *night.* The main meal was normally eaten in the late afternoon, but the Passover meal was always at night (Jeremias, EWJ, pp. 44–46). That the Last Supper was eaten at night seems to be confirmed by I Cor xi 23: "The Lord Jesus, on the night when he was handed over, took bread. . . ." The mention of "night" and of "supper" (NOTE on vs. 2), shared by I Cor xi and John xiii but not by the Synoptics, is used by Wilcox, pp. 144, 155, to suggest that Paul and John (also John vi) may be reflecting an ancient eucharistic tradition not preserved in Mark.

COMMENT

Having performed a prophetic action in the footwashing, Jesus now utters a verbal prophecy about his betrayer. This prophecy is also recorded by the Synoptics, but there is no real evidence that John is dependent on their narratives. Both Bultmann, p. 366, and Dodd, *Tradition*, pp. 52–54, maintain that the Johannine account is based on an independent tradition. Wilcox, pp. 155–56, finds three strata of tradition combined in vss. 21–30, one of which is close to Paul (see NOTE on 30), and one of which is close to the Marcan tradition. The third stratum, the material peculiar to John, is most obvious in 23–25 and 28–29. It is noteworthy that if these verses are taken out, there remains a consecutive story in which Semitisms are common (see NOTE on "declared" in 21). Wilcox, however, thinks that there are some signs of an early date in the peculiarly Johannine stratum as well. The details in John's scene that cannot be verified from the Synoptics are dramatic but not really implausible.

Verse 21 mentions that Jesus was troubled. In John the troubling of Jesus is related to the presence of Satan in death, as we saw in our discussion of Jesus' being troubled at the death of Lazarus (vol. 29, p. 435).

A passage that has much in common with xiii 21 is xii 27 where Jesus is troubled at the coming of the hour. In vol. 29, p. 470, we pointed out that xii 27 has a parallel in the Synoptic scene of the agony in Gethsemane where Jesus is sorrowful as he waits for Judas to come to hand him over to his enemies. Both John xii 27 and the Synoptic garden scene seem to cite Ps xlii 6(5): "Why are you sorrowful, my soul [=Synoptic scene, Mark xiv 34], and why do you trouble me [=John xii 27]?" It is noteworthy that here in xiii 21 John seems to cite the next verse of the same psalm: "My soul has been troubled." (Because of this Boismard theorizes that John xii 23, 27–29 originally belonged to the context we are now considering, and that the verses were moved to ch. xii when xi–xii were introduced into the plan of the Gospel—see vol. 29, p. 414.) In any case, if xii 27 shared with the Synoptic agony scene the troubling of Jesus at the coming of the hour, in xiii 21, as in the Synoptic agony scene, the dark shadow of Judas' betrayal covers Jesus' soul and throws him into gloom.

Jesus' statement in 21, "Let me firmly assure you [=Amen, amen], one of you will betray me," is found (with only one "Amen") in Matt xxvi 21 and Mark xiv 18, although Mark adds the words "one who is eating with me," which, as we saw, have their parallel in John xiii 18. But in what follows the parallels with the Synoptics are not so close. All the Gospels agree that the disciples raised the question as to what Jesus meant, but the questioning is reported in different ways in John xiii 22, Luke xxii 23, and Mark xiv 19 (=Matt xxvi 22). Mark relates that the first thought of each disciple was that he himself might be the betrayer; in Luke and John the disciples wonder in general who the betrayer is. In Mark they put their question directly to Jesus; in Luke they ask one another; John has elements of both (22 and 24).

The incidents described in 23–24 are peculiar to John. This is not surprising since they concern the Beloved Disciple, and this Gospel claims to preserve the testimony of that Disciple (xix 35, xxi 24). This first description of the Beloved Disciple is typical in its emphasis on his closeness to Jesus and on his friendship with Peter. He is resting on Jesus' bosom, just as in i 18 Jesus is described as in the Father's bosom. In other words, the Disciple is as intimate with Jesus as Jesus is with the Father. One can see why scholars suggest that he is the Johannine symbol for the Christian, since in xvii 23 Jesus will pray to his Father that Christians may enjoy just such an intimacy: "I in them and You in me." (There is no real evidence here, however, that he is a symbol for *Gentile* Christianity, as Bultmann, p. 369, suggests.) Perhaps the reason we have not heard of him before (yet see NOTE on "two disciples" in i 35) is that the evangelist wished to introduce him as an antithesis to Judas, showing the good and bad extremes in the spectrum of discipleship. But John does not present the Disciple as a pure symbol without historical reality. There is nothing symbolic in Peter's signal to him to ask Jesus about the betrayer. For the theory that he is John son of Zebedee, see vol. 29, p. xcvi.

In Mark xiv 20 (Matt xxvi 23), in response to the question of the disciples, Jesus identifies the traitor as one who is or has been dipping for food with him in the common dish. The picture is that of stretching forth one's hand to select a morsel from a central plate. The word *psōmion*, "morsel," generally refers to bread but not necessarily so. Those interested in the Passover aspect of the meal have suggested that John is describing the dipping of the herbs in the *ḥaroseth* sauce, an action that took place early in the Passover meal before the main course with its blessings of the bread and of the third cup of wine (the blessings generally associated with the Eucharist—Jeremias, EWJ, pp. 86–87). Obviously this cannot be proved. What John describes is a basic gesture of Oriental hospitality, as can be seen from Ruth ii 14. Indeed, Jesus may be extending to Judas a special act of esteem whereby a host singles out a guest whom he wishes to honor and picks out for him from the common plate a choice morsel of food. But this sign of Jesus' affection, like the act of love that brought him into the world, brings Judas to the decisive moment of judgment (see iii 16–21). His acceptance of the morsel without changing his wicked plan to betray Jesus means that he has chosen for Satan rather than for Jesus.

We note that only in John do we hear that the morsel was given to Judas, although at this moment in the narrative Matthew (like John, but unlike Mark and Luke) does identify Judas as the betrayer. John xiii 27 agrees verbally with Luke xxii 3 where we also hear that Satan entered into Judas; but, as already mentioned, the Lucan passage is closer to John xiii 2 in detecting a diabolic influence on Judas even before the meal began. We have noted the possibility that John xiii 2 and 27 are doublets. Some have thought of vss. 27–29 as an editorial addition interrupting the sequence of 26 and 30; but closer examination suggests that only 28–29 are an addition and that 27 should be recognized as essential to the narrative (Bultmann, p. 366).

Following the eating of the morsel, Judas is said (vs. 30) to have gone out. It is usually supposed that he went to the authorities to betray Jesus, for the next time he appears (xviii 2–5) he comes with police from the priests and the Pharisees to arrest Jesus. In the Synoptic tradition there was contact between Judas and the authorities before the Last Supper (Mark xiv 10–11), and John xiii 2 is probably in harmony. By having Judas depart from the Supper only after Jesus has told him to leave, John stresses Jesus' control over his destiny; no one can take Jesus' life from him unless he consents (x 18). Indeed, having recognized the irrevocability of Judas' malice, Jesus hastens him on. One is reminded of Luke xii 50: "I have a baptism to be baptized with, and I am constrained until it is accomplished."

As we have seen in the NOTES, J. Jeremias uses the data of vss. 28–30 to substantiate his thesis that not only does the Johannine Last Supper have Passover characteristics (which we admit) but also that it was eaten on the feast of Passover, i.e., on the night that began the 15th of Nisan (even though John makes it clear that on Friday Passover had not begun: xviii 28, xix 14). Such proof is not without difficulty. If vss. 28–29 are an editorial explanation, it is not clear whether they contain genuine tradition or an editorial surmise. Although the statement, "It was night," may also have chronological importance, there can be no doubt that the evangelist included it because of its dramatic theological import. Thus we are not certain how much such data contribute to the historical problem.

With Jesus' permission to Judas and the solemn entrance of Satan into the drama, the hour of darkness (night) has come. In the closing days of his ministry Jesus had warned: "Night is coming" (ix 4); "If a man goes walking at night, he will stumble because he has no light in him" (xi 10). Judas is one of those who "have preferred darkness to light because their deeds were evil" (iii 19). John's "It was night" is the equivalent of the words of Jesus reported in Gethsemane by Luke xxii 53: "This is your hour and the power of darkness." Yet even at this tragic moment in Jesus' life as the darkness envelops him, there is the assurance of the Prologue: "The light shines on in the darkness, for the darkness did not overcome it" (i 5). If this optimistic note was true of the situation caused by the first sin in the world, it was also true in the night of Jesus' passion. The long night that now descended upon the earth would have its dawn when "early on the first day of the week, while it was still dark, Mary Magdalene came to the tomb" (xx 1).

BIBLIOGRAPHY
(xiii 1–30)

Boismard, M.-E., "Le lavement des pieds (Jn, XIII, 1–17)," RB 71 (1964), 5–24.
Braun, F.-M., "Le lavement des pieds et la réponse de Jésus à saint Pierre (Jean, XIII, 4–10)," RB 44 (1935), 22–33.
Dodd, C. H., "Some Johannine 'Herrnworte' with Parallels in the Synoptic Gospels," NTS 2 (1955–56), especially pp. 75–78 on xiii 16 and pp. 81–85 on xiii 20. Reprinted in *Tradition*, pp. 335–38, 343–47.
Fridrichsen, A., "Bemerkungen zur Fusswaschung Joh 13," ZNW 38 (1939), 94–96.
Grelot, P., "L'interprétation pénitentielle du lavement des pieds," in *L'homme devant Dieu* (Mélanges H. de Lubac; Paris: Aubier, 1963), I, 75–91.
Grossouw, W. K., "A Note on John xiii 1–3," NovT 8 (1966), 124–31.
Haring, N. M., "Historical Notes on the Interpretation of John 13:10," CBQ 13 (1951), 355–80.
Knox, W. L., "John 13. 1–30," HTR 43 (1950), 161–63.
Lazure, N., "Le lavement des pieds," *Assemblées du Seigneur* 38 (1967), 40–51.
Lohmeyer, E., "Die Fusswaschung," ZNW 38 (1939), 74–94.
Michl, J., "Der Sinn der Fusswaschung," *Biblica* 40 (1959), 697–708.
Richter, G., "Die Fusswaschung Joh 13, 1–20," MüTZ 16 (1965), 13–26. English summary in TD 14 (1966), 200–5.

—— *Die Fusswaschung im Johannesevangelium* (Regensburg: Pustet, 1967).

Robinson, J. A. T., "The Significance of the Foot-washing," NTPat, pp. 144–47.

Schwank, B., "Exemplum dedi vobis. Die Fusswaschung (13, 1–17)," SeinSend 28 (1963), 4–17.

—— " 'Einer von euch wird mich verraten' (13, 18–30)," SeinSend 28 (1963), 52–66.

Sparks, H. F. D., "St. John's Knowledge of Matthew: The Evidence of Jo. 13, 16 and 15, 20," JTS n.s. 3 (1952), 58–61.

von Campenhausen, H., "Zur Auslegung von Joh 13, 6–10," ZNW 33 (1934), 259–71.

Weiser A., "Joh 13, 12–20—Zufügung eines späteren Herausgebers?" BZ 12 (1968), 252–57.

Wilcox, M., "The Composition of John 13:21–30," *Neotestamentica et Semitica*, in honor of M. Black, eds. E. E. Ellis, M. Wilcox (Edinburgh: Clark, 1969), pp. 143–56.

48. THE LAST DISCOURSE:
GENERAL REMARKS

In general the question of how to divide the parts of the Book of Glory (p. 542 above) is not nearly so difficult as was the question of the division of the Book of Signs. This difference is exemplified in an article on the structure of John by D. Deeks, NTS 15 (1968–69), 107–29: while Deeks' analysis of the structure of John i–xii differs in many details from the one we gave in vol. 29, pp. CXXXVIII–CXLIV (of which he seems unaware), an almost identical analysis is proposed for John xiii–xx. The only major problem in the structure of the Book of Glory is the division of the long discourse that runs, with occasional short interruptions, from xiii 31 to xvii 26. The origin, composition, and division of this Last Discourse requires an extended discussion.

In the Book of Signs we noted John's tendency to narrate first the story of Jesus' sign and to follow this with a discourse that would interpret the sign, for example, chs. v, vi, and ix. In the Book of Glory the pattern is reversed. The Last Discourse explains the significance and implications of the greatest of Jesus' deeds, namely, his return to his Father; but it precedes what it explains. The reason for this change of pattern is easy to see: it would be awkward to interrupt the action of the passion, death, and resurrection; and it would be anticlimactic to place so long a discourse after the resurrection. Moreover, in the psychology guiding the evangelist's presentation, since the disciples would be affected by Jesus' passion and death, they had to be prepared for this by Jesus' explanation and consolation. (We shall mention below the possibility that the evangelist was guided by an older tradition of a discourse by Jesus at the Last Supper.)

Yet the Last Discourse is not simply another discourse interpreting a sign. Jesus' death and resurrection break out of the category of sign into the realm of glory; now he makes present and available to men the heavenly realities signified in the miracles of the ministry. Correspondingly the Last Discourse partakes of the glory of "the hour" and surpasses in nobility and majesty even the most solemn discourses of the ministry. The latter were often directed to hostile audiences ("the Jews") and were delivered against a background of rejection by the world. But in the Last Discourse Jesus speaks to "his own" (xiii 1) for whom he is willing to lay down his life, so intense is his love (xv 13). The Jesus who speaks here transcends time and space; he is a Jesus who is already on his way to the Father, and

his concern is that he shall not abandon those who believe in him but must
remain in the world (xiv 18, xvii 11). Although he speaks at the Last
Supper, he is really speaking from heaven; although those who hear him
are his disciples, his words are directed to Christians of all times. The
Last Discourse is Jesus' last testament: it is meant to be read after he has
left the earth. Yet it is not like other last testaments, which are the recorded words of men who are dead and can speak no more; for whatever
there may be of *ipsissima verba* in the Last Discourse has been transformed
in the light of the resurrection and through the coming of the Paraclete
into a living discourse delivered, not by a dead man, but by the one who
has life (vi 57), to all readers of the Gospel.

Because of this it has been wisely said that the Last Discourse is best
understood when it is the subject of prayerful meditation and that scientific
analysis does not really do justice to this work of genius. Just as a great
painting loses its beauty when the individual parts are studied under a mi-
croscope, so the necessary discussion of the composition and division of the
Last Discourse may tend to mar the over-all realization that one is dealing
with a masterpiece. We shall have to point out its monotony of style,
repetitions, confusing time perspective, and almost irreconcilable variety of
expectations about the post-resurrectional presence of Jesus with his disciples. Yet none of this should prevent the reader from recognizing that the
Last Discourse is one of the greatest compositions in religious literature.
The one who speaks here speaks as no man has spoken.

The Composite Nature of the Discourse

There can be no doubt that the chapters that form the Last Discourse
were not always united. Already in Luke we see at work the tendency to
incorporate into the Last Supper material from the ministry proper (compare Luke xxii 24–26 with Mark x 42–45). The Christian Eucharist, which
recalled the Last Supper, provided an opportunity for preaching and teaching; and the use of this occasion to gather together traditional sayings of
Jesus may have had its effect on the narrative of the Supper itself. Such a
tendency would be at work especially in John's Gospel; for the fact that
the public ministry was consistently portrayed as an encounter with unbe-
lievers or partial believers would give impetus for bringing sayings directed
toward believers into the Book of Glory where Jesus is dealing with "his
own." Thus the Last Discourse is undoubtedly composed of varied material
suitable to a setting in which Jesus is speaking to his disciples.

Let us list the details that call into question the consecutiveness of
the Discourse and betray the artificial character of the present organization:

(a) The words of xiv 30–31 ("I shall no longer speak [much] with
   you. . . . Get up! Let us leave here and be on our way.") clearly
   mark the end of a discourse and Jesus' departure from the table.

Yet Jesus continues to speak for three more chapters, and only in xviii 1 does the departure seem to have been accomplished.

(b) One part of the Discourse does not agree with another part. In xiii 36 Simon Peter asks, "Lord, where are you going?" Yet in xvi 5 Jesus complains to the disciples, "Not one of you asks me, 'Where are you going?'"

(c) There are duplications and repetitions in the Last Discourse. We shall give below a chart (I) of the parallels between xiii 31 – xiv 31 and xvi 4b–33. Such repetition is hard to explain if these sections were originally consecutive parts of the same Discourse.

(d) Some of the material that appears in the Last Discourse resembles closely material that the Synoptic Gospels place in the public ministry. For the parallels between xv 18 – xvi 4a and Matt x 17–25 see p. 694 below. Of course the Synoptic localization of such material is not necessarily more original, but the difference in localization suggests that at least some of the parallel material was not always associated with the Last Supper.

(e) Some of the material in the Discourse, like the allegorical parable of the vine in xv 1–6, has no necessary connection with the theme of Jesus' departure that is characteristic of the Last Supper (see p. 666 below).

(f) The variety of theological outlook found in the Last Discourse is most difficult to explain if all the sayings were delivered at the same time. The different expectations about how Jesus will return are a good example of this difficulty; see pp. 602–3 below.

Various Theories about the Composition of the Discourse

How then did the Last Discourse take its present form if it was not originally a unity? A very conservative solution has been suggested for problem (a) above. Some have proposed that Jesus really did leave the supper room after what he said in xiv 30–31 and that the rest of the Discourse was spoken on his way to the garden of Gethsemane on the other side of the Kidron (xviii 1). Thus his remarks about the vine and the branches were suggested by the sight of vineyards dotting the slopes leading down into the Kidron valley, and the warning in xv 6 ("a branch . . . which they collect and throw into the fire to be burned") was prompted by the sight of pyres of dead branches being burned by the vinedressers. Such a romantic approach, dependent on unrecorded stage directions, has been almost universally abandoned today. Not only does it fail to solve the other problems about the Last Discourse, but it does not even do justice to xviii 1 which says that only after the words in xvii did Jesus go *out*.

Rearrangement is an approach to solving problems (a) and (b). If xiv 30 and 31 are moved to the end of the Discourse, then naturally these verses can serve as an appropriate conclusion for the whole. If xvi 5 is replaced so that it comes before xiii 36, the seeming contradiction disappears. Bernard, for instance, proposes the following arrangement: xv, xvi, xiii 31–38, xiv, xvii. Moffatt agrees substantially but moves the half-verse xiii 31a to the front; and in the light of xiv 31 he proposes that ch. xvii was spoken by Jesus standing, before he left the room. Bultmann has a different arrangement: xvii, xiii 31–35, xv, xvi, xiii 36–38, xiv. We have already expressed our misgivings about rearrangement as an adequate solution for the difficulties found in John (vol. 29, pp. XXVI–XXVII). If one were to object that the Last Discourse is a special problem and that rearrangement might work at least here, he would still have to tell us how the present sequence with its presumed displacements came into being and why the obvious lack of sequence did not disturb the final redactor of the Gospel. If we say that a 1st-century redactor erroneously put displaced fragments into the present order, can we seriously suppose that he did not see that xiv 30–31 marked the end of the Discourse and could not be put in the middle? Moreover, rearrangement does nothing to solve the other problems listed above under (c) to (f) and so at best can be only a partial solution.

Many today think of the Last Discourse as composed of independent smaller discourses or even of individual sayings, some of which were uttered by Jesus on another occasion. But within this view there is a wide spectrum of theories ranging from the very radical to the very conservative. At one extreme, some scholars would suggest that the evangelist developed his Discourse on the basis of a few authentic sayings of Jesus borrowed from the Synoptic tradition; the rest was the evangelist's creative commentary. Bultmann has a different approach: the backbone of the Discourse came from the early Gnostic, non-Christian, Revelatory Discourse Source (vol. 29, p. XXIX; for Bultmann's reconstruction of this borrowed material see Smith, pp. 30–34). At the other extreme, conservative commentators propose that the Discourse is composed from a speech given verbatim by Jesus at the Last Supper and speeches given verbatim on other occasions. For instance, W. J. P. Boyd, *Theology* 70 (1967), 207–11, proposes that the original context of John xiv–xvii was post-resurrectional, for these chapters belong to the literary genre known as "Conversations between Jesus and his disciples after the resurrection." More specifically, J. Hammer (*Bibel und Kirche* 14 [1959], 33–40) thinks that chapters xv–xvi represent what was said by the risen Jesus when he appeared to the five hundred brethren (I Cor xv 6), while xvii was spoken in Jesus' final appearance just before he ascended into heaven. Hammer is attempting to deal with a real problem, namely, the strange use of tenses in the Discourse, especially in xvii, whereby Jesus seems to be looking back on his return to his Father as something already accomplished (xvii 11: "I am no longer in the world"). That parts of the Last Discourse do have a post-resurrectional air is reflected in the ancient liturgical practice of the Greek, Syrian, and Latin churches of reading pericopes from the Discourse in the season after Easter.

Yet Hammer's solution is oversimplified and does not answer the acute problem mentioned under (c) above.

As a general guideline we think that literary criticism makes it most implausible that the Last Discourse consists to any great extent of complete speeches given on other occasions and simply transferred to the setting of the Last Supper. The largest blocks of material that have come as substantial units into the Discourse from other contexts are, in our judgment, the allegorical parable in xv 1–6 and the unit that deals with the world's hatred of the disciples in xv 18–xvi 4a, although the latter has accretions adapting to its present setting. Otherwise the atmosphere shared by all parts of the Discourse means that whatever material has been taken from elsewhere has been reworked and amalgamated with material traditionally belonging to the Last Supper context. We cannot exclude the possibility that some of the independent sayings incorporated into the Last Discourse may have originally been transmitted in a post-resurrectional context, but we regard any regular recourse to such a possibility as an inadequate solution to the problem of the peculiar time-perspective of the Discourse. There are different temporal standpoints in the Last Discourse: sometimes Jesus looks ahead to his departure and union with the Father; sometimes he looks back on it. But instances of the latter are not necessarily post-resurrectional sayings; rather they reflect the incursion of the temporal viewpoint of the composer. For the evangelist, Jesus' return to the Father had been accomplished long before; he and his readers were living in the era when Jesus had come back to men in and through the Paraclete. Since he thinks in the gospel of Jesus as speaking to the readers, their viewpoint has become part of the historical setting. Dodd, *Interpretation*, p. 397, describes the situation thus: "The whole series of discourses, including dialogues, monologues, and the prayer in which it culminates, is conceived as taking place within the moment of fulfillment. It is true that the dramatic setting is that of 'the night in which he was betrayed', with the crucifixion in prospect. Yet in a real sense it is the risen and glorified Christ who speaks."

The parts of the Last discourse were probably formed in the same manner as other Johannine discourses (vol. 29, pp. xxxiv–xxxv; Stage 2); traditional sayings of Jesus directed to his disciples, which had been preserved in various contexts, were woven into connected speech on a particular theme; then the units of speech were woven into larger compositions. At times we can still see the seams where disparate units were joined, for example, between xiv 1–4 and xiv 6 ff. Perhaps the guiding themes of the compositions were supplied by a core of material that from its earliest formation was associated with the context of the Last Supper. It is true that there is no tradition in Mark and Matthew of a discourse delivered by Jesus at the Supper, but Luke xxii 21–38 has a post-eucharistic collection of sayings, some of which may have belonged originally to this setting. Moreover, the Synoptics have the tradition of Jesus' praying to his

Father in Gethsemane, corresponding to the prayer that John has at the conclusion of the Discourse. In discussing John vi (vol. 29, pp. 275, 238), we saw that while the Synoptics had only slight traces of an explanation of the multiplication of the loaves, John had a fully developed explanatory Discourse; and the same phenomenon may be present here. At any rate, themes adapted to the Supper context (departure and return; a legacy of commandments and love; intercession before the Father) have colored and modified all the other traditional sayings that were brought into the present context. In this manner *several independent last discourses* were formed, and eventually these were combined into the Last Discourse as we know it. These independent last discourses supply the key to the division of xiii 31 – xvii 26.

The Divisions of the Last Discourse (see Outline, pp. 545–47 above)

(What follows is proposed in light of the theory of Gospel composition advanced in vol. 29, pp. XXXV–XXXIX; Stages 3–4–5.) The first, or at least an early, written form of the Gospel (Stage 3) probably contained a last discourse consisting of an introduction (xiii 31–38) and a final address of Jesus to his disciples substantially similar to what is now xiv. This last discourse would have been concluded with the signal for the end of the Supper in xiv 31. However, we cannot be certain that all the sayings now found in xiii 31 – xiv 31 were in this primitive last discourse, for some modifications of this material may have been introduced in the evangelist's own editing of the Gospel (Stage 4) or in the final redaction of the Gospel (Stage 5). Nevertheless, this early last discourse remains substantially as **Division 1** of the final Last Discourse. We call attention to the fact that, along with Dodd, we treat xiii 31–38 as the introductory part of Division 1 rather than as an introduction to the whole Discourse (xiv–xvii). The latter position is taken by many scholars (Lagrange, Schneider, Barrett), and we shall discuss the question in detail on pp. 608–9 below.

Additional discourse material was joined to the primitive last discourse by the final redactor. Not feeling free to rewrite the evangelist's own work, he did not change the ending of xiv; rather he tacked more discourses on to what already was part of the Gospel. The material in these added discourses is not necessarily inferior to or later than the material of Division 1; for in our theory of Gospel composition we have insisted that the redactor was incorporating other genuinely Johannine material, some of it ancient, some of it stemming from the evangelist himself, but for one reason or another not previously made part of the Gospel in stages 3 and 4.

The longest addition constituted what is now **Division 2** of the Last Discourse (xv–xvi), a larger collection of material than that contained in Division 1. The origins of the material in Division 2 were quite diverse and we shall distinguish three subdivisons:

(a) *The first subdivision* is xv 1–17. This consists of an allegorical parable on the vine and the branches (xv 1–6) with an accompanying explanation of which traces appear in xv 7, 16. But the explanation has been adapted to the context of the Last Supper by the addition of appropriate departure themes, forming the beautiful complex in xv 7–17. The dominant theme is that love should unite the disciples to Jesus and to one another.

(b) *The second subdivision* is xv 18 – xvi 4a. The dominant theme here is the hatred of the world for Jesus and his disciples. The material was largely taken from a body of independent tradition about future persecution very similar to the tradition found in Matt x 17–25 and in the Synoptic Eschatological Discourse (Mark xiii and par.).

(c) *The third subdivision* is xvi 4b–33. It is very closely parallel in content and organization to the form of the last discourse found in xiii 31 – xiv 31. We shall discuss this similarity in a chart, but we may point out that this subdivision is the only part of Division 2 that has interruptions by the disciples, a feature found in Division 1. Consequently only in this subdivision, as in Division 1, is there any reference to a setting where the disciples were Jesus' audience at a supper table; in the first and second subdivisions of Division 2 we have straight discourse spoken to the disciples without any indication of setting.

The reader may wonder why we suggest that the three parts, (a), (b), and (c), should be treated as subdivisions of one discourse (Division 2), rather than as separate discourses. The reason is that while these units had independent origins, there has been a real editorial effort to bind them together. The theme of choosing the disciples in (a) overlaps into (b); cf. xv 16 and 19. The theme of love in (a) is matched by the theme of hatred in (b). The theme of the world's opposition in (b) prepares the way for the description of the Paraclete as the prosecutor of the world in (c).

Turning to **Division 3** of the Last Discourse, the great sacerdotal prayer in xvii, we find a tightly knit whole. If material of diverse origin has gone into xvii, that material has been welded together more smoothly than in any other division or subdivision of the Discourse. Chapter xvii is Jesus' prayer in the hour of his return to his Father, and the redactor showed a touch of genius in putting it at the end of the Discourse. Its soaring, lyrical quality provides a perfect climax, whereas almost any other unit that could have been added here might have been flat and anticlimactic. Of course, in localizing the prayer at the end, the redactor may have been guided by the traditional pattern seen in the Synoptics which reported Jesus' prayer to his Father (in Gethsemane) just before his arrest. The following features in the Synoptic tradition of this prayer (Mark xiv 35–36) have parallels in John: the address, "Father"; the theme of "the hour"; the theme of conformity to the Father's will (John xiv 31).

By way of concluding our discussion of the divisions of the Last Discourse, we may compare our results with those of two quite different approaches to the problem. Zimmermann, *art. cit.*, finds a difference of theme in xiii–xiv and xv–xvi respectively: chs. xiii–xiv are concerned with Jesus' departure, while chs. xv–xvi are concerned with Jesus' enduring presence among his disciples. Zimmermann thinks of two discourses: chs. xiii–xiv situated in the perspective of the period before Jesus' departure, and chs. xv–xvi situated in the perspective of the period after Jesus has gone to the Father. The prayer of ch. xvii is uttered by Jesus as a heavenly Paraclete or intercessor with the Father, appealing on behalf of his own who are still in the world. Richter, *art. cit.*, detects two thematic strains in the material under discussion. The first is the christological or soteriological theme wherein Jesus effects salvation by carrying out the will of his Father, and his death on the cross shows him to be the Messiah and Saviour. The atmosphere is apologetic and confessional, underlining faith in Jesus as the Messiah in order both to answer the objections of outsiders and to strengthen the wavering faith of insiders. Since this theme matches the statement of purpose in xx 31, the evangelist himself is responsible for the parts of the Last Supper scene in which it is found (xiii 2–10, 21–33, 36–38, xiv, xvii 1–5). The second theme, prominent in the work of the editor or redactor, is paraenetic or morally exhortatory: Jesus lays down his life in death out of love for his own, and his example should be imitated. Here the appeal is not primarily for faith but for love and the living out of the commandments. This theme, which is harmonious with the spirit of I John, marks xiii 1, 12–20, 34–35, xv–xvi, xvii 6–26. It is characteristic of a later stage in the development of the Johannine community once it had become more settled doctrinally. We note that in the theories of both Zimmermann and Richter the substance of xiii 31 – xiv 31 is attributed to a different discourse or stage of composition from that represented by the substance of xv–xvii. Both authors allow for difference of perspective in the two bodies of material.

The Special Relationship between xiii 31 – xiv 31 and xvi 4b–33

Having considered the three main divisions of the Last Discourse, let us give more attention to the relationship between Division 1 and the third subdivision of Division 2. The accompanying Chart I will show how many verses are parallel in these two units. By way of general parallels, we note that the over-all structure of the two is roughly the same. Both begin with the theme of Jesus' imminent departure. The question of where he is going and the motif of the sorrow of the disciples soon appear. Each unit has two Paraclete passages; each promises that shortly the disciples will see Jesus again and that the Father will love the disciples; each assures the disciples in Jesus' name that whatever is asked will be granted. In each Jesus is interrupted by questions from the disciples, and in each

CHART I: THE PARALLELS BETWEEN xvi 4b–33 AND xiii 31–xiv 31

xiii 31 – xiv 31	xvi 4b–33	OTHER PERTINENT PARALLELS
xiv 28: "You have heard me tell you, 'I am going away'. . . . If you loved me, you would rejoice that I am going to the Father"	5–7: "Now I am going to Him who sent me. . . . Just because I have said this to you, your hearts are full of sadness. . . . it is for your own good that I go away"	
xiii 36: "'Lord,' said Simon Peter, 'where are you going?'" xiv 5: "'Lord,' said Thomas, 'we don't know where you are going'"	5: "Yet not one of you asks me, 'Where are you going?'"	
xiv 1: "Do not let your hearts be troubled" Also xiv 27.	6: "Your hearts are full of sadness"	
xiv 15–17: *First Paraclete Passage*	7–11: *First Paraclete Passage*	
xiv 16: "The Father will give you another Paraclete" xiv 26: "The Father will send (him) in my name"	7: "I shall send him to you"	xv 26: "I shall send (him) to you from the Father"
xiv 17: "The world cannot accept (him)"	8: "He will prove the world wrong"	
xiv 12: "I am going [poreuesthai] to the Father"	10: "I am going [hypagein] to the Father." Also 28 with poreuesthai	
xiv 30: "The Prince of the world is coming"	11: "The Prince of this world has been condemned"	xii 31: "Now will the Prince of this world be driven out"
xiv 30: "I shall no longer speak [much] with you"	12: "I have much more to tell you, but you cannot bear it now"	

xiii 31 – xiv 31	xvi 4b–33	Other Pertinent Parallels
xiii 31: *Second Paraclete Passage*	13–15: *Second Paraclete Passage*	
xiv 26: "The Paraclete, the Holy Spirit, that the Father will send" xiv 17: "He is the Spirit of Truth"	13: "When he comes, however, being the Spirit of Truth"	xv 26: "When the Paraclete comes, the Spirit of Truth"
xiv 26: "(He) will teach you everything" (xiv 6: Jesus says: "I am the way and the truth") (xiv 10: Jesus says: "The words that I say to you men are not spoken on my own")	13: "He will guide you along the way of all truth" 13: "He will not speak on his own" 14: "It is from me that he will receive what he will declare to you"	Synoptic Eschatological Discourse (Mark xiii 11; Matt x 20): The Holy Spirit ("of your Father") will speak through the disciples in times of trial
xiv 26: "(He will) remind you of all that I told you [myself]"		xv 26: "He will bear witness on my behalf"
xiv 19: "In just a little while the world will not see me any more; but you will see me"	16: "In a little while you will not see me any more, and then again in a little while you will see me"	
	No real parallels elsewhere to 17–22, with the possible exception of 22: "I shall see you again"	
xiv 18: "I am coming back to you"		
xiv 20: "On that day"	23: "On that day." Also 26	
xiv 14, 13: "If you ask anything of me in my name, I will do it. Whatever you ask in my name, I will do"	23–24: "If you ask anything of the Father, He will give it to you in my name. Until now you have asked nothing in my name. Ask and you shall receive"	xv 7: "Ask for whatever you want and it will be done for you" xv 16: "The Father will give you whatever you ask Him in my name." See pp. 634–35 for Synoptic parallels
No mention of joy, but of peace (xiv 27)	24: "that your joy may be full"	xv 11: "that my joy may be yours and your joy may be fulfilled" xvii 13: "that they may share my joy to the full"

xiii 31 – xiv 31	xvi 4b-33	Other Pertinent Parallels
xiv 25: "I have said this to you"	25: "I have said this to you"	xv 11: "I have said this to you." Also xvi 1, 4 below
xiv 9: "Whoever has seen me has seen the Father"	25: "I shall tell you about the Father in plain words"	
See above on xiv 14, 13	26: "You will ask in my name"	See above on xv 16
xiv 21: "The man who loves me will be loved [agapan] by my Father" xiv 23: "If anyone loves me, he will keep my word. Then my Father will love [agapan] him"	27: "The Father loves [philein] you Himself because you have loved me"	
xiv 12: "I am going to the Father"	28: "I am going to the Father." See above on 10	
	No real parallels elsewhere for 29-31, although there is a similar pattern of interruption by disciples in xiv	No interruptions in the other parts of the Last Discourse (xv, xvii)
xiii 38: To Peter: "The cock will not crow before you deny me three times"	32: "An hour is coming . . . for you to be scattered, each on his own"	In Mark xiv 27-31 (Matt xxvi 31-35) the equivalents of the two Johannine passages are joined together
xiv 29: "I have told you this even before it happens so that . . . you may believe" xiv 27: "'Peace' is my farewell to you"	33: "I have said this to you so that in me you may find peace"	xvi 1: "I have said this to you to prevent your faith from being shaken" xvi 4: "I have said this to you, so that . . . you may remember that I told you"
	33: "In the world you find suffering"	xv 18 – xvi 4a: On the world's hatred for and persecution of the disciples
xiv 27: "Do not be fearful"	33: "Have courage"	
xiv 30: "The Prince of the world . . . has no hold on me"	33: "I have conquered the world"	xii 31 above. Also I John v 4-5

CHART II: SECTIONS OF xiii 31–xiv 31 FOR WHICH THERE ARE NO PARALLELS IN xvi 4b–33.

xiii 31 – xiv 31	PARALLELS ELSEWHERE IN LAST DISCOURSE	OTHER PERTINENT PARALLELS (In John, unless otherwise indicated)
xiii 31-32: Glorification of the Son of Man	xvii 1-5: Glorification of the Son	xi 4: Glorification of the Son [of God]; xii 23, 27-28: Glorification of the Son of Man
xiii 33: "I am to be with you only a little longer"		vii 33; xii 35
xiii 33: "Little children"		Common in I John (ii 1, 12, 28, etc.)
xiii 33: Theme of looking (and not finding) and of inability to follow Jesus		vii 33–34, viii 21
xiii 34–35: New commandment to love one another	xv 12–13, 17	I John ii 7, iii 11, iv 21
xiv 1b–4: Jesus is going to prepare a place; then he will come back to take the disciples along with him	xvii 24: "Where I am, I wish them also to be"	
xiv 6–11: Jesus the way, truth, life		
7: Knowing Jesus=knowing the Father		viii 19
9: Seeing Jesus=seeing the Father		xii 45
10: "I am in the Father and the Father is in me"	xvii 21	x 38
10: Words are not spoken on Jesus' own		xii 49
10: The Father performs Jesus' works		v 19
11: "Believe [me] because of the works"		x 37–38

xiii 31 – xiv 31	PARALLELS ELSEWHERE IN LAST DISCOURSE	OTHER PERTINENT PARALLELS (In John, unless otherwise indicated)
xiv 12: The man with faith performing greater works, combined with theme of asking and receiving in 13–14		Mark xi 23–24: Man of faith can move mountains (combined with theme of asking and receiving)
xiv 15: Loving Jesus and keeping his commandments	xv 10, 14	I John ii 3, iii 24, v 3: Keeping His commandments
xiv 17: The Spirit of Truth "remains with you and is within you"		I John ii 20, 27: The anointing from the Holy One "remains in your hearts"—no need for another teacher. Also II John 2
xiv 20–21: "I am in my Father, and you are in me and I in you," plus the themes of keeping the commandments and of love		I John iii 24, iv 11–13
xiv 24: The word is not Jesus' own, "but comes from the Father who sent me"	vii 16	
xiv 29: "Now I have told you this even before it happens so that, when it does happen, you may believe"	xiii 19	
xiv 31: "I do exactly as the Father has commanded me. . . . Get up! Let us leave"		Gethsemane: Mark xiv 36, 42

there appears the theme of the infidelity of the disciples to Jesus during the passion. We note, of course, that there are some sections in one that have no parallel in the other, whence the value of Chart II.

In vol. 29, pp. xxv, xxxvii, we discussed the phenomenon of duplicate discourses in John, and here seemingly we are dealing with another instance of this phenomenon. The same themes and even the same sayings have been preached, gathered, and written down in two different collections that may stem from different periods in the history of the Johannine tradition or from different circles in the Johannine community. We saw the same process at work in v 19–25 and 26–30, and again in vi 35–50 and 51–58.

Which is the earlier collection? Probably no over-all answer is possible. On the basis of the conclusion supplied by xiv 30–31 we have already suggested that xiii 31 – xiv 31 represents substantially the discourse that stood in the early written form of the Gospel (Stage 3, perhaps with some additional editing in Stage 4) and that xvi 4b–33 was added along with the rest of xv–xvi by the final redactor (Stage 5). But again, we must insist that this does not mean that the material in xvi 4b–33 is necessarily later, since the redactor was preserving and adding Johannine material from all periods, early and late. (Lagrange, pp. 399, 434, thinks that xvi 4b–33 is less developed than xiv 1–31.) Each of the two collections has its share of early traditional sayings of Jesus and each has later developments. Therefore, the two must be compared verse by verse; and a decision as to which is older in each verse is not always possible. For instance, many scholars will suggest that the Paraclete passages in xiv are older than those in xvi because in xiv 16, 26 the Father gives or sends the Paraclete, while in xvi 7 it is Jesus who sends the Paraclete. (Yet how sharp a difference is there between the Father's sending the Paraclete *in Jesus' name* and Jesus' sending him?) Using the same argument, however, one would have to attribute priority to xvi 23–24 (the Father will give what the disciples ask for) over xiv 13–14 (Jesus will do what the disciples ask for). In another comparison, how can one decide whether xvi 5 (none of the disciples ask where Jesus is going) is earlier than xiii 36 and xiv 5 (Peter asks where Jesus is going; Thomas says they do not know where Jesus is going)?

Leaving aside the question of the priority of one of these two collections over the other, we would still maintain that, if they represent last discourses formed independently in different Johannine circles at different times, they may be very helpful guides to the type of material that is most original in the context of the Last Supper. Scholars have often tried to isolate this material using various criteria. Dodd, *Interpretation*, pp. 390–400, has sought, for instance, to distinguish in the present Last Discourse: (I) material that has parallels in the Synoptic Gospels and (II) material that is peculiarly Johannine. Let us follow this method, paying particular attention to instances drawn from the two collections we are now considering.

(I) The material in John's Last Discourse that has Synoptic parallels and similarities may be subdivided according to whether the parallels appear: (A) in the Synoptic accounts of the Last Supper and Gethsemane scenes or (B) elsewhere in the Synoptic Gospels. As for (A), the list of parallels given above on p. 557 will serve; numbers 2–7 in that list are applicable here; and with the exception of 3, these parallels are drawn from xiii 31–xiv 31 or from xvi 4b–33. We would add to that list three parallels between John and the Gethsemane scene:

- The prayer of Jesus in John xvii 1 and Mark xiv 36.
- The coordination of Jesus' will and that of the Father in John xiv 31 and Mark xiv 36.
- The words "Get up! Let us leave" in John xiv 31 and Mark xiv 42.

As for (B), the following parallels and similarities may be given:
- The persecution of the disciples: John xv 18–xvi 4a (also xvi 33); Matt x 17–25: Mark xiii 9–13 (Eschatological Discourse).
- The mention of the Paraclete as one who bears witness through the disciples (John xv 26–27) resembles the mention of the Holy Spirit's speaking through the disciples who will bear witness (Matt x 20; Mark xiii 9–11).
- The theme of asking and receiving (see pp. 634–35 below).
- The idealism of John xv 13 ("to lay down his life for those he loves") resembles Mark x 45: "The Son of Man came . . . to give his life as a ransom for many."
- The Johannine promises that Jesus will return (xiv 3, 18–19, xvi 22) vaguely resemble in theme the Synoptic predictions of the resurrection (Mark viii 31, ix 31, x 34).
- The apocalyptic theme of the coming of the Son of Man found in the Synoptic Gospels seems to be reinterpreted in terms of realized eschatology in John (see discussion of xiv 2–4).
- The confession of Jesus as the one who has come forth from God (xvi 30) has a distant resemblance to Peter's confession in Mark viii 29; but there are better parallels to that confession in John i 41–42, vi 68–69.

Evaluating these similarities between John and the Synoptics is difficult. They certainly help to show that John is drawing on traditional material, but it is more difficult to use them to determine themes that were original in the Last Supper setting. Only those under (A) are much help in this regard, and it is interesting that most of those are parallels to xiii 31–xiv 31 or to xvi 4b–33, the units that we suggest as the key to the Last Discourse. As for the parallels under (B), we note that the last three similarities to material in John xiii 31–xiv 31 and xvi 4b–33 are very weak, while the preceding similarities to material in John xv are much stronger. This is probably because xv 1–xvi 4a is a composite largely made up of material not originally related to the Last Supper.

(II) We can also subdivide the material that is peculiarly Johannine and without Synoptic parallels:

(A) Material that xiii 31 – xiv 31 and xvi 4b–33 have in common. See Chart I.

(B) Material found only in one of the two collections but with parallels elsewhere in the Last Discourse. See Charts I and II.

(C) Material found only in one of the two collections but with parallels elsewhere in Johannine writings, for example, in the discourses of the Book of Signs or in the Johannine Epistles. See Chart II.

(D) Material found only in one of the two collections and with no other Johannine parallels, for example, the statement in xvi 29 that Jesus is now speaking plainly without figures of speech.

There is no way to decide scientifically if the (D) material is original in the Last Supper setting, and obviously (C) material has less chance than either (A) or (B) of being original in this setting. If a small core of sayings traditionally connected with the Last Supper was being expanded by the evangelist or others into a formal last discourse, the addition and readaptation of material from discourses of the ministry would be likely. Boismard would maintain, for instance, that xiv 6–11 is posterior in composition to the parallel material in the earliest form of viii. He also suggests (RB 68 [1961], 519–20) that in xiv 15–23 there has been much rewriting of earlier material under the influence of I John.

Even within the (A) and (B) material some choice may have to be made as to what is original in the Last Supper context. The eschatology of xiv 2–3 seems to be the final eschatology of the expectation of the parousia in glory, while xiv 18 ff. seems to refer to realized eschatology and divine indwelling. If the latter is a later stage of Johannine thought than the former (vol. 29, pp. cxvi–cxxi), the sayings cannot both be original in the last discourse. A special attempt has been made by J. Schneider, art. cit., to isolate the more primitive nucleus of material in xiv from a later stratum of material (both the work of one hand). He suggests that the two Paraclete passages (xiv 16–18, 26) are later and also xiv 19–20 (because 15 should be followed by 21). This method depends on the interpreter's feeling for what is consecutive in John: obviously xiv 15 and 21 are related, but is the relation so close that all that is between must be regarded as secondary? One may agree that the Paraclete passages as they now stand represent a late level of Johannine thought; nevertheless, since they appear in two presumably independent last discourses (xiii 31 – xiv 31, xvi 4b–33), one may well wonder if some tradition about the Spirit was not part of the Johannine tradition of the last discourse from very early times. If we had to select from (A) and (B) the material most likely to be original in the Last Supper context, it would have to include the themes of departure (*hypagein, poreuesthai, erchesthai*), of the consolation of the disciples, and of the promises for the future after the departure. (See Dodd, *Interpretation*, p. 403; Schneider, *art. cit.,* p. 108.)

These themes, combined with the material given above in (I) under (A), should appear in any reconstruction of the primitive last discourse.

The Literary Genre of the Last Discourse.

If the final redactor of the Gospel produced the present Last Discourse by adding discourses to the last discourse that he found already in an early form of the Gospel, was he guided by any literary plan? For those who see patterns of sevens in the Fourth Gospel (vol. 29, p. cxlii), it is noteworthy that there are seven references to the disciples' asking or receiving "in my name" (xiv 13, 14, 26, xv 16, xvi 23, 24, 26). Others who are partial to chiastic patterns (vol. 29, p. cxxxv) may be able to detect one in the final form of the Last Discourse:

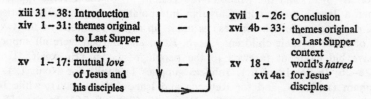

    xiii 31 – 38: Introduction   xvii 1 – 26: Conclusion
    xiv 1 – 31: themes original   xvi 4b – 33: themes original
                 to Last Supper   to Last Supper
                 context   context
    xv   1 – 17: mutual *love*   xv 18 –   world's *hatred*
                 of Jesus and   xvi 4a: for Jesus'
                 his disciples   disciples

However, both in the instances of the sevens and in the discovery of this chiastic pattern we may be dealing more with the interpreter's ingenuity than with the final redactor's intent. For instance, the similarity between the introduction and conclusion is scarcely obvious.

Laying aside the question of literary plan and turning to that of literary genre, we have mentioned the possibility that in the pre-Gospel tradition on which the evangelist drew there may have been a short address delivered by Jesus to his disciples on the night before he died. However, the idea of composing a solemn discourse before death, attested in the various independent discourses that we have posited (xiii 31 – xiv 31, xiv–xvi, xvii) and in the final composite Last Discourse, was probably prompted by more than historical reminiscence. Some have thought that the idea of combining the description of the meal with an esoteric discourse and an intercessory prayer (xvii) was suggested by the liturgy. Schneider, *art. cit.*, and W. Grundmann, NovT 3 (1959), 63, suggest that John xiii–xvii reflects an early Christian Last Supper liturgy. Hoskyns, p. 495, says: "It may be that the structure of chs. xiii–xvii corresponds with the structure of Christian worship at the time when the gospel was written, in which the scene in the Upper Room was reproduced and creatively interpreted by spiritual teachings (chs. xiv–xvi) and finally summed up in a comprehensive Eucharistic prayer (ch. xvii)." Such a hypothesis is interesting but difficult to prove.

We prefer an approach that can be verified by contemporary evidence and join those scholars (W. Bauer, O. Michel, Käsemann, etc.) who think that the Last Discourse exemplifies the well-established literary pattern of attributing to famous men farewell speeches delivered before death. This literary genre has been carefully studied (see Bibliography); in particular we are dependent here on Munck's analysis of the development of the farewell speech within Judaism and by Stauffer's tables of parallels.

The farewell speech had already made its appearance in the earlier books of the OT, for instance, the farewell and blessings of Jacob to his children in Gen xlvii 29 – xlix 33; Joshua's farewell to Israel in Josh xxii–xxiv; David's farewell in I Chron xxviii–xxix. Perhaps the most important example from the pre-exilic period would be Deuteronomy where the whole book is made up of Moses' farewell speeches to Israel. This literary genre became even more popular in the late biblical and the intertestamental periods. Tobit's deathbed farewell to Tobias is recorded in Tob xiv 3–11, and the whole of the *Testaments of the Twelve Patriarchs* (either a Jewish work with Christian interpolations or an early Christian work drawing on Jewish sources) is made up of the farewells of the twelve sons of Jacob to their children. Enoch, Ezra, and Baruch were all supposed to have bid eloquent farewell to the people of Israel (En xci ff.; II Esd xiv 28–36; II Bar lxxvii ff.). Jubilees supplies farewells for Noah (x), for Abraham (xx–xxii), and for Rebecca and Isaac (xxxv–xxxvi), while Josephus supplies one for Moses (*Ant.* IV.viii.45–47;⌗309–26). In the NT the speech of Paul to the elders of Ephesus (Acts xx 17–38) is a type of farewell speech. This genre is also attested in the epistolary literature; for instance, the Pastorals are a form of Pauline farewell (especially II Tim iii 1 – iv 8), and II Peter is a form of Petrine farewell (even if pseudonymous). The eschatological discourses in the Synoptic Gospels have certain elements in common with this literary genre, but we shall discuss them separately below.

We shall now list the features of these biblical and post-biblical farewell speeches that are found also in John's Last Discourse. The common situation is that of a great man who gathers together his followers (his children, his disciples, or the people) on the eve of his death to give them instructions that will help them after his departure. In John this occurs in the setting of a final meal; and a meal precedes death also in Jub xxxv 27 (Rebecca), xxxvi 17 (Isaac), and *Testament of Naphtali* i 2.

■ The speaker announces the imminence of his departure. In Jub xxxvi 1, Isaac says, "My sons, I am going the way of my fathers to the eternal house where my fathers are." Zebulun (*Testament of Zebulun* x 4) says, "I am now hastening away to my rest." The theme of "I am going away" is a recurring one in the Johannine Last Discourse. In particular, in xiv 2–3 Jesus speaks of going to his Father's house, and in xiii 33 and xvi 16 he stresses that his departure will come after only a little while.

■ Occasionally this announcement produces sorrow, and some form of reassurance is necessary. In Jub xxii 23, Abraham tells Jacob, "Do not be fearful"; and Enoch (xcii 2) advises his children, "Let not your spirit be troubled." In *Testament of Zebulun* x 1–2, the patriarch says, "Grieve not that I am dying . . . for I shall rise again in the midst of you . . . and I shall rejoice." On several occasions in John (xiv 1, 27, xvi 6–7, 22) Jesus tells his disciples not to be troubled or sad, and in xiv 27 he adds, "Do not be fearful." He assures them that if he is going away, he is also coming back (xiv 3, 18, xvi 16), and this return will be an occasion of joy for them (xv 11, xvi 22).

▪ In the earlier OT farewells the speaker tends to support his instructions by recalling what God has done for Israel, but in the later Jewish examples it became more customary for the speaker to recall his own past life, for example, *Testaments*. In his farewell speech Mattathias, father of the Maccabees, reminds his sons of what he has done for Israel and urges them to emulate his deeds (*Ant.* XII.vi.3;※279–84). In John, Jesus recalls some of the specific things he has said (xiii 33, xv 20) and recalls his words and works in general (xiv 10, xv 3, xvii 4–8). In particular, Jesus speaks of the Paraclete/Spirit whose task it will be to interpret for the disciples what Jesus has said and done (xiv 26, xvi 14–15). In xiv 12 Jesus promises, "The man who has faith in me will perform the same works that I perform. In fact, he will perform far greater than these."

▪ The directive to keep God's commandments is often part of the advice passed on by the speaker, for instance, by Abraham in Jub xxi 5. Moses (Deut xxx 16) insists on this as a necessary condition: "If you obey the commandments of the Lord your God, which I command you this day, by loving the Lord your God. . . ." Sometimes the speaker mentions his own commandments or word. Enoch xciv 5 has the command: "Hold fast my words." In John, Jesus frequently repeats the condition: "If you love me and keep my commandments . . ." (xiv 15, 21, xv 10, 14). In xiv 23 he says, "If anyone loves me, he will keep my word."

▪ In particular, the speaker often commands his children to love one another, for instance, Abraham in Jub xx 2. In Jub xxxvi 3–4, Isaac says to Esau and Jacob: "And this I command you, . . . love one another, my sons, . . . as a man loves his own life." In John xiii 34, xv 12, Jesus speaks of the new commandment to love one another; and in xv 13 he sets a standard, "No man can have greater love than this: to lay down his life for those he loves." See p. 611 below.

▪ Unity is another frequent theme in the later forms of the farewell speeches. In Jub xxxvi 17, Isaac rejoices that there is one mind between his children; also see Mattathias in *Ant.* XII.vi.3;※283. Baruch stresses the unity among the tribes, "bound by one bond" (II Bar lxxviii 4). In the *Testaments*, Zebulun viii 5–6 urges Zebulun's children to love one another, for evil done to one's brother violates unity; and *Joseph* xvii 3 says, "God delights in the unity of the brethren." This same theme of unity appears on the lips of Jesus in John xvii 11, 21–23.

■ The speaker tends to look into the future and to see the fate that will befall his children. Enoch (xci 1) says, "The spirit is poured out on me that I may show you everything that shall befall you forever." In John, although Jesus himself makes general predictions about the future, it is the Paraclete/Spirit that Jesus will send who will declare to the disciples the things to come (xvi 13).

■ In looking to the future the speaker curses those who persecute the just and rejoice in their tribulation (En xcv 7, xcviii 13, c 7). Correspondingly Jesus predicts that the world will hate and persecute the disciples (John xv 18, 20; xvi 2–3) and will rejoice at his own death (xvi 20).

■ The speaker may call down peace upon his children (Jub xxi 25: "Go, my son, in peace") and promise ultimate joy in the next life (En ciii 3; *Testament of Judah* xxv 4). Jesus also gives his disciples his peace (John xiv 27, xvi 33) and promises them joy that no one can take from them (xvi 22).

■ The speaker may promise to his children that God will be close to them if they are faithful. With the caution that there are Christian interpolations in the *Testaments,* we should note *Joseph* x 2, "If you follow modesty, . . . the Lord will dwell in you," and xi 1, "For everyone who observes the Law of the Lord shall be loved by Him." One is reminded of John xiv 23, "If anyone loves me, he will keep my word. Then my Father will love him, and we shall come to him and make our dwelling place with him."

■ It is natural for a dying man to worry about the endurance of his name. In Jub xxii 24, Abraham says in reference to his descendants, "This house I have built for myself that I might put my name upon it on the earth. . . . You will build my house and establish my name before God forever." The Johannine Jesus also speaks of the name that God has given to him (xvii 11–12); and he says, "I revealed your name to the men whom you gave me out of the world" (xvii 6). These men will pray and make requests of God in Jesus' name (xiv 13, 14, xv 16, xvi 24, 26) and thus keep his name alive upon the earth.

■ As part of Moses' farewell to Israel, he picks as a successor Joshua who in many ways will be another Moses (Deut xxxi 23). We shall point out in Appendix V that this tandem relationship resembles the relationship between Jesus and the Paraclete. The Paraclete about whom Jesus speaks in the Last Discourse is his successor and carries on his work.

■ Finally the speaker often closes his farewell address with a prayer for his children or for the people he is leaving behind. In Deut xxxii Moses calls down God's blessing on the tribes, and in Jub xxii 28–30 Abraham prays to God to protect Jacob. So also the Johannine Last Discourse is terminated by chapter xvii where Jesus prays for himself, for his disciples, and for all those who will come to believe in him through his disciples' word.

From this survey of parallel themes it seems certain that the Last Discourse of the Fourth Gospel belongs to the literary genre of the farewell speech. Dodd, *Interpretation*, pp. 420–23, has compared the Last Discourse to the dialogue in the Hermetic tractates (see vol. 29, pp. LVIII–LIX), and he believes that the readers of the Gospel would have interpreted this Discourse against such a Hellenistic background. It is very difficult to be certain about the mentality of the readers, but we think that the composition of the Discourse can be better explained as an imitation of models well known in Judaism, without necessary recourse to pagan models.

The Last Discourse and Eschatology

Among the Synoptic Gospels only Luke (xxii 24–34) has a collection of sayings of any length at the Last Supper. However, in the Synoptic tradition of the public ministry there is a long final speech of Jesus, namely, the Eschatological Discourse (or the Synoptic Apocalypse: Mark xiii; Matt xxiv–xxv; Luke xxi). There, often in apocalyptic language, Jesus turns his attention to the future. He warns of perils and persecutions to come and of dangers to faith, and he stresses the necessity to keep watch. All will be concluded when the Son of Man comes on the clouds and sends out angels to gather his elect from the four winds (Mark xiii 26–27). In Matt xxiv 45–51 there is an assurance of the graciousness of the master to those whom he finds watching. Finally, Matt xxv 31–46 paints the dramatic scene of judgment where the wicked will be consigned to eternal punishment, while the just will be rewarded with eternal life. This Eschatological Discourse is not exactly a farewell speech, although the farewell speeches in Enoch and II Baruch cited above are interlaced with apocalyptic visions of the endtime.

It has been suggested that the Last Discourse is a Johannine substitute for the Synoptic Eschatological Discourse. With proper modification this thesis touches on truth. One whole subdivision of the Last Discourse, xv 18 – xvi 4a, contains material very similar to that which is found in the Eschatological Discourse (see p. 694 below). A refrain like that of John xiv 29, "But now I have told you this even before it happens so that, when it does happen, you may believe" (also xvi 1, 33) is reminiscent of Mark xiii 23 (Matt xxiv 25): "Take heed, I have told you all things beforehand." But even more important, the theme of Jesus' return, which occurs in many forms in the Last Discourse, may represent a non-apocalyptic Johannine form of the theme of the coming of the Son of Man that we find in the Synoptic Apocalypse. We have already noted that some of the futuristic eschatological elements found in the farewell speeches of Jewish apocalyptic writings appear in John in an atmosphere of realized eschatology. For example, the *Testament of Judah* xxv 4 and En ciii 3 mention joy in the next life as a reward for those who have died in a state of justice; but in John xv 11, xvi 24 this joy seems to be characteristic of Christian life in this world after the resurrection of Jesus.

Let us study in more detail what the Last Discourse says about the return of Jesus. According to the Johannine setting of the Discourse, Jesus is speaking on the eve of his death about what will happen after his death. The Christian reader has a definite belief about what happened after that death, namely, that there was a brief period of post-resurrectional appearances which was followed by a longer period, still continuing, when Jesus was (and is) present through his invisible Spirit, and that the culmination of all this will be the parousia or second coming of Jesus. This belief often unconsciously guides the Christian reader as he interprets the sayings of Jesus about returning that are reported in the Last Discourse; consequently he applies some sayings to the resurrectional appearances, some to the presence of the Spirit, and some to the parousia. But can we assume that this neat sequence was known or predicted during Jesus' lifetime or understood in the first few years of Christianity? If one accepts the evidence of the Gospels that Jesus predicted that he would be victorious over death, one is still not certain how he conceived the victory. The Synoptic Gospels portray Jesus as predicting a resurrection after three days (Mark viii 31, ix 31, x 34, and par.); they picture him as predicting an era when men will be moved by the Holy Spirit (Matt x 20; Luke xi 13; cf. Matt iii 11); they picture him as predicting the coming of the Son of Man (Matt xvi 27–28; xxiv 27, 30, 37, 39). Even if we were to accept all these statements in their present form as stemming from the ministry of Jesus (a difficult presupposition), we would not know how Jesus combined them. If Jesus spoke of the resurrection of the Son of Man, he seems also to have spoken of the coming of the Son of Man shortly after his own death (Mark xiv 62—to be seen by the high priest); do these statements refer to the same event? John xx 22 pictures the era of the Spirit as having begun immediately after the resurrection; Acts ii 1 pictures an interval of fifty days.

The confused character of the predictions that have come down to us is most apparent in the Last Discourse. Here Jesus speaks of coming back to take his disciples along with him (xiv 3); he speaks of the coming of the Paraclete (see App. V); he speaks of coming with his Father to make a dwelling place in the believer (xiv 23); he speaks of the disciples' seeing him no more because he will be with the Father (xvi 10); he speaks of their seeing him again after a little while (xvi 16, 22); he expresses a wish that the disciples be with him where he will be that they may see his glory (xvii 24). Is he speaking of his resurrectional appearances? Of a presence through the Spirit? Of another type of indwelling? Of his coming at the death of the Christian? Of the parousia (cf. v 28–29)?

To illustrate the confusion more particularly, let us concentrate on the various types of indwelling promised in the Last Discourse and the Johannine Epistles:

■ Indwelling involving the Father, Jesus, and the disciples:
The Father and Jesus in the disciples: xiv 23.

Mutual *koinōnia* or common life: I John i 3.

The disciples in the Father and Jesus: xvii 21; I John v 20.

■ Indwelling involving Jesus and the disciples:

Jesus in the disciples: xvii 23, 26.

Mutual indwelling: xiv 20, xv 4, 5(7); see also vi 54, 56.

The disciples in Jesus: xv 6, 7; I John v 20.

■ Indwelling involving the Spirit and the disciples:

The Paraclete/Spirit in the disciples: xiv 17, xvi 7–8.

Commentators have sought to draw a consistent historical and theological sketch from the various predictions and references to indwelling found in the Last Discourse, but we must admit that without considerable reinterpretation these predictions and references seem to be quite diverse. However, the final redactor and perhaps even the evangelist apparently saw no contradiction in this diversity, since these predictions and references were left side by side without an attempt at reconciling them. It is not always easy to be sure how the redactor interpreted the predictions; and it is even more difficult to guess what they meant when they were first reported, especially if they originally belonged to a context other than that of the Last Supper. The theory of the composition of the Last Discourse espoused here warns the reader to expect to find in the Discourse a collection of sayings composed or rephrased at various stages in the history of Johannine eschatological thought, as well as early sayings reinterpreted in a way consonant with later thought.

BIBLIOGRAPHY

General Treatments of the Last Discourse

Behler, G.-M., *The Last Discourse of Jesus* (Baltimore: Helicon, 1965).

Corssen, P., "Die Abschiedsreden Jesu im vierten Evangelium," ZNW 8 (1907), 125–42.

Dodd, *Interpretation*, pp. 390–423.

Durand, A., "Le discours de la Cène (Saint Jean xiii 31–xvii 26)," RSR 1 (1910), 97–131, 513–39; 2 (1911), 321–49, 521–45.

Gächter, P., "Der formale Aufbau der Abschiedsreden Jesu," ZKT 58 (1934), 155–207.

Hauret, C., *Les adieux du Seigneur (S. Jean XIII–XVII)* (Paris: Gabalda, 1951).

Holwerda, D. E., *The Holy Spirit and Eschatology in the Gospel of John* (Kampen: Kok, 1959).

Huby, J., *Le discours de Jésus après la Cène* (2nd ed.; Paris: Beauchesne, 1942).

Könn, J., *Sein letztes Wort* (Einsiedeln: Benziger, 1954).

Kundsin, K., "Die Wiederkunft Jesu in den Abschiedsreden des Johannesevangeliums," ZNW 33 (1934), 210–15.

Richter, G., "Die Deutung des Kreuzestodes Jesu in der Leidensgeschichte des Johannesevangeliums (Jo 13–19)," BiLeb 9 (1968), 21–36.

Schneider, J., "Die Abschiedsreden Jesu," *Gott und die Götter* (Festgabe E. Fascher; Berlin: Evangelische Verlagsanstalt, 1958), pp. 103–12.

Stagg, F., "The Farewell Discourses: John 13–17," RExp 62 (1965), 459–72.

van den Bussche, H., *Le discours d'adieu de Jésus* (Tournai: Casterman, 1959).

Zimmermann, H., "Struktur und Aussageabsicht der johanneischen Abschiedsreden (Jo 13–17)," BiLeb 8 (1967), 279–90.

Farewell Speeches

Munck, J., "Discours d'adieu dans le Nouveau Testament et dans la littérature biblique," *Aux sources de la tradition chrétienne* (Mélanges M. Goguel; Neuchâtel: Delachaux, 1950), pp. 155–70.

Randall, J., *The Theme of Unity in John XVII:20–23* (Louvain University, 1962), pp. 42–98.

Schnackenburg, R., "Abschiedsreden Jesu," *Lexikon für Theologie und Kirche* 1 (1957), 68–69.

Stauffer, E., "Abschiedsreden," *Reallexikon für Antike und Christentum* 1 (1950), 29–35.

——— "Valedictions and Farewell Speeches," in *New Testament Theology* (New York: Macmillan, 1955), pp. 344–47.

49. THE LAST DISCOURSE:
—DIVISION ONE (INTRODUCTION)
(xiii 31–38)

Jesus' departure; his commandment of love; Peter's denial

XIII 31 Then, when Judas had gone out, Jesus said:

"Now has the Son of Man been glorified,
and God has been glorified in him.
32 [If God has been glorified in him,]
God will, in turn, glorify him in Himself
and will glorify him immediately.
33 My little children,
I am to be with you only a little longer.
You will look for me;
but, as I told the Jews
and now I tell you too,
'Where I am going, you cannot come.'
34 I am giving you a new commandment:
Love one another.
As I have loved you,
so you too must love one another.
35 By this will all identify you as my disciples—
by the love you have for one another."

36 "Lord," said Simon Peter, "where are you going?" Jesus answered,

"Where I am going, you cannot follow me now;
but you will follow me later."

37 "Lord," said Peter, "why can't I follow you now? I will lay down
my life for you." 38 "So you will lay down your life for me?" Jesus
answered. "Let me firmly assure you, the cock will not crow before
you deny me three times!"

31: *said;* 36: *said;* 37: *said;* 38: *answered.* In the historical present tense.

NOTES

xiii 31. *God has been glorified in him.* Caird, *art. cit.*, lists four possible ways to understand this clause:

(a) "Through Jesus God is held in honor by men." This interpretation is not impossible but is unlikely, for it requires the "Now" that prefaces the verse to refer not only to "the hour" of Jesus' passion, death, resurrection, and ascension, but also to the future moment of the appreciation of those events by the Christian community. Such an extension of time makes otiose the next verse which professedly deals with the future.

(b) "God is honored by Jesus," for example, by his obedience. While this concept is Johannine (xvii 4: "I glorified you on earth"), Caird finds difficulty in the fact that nowhere else does John use the preposition *en* with the dative of personal agency. Moreover, such an interpretation does not fit the nearly parallel clause in xiv 13: "Whatever you ask in my name I will do, so that the Father may be glorified in the Son."

(c) "God has won honor for Himself in Jesus." This interpretation has the more acceptable local use of *en* but is open to the same objection raised against the first interpretation above.

(d) "God has revealed His glory in Jesus." This is the interpretation that Caird accepts, pointing out that the passive of *doxazein* here is really intransitive, as regularly in LXX when it renders the *niphal* of Heb. *kābēd*, used in the sense of manifesting glory.

In vol. 29, p. 503, we stressed that glory involves a *visible* manifestation of God's majesty in *acts of power*. Both these qualities are verified in Jesus' death and resurrection, which is an action of his own power (x 17–18). Since Jesus' power is at the same time God's power (see vol. 29, p. 407), the full meaning here is to be found in a combination of Caird's second and fourth interpretations. (The preposition *en* in the NT has some of the wider sense of Heb. *bᵉ*.) M. Martínez Pastor (*Miscelánea Comillas* 42 [1964], 173–82) has analyzed the concept of glory in Origen's exegesis of this verse. Origen has hellenized the concept of glory in the direction of Christian Gnosticism, for he associates glory with knowing God and being known by God. The Hebrew concept did not stress contemplation.

32. [*If God . . .*]. This clause is missing in some very important textual witnesses, including P66 and Codex Vaticanus, but perhaps by homoioteleuton. It is easier to explain why it may have been lost than why it would have been added. Bernard, Lagrange, Bultmann, and Thüsing are among those who accept the clause.

in Himself. By contrast with vs. 31 which states that God is glorified in Jesus, this verse means that Jesus is glorified in God. (Yet many, including Cyril of Alexandria, Lagrange, and Behler, think that the reference is to Jesus' being glorified in himself.) The same thought is found in xvii 5: "Glorify me, Father, in your presence."

immediately. The passion, death, resurrection, and ascension are looked on as one brief action (also the "only a little longer" of vs. 33) leading to future glory in the Father's presence.

33. *My little children.* This address (*teknia*) appears seven times in I John

but only here in John. In which direction has the influence gone? Has the writer of I John patterned himself on an occasional usage of Jesus, or has that writer's own way of speech been read back into the Discourse? No definitive answer is possible, but there is evidence that a Jewish teacher might well address his disciples as "children" (StB, II, 559). Moreover, in Mark x 24 Jesus calls the disciples "My children" (*tekna*, instead of the Johannine diminutive *teknia*); and in Matt xviii 3, xix 14, Jesus admonishes the disciples to be like children. See NOTE on "Lads" in xxi 5.

only a little longer. In the Book of Signs we had two instances of the expression *eti mikron chronon*: "I am to be with you only a little while longer" (vii 33); "The light is among you only a little while longer" (xii 35). In the Last Discourse *chronos*, "time, while," is omitted and the neuter *mikron* is used as a substantive. We find *eti* ("only, just") *mikron* here and in xiv 19; but *eti* is omitted in xvi 16. Bultmann, p. 445[1], points out the Semitic flavor of this expression which is not normal Greek. That the expression tells us little about chronological duration is seen in the fact that it can be used both in vii 33, when Jesus had at least six months more to live, and in the present context when Jesus has only a few hours to live. It is an OT expression used by the prophets to express optimistically the shortness of time before God's salvation would come (Isa x 25; Jer li [xxviii] 33).

as I told the Jews. The reference is to the scenes in vii 33 and viii 21 (see COMMENT) which occurred at least six months before. We need not worry whether the disciples would have recalled the saying after so long a time; as always (see vol. 29, p. 316) such recall is meant for the Christian reader of the Gospel.

34. *I am giving.* Some witnesses take the "now" of 33 (next-to-the-last line) with 34: "Now I am giving. . . ."

commandment. The theme of the commandment(s) recurs frequently in the Last Discourse (six or seven times) and in the Johannine Epistles (eighteen times). From the Latin for "commandment" (*mandatum*) we get the name Maundy Thursday.

Love one another. This clause is preceded by *hina* which we have translated epexegetically, so that "Love one another" constitutes the commandment. ZGB, §415, mentions the possibility of an imperative *hina*. Jerome (*Ad Galat.* III 6:10; PL 26:433) relates the story that in John's old age his message was reduced to this: "My little children, love one another"—a combination of phrases from 33 and 34. For the love that should exist among the disciples of Jesus, John always uses the verb *agapan;* however, elsewhere in John *agapan* and *philein* seem to be interchangeable (vol. 29, p. 498).

As I have loved you. In the context of "the hour," Jesus' demonstrable love includes the laying down of his life and taking it up again (see xiii 1, xv 13).

so you too must love. This is a *hina* clause, and some interpreters would give it full final force: "I have loved you in order that you also love one another."

35. *by the love you have for one another.* Loisy, p. 402, points out that the evangelist is writing of something that has long been experienced, and very soon after his time the Christian apologists would call upon the impact made by Christian love as a standard argument for the superiority of Christianity.

36. *where are you going?* In Latin this is *"Quo vadis?"* In the late 2nd-century apocryphal *Acts of Peter* xxxv (=*Martyrdom of Peter* III) the words

reappear. As Peter flees from Rome and from the danger of martyrdom, he meets Jesus and asks, "Lord, where are you going?" Jesus tells Peter that he is going into Rome to be crucified again (in Peter's place). Shamed by his master, Peter returns to the city to die.

37. *Lord.* There is some ancient evidence for omitting this.

lay down my life. Although John shares this scene with the Synoptics (see COMMENT), the language is peculiarly Johannine (NOTE on x 11).

38. *So you will lay down your life.* In Jesus' response there is a note both of irony and of being resigned to human weakness.

the cock will not crow. John, like the Synoptics, is careful to narrate the fulfillment of this prediction in xviii 17–18, 25–27.

COMMENT: GENERAL

We consider xiii 31–38 to be the introduction to Division 1 of the Last Discourse. Yet the very fact that we treat xiii 31–38 separately from xiv 1–31 implies a certain distinction between the introduction and the body of Division 1, so that they do not form a perfect unit. One indication of shift in focus between the end of xiii and the beginning of xiv is seen in the change of audience: in xiii 38 Jesus is speaking to Peter, while in xiv 1 he is speaking to all the disciples. Never again in the Discourse, despite the interruptions in xiv by individual disciples (Thomas, Philip, and Judas [not Iscariot]), does Jesus center attention on the fate of one disciple, as he does with Peter in xiii 36–38. If he answers the questions of individuals, he soon turns to speak to all the disciples, for example, see the "you men" in xiv 7, 10. (The duplicate discourse in xvi 4b–33 reflects this attitude by having the disciples *as a body* interrupt Jesus.) Moreover, the nature of xiv 1–31 as a unit separate from xiii 31–38 is indicated by the inclusion between xiv 1–3 and 27–28 (being fearful; going and coming back), marking the beginning and end of a section.

Yet, if there is a demarcation between xiii 31–38 and xiv 1–31, one may wonder whether xiii 31–38 should not be separated completely from xiv and treated as the introduction to the whole Last Discourse (so Schneider, p. 106; also Lagrange, Barrett). The real objection to this is that xvi 4b–33, which is a duplicate of xiv, also has parallels to xiii 31–38. The question about where Jesus is going is asked in xiii 36 and discussed in xvi 5. The predictions of the denial by Peter in xiii 36–38 and of the desertion by the disciples in xvi 32 are related; for they are joined in the Synoptic parallels (Mark xiv 27–31; Matt xxvi 31–35), but in inverse order. On the analogy of xvi 4b–33, then, it would seem that xiii 31–38 belongs with xiv 1–31. The most plausible suggestion remains that at the stage when what is now xiv 1–31 substantially constituted the whole Last Discourse, xiii 31–38 served as the introduction to that Discourse. Like an overture, it blended brief echoes of the two themes that were heard prominently in the original Last Discourse (and, of course,

are heard throughout the much longer final form of the Last Discourse):
the themes of love and of Jesus' imminent departure. The less structured
duplicate in xvi 4b–33 has no introduction, even though it repeats in
scattered fashion elements present in xiii 31–38.

Considered in itself, xiii 31–38 is obviously a composite. It combines
material that the Synoptic Gospels also place at the Last Supper (prediction
of Peter's denial in 36–38) with themes peculiar to John, for example,
glorification, departure, fraternal love. As for the verses containing the
latter themes, Loisy, p. 402, is perfectly correct in his contention that
31–32, 33, 34–35, are more juxtaposed than connected. Moreover, they
have parallels elsewhere in John (31–32=xii 23, 27–28; 33=vii 33,
viii 21; 34–35=xv 12), so that it is difficult to determine how much of
the material in 31–35 belongs in the historical setting of the Last Supper
and how much has been imported from the public ministry.

Nevertheless, one can trace the logic that led to the union of these
disparate elements. Jesus' glorification (31–32), which is the goal of "the
hour," is an appropriate opening theme for the great Discourse explaining the hour. This glorification involves his return to his Father and,
therefore, his departure from his disciples (33). The command to love
(34–35) is Jesus' way of ensuring the continuance of his spirit among his
disciples. Peter, failing to understand the nature of this departure, wishes
to follow Jesus: the "Where are you going?" of 36 picks up the "Where I
am going" of 33. Going beyond this chain of ideas, L. Cerfaux, *art. cit.*,
has proposed a more subtle analysis of the relationships in these verses.
He suggests that the theme of love (34–35) is related to the theme of
Jesus' return hinted at in 33 where Jesus speaks of his departure. The
basis for this suggestion is that the theme of love or charity appears in
sections of the Synoptic Gospels dealing with Jesus' return in the parousia,
for example, in the parables of Matt xxv. Now it is quite normal for a
parable to be misunderstood, and Cerfaux would see Peter's question in
36–37 as a misunderstanding of the ideas of 33–35. We do not find this
analysis particularly convincing, although Cerfaux may be right in stressing
that there is more traditional relationship in 31–38 than appears on the
surface.

COMMENT: DETAILED

Verses 31–32: Glorification

The Last Discourse opens with a proclamation of the glorification
of the Son of Man. After the Greeks appeared on the scene in xii 20–22,
Jesus announced that the hour had come and began to speak of the
glorification of the Son of Man (xii 23, 28–29). We have pointed out (vol.
29, p. 477) that some scholars would join that section of xii to xiii 31.

It is even possible that we are dealing with a doublet, especially since chapters xi–xii may have had an independent history and have been added to the Gospel proper only at a late stage of editing (vol. 29, pp. 414, 427–28). Be that as it may, there is no contradiction in having two proclamations of the glorification of the Son of Man. On the one hand, the coming of the Greeks heralded the beginning of the glorification, for they foreshadowed all the men who would be drawn to Jesus once he had been lifted up to the Father (xii 32). On the other hand, the treachery of Judas, accepted by Jesus (xiii 27), actually inaugurated the process of Jesus' passing from this world to the Father. It has been suggested that the "now" of vs. 31 refers primarily to the footwashing with its symbolism of the self-sacrificial death of Jesus; but more directly it refers to the situation produced by Judas' departure from the Last Supper, as he goes to bring the police and soldiers who will arrest Jesus and eventually put him to death.

We have already stressed that John's interpretation of Jesus' glorification as related to his suffering and death is foreshadowed in Isa lii 13 (vol. 29, p. 478). D. Hill, NTS 13 (1966–67), 281–85, suggests that the same relationship of glory and death appears in the Synoptic tradition in Mark x 35. There James and *John* are told figuratively that sharing Jesus' glory is possible only through suffering unto death ("Are you able to drink the cup that I drink, or to be baptized with the baptism with which I am baptized?").

The shift from a past tense in 31 ("has been glorified") to a future tense in 32 ("will glorify") has provoked much comment. Indeed, the idea in 31 that Jesus has already been glorified illustrates that beginning with the first verse of the Last Discourse there is a problem of time perspective, discussed above (p. 585). Bultmann, p. 401, has used the past tense of vs. 31 to support his rearrangement whereby xvii precedes xiii 31, for he says that 31 fulfills Jesus' prayer for glorification in xvii 1. However, as Bultmann himself recognizes, the theme of glory that dominates the second half of the Gospel (The Book of Glory) is past, present, and future, since the whole process is viewed from an eternal viewpoint (perhaps produced by mixing the viewpoint of the night before Jesus died and the viewpoint of the later period of Gospel composition). The same mixture of past and future that we encounter in xiii 31–32 was seen in xii 28: "I have glorified it and will glorify it again" (see discussion in vol. 29, pp. 476–77). Once again we find attractive the suggestion of Thüsing: the past tense (aorist in 31) is complexive, referring to the whole passion, death, resurrection, and ascension that takes place in "the hour"; the future in 32 refers to the glory that will follow when the Son returns to the Father's presence (cf. xvii 5).

These two verses are also of interest since they refer to "the Son of Man," a title occurring only here in the Book of Glory, as compared to twelve instances in the Book of Signs. We mentioned in the NOTE on i 51 that there are three types of Son of Man sayings in the Synoptic tradition. Verse 31 (also iii 14) would be an example of the second type of saying that refers to the suffering of the Son of Man. The idea that the Son of Man has been glorified in the process of death and resurrection may be compared to Mark viii 31: "The Son of Man must suffer many things and after three days rise again." Verse 32, on the other hand, since it speaks of future glorification (which will be seen by Jesus' followers: xvii 24), would be an example of the third type of saying and may be compared to Mark xiii 26: "Then they will see the Son of Man coming in clouds with great power and *glory*." Perhaps, however, it is somewhat deceptive to interpret John's usage of the title in light of the Synoptic usage; for a comparison of the present verse with xvii 1 ("Glorify your Son that the Son may glorify you") suggests that for John the title "Son of Man" had become interchangeable with "the Son [of God]." Compare also these two titles in iii 13–17, and see the articles in this vein by E. D. Freed, JBL 86 (1967), 402–9, and H.-M. Dion, ScEccl 19 (1967), 49–65. A new analysis of the Johannine Son of Man sayings has been done by S. S. Smalley, NTS 15 (1968–69), 278–301.

Verse 33: Departure

The endearing salutation, "My little children" (see NOTE), is particularly appropriate if the Last Supper is thought of as a Passover meal, for the small groups that banded together to eat the paschal meal had to pattern themselves on family life, and one of the group had to act as a father explaining to his children the significance of what was being done. The address is also very fitting if the Last Discourse is thought of as a farewell speech, for in this literary genre the scene is often that of a dying father instructing his children. Examples of particular interest in view of the context in John (vs. 34 mentions the commandment of love for one another) are found in the *Testaments of the Twelve Patriarchs,* a Jewish work with Christian interpolations, or perhaps a Christian work dependent on Jewish sources. "My children, beware of hatred . . . for hatred is not willing to hear the words of God's commandments concerning the love of one's neighbor" (*Gad* iv 1–2). "Now, my children, let each one of you love his brother . . . loving one another" (*Gad* vi 1). See also *Zebulun* v 1, viii 5: *Joseph* xvii 1–2; *Issachar* vii 6–7; *Simeon* iv 7. The affirmation in John, "My little children, I am to be with you only a little longer," is not unlike *Reuben* i 3, "My little children, I am dying and I go the way of my fathers." And just as the departing Jesus gives a commandment to his little children, so we hear in *Reuben* iv 5: "My children, observe all that I have commanded you."

The theme of departure in vs. 33 echoes vii 33–34 and viii 21:
■ "I am to be with you only a little longer"=vii 33 (but the latter has the word *chronon* that is missing here);

■ "You will look for me" (without the clause "and not find me")=viii 21 (vii 34 has "and not find me");

■ "Where I am going, you cannot come"=viii 21 (vii 34 has "where I am").

In vii and viii Jesus was warning "the Jews" that they could not find him because they did not believe in him; but in the present passage the same words spoken to his disciples are a preparation for his departure *and return*. (The disciples cannot come where Jesus is going, but subsequently Jesus and the Father will come to them [xiv 23].) The idea that 33 is also a warning because it prepares for the prediction of Peter's denial in 36–38 is hardly correct. The salutation, "My little children," gives the verse a tone of tenderness; and certainly Jesus' words in 36 interpret the statement of 33 as a promise of ultimate happiness ("you will follow me later"). See also the parallel passage in xvi 4 ff. which promises a return and continued presence through the Paraclete. The similarity of xiii 33 to vii 33–34 and viii 21 is not in the fact that all are warnings, but in the misunderstanding that greets both the promise of xiii 33 and the warning of vii and viii. In xiii 37 Peter shows that he does not understand why he cannot come with Jesus.

Verses 34–35: Commandment of Love

Since the disciples cannot follow Jesus as he leaves this life, they receive a command that, if obeyed, will keep the spirit of Jesus alive among them as they continue their life in this world. The commandment of loving one another appears again in the Last Discourse in xv 12 and 17, and is the subject of discussion in I John ii 7–9, iii 23, iv 21, v 2–3; II John 5. The very idea that love is a commandment is interesting. In the OT the Ten Commandments have a setting in the covenant between God and Israel at Sinai; traditionally they were the stipulations that Israel had to observe if it was to be God's chosen people. In speaking of love as the new commandment for those whom Jesus had chosen as his own (xiii 1, xv 16) and as a mark by which they could be distinguished from others (vs. 35), the evangelist shows implicitly that he is thinking of this Last Supper scene in covenant terms. The Synoptic accounts of the Eucharist make this specific (Mark xiv 24: "my blood of the covenant"; Luke xxii 20: "the *new* covenant in my blood"; also I Cor xi 25).

Yet love is more than a commandment; it is a gift, and like the other gifts of the Christian dispensation it comes from the Father through Jesus to those who believe in him. In xv 9 we hear, "As the Father has loved me, so have I loved you"; and in both xiii 34 and xv 12 the "as I have loved you" emphasizes that Jesus is the source of the Christians' love for one another. (Only secondarily does it refer to Jesus as the standard of Christian love.) The love that Jesus has for his followers is not only affective but also effective: it brings about their salvation. It is expressed in his laying down his life, an act of love that gives life to men. This is well expressed in Rev i 5: ". . . the one who loves us and has delivered [or washed] us from our sins." We should also stress that the "love of one another" of which the Johannine Jesus speaks is love *between Christians*. In our own times a frequent ideal is the love of all men, enunciated in terms of the fatherhood of God and the brotherhood of man. Such a maxim has some biblical base in the creation of all men by God (see Matt v 44), but the idea is not Johannine. For John, God is a Father only to those who believe in His Son and who are begotten as God's children by the Spirit in Baptism. The "one another" that the Christian is to love is correctly defined in I John iii 14 as "our brothers," that is, those within the community (see usage of "brothers" in John xxi 23). In this stress John is not far from the thought of Qumran (see our discussion in CBQ 17 [1955], 561–64, reprinted in NTE, pp. 123–26 or 163–67). While the Qumran sectarians had little use for outsiders, their emphasis on fraternal love was edifying. They were instructed "to love all the sons of light, each according to his lot in God's designs, and to hate all the sons of darkness, each according to his guilty place in God's vengeance" (1QS i 9–11). Yet, while for Qumran love is a duty consequent upon one's belonging to the community, for John, Jesus' love for men is constitutive of the community.

In what sense is the commandment to love one another a *"new commandment"*? Christian scholars have often sought to explain the newness by contrast with the OT attitude toward love of neighbor. To the commandment of loving one's Israelite neighbor as oneself (Lev xix 18) there was added in the OT a similar command to love the foreigner dwelling among the Israelites (xix 34); but there is no clear evidence in the OT that these commands received special emphasis. Yet an emphasis on love of neighbor is attested in intertestamental Judaism, for example, on the part of Hillel (*Pirqe Aboth* i 12). The newness of Jesus' teaching has been credited to his giving the commandment of love of neighbor a status second only to the commandment of love of God (Mark xii 28–31; Matt xxii 34–40) and to his defining "neighbor" in a very wide sense (Luke x 29–37). Whether this approach is valid for the Synoptic tradition we cannot discuss here (Luke x 25–28 has a scribe, not Jesus, associate the two commandments). But such a contrast with the OT casts little light on the newness of the commandment to love in John; for the Johannine Jesus does not mention two commandments (see NOTE on I John iv 21) and, as we have seen, his concept of "one another" is not wide. The phrasing of the Johannine command, "Love one another," does not spontaneously recall Lev xix 18, as does the Synoptic phrasing. This fact also renders dubious the suggestion that the newness consists in the fact that Jesus commands the Christian to love "as I have loved you," while the OT commands the Israelite to love his neighbor *as himself*. B. Schwank, "Der Weg," 103–4, in thoroughly refuting the idea that the Johannine commandment is new by contrast with the OT commandment, points out that in arguing for the necessity of loving one another I John iii 11–12 takes a negative example from the OT, as if the commandment to love were binding in OT times.

The newness of the commandment of love is really related to the theme of covenant at the Last Supper—the "new commandment" of John xiii 34 is the basic stipulation of the "new covenant" of Luke xxii 20. Both expressions reflect the early Christian understanding that in Jesus and his followers was fulfilled the dream of Jeremiah (xxxi 31–34): "Behold, the days are coming when I will make a new covenant with the house of Israel and the house of Judah." (For Jeremiah this was more a renewed covenant than a totally new covenant, and this was probably the earliest Christian interpretation as well, with emphasis on the radical and eschatological nature of the renewal.) This new covenant was to be interiorized and to be marked by the people's intimate contact with God and knowledge of Him—a knowledge that is the equivalent of love and is a covenantal virtue. The themes of intimacy, indwelling, and mutual knowledge run through the Last Discourse. We pointed out above the Qumran parallels for the Johannine theme of brotherly love; it is no accident that the Qumran community speaks of itself and its life as "the covenant of mercy [grace]" (1QS i 8), "the covenant of eternal fellowship [unity]" (iii 11–12), and "the new covenant" (CD vi 19, xx 12).

The mark that distinguishes God's love expressed in the covenant from even the noblest forms of human love is that it is spontaneous and unmotivated, directed to men who are sinners and unworthy of love—a theme beautifully expounded in Anders Nygren's classic *Agape and Eros*. The generosity of God's love was already realized by Israel (Deut vii 6–8), and therefore in one way the Christian concept of love is not new (cf. I John ii 7–8). Yet because the generosity of God's love could not be fully known until He had given His own Son, in another way the Christian concept of love stemming from Jesus is new. Verse 35 says that even outsiders will recognize the distinctiveness of Christian love. The same theme is found in xvii 23 where it is said that the world's attention will be caught by the love and union that exists between the Father, the Son, and the Christian disciples. Such a love challenges the world even as Jesus challenged the world, and leads men to make their choice for the light. Thus, as long as Christian love is in the world, the world is still encountering Jesus; and so we can see that the commandment to love in 34–35 is a response to the problem raised by Jesus' physical departure in 33.

Verses 36–38: Prediction of Peter's Denial

We have mentioned that Peter's question "Where are you going?" in 36 has a certain parallelism with xvi 5: "Not one of you asks me, 'Where are you going?'" They are probably variant forms of the same incident.

Bultmann's rearrangement whereby xiii 36 follows xvi is not really helpful, for then the question "Where are you going?" would follow shortly after xvi 28 ("I am going to the Father") and a new illogicality would be created. In its present sequence vs. 36 picks up the theme of Jesus' departure from 33.

It is interesting to compare the Johannine scene with Luke xxii 31–34, where the prediction of Peter's denial is set during the Last Supper in a short discourse following the Eucharist, and with Mark xiv 26–31 and Matt xxvi 30–35, where the prediction is given by Jesus on the way to the Mount of Olives.

	Mark/Matthew	Luke	John
Preliminaries	Jesus warns that the disciples will fall away and be scattered.		See xvi 32.
		Jesus warns Peter that Satan will shake him but he will survive.	Peter asks where Jesus is going. Jesus tells him he can follow only later.
Prediction	Peter says he will not fall away even if others do. Jesus predicts Peter will deny him before cockcrow (Mark: second cockcrow). Peter says he will die rather than deny Jesus. The others say the same.	Peter says he is ready to go to prison and to death. Jesus predicts Peter will deny him before cockcrow.	Peter says he is willing to lay down his life in order to follow. Jesus predicts Peter will deny him before cockcrow.

The preliminaries are different in the three accounts; John xvi 32 has a similarity to Mark/Matthew, and John xiii 36 has a slight similarity to Luke. In the actual prediction, there are two general points in common: Peter's willingness to die and the prediction of denial before cockcrow. But if we examine these common points, there are still many differences of detail.

First, Peter's willingness to die. In Mark/Matthew this follows Jesus' prediction of denial; in Luke and John it precedes. The wording of Peter's statement is quite varied:

Mark/Matthew: "Even if I must die with you, I shall not deny you."
Luke: "I am ready to go with you to prison and to death."
John: "I will lay down my life for you."

In the first two forms of the statement Peter is ready to accompany

Jesus to death; in John's form Peter will sacrifice his own life to save Jesus' life. The scene in John has definite theological overtones. The Johannine Peter speaks as a disciple who has heard Jesus insist that the model shepherd is willing to lay down his life for his sheep (x 11), and by his outburst Peter implicitly proclaims his willingness to live up to this demand. But Jesus rejects Peter's offer, for Peter is overconfident. (There is an element of overconfidence on the part of all the disciples in the related scene in xvi 29–32—see COMMENT there.) Peter does not estimate correctly his own weakness or the difficulty of following Jesus, for the death to which Jesus goes involves a struggle with the Prince of this world. Only when Jesus has overcome him can others follow. After the resurrection Jesus will offer the role of shepherd to Peter and at the same time predict how Peter will actually lay down his life (xxi 15–19). Then Jesus' words to Peter, "Follow me," will fulfill the promise given in xiii 36: "You will follow me later." As Bultmann, p. 461, observes, the "later" of vs. 36 is the same as the "afterwards" of xiii 7—they both refer to the period after "the hour." In light of this implicit Johannine shepherd theme it is interesting that Mark/Matthew tell us that before Jesus predicted Peter's denial, he cited Zech xiii 7: "I will strike the *shepherd* and the sheep will be scattered."

Second, the prediction of Peter's denial before cockcrow:

Mark/Matthew: "Let me assure you, [Mark: today] this very night before the cock crows [Mark: twice], you will disown (*aparneisthai*] me three times."

Luke: "I assure you, Peter, today the cock will not crow until three times you disown [*aparneisthai*] knowing me."

John: "Let me firmly assure you, the cock will not crow before you deny [*arneisthai*] me three times."

The Johannine form of the saying has none of the peculiar Marcan details but shares common features with Matthew and with Luke. Yet there remain differences inexplicable in a theory of borrowing; probably a saying of Jesus has been passed down in slightly variant forms. Granted all the other differences we have seen, we have no reason to doubt that Dodd, *Tradition*, pp. 55–56, is correct in insisting that John's account of the scene is independent of the Synoptic accounts. No over-all judgment can be passed on which account is more original (although John's account is closely integrated into Johannine theological interests); perhaps elements of what was once a larger scene have been transmitted in each of the various traditions.

[The Bibliography for this section is included in the Bibliography found at the end of §52.]

50. THE LAST DISCOURSE:
—DIVISION ONE (UNIT ONE)
(xiv 1–14)

Jesus is the way to the Father for those who believe in him

XIV 1 "Do not let your hearts be troubled.
You have faith in God; have faith, then, in me.
2 There are many dwelling places in my Father's house;
otherwise I would have warned you.
I am going off to prepare a place for you;
3 and when I do go and prepare a place for you,
I am coming back to take you along with me,
so that where I am, you also may be.
4 And you know the way to where I am going."

5 "Lord," said Thomas, "we don't know where you are going. So how can we know the way?" 6 Jesus told him,

"I am the way and the truth and the life:
no one comes to the Father except through me.
7 If you men really knew me, then you would recognize my
|Father too.
From now on you do know Him and have seen Him."

8 "Lord," said Philip, "show us the Father. That's enough for us."
9 "Philip," Jesus replied, "here I am with you all this time, and you still don't know me?

Whoever has seen me has seen the Father.
So how can you say, 'Show us the Father'?
10 Do you not believe that I am in the Father
and the Father is in me?
The words that I say to you men are not spoken on my own;
it is the Father, abiding in me, who performs the works.

5: *said;* 6: *told;* 8: *said;* 9: *replied.* In the historical present tense.

11 Believe me that I am in the Father
   and the Father is in me;
   otherwise believe [me] because of the works.
12 Let me firmly assure you,
   the man who has faith in me
   will perform the same works that I perform.
   In fact, he will perform far greater than these,
   because I am going to the Father,
13 and whatever you ask in my name
   I will do,
   so that the Father may be glorified in the Son.
14 If you ask anything of me in my name,
   I will do it."

NOTES

xiv 1. *Do not*. Codex Bezae, the OL, and OS[sin] have an introductory line
not preserved in the majority of textual witnesses: "And he said to his disciples."
If this were original, it would confirm a demarcation between xiii 38 and xiv 1,
as suggested on p. 608 above. However, it is probably only a liturgical
interpolation to facilitate reading in public. "Jesus said to his disciples" is
prefixed to many Gospel pericopes selected for reading in the Roman liturgy, for
example, to this pericope (xiv 1–13) on May 11 (Feast of Saints Philip and
James).

hearts. The singular is used, as also in xiv 27, xvi 6, 22. MTGS, p. 23,
remarks: "Contrary to normal Greek and Latin practice, the NT follows the
Aramaic and Hebrew preference for a distributive sing[ular]." In the OT and the
Synoptic Gospels "heart" is generally the seat of decisions; in most Johannine uses
it has an affective role.

be troubled. This verb *tarassein* was used to describe Jesus' emotions when
confronted with Lazarus' death in xi 33 ("he shuddered") and with his own
betrayal to death by Judas in xiii 21.

You have faith. We have translated this as an indicative, although it is
equally possible to translate it as an imperative ("Have faith"), as did the OL.
The difference of meaning is not great, for the imperative translation would
really mean: "If you have faith in the Father, have faith in me" (BDF, §387[2]).
A thematic parallel appears in Mark xi 22–24, where during his last days in
Jerusalem Jesus tells his disciples to have faith in God and not to doubt in their
hearts. The Hebrew word for "faith," from the root *'mn*, has the concept of
firmness; to have faith in God is to participate in His firmness—an appropriate
note in the present context.

2. *dwelling places*. The significance of the Greek term *monē* is disputed.
Many have thought that it represents Aram. *'wn'* (*'ōnâ*, or sometimes *'awawnâ*),
a word that can refer to a night-stop or resting place for a traveler on a journey.
Monē has a similar meaning in secular Greek; and Origen (*De principiis* II xi 6;
PG 11:246) understands John to refer to stations on the road to God. This may

also have been the understanding of the Latin translators who rendered *monē* by *mansio*, a halting place. (The standard English rendition "many mansions" stems from Tyndale, but in Old English "mansion" meant dwelling place, and not necessarily a palatial dwelling. It has no connotation of a stopping place.) Such an interpretation would also have suited the Gnostic theory that the soul in its ascent passes through stages wherein it is gradually purified of all that is material. Westcott, p. 200, accepts "stations" as the meaning, but see the strong dissent of T. S. Berry, *The Expositor*, 2nd series, 3 (1882), 397–400. It would be much more in harmony with Johannine thought to relate *monē* to the cognate verb *menein*, frequently used in John in reference to staying, remaining, or abiding with Jesus and with the Father. J. C. James, ET 27 (1915–16), 427–29, points to a Nabatean inscription from the beginning of the Christian era which uses *'wn'* in apposition to "tomb," with the sense of a resting place or a place to dwell in peace after the struggles of life. And so in using *monē* John may be referring to places (or situations) where the disciples can dwell in peace by remaining with the Father (cf. xiv 23). An interesting parallel to such a picture is found in a later work, *Slavonic Enoch* xli 2: "In the world to come . . . there are many dwelling places prepared for men, good for the good, evil for the evil."

in my Father's house. There is considerable patristic evidence for reading "with my Father"; Boismard, RB 57 (1950), 388–91, argues that it is the original reading. The two Greek readings could be alternative translations from the same Semitic phrase (b)*bēt 'abbâ;* see Boismard, ÉvJean, p. 52. However, "with my Father" may also represent a theological reinterpretation of "in my Father's house": see COMMENT. Irenaeus (*Adv. Haer.* v.36:2; PG 7:1223) cites the words "In my Father's (house) there are many dwelling places" seemingly as a saying of the Lord *reported by the elders.* Almost certainly he is referring to the elders mentioned by Papias (see vol. 29, p. xc); yet it is curious that he would attribute the saying to them rather than to the Fourth Gospel which he knew. Some have seen here confirmation that the Gospel was composed by Elder John (John the Presbyter); others have argued that Irenaeus was citing from an independent tradition rather than from the Gospel. See B. W. Bacon, ET 43 (1931–32), 477–78.

I would have warned you. Literally "I would have told you" or possibly "Would I have told you?". There is excellent, but not conclusive, ms. evidence for reading the conjunction *hoti,* "that" or "because," after the verb "to tell." (This may have been an attempt of the scribes to clarify John's parataxis.) This reading with *hoti* makes possible four different translations of the line:

(a) "otherwise I would have told [=warned] you, because I am going off to prepare. . . ."

(b) "otherwise would I have told you so, because I am going off to prepare . . . ?"

(c) "otherwise I would have told you that I am going off to prepare. . . ."

(d) "otherwise would I have told you that I am going off to prepare . . . ?"

One can make sense of (a) only if "otherwise I would have told you" is put in parentheses, and the real sequence is: "There are many dwelling places in my Father's house (. . .) because I am going off to prepare a place for you." Both (b) and (d) depend on previous statements of Jesus; yet Jesus has *not* previously told his disciples that there are many dwelling places in his Father's house (b) or that he was going off to prepare a place for them (d). One can make sense of (c): if there were not dwelling places, Jesus would have told them that he would go off to make places. Yet, as vs. 3 indicates, it is not really a question of Jesus' *telling* them that he was going off, but of his actual going. All in all, the translation without *hoti* makes the best sense.

I am going off. Here and in vs. 3 the verb is *poreuesthai;* in vs. 4, as in xiii 33, 36, the verb is *hypagein.* For further variation see NOTE on xvi 5.

a place. Topos is used for a place in heaven in Rev xii 8. Some would compare Jesus' role in going to prepare a place for his disciples to Heb vi 20 which says that Jesus has gone into the inner shrine of the heavenly temple "as a forerunner on our behalf." Others have seen a resemblance to the portrait of the Gnostic savior who leads chosen souls from earth to heaven. The latter comparison always suffers from the weakness of the over-all difference between the Gnostic myth of the divinization of man and the Christian gospel of the historical career of Jesus.

for you. The sequence of this phrase varies in a few of the Greek witnesses for vs. 2 and in many more for vs. 3. Perhaps one of the two instances of its occurrence is a scribal clarification.

3. *when I do go.* For *ean,* "if," with the meaning "when" see BAG, p. 210, §1d.

I am coming back. In some NT books the parousia is *the* coming of Jesus for which his ministry was only a preparation. John is much closer to understanding the parousia as a second coming ("back" or "again").

to take you along with me. Literally "take you to myself." A. L. Humphries, ET 53 (1941–42), 356, argues for the connotation "take along with me *to my home.*" *Pros* with a reflexive pronoun has a similar connotation in xx 10; Luke xxiv 12; I Cor xvi 2.

4. Another well-attested reading (including P66*) is: "You know where I am going and you know the way"; it is smoother Greek but for that very reason suspect as a scribal improvement. It may have been suggested by the division found in Thomas' statement in vs. 5. Dodd, *Interpretation*, p. 412[1], thinks that this alternative reading misinterprets vs. 4; for Jesus means, "You know the way [I am the way], but you do *not* know where it leads." Peter's question in xiii 36 concerned destination, and no answer was given. According to Dodd, Thomas' objection in 5 means: "If we do not know the destination, how can we know the way?"

5. *Thomas.* Codex Bezae adds, "This name means 'Twin,'" as in xi 16 (see NOTE there) and xx 24. Barrett, p. 382, remarks, "Thomas appears in John as a loyal but dull disciple, whose misapprehensions serve to bring out the truth."

So how can we know. There are many unimportant variants; some major witnesses read: "*do* we know." The "so" is implicit in the tone of the question whether or not the initial *kai,* found in many witnesses, is original.

6. *the way and the truth and the life.* There is an interesting passage in the *Gospel of Truth* (mid 2nd-century A.D. Gnosticism) that may echo this: "It [the Gospel] gave them a way, and the way is the truth which it showed them" (xviii 18–21). It is noteworthy that *zōē,* "life," which occurs thirty-two times in the Book of Signs, occurs only four times in the Book of Glory. Now that "the hour" is at hand, life is actually being given and need not be talked about.

The most difficult problem concerns the relationship of these three nouns to one another. De la Potterie, pp. 907–13, has provided a summary of opinions: (A) Explanations wherein *the way* is directed toward a goal that is *the truth* and/or *the life:* (1) Most of the Greek Fathers, Ambrose, and Leo the Great [Leo I] understood the way and the truth to lead to the life (eternal life in heaven). Maldonatus had a modification of this, since he saw behind the Greek a Hebraism wherein the truth is just an adjectival description of the way: "I am the true way to life." (2) Clement of Alexandria, Augustine, and most of the Latin Fathers understood that the way leads to both the truth and the life. In this interpretation both truth and life are eschatological, divine realities (the truth is the mind of God, the *Logos*). Thomas Aquinas held a medieval form of the theory wherein Christ was the way according to his humanity, but the truth and the life according to his divinity. Many modern scholars still hold a modification of the theory (De la Potterie lists Westcott, E. F. Scott, V. Taylor, Lagrange, and Braun). (3) Other modern scholars (W. Bauer, Bultmann, and Dodd) interpret John against the background of Gnostic dualism, Mandean, or Hermetic thought (vol. 29, pp. LIV ff. and LVIII ff.). They think of the ascent of the soul along the way to the heavenly sphere of truth, light, and life. Bultmann, pp. 467–68, maintains that John has demythologized the Gnostic picture, so that in Jesus the disciples encounter their Saviour, and the way is no longer spatially separated from the goal of truth and life. Their way is already their goal. The truth is the manifested divine reality, and the life is that reality shared by men.

(B) Explanations wherein *the way* is the primary predicate, and *the truth* and *the life* are just explanations of the way. Jesus is the way because he is the truth and the life. Among the advocates of this view are De la Potterie, Bengel, B. Weiss, Schlatter, Strathmann, W. Michaelis, Tillmann, and Van den Bussche. That "the way" is the dominating phrase in 6 is suggested by the fact that Jesus is reaffirming his statement about the way in 4, in response to Thomas' question about the way in 5. Moreover, the second line of 6 leaves aside the truth and the life and concentrates on Jesus as the way: "No one comes to the Father except *through me*." This view seems the best to the present writer. If the three phrases, "the way," "the truth," and "the life" are joined by "and," the *kai* between the first and the second may be epexegetical or explanatory (="that is to say"; BDF, §442[9]).

to the Father. This is the goal of "the way."

7. *If you men really knew me.* This is no longer addressed to Thomas alone but to all the disciples. The ms. evidence is almost evenly divided on what type of condition is meant: (a) Contrary-to-fact, implying that they have not come to know him; this receives some confirmation from vs. 9; cf. also 28: "If you loved me"; (b) Real ("If you know me"), implying that they have come to know him and promising them knowledge of the Father. The latter fits the second half of the verse better, but for that very reason is suspect as an amelioration of a difficulty. Yet, if we incline toward the first reading on the principle of choosing the more difficult reading, we recognize the possibility that there has been a cross influence from viii 19 ("If you recognized me, you would recognize my Father too"), which is clearly contrary to fact.

From now on. Not from this precise moment at the Last Supper but from the supreme "hour" of revelation that runs from the passion to the ascension. This is clearer in xvi 25: "An hour is coming when I shall no longer speak to you in figures but shall tell you about the Father in plain words."

seen Him. Here and in 9 the verb is *horan;* in xii 45 we had the same thought expressed with *theōrein;* in both instances spiritual insight is involved (see vol. 29, pp. 501-3). The "Him" is omitted in Codex Vaticanus; it may represent a scribal addition to spell out what is implied.

8. *Philip.* See NOTE on i 43.

9. *seen the Father.* P[75] and some Latin witnesses add "too," perhaps in imitation of 7.

So. See NOTE on 5 above.

10. *you men.* In mid-verse the "you" suddenly becomes plural, and what follows is addressed not only to Philip but to all the disciples.

performs the works. The textual witnesses have variants: "His works"; "the works Himself"; so also in 11: "His works"; "the works themselves." Probably these are attempts to improve on the terseness of the original and have been influenced by x 37-38. The relation of "the words" in 10c to "the works" in 10d is not clear. Patristic writers, like Augustine and Chrysostom, tended to identify them on the grounds that Jesus' words were works. Bultmann, p. 471, on the other hand, seems to understand "works" in 10-14 primarily as words. More likely the terms are complementary but not identical; the parallelism is progressive rather than synonymous. Against Bultmann's view we call attention to the emphasis here on *performing* works, to the implicit contrast between word and work in 11, and to the context in 12 which seems to demand a reference to deeds. From Jesus' point of view both word and work are revelatory, but from the audience's point of view works have greater confirmatory value than words.

11. *Believe me.* This forms an inclusion with the imperative "have faith [believe], then, in me" of vs. 1. Here "believe" (*pisteuein*) is followed by the dative pronoun; in 1 and again in 12 it is followed by the prepositional phrase "in me" (vol. 29, p. 513).

[*me*]. P[66] and P[75] lend support to the witnesses omitting the pronoun, which may have been added by scribes in imitation of the first line of the verse.

13. *you ask.* Instead of an aorist subjunctive, Codex Vaticanus and probably P[75] have a present tense which would give a continued character to the request. The Clementine Vulgate and some other witnesses add "the Father" and thus specify the direction of the request. The addition is probably under the influence of xv 16, xvi 23.

14. The whole verse is omitted in some important witnesses including OL and OS, but both P[66] and P[75] have it. Its repetitive character may have caused the omission. There is some evidence for another reading: "If you ask anything [omit "of me"] in my name, *this* will I do." This is probably an attempt to soften the awkwardness of the original, for example, in the sequence "of me in my name." Lagrange, p. 380, points out that there is nothing too illogical about petitioning Jesus in his own name, for in the OT the psalmist petitioned Yahweh for His name's sake (Ps xxv 11). It is even less illogical if "in my name" means "in union with me."

COMMENT: GENERAL

The Introduction (xiii 31-38) announced the theme of Jesus' departure; what follows in the Last Discourse is concerned with answering the problems raised by this departure—not the problems of what will happen to Jesus (his glorification is only mentioned), but the problems of what will happen to the disciples he leaves behind. Yet ch. xiv (Division 1) and its duplicate xvi 4b–33 (Division 2, Subdivision 3) tackle these problems more directly than do the other parts of xv and xvi. Chapter xiv begins with the note of reassurance that the disciples will not be separated from Jesus. He will return to take them along with him (3); their requests will be answered by his Father and by him (12–13); the Paraclete will come to them as a form of Jesus' continued presence (16–17, 26); Jesus himself will come back to them (18); and so will his Father come to them (23). Finally (27–29) the chapter returns to the theme of reassurance. Whether or not all these sayings were originally uttered on this occasion, they are now completely steeped in the Last Supper atmosphere of imminent departure.

The internal organization of ch. xiv is not easy to discern. Lagrange, for instance, suggests a division into 1–11, 12–26, 27–31, while Bultmann suggests 1–4, 5–14, 15–24, 25–31. A point of demarcation seems to occur between 14 and 15, for in 15–16 the new theme of the Paraclete is introduced. But even this break is not sharp; for the Paraclete comes at Jesus' request (erōtan), and vss. 13–14 have been concerned with asking (aitein) in Jesus' name. The inclusion that exists between the beginning and ending of 1–14 lends support to the suggestion that these verses are a unit: the challenge to believe in Jesus is shared by 1 and 11–12; the theme that Jesus is going to the Father is shared by 2 and 12. Verses 13–14 are a problem: they are related to 12 and probably should be kept with that verse, but they also offer a transition to 15. We may have here an instance of the Johannine technique of overlapping, where the conclusion of one unit is the beginning of the next (vol. 29, p. cxliii). The next unit seems to consist of 15–24, for there is an inclusion between 15 and 23–24 in the theme of loving Jesus and keeping his commandments and words. This leaves a third unit of 25–31. These three units, 1–14, 15–24, 25–31, however, are not major subdivisions such as we shall find in chs. xv–xvi, for the train of thought is reasonably consecutive throughout. If we treat them in separate sections in this commentary, it is really a question of practicality.

Let us analyze the first unit, vss. 1–14. Burney, *The Poetry of Our Lord*, pp. 126–29, thinks that behind xiv 1–10 there lies an Aramaic poetic original in four-beat rhythm, and so he sees a tight unity in at least this group of verses. Many would not agree. Boismard, RB 68 (1961), 519, following the lead of Spitta, thinks that 1–3 and 4 ff. were once independent complexes of thought. In 3 Jesus announces that he is going off to prepare a place for his disciples and then coming back to take them along with him; but in 6 Jesus himself is the way to the Father. Certainly this is a change in the direction of thought; yet one must also admit that the connection between the two parts is smooth enough on first reading. How difficult the problem is can be seen in the fact that Bultmann, unlike Boismard, would put 4 with 3. (The difficulty is centered on the meaning of "the way" in 4: Does it mean Jesus' own way to where he is going [an idea closer to 2–3], or the disciples' way to the Father [closer to 6]?)

De la Potterie, pp. 927–32, would argue that 2–6 are a subunit, with no sharp break between 3 and 4. For him the second subunit would be 6–11, with 6 as a hinge to the previous subunit (yet on p. 914 he seems to speak of 7–14). To support his claim he advances a complicated theory of chain words that this writer does not find convincing. (Some of the words that he uses to support the unity of 6–11 also appear in 12–14 with about the same frequency, so why should the latter verses not be included?) But he is right in pointing out that in the first verses the theme has concerned the departure and return of Jesus and has been strongly eschatological, while in 6–11 the verb tenses and the thought concern the present time in which the Christians are living; only in 12–14 is there a reappearance of the departure theme and of the future tenses.

With hesitancy we propose the following division into subunits: 1–4, 6–11, and 12–14. The inserted question in 5 serves to change the train of thought; the question and answer in 8–9a merely move the discourse along.

COMMENT: DETAILED

Verses 1–4: Jesus' Departure and Return

Jesus begins by a reference in vs. 1 to the troubling of heart that his departure is causing his disciples. Previously we have heard that Jesus himself was *troubled* in facing death (see NOTE), seemingly because death belongs to the realm of Satan. Putting Jesus to death will be the final act of hostility on the part of the world and of Satan, its Prince; and because of Jesus' death there will remain implacable hostility between the world and the disciples who follow Jesus (xv 18, xvii 14). Thus, the troubling of the disciples' hearts in face of Jesus' departure (also xvi 6: "Your hearts are full of sadness") is not mere sentiment but is part of the dualistic struggle between Jesus and the Prince of this world. In this light Jesus' demand that they have faith in him is more than a request for a vote of confidence: the disciples' faith conquers the world (I John v 4) by uniting them to Jesus who has conquered the world (John xvi 33). In Jesus' death the Prince of this world is driven out (xii 31), but this victory will be made apparent by the Paraclete only to those who have faith (xvi 8–11, xiv 17). It is interesting to note that in the Synoptic tradition (Mark v 35–36; Matt viii 25–26), in entirely different contexts, we find similar instances of fear in face of death and the same suggestion that faith is the remedy.

The theme in vs. 1 that faith in God has as its counterpart faith in Jesus reappears in terms of knowing and seeing in vss. 7 and 9. John does not mean that the Christian's faith in Jesus is a criterion of the Christian's faith in God; rather one and the same faith is involved. The same idea is found in xii 44: "Whoever believes in me is actually believing, not in me, but in Him who sent me"; it is negatively phrased in I John ii 23: "Anyone who denies the Son does not possess the Father."

In order to reassure his disciples about his departure, Jesus tells them that there are many dwelling places (monē—vs. 2) in his Father's house, that he is going off to prepare a place (topos—vss. 2–3) for them, and that he will come back to take them to himself so that they will be where he is. These two verses are extraordinarily difficult. The saying (if it is one saying) would not have been reported if the promise were not thought to have been realized or to be realizable. Yet it is not apparent that Jesus ever did return to take his disciples along with him; and if the reference is thought to be to a coming at the end of time (which we now know to have been far from imminent), how was this to console the disciples who would never see it? Moreover, this promise seems to clash with many other statements in the Last Discourse that Jesus would come back, not to take the disciples along with him, but to be with the disciples here below. See pp. 602–3 above on this problem.

We may begin our discussion by noting that Jesus is using traditional terminology. Taken against the Jewish background, "my Father's house" is probably to be understood as heaven. Philo (De somniis I 43; #256) speaks of heaven as "the paternal house." As for the "many dwelling places," we must reject the patristic tradition, going back at least to Irenaeus (see NOTE), that they refer to different degrees of heavenly perfection, that is, to higher and lower places in heaven. The "many" simply means that there are enough for all; the "dwelling places" reflects the type of Jewish imagery found in En xxxix 4 which speaks of "the dwelling places of the holy and the resting places of the just" that are situated in the extremities of the heavens (also xli 2, xlv 3). In II Esd vii 80 and 101 a distinction is made between the souls of the wicked who cannot enter into habitations and must wander and the souls of the just who will enter into their habitations. In the NT the imagery of eternal habitations (skēnē) is found in Luke xvi 9, while Mark x 40 speaks of heavenly chairs (prepared by the Father, not by Jesus). The Johannine Jesus' promise to his disciples that there would be dwelling places for them in his Father's house is somewhat similar to the promise made to them in Luke xxii 29–30 (a Last Supper saying): "So I appoint for you that you may eat and drink at my table in my kingdom and sit on thrones. . . ." The language that appears in John xiv 2–3 of going and preparing a place may stem from the typology of the Exodus (the Last Supper is situated in the night before Passover). In Deut i 33 God says that He will go before Israel in the way to choose for them a place; Deut i 29 reads: "Do not be in dread or afraid of them" —a command not unlike Jesus' "Do not let your hearts be troubled." In this typology Jesus would be going before the disciples into the Promised Land to prepare a place for them.

If we assume that the "many dwelling places [*monē*]" in Jesus' Father's house are the same as the place (*topos*) that Jesus is going off to prepare for his disciples, what does Jesus mean when he says he will return to take the disciples along with him, seemingly to the places he has prepared? These verses are best understood as a reference to a parousia in which Jesus would return soon after his death to lead his disciples triumphantly to heaven. (The idea of a parousia soon after death may underlie Matt xxvi 29 where at the Last Supper Jesus says: "I shall not drink again of this fruit of the vine until that day when I drink it new with you in my Father's kingdom.") A reference to the parousia is found in John xxi 22 which employs the same verb "to come" as that used in xiv 3; cf. also Rev iii 20. For the parousia as the moment when Jesus will take his followers to himself see I Thess iv 16–17: "For the Lord himself will descend from heaven. . . . Then the dead in Christ will rise first; then we who are alive and survive shall be caught up together in the clouds to meet the Lord in the air; and so we shall always be with the Lord"; note how the last clause resembles John's "so that where I am, you also may be."

Some scholars think that xiv 2–3 refer to Jesus' coming to his disciples at the hour of their death to take them to heaven. We would see this as a possible reinterpretation of the parousia theme when it was realized that the parousia had not occurred soon after the death of Jesus and when the disciples began to die. (The same double outlook may be involved in xvii 24; see p. 780 below.) When we studied xiii 36–37 in the light of xxi 15–19, we saw that Jesus' promise to Peter, "You will follow me later," was subsequently related to Peter's death. The idea that through death Christians are taken to the Father's house seems to be reflected in II Cor v 1: "For we know that if our earthly tent-house is destroyed, we have a building from God, a house not made with hands, that is eternal in the heavens."

If we think that xiv 2–3 originally referred to the parousia and possibly was reinterpreted in terms of the death of the Christian, we cannot overlook the tension between such a view in 2–3 and the realized eschatology of the rest of the chapter, for example, the thought in 15–17 (also xvi 7) that Jesus comes back to the believer in and through the Paraclete who dwells in the Christian, or the thought in 23 (only other NT use of *monē*) that Jesus and the Father shall make their dwelling place in the Christian. (Boismard, *art. cit.*, brings out well the difference between the two perspectives.) We have insisted that there are elements both of final and of realized eschatology in John (vol. 29, pp. cxvi ff.) and that they can be found even in contiguous passages (v 19–25, 26–30). Yet some commentators find it difficult to think that two such different pictures of heavenly dwelling with Jesus and of earthly divine indwelling could have been put side by side in xiv as promises of how the disciples would be consoled after Jesus' departure without some attempt at reconciliation or harmonization. It is obvious from our discussion that the phraseology of vss. 2–3 did not originally refer to Jesus' return in the form of indwelling, but could the phraseology have been secondarily reinterpreted to make it harmonious with the indwelling theme of the rest of the chapter?

Schaefer, *art. cit.*, has proposed a possible understanding of "my Father's house" that may be helpful in this regard. The phrase occurred in ii 16 in reference to the Jerusalem Temple, but John reinterpreted the Temple so that it was Jesus' body (ii 19–22). Even more significant is the parabolic saying about the house in viii 35: "While no slave has a permanent place [*menein*] in the household [or family: *oikia* as in xiv 2], the son has a place there forever." This special house or household where the son has a permanent dwelling place suggests a union with the Father reserved for Jesus the Son and for all those who are begotten as God's children by the Spirit that Jesus gives. Thus there would be some precedent for reinterpreting "many dwelling places in my Father's house" parabolically as possibilities for permanent union (*monē/menein*) with the Father in and through Jesus. (Gundry, *art. cit.*, has independently proposed a similar interpretation: ". . . not mansions in the sky, but spiritual positions in Christ.") Jesus is on his way to be reunited with the Father in glory (xiii 1) and to make it possible for others to be united to the Father—this is how he prepares the dwelling places. The variant reading for "in my Father's house" is "with my Father" (see NOTE), and that is just the meaning that the phrase may have taken on as it was integrated into the over-all Johannine theology of ch. xiv. Jesus' return after the resurrection would be for the purpose of taking the disciples into union with himself and with the Father, without any stress that the union is in heaven—his body is his Father's house; and wherever the glorified Jesus is, there is the Father. In the Greek of 3, Jesus says literally, "I am coming back to take you to myself"; in the reinterpretation this statement may have lost its original meaning of a heavenly locale. The *monē* or "dwelling place" may have become the *monē* of xiv 23—an indwelling place.

It is perhaps in this reinterpreted sense that vss. 2–3 are related by the Johannine writer to vss. 6 ff., while 4 serves as a transition by way of the Johannine technique of misunderstanding. If by his death, resurrection, and ascension Jesus is to make possible a union of the disciples with his Father, he must prepare his disciples for the union by making them understand how it is to be achieved. Augustine (*In Jo.* LXVIII 2; PL 35:1814) expresses this cleverly: "He prepares the dwelling places by preparing those who are to dwell in them." Thus, vs. 4 seeks to involve the disciples, as Jesus assures them that they know the way to where he is going (—to the Father, because they know Jesus). But just as "the Jews" of vii 35 and viii 22 could not understand where he was going, neither can Thomas. To answer, Jesus must now explain clearly that he is going to the Father and that he represents the way to get to the Father (vs. 6).

Verses 6–11: Jesus as the Way

These verses simply explain how Jesus is the way to the Father. He is the way because he is the truth or revelation of the Father (see NOTE on how to interpret the three nouns in 6a), so that when men know him they know the Father (7) and when men see him they see the Father (8). He is the way because he is the life—since he lives in the Father and the Father lives in him (10–11), he is the channel through which the Father's life comes to men.

What is the background from which this concept of Jesus as "the way" was drawn? Both Hermetic and Mandean parallels have been proposed; in these writings generally "the truth" is the sphere of divinity and "the way" is the route to the divinity (although in the Mandean texts the redeemer is never called "the way"). In particular the Mandean expression "the way of truth" has been noted. W. Michaelis (*"Hodos,"* TWNTE, V, 82–84) and De la Potterie (pp. 917–18) have rejected these parallels. They point out that John's concept of the way is not really spatial in the same way that these Gnostic concepts are spatial. Moreover, much of what is interesting in such parallels had to some extent already existed in Judaism. In OT passages (Ps cxix 30; Tob i 3; Wis v 6) "the way of truth" is a way of life in conformity with the Law. Psalm lxxxvi 11 puts "way" and "truth" in parallelism: "Teach me your way, O Lord, that I may walk in truth." We note that in these OT texts there is no question of a way to truth, as found in the Gnostic writings; rather the way is a way of truth (and this seems closer to John's meaning—see NOTE). This way in the OT sometimes has eschatological overtones, for it leads from death to life: "The wise man's way leads upward to life that he may avoid Sheol below" (Prov xv 24). The way of life and the way of death are contrasted in Jer xxi 8. Psalm xvi 11 says that the way of life is revealed by God to man; this comes close to combining John's three notions of way, truth, and life. At Qumran the way of (the Spirit of) truth is opposed dualistically to the way of the Spirit of iniquity (1QS iv 15–16; see also II Pet ii 2 and 15 which contrast "the way of truth" and "the way of Balaam").

To what extent does this Jewish material offer background for John xiv 6? In John there is no stress on the moral aspect of the way such as is found in the OT concept of "the way of truth"; rather, for John, Jesus is the way because he is the revelation of the Father. Yet we must not create a dichotomy between the revelatory aspect and the moral aspect of Jesus as the way. McCasland, *art. cit.*, stresses that Jesus is the way in a twofold sense: first, as a mediator of salvation; second, as a norm of life. For John truth is a sphere of action as well as one of believing and knowing; for instance, he can speak of acting in the truth (iii 21). If we may call upon a Synoptic passage, in Mark xii 14 the Pharisees admit that Jesus teaches "the way of God in truth."

Another objection to finding the background of the Johannine concept of "the way" in Judaism is that there is in the OT no example of the absolute use of "the way." But with the discovery of the Dead Sea Scrolls we can dispense with this objection, for the Qumran community designated itself absolutely as "the Way" (*ha-derek*). Those who entered the community were "those who have chosen the Way" (1QS ix 17–18), while those who apostatized were "those who turn aside from the Way" (CD i 3). The regulations of community life were "the regulations of the Way" (1QS ix 21). For Qumran "the Way" consisted in the strict observance of the Mosaic Law as it was interpreted by the great Teacher of the community, and there can be no doubt that this usage is the heir of the OT background mentioned above (with the added factor of dualism). In particular the absolute use of "the Way" at Qumran seems to have originated from reflection on Isa xl 3. We find such reflection in 1QS viii 12–16, a text of major importance for understanding the community's conception of itself:

> When men [who have been tested] become members of the community in Israel according to all these rules, they shall separate themselves from the places where wicked men dwell in order to go into the desert to prepare there the way of Him, as it is written, "Prepare the way of the Lord in the desert; make straight a highway for our God in the wilderness." This (way) is the study of the Law which He commanded through Moses, that they may act according to all that has been revealed from age to age, and as the prophets have revealed through His holy spirit.

If the Qumran community was living "the way of the Lord in the desert," John the Baptist too had this ideal of preparing the way of the Lord. The Christian community, which resembled the Qumran community in some basic practices and organization, seems also to have looked on itself as "the Way" (Acts ix 2, xix 9, 23, xxii 4, xxiv 14, 22), perhaps because its life was the way that prepared for the ultimate coming of Christ, a way of life commanded by Jesus and motivated by the Spirit. Now we suggest that John xiv 6 reflects this whole chain of usage of the imagery of "the way," originating in the OT, modified by sectarian Jewish thought illustrated at Qumran, and finally adopted by the Christian community as a self-designation. It is not unusual for the Johannine Jesus to take terminology once applied to Israel (and subsequently adopted by the Christian community) and to apply it to himself. If the Christian community is the temple (Eph ii 19–21; I Pet ii 5, iv 17), for John, Jesus is the temple (ii 21). The "I am . . ." sayings of the Johannine Jesus take the place of the Synoptic "The kingdom of God [heaven] is like . . ." sayings (vol. 29, p. cx), and in some instances the kingdom of God seems to have been partially identified with the Church. The imagery of the sheepfold and vineyard, applied in the OT to Israel and in the Synoptic Gospels to the kingdom of God, is applied in John to Jesus, the shepherd and the vine. The same process seems to be at work in calling Jesus rather than the Christian community "the way." If the Baptist came to make straight "the way of the Lord," his mission in the Johannine view was to reveal Jesus to Israel (i 23, 31), for Jesus is the way given to men by God.

Such transformation of terminology may have been encouraged by the Johannine understanding of Jesus as personified divine Wisdom (vol. 29, pp. cxxii ff.). In Prov v 6 it is implied that Wisdom offers the way of life to men (see also Prov vi 23, x 17). There is a very perceptive Christian interpolation into the words of Lady Wisdom in the Latin of Sir xxiv 25. Wisdom says, "In me is the gift of every *way* and *truth;* in me is every hope of *life* and virtue." It is almost as if the interpolator has associated the Johannine description of Jesus in xiv 6 with the claims of Wisdom. Concluding this discussion of the background of the Johannine concept of Jesus as the way, we wish to emphasize that we recognize that the material drawn from Jewish sources has been greatly transformed in the light of Johannine christology, but we do insist that the Jewish sources offer ample raw material so that it is not really necessary to wander farther afield in the search for background.

When we turn to the exegesis of John xiv 6, we find that in saying "I am THE WAY," Jesus is not primarily presenting himself as a moral guide, nor as a leader for his disciples to follow (as in Heb ii 10, vi 20). The emphasis here is different from that of xvi 13 where the Paraclete/ Spirit is said to guide the disciples along the *way* of all *truth.* Rather Jesus is presenting himself as the only avenue of salvation, in the manner of x 9: "I am the gate. Whoever enters through me will be saved." This is so because Jesus is THE TRUTH (*alētheia*), the only revelation of the Father who is the goal of the journey. No one has ever seen the Father except Jesus (i 18); Jesus tells us what he saw in the Father's presence (viii 38); and Jesus makes men the children of God whom they can then call Father (see COMMENT on xx 17). In calling himself the truth, Jesus is not giving an ontological definition in terms of transcendentals but is describing himself in terms of his mission to men (cf. NOTE on iv 24). "I am the truth" is to be interpreted in light of xviii 37: "The reason I have come into the world is to testify to the truth." Yet, De la Potterie, p. 939, is correct in insisting that the Johannine formula does more than tell us what Jesus does: it tells us what Jesus *is* in relation to men. Furthermore, it reflects what Jesus is *in himself;* the whole Johannine emphasis on "the real" (*alēthinos:* the real bread, the real vine) would be in vain if what Jesus is in relation to men was not a true indication of what he is in himself.

If Jesus is the way in the sense that he is the truth and enables men to know their goal, he is also the way in the sense that he is THE LIFE (*zōē*). Once again this is a description of Jesus in terms of his mission to men: "I came that they may have life and have it to the full" (x 10). The destination of the way is life with the Father; this life the Father has given to the Son (v 26), and the Son alone can give

it to men who believe in him (x 28). The gift of natural life to Lazarus
was a sign of the eternal realities behind Jesus' claim to be the resurrection
and the life (xi 25–26): "Everyone who is alive and believes in me shall
never die at all."

If Jesus is the way because he is the truth and the life, "truth"
and "life" are not simply coordinate: life comes through the truth. Those
who believe in Jesus as the incarnate revelation of the Father (and that
is what "truth" means) receive the gift of life, so that the words of
Jesus are the source of life: "The words that I have spoken to you
are both Spirit and life" (vi 63); "The man who hears my word and
has faith in Him who sent me possesses eternal life" (v 24). The use of
the definite article before the three nouns in vs. 6 implies that Jesus
is the only way to the Father. Bultmann, pp. 468–69, is correct in
insisting that when a person comes to Jesus for the truth, it is not
simply a matter of learning and going away. One must belong to the
truth (xviii 37). Thus, not only at the moment of first belief but always
Jesus remains the way.

The verses that follow (7–11) are simply a commentary on Jesus'
relationship to the Father that has been expressed in lapidary form in
vs. 6. No matter what type of condition is read in 7 (see NOTE), the
theme is that the knowledge of Jesus is the knowledge of the Father.
(B. Gärtner, NTS 14 [1967–68], 209–31, sees in this theme a reflection
of the Greek principle of knowledge of like by like.) The disciples have
not failed completely to know Jesus (as "the Jews" had done: viii 19);
yet their questions indicate that they do not know him perfectly. All
of this will be changed "from now on" (see NOTE); after "the hour"
the author of I John (ii 13) will be able to say with assurance to his
Christian audience: "You have known the Father." The theme of knowing
Jesus and thus knowing the Father in John xiv 7 is also found in the
so-called Johannine logion of the Synoptic Gospels (Matt xi 27; Luke
x 22): "No one knows the Son except the Father, and no one knows the
Father except the Son and anyone to whom the Son chooses to reveal
Him."

The appearance of this theme in the Last Discourse reflects the
covenant atmosphere of the Last Supper (p. 614 above). H. B. Huffmon
(BASOR 181 [1966], 31–37) has shown that the verb "to know," in the
sense of "acknowledge," belonged to Near Eastern covenantal language.
It is used in the Bible for Israel's acknowledgment of Yahweh as its sole
God and suzerain (Hos xiii 14); and Jeremiah (xxiv 7, xxxi 34) makes
true knowledge or acknowledgment of Yahweh part of the new covenant.
The Johannine Jesus, as author of the new covenant with the disciples,
insists that they must know him even as Israel knew Yahweh, for "from
now on" it is Jesus who will be acknowledged by Christians as "My
Lord and my God" (xx 28).

The disciples still misunderstand: Jesus is talking about knowing and seeing the Father, but they have never seen the Father (vs. 8). Exactly what Philip expects by way of vision is difficult to say. Perhaps, in the historical setting before Passover, we are to think that Philip is reflecting on the great theophanies on Sinai to Moses and Elijah. (In the Greek of Exod xxxiii 18 Moses says to God: "Show yourself to me.") Or is he thinking of the visions of the heavenly court enjoyed by the prophets? In the context of the evangelist's own time, perhaps Philip is made the innocent spokesman of those heretical Christians who seek after or claim a mystical vision of God (see vol. 30 on I John).

In any case, the question causes Jesus to explain clearly (vs. 9) that such theophanies or visions are otiose now that the Word who is God has become flesh. In seeing Jesus one sees God. This is very high christology, even though, as we have insisted before (vol. 29, p. 407), the Johannine stress on the oneness of Jesus and the Father is primarily related to the Son's mission to men and has only secondary metaphysical implications about life within the Godhead. We have also suggested that much of the equivalence between Father and Son is phrased in language that stems from the Jewish concept that the one who is sent (šālīaḥ) is completely the representative of the one who sends him. This idea has now been admirably developed by P. Borgen, "God's Agent in the Fourth Gospel," in *Religions in Antiquity* (Goodenough Volume; Leiden: Brill, 1968) pp. 137–48. He points to the rabbinic halakic or legal principle: "An agent is like the one who sent him," or, as it is phrased in TalBab *Qiddushin* 43a: "He ranks as his [master's] own person." Because Jesus is an agent who is God's own Son, John deepens the legal relationship of agent and sender to a relationship of likeness of nature (still not in philosophical terms, however). Borgen's study of the Jewish background of the type of language we find in xiv 9 is most important because of the oft-made claim that the NT passages which describe Jesus in divine language are ultimately pagan in origin. We may add that there are similarities between the description of Jesus in vs. 10 and that of the Prophet-like-Moses in Deut xviii 18 of whom God says, "I shall put my words in his mouth, and he shall speak to them all that I command him." Of Moses himself Deut xxxiv 10–12 says that the Lord sent him to do signs and works.

In its two themes of Jesus' union with the Father and of the ability of his "works" to reveal that union, vs. 10 is quite close to x 38: "Put your faith in these works so that you may come to know [and understand] that the Father is in me and I am in the Father." In complementary parallelism the last two lines of 10 bring together words and works as witnesses to Jesus' union with the Father. In xii 49–50 and in viii 28 we have heard Jesus claim that he *says* only what the Father told or taught him to say; in viii 28 he stated, "I *do* nothing by myself." Thus, precisely because neither his words nor his deeds are his own, these words and deeds tell men that Jesus is intimately related to the

Father. This attitude is best phrased in xvii 4 where the whole ministry of Jesus, words and deeds, will be called the "work" given him by his Father to do.

Verse 11 repeats 10 with a more direct appeal to believe. The two motives of belief that are offered ("believe me"; "believe [me] because of the works") are not totally distinct, for there is no appeal to miraculous works merely as extrinsic credentials for Jesus' mission (vol. 29, pp. 411–12). Real belief in the works involves the ability to understand their role as signs—the ability to see through them to what they reveal, namely, that they are the work both of the Father and of the Son who are one, and thus that the Father is in Jesus and Jesus is in the Father.

Verses 12–14: The Power of Belief in Jesus

Verse 12 serves as a transition from the theme of belief (10–11) to the theme of receiving help from God (13–14). Belief in Jesus will bring to the Christian power from God to perform the same works that Jesus performs, because, by uniting a man with Jesus and the Father, belief gives him a share in the power that they possess. The additional promise that the believer "will perform (works) far greater than these" is explicable in the changed situation of the post-resurrectional period. After Jesus has been glorified (xvii 1, 5), the Father will perform in His Son's name works capable of manifesting the Son's glory (notice the last line of vs. 13). There was another reference to "greater works" in v 20 (cf. also i 50) in a context referring to judging and giving life, and perhaps a share in these two works is included in what the disciples are now being promised. They will share in judgment, for the risen Jesus will give them power over sin (xx 21–23) and will give them the Paraclete who will prove the world wrong about judgment (xvi 8, 11). They will also have a mission to bring a share in Jesus' life to others ("bear fruit": xv 16). The idea that the disciples will be given the power to perform marvelous works is found in many NT writings. Verse 12 with its firm assurance that the man who has faith will perform greater works than those done by Jesus is somewhat similar to Matt xxi 21: "I assure you, if you have faith and never doubt, you will not only do what was done to the fig tree, but even if you say to this mountain, 'Be taken up and cast into the sea,' it will be done." The long ending of Mark (xvi 17–18) lists a group of miracles that believers will be able to do in the name of Jesus. And, of course, Acts shows the disciples working great miracles in his name, including the taking away of life (v 1–11) and the granting of life and healing (iii 6, ix 34, 40)—the works of judging and giving life. John's thought, however, differs from these other NT examples in that in John there is less emphasis on the marvelous character of the "greater works" that the disciples will do: the "greater" refers more to their eschatological character.

Statements such as those in vss. 13 and 14 that Jesus will do whatever is requested in his name are frequent in the Last Discourse. Let us study carefully four variant patterns:

(a) xiv 13: "Whatever you ask in my name I will do [*poiein*]."

     xiv 14: "If you ask anything of me in my name, I will do [*poiein*] it."

(b) xv 16: "Whatever you ask the Father in my name He will give you."

     xvi 23: "If you ask anything of the Father, He will give it to you in my name."

(c) xvi 24: "Ask and you shall receive."

     xv 7: "Ask for whatever you want and it will be done [*ginesthai*] for you."

(d) A free form (found also in I John):

     xvi 26: "On that day you will ask in my name; and I do not say that I shall have to petition the Father for you."

     I John iii 21–22: "If conscience [heart] knows nothing damaging, we can have confidence before God and receive from Him whatever we may ask, because we are keeping His commandments and doing what is pleasing in His sight."

     I John v 14–15: "Now we have confidence in God that He hears us whenever we ask for anything according to His will. And since we know that He hears us whenever we ask, we know that what we have asked Him for is ours."

In the (*a*) sayings of ch. xiv the request is (seemingly in 13, certainly in 14) addressed to Jesus and he grants it; in the (*b*) sayings of chs. xv and xvi the request is addressed to the Father and He grants it in Jesus' name. (Curiously enough, if we compare the Paraclete sayings in the respective chapters, the situation is reversed: in xiv the Father gives or sends the Paraclete in Jesus' name or at Jesus' request, while in xv and xvi Jesus sends the Paraclete.) In the (*d*) sayings the request is granted by God without any mention of Jesus' name. In the (*c*) sayings neither the addressee nor the donor is expressly mentioned, but in the context following each saying the Father is indicated.

The pattern in the (*a*) and (*b*) sayings, and to some extent in the (*d*) sayings, involves a condition with a "whatever" or "if" clause of asking; in the (*c*) sayings an imperative is used (present tense in xvi 24; aorist in xv 7).

In the (*a*) sayings the verb "do" (*poiein*) appears in the apodosis; in (*b*) the verb "give" appears; (*c*) and (*d*) have varied vocabulary, but "receive" is popular.

There are parallels in vocabulary and pattern in a group of Synoptic sayings:

■ Matt vii 7 (Luke xi 9): "Ask and it will be given to you." The (present) imperative is used as in John's class (*c*), but the verb "give" appears as in (*b*).

■ Matt vii 8 (Luke xi 10): "Everyone who asks receives." While this structural pattern is not found in John's sayings, there is a similarity to (c) in the verb "receive" and in the fact that the agent is not named. Notice that these sayings are bunched in consecutive verses, as also in John xiv 13–14, xvi 23–24.

▪ Matt xviii 19: "If two of you agree on earth about anything they ask, it will be done [ginesthai] for them by my Father in heaven." The saying contains an "if" conditional clause as in (a); the Father is the agent as in (b) and (d); the verb ginesthai is used as in (c).

▪ Matt xxi 22: "Whatever you ask in prayer, you will receive if you believe" (see variant in Mark xi 24). The patterning of the first part of the sentence is close to (a) or (b), but the lack of indication of agency and the use of the verb "receive" resemble (c).

It is clear that there are many similarities between John's patterns and those of the Synoptics, especially those of Matthew (though it is unusual for John and Matthew to have particular parallels: vol. 29, p. XLIV). Yet it is also clear that there are many variations and different combinations, and no one of John's sayings is exactly the same as a Synoptic saying. Dodd, *Tradition*, pp. 349–52, is probably correct once more in maintaining that John and the Synoptics preserve independent echoes of older sayings. Some of the variations in mood (imperative or conditional) and vocabulary ("be given," "receive," various verbs of doing) and voice (active or passive) may be attributable to different attempts to translate original Aramaic sayings into Greek.

There are two points that deserve brief notice. The last two sayings in (d) and the last two sayings in Matthew carry with them conditions for having the request granted—conditions of keeping the commandments, of asking in accordance with God's will, of having the agreement of several Christians on what should be asked, and of believing. The last mentioned condition, that of faith upon the part of the person requesting, is really implicit in all forms of the saying. But the other conditions may have been dictated by the realistic experience in the life of the community that not all requests were granted. The unconditioned forms of the sayings are more original, and it is interesting that in the Johannine tradition the conditioned forms are not attributed to Jesus.

The other point to be considered is that five of the Johannine sayings mention asking (or giving—xvi 23) "in my name." While John stresses this motif, it is not original with John. The saying in Matt xviii 19 cited above is immediately followed by a statement that supplies the basis for confidence that the request will be granted: "For where two or three are gathered together *in my name,* there I am in the midst of them." In prayer the Jews frequently recalled the Patriarchs in the hope that God would be touched by the remembrance of those holy men, and prayer in Jesus' name may have originated in similar manner. See also Mark ix 41 and the idea of giving in the name of Jesus. The Eucharist which was done in remembrance of Jesus may have contributed to the custom of praying in his name, especially since early Christian prayers would frequently be voiced on the occasion of the Eucharist (so Loisy, p. 409). But Johannine theology has introduced into prayer in Jesus' name an emphasis that goes beyond the use of a formula. A Christian prays in Jesus' name in the sense that he is in union with Jesus. Thus, the theme of asking "in my name" in xiv 13–14 continues and develops the indwelling motif of 10–11: because the Christian is in union with Jesus and Jesus is in union with the Father, there can be no doubt that the Christian's requests will be granted. This context of union with Jesus also suggests that the requests of the Christian are now no longer thought of as requests concerning the petty things of life—they are requests of such a nature that when they are granted the Father is glorified in the Son (13). They are requests pertinent to the Christian life and to the continuation of the work by which Jesus glorified the Father during his ministry (xvii 4).

[The Bibliography for this section is included in the Bibliography at the end of §52.]

51. THE LAST DISCOURSE:
—DIVISION ONE (UNIT TWO)
(xiv 15–24)

The Paraclete, Jesus, and the Father will come to those who love Jesus

XIV 15 "If you love me
     and keep my commandments,
   16 then at my request
      the Father will give you another Paraclete
      to be with you forever.
   17 He is the Spirit of Truth
      whom the world cannot accept
      since it neither sees nor recognizes him;
      but you do recognize him
      since he remains with you and is within you.
   18 I shall not leave you orphans:
      I am coming back to you.
   19 In just a little while the world will not see me any more;
      but you will see me
      because I have life and you will have life.
   20 On that day you will recognize
      that I am in the Father,
      and you are in me, and I in you.
   21 Whoever keeps the commandments that he has from me
      is the man who loves me;
      and the man who loves me will be loved by my Father,
      and I shall love him
      and reveal myself to him."

22 "Lord," said Judas (not Judas Iscariot), "what can have happened
that you are going to reveal yourself to us and not to the world?"
23 Jesus answered,

      "If anyone loves me,
       he will keep my word.

22: *said.* In the historical present tense.

Then my Father will love him,
and we shall come to him
and make our dwelling place with him.

24 Whoever does not love me does not keep my words;
yet the word that you hear is not my own
but comes from the Father who sent me."

NOTES

xiv 15. *and keep.* We have read this verb in the subjunctive (*tērēsēte*) as part of the protasis, along with P66 and Codex Sinaiticus. Other readings are well attested: (a) Codices Alexandrinus and Bezae have an imperative (*tērēsate*): "If you love me, keep my commandments"; (b) Codex Vaticanus has the future (*tērēsete*): "If you love me, you will keep my commandments." The reading we have followed closely relates 15 to 16. Reading (b) may represent a scribal harmonization with the pattern in 23. Reading (a) and, to a lesser extent, reading (b) isolate this verse from 16, establishing no grammatical relationship between the stipulations of 15 and the giving of the Spirit in 16. K. Tomoi (ET 72 [1960–61], 31) feels this lack of connection so sharply that he suggests that 15 is out of place and belongs between 20 and 21. Such a rearrangement destroys the triadic pattern of the section (see COMMENT) and is unnecessary if our translation is accepted.

keep my commandments. The verb *tērein* ("keep" in the sense of "fulfill") is used in John for observing Jesus' commandments (xiv 21, xv 10); elsewhere it is used for observing the Ten Commandments of God (Matt xix 17; I Cor vii 19). In I John too (ii 3–4, iii 22–24) the verb is used for God's commands; a close parallel to the present verse is found in I John v 3: "For the love of God consists in this: that we keep His commandments." It will be noted that here and in vs. 21 below Jesus speaks of his commandments in the plural, in contrast with the "new commandment" (singular) of xiii 34. The same variation of plural and singular is found in speaking of Jesus' commandment(s) in xv 10 and 12. His commandments are not simply moral precepts: they involve a whole way of life in loving union with him.

16. *request.* Bernard, II, 545, maintains that in general this verb *erōtan* is used to describe the prayers of Jesus, while *aitein* is used for the prayers of the disciples (as in 13, 14). But there are many exceptions.

the Father will give. In xiv 26 we hear that "the Father will send" the Paraclete; but in xv 26 and xvi 7 the sending is done by Jesus. Attribution of the action to the Father may be more original. We should not exaggerate the Johannine character of this variation, for one finds it also in Luke/Acts (Jesus sends or pours out the Spirit in Luke xxiv 49; Acts ii 33; yet these very passages show that the Father is the source of the Spirit). The verb "to give" is often associated in the NT with the Holy Spirit (Rom v 5), so that "gift" has become a designation of the Spirit (Acts ii 38, viii 20, x 45, xi 17).

another Paraclete. The Greek could be rendered: "another, a Paraclete," a translation that removes the implication that there had been an earlier Paraclete; and the OSsin supports this. However, it is not the obvious meaning (cf. x 16: "I have other sheep"; not "I have others—sheep"), and I John ii 1 shows that

Johannine thought is not loath to present Jesus as a Paraclete. Johnston, p. 33, takes the phrase as an adjectival modifier of "the Spirit of Truth" in the next verse: "the Father will give as another Paraclete . . . the Spirit of Truth whom the world cannot accept. . . ."

to be with you. Those who think of an Aramaic original underlying John suggest that *hina,* the Greek conjunction expressing purpose, is a mistranslation of the Aramaic relative *d^e* (="who will be with you"). Such a hypothesis is unnecessary, for there is truly an element of purpose in the sentence. The mss. that have the verb "to be" exhibit considerable variance in the word sequence, and there is also strong evidence for reading the verb "to remain" (*menein*). Once more some find support in this for a Semitic original, for Hebrew often uses the verb "to be" in the sense of remaining, for example, the Greek of Matt ii 13 reflects Hebrew usage: "Be [i.e., remain] there until I tell you." For the Johannine use of *menein,* see vol. 29, pp. 510–12.

17. *the Spirit of Truth.* In Johannine thought the genitive is objective: the Spirit communicates truth (see xvi 13), although there might also be an element of the appositive genitive (I John v 6[7]: "the Spirit is truth"). The phrase does not give an essential or ontological description of the Spirit; for the background see App. V.

whom . . . him. The Greek pronouns in this verse referring to the Spirit are neuter, for *pneuma* is neuter. However, the masculine pronouns *ekeinos* and *autos* are used of the Spirit/Paraclete in xv 26, xvi 7, 8, 13, 14. As the Paraclete, the Spirit takes on a more personal role than in many other sections of the NT.

since it neither sees nor recognizes. The failure to see is not really a reason or cause for the world's failure to accept the Spirit of Truth. The failure to accept and the failure to see or recognize constitute one attitude. The verb of seeing, *theōrein,* can be used of bodily sight (ii 23, xiv 19) or of spiritual sight (xii 45; see vol. 29, p. 502). The world cannot physically see the Paraclete because the Paraclete is not corporeal; nor does the world have the spiritual insight to divine his presence in the disciples. For Paul's attitude on the same question see I Cor ii 14.

you do recognize. This verb and the verb "remains" in the next line are in the present tense; in the other Paraclete passages the actions of the Paraclete are described in the future tense. Probably we are to consider the present tenses here to be proleptic (BDF, §323). But some authors would take the present tenses literally and argue either that the Paraclete was already indwelling at the Last Supper or that the verse is written from the evangelist's standpoint in time. W. R. Hutton (ET 57 [1945–46], 194) thinks that these lines are a parenthetical comment added to Jesus' words by the evangelist as a footnote. See vol. 29, p. 149, for our general attitude toward such an approach to the Johannine discourses.

since he remains with you. Again this is not really a reason or cause: the indwelling and recognition are coordinate. As Bengel has put it: the lack of recognition rules out indwelling, while indwelling is the basis of recognition. Here it is said that the Spirit of Truth *remains* with the disciple, while 16 spoke of the Paraclete's *being* with the disciple. II John 2 uses this twofold vocabulary in reference to truth itself: ". . . the truth that abides [remains] in us and will be with us forever." The interchangeability of "truth" and "Spirit of Truth" has a certain parallel at Qumran (1QS iv 23–24): "Until now the spirits of truth and of falsehood struggle in the hearts of men. . . . According to his portion of truth does a man hate falsehood."

is within you. The textual witnesses are divided on whether to read a present or a future form of the verb. The future may be a scribal correction to avoid the idea of an indwelling already at the Last Supper; or the future may be preferred as a *lectio difficilior* after two verbs in the present tense (so Rieger, *art. cit.*, p. 20) —unless the scribe introduced the future to emphasize the proleptic quality of the two preceding verbs. Rieger thinks that in this verse lines 2 to the last part of 5 are a parenthesis, while the last part of 5 continues line 1: "He is the Spirit of Truth (. . .) and he will be within you." The parenthetical lines, in his view, deal with the presence of the Paraclete/Spirit during the ministry of Jesus. The latter part of his theory seems untenable, since for John the Paraclete can only come when Jesus has gone (xvi 7); during Jesus' ministry there is no Spirit given to men (vii 39).

18. *orphans.* This figure of speech is not unusual: the disciples of the rabbis were said to be orphaned at their death (StB, II, 562), as were the disciples of Socrates at his death (*Phaedo* 116A). In the Last Discourse the image fits in with Jesus' addressing his disciples as "Little children" (xiii 33). Whether here "orphan" means fatherless or, more generally, one deserted without anyone to care for him is hard to say; yet Schwank, "Vom Wirken," p. 152, points to this verse as a basis for calling Christ "Father" in prayer.

coming back. While "back" (*palin*) was expressed in vs. 3, it is only implied here and in 28.

19. *just a little while. Eti mikron;* see Note on xiii 33. That it refers to the interim before the eschatological period is seen by the reference in the next verse to the fulfillment of the promise of seeing Jesus "on that day."

will see. A present tense used proleptically to convey the certainty of the future. *Theōrein* is used here, while *horan* is used in the parallel passage in xvi 16.

because I have life and you will have life. Literally "because I live and you will live." Once again the relation of this line to the preceding line is more coordinate than causal: sight of the risen Jesus and life are the one gift. Actually this last line of 19 could be made a separate sentence: "Because I have life, you also will have life."

20. *On that day.* This expression occurs three times in John: here, xvi 23, 26. Although in the OT "that day" is a traditional formula to describe the time of God's final intervention (also in Mark xiii 32), in the final form of Johannine thought the term seems to be applied to the period of Christian existence made possible by "the hour" of Jesus. Compare "on the last day" in vi 39, 40, 44, 54.

you will recognize. This could be translated "you yourselves" if the expressed pronoun for "you" is emphatic (so Bernard, II, 548); but Bultmann, p. 479[5], is probably right in maintaining that it is not (BDF, §277[2]).

21. *Whoever.* There is a shift to the third person in 21, 23–24a (perhaps under the impact of the Wisdom motif—see Comment). Verses 1–20 have been directed to the disciples in the second person; the duplicate discourse in xvi remains in the second person throughout.

keeps the commandments that he has from me. Literally "has my commandments and keeps them." There is no real difference between having the commandments (only here, but with rabbinic parallels) and keeping them, even though Bernard, II, 548, would see keeping the commandments as a further step (so also Augustine).

will be loved by my Father. P[75] reads "kept safe" (*tērein;* cf. xvii 11) for "loved"; and C. L. Porter, in *Studies in the History and Text of the New Testament,* ed. by B. L. Daniels and M. J. Suggs (Salt Lake City: University of Utah, 1967), p. 74, theorizes that this may be the earlier reading. Barrett, p. 388, says that John does not mean that God's love is conditional upon man's obedience; rather he is concentrating on the mutuality of love. Yet one must recognize that in Johannine dualism, since God's spontaneous love is expressed in the gift of His Son, if one turns away from the Son, one forfeits God's love.

22. *"Lord," said Judas.* All three of the interrupting questions posed by the disciples in this chapter (here, vss. 5 and 8) start in the same way. Obviously there is some editorial artificiality; yet if pure invention were involved, why would such an obscure disciple as this Judas be introduced?

Judas (not Judas Iscariot). The original may simply have had "Judas"; and the parenthesis, as well as the versional variants may be scribal attempts to clarify. The departure of Judas Iscariot in xiii 30 could have indicated to a scribe that this Judas was not Iscariot. The English form of this man's name is sometimes given as Jude, precisely to distinguish its bearer from Iscariot; but this distinction in the form of the name is not warranted by the Greek. Besides Iscariot there were at least two other important men named Judas (=Judah) who had contact with Jesus. The *first* was Judas or Jude, the relative or brother of Jesus (Mark vi 3; Matt xiii 55). He was the brother of James of Jerusalem and is traditionally identified as the author of the Epistle of Jude. The *second* was Judas of James (i.e., presumably, the son of James, not the brother of James, as some translations have it). His name appears in the two Lucan lists of the Twelve (Luke vi 16; Acts i 13), but not in the Marcan or Matthean lists. We know nothing of him, but in later hagiography there was an attempt to identify him with the Thaddaeus or Lebbaeus whose name appears in the Marcan and Matthean lists of the Twelve (Mark iii 18; Matt x 3) but is missing from the Lucan lists—an identification that is presumably the product of a guess by someone comparing the lists. Usually it is suggested that the Judas mentioned in the present verse by John is Judas of James and that he was one of the Twelve (thus Luke and John vs. Matthew and Mark on the constituency of the Twelve).

The Sahidic of this verse reads "Judas the Cananean," perhaps an attempt to identify Judas with Simon the Cananean of the Marcan and Matthean lists. The OS reads "[Judas] Thomas," and this tradition of identifying Judas with Didymus Thomas (see NOTE on xi 16, which mentions the legend that Thomas was the twin brother of Jesus) recurs in works of Syriac origin and in the *Gospel of Thomas.* H. Koester, HTR 58 (1965), 296–97, suggests that the Syriac tradition is correct and that the Judas in question was the brother of Jesus and the apostle of Edessa. This is quite speculative, however, going beyond the evidence and even beyond the traditions of the church of Edessa. Cf. G. Quispel, NTS 12 (1965–66), 380. We may note that these attempts in the versions to identify Judas work against identifying him with the Lucan "Judas of James," for the Lucan lists distinguish this disciple from Simon the Zealot and from Thomas. In the face of such confused evidence, no decision is possible.

23. *keep my word.* The expression is used in vss. 23, 24, viii 51, and xv 20; the theme of keeping God's word appears in I John ii 5. Above in 15 and 21 we had the expression "keep my [the] commandments." The plural and singular of "word" appear in 24 without apparent distinction of meaning; and so the variation between singular and plural in the use both of "word" and "commandment" (NOTE on 15) is not of clear theological significance. The equivalence

between "word" and "commandment" stems from the OT where the Ten Commandments are referred to as the "words" of God (Exod xx 1; Deut v 5, 22—indeed "word," Heb. *dābār,* may be a technical term for covenant stipulation); see also the interchangeability of "commandments," "word," and "words" in the Greek of Ps cxix 4, 25, 28. In the light of this OT background, we do not accept Bultmann's contention (p. 475[2]) that, because "keeping the commandments" is the same as "keeping the word," the expression simply involves faith and therefore there is no sign in John of "the legalism of the incipient Catholic Church." Throughout NT thought there is a strong legacy of law and precept stemming from the OT. I John binds together faith and a carefully regulated moral life.

Then my Father will love him, and we shall come to him. In RB 57 (1950), 392–94, Boismard gives evidence for a shorter form: "Then I and the Father shall come." For the difference between John's notion of divine indwelling and Philo's notion see Lagrange, pp. 389–90.

24. *the word you hear is not my own.* The Western witnesses read: "my word is not my own." Perhaps this reading has been introduced by analogy with vii 16: "My doctrine is not my own but comes from Him who sent me."

comes from. Literally "is of."

COMMENT

Many authors, including Bultmann, Wikenhauser, and Boismard, have found an interesting triadic pattern in this second unit of Division 1. If the command, "Have faith in [believe] me," dominates the first unit (xiv 1, 11), the idea of "love me" dominates the second unit. A statement about loving Jesus and keeping his commandments/word(s) occurs three times (15, 21, 23); and in each instance there is a promise that a divine presence will come to those who meet the demand. In 15–17 it is the Paraclete/Spirit who will come to dwell within the disciples. In 18–21 it is Jesus who will come to dwell within the disciples. In 23–24 (22 is transitional) it is the Father who will come along with Jesus to make a dwelling place within the disciples. Thus seemingly there is a triadic pattern here placing in rough parallelism the Spirit, Jesus, and the Father (with Jesus). Such a pattern would not be unusual; for instance, brief triadic patterns are frequent in the Pauline writings (I Cor xii 4–6; II Cor xiii 14: Eph iv 4–6). If one accepts this pattern in John xiv 15–24, the most plausible theory of its origin is that once-independent sayings about divine presence have been joined together, and that these sayings stemmed from different periods within the history of Johannine tradition. (Often the sayings about God's presence through and in the Paraclete are thought to be the latest.)

However, without necessarily denying the validity of the triadic pattern, one should note that it glosses over difficulties. The third subunit does not concern the Father alone, but the Father and Jesus. Actually the Father is already mentioned in 21, in the second subunit, although the Father's indwelling is not specified there. In fact, one can make a case for a certain unity in 21–24, since those verses speak of the Christian disciple in the third person, while 15–20 address the disciples in the second person (NOTE on "Whoever" in 21). Moreover, the question and answer pattern in 22–23a really serves better as a connective between 21 and 23–24 than as a divider between two of the triadic subunits.

But, whether or not one accepts the perfect triadic pattern, there is certainly mention of three types of divine indwelling. Despite their presumably independent origins, the sayings about these indwellings have been woven together into a unit that begins and ends on the theme of loving Jesus and keeping his commandments. Probably, in the final stage of Johannine theology, all these indwellings were thought to be accomplished through and in the Paraclete. The Paraclete is the presence of Jesus while Jesus is absent, so that the "I am coming back to you" in 18 is no contradiction to the idea that the Paraclete is being sent. And since the Father and Jesus are one, the presence of the Father and Jesus (23) is not really different from the presence of Jesus in the Paraclete.

Finally we may note that in xvi 4b–33, the discourse that is a duplicate of xiv, there is no closely worked out triadic pattern. There is no recurrence of a refrain about loving Jesus and keeping his commandments. The coming of the Paraclete in xvi 13–15 is followed by a section promising that the disciples will see Jesus again (=xiv 19); but it is not said that Jesus will dwell in the disciples, nor is it said that the Father will dwell in them (although the Father is said to love the disciples in xvi 27). Boismard, art. cit., argues that xiv closely resembles the Johannine Epistles, even though xiv is christocentric while I John is theocentric. To the verses in xiv (15, 21, 23–24) that speak of loving Jesus there correspond verses in I John (iv 20–21, v 2–3) that speak of loving God. In the NOTE on 15 we pointed out that the insistence in this unit of John on keeping Jesus' commandments is matched in I John by an insistence on keeping God's commandments, an observance that leads to God's indwelling within the Christian (I John iii 24, iv 12–16).

Verses 15–17: The Coming of the Paraclete

Verse 15 begins with a demand to love Jesus. While the love of God is a well-attested theme in both Testaments, surprisingly the theme of the Christian's love of Jesus is not overly common—belief in Jesus is a more frequent motif. The love of Jesus is mentioned chiefly in the later NT books: *agapan* is the verb used in this unit of John xiv, in viii 42, xxi 15, 16; Eph vi 24; I Pet i 8; and *philein* is used in John xvi 27, xxi 17; Matt x 37 (but cf. Luke xiv 26); I Cor xvi 22. The understanding that the Christian must love Jesus even as he loves the Father may be a facet of a gradual theological development in the realization of who Jesus is, but we cannot discount the fact that Jesus' demand to be loved is perfectly at home in the covenant atmosphere of the Last Discourse and the Last

Supper. N. Lohfink (GeistLeb 36 [1963], 271–81) has pointed out a parallelism between the demand of the covenant God of Sinai to be loved exclusively by His people (Deut vi 5) and the demand for exclusive love on the part of Jesus who is God's visible presence among men, establishing a new covenant with them.

The introduction of the theme of the Paraclete in 16–17 is not too abrupt when the gift of the Paraclete is associated with the theme of having one's prayers answered by God (13–14). We get the same sequence in Luke xi 9–13: "Ask and it will be given to you. . . . How much more will the Father in heaven give a Holy Spirit to those who ask Him!" Verses 16–17 constitute the first of five Paraclete passages in the Last Discourse, which we shall treat together in App. V, mentioning here only features peculiar to this particular passage. Two of the passages occur in xiv, and two occur in the duplicate discourse of xvi 4b–33; and in each case the first passage concerns the opposition between the Paraclete and the world. The reference in 16 to the Paraclete as "another Paraclete" (see NOTE) has the obvious implication that Jesus has been a Paraclete, since the other Paraclete is coming when Jesus departs. I John ii 1 presents Jesus as a Paraclete in his role as a heavenly intercessor in the Father's presence after the resurrection; yet John would seem to imply that Jesus has been a Paraclete during his earthly ministry. (The suggestion that Jesus is a Paraclete because he will utter the great intercessory prayer of ch. xvii is scarcely adequate to explain the implication of xiv 16–17 where no intercessory function is attributed to the Paraclete.) We shall see in App. V that the Spirit of Truth is a Paraclete precisely because he carries on the earthly work of Jesus. The Paraclete/Spirit will differ from Jesus the Paraclete in that the Spirit is not corporeally visible and his presence will only be by indwelling in the disciples. The OT theme of "God with us" (the Immanuel of Isa vii 14) is now to be realized in the Paraclete/Spirit who remains with the disciples forever.

Verses 18–21: The Coming (Back) of Jesus

There is a parallelism between the first and second subunits of the triadic pattern, those that deal respectively with the coming and indwelling of the Paraclete/Spirit and the coming (back) and indwelling of Jesus:

	15–17	18–21
Necessary conditions: love Jesus; keep his commands	15	21
Giving of Paraclete; coming back of Jesus	16	18
World will not see Paraclete or Jesus	17	19
Disciples will recognize Paraclete and see Jesus	17	19
Paraclete and Jesus will dwell in the disciples	17	20

(John seems to have two patterns of parallelism. One is chiastic where there is an inverse sequence in the two sections so that together they form a parabolic curve; see vi 36–40 in vol. 29, p. 276; also xv 7–17 on p. 667 below. In the other pattern the sequence is the same in both sections, often with the exception that the first verse in one section matches the last verse in the other; see v 19–30 in vol. 29, p. 219. The latter is involved here.) Such parallelism is John's way of telling the reader that the presence of Jesus after his return to the Father is accomplished in and through the Paraclete. Not two presences but the same presence is involved.

Since we have already called attention to the resemblances between John xiv and I John, it is of interest to point out that the five features noted above are found in I John, generally in descriptions of the Father (it is not always possible to say to whom the "he" and "his" of I John refer):

		I John
Necessary conditions: love one another; keep His commandments		iii 23–24
Revelation of God		iii 2
Opposition between the Father and the world		ii 15–17
Christians shall see Him as He is		iii 2
God abides in Christians		iii 24

Commenting on the individual verses of this subsection, we find in the first line of 18 a bridge between the reference to the Paraclete and the reference to Jesus' own post-resurrectional work. In fact, it is difficult to be sure which type of indwelling supplies the basis for "I shall not leave you orphans." Even though in the present sequence "I am coming (back) to you" is probably to be interpreted in terms of the coming of the Paraclete, we must ask about the original reference of these words if, as probable, they once existed independently of the promise of the Paraclete. The Latin Fathers thought that the reference was to the parousia promised in xiv 2–3. The implication in 19 that the coming will occur after a little while is no obstacle to this interpretation since that phrase is not a chronological indication (NOTE on xiii 33), and the words "On that day" in 20 might favor the thought of the parousia. But the statement in 19 that the world will not see Jesus does not fit the parousia at all. The Eastern Fathers generally understood a reference to the post-resurrectional appearances of Jesus, an interpretation that takes "a little while" literally. This fits in well with the idea that the world will not see Jesus (Acts x 40–41: "God made him manifest, not to all the people, but to us who were chosen as witnesses"). Also the statement in 19 "I have life" seems to be characteristic resurrection terminology: Luke xxiv 5, "Why do you seek the living one among the dead?", 23, ". . . angels who said that he was alive"; also Mark xvi 11; Acts i 3; Rev i 18.

Yet it is obvious that Jesus is speaking of a more continued presence than was possible in the brief period of post-resurrectional appearances—not only the words "I shall not leave you orphans" but the whole tone of his remarks imply permanency. Therefore, if originally these verses referred to Jesus' coming back in a series of post-resurrectional appearances, they were soon reinterpreted in Johannine circles to refer to a more abiding and non-corporeal presence of Jesus after the resurrection. (And seemingly this happened before they were associated with the promise of the Paraclete and still further reinterpreted to refer to Jesus' presence in his Spirit.) This reinterpretation grew out of the profound insight that the real gift of the post-resurrectional period was a union with Jesus that was not permanently dependent on bodily presence. This does not mean that passages such as this strip the Easter event of its external, miraculous character (Bultmann, p. 479), and that there is no difference between post-resurrectional appearances and indwelling. Rather, the Fourth Gospel (xx 27) goes out of its way to insist on the external character of the appearances and the bodily reality of the risen Jesus. But John has also realized that the appearances are not an end in themselves; they initiate and point to a deeper type of presence. (We saw the same approach to the miracles of Jesus: the Fourth Gospel does not dispense with the reality of the miracles but insists on their spiritual significance.) This insight is not peculiar to John; for in Matt xxviii 20 the risen Jesus says, "I am with you always until the end of time." (It is possible, however, that Matthew is not speaking of Jesus' presence in individual Christians but in the Christian community as a community.) It should be noted that none of these passages is concerned with the presence of Jesus encountered by mystics; the presence of Jesus is promised, not to an ascetical elite, but to Christians in general.

The theme in the last line of 19 that Jesus' life is the basis and source of Christian life is common NT doctrine (Rom v 10; I Cor xv 22). In 20 John moves ahead to the idea that, once Christians have received life from Jesus, they will be able to recognize that it is a life mutually shared by Father and Son (see also v 26, vi 57). We have already pointed out how many types of indwelling formulas there are involving Jesus, the Father, and the disciples (pp. 602–3 above).

The mention of indwelling in 20 is followed in 21 by the condition on which that indwelling depends: keeping Jesus' commandments and thus loving him. The first two lines of 21 restate 15 in inverse fashion and show that love and keeping the commandments are but two different facets of the same way of life. Love motivates the keeping of the commandments, and indeed love is the substance of Jesus' commandments. The statement in 21 that whoever loves (*agapan*) Jesus will be loved by the Father has a parallel in the duplicate discourse of xvi (27): "For the Father loves [*philein*] you Himself because you have loved me." The OT Sapiential background of Johannine thought and vocabulary comes very much to the fore in 21. For instance, Wis vi 18 speaks of Lady Wisdom, "Love [*agapē*] is the keeping of her laws"; also vi 12, "She is easily seen [*theōrein*] by those who love her." If Jesus says, "I shall reveal myself to him [who loves me]," Wis i 2 says that the Lord will reveal Himself to those who trust Him.

The question posed in 22 ties in the end of the second subunit (18–21) with the beginning of the third subunit (23–24)—unless one should take more seriously the possibility mentioned above (p. 643) that 21–24 belong together. The problem that bothers Judas is disturbingly like the problem posed long before in vii 4 when the "brothers" of Jesus pointedly suggested that he should display his miracles to the world. We might have expected that by this time Judas would have had more faith in Jesus than the disbelieving brothers, but evidently the nature of the messianic expectations of the disciples has not changed greatly (cf. Luke xxii 24, at the Last Supper). Jesus had spoken of *revealing* himself to his disciples. He meant that he would do this by indwelling (if we speak on the level of the present context); but this same term had been used in LXX descriptions of the theophany to Moses on Sinai (Exod xxxiii 13, 18). It would seem then that Judas, perhaps not unlike Philip in 8, is looking for another theophany that will startle the world and cannot understand Jesus' statement in 19 that the world will not see him any more. (If at an earlier period the "coming back" of 18–21 referred to post-resurrectional appearances, then this question may have originally been centered on the fact that the risen Jesus did not show himself to all men, a problem reflected in Acts x 40–41 and still being discussed in Origen's time. Origen [*Celsus* II 63–65; GCS 2:185–87] gave the answer that not all eyes could have tolerated the glory of the Risen One. John's answer would seem to have been that love of Jesus and keeping the commandments were necessary for sharing Jesus' presence in any form.)

Verses 23–24: The Coming of the Father (with Jesus)

As has happened frequently before (iii 5, iv 13), Jesus does not answer directly the question posed by Judas, although, when properly understood, what he says is an answer. He takes the opportunity to explain once again what it really means to see him and, therefore, implicitly explains why the world cannot see him. He told Philip in 9, "Whoever has seen me has seen the Father"; now he points out that his presence after the resurrection will also mean the Father's presence. Above we pointed out five features that were common to the descriptions of the presence of the Paraclete and of Jesus; three of these reappear here in vs. 23 in relation to the Father's presence: the necessary conditions of loving Jesus and keeping his word; the statement that the Father (and Jesus) will come to the disciple; and a reference to the indwelling of the Father (and Jesus) within the disciple. Of the remaining two features, there is no specific mention of the world's inability to see the Father, as was the case with the Paraclete and with Jesus; but the verses dealing with the Father's presence are in answer to Judas' question of why there will be no revelation to the world. As for the special ability of the Christian to see or recognize the Father, we heard in 7: "If you men really knew me, then you would recognize my Father too. From now on you do know Him and have seen Him." Thus the similarities shared by the subunits of the triadic pattern are truly impressive.

In 23 Jesus emphasizes that divine indwelling flows from the Father's love for the disciples of His Son. In iii 16 we heard that God loved the world so much that He gave the only Son—if the incarnation (and death) of the Son was an act of the Father's love for the world, the post-resurrectional indwelling is a special act of love for the Christian. In 2 we found the word "dwelling place" (*monē*) used for the heavenly abode with the Father to which Jesus would take his disciples; here it is used for the indwelling of the Father and the Son with the believer. Although Jesus' words do not exclude a parousia or revelation in glory such as Judas expected, he is implicitly saying that in indwelling are fulfilled some of the expectations of the last period. A prophet like Zechariah (ii 14 [10]) had promised on behalf of Yahweh: "For look, I come to dwell in the midst of you." Israel had expected this to take place in the Temple, the house of God (cf. Exod xxv 8; I Kings viii 27 ff.); but in Johannine thought this was now the hour when men would worship the Father neither on Mount Gerizim nor in the Jerusalem Temple, but in Spirit and truth (iv 21–24).

Verse 24 comes back obliquely to the reason why the world cannot see the Father, namely, that it refuses to hear the word of Jesus since it does not love Jesus. As Augustine (*In Jo.* LXXVI 2; PL 35:1831) puts it, "Love separates the saints from the world." The theme in 24 is very similar to what Jesus said in xii 48–49. There he promised that the word he spoke would condemn the disbeliever on the last day. We see here that it does this by cutting him off from the source of life that the true disciple of Jesus enjoys.

[The Bibliography for this section is included in the Bibliography at the end of §52.]

52. THE LAST DISCOURSE:
—DIVISION ONE (UNIT THREE)
(xiv 25–31)

Jesus' final thoughts before departure

XIV 25 "I have said this to you while I am still with you.
26 But the Paraclete, the Holy Spirit
    that the Father will send in my name,
    will teach you everything
    and remind you of all that I told you [myself].
27 'Peace' is my farewell to you.
    My 'peace' is my gift to you,
    and I do not give it to you
    as the world gives it.
    Do not let your hearts be troubled,
    and do not be fearful.
28 You have heard me tell you,
    'I am going away,' and 'I am coming back to you.'
    If you loved me,
    you would rejoice that I am going to the Father,
    for the Father is greater than I.
29 But now I have told you this even before it happens
    so that, when it does happen, you may believe.
30 I shall no longer speak [much] with you,
    for the Prince of the world is coming.
    Actually, he has no hold on me;
31 but the world must recognize that I love the Father
    and that I do exactly as the Father has commanded me.
    Get up! Let us leave here and be on our way."

NOTES

xiv 25. *I have said this to you.* Literally "these things." These words will recur as a refrain six times in Division 2 of the Last Discourse (xv 11, xvi 1, 4a, 6, 25, 33). In two instances (xvi 4a, 33) the refrain marks the end of a subdivision; in three instances (xv 11, xvi 1, 25) it comes a few verses before the end as Jesus summarizes. Bernard, II, 485, points out that a refrain of this sort is not unusual in the prophets: "I, the Lord, have spoken" occurs many times in Ezekiel (e.g., v 13, 15). There is a functional parallel in the refrain with which Matthew marks the end of each of his five great discourses: "When Jesus had finished these words [or these parables or instructing] . . ." (vii 28, xi 1, xiii 53, xix 1, xxvi 1).

I am still with you. Literally "remaining with you"; for the interchangeability of the ideas "to remain" and "to be" see NOTE on 16 ("to be with you"). If John uses the verb *menein* here to describe Jesus' presence at the Last Supper with his disciples, the verb was previously used in 17 to describe the future presence of the Paraclete/Spirit with the disciples, and the cognate noun *monē* was used in 23 to describe the future presence of the Father and the Son with the disciples.

26. *But.* Verse 26 is related to 25; the Paraclete takes Jesus' place (explicitly in xvi 7).

the Holy Spirit. This is a very well attested reading. There is minor support for "the Spirit of Truth," but this is probably a harmonization with other Paraclete passages (xiv 17, xv 26, xvi 13). Simply "the Spirit" is read by OS[sin]; Barrett, p. 390, points out that it is not impossible that such a short reading was original and that both "holy" and "of truth" are scribal clarifications. It should be noted that this is the only instance in John of the fullest Greek form of "Holy Spirit" (*to pneuma to hagion*), so that even some who think it is the genuine reading suggest that in the process of Johannine editing it was introduced into a passage that originally mentioned only the Paraclete. The question is of importance because there are some scholars who question the traditional identification of the Paraclete with the Holy Spirit (see App. V), and this is the only passage that makes that identification explicit.

will send. See NOTE on "will give" in 16.

will teach you everything. A masculine pronoun is the subject of the verb (see NOTE on "him" in 17). While we must beware of reading 4th-century Greek theological discussions about person and nature back into this pronoun, Bernard, II, 500, is correct in saying that the use of masculine pronouns shows that for the writer the Spirit was more than a tendency or influence. The "everything" sets up a contrast with the "this" ("these things") of 25, but not necessarily in the sense that the Paraclete will teach more quantitatively than Jesus did during his ministry. Rather, as we gather from xvi 13, the Paraclete will enable the disciples to see the full meaning of Jesus' words. In I John ii 27 the Christian is told that the anointing that he has from God "teaches you about everything" and that he needs no new teaching (also II John 9). The present passage and its parallel in xvi 13 ("He will guide you along the way of all truth") are a divided echo of Ps xxv 5: "Guide me along the way of your truth and teach me."

remind. The verb is used in Luke xxii 61 for recalling the words of Jesus. Bultmann, p. 485[1], points out that teaching and reminding are not two different functions of the Paraclete but aspects of the same function. Thus the last two lines of 26 are in synonymous parallelism.

[myself]. The personal pronoun is found in Vaticanus and a few other witnesses; if original, it is emphatic.

27. 'Peace' is my farewell to you. Literally "Peace I leave to you." The verb "to leave" can have the sense of bequeathing, although it is not a technical juridical term. There is a play here on the traditional Hebrew salutation "Shalom" (šālōm, "peace"), e.g., I Kings i 17. In departing Jesus says "Shalom" to his disciples; but his "Shalom" is not the thoughtless salutation of ordinary men—it is the gift of salvation (see COMMENT). "Peace," along with "grace," became part of the traditional greeting from one Christian to another (Rom i 7; I Cor i 3); but despite frequent usage it retained its deeply religious meaning: "Let the peace of Christ reign in your hearts" (Col iii 15).

hearts. See NOTE on xiv 1.

fearful. Rev xxi 8 curses the fearful along with the other wicked; for early Christians fear represented lack of faith in Jesus.

28. You have heard me tell you, 'I am going away.' The verb is hypagein. Jesus said this obliquely in xiii 33 ("Where I am going [hypagein], you cannot come") and in xiv 4 ("You know the way to where I am going [hypagein]"). Seemingly it is to the latter that Jesus is referring.

'I am coming back to you.' The verb is erchesthai. Jesus said this verbatim in xiv 18, but see also the palin erchesthai of xiv 3. Only in xiv 3–4 do the two statements cited in 28 appear together, but there neither one is verbatim the same as in 28.

If you loved me. Some witnesses soften the unreal condition to a real one, implying that the disciples do love Jesus. For the use of the aorist in the apodosis of this unreal condition see ZGB, §317.

going to the Father. Here the verb is poreuesthai; see NOTE on "going off" in 2.

for the Father is. The OS reads "who is."

29. See NOTES on xiii 19.

30. [much]. The evidence for omission is weak (OSsin); yet a scribe, thinking the statement "I shall no longer speak with you" strange when three chapters of discourse were yet to follow, may have inserted the word. Without "much" the statement would have made perfect sense when Division 1 was the whole Last Discourse.

the Prince of the world. See NOTE on xii 31. In the duplicate discourse in xvi he is mentioned in 11.

he has no hold on me. Literally "in me he has nothing"; for our translation see BAG, p. 334, §I,7. There is evidence, both versional and patristic, for another reading: "in me he finds nothing" (by conflation Codex Bezae has both verbs). This may be a scribal attempt at an easier reading, but Boismard suggests that the two verbs represent alternative renderings of an Aramaic verb ('aškaḥ) that means both "to be able" and "to find"—see full discussion in ÉvJean, pp. 54–55.

31. but the world must recognize. Literally "in order that the world recognize"—an elliptical construction similar to the ones in ix 3, xiii 18. Some would connect it to what follows so that it supplies the reason for the command to get up and leave (perhaps understood as a reference to his ascension to the Father). More likely the clause is to be related to the complex of ideas that has

preceded and explains why Jesus is entering the struggle against the Prince of the world.

has commanded me. Jesus' obedience to the Father's command is a Johannine theme: "Doing the will of Him who sent me . . . that is my food" (iv 34); "I keep His word" (viii 55).

COMMENT

In ch. xiv it is difficult to know where one unit ends and another begins. For instance, vss. 25–26 might be treated as the ending of the unit 15–24 (so Schwank), with the reference to the Paraclete in 26 serving as an inclusion to the earlier Paraclete section in 15–17. However, from another point of view, 25–26 can be put with 27–31, for these verses collect the various themes that have been scattered through the whole of Division 1 of the Last Discourse and the Last Supper scene that prefaced it:

26: The Paraclete=xiv 16–17
27: Do not let your hearts be troubled=xiv 1
28: I am going away=xiv 2
28: I am coming back to you=xiv 3
28: If you loved me (contrary to fact condition)=xiv 7 (If you really knew me)
29: I have told you this even before it happens=xiii 19
30: The Prince of the world=xiii 27 (Satan)

Since the refrain in 25, "I have said this to you," is used elsewhere in the Last Discourse to introduce concluding remarks (see NOTE), it seems best to treat 25–31 as the conclusion of the Last Supper scene and of the original form of the Last Discourse (pp. 583–86 above). The remarks have an air of finality and farewell, and vs. 31 is the signal for departure from the supper room.

Verses 25–26: The Sending of the Paraclete to Teach

The refrain in vs. 25 differs from the other instances of its use in that it is modified by the clause "while I am still with you," an unhappy reminder that Jesus' time with his disciples is running out. This prepares the way for another reference to the Paraclete. The second Paraclete passage in both xiv and xvi (13–14) treats of his function as a teacher. Both are introduced by a statement about the limitations that time has put on what Jesus himself could teach (xiv 25, xvi 12), and the teaching of the Paraclete is clearly related to Jesus' own teaching. "He will not speak on his own, but will speak only what he hears . . . because it is from me that he will receive what he will declare to you" (xvi 13–14).

If the first Paraclete passage (xiv 16) said that the Father would give the Paraclete *at Jesus' request,* this passage says that the Father will send the Paraclete *in Jesus' name.* The two phrases are related (remember that in 13–14 Christians were told to make their requests in Jesus' name); but, as we have pointed out (p. 636 above), "in my name" carries with it an implication of union with Jesus. When the Father acts in Jesus' name, this action flows from the union of Father and Son (a union that was the topic of vss. 20, 23–24). Here "in my name" may also refer to the conduct of the mission: the Paraclete's mission is the completion of Jesus' mission. Jesus bore God's name (xvii 11, 12) because he was the revelation of God to men; the Spirit is sent in Jesus' name because he unfolds the meaning of Jesus for men. If Jesus could say in 24, "The word that you hear is not my own," so too the teaching that the Paraclete will communicate is not his own.

Verse 27ab: The Parting Gift of Peace

The first four lines of this verse are a majestic promise made by Jesus to the disciples he leaves in the world. The peace of which Jesus speaks has nothing to do with the absence of warfare (indeed it will come only after the world has been conquered: xvi 33), nor with an end to psychological tension, nor with a sentimental feeling of well-being. Cyril of Alexandria identified peace with the Holy Spirit mentioned in the previous verse; his exegesis is wrong, but it is closer to the truth than many of the modern oratorical distortions of this verse, for it recognizes correctly that the peace of Jesus is a gift that pertains to man's salvation. Barrett, p. 391, points out that already in many OT passages "peace" had acquired more than conventional meaning, for example, as a special gift of the Lord in Ps xxix 11; Isa lvii 19. In Johannine language "peace," "truth," "light," "life," and "joy" are figurative terms reflecting different facets of the great gift that Jesus has brought from the Father to men. " 'Peace' is my gift to you" is another way of saying "I give them eternal life" (x 28). The "my peace" of which Jesus speaks here is the same as the "my joy" of xv 11, xvii 13.

The use of the term "peace" here is particularly appropriate since a farewell is involved (see NOTE). In 20 Jesus used the OT phrase "on that day," implying that his indwelling with his disciples after the resurrection would fulfill the eschatological dreams of the prophets. For these prophets the messianic king sent by God was to be a prince of peace (Isa ix 6) who would "command peace to the nations" (Zech ix 10). The bringer of good tidings was to be one who announces peace and salvation (Isa lii 7). The theme of peace also belongs to the covenant mentality we have seen exhibited at the Last Supper. In Ezek xxxvii 26, Yahweh says to Ezekiel: "I will make a covenant of peace with them." (Ezekiel makes it clear that an essential part of the covenant is that Yahweh would set His sanctuary in the midst of His people forever; so also Jesus' covenant with his followers involves his indwelling forever.) According to Wis iii 1, 3 peace is one of the blessings of the souls of the just who are in the hand of God, but in Johannine realized eschatology peace is enjoyed by Christians even during this life.

Verses 27c–29: Jesus' Departure

The last two lines of 27 repeat the opening counsel of ch. xiv that the disciples are not to be fearful or troubled at Jesus' departure. While this thought flows smoothly after the mention of peace, its prime function is to prepare the way for 28–29 where that departure will be stressed and explained. Once again we are in the atmosphere of the farewell speech, for Moses' parting counsel in Deut xxxi 8 is "Do not fear." Such advice is especially appropriate as Jesus departs, for this departure involves a combat with the Prince of the world (30–31).

In 28 Jesus recalls what he said in 3–4 (see NOTE) about going away and coming back, an inclusion binding together the beginning and ending of the body of Division 1. The unreal condition, "If you loved me . . . ," is meant not to deny that the disciples love him, but to indicate that their love is possessive instead of generous. The Johannine Jesus represents the Father and leads to the Father, and so in going to his Father he is accomplishing his life's purpose; any love that would fail to recognize and respect that is not real love. Thus implicitly faith and love are closely associated here. The thought is carried even further in xvi 7: "It is for your own good that I go away," for in that statement are envisaged both the glorification of Jesus with the Father and the results of that glorification for men.

The last line of 28, "for the Father is greater than I," has been the subject of much christological and trinitarian debate. The Arians called upon this statement to justify their christology, and subsequently it has often been used as an argument against the divinity of Jesus. (But here Loisy, p. 415, is very perceptive: "From the very fact that Christ compares himself to the Father, it is taken for granted that he is of divine nature by reason of his heavenly origin." For other texts that seem to make Jesus less than God the Father, see vol. 29, p. 24.) There have been two classic orthodox interpretations. One group of Fathers (Origen, Tertullian, Athanasius, Hilary, Epiphanius, Gregory of Nazianzus, John Damascene) have explained the text as expressive of the distinction between the Son and the Father: the Son is generated while the Father is not. However, this interpretation stems from later dogmatic reflection upon Scripture rather than from literal exegesis. It is anachronistic to imagine that John had Jesus speaking to his disciples of inner trinitarian relationships. Another group of Fathers (Cyril of Alexandria, Ambrose, Augustine) have explained that *as man* the incarnate Son was less than the Father.

This explanation seems on first glance to be more plausible exegesis than the previous one. Yet while John offers the basis on which was built the subsequent theology of the distinction of natures in Jesus (compare the statement under consideration with x 30; "The Father and I are one"), we must not interpret John as if such formal theology was in the author's mind. Would the evangelist think of a distinction between Jesus speaking as man and Jesus speaking as God? More particularly is such a distinction appropriate in the Last Discourse where more than anywhere else the Jesus who speaks transcends time and space (see pp. 581–82 above)?

If we seek to explain the passage without the intervention of the formal dogmatics of a later period, the key probably lies in a similar statement made in xiii 16: "No messenger is more important than the one who sent him." We have already explained that statements like "The Father and I are one" (x 30) and "Whoever has seen me has seen the Father" (xiv 9) have their background in the Jewish concept of the relationship between a messenger or agent and the one who sent him. (See p. 632 above and the article of P. Borgen cited there.) Borgen, p. 153, points out the subordination of the agent to the sender: "The sender is greater than the one sent" (Midrash Rabbah lxxviii 1 on Gen xxxii 27). In addition, the statement in John xiv 28 must be related to its context: the disciples should rejoice that Jesus is going to the Father, for the Father is greater than Jesus. Neither of the classic dogmatic explanations explains why the disciples should rejoice. The idea is probably the same as in xvii 4–5: Jesus is on the way to the Father who will glorify him. During his mission on earth he is less than the One who sent him, but his departure signifies that the work that the Father has given him to do is completed. Now he will be glorified with that glory that he had with the Father before the world existed. This is a cause of rejoicing to the disciples because when Jesus is glorified he will glorify his disciples as well by granting them eternal life (xvii 2).

The "I have told you this even before it happens" of 29 refers to the whole process of death, resurrection, ascension, and giving of the Spirit. When it does happen, the disciples will be able to recognize it as the fulfillment of what Jesus had said precisely because they will have the Paraclete who reminds them of all that Jesus told them (xiv 26). Until they had the enlightenment of the Paraclete, they would not understand the death of Jesus (Luke xxiv 20–21) nor would they be prompt to believe in his resurrection (John xx 25; Matt xxviii 17).

Verses 30–31: Struggle with the Prince of the World

Here, just as at the end of the duplicate discourse in xvi, there is an allusion to the impending struggle with the world, personified in vs. 30 in its Prince. In both instances Jesus is confident of his victory (xvi 33: "I have conquered the world"). Some have suggested that the statement that the Prince of the world has no hold on Jesus refers to the fact that Jesus lays down his life of his own choice and no one takes it from him (x 18). However, we are actually past the moment when Jesus submitted himself to death; for in xiii 27 after Satan entered into Judas, Jesus told Judas to do what he was going to do. Now a more likely source of confidence is that no one will be given power over Jesus except by the Father's permission (xix 11). The contention in 31 that the struggle with the Prince of the world will show that Jesus does as the Father has commanded him indicates that the Father's control of what is happening will prevent the Prince of the world from gaining any hold over Jesus. Once again we are not to think that the results of the struggle will be immediately evident to the world. If from the struggle the world must come to recognize Jesus' relation to the Father (31), it will be the task of the Paraclete to prove this to the world (xvi 8–11).

Verse 31 is the only passage in the NT that states that Jesus *loves* the Father. What this love consists in is made clear by the second line, for the "and" that joins the second line to the first is epexegetical (Bultmann, p. 488[4])—the love consists in doing what the Father has commanded, just as the Christian's love for Jesus consists in doing what Jesus has commanded. No one can accuse the evangelist of not being a realist!

In vol. 29, pp. 470–71, we showed that while John does not describe the agony in Gethsemane, elements parallel to that scene are scattered through John. Some of these are found in 30–31. The mention of the coming of the Prince of the world resembles Luke xxii 53 where Jesus acknowledges that the moment of his arrest is the hour of "the power of darkness." The directive in 31 to get up and leave is the same directive given by Jesus in Mark xiv 42 as Judas approaches the garden: "Get up! Let us leave." In this context we may compare John's "I do exactly as the Father has commanded me" with Luke xxii 42: "Father . . . not my will but yours be done." Mark xiv 42, just cited, ends with these words: "See, the one who hands me over is at hand." This is a reference to Judas' approach; John is more interested in the approach of Satan who is the real force acting in Judas (xiii 2, 27).

The last line of 31 was the ending of the original Last Discourse. We have suggested that the final editor did not want to tamper with this ending and so, despite the fact that he was creating an awkward sequence, added additional forms of the Last Discourse after 31. Dodd, *Interpretation*, pp. 407–9, although he recognizes the possibility of such editing, thinks that "Get up! Let us leave here and be on our way" must be intelligible even in its present position where several chapters follow. He understands it in terms of encouragement to march to meet the Prince of this world in death and resurrection and contends that "a movement of the spirit," rather than a physical movement, takes place in 31, so that the next stage of the Last Discourse is from a standpoint beyond the cross after death (so also Zimmermann, *art. cit.*). This seems farfetched and unnecessary. It is more plausible that the final editor simply made the best of a difficult situation and did not seek to force a new meaning on 31.

BIBLIOGRAPHY
(xiii 31 – xiv 31)

See the general bibliography on the Last Discourse at the end of §48 and the Bibliography on the Paraclete in App. V.

Boismard, M.-E., "L'évolution du thème eschatologique dans les traditions johanniques," RB 68 (1961), especially 518–23.

Caird, G. B., "The Glory of God in the Fourth Gospel: An Exercise in Biblical Semantics," NTS 15 (1968–69), 265–77. A study of xiii 31.

Cerfaux, L., "La charité fraternelle et le retour du Christ (Jn. xiii 33–38)," ETL 24 (1948), 321–32. Also RecLC, II, 27–40.

de la Potterie, I., " 'Je suis la Voie, la Vérité et la Vie' (Jn 14, 6)," NRT 88 (1966), 907–42. Condensed in English in TD 16 (1968), 59–64.

Gundry, R. H., " 'In my Father's House are many *Monai*' (John 14,2)," ZNW 58 (1967), 68–72.

Kugelman, R., "The Gospel for Pentecost (Jn. 14:23–31)," CBQ 6 (1944), 259–75.

Leal, J., " 'Ego sum via, veritas, et vita' (Ioh. 14, 6)," VD 33 (1955), 336–41.

McCasland, S. V., "The Way," JBL 77 (1958), 222–30.

Rieger, J., "Spiritus Sanctus suum praeparat adventum (Jo 14, 16–17)," VD 43 (1965), 19–27.

Schaefer, O., "Der Sinn der Rede Jesu von den vielen Wohnungen in seines Vaters Hause und von dem Weg zu ihm (Joh 14, 1–7)," ZNW 32 (1933), 210–17.

Schwank, B., "Der Weg zum Vater (13, 31–14, 11)," SeinSend 28 (1963), 100–14.

———— "Vom Wirken des dreieinigen Gottes in der Kirche Christi (14, 12–26)," SeinSend 28 (1963), 147–59.

———— " 'Frieden hinterlasse ich euch' (14, 27–31)," SeinSend 28 (1963), 196–203.

53. THE LAST DISCOURSE:
—DIVISION TWO (SUBDIVISION ONE)
(xv 1–17)

The vine and the branches

XV 1 "I am the real vine
and my Father is the gardener.

2 He cuts off
any of my branches that does not bear fruit,
but any that bears fruit
he trims clean
to make it bear more fruit.

3 You are clean already,
thanks to the word I have spoken to you.

4 Remain in me as I remain in you.
Just as a branch cannot bear fruit by itself
without remaining on the vine,
so neither can you bear fruit
without remaining in me.

5 I am the vine; you are the branches.
He who remains in me and I in him
is the one who bears much fruit,
for apart from me you can do nothing.

6 If a man does not remain in me,
he is like a branch, cast off and withered,
which they collect
and throw into the fire to be burned.

7 If you remain in me
and my words remain in you,
ask for whatever you want
and it will be done for you.

8 My Father has been glorified in this:
in your bearing much fruit
and becoming my disciples.

9 As the Father has loved me,
  so have I loved you.
  Remain on in my love.

10 And you will remain in my love
   if you keep my commandments,
   just as I have kept my Father's commandments
   and remain in His love.

11 I have said this to you
   that my joy may be yours
   and your joy may be fulfilled.

12 This is my commandment:
   Love one another
   as I have loved you.

13 No man can have greater love than this:
   to lay down his life for those he loves.

14 And you are the ones I love
   when you do what I command you.

15 No longer do I call you servants,
   for a servant does not understand what his master is doing.
   Rather, I have called you my beloved,
   for I revealed to you everything I heard from the Father.

16 It was not you who chose me;
   it was I who chose you.
   And I appointed you
   to go and bear fruit—
   fruit that will remain—
   so that the Father will give you
   whatever you ask Him in my name.

17 This I command you:
   Love one another."

NOTES

xv. 1. *I am.* We have discussed the "I am" statements with a predicate nominative in vol. 29, p. 534. Only in the present instance (vss. 1 and 5) is there a development of the affirmation by further predication—"my Father is the gardener"; "you are the branches." Especially in vs. 1, however, it is clear that the emphasis is on Jesus as the real vine and not on the Father as the gardener. The latter was a common image to those familiar with the OT and did not need to be emphasized. The mention of the Father really helps to qualify the kind of vine that Jesus is—a vine belonging to the heavenly order (Borig, p. 36).

real. Hitherto we have consistently rendered attributive *alēthinos* as "real" (vol. 29, pp. 500–1), and we shall adhere to this translation, although "true" (which we have used to render *alēthēs*) would sound better in English here. See COMMENT for meaning.

vine. The OL, OS^cur, Eth. Tatian, and some of the Fathers read "vineyard." Sometimes in the popular Greek attested in the papyri *ampelos*, "vine," takes on the meaning of *ampelōn*, "vineyard." See NOTE on "cast off" in 6 below.

gardener. Basically *geōrgos* is one who tills the soil; and Lagrange, p. 401, remarks that often in Palestine little more is done for the vineyard than tilling the soil. Yet the term can refer in a specialized way to a vinedresser; for example, it is used for the wicked tenant farmers who work God's vineyard in Mark xii 1 ff. In John, God does his own vinedressing. (Pressing the allegorical details too far, the Arians argued that just as there was a difference of nature between the gardener and the vine, so there was a difference of nature between the Father and the Son.) One of the main points of this allegorical parable is that the branch gets its life from the vine, that is, that the disciple gets his life from Jesus. Normally in John this would lead to the idea that Jesus gets his life from the Father (vi 57), but here the role of the Father is to tend the vine, not to give it life.

2. *cuts off . . . trims clean.* In Greek there is a play on two similar sounding verbs (paronomasia), respectively *airein* and *kathairein*. (Thus, despite the possible Semitic roots of this allegorical parable, the Greek phrasing has become an essential vehicle.) An adjective, *katharos*, "clean," corresponding to the second verb, *kathairein*, "to cleanse," appears in the next verse as part of a chain of ideas. *Kathairein* itself is not frequent in the Greek Bible; its use for agricultural processes is well attested in secular Greek, although there is some doubt whether, taken alone, it has the meaning "to prune" that is demanded by the context here. (In the examples that commentators usually give from Philo, *kathairein* is accompanied by another verb meaning "to cut.") The use of *airein*, "to take away," for cutting off branches is even more awkward. And so it would seem that both verbs were chosen not because of their suitability for describing vineyard practices but for their applicability to Jesus and his followers (Dodd, *Interpretation*, p. 136). Some of the Latin witnesses read these verbs in the future—a scribal attempt to conform the parable to the futuristic outlook appropriate in the Last Discourse.

any of my branches that does not bear fruit. Literally "every branch in me not bearing fruit, he cuts it off." This construction would seem to be a nominative pendens after *pas*, "all, every," a construction that is often a Semitism (BDF, §466³; ZGB, §31; yet Barrett, p. 395, states that it is not a Semitism here). A Semitism would be interesting in light of the Greek paronomasia seen above!

3. *You.* The indirect parabolic symbolism yields to direct address here.

thanks to. The preposition is *dia* with the accusative which generally means "because of," but sometimes "through." Bernard, II, 480, argues strongly for the former meaning here. It does not mean that through or by his word Jesus declares his disciples clean, an interpretation supported by Cyril of Alexandria, Augustine, and some modern authors like Schlatter, p. 305. It is more a question of the working of the word of Jesus within the disciple. See COMMENT.

word. Logos here means Jesus' whole teaching. Cf. v 38: "His word you do not have abiding [*menein*] in your hearts, because you do not believe the one He sent"; I John ii 24: "If what you have heard from the beginning abides in your hearts, then you will abide in the Son and [in] the Father."

4. *remain in . . . remaining on.* These translations represent the same

Greek expression *menein en* which is used ten times in vss. 4–10. It is most difficult to find a consistent translation suitable to the relations both between a vine and its branches and between Jesus and his disciples. The branches are to remain *on* the vine; the disciples are to remain *in* Jesus.

Remain in me as I remain in you. There are other possible ways of translating the idea in this phrase (Barrett, pp. 395–96): "If you remain in me, I shall remain in you"; "Remain in me and I remain in you." The various translations are not really exclusive; in vs. 5 we shall adopt the last mentioned, as we did in vi 56.

without remaining. The Greek witnesses vary between an aorist and a present subjunctive. The latter would give more stress to the continuous character of the action, but this is obvious in any case with the verb "to remain." The imagery breaks down here and yields to the reality that is symbolized: a branch has no exercise of choice about remaining on the vine.

5. *much fruit.* The Greek here and in 8 is *karpos polys.* In ET 77 (1965–66), 319, J. Foster has made the suggestion that Polycarp, bishop of Smyrna in the early 2nd century and a disciple of John (according to Irenaeus: see vol. 29, pp. LXXXVIII ff.), received his name in light of the challenge of these verses. He was a disciple bearing *much fruit.*

apart from. The Gr. *chōris* has the meanings "without" and "apart from"; while John may intend both connotations, the pictorial image requires the latter. See NOTE on i 3: "Apart from him not a thing came to be."

you can do nothing. The same idea is found in II Cor iii 5: "Not that we are sufficient of ourselves to claim anything as coming from us; our sufficiency is from God."

6. *If a man does not remain.* This is the negative counterpart of "He who remains" in 5.

he is like a branch, cast off and withered. Literally "he was cast *out* like a branch and he withered." There is an inversion of the symbolic pattern: we would have expected to find a description of what happened to the branch with an implication that the fate of the disciples would be similar; but here the picture is subordinate to the reality. When a man is made the immediate subject of these verbs, it is very awkward. Both verbs are in the aorist, and there have been various attempts to explain this. W. Bauer thinks that the aorist stresses the immediacy of the sequence: the moment a man is no longer united to Jesus is the moment that he has been cast out and has withered. Or we may be dealing with a proleptic aorist after an implied condition: the result is so certain that the future is expressed as if it had come to pass (Lagrange; Bernard; MTGS, p. 74; ZGB, §257—the Vulgate has future tenses). Or we may have a gnomic aorist used to express what is valid for all times: he is always cast out and withers—such an aorist is not unusual in a parable where the author is generalizing on the basis of a specific case that he remembers (BDF, §333[1]; MTGS, p. 73). We should also notice the expression "cast out"; this would fit the image of a vineyard better than that of a vine where we might expect "fallen off."

they collect. Bernard, II, 481, probably thinking of the Synoptic parables of the vineyard, suggests that the "they" refers to unnamed servants. More likely we have here the Semitic custom of using the third person plural for the passive. The verb is the one that was used for gathering the fragments (vi 12–13) and for gathering the dispersed children of God in xi 52. The fact that this verb and the following verb "to throw" are in the present tense suggests to

Lagrange, p. 404, an interval between the moment when the branches were cast off (aorist) and the moment when they are collected. The grammatical argument is not convincing, for this is probably an instance of the general present, describing what people ordinarily do in the situation envisaged in the parable. This interpretation is very appropriate if the preceding aorists are gnomic.

the fire. The use of the article (contrast Matt iii 10) may be an instance of the tendency to use the definite article in parabolic style, or else the author may be referring to the well-known fire of eschatological punishment (see COMMENT). Westcott, p. 216, implausibly theorizes that if this part of the Last Discourse was spoken on the way to the Mount of Olives, the fires of the vine-prunings in the Kidron valley may have been the origin of the imagery.

7. *If you remain in me.* Some scholars who do not see a division between 6 and 7 suggest that this clause in 7 is the positive counterpart to "If a man does not remain in me" in 6. But we have pointed out that the positive counterpart for 6 is in 5. In 7 there is a change to the second person, and the vine imagery is gone.

my words remain in you. In 4–5 Jesus spoke of his own remaining in the disciples (also xiv 20); here it is his words that remain in the disciples. Jesus and his revelation are virtually interchangeable, for he is incarnate revelation (the Word). Cf. vi 35, "I myself am the bread of life," where bread symbolizes his revelation. It is dubious that the plural "words" (*rēmata*) is to be distinguished from the singular "word" (*logos*) of 3; see NOTE on "keep my word" in xiv 23.

ask. This could be translated as a future ("you will ask"), but the imperative seems preferable; see pattern (*c*) on p. 634 above.

it will be done. The passive is a circumlocution for describing the actions of God without mentioning his name; cf. 16: "The Father will give you whatever you ask Him in my name."

for you. Omitted in P66* and some Western witnesses.

8. *has been glorified.* The aorist may be proleptic ("will have been glorified") or gnomic ("is always glorified")—see NOTE on "cast off" in 6. Yet it is possible that there is an element of the once-for-all in this aorist. Since the disciples continue the work of the Son and remain united to him, there is only one mission shared by the Son and his disciples. In this one mission the Father has been glorified. (Cf. xvii 4: "I glorified [aorist] you on earth by completing the work you have given me to do.") It is also possible that the past tense represents the evangelist's standpoint in time.

in this. The phrase refers to what follows in the second and third lines of 8, rather than to what precedes in 7. The *hina* that introduces the second line of 8 is epexegetical of "this" (ZGB, §410). The Father is glorified in that the disciples become like Jesus and carry on his work.

and becoming. P66 seems to add its support to reading a subjunctive here, thus making "becoming" part of the *hina* clause, grammatically coordinate with the preceding subjunctive, "bearing." Other good witnesses read a future indicative, and this could favor the translation: "and then you will become my disciples" (so BDF, §369³). While we judge the future the more probable reading, in meaning it is coordinate with the preceding subjunctive (ZGB, §342). Thus, "bearing much fruit" and "becoming my disciples" are not really two different actions, one consequent upon the other. The sense is not that when the hearers bear fruit, they will become his disciples, but that in bearing fruit they show they are disciples. Becoming or being a disciple is the same as being or remaining in Jesus.

9. *As.* For John *kathōs* is not only comparative but also causative or constitutive, meaning "inasmuch as" (BDF, §453[2]; NOTE on xvii 21). The Father's love for Jesus is the basis of Jesus' love for his disciples both as to origin and intensity. The Son loves his disciples with the same divine love the Father has for him.

the Father has loved me. The vocabulary for love in 9, 10, 12, 13a, and 17 is *agapan/agapē*, while in 13b, 14, and 15 there are instances of *philos* (see NOTE on 13). In iii 35, x 17 (*agapan*) and in v 20 (*philein*) the Father's love for Jesus is expressed in the present tense, an indication of its continuous character. Here and in xvii 24, 26 the tense is aorist, and the emphasis is on the expression of the love in Jesus' giving himself for men—a supreme act of love well expressed by the aorist. Of course, this emphasis does not exclude the continuity of love, as may be seen in the last line of 10. Spicq, RB 65 (1958), 358, contends that in the 1st century *agapan* had the connotation of love made manifest. Thus, the Father loved the son before the creation of the world (xvii 24) and this love became manifest when He sent the Son into the world (iii 16).

Remain. Aorist imperative; see NOTE on "without remaining" in 4. The abruptness gives an air of authority; Abbott, JG, §2438, says that this "is perhaps the nearest approach to an authoritative command (in John) to obey a moral or spiritual precept."

my love. This means "my love for you," although the disciples' love for Jesus is not excluded (cf. xiv 15, "If you love me")—for the possibility of a secondary meaning in such phrases see NOTE on v 42. An interesting parallel to this idea in John is Jude 21: "Keep yourselves in the love of God."

10. *If you keep my commandments.* We have seen this expression in xiv 15, 21, 23–24 ("keep my word[s]"). See NOTE on xiv 15.

I have kept. The perfect tenses in these verses give an air of completed action; contrast viii 29: "I always do what pleases Him." The perfect tense is not out of place in the context of the Last Discourse when "the hour" has begun and the ministry is over, but the tense may be attributable to the evangelist's standpoint in time.

my Father's commandments. We saw in a NOTE on xiv 15 that the alternation between singular and plural in speaking of Jesus' commandment(s) had no particular significance; the same seems to be true of the Father's commandment(s), plural here, singular in xiv 31; see also the alternation in I John iii 22–23.

11. *this.* Literally "these things"; more than what was said in 10 is included, for the statement "I have loved you" in 9 is the real basis of the joy in 11.

my joy. Stanley, p. 489, points out that Jesus has spoken of "my peace" which is the Hebrew salutation "Shalom" (NOTE on xiv 27), and here he speaks of "my joy" (*chara*) which is akin to the Greek greeting *chaire*. The risen Christ will fill the disciples with joy as he greets them with "Peace" (xx 19–21).

yours. Literally "in you."

12. *Love one another.* The use of the present subjunctive suggests that their love for one another should be continuous and lifelong.

as I have loved you. The aorist tense prepares the way for the supreme act of Jesus' love to be mentioned in the next verse. The Pauline writings also call upon Christ's death as a sign of love: "God demonstrates His love for us in that while we were yet sinners Christ died for us" (Rom v 8); "Walk in love, as Christ loved [aorist] us and gave himself for us" (Eph v 2).

13. *to lay down his life.* This is an epexegetical *hina* clause (BDF, §394) explaining the "this" of the first line. But, as Spicq (RB 65 [1958], 363) points out, there is a finality as well: Christian love does not simply *consist* in laying down one's life; but because it stems from Jesus, there is a tendency in Christian love that produces such self-sacrifice. That is why John xv 13 has left a greater mark on subsequent behavior than, for example, a similar sentence in Plato (*Symposium* 179B): "Only those who love wish to die for others." For the expression "lay down one's life" see NOTE on x 11.

for those he loves. The same preposition, *hyper,* occurs in the eucharistic formulas for the blood of the convenant which is shed "for many" (Mark xiv 24) or "for you" (Luke xxii 20). The noun in 13–15 that we have translated as "those he loves" is *philos,* "friend," a cognate of the frequent Johannine verb *philein,* "to love." The English word "friend" does not capture sufficiently this relationship of love (for we have lost the feeling that "friend" is related to the Anglo-Saxon verb *frēon,* "to love"). In Johannine thought Jesus is not addressing the disciples here as casually as he addresses them in Luke xii 4: "I tell you, my friends, do not fear those who kill the body"— the only Synoptic use of *philos* for the disciples. Rather vs. 14 is similar to 10, and the "You are my *philoi*" of 14 is the equivalent of the "You will remain in my love" of 10. Lazarus is the *philos* of Jesus (xi 11) because Jesus loves him (*agapan* in xi 5: *philein* in xi 3). Sometimes in relation to this verse of John, the title of Abraham as "the friend of God" is recalled (*philos* in James ii 23). However, it should be noted that the LXX of Isa xli 8 speaks of Abraham as the one "whom God loved" (*agapan*). Thus the title of Abraham becomes another example of our thesis that *philos* means "the beloved" (see also NOTE on III John 15 in vol. 30). See the synonymous use of *philia* and *agapē* in Justin *Trypho* XCIII 4: PG 6:697C.

15. *servants. Doulos* covers both slave and servant. In one way "slave" might be more appropriate here when the servile condition of the *doulos* is stressed—he follows orders without comprehending. Yet the implication that hitherto Jesus had treated his disciples as slaves seems too harsh. The contrast between *doulos* and *philos* was not unfamiliar to the Jews; it appears in Philo (*De sobrietate* XI; ¾55) who says that Wisdom is God's *philos,* not His *doulos.*

I revealed. Even though "the hour" is not over, the aorist is used of the completed work of Jesus. It is the revelation of the whole "hour" that changes the disciples' status, not simply the words of the Last Discourse. The statement that Jesus has revealed to the disciples *everything* he has heard from the Father seems to contradict xvi 12: "I have much more to tell you, but you cannot bear it now." Yet the latter is said in the context of the coming of the Paraclete, and we have pointed out that the Paraclete does not reveal anything new but gives greater insight into what Jesus has revealed.

16. *I appointed.* This is the verb *tithenai,* the same verb used in 13 in the expression "to lay down one's life," so that in the Greek the connection between the commission of the disciples and the example of love that Jesus

gave them would be quite apparent. The use of the verb here is awkward Greek. In NT quotations from the OT (Rom iv 17; Acts xiii 47), *tithenai* reflects the Hebrew verb *nātan*, "to give," thus the literal idea might be: "I have given you to go." However, Barrett, p. 399, suggests that the Greek verb may reflect Heb. *sāmak*, "to lay [hands] on, ordain," the verb used in later Judaism of the ordination of a scholar or rabbi. *Sāmak/epitithenai* are used respectively in the MT and LXX of Num viii 10 for the ordination of the Levites and in Num xxvii 18 for Moses' commission of Joshua.

to go. For Bultmann, p. 420[2], and others the verb *hypagein* here is merely a Semitic pleonastic expression and could be omitted as far as meaning goes. But Lagrange, p. 408, and Barrett, p. 399, plausibly see here a reference to the apostolic mission to the world. Luke x 3 uses the same verb in describing the mission of the seventy.

so that. After *appointed* there are two *hina* clauses; literally "in order that you go and bear fruit . . . , in order that whatever you ask the Father in my name He will give you." Grammatically these are coordinate; but commentators are divided on whether the second is logically subordinated to the first, so that the bearing of fruit disposes the Father to grant the request.

17. *This I command you.* The "this" (literally "these things") does not refer to what has preceded but to what follows. In most witnesses (not P[66] or Codex Bezae) the second line is preceded by a *hina* that is almost certainly epexegetical, making the "Love one another" the command. The *hina* could be final: "I command these things in order that you may love one another"; but the omission in some witnesses seems to indicate that the respective scribes interpreted it as epexegetical and not necessary to the sense.

COMMENT: GENERAL

The Structure of the Subdivision

Generally xv 1–17 is recognized by scholars to be a unit; for the last mention of the imagery of the vine ("bear fruit") appears in 16, and there does seem to be a change of subject between 17 and 18. (Strachan is an exception among the commentators on John xv; he puts the break between 16 and 17.) If one seeks subunits within 1–17, many scholars suggest 1–8, dealing with the vine and the branches, and 9–17, dealing with the disciples' love. (Borig, p. 19, is an exception, for he sees 1–10 as the first subunit.) Some even suggest that two independent blocks of matter have been juxtaposed. Bultmann, p. 415, sees the two parts as parallel, the first having the theme "Remain in me" and the second having the theme "Remain in love." Boismard in his Jerusalem lectures has perhaps phrased the relationship best when he speaks of the second part as a paraenetic or exhortatory commentary on the first.

Moreover, it may be better to divide the parts thus: 1–6, the figure of the vine and the branches; 7–17, an explanation of this figure in the context of Last Discourse themes. We remind the reader of the structure we proposed for x 1–21. In x 1–5 there were figurative sayings about the shepherd and the sheep, drawn from pastoral life; in x 7–18 there were several developments or explanations of these figures, for example, two developments of the gate and two of the shepherd. We propose a somewhat similar structure for xv 1–17 (with the notable exception that in ch. x the "I am" passages are not in the figurative description [1–5] but in the section that develops the figures [7–17], while here in ch. xv they are in the figurative description itself). It is perhaps worth noting that I Cor ix 7 juxtaposes the images of the vineyard and the tender of flocks.

Let us begin with 1–6. If we compare what is said here with other parts of the Last Discourse, one distinctive feature is apparent: there is nothing futuristic in the description of the union between the branches and the vine. In many other passages of the Last Discourse union with Jesus is described as belonging to the future (xiv 3, 20–22, xvi 22, the Paraclete passages). But in xv 1–6 the disciples are already in union with Jesus, and the emphasis is on remaining in that union. There is not the slightest reference to imminent departure; nor do the other themes characteristic of the Last Supper appear. (The suggestion that originally vss. 1–6 were spoken immediately after the distribution of the eucharistic cup when the emphasis would be on the existing eucharistic union with Jesus is interesting but totally lacking in proof.)

The situation is quite different in xv 7–17; the themes of the Last Supper are found in every line. In 7 and 16 there is the theme of asking and having the request granted (xiv 13–14, xvi 23–24, 26). In 8 there is the theme of the glorification of the Father (xiii 31–32, xiv 13, xvii 1, 4). In 9 there is the theme of the Father's love for Jesus (xvii 23) and of Jesus' love for the disciples (xiii 1, 34, xiv 21). In 10 and 14 there is the combination of love and keeping the commandments (xiv 15, 21, 23–24). In 11 there is the refrain "I have said this to you" (xiv 25, xvi 1, 4a, 6, 25, 33). In 12 and 17 there is the command to love one another (xiii 34). In 13 there is an implied reference to the disciple's laying down his life (xiii 37). In 15 there is the analogy of the servant/master relationship (xiii 16, xv 20). In 16 there is the theme of choosing the disciples (xiii 18, xv 19). If, then, vss. 7–17 have many echoes of Last Supper themes, there are, on the other hand, only a few echoes of the imagery of the vine and the branches (7: "remain in me"; 8: "bearing much fruit"; 16: "bear fruit").

We suggest that the figure of the vine and branches found in xv 1–6 originally belonged to another context. (We would not attempt, however, to specify that context, as does J. E. Roberts, ET 32 [1920–21], 73–75, who suggests that it was spoken on the road between Bethany and Jerusalem in conjunction with the cursing of the fig tree—he points to the idea of not bearing fruit [John xv 4] in Matt xxi 19, and that of having requests granted [John xv 7] in Matt xxi 22.) When it was brought into the Last Discourse, it was supplied with a paraenetic development and application. This development, now found in 7–17, was formed by combining some imagery drawn from the figure of the vine and branches with sayings and themes traditional in the Johannine Last Discourse material. (We need not think of this as a purely literary process; such combination may have taken place in the course of preaching.) The thesis that there is a division between 1–6 and 7–17, based on the lack of Last Discourse parallels in the former and their presence in the latter, is supported by other arguments. While 1–6 has some use of the second person, the third person dominates the imagery; but the use of the second person in 7–17 is consistent, even when the imagery of the vine and the branches is recalled. In 1–6 there is an inclusion between 1 and 5 ("I am the vine"); in 7–17 there are inclusions between 8 and 16 (bearing fruit) and between 7 and 16 (asking and having it granted).

In particular, 7–17 has a rather interesting internal structure. One can subdivide it further into 7–10 and 12–17, with 11 as a transition that summarizes the import of 7–10. There are minor inclusions that justify this further subdivision. In 7–10, vs. 7 shares with 9 and 10 the emphasis on remaining in Jesus or in his love. Verse 7 stresses that Jesus' words must remain a part of the disciples, while 10 stresses that Jesus' commandments must be kept by the disciples (for the equivalence between word and commandment see NOTE on xiv 23). In 12–17, vs. 17 repeats 12 almost verbatim. If we put 7–10 and 12–17 side by side we find an interesting chiastic pattern:

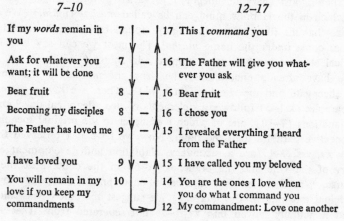

	7–10			12–17
If my *words* remain in you	7	—	17	This I *command* you
Ask for whatever you want; it will be done	7	—	16	The Father will give you whatever you ask
Bear fruit	8	—	16	Bear fruit
Becoming my disciples	8	—	16	I chose you
The Father has loved me	9	—	15	I revealed everything I heard from the Father
I have loved you	9	—	15	I have called you my beloved
You will remain in my love if you keep my commandments	10	—	14	You are the ones I love when you do what I command you
			12	My commandment: Love one another

11: I have said this to you
that my joy may be yours

It is always difficult to be sure that the discovery of such an elaborate chiastic structure does not reflect more of the ingenuity of the investigator than of the intention of the Johannine writer. (Borig, pp. 68 ff., uses chiastic pattern to defend a different division of verses.) Nevertheless, here there are too many correspondences to be coincidental.

Verses 1–6 as a Mashal

We turn now to the literary genre of xv 1–6. We have already discussed the question of allegory and parable in John (vol. 29, pp. 390–91). Certainly there are allegorical features in 1–6, for example, the identification of the vine, the gardener, and the branches; but Van den Bussche, p. 102, is correct in insisting that there is no careful allegory in which all the details have significance. The reality that John is describing, namely, the relation of Jesus and his disciples, keeps breaking through the figurative language; and indeed some of the vocabulary is more appropriate to this relationship than it is to viticulture. (Incidentally, we may recall that there is an allegorical cast to the Synoptic Parable of the Vineyard [Mark xii 1–11 and par.], where the owner is God, the tenants are the Jewish authorities, the son is Jesus, etc.) Bultmann, pp. 406–7, is accurate when he says that what we have in the description of the vine and the branches is neither allegory nor parable. But he does not go far enough; for he does not emphasize that the problem of classification is complicated and even falsified by the attempt to apply precise categories derived from the Greek rhetoricians (parable, allegory) to varied Semitic imagery patterns, all of which in the Hebrew mind can be called *mashal* (*māšāl*). We must recognize that the illustrations and figures found both in John and in the Synoptics come under the name *mashal*. The most we can say is that the allegorical element receives more emphasis in John.

We have already encountered the genre of *mashal* in the imagery of the sheepgate and the shepherd in x 1–18. There we saw a pattern of basic parables (x 1–5) followed by elements of *two* allegorical developments or explanations (7–18), one of which was closer to the original meaning of the respective parables than the other. Now we have just observed that in chapter xv, vss. 7–17 are a secondary adaptation and development of the imagery of the vine and the branches (1–6) in the context of the Last Discourse. Was there another allegorical development that was closer to the original meaning of the imagery? We suggest that there was and that we find it actually woven into xv 1–6 (not separated from it as in the instance of x 8 and 14–16). In chapter x the allegorical developments came in the form "I am the gate" and "I am the model shepherd" (each twice). We find similar statements in xv 1–6: "I am the (real) vine" (1 and 5); "My Father is the gardener" (1); "You are the branches" (5). Verse 3, "You are clean already," is a development related to the imagery of trimming the branches clean in 2. The lapse into the second person in the last line of 5 is another sign that the imagery is being explained. In discussing chapter x we insisted that there is good reason to believe that Jesus did explain or develop his parables for his disciples and that, although such developments had often been "modernized" by the time they were written down in the Gospels, some elements of the original explanations were usually retained. This may well be the case in John xv 1–6.

The Background of the Imagery of the Vine and the Branches

As with so many other instances where there is a problem about the background of Johannine thought, some scholars turn to Gnostic and Mandean sources (W. Bauer, Bultmann), while others (Behm, Büchsel, Jaubert) stress the OT and Jewish writings. In particular, Bultmann, p. 407[6], maintains that John's imagery reflects the Oriental myth of the tree of life, sometimes represented as a vine; and he offers some impressive parallels from the semi-Gnostic *Odes of Solomon* (vol. 29, p. 21—yet see J. H. Charlesworth, "The Odes of Solomon—Not Gnostic," CBQ 31 [1969], 357–69) for the association of themes of love and joy with the vine imagery. S. Schulz, *Komposition und Herkunft der johanneischen Reden* (Stuttgart: Kohlhammer, 1960), pp. 114–18, although he is more appreciative than Bultmann of Jewish parallels for John, thinks that in this case the best parallels are in the Mandean and Gnostic literature, even if there are OT elements intermixed. This was also the contention of E. Schweizer in *Ego Eimi* (Göttingen: Vandenhoeck, 1939), pp. 39–41, although he seems to have modified his views since (in NTEM, pp. 233–34). Borig, *op. cit.*, has made a careful study of these varied suggestions, but he finds the OT and Jewish background for the Johannine symbolism far more plausible than any of the others. For instance, he recognizes (pp. 135–87) that the Mandean documents offer parallels to John in that the vine symbolism is used to describe individuals and used in combination with "I am" sayings, but the general Mandean and Johannine emphases in the vine symbolism are quite different. The Mandean symbolism is highly mythical; it does not concentrate on the branches; moreover, while, especially in the later Mandean writings, the vine is a tree of life (note that John does not directly mention "life" in his description), the life-giving function of the vine in relation to the branches, which is important in John, does not come to the fore in the Mandean picture (Borig, p. 172).

Let us then survey the possible OT and Jewish background to see if it is applicable. In the OT the vineyard is a frequent symbol for Israel. Occasionally the symbol is one of fruitfulness (Isa xxvii 2–6); more often the vineyard is unproductive or desolate and disappointing to Yahweh (Jer v 10, xii 10–11). In the Synoptic tradition Jesus draws on the OT vineyard symbolism: his Parable of the Vineyard (Mark xii 1–11 and par.) implicitly cites Isaiah's "Song of the Vineyard" (Isa v 1–7). See also the

Parables of the Workers in the Vineyard (Matt xx 1–16), of the Obedient and Disobedient Sons (Matt xxi 28–32), and of the Fig Tree Planted in the Vineyard (Luke xiii 6–9). Now in John we are dealing with a vine rather than a vineyard. That this distinction is not as sharp as some would contend is suggested by the variant reading in vs. 1 and by the verb in vs. 6 (see NOTE on "cast off," literally "cast out"). Moreover, in the OT the imagery sometimes shifts back and forth from vine to vineyard (cf. Ps lxxx 9[8] and 13[12]). Annie Jaubert, p. 94, is correct in suggesting that the whole symbolism of Israel as a plant or tree, frequent in the OT, the Apocrypha, and Qumran, should also be brought into play here. But even if we confine ourselves to the use of the vine as a symbol, we may cite Hos x 1, xiv 8(7); Jer vi 9; Ezek xv 1–6, xvii 5–10, xix 10–14; Ps lxxx 9(8) ff.; and II Esd v 23. These passages offer many close parallels with John, especially in the themes of fruitfulness, taking off the bad branches, etc.

The real objection to calling on this imagery as background for John is that the vineyard or vine stands for Israel, while John identifies the vine with Jesus and not with a people. But, as we pointed out above (p. 629) in dealing with "the way" in xiv 6, it is a feature of Johannine theology that Jesus applied to himself terms used in the OT for Israel and in other parts of the NT for the Christian community. This is part of the Johannine technique of replacing "the kingdom of God is like . . ." with "I am. . . ." In the present instance, however, we should note that the element of the collective is not absent. Jesus is not the stalk but the whole vine, and the branches remain part of the vine. Since John (i 47) sees the Christian believers as the genuine Israelites, the vine as a symbol of Jesus and the believers is, in a certain way, the symbol of the new Israel. (We remember that the vine has often been suggested as the Johannine equivalent of Paul's notion of the body. The equivalence is not total; for example, there is nothing in John's imagery matching Paul's stress on the diversity of members; and the resemblance is to the earlier Pauline view where Christians are members of the physical body of Christ rather than to the later Pauline view where Christ is the head of the body. But granted these reservations, the idea of Christians being in Jesus with the resultant corporate image is quite similar.)

Some specific passages from the OT and Jewish background have been offered for consideration as closely related to John's thought. Dodd, *Interpretation*, p. 411, points to Ps lxxx 9(8) ff., where there is a description of Israel as a vine. Commentators on the psalm have often regarded the last part of vs. 16(15) as an incorrect duplication of 18(17); but if 16(15) is read as it stands, especially in LXX, it seems to identify the vine of Israel with the suffering "son of man." The whole passage is worth citing: "Take care of this vine and protect [?] what your right hand has planted, the son of man whom you yourself made strong; for they have burned it with fire and cut it down." Whether this reading came about by accident or by theological reflection, one can see how it might have led to symbolizing Jesus, the Son of Man, as the vine. Yet the connection is highly speculative.

E. M. Sidebottom, ET 68 (1956–57), 234, points out correctly that from the viewpoint of vocabulary John xv is quite close to the *mashal* of the vine in Ezek xvii. This *mashal* was propounded to the house of Israel by the "son of man," a form of address that God frequently used to refer to Ezekiel. Could meditation upon Ezekiel have led to the association of the new Son of Man with the vine? This connection seems far-fetched, but what is significant is that the vine imagery of Ezek xvii refers to a king of the house of David. As Borig, p. 101, states: "In the OT the imagery of the vine was already associated not only with the community of Israel but also with the picture of an individual person, so that the Johannine transferal of a collective image to a person is already anticipated in Ezekiel's vine symbolism." It is noteworthy that Ezek xxxiv offered the closest parallel to the shepherd passages of John x, so that we may claim a relationship between John's imagery and Ezekiel's imagery. Other possible parallels between the two are pointed out by B. Vawter, "Ezekiel and John," CBQ 26 (1964), 450–58. For the idea that the vine represents a person some have also pointed to II Bar xxxix 7 ff. which seems to speak of the Messiah or his principate as a vine uprooting the evil powers of the world. Although this may be helpful in showing that it was acceptable within Judaism to portray the Messiah as a vine, certainly the thrust of the imagery is quite different from the lesson that John draws.

Another objection to attempts to find an OT background for the Johannine vine and branches is that none of the OT vine passages stresses the vine as the source of life for the branches, the point that is capital in John. (In Ps lxxx discussed above, along with the plea to take care of the vine [=son of man], there is a plea, "Give us life" [19(18)], but there is no suggestion that the vine is the source of life.) However, Annie Jaubert, p. 95, argues that in post-biblical Judaism there had been a certain assimilation of the vine to the tree of life. In later Jewish iconography the tree of life was pictured as a vine (Z. Ameisenowa, *Journal of the Warburg Institute* 2 [1938–39], 340–44). Such an assimilation may have taken place in the realm of sapiential thought as a means of symbolizing the life-giving power of wisdom, the Law, or the word of God. A. Feuillet, NRT 82 (1960), 927 ff., has drawn attention to the parallels that the Wisdom Literature offers to John xv. In Sir xxiv 17–21 personified Wisdom speaks as follows: "I bud forth delights like the vine; my blossoms become fruit fair and rich. Come to me, all you who desire me, and be filled with my fruits. . . . He who eats of me will hunger still; he who drinks of me will thirst for more." This passage seems to have been known in Johannine circles (see NOTE on vi 35), and we have mentioned above (p. 630) that an early Christian glossator saw its connection with John xiv 6. The imagery of eating the fruit of the vine is different from that of John, but the vine is presented as giving life. Certainly the tree of life figured in Johannine thought (explicitly in Rev xxii 2; implicitly perhaps as part of the background of John vi—see vol. 29, p. 279), and John's notion of the vine and the branches may stem from a combination of the imagery of Israel as the vine and the imagery of Wisdom as a life-giving tree or vine. (We see how complicated such mixed imagery can get in Ignatius *Trallians* xi 1–2, which seems to combine the vine, the tree of the cross, and the tree of life: "Flee from these wicked offshoots that bear deadly fruit. . . . For these are not the planting of the Father. If they were, they would appear as branches of the cross, and their fruit would be incorruptible.")

In conclusion, it is clear that John's *mashal* of the vine and the branches has a unique orientation, consonant with Johannine christology. This orientation is not found in the OT or in Jewish thought, but many of the images and ideas that have been blended together under this orientation are found there. Granting the originality of John's thought, we suggest that the OT and Judaism supplied the raw material from which this *mashal* was composed, even as they supplied the raw material for the *mashal* of the sheepgate and the shepherd (vol. 29, pp. 397–98).

The Vine as a Eucharistic Symbol?

The basic meaning of the vine is quite clear. Just as Jesus is the source of living water and is the bread from heaven that gives life, so is he the life-giving vine. Hitherto the metaphors that concern the receiving of Jesus' gift of life have involved external actions: one has had to drink the water or eat the bread to have life. The imagery in the *mashal* of the vine is more intimate, as befits the general theme of interiorization in the Last Discourse: one must remain in Jesus as a branch remains on a vine in order to have life. Drinking water and eating bread were symbols of believing in Jesus; the explanation in xv 7–17 makes it clear that remaining on the vine is symbolic of love. We have suggested that on a secondary level the water and the bread were sacramental symbols, respectively of Baptism and the Eucharist. Is it possible that the vine is also symbolic of eucharistic union and eucharistic life-giving, inasmuch as it is a figure related to the eucharistic cup of wine?

As might be expected, Bultmann, p. 407, curtly dismisses the possibility by pointing out that there is no emphasis on wine in the *mashal*. This objection certainly excludes a reference to the Eucharist as the primary symbolism—a conclusion that would also be dictated by our contention that the *mashal* was not originally spoken in the Last Supper context. Yet we must still ascertain whether or not the *mashal* of the vine, set in the context of the Last Supper and the institution of the eucharistic cup, would not have immediately evoked eucharistic thoughts and thus have acquired a secondary eucharistic symbolism. The absence of the institution of the Eucharist in John's account of the Last Supper is not really an insurmountable obstacle to this suggestion—not only because there may once have been a Johannine institution account (see vol. 29, pp. 287–91), but also because an early Christian audience would certainly have known of the tradition of the institution at the Last Supper (for seemingly it was part of the standard preaching: I Cor xi 23–26). That the readers of the Gospel would easily associate the imagery of the vine with the eucharistic cup in the context of the Last Supper is suggested by the designation of the contents of that cup as "the fruit of *the vine*" in Mark xiv 25; Matt xxvi 29. In the very early liturgical practice preserved for us in the *Didache* ix 2, the following words were spoken as part of the eucharistic blessing: "We thank [*eucharistein*] you, our Father, for the holy *vine* of David your servant, which you revealed to us through Jesus your servant." This citation from the *Didache* is important because of the close similarity we saw between the *Didache*'s words concerning the eucharistic bread and John's account of the multiplication of the loaves (vol. 29, p. 248).

Let us look at some of the ways that the *mashal* of the vine and the branches may be related to the Eucharist. This *mashal* is narrated just before the death of Jesus, and indeed the explanation (xv 13—see NOTE on "for those he loves") mentions sacrificial death. The importance of bearing fruit is brought out in the *mashal;* and the only other place in the Gospel that bearing fruit is mentioned is in xii 24 where it is stressed that the seed must die to bear fruit. This motif of the death of Jesus is, of course, part of all the accounts of the institution of the Eucharist. The theme of intimate union with Jesus would also be shared both by the *mashal* of the vine (remaining in Jesus) and by the eucharistic theology of the early Church (I Cor x 16–17).

It is very interesting to compare xv 1–17 with the eucharistic section in John vi 51–58. In general, the same Wisdom background seems to underlie both passages. In particular, xv 5 with its "He who remains in me and I in him" echoes vi 56: "The man who feeds on my flesh and drinks my blood remains in me and I in him." In xv it is implied that life comes to the branch through the vine; so in vi 57 we hear: "The man who feeds on me will have life because of me." In xv 13 Jesus speaks of one's laying down his life for those he loves; in vi 51 he says: "The bread that I shall give is my own flesh for the life of the world." The "I am the living bread" of vi 51 and "I am the real vine" of xv 1 form a Johannine diptych not unlike "This is my body" and "This is my blood."

Thus, it seems likely that the *mashal* of the vine and the branches has eucharistic overtones. This is a thesis supported both by Protestants (Cullmann) and Roman Catholics (Van den Bussche, Stanley). Sandvik, *art. cit.*, has argued strongly for it, although we are dubious about the added eucharistic dimension he introduces whereby the vine represents the Temple which is the *body* of Jesus (ii 21—see vol. 29, p. 125). Nor would we be able to accept literally Cullmann's evaluation of the primacy of this eucharistic reference: "The relation between the branch and the vine is, therefore, above all, the eucharistic communion of believers with Christ" (ECW, p. 113). The relation is primarily one of love (and faith) and only secondarily eucharistic. Perhaps, when it was brought into the context of the Last Supper, the *mashal* of the vine served in Johannine circles the paraenetic purpose of insisting that eucharistic union must last and bear fruit and must deepen the union between Jesus and his disciples already existing through love.

COMMENT: DETAILED

Verses 1–6: The Mashal *of the Vine and the Branches*

In vs. 1 Jesus insists that he is the *real* vine (for *alēthinos* as "real" see vol. 29, pp. 500–1), and he mentions his Father to justify this claim. We saw the same mentality in vi 32: "It is my Father who gives you the real bread from heaven." It does not seem that in claiming to be the real vine Jesus is directly polemicizing against a false vine; rather he is emphasizing that he is the source of "real" life, a life that can come only from above and from the Father. Jesus is the vine in a sense in which only the Son of God can be the vine. "Real" here is the language of Johannine dualism distinguishing what is below from what is above. Nevertheless, we may ask if on a secondary level there may not be by implication a reference to a false vine. Occasionally the contrast in "real" is not only heavenly vs. earthly but also NT vs. OT (or Christian vs. Jewish), for example, in the instance of the bread from heaven or manna. We have seen that in the OT the vineyard or vine frequently stands for Israel and that in the Synoptic tradition Jesus draws on Isaiah's Song of the Vineyard to form a parable (Mark xii 1–11) that warns of the rejection of the Jewish leaders. At the conclusion of the parable Matt xxi 43 reports these words: "The kingdom of God will be taken from you and given to a nation producing its fruits." In the *mashal* of the vine and the branches is John contrasting Jesus and his followers as the real vine with the false vine represented by the Jewish Synagogue? Such a motif would fit in with one of the main purposes for which the Gospel was written, namely, apologetic against the Synagogue (vol. 29, pp. LXX–LXXV). It is quite possible that the vine as a symbol would suggest Judaism. One of the notable ornaments of the Jerusalem Temple was a golden vine with clusters as tall as a man (Josephus *Ant.* XV.xi.3; ⚹395; *War* V.v.4; ⚹210; Tacitus *Hist.* v.5; Mishnah *Middoth* 3:8); and on the coins of the First Jewish Revolt (A.D. 66–70), struck to honor Jerusalem the holy, there was an outline of a vine and branches. After the fall of the Temple the regroupment of rabbinical disciples at Jamnia under Rabbi Johanan ben Zakkai was known as a vineyard (Mishnah *Kethuboth* 4:6). Moreover some of the Johannine description of the vine and the branches echoes OT passages dealing with the chastisement of Israel.

The expression "real vine" (*ampelos alēthinē*) occurs in the LXX of Jer ii 21: "I planted you as a fruitful vine, entirely *genuine*. How have you become a wild vine, turned to bitterness?" Just as John says that the Father is the gardener of the vine, Isaiah's Song of the Vineyard, which is the background of the Synoptic parable mentioned above, stresses that Yahweh spaded, cleared, planted, and took care of the vineyard only to be rewarded with sour grapes. In return Yahweh says he will make a ruin of the vineyard (Isa v 1–7). And so, in presenting Jesus as the real vine, the Johannine writer may well have been thinking that God had finally rejected the unproductive vine of Judaism still surviving in the Synagogue. (For a suggestion about the modern Christian attitude toward such anti-Synagogue polemic see vol. 29, p. 368.)

Verse 2 describes two different actions of the gardener or vinedresser. The first, that of cutting off branches that cannot bear fruit, takes place in February–March. Sometimes the vines are so completely cut back that one sees in the vineyards only the stalks bereft of branches (F. G. Engel, ET 60 [1948–49], 111). Later (August), when the vine has put forth leaves, comes the second stage of pruning, as the vinedresser pinches off the little shoots so that the main fruit-bearing branches get all the nourishment (G. Dalman, *Arbeit und Sitte in Palästina* [Gütersloh: Bertelsmann, 1935], IV, 312–13, 331). This verse, then, introduces a somber note; for it recognizes both that there are branches on the vine (literally "in me") that do not bear fruit and that even the fruit-bearing branches need pruning.

What does the symbolism of bearing and not bearing fruit mean? Spontaneously one tends to interpret the imagery in terms of good works and a virtuous way of life (so Lagrange, p. 401), but we must remember that John does not make the distinction that later Christian theologians would make between the life that comes from Christ and the translation of that life into virtue. For John love and keeping the commandments are so much a part of the life coming from faith that one who does not behave in a virtuous manner does not have life at all. Life is committed life. Therefore, a branch that does not bear fruit is not simply a living, unproductive branch, but a dead branch. Some may find this interpretation harsh since it holds out no hope for the unproductive branches; yet in Johannine dualism there is not much room for an intermediate stage: there are only living and dead branches. Augustine (*In Jo.* LXXXI 3; PL 35:1842) captures this dualism in his rhyming Latin epigram, *"Aut vitis, aut ignis."* Thus, John's thought is different from that implied in Matt iii 8 where the Baptist tells the Jewish leaders, "Put forth fruit that befits repentance"; for John is speaking of Christians who have already been converted and are in Jesus but are now dead. The attitude is much closer to Jeremiah's words (v 10) about the vineyard of Judah: "Go through her rows of vines and destroy . . . strip away her branches, for they are not the Lord's." In the atmosphere of the Last Supper Judas may be thought of as a branch that did not bear fruit; he is now a tool of Satan and belongs to the realm of darkness (xiii 2, 27, 30). In the atmosphere of the evangelist's own time perhaps the "antichrists" of I John ii 18–19 were thought of as branches in Jesus that did not bear fruit; they went out from the ranks of the Christians because they did not really belong and could not remain united to the Christian community. Is there also polemic against the Synagogue here? Certainly many of the OT passages referring to cut off branches and to unfruitfulness (Ezek xvii 7 ff.) deal with the unworthiness and rebelliousness of Israel, and the same may be said of some NT passages (the unfruitful fig tree in Mark xi 12–14; the branches broken off the olive tree in Rom xi 17). However, John could scarcely compare the Jews of the Synagogue to branches that are in Jesus. If there is any polemic here it would have to be against Jewish Christians who had not yet publicly professed their faith and still remained in the Synagogue, but such a reference is very speculative.

The end of vs. 2 mentions that the gardener trims clean the branches that do bear fruit in order that they may bear more fruit. It is not clear what this symbolizes. Since bearing fruit is symbolic of possessing divine life, the passage concerns growth in that life and growth in union with Jesus. Does increased fruit-bearing also imply the communication of life to others? The explanation of the *mashal* emphasizes strongly love for others (xv 12–13) and seems to relate bearing fruit to the apostolic ministry (16). In xii 24 it is implied that Jesus himself "bears fruit" only when through his death and resurrection he can communicate life to others. In the agricultural *mashal* involving harvest and fruit (iv 35–38) the focus was very much on missionary enterprise. Seemingly, then, the imagery of trimming clean the branches so that they bear more fruit involves a growth in love which binds the Christian to Jesus and spreads life to others. As Van den Bussche, p. 108, points out, it may be false to think that the Johannine writer would have been aware of a distinction between a Christian's internal vitality and his apostolic activity directed toward others, for he would not have thought of the "life" of a Christian as something bent in upon itself in an unproductive seclusion. The sense that there were others who had to be brought into the flock (x 16) was too strong in the 1st century to have been left out of any understanding of what it meant to be united to Jesus.

Verse 3, which is certainly a development or explanation of the original imagery, breaks into the *mashal* (see first NOTE on 3) to reassure the disciples that they are already clean and need not be trimmed clean by the Father. If this is meant as a consolation to the already fearful disciples (xiv 1, 27), then it is the only line in the *mashal* that directly envisages the Last Supper setting and was probably added at the time that the *mashal* was placed in its present context. Being "clean" in 3 refers primarily to being clean not from sin but from all that prevents fruit-bearing (Borig, p. 42). The editor may have wished to recall xiii 10 where in reference to the footwashing Jesus told his disciples, "And now you men are clean." We suggested that that meant the disciples were cleansed through Jesus' parabolic action foreshadowing his death (and on a secondary level Christians were cleansed through Baptism). Here, however, it is the word of Jesus that cleanses the disciples. (Bultmann uses xv 3 to interpret the footwashing as a symbol of the cleansing power of the word; and on p. 410, he points to this verse as indicating that the Christian is cleansed not by church institutions or sacramental means of salvation but by the revealer's word alone!) The two ideas are not contradictory. The Johannine writer certainly does not think of the disciples at the Last Supper as already fully united to Jesus and abundantly bearing fruit. All the questions attributed to them stress the imperfection of their understanding. But when "the hour" has been completed and the Paraclete/ Spirit has been given to the disciples, he will bring the work of Jesus' word to fruition. Thus Jesus' word may be said to make them clean already because they have received his word and they are in the context of "the hour" which will make the working of that word possible. So also the footwashing cleansed them precisely because it was a parabolic action capturing in itself Jesus' subjection in death. A dichotomy between the salvific action of Jesus and his salvific word is not true to John. Nor was there any necessary dichotomy in the mind of the Johannine writer between Baptism and the working of the word of Jesus through the Paraclete. The Christians to whom this *mashal* was addressed would have become branches in Jesus through Baptism. This would make them fruit-bearing because it would give them life begotten from above and would make them clean according to the symbolism of xiii 10. But to make them bear more fruit it was necessary that Jesus' commandment of love gradually express itself more and more in their lives. We may mention that the power attributed here to Jesus' word is perfectly consonant with other Johannine statements about this word: it is an active force that condemns the unbeliever on the last day (xii 48), but for the believer it is both Spirit and life (vi 63). Nor is this thought peculiarly Johannine. In what may well be a baptismal context I Pet i 23 attributes to the abiding word of God the power to beget men anew. John xv 3 is not too far in thought from Acts xv 9: "God cleansed their hearts by faith."

Although 3 was probably inserted into the *mashal*, the verse as it now stands provides a transition to 4–5. If the disciples are made clean, they must respond and live out this state by remaining in Jesus (4). Hoskyns, p. 475, sees a double element in the purification of the disciples: the initial purgation occasioned by the word of Jesus, and its conservation through the maintaining of a permanent union with him. This may be a more formal division than the Johannine writer intended, but at least it is clear that in Johannine thought being made clean is not static nor a goal in itself.

Verse 4 begins "Remain in me as I remain in you." This is not a simple comparison between two actions, nor is one part of the command the causal condition of the other—rather one cannot exist without the other. Remaining in Jesus and having Jesus remain in the disciple are parts of the whole, for there is only one personal relationship between Jesus and his disciples: if they remain in Jesus through faith, he remains in them through love and fruitfulness (Borig, pp. 45–46). That is why 4 and 5 insist that in order to bear fruit one must remain in Jesus; all who remain in Jesus bear fruit and only those. (Verse 2 made bearing more fruit dependent on being pruned by the Father—evidently all this symbolism is concerned with the same thing.) Verse 5 simply says positively what 4 says negatively. This theme of indwelling fits in well with the general theology of the Last Discourse and may have been the key factor that led to the inclusion of the *mashal* in its present context. The total dependence of the Christian upon Jesus, which is a leitmotif of Johannine thought, is expressed nowhere more eloquently than here. The last line of 5, "Apart from me you can do nothing," has played an important role in the history of the theological discussion of grace. Augustine used it to refute Pelagius who stressed man's natural power to do good works worthy of eternal reward; and the text was cited in 418 by the Council of Carthage (DB 227) against the Pelagians and again in 529 by the Second Council of Orange (DB 377) against the Semi-Pelagians who defended man's natural power to do good works that were in some sense deserving of grace. The text appeared again in the Council of Trent (DB 1546) in the arguments of Rome against the Reformers, defending the meritorious quality of good works done in union with Christ. While these theological debates go beyond the meaning clearly envisaged by the Johannine writer, we can see how the theology of grace and merit is an attempt to systematize insights provided by John (see Leal, *art. cit.*).

In vs. 6 the *mashal* turns to deal with the fate of the branches that were cut off. We have pointed out that many of the OT vineyard/ vine passages involve a rejection of Israel and come to an end on a note of divine judgment wherein the vineyard is trampled or the vine laid waste. The imagery of these passages seems to have influenced John. In Ezek xv 4–6 the wood of the vine is given to the fire as fuel (in the LXX of 4 it is stated that the fire consumes what is *trimmed clean* every year—cf. John xv 2); in Ezek xix 12 we hear that the stem of the vine is withered and the fire consumes it. For the picture of the withering of the branches that do not bear fruit Isa xl 8 is interesting: "The grass withers; the flower fades; but the word of our God will stand forever," especially when we recall that for John the fruitful branches have been made clean by Jesus' word (xv 3). Ending a *mashal* on the theme of judgment has a parallel in the Matthean Parable of the Weeds among the Wheat; in Matt xiii 30 we hear: "Gather together the weeds first and bind them in bundles to be burned." The explanation of the parable (xiii 41) interprets the weeds as evildoers who have been within the kingdom of the Son of Man. So also in John the branches that are burned were once united to Jesus the vine. The expression "withered" occurs in Mark iv 6 in the Parable of the Sower to describe the fate of the seed that falls on rocky ground and begins to grow, only to be scorched by the sun.

How much of the description in vs. 6 is meant simply as parabolic imagery, i.e., a description of a fate fitting for branches? How much is descriptive of the actual punishment envisaged for the men represented by the branches? (Some think the picture was suggested by Judas' behavior; for in xiii 10 the theme of being clean [also found in xv 3] leads into a reference to Judas.) Naturally the scholars who refuse to see any final eschatology in John are reluctant to see here a reference to eschatological punishment, but it would not lie beyond the range of Johannine thought to suggest that those fallen away from Jesus are to be punished by fire (cf. v 29). The Synoptic Gospels offer some interesting points of comparison; see Mark ix 43; Matt xxv 41; and particularly Matt iii 10: "Every tree that does not produce good fruit is cut down and thrown into the fire." John's strange use of "cast off [literally 'out']," which does not fit the imagery, may have been suggested by the frequent use of this verb in eschatological descriptions: "The children of the kingdom will be cast out into the exterior darkness" (Matt viii 12). The suggestion that "cast out" is a reference to excommunication from the Christian community is harder to prove, but see I John ii 19.

Verses 7–17: Development of the Mashal *in the Context of the Last Discourse*

Verses 5–6 offered the dualistic choice of remaining or not remaining in Jesus; but in 7 ff. only the positive side of the *mashal* is developed, for we are now in the context of the Last Discourse and Jesus is speaking to his own, i.e., to those who remain in him (notice that the disciples of Jesus are clearly specified in vs. 8). Thus 7–17 unfold the implications of the indwelling that was the theme of the *mashal* in 1–6. (For the subdivision and chiastic arrangement of 7–17, see pp. 666–67 above.) Notice that the second line of 7 explains the first line: indwelling involves a life lived in harmony with Jesus' revelation (see NOTE on "words") and in obedience to Jesus' commands (compare "my words" in 7 with "my commandments" in 10). The requests of those who have conformed themselves to Jesus will be harmonious with what Jesus wants, and so they will always be granted by the Father (last part of 7). Jesus does not specify that the request must be "in my name," a condition that appears in most of the other Johannine forms of this saying (see pp. 634–35 above); but such a specification is not necessary since the request is made by one who remains in Jesus.

Verses 7 and 8 belong together, and the requests mentioned in 7 are probably to be interpreted in the light of 8: they are requests involving the growth of Christian life, namely, bearing fruit and becoming disciples. We reach the same conclusion if we study 16, which is an inclusion with 7–8: there too the requests of the Christians are associated with going and bearing fruit. (Incidentally, how closely 8 is related to 7 is illustrated by studying viii 31, "If you abide [remain] in my word, you are truly my disciples"—that verse joins the "becoming my disciples" of 8 with the "If my words remain in you" of 7.) By their requests Christians take an active part in God's plan. In the *mashal* the Father was mentioned as the gardener who helped the branches to bear more fruit; the development of the *mashal* shows how the Father exercises His role (vs. 8). We have heard in John (xii 28, xiii 31–32, xiv 13) that the Father was glorified in the mission of the Son; but now that the Son has completed his mission of bringing life to men, the Father is glorified in the continuation of that mission by His Son's disciples. In Matt v 16 it is stated that men will see the good works of the disciples and give glory to the Father in heaven. However, in Johannine thought the glorification of the Father in the disciples is not merely a question of praise by others; it is rooted in the life of the disciples as a sharing in Jesus' life (cf. xvii 22: "I have given to them the glory which you have given me"). We suggested in discussing the *mashal* that "bearing fruit" was symbolic of possessing divine life and that secondarily it involved communicating that life to others. This aspect of sharing life comes more strongly to the fore in the development of the *mashal*. "Becoming my disciples" involves love of Jesus (9–10) and love of one another (12–17). The love of the disciple for his fellow Christian must be so great that he is willing to lay down his life (13). Ignatius of Antioch (ca. 110) truly exemplified the Johannine notion of becoming a disciple of Jesus when on the road to martyrdom he exclaimed, "Now I am beginning to be a disciple" (*Romans* v 3).

Thus vss. 9–17 with their theme of love are really an interpretation of the idea of bearing fruit in 8 (even though this connection may not have been original); and although the imagery of the vine and the branches occurs again only in 16, the whole of 9–17 is still very much related to that imagery. We have frequently observed parallels between parts of the Last Discourse and I John; certainly the theme of love is more strongly developed in 9 ff. than anywhere else in the Gospel, and we are very close to the motifs of I John. (Was the writer of I John the editor who brought the *mashal* into the context of the Last Discourse and supplied it with an explanation made up of Last Discourse themes?) Elsewhere (vi 57) we heard that life was passed from the Father to the Son so that the Son might communicate it to others; now (xv 9) it is love that is passed on. This is fitting because Jesus is speaking in "the hour" when "he showed his love for his own to the very end" (xiii 1). Yet the partial interchangeability of "life" and "love" cautions us against thinking that by "love" John means something primarily emotional—besides being ethical, "love" is at times close to being something metaphysical (Borig, p. 61). Dibelius, p. 174, observes that love is not a question of unity of will existing by virtue of an affective relationship but a unity of being by virtue of a divine quality. For John love is related to being or remaining in Jesus. The last line in 9, "Remain on in my love," puts a demand on the disciples to respond to Jesus' love for them, even as the first line of 4, "Remain in me," puts a demand on them to respond to Jesus' cleansing them by his word.

The theme of love introduced in 9 is developed in 10 (Borig, p. 68, detects a chiastic arrangement in the Greek of these two verses binding them together). In particular, 10 associates love and commandment(s), an association already encountered in xiii 34, xiv 15, 21, 23–24. Barrett, p. 397, observes, ". . . love and obedience are mutually dependent. Love arises out of obedience, obedience out of love." This is in marked difference from the concept of love in many of the Gnostic parallels adduced for the image of the vine; there the love is far more mystical.

In vs. 11 there reappears the refrain "I have said this to you" (see NOTE on xiv 25); here it marks the transition from 7–10 to 12–19 (diagram on p. 667 above). The theme of joy, seen in passing in xiv 28, is mentioned briefly in 11; it will be the subject of prolonged treatment in xvi 20–24. Joy is presented as flowing from the obedience and love of which Jesus has spoken. Jesus' own joy springs from his union with the Father which finds expression in obedience and love (xiv 31: "I love the Father and I do exactly as the Father has commanded me"). The obedience and love to which in turn Jesus calls his disciples both constitute and witness their union with him; and it is this union that will be the source of their joy. Thus "my joy," like "my peace" (p. 653 above), is a salvific gift. It is interesting to see how often in the Gospel "joy" is associated with the saving work of Jesus:

- iii 29: The full or complete joy of the Baptist consists in his hearing the voice of Jesus, the bridegroom.
- iv 36: The sower and the reaper rejoice together over the fruit that is gathered for eternal life.
- viii 56: Abraham rejoiced at seeing Jesus' day.
- xi 15: Jesus rejoices that he was not there when Lazarus died so that his disciples will believe.
- xiv 28: The disciples should rejoice to have Jesus go to the Father.

So also in the present instance, if joy flows from the disciples' union with Jesus, it comes to fulfillment in their continuing his mission and bearing fruit.

Verse 12 (repeated in 17) is related to and perhaps a duplicate of xiii 34: "I am giving you a new commandment: Love one another." In xv 10 Jesus had said that they would remain in his love if they

kept his commandments; now the disciples are told that the basic commandment is love. Love can subsist only if it produces more love. Notice the
chain of love that is found in vss. 9 and 12: the Father loves Jesus;
Jesus loves the disciples; they must love one another. While this is
thoroughly Johannine, Matt v 44–45 offers an interesting comparison:
"Love your enemies . . . so that you may be sons of your Father
who is in heaven." The model of the disciples' love is Jesus' supreme
act of love, his laying down his life (the "as I have loved you" is
specified by 13). In x 18 and in xiv 31 this laying down of life was
spoken of as a command from the Father—thus again the combination
of love and commandment. In what way is Jesus' death for others held
up as an example for (and the source of) the disciples' love? It is clearly
to be a model of the *intensity* of their love, but I John iii 16 would
seem to interpret it also as a model for the *way of expressing* love:
"The way we came to understand what love means was that he laid
down his life for us; so must we too lay down our lives for our brothers."
Verses 12–13, taken in an expanded sense, became one of the great
justifications for the Christian martyrs. In discussing vs. 13, L. Jacobs,
art. cit., points out that modern Jewish teachers have been fairly unanimous
in rejecting this sweeping demand of self-sacrifice, and it constitutes one
of the classical distinctions between Christianity and Judaism. Of course,
both the OT and the rabbis recognized the sanctity of risking one's
safety for another, but Jacobs says that they did not command it. It
will be noted that we have been interpreting 12 and 13 together, for
we agree with Bultmann, p. 417, that 13 is connected to what precedes
as well as to what follows. On the other hand, Dibelius, *art. cit.*,
has argued that 13–15 form a type of midrashic excursus interrupting
the unity between 12 and 17, with 16 as a gloss. This criticism seems
too trenchant: at one time 13 may have been an independent logion, but
now it is very well built into its context.

In vs. 14 we are told that the act of love of which 13 speaks
is constitutive of the group of those whom Jesus loves (the *philoi;* see
Note). This is no esoteric group within the wider Christian community.
Jesus' death, which is his act of love, will make possible the giving of
the Spirit to all who would believe in him and this Spirit will beget
all believers as children of God. Therefore the *philoi* or beloved of
Jesus are all Christian believers. In the words of I John iv 19, "He
loved us first"; and his love makes the Christian beloved. In making men
his *philoi* through his union with them Jesus is acting in the manner of
divine Wisdom: "In every generation she passes into holy souls and makes
them the beloved [*philoi*] of God" (Wis vii 27). The second line of 14
describes the way one acts as a *philos* of Jesus. We should not understand
this verse to mean that obeying Jesus' commandments makes one a
philos—such obedience is not a test of whether or not one is loved by
Jesus but naturally flows from being loved by Jesus. Verse 14 really

repeats 10 in another way: "You will remain in my love if you keep my commandments."

Verse 15 explains more fully the state of being a *philos* of Jesus. We should not take the exclusion of the servant (*doulos*) status too literally. Just as in the OT the prophets spoke of themselves as the servants of God (Amos iii 7), Christians thought of themselves as servants. In Luke xvii 10 Jesus instructs the disciples to say, "We are unprofitable servants." In John xiii 13 the disciples were commended for addressing Jesus as "Lord," an address that has the implication that they are his servants; see also xiii 16, xv 20. Paul calls himself the "servant of Jesus Christ" (Rom i 1); yet in Gal iv 7 he asserts that the Christian is no longer a servant but a son. Thus, in NT thought the Christian remains a *doulos* from the viewpoint of service that he should render, but from the viewpoint of intimacy with God he is more than a *doulos*. So also here in John xv 15, from the viewpoint of the revelation given to him the Christian is no mere servant. If Jesus' act of love in dying for them has made the disciples his beloved, the same effectiveness may be attributed to his word which he has received from the Father—notice once more the intimate relation between Jesus' deed and word. Those scholars who see Gnostic influence on John xv 1–17 naturally think here of the beloved or *philoi* of Jesus as an elite group who claim to have had special revelation. We need not go so far afield for the idea in vs. 15. In the OT the supreme revelation of Yahweh to Moses on Sinai was as intimate as a man speaking to his *philos* (Exod xxxiii 11). And even closer to John's thought is the passage from Wis vii cited above in COMMENT on 14.

The constitution of the disciples as his beloved is part of their election by Jesus (vs. 16). In speaking of those whom he has chosen the Johannine Jesus is undoubtedly addressing himself to all Christians who are the "elect" or "chosen" of God (Rom viii 33; Col iii 12; I Pet ii 4). Some scholars would press this to the point of having John deny any special significance to the Twelve. Yet it is far more consonant with Johannine thought to present the Twelve who were the most intimate disciples of Jesus as the models of all Christians, both in their having been chosen and in their having been sent to bring the word to others. In vi 70 and xiii 18 Jesus speaks of having chosen the Twelve (and indeed the verb "to choose, elect" is used of the selection of the Twelve in Luke vi 13; Acts i 2). As John xv 27 makes clear, Jesus' words here are directed to those who have been with him from the beginning. That apostles, "ones sent," are particularly in mind in the "I chose you" of vs. 16 is suggested by what follows: "I appointed you to go and bear fruit." Both the notions of going (see NOTE) and of bearing fruit (see above) have connotations of a mission to others. The use of the Greek verb "to appoint" (see NOTE) in OT passages for commission and ordination lends another hint of mission to this verse. *If* elsewhere in Johannine thought the Twelve are apostles par excellence (Rev xxi 14: "the Twelve Apostles of the Lamb"), the Twelve are being given a mission that all Christians must fulfill. By stressing that the *fruit* that they bear must *remain*, John achieves in 16 an inclusion with the themes of 7 and 8, and at the end of the explanation of the *mashal* brings back once more the prominent vocabulary used to describe the vine and the branches. The theme of asking and having it granted at the end of 16 is also by way of inclusion with 7. Verse 7 gave assurance that God would hear those united to Jesus; vs. 16 gives assurance that God will hear Jesus' chosen and loved ones. They are the ones commissioned by Jesus, and so they can make their petitions in Jesus' name (notice Luke x 17 where the seventy[-two] who have been sent out by Jesus expel demons in his name).

The "This I command you" of vs. 17 is not only an inclusion with 12; it is also a variant of the refrain "I have said this to you" with which, as we have seen, John closes several of the units or subdivisions of the Last Discourse. The "Love one another" is a fitting ending for a section so concerned with love; it stands in striking contrast with the message of the world's hate that is to follow.

BIBLIOGRAPHY
(xv 1–17)

See the general bibliography on the Last Discourse at the end of §48.

Borig, R., *Der wahre Weinstock* (Munich: Kösel, 1967).

Dibelius, M., "Joh. 15:13. Eine Studie zum Traditionsproblem des Johannesevangeliums," in *Festgabe für Adolf Deissmann zum 60. Geburtstag* (Tübingen: Mohr, 1927), pp. 168–86. Reprinted in Dibelius' *Botschaft und Geschichte* (Tübingen: Mohr, 1953), I, 204–20.

Grundmann, W., "Das Wort von Jesu Freunden (Joh. xv 13–16) und das Herrenmahl," NovT 3 (1959), 62–69.

Jacobs, L., " 'Greater Love Hath No Man . . .' The Jewish Point of View of Self-Sacrifice," *Judaism* 6 (1957), 41–47.

Jaubert, A., "L'image de la Vigne (Jean 15)," in *Oikonomia* (Cullmann Festschrift; Hamburg: Reich, 1967), pp. 93–99.

Leal, J., " 'Sine me nihil potestis facere' (Joh. 15, 5)," in *XII Semana Bíblica Española* (Madrid, 1952), pp. 483–98.

Sandvik, B., "Joh. 15 als Abendmahlstext," TZ 23 (1967), 323–28.

Schwank, B., " 'Ich bin der wahre Weinstock' (15, 1–17)," SeinSend 28 (1963), 244–58.

Stanley, D. M., " 'I Am the Genuine Vine,' (John 15:1)," BiTod 8 (1963), 484–91.

van den Bussche, H., "La vigne et ses fruits (Jean 15, 1–8)," BVC 26 (1959), 12–18.

54. THE LAST DISCOURSE:
—DIVISION TWO (SUBDIVISION TWO)
(xv 18–xvi 4a)

The world's hatred for Jesus and his disciples

XV 18 "If the world hates you,
    bear in mind that it has hated me before you.
19 If you belonged to the world,
    the world would love its own;
    but the reason why the world hates you
    is that you do not belong to the world,
    for I chose you out of the world.
20 Remember what I told you:
    'No servant is more important than his master.'
    If they persecuted me,
    they will persecute you;
    if they have kept my word,
    they will keep yours too.
21 But they will do all these things to you because of my
    for they do not know the One who sent me. |name,
22 If I had not come and spoken to them,
    they would not be guilty of sin;
    but as it is, they have no excuse for their sin—
23 to hate me is to hate my Father.
24 If I had not done works among them
    such as no one has ever done,
    they would not be guilty of sin;
    but as it is, they have seen
    and still have hated both me and my Father.
25 However, this is to fulfill the text in their Law:
    'They hated me without cause.'

26 When the Paraclete comes,
    the Spirit of Truth who comes forth from the Father

and whom I shall send to you from the Father,
he will bear witness on my behalf.
27 You too should bear witness
because you have been with me from the beginning.
XVI 1 I have said this to you
to prevent your faith from being shaken.
2 They are going to put you out of the Synagogue.
In fact, the hour is coming
when the man who puts you to death
will think that he is serving God!
3 And they will do such things [to you]
because they never knew the Father nor me.
4a However, I have said this to you
so that, when the[ir] hour comes,
you may remember that I told you so."

NOTES

xv 18. *If the world hates.* P⁶⁶* reads an aorist tense: "hated." Grammatically
this is a real condition; the world does hate the disciples. Here "hate" has
its literal sense, unlike Matt vi 24 where, by Semitic exaggeration, it means
"to love less."

bear in mind. Literally "know." This may be an indicative, but the
older versions understand it as an imperative—there is no significant difference
of meaning. The almost parenthetical presence of a form of the verb "to know"
is characteristic of Johannine style, for example, ". . . the testimony that
He gives for me I know can be verified" (v 32; cf. also xii 50).

has hated. The perfect tense indicates that the hatred endures.

me before you. "Before" is *prōtos,* "first," used as a comparative, as in
i 30 (BDF, §62). Codex Sinaiticus and some Western witnesses omit the "you,"
leading to the translation: "hated me first"; this probably represents a scribal
attempt at grammatical improvement.

19. *If you belonged to.* This is a contrary-to-fact or unreal condition.
"Belonged to" is literally "were of"; the preposition *ek* used in this way
expresses membership in a certain group (ZGB, §134).

its own. The expression is neuter in gender—an example of the Johannine
tendency to use a neuter for persons taken as a group. See NOTE on vi 37.

the world hates you. The idea is echoed in the majestic statement of
Ignatius of Antioch (*Romans* iii 3): "Christianity is not a matter of per-
suasiveness but of true greatness when it is hated by the world."

I chose you out of the world. This composite idea of election and of
separation is awkward to translate. D. Heinz, ConcTM 39 (1968), 775, prefers
"from this world," for he thinks of the *ek* as partitive. See COMMENT.

20. *Remember what I told you.* Literally "Remember the word that I
said to you." Codex Bezae and OL have "words"; Sinaiticus has "spoke"; Tatian
and some minor witnesses have "my word"; OSˢⁱⁿ omits "the word." The

number of variants makes one suspect that a shorter text has been expanded by scribes. This line may form an inclusion with xvi 4a, the end of the subdivision: ". . . that you may remember that I told you so."

'No servant . . . master.' This is a literal citation of xiii 16 (see NOTE there). Yet in xiii the saying is an encouragement to imitate the humility of the master; here it concerns the necessity of undergoing the master's fate. The reappearance of the figure of the servant and the master is somewhat awkward following xv 15: "No longer do I call you servants."

If they persecuted me. Like vs. 18 this is a real condition. Acts ix 4 ("Saul, Saul, why do you persecute me?") carries the equation further: the persecution of the Christians is not only patterned upon the persecution of Jesus, but the persecution of the Christians is the persecution of Jesus.

if they have kept my word. The three preceding conditions in vss. 18–20 have been negative in tone in describing the world's attitude toward Jesus and his disciples, but suddenly the possibility of a positive reaction on the part of the world is suggested. A positive tone here is also contrary to the thrust of the next verse which supposes the world's hostility. Thus, with a certain logic but without textual support, some scholars would introduce negatives into this condition: "If they have *not* kept my word, they will *not* keep yours either." Yet such an introduction destroys the parallelism in form of the two conditions in vs. 20. Perhaps it is best to settle for a negative implication: they will keep your word to the extent they have kept mine (and they have not kept mine). Dodd, *Tradition*, p. 409, sees an unspoken *per impossibile* behind the statement; Lagrange, p. 411, speaks of a hypothesis that is negated by the sad reality. In any case, it is most unlikely that vs. 20 is presenting an equal choice between the two alternatives facing men, namely, of persecuting Jesus and his disciples or of accepting their teaching. It is not so neutral as I John iv 6: "Anyone who had knowledge of God listens to us, while anyone who does not belong to God refuses to listen to us."

21. *will do.* P66 reads a present tense.

all these things. Those who think that the last clause in 20 has a positive tone find difficulty with this verse. Bernard, II, 493, points out that the sequence would read more smoothly without 21, and we note that the substance of 21 is repeated in xvi 3. The verse may be an insertion designed to connect what were once independent groups of sayings (18–20 and 22–25). "All" is omitted by Codex Bezae and some minor witnesses.

to you. There is a division among the witnesses whether to read a dative or *eis* with the accusative; the latter is better attested, and the dative may be a scribal grammatical improvement over the strange use of *eis* (which is unexpected; MTGS, p. 256). But it is also possible that, in either form, the phrase "to you" has been added by scribes.

because of my name. Barrett, p. 401, suggests that this simply means on Jesus' account and cites the use of Heb. *lᵉšēm*, Aram. *lᵉšēmâ*, "for the sake of." But it seems more likely that this is a play on the Johannine theological theme that Jesus bears the divine name; see COMMENT. The phrase "because of God's [great] name" occurs in the OT (I Sam xii 22; II Chr vi 32; Jer xiv 21) where it means because of what God is, i.e., His goodness, might, fidelity, etc. Other instances of this formula in Johannine writing are I John ii 12: "Your sins have been forgiven because of his name"; Rev ii 3: "I know that you are enduring patiently and bearing up because of my name."

22. *If I had not come . . . they would not be guilty.* This is an unreal or contrary-to-fact condition with mixed tenses. Instead of the use of imperfect tenses in both parts to express what might be now ("were . . . would be"), or the use of aorist tenses in both parts to express what might have been in the past ("had . . . would have"), we have an aorist in the protasis (Jesus did come and speak) and an imperfect in the apodosis (they were and *are still* guilty). The same pattern is found in vs. 24.

and spoken. The parallel in 24 is: "If I had not done works." Once again we encounter the Johannine theme of the revelatory words and works of Jesus; cf. xiv 10. A comparison of 22 and 24 does not suggest that here the works are looked on as more persuasive than the words. The combination "come and spoken" is not a real coordination, as if two equal and separate actions were involved; the Semitic tendency to coordinate what is logically subordinate is involved. Lagrange, p. 411, suggests that the sense is: "If, having come, I had not spoken."

guilty of sin. The basic sin is the refusal to believe in Jesus (xvi 9); hatred is the necessary concomitant to that refusal, for men must decide either for or against Jesus.

but as it is. Here *nyn,* "now," combined with *de,* does not have true temporal significance; it means "in reality." The expression is repeated in 24.

23. *to hate me.* Literally "he who hates me hates my Father too." Pointing out that 22 and 24 are parallel in structure, Bultmann, p. 424[1], suggests that 23, which breaks up the structure, has been added from elsewhere. Yet, by connecting 23 to the sentence in 22, as we have done, we find that the last line of 22–23 matches the last line of 24.

24. *they have seen and still have hated.* Literally "both have they seen and have they hated both me and my Father." Bernard, II, 495, insists that each of the verbs covers the two objects, so that John is saying: they have seen me and my Father, and they have hated me and my Father. However, would the Johannine Jesus say that those who belong to the world have seen his Father? (Some cite xiv 9: "Whoever has seen me has seen the Father"; yet this is addressed to the disciples and presupposes the acceptance of Jesus in faith.) The world has seen Jesus but has not had the faith to see the Father in him. In a few verses (xvi 3) Jesus will say of the men of the world, "They never knew the Father nor me." Perhaps we should understand the seeing in 24 to refer to the works that Jesus has just mentioned: "They have seen (the works that I did among them) and still they have hated both me and my Father." That such an interpretation is possible for the first "both . . . and" construction is verified by BDF, §444[3]. The perfect tense in "have hated" hints at a deliberate, enduring hatred.

25. *However, this is to.* The Greek is simply *alla hina.* The *alla* is hard to render; Bultmann, p. 424[8], points out that we should understand something like this: The fact that they have seen and still have hated is almost incredible; however, ... The *hina* clause can be translated as an imperative construction: "However, let the text in their law be fulfilled" (ZGB, §415). More likely the sentence is elliptic (BDF, §448[7]), and we have to supply "this is"; cf. ix 3: "Rather, *it was* to let God's work be revealed in him" (also xiii 18).

in their Law. As in x 34 and xii 34, "Law" refers to a larger complex than the five books of Moses, for the citation is from a psalm. For the dissociation of Jesus from the Jewish heritage seemingly implied in the use of "their," see NOTES on vii 19, viii 17. Here the idea is that the very books that "the Jews" claim as their own convict them. Freed, OTQ, p. 94, says that the formula used here to introduce Scripture is the longest in John and perhaps in the NT.

'They hated me without cause.' In Ps xxxv 19 the psalmist prays that God will not give joy to "those who have hated me without cause"; in Ps lxix 5(4) the persecuted psalmist complains that more numerous than the hairs of his head are "those who have hated me without cause." In the Hebrew and Greek of both passages the construction is participial; John uses a finite verb. (Of interest is *Psalms of Solomon* vii 1 where the psalmist asks God to be nearby lest "they assail us who hate us without cause"; here the verb is finite. Cf. also Ps cxix 161: "Princes persecute me without cause.") J. Jocz, *The Jewish People and Jesus Christ* (London: SPCK, 1962), p. 43, points to TalBab *Yoma* 9b where Rabbi Johanan ben Torta gives as one of the causes of the destruction of the Temple: "Because therein prevailed *hatred without cause.*" Jocz thinks that this rabbi, who lived ca. A.D. 110, may have been influenced by Hebrew Christian tradition echoing the present verse in John (for Christians did explain the destruction of the Temple as flowing from the Jewish leaders' rejection and hatred of Jesus). This theory goes considerably beyond the evidence.

26. *who comes forth from the Father.* The verb is *ekporeuesthai,* while the verb *exerchesthai* will be used of Jesus in xvi 27–28. This description made its way into the 4th-century creeds to describe the eternal procession of the Third Person of the Trinity from the Father. Many of the Greek Fathers thought that John was referring to eternal procession, and Lagrange, p. 413, still argues for this interpretation. However, even though the tense of the verb is present, the coming forth is in parallelism with the "I shall send" in the next line and refers to the mission of the Paraclete/Spirit to men (see NOTE on xvi 28). The writer is not speculating about the interior life of God; he is concerned with the disciples in the world.

whom I shall send. Some Western witnesses read a present tense in an attempt to harmonize with the present ("comes forth") in the preceding line. In xiv 26 Jesus spoke of the *Father's* sending the Paraclete. Whether or not the difference of agency in sending the Paraclete reflects different stages in the development of Johannine thought, the variation is not really significant on the theological level, for in Johannine thought the Father and Jesus are one (x 30). "They are variant formulas, not variant ideas," says Loisy, p. 427, "and they do not prove that the passages are not from the one hand." The fact that *Jesus* sends the Paraclete is stressed here because the theme concerns Jesus and the world.

he will bear witness. That the Spirit is personal is strongly implied here.

27. *You too.* Superficially this gives the impression of a witness in addition to that of the Paraclete/Spirit; but, as Hoskyns, p. 481, indicates, the idea is: "And, moreover, it is you who must do and bear the witness (of the Spirit)." A similar coordination in Johannine writing about the Spirit is found in I John iv 13–14: "He has given us of His own Spirit, and we . . . can testify" (cf. also III John 12).

should bear witness. As in 18 the verb form in the present tense can be indicative or imperative; there is not much distinction of meaning so long as Jesus is understood to be describing a role the disciples shall play after they receive the Spirit. But Bernard, II, 500, thinks that the present tense used of the disciples stands in contrast with the future used in 26 of the Spirit—the disciples' ministry of witness has already begun, while the Spirit's is still to come. This interpretation fails to recognize that the disciples' witness is simply the exteriorization of the Spirit's witness (see COMMENT). In Johannine as in Lucan thought the witness-bearing of the disciples begins in the post-resurrectional period when the Spirit has been given; the words here are equivalent to the words of the *risen* Jesus in Luke xxiv 48: "You are witness of these things." Acts i 8 clarifies how this will take place: "You shall receive power when the Holy Spirit has come upon you; and you shall be my witnesses."

have been with me. Literally "are"; the present tense is used with a perfect meaning (MTGS, p. 62) because the action is conceived as still in progress. (This is true even if the statement is looked at from the evangelist's point in time: the Christians are still with Jesus because they possess the Paraclete who is the presence of Jesus.) In xiv 9 the relationship was seen from the other direction: "Here I am with you all this time." If we combine the phrase "with me" of this verse with the "I chose you" of 19, we are not far from the idea in Mark iii 14 where we are told; "He appointed Twelve to be with him."

from the beginning. In the setting of the Last Supper, *ap' archēs* means from the beginning of Jesus' ministry when disciples began to follow him; see NOTE on xvi 4b. The theme that those who were with Jesus during his ministry were privileged witnesses is found also in the Lucan writings: Luke i 2 speaks of "those who from the beginning were eyewitnesses"; Acts i 21 specifies that the place of Judas had to be filled from "the men who accompanied us during all the time that the Lord Jesus went in and out among us." When the statement in John is considered from the evangelist's standpoint in time, Hoskyns, p. 482, points out that it can refer to Christians who have been faithful to Jesus *since their conversion* ("beginning" in I John ii 13, 14, 24, etc.).

xvi 1. *I have said this to you.* Literally "these things"; the reference is to the content of 18–27 and not merely to the promise of the Paraclete in 26–27. For this statement as a refrain in the Last Discourse see NOTE on xiv 25.

to prevent your faith from being shaken. Literally "lest you be scandalized." According to Matt xxvi 31 the first words that Jesus spoke after he went out from the Supper to the Mount of Olives were: "This night you will all be scandalized because of me." For Johannine thought (vi 61; I John ii 10) "scandal" is what trips up a disciple and takes him from Jesus' company; or if we transfer the scene from Jesus' ministry to the lifetime of the Johannine church, "scandal" is what causes one to give up the true Christian faith and withdraw from the community. The same usage is found in early Christian writings, for example, *Didache* xvi 5 distinguishes between two groups at judgment: the many who shall be "scandalized" and lost, and those who endure in their faith.

2. *put you out of the Synagogue.* See NOTE on ix 22. It is impossible from the adjective *aposynagōgos* to be certain that John is not referring to one local synagogue. But the whole context of the introduction into synagogue prayer of the curse against the Jewish Christians (vol. 29, p. LXXIV), plus John's sweeping condemnations of "the Jews" and the hostile references to different syn-

agogues in Rev ii 9, iii 9, makes us think that he is referring to the Synagogue in general and fighting a policy that is, at least, in effect in all the synagogues of the area he knows.

In fact. Alla ("but") is not used adversatively here; BDF, §448⁶, points out that *alla* has the function of introducing an additional point in an emphatic way, while MTGS, p. 330, suggests the meaning, "Yes, indeed" (cf. Luke xii 7).

hour. It is not certain that here and in 4a there is a play on the Johannine symbolism of "the hour" of Jesus (vol. 29, pp. 517–18), although Hoskyns, p. 483, thinks that "the hour" that involved Jesus' suffering has been extended to the future hour of the disciples' suffering. (But in John's concept of "the hour," suffering and crucifixion are subordinate to Jesus' return to his Father.)

serving God. The Greek has "to offer *latreia* to God," a somewhat redundant expression, for *latreia* by itself means the service of offering worship to the deity. In stating that the killing of Christians would be considered a service to God is John referring to Roman persecutions, such as those which formed the background of the Book of Revelation? We are told that at a slightly later period Trajan's gratitude to the gods for victories over the Dacians and Scythians led him to persecute the Christians who refused to acknowledge these gods. Yet elsewhere in the NT (Rom ix 4; Heb ix 1, 6) *latreia* refers to Jewish worship. Moreover, in vs. 2 this killing of Christians is associated with expulsion from the Synagogue. Therefore, it seems likely that the writer is thinking of Jewish persecution of Christians rather than of Roman persecution. Did Jews of the 1st century put Christians to death (Jewish Christians— scarcely Gentiles), thinking that in so doing they were serving God? Certainly Christian literature makes this charge. We hear in Acts of Jewish responsibility for the martyrdom of Stephen (vii 58–60) and for the death of James the brother of John (xii 2–3). That Jewish authorities might act thus is confirmed by Josephus (*Ant.* XX.ix.1;※200) who makes the high priest Ananus II responsible for the stoning of James the brother of Jesus. The reason that Ananus gave to the judges of the Sanhedrin was that James had transgressed the Law. Paul, who was a witness at the execution of Stephen (Acts viii 1), says that his reason for persecuting the Church violently was zeal for his ancestral Jewish traditions (Gal i 13–14; also Acts xxvi 9). The 2nd-century Christian writer Justin, who had been born in Palestine, accused his Jewish opponents thus: "Though you have slain Christ, you do not repent; but you hate and murder us also . . . as often as you get authority" (*Trypho* cxxxiii 6, xcv 4). The *Martyrdom of Polycarp* (xiii 1) says that "the Jews were extremely zealous, *as is their wont,*" in preparing the material for burning the saint. Some of these statements are undoubtedly polemic exaggeration, but they represent a continuation of the attitude referred to by John. J. L. Martyn, *History and Theology in the Fourth Gospel* (New York: Harper, 1968), pp. 47 ff., argues persuasively that much of the hostile action taken against Jesus in John (attempts to arrest and kill him) really reflects action taken against the Jewish Christians of the Johannine community by the authorities of the local synagogue, so that the situation envisaged in the present passage has actually come to pass in John's time. It has been pointed out that there are passages in Jewish literature that *might* be taken to exemplify the attitude of which John speaks. For example, the Mishnah *Sanhedrin* 9:6 allows certain instances where zealots may slay people for religious offenses. In relation to Phinehas' slaying of an Israelite who was contaminated with idolatry, Midrash Rabbah xxi 3 on Num xxv 13 remarks: "If a man sheds the blood of the wicked, it is as though he had offered a sacrifice." (Need we add that, on the Christian side, there are passages in the patristic literature that make hatred of the Jews a duty owed to God. Neither religion can pretend that it has not made the other suffer in the name of the God that both serve. Yet, in fact, on the ethical plane, because of Christianity's profession of the necessity of loving one's enemies, Christians are especially culpable in conducting persecution of any sort; and, on the historical plane, the tragedy is that Christians have had the political power to do infinitely more harm to the Jews than vice versa.) As for vs. 2, Barrett, p. 404, sees here an example of Johannine irony: the persecutors think that they are serving God while the real *latreia* comes from the Christian martyr victims. Yet it is not certain that the writer intended such an ironic play.

3. *will do.* A few witnesses among the versions have a present tense. The whole verse is omitted in OS^sin, perhaps because it is repetitious, duplicating xv 21.

[*to you.*] Codex Sinaiticus and many of the Western witnesses have this phrase. It is difficult to decide whether it is original or an addition in imitation of xv 21 (cf. also "said this to you" in xvi 1, 4a).

never knew. This is the aorist of *ginōskein;* cf. the perfect of *eidenai* (*oida*) in xv 21: "They do not know the One who sent me." (See vol. 29, p. 514, for these two verbs.) MTGS, p. 71, cites this is an example of the inceptive or ingressive aorist, meaning that they did not begin to recognize.

4a. *However.* Some Western witnesses omit the initial *alla*, as would BDF, §448³. The omission suggests that the scribes found an adversative awkward here, but the conjunction has a resumptive implication that is legitimate in the present instance.

I have said this to you. Literally "these things"; see vs. 1 above.

the[*ir*] *hour.* The possessive pronoun is omitted by very important witnesses, but the omission may be an attempt to conform the phrase to the more usual "the hour." Although one could understand the "their" to mean the hour for these things, more probably it means the hour of the persecutors. In Luke xxii 53 Jesus says to the chief priests and those who have come out to arrest him at Gethsemane: "This is your hour."

remember that I told you so. Literally "remember these things—that I told you."

COMMENT: GENERAL

The first subdivision (xv 1–17) of Division Two of the Last Discourse stressed Jesus' love for his disciples; the second subdivision (also entirely a monologue) stresses by contrast the world's hate for these disciples. Jesus loves his disciples because they remain or abide in him; the world hates them for the same reason. As Hoskyns, p. 479, says so well, "The implacable hatred of the World for the friends of Jesus is the sign of the verity of that friendship." To belong to Jesus is not to belong to the world, and the world can love only what belongs to it. Besides being related to

the first subdivision by way of contrast, the second subdivision repeats in
vs. 19 the theme of Jesus' having chosen his disciples (found in xv 16).

We saw that there was general agreement among scholars that xv
1–17 constituted a unit or subdivision. There is far less agreement about
where the subdivision that begins in xv 18 should terminate. Some would
bring the unit to a close within ch. xv. For example, Hoskyns and Filson
suggest a break after xv 25. This has in its favor an inclusion between xv
18 and 25, both of which share the theme of hating Jesus; moreover the
introduction of the Paraclete in xv 26–27 seems a new step. While we
accept a minor break between 25 and 26, we would not put a major line
of division here because, as we shall see below, we believe that the theme
of the Paraclete is intimately related to that of facing the world's hatred.
Another group of scholars treat xv 18–27 as a unit and put the break
between xv 27 and xvi 1 (thus Barrett and Strachan [xv 17–27]). But
the "I have said this to you" of xvi 1 implies a relationship to what
precedes, and the persecution motif in xvi 1–4a is similar to that of xv
18–25 (as we see in the table below, both passages have parallels in Matt
x 17–25). We think that Maldonatus was correct when he stated that it
was a mistake to have begun a new chapter with xvi 1. (Schwank, "Da sie,"
p. 299, suggests that a chapter was begun here because, by analogy with
Matt xxvi 31 [see second NOTE on xvi 1], it was thought that at last Jesus
had reached the Mount of Olives.)

On the other hand, there are scholars who would carry the subdivision deep into ch. xvi (Dodd suggests xv 18 – xvi 11; Loisy suggests xv
18 – xvi 15). We prefer to join Lagrange, Strathmann, Buchsel, Bultmann,
Van den Bussche, and others in placing the end of the subdivision in the
first part of xvi 4. The theme of persecution ends there, and the "I have
said this to you" of xvi 4a is a fitting conclusion (a role it plays also in xvi
33). The recognition that xv 18 – xvi 4a constitutes a unit is confirmed by
the fact that these verses have parallels to Matt x 17–25, while xvi 4b–33
is a unit that duplicates xiii 31 – xiv 31, Division One of the Last Discourse.
(See Chart I on pp. 589–91 above.)

This subdivision is the Johannine equivalent of the threat of persecution that plays such an important role in the Synoptic Eschatological
Discourse (Mark xiii; Matt xxiv–xxv, plus x 17–25; Luke xxi). It is interesting that both the Johannine and Synoptic traditions place this warning
among the last words spoken by Jesus. In the table that we give below, it is
evident that while John has many parallels to Mark xiii 9–13 and to Luke
xxi 12–17, the best parallels are to Matt x 17–25, xxiv 9–10. Many
critics believe that Matt x 17–25 has been displaced from a more original
context contiguous to xxiv 9–10, the place where Matthew's general similarity to Mark and Luke would cause us to expect to find this material.
(It is interesting that, if John xv 18 – xvi 4a has these parallels to Matthew,
John xvi 33 also seems to echo the theme of *thlipsis* or suffering of Matt
xxiv 9–10.) The similarities between John and Matthew are not such to

694

CHART SHOWING THE PARALLELS BETWEEN John xv 18 – xvi 4a AND THE SYNOPTIC ESCHATOLOGICAL DISCOURSE

John xv 18 – xvi 4a	Matt x 17-25, xxiv 9-10	Mark xiii 9-13; Luke xxi 12-17
xv 18: "The world hates you . . . has hated me before you"	x 22: "You will be hated by all because of my name"; also xxiv 9	Mark xiii 13; Luke xxi 17: same as Matthew
20: "No servant is more important than his master"	x 24: "No servant is above his master"	
20: "They will persecute you"	x 23: "When they persecute you"; cf. also xxiii 34	Luke xxi 12: "They will persecute"
21: "They will do all these things to you because of my name"	See first parallel above	See first parallel above
26: "The Paraclete . . . will bear witness on my behalf"	x 20: "The Spirit of your Father speaking through you"	Mark xiii 11: "The Holy Spirit (speaking)"; cf. Luke xii 12
27: "You too should bear witness"	x 18: "You will be dragged before governors and kings . . . to bear witness"	Mark xiii 9; Luke xxi 12-13: almost the same as Matthew
xvi 1: "To prevent your faith from being shaken"	xxiv 10: "The faith of many will be shaken"	
2: "They are going to put you out of the Synagogue"	x 17: "They will flog you in their synagogues"	Mark xiii 9: "You will be beaten in synagogues"; Luke xxi 12: "Delivering you up to the synagogues"; cf. also Luke vi 22
2: "The man who puts you to death"	xxiv 9: "They will put you to death"	Mark xiii 12: "Children will rise against parents and will put them to death" (=Matt x 21); Luke xxi 16: "Some of you they will put to death"

make us think that one evangelist copied from the other (see Dodd, *Tradition*, pp. 406–13); in particular if the fourth evangelist had copied from Matthew, he would have had to anticipate the era of modern criticism by recognizing that Matt x 17–25 and xxiv 9–10 belong together. Both Gospels independently preserve early tradition, and John has kept the material more closely together than did Matthew. (Indeed it is John's desire to keep the material together that probably explains the appearance of "No servant is more important than his master" in xv 20, even though it has already been used in xiii 16.) Although this traditional material has been shaped into Johannine thought patterns, no other long section of Johannine discourse resembles a section of Synoptic discourse so closely as does John xv 18–xvi 4a.

Mark and Luke have the warnings about persecution in the Eschatological Discourse where the persecutions are treated as preliminary to the apocalyptic signs that will mark the end. Matthew, by moving the bulk of the material to ch. x and to the setting of a discourse on the Christian mission (see Matt x 5), gives the impression that persecution will be the normal accompaniment of Christian preaching in the world. John uses the material with partially the same realized outlook as Matthew.

We shall distinguish four groupings of verses in this subdivision. The first (xv 18–21) and the last (xvi 1–4a) treat directly of the world's hatred for and persecution of the disciples. Each traces this hatred to the fact that the world has not known the Father (xv 21, xvi 3). The second grouping (xv 22–25) analyzes the world's guilt and sin; the third grouping (xv 26–27) treats of the Paraclete who, as we shall discover in xvi 8–11, is the one who points out the world's guilt and sin. Thus there is a rough chiastic pattern in the subdivision.

COMMENT: DETAILED

Verses 18–21: The World Hates and Persecutes the Disciples

John makes clear that the world's hatred of the Christian is not a passing phenomenon; hate is just as much of the essence of the world as love is of the essence of the Christian. The world is opposed to God and His revelation; it can never have anything but hate for those who recognize that revelation in His Son. In a series of four conditional sentences it is repeated that the world's hatred for Christians is basically a refusal of Jesus himself. Love of Jesus has made the true Christian so much like Jesus that he is treated in the same manner as Jesus. We may remember that by the time the Fourth Gospel was in its final form, persecution by the Romans and the expulsion of Jewish Christians from synagogues were already accomplished facts and no longer morose forebodings.

The idea in vs. 18 is found elsewhere in John. In vii 7 Jesus said to his disbelieving brothers who were tempting him to show off his miraculous power in Jerusalem: "The world cannot possibly hate you, but it does hate me." This is implicitly saying that the world hates all who are not its own. That this hate is extended to the Christians is stated in I John iii 13: "No need then, my brothers, to be surprised if the world hates you."

The distinction between the realm of Jesus and that of the world which is implied in 19 had already been sharply delineated in viii 23, spoken to "the Jews": "You belong to what is below; I belong to what is above. You belong to this world—this world to which I do not belong." As for Jesus' disciples, in xv 16 Jesus has said, "It was not you who chose me; it was I who chose you." But now the theme of the call of the disciples is elaborated by the idea that Jesus is taking them out of the world, at least in the sense that while they will be in the world, they will not belong to it (xvii 15–16). The idea is not simply that the disciples should withdraw from the sinful elements of a pagan world (as in I Pet iv 3–4); rather the fact that they have been called means that they shall be bearers of the word of God and thus stand in dualistic opposition to the world. This will be reiterated in xvii 14: "I have given to them your word, and the world has hated them because they do not belong to the world [any more than I belong to the world]." The same dualistic theme appears in I John iv 5–6: "Those others belong to the world; that is why theirs is the language of the world and why the world listens to them. We belong to God; and anyone who has knowledge of God listens to us, while anyone who does not belong to God refuses to listen to us."

The first two lines of 20 give figurative expression to the thesis that the disciples will fare no better than Jesus. This is followed by two conditional sentences. The first corresponds to the theme of persecution in the Synoptic Eschatological Discourse; the second is even more sweeping, for it implies that the word of Jesus' disciples will have the same effect as the word of Jesus himself. The "I chose you" of 19 (and of 16) has a missionary cast: the word of Jesus will now be communicated through the preaching and teaching of the disciples. In the OT the prophets bore the word of God, and as Yahweh pointed out to Ezekiel, "They will not listen to you because they will not listen to me" (Ezek iii 7). The same will be true in the instance of the disciples. There is a good parallel for this idea in Matt x 14 (the same missionary discourse in which we have found parallels for the persecution theme): Jesus instructs his missionaries, "If anyone will not receive you or listen to your words, shake off the dust from your feet as you leave that house or town." Jesus then promises judgment on such a town; later in x 40 he says: "He who receives you receives me, and he who receives me receives Him who sent me" (see p. 572 above on John xiii 20 which is a parallel to Matt x 40).

Verse 21 summarizes the theme of persecution and explains its cause. John uses a standard formula, "because of my name" (Synoptic parallels in chart; I Pet iv 14; Acts v 41), used by Christians to describe those who were being persecuted because they professed Jesus. Jews would resent the name "Christ" by which Christians professed Jesus as the Messiah; the Romans would resent the exclusive claim that he is "Lord" or *kyrios*, a title by which the Emperor (Domitian) was known. But in Johannine thought "because of my name" means more than such profession of Jesus and leads us to the basic reason of why Jesus is unacceptable to the world. Jesus bears the divine name (see pp. 754–56 below); the Father has given it to him (xvii 11–12); and this means that he is the incarnate revelation of God to men. To persecute Jesus' followers because of Jesus' name is to reject the revelation of God in Jesus. This becomes clear in the second line of 21 which traces the persecution to ignorance of the Father who sent Jesus. In viii 19, x 30, xii 44, xiv 9 (cf. I John ii 23) Jesus claimed that only those who knew him would know the Father, so that ignorance of him was ignorance of the Father. Here the claim is inverted: ignorance of the Father leads to ignorance of Jesus. This inversion is not startling if we remember that only those whom the Father has given to him can come to Jesus (vi 37, 39); therefore a certain openness to the Father is required before one can be open to Jesus. This openness to the Father which is demonstrated in a good life is precisely what the world lacks (iii 19–20). Thus Jesus is extending to the world the charge of ignorance of the Father that he has already hurled at "the Jews" (v 37, vii 28). Indeed the exchange with "the Jews" in viii 54–58 illustrates well the ideas found in xv 21. In viii 54–55 Jesus tells "the Jews" that they do not know the Father whom they claim as their God; then in 57 Jesus speaks the divine name, saying "I AM," and because of his use of the divine name "the Jews" try to stone him. In the words of xv 21, they did these things to Jesus because of his name, showing that they did not know the One who sent him.

Verses 22–25: The Guilt of the World

The reference to not knowing in 21 leads into the theme of guilt (thus 21 not only summarizes 18–20 but also introduces 22–25). There are several instances in the NT where those responsible for the suffering of Jesus are said to have been ignorant (Luke xxiii 34; Acts iii 17); yet when in John xv 21 and again in xvi 3 Jesus says that those who persecute his disciples have not known the Father (nor himself), there is no suggestion that such ignorance lessens culpability. Rather the ignorance itself is culpable. Jesus has come to these men both with words (22) and with works (24); yet they have refused to know him, and this refusal to believe is the root of sin. Because the words and works of Jesus are the words and works of the Father (v 36, xiv 10), rejection and hatred of Jesus are rejection and hatred of the Father, as 23 makes clear. (This attitude resembles the respect that God demands for the Prophet-like-Moses of Deut xviii 18–19: "I shall put my words in his mouth. . . . I shall hold responsible anyone who will not listen to my words which he shall speak in my name.") In the ministry there were some who saw Jesus' signs and reacted with enthusiasm, mistaking him for a wonder-worker; this imperfect under-standing opened the way for further growth (iv 46–54). But those about whom Jesus is speaking here are those who refused even this initial step (see vol. 29, pp. 530–31). They are like "the Jews" who would not be-lieve that the blind man had been healed (ix 18) and to whom Jesus said: "If only you *were* blind, then you would not be guilty of sin. But now that you claim to see, your sin remains" (ix 41).

In xii 38–39, in order to explain such culpable failure to believe, the Johannine writer resorted to Scripture—it was to fulfill the words of Isaiah that predicted disbelief. So also in xv 25, in order to explain the hatred of Jesus that stems from disbelief, the author turns to a psalm that predicted hatred without cause. Although there are two psalms from which the citation may have been taken (see NOTE), Ps lxix 5(4) is the more likely candidate; for elsewhere in the Gospels this psalm is associated with Jesus' passion and death (Ps lxix 22[21] in John xix 29 and Mark xv 36; Ps lxix 10[9] in John ii 17; also there is frequent reference to Ps lxix in Revelation [iii 5, xiii 8, xvi 1, xvii 8]). Moreover the context of Ps lxix is better for the meaning that John gives to the citation.

It is worth noting that, while vss. 22–25 develop the theme of per-secution, they do so in a peculiarly Johannine way; and there is no parallel for these verses in the treatment of persecution found in the Synoptic Eschatological Discourse. They represent a good example of the develop-ment that the Johannine writers have given to traditional material common to John and the Synoptics by combining it with material that is peculiar to the Johannine tradition.

Verses 26–27: The Witness of the Paraclete

Against the background of Jesus' charge that the world's hatred means that it is guilty of sin, the theme of the Paraclete is introduced to prepare the way for the very forensic description of the Paraclete in xvi 8–11, where fittingly the role of the Paraclete will be to establish the guilt and sin of the world. The world has rejected the truth of Jesus' words and works, and the Spirit of Truth will demonstrate this. The world will persecute the disciples because of Jesus' name, and to counter this the Paraclete will be sent in Jesus' name (xiv 26). In this persecution the Christian disciple is not to be a passive victim; the Paraclete dwells within him (xiv 17), and he is to give voice to the Paraclete's witness against the world. This aggressive witness-bearing will produce further hostility on the world's part (xvi 1–4a). The Paraclete passage in xv 26–27 not only looks forward to the passages that follow, but is also related to what has just been said by Jesus, for the coming of the Paraclete gives a profound explanation of why the world treats Jesus' disciples the same way it treated him. The Paraclete represents Jesus' presence among men (App. V); and in hating the disciples who are the dwelling place of the Paraclete, the world is striking at Jesus' continued presence on earth. Through the Paraclete's indwelling, the disciples represent Jesus *contra mundum*.

Scholars like Windisch have maintained that the Paraclete passages represent an extraneous addition to the Last Discourse; in particular many have thought it easy to demonstrate that xv 26–27 is an interpolated passage. (Already Maldonatus recognized that xvi 1 follows xv 25 more easily than it follows xv 26–27.) On the other hand, Barrett, p. 402, argues, "The whole paragraph bears such strong marks of unity that it seems very improbable that the verses about the Paraclete have been inserted into already prepared material." We suggest that the present passage may be the key to how the figure of the Paraclete came to play such an important role in the Johannine Last Discourse. If we accept the evidence of our chart that xv 18 – xvi 4a contains traditional material parallel to what is now found in the Synoptic Eschatological Discourse, it is of importance that in Matt x 20 (cf. Mark xiii 11) there is a reference to the Spirit of the Father speaking through the disciples. In Appendix V we shall stress that the Johannine portrait of the Paraclete cannot be simply equated with the general NT picture of the Spirit—the Paraclete is the Spirit under a particular aspect, and into the formation of the concept have gone extraneous elements, for example, elements stemming from angelology and dualism. Yet it is precisely this mention of the Spirit in the context of facing the persecution of the world that may have been the principal catalyst for the development of John's understanding of the Paraclete. We note that the Paraclete is given the title of "the Spirit of Truth" in xv 26, a title that Qumran gives to the leader of the forces of good against the forces of evil (see App. V). Moreover, the Paraclete has more in common with the description of the Spirit in the Synoptic Eschatological Discourse than it has with most of the other Synoptic descriptions of the Spirit. The Paraclete is given by the Father (John xiv 16); the Synoptic mention of the Spirit in the hour of persecution is in a context where Jesus promises that what the disciples are to say will be *given* to them (Matt x 19–20; Mark xiii 11). Undoubtedly we are to understand that God is the giver, for the passive is frequently a circumlocution to avoid mentioning the divine name. (Matt x 20 confirms this by speaking of "the Spirit *of your Father*." It is interesting that Luke xxi 15 makes Jesus the giver of "a mouth and wisdom" in this moment of persecution—John also alternates between the Father and Jesus as the sender of the Paraclete.) The Synoptics clarify for us this gift that will communicate to the disciples what they are to say: "For it is not you who speak but the Spirit of your Father speaking through you" (Matt x 20; Mark xiii 11 has "the Holy Spirit"). The role of bearing witness in times of persecution and of doing so through the disciples' witness is precisely the role attributed to the Paraclete in John xv 26–27. The Lucan parallel for this statement in Matthew and Mark is not found in the Eschatological

Discourse but in Luke xii 12: "For the Holy Spirit will *teach* you in that very hour what you ought to say"; and in John xiv 26 we find that the Paraclete "will teach you everything." Of course, the Synoptics describe the Spirit as defending the disciples before various authorities, while John pictures the Paraclete as accusing the world. But this difference is part of the new orientation in the Johannine development; it does not vitiate the similarities, including that of forensic setting. In conclusion, then, there is a possibility that when the traditional material about persecution now found in xv 18 – xvi 4a was introduced into the context of the Last Discourse, the forensic description of the Spirit in that material was a catalyst to the formation of the Johannine picture of the Paraclete that found its way into the other divisions and subdivisions of the Last Discourse. The process would have been facilitated if there was already a mention of the Spirit in the earliest forms of the Last Discourse, something suggested by the presence of two Paraclete passages in xiii 31 – xiv 31 and in xvi 4b–33, the duplicate discourses that we have used as a guide to the original form of the Last Discourse. This (hypothetical) original mention of the Spirit would then have been reshaped into the present description of the Paraclete. Thus the question of whether the Paraclete passages were originally part of the Last Discourse may require a very nuanced answer.

Berrouard, *art. cit.*, has argued persuasively that the witness of the Paraclete (xv 26) and the witness of the disciples (27) are not two separate witnesses. This is in harmony with Matt x 20 which envisions the Spirit speaking through the disciples. The coordination of the witnesses in 26 and 27 resembles that of Acts v 32: "We are witnesses to these things, and so is the Holy Spirit whom God has given to those who obey him," when that verse is interpreted in the light of Acts vi 10: "They could not withstand . . . the Spirit *with which* he spoke." (See also Acts xv 28: "It has seemed good to the Holy Spirit and us.") The Paraclete/ Spirit is invisible to the world (xiv 17), so that the only way his witness can be heard is through the witness of the disciples. Augustine understood this well: "Because he will speak, you will also speak—he in your hearts, you in words—he by inspiration, you by sounds" (*In Jo.* xciii 1; PL 35: 1864). The witness of the Spirit and the witness of the disciples stand in relation to each other much in the same way that the witness of the Father is related to the witness of the Son. In viii 18 Jesus said, "I am one who gives testimony on my behalf, and the Father who sent me gives testimony for me"; but the statement in the next verse ("If you recognized me, you would recognize my Father too") shows that only one testimony or witness is involved, namely, that of the Father given through Jesus.

The last line of vs. 27 hints at what will be the subject matter of the witness borne by the Spirit through the disciples. They are the unique witnesses because they have been with Jesus, and it is his word that must be brought to the world. This agrees with what we hear of the Paraclete in xiv 26 ("He will remind you of all that I told you [myself]") and in xvi 13–14 ("He will not speak on his own. . . . It is from me that he will receive what he will declare to you"). Moreover, it agrees with other Johannine references to the witness of the disciples in the post-resurrectional period: in I John i 2 and iv 14 bearing witness is combined with the claim "We have seen for ourselves." Jesus is the supreme revelation of God to men; there can be no witness to the world other than the witness he bore. All other witness by the Paraclete through the disciples simply interprets that.

Verses xvi 1–4a: The Persecution of the Disciples

By way of inclusion the theme of vss. 18–21 recurs here, but now the author makes clear that he sees the hatred of the world for the Christian disciples particularly verified in their treatment by the Synagogue (a polemic narrowing down of the councils, synagogues, prisons, governors, and kings who constitute the persecutors in the Synoptic accounts). By dividing the material about persecution so that some of it comes at the beginning of the subdivision and some of it comes at the end, the author may have intended a development of thought. The first group of verses (xv 18–21) follows xv 1–17 which speaks of Jesus' love for his disciples, so that the general hatred of the world stands in contrast to Christian love. The second grouping (xvi 1–4a) follows the mention of the Paraclete and concerns the specific means of persecution that will be adopted to prevent Christians from giving voice to the witness of the Paraclete.

Twice (1 and 4a) in these last verses Jesus explains why he has been telling the disciples about future persecution. The reason is to prevent their faith from being shaken ("scandal"; see NOTE). This theme of scandal appears in Jesus' words at the Last Supper in Mark xiv 27 (Matt xxvi 31) where he predicts that when he is acted against, they will all fall away, i.e., "be scandalized." (While John has the scandal theme here, the falling away of the disciples does not appear until xvi 32.) In John, the fear about scandal among the disciples goes beyond their reaction to the immediate arrest of Jesus and stretches out to their reaction to persecution by way of disillusionment. There may have been a tendency to expect messianic bliss after Jesus' victory, and perhaps some were beginning to think their faith in Jesus vain when they encountered war with the world rather than peace. Recalling that Jesus had foretold this might eliminate the element of scandal (cf. the psychology in I Pet iv 12). But, of course, beyond this motive of anticipating and avoiding shock, the Johannine Jesus' main desire is to explain clearly that conflict with the world is inevitable, for it stems from the world's natural attitude toward God.

The words in vs. 2 show that the evangelist had a practical reason for writing down these words of Jesus, namely, that the Christian community was locked in combat with the Synagogue (vol. 29, pp. LXX–LXXV). That in Johannine thought the Synagogue could be identified with the evil, hostile world is seen by the epithet "synagogue of Satan" in Rev ii 9, iii 9. John does not refer to the Christians being beaten or flogged in the synagogues (so Mark xiii 9; Matt x 17) but to their expulsion from the synagogues; this indicates that the situation is that of the late 80s and 90s when excommunication was being invoked against Jews who professed Jesus as Messiah. See the NOTE for the possibility that Jews were putting Jewish Christians to death, thinking that in so doing they were serving God. What has probably happened is that more general predictions by Jesus of future persecutions before the complete messianic victory have been specified in terms of the contemporary situation. Paul, who suffered in many a synagogue, remained hopeful that all Israel would be saved (Rom xi 26); but for John the Jews of the Synagogue represent the world in its opposition to the Father: "They never knew the Father nor me" (xvi 3). Once again we remind the reader, as we have already done in vol. 29, p. 368, that the Johannine attitude toward the Synagogue must be evaluated in the light of the polemic context of the times.

We have already noted the similarity between xvi 3 and xv 21. Having separated the material pertaining to persecution into two groupings, one at the beginning, the other at the end of the subdivision, the writer may have wished to reiterate the cause of this persecution. As it stands, 3 is almost parenthetical, interrupting the flow of thought from 2 to 4.

Verse 4a repeats in a slightly more positive way what was said in 1. The phrasing "so that . . . you may remember that I told you so" is particularly fitting after the Paraclete theme of xv 26–27, for one of the functions of the Paraclete will be to remind the disciples of all that Jesus has told them (xiv 26). Indeed, in the author's mind, the reapplication of Jesus' traditional sayings about persecution to the situation of Church-Synagogue polemic at the end of the century is precisely the work of the Paraclete, for this Spirit recalls in a living way and adapts the tradition of Jesus' words to an existential situation. In his "I have said this to you" Jesus is speaking to a new generation, speaking through the Paraclete who is now his presence among men.

[The Bibliography for this section is included in the Bibliography for ch. xvi, at the end of §56.]

55. THE LAST DISCOURSE:
—DIVISION TWO (SUBDIVISION THREE)
Unit One (xvi 4b–15)

Jesus' departure and the coming of the Paraclete

XVI 4b "At the beginning I did not tell you this
    because I was with you;
  5 but now I am going to Him who sent me.
    Yet not one of you asks me, 'Where are you going?'
  6 Just because I have said this to you,
    your hearts are full of sadness.
  7 Still I am telling you the truth:
    it is for your own good that I go away.
    For if I do not go away,
    the Paraclete will never come to you;
    whereas, if I do go,
    I shall send him to you.
  8 And when he does come,
    he will prove the world wrong
    about sin,
    about justice,
    and about judgment.
  9 First, about sin—
    in that they refuse to believe in me.
  10 Then, about justice—
    in that I am going to the Father
    and you can see me no longer.
  11 Finally, about judgment—
    in that the Prince of this world has been condemned.
  12 I have much more to tell you,
    but you cannot bear it now.
  13 When he comes, however,
    being the Spirit of Truth,
    he will guide you along the way of all truth.
    For he will not speak on his own,

but will speak only what he hears
and will declare to you the things to come.
14 He will glorify me
because it is from me that he will receive
what he will declare to you.
15 Everything that the Father has is mine;
that is why I said:
'It is from me that he receives
what he will declare to you.'"

NOTES

xvi 4b. *At the beginning. Ex archēs,* found also in vi 64, is literally
"from the beginning"; like *ap' archēs* in xv 27, it means from the beginning of
the ministry.

I did not tell you this. Literally "these things," namely, the inevitability of
persecution in the world, as just discussed in xv 18 – xvi 4a. Jesus made
parabolic reference to the necessity of suffering and dying in xii 24–26, but
that passage was already under the rubric of "the hour" (xii 23). In the
Synoptics too the threat of future persecution for the disciples tends to come
late in Jesus' life, for example, in the Eschatological Discourse. Often we cannot
depend on the chronology of Gospel sayings, but it is not implausible in this
instance.

because I was with you. A logical reason for not speaking of persecution
at the beginning (John presupposes that Jesus foresaw it from the beginning)
would have been the desire not to frighten the disciples away before they
had begun to understand and to believe. But this is not the reason that Jesus
offers. Perhaps the idea is that as long as he was with them, all persecution
was directed against him. Only when he departs is there a problem for his
disciples who will become the chief spokesmen of the word of God.

5. *but now.* In "the hour" as contrasted with "at the beginning."

I am going to Him who sent me. In vii 33 Jesus told the crowds,
"I am to be with you only a little while longer; then I am going [*hypagein*]
to Him who sent me." Notice how the theme of return to the Father dominates
his attitude toward death. The departure of Jesus was a frequent theme
in xiv, phrased in a varied vocabulary (NOTE on xiv 2). Similarly here in
xvi: in 5 and 10 "go" is *hypagein* (also xiii 33, 36, xiv 4, 5, 28); in 7
"go away" is twice expressed by *aperchesthai,* while "go" is *poreuesthai* (also
xiv 2, 3, 12, 28).

6. *this.* Literally "these things."

your hearts are full of sadness. Literally "sadness has filled your heart";
for the singular "heart" see NOTE on xiv 1. The theme of sadness (*lypē*) is strong
in this chapter, appearing again in vss. 20, 21, and 22. In xiv it is implied
in vs. 1: "Do not let your hearts be troubled." For "full of sadness" the Gothic
version reads "made numb with sadness" (cf. xii 40).

7. *I am telling you the truth.* Jesus used this expression in speaking
to "the Jews" in viii 45–46 (cf. the assurance in Rom ix 1; I Tim ii 7).

Is this merely an assurance, or does "truth" have its special Johannine connotation of divine revelation? What follows in the chapter is part of what Jesus has come to reveal.

for your own good. This expression occurred in xi 50 ("more to your advantage"; to be repeated in xviii 14), and there too it concerned Jesus' death.

will never come to you. The negative (*ou mē* plus the subjunctive) is emphatic. *Perhaps* the milder negative (*ou* plus the future) that appears in the Byzantine tradition may represent a theological modification; cf. NOTE on vii 39, "there was as yet no Spirit."

if I do go. This whole last condition is omitted in P⁶⁶* by homoioteleuton.

I shall send. Here, as in xv 26, Jesus sends the Paraclete; in xiv 26 the Father sends him.

8. *prove . . . wrong about.* There has been much discussion about the possible meanings of *elenchein peri* (Barrett, p. 406; De la Potterie, "Le paraclet," pp. 51–52). We shall seek an interpretation appropriate to all three phrases governed by the verb in this verse, although some have experimented with the idea that the meaning shifts from phrase to phrase (cf. A. H. Stanton, ET 33 [1921–22], 278–79). The verb means both "to bring to light, expose" and "to convict someone of something" (also "to correct, punish," but such a meaning is not apropos here). Barrett chooses the second meaning on the analogy of viii 46 where Jesus challenges "the Jews" to convict him of sin. But if we examine the three elements governed by the preposition *peri* in xvi 8, we find that "convict of" is appropriate only for the first element, precisely because there it is a question of the *world's* sin. But "convict of" is less appropriate for the second and third elements, for it is not the world's justice, nor the world's judgment. The idea is that, in a reversal of the trial of Jesus, the world is found guilty of *sin* in that it has not acknowledged the *justice* of God in the glorified Jesus, and this very conviction is a *judgment* on the Prince of this world who accused Jesus and put him to death. Thus, "convict the world of justice and of judgment" is not too satisfactory a rendering. A translation in terms of exposing the guilt of the world in relation to the three elements seems better able to catch the broadness of the concept. (The *Testament of Judah* xx 5 has an interesting parallel: "The spirit of truth will accuse all"; but there the verb is *katēgorein*.) In the use of *elenchein peri* and of the coordinating *men . . . de . . . de* to set up a pattern in 9, 10, and 11 respectively, John shows an almost classical elegance of style. The "catchy" paraphrase in NEB is worth noting: "show where wrong and right and judgment lie." Bultmann thinks that in the Revelatory Discourse Source vs. 8 with its legal language once stood in direct sequence to xv 26, so that the proving of the world wrong constitutes the witness that the Paraclete is to bear on Jesus' behalf. This interpretation of the meaning is correct whether or not one accepts the reconstructed sequence.

about sin. All three nouns, "sin," "justice," "judgment," lack the article— the author is dealing with basic ideas rather than with individual instances. This effect is heightened by the lack of any clarifying genitives ("sin of the world"; "justice of God in Jesus"; "judgment of the Prince of the world"— there is an attempt to supply these in OS^sin, on the basis of information in 9, 10, and 11). The question is not primarily who sinned but in what sin consists (Bultmann, p. 434).

about justice. The word *dikaiosynē*, so important in the Pauline letters, occurs in John only in these verses. The general NT problem of whether it is best translated as "righteousness" or as "justice" is well known, but the trial atmosphere here seems to make "justice" more appropriate. Of course, the word has a larger context than legal justice; in particular, the "justice of God" involves His holiness and majesty as well. Papyrus Bodmer III, a recently discovered 4th-century Bohairic version of John, has "truth" instead of "justice." E. Massaux, NTS 5 (1958–59), 211, suggests that this may be a Gnostic reading, for in Gnostic thought truth was more important than justice.

about judgment. Krisis, here condemnatory, as we see from vs. 11. See NOTE on iii 17, "condemn."

9. *First.* We render the *men . . . de . . . de* construction of 9, 10, and 11 by "first . . . then . . . finally."

in that. Hoti can also be translated "because" (Barrett, p. 406), but the main emphasis seems to be explicative rather than causative (Bultmann, p. 434[3]).

refuse to believe. The present tense (literally "do not believe") indicates prolonged incredulity. A few Greek witnesses and the Vulg. read an aorist which would emphasize the once-for-all nature of the decision not to believe. The stubbornness of the disbelief has already been indicated in xv 22.

10. *justice—in that I am going to the Father.* Elsewhere in the NT Jesus is called just in the sense that he is morally virtuous (I John ii 1, 29, iii 7), but here Jesus is just in the sense of one who has been vindicated in court (cf. Deut xxv 1 where the judges acquit the *ṣaddîq*). He stands in the Father's presence and so partakes of the justice of God, before whom there can be nothing unjust.

the Father. The Byzantine tradition has "my Father."

you can see me no longer. The present tense of *theōrein.* In xiv 19 Jesus said, "In just a little while the world will not see me any more, but *you will see [theōrein]* me." On pp. 645–47 above we suggested that, while xiv 19 may have originally referred to post-resurrectional appearances, it was reinterpreted in Johannine circles to refer to a more abiding and non-corporeal presence of Jesus after the resurrection, especially to his presence in the Paraclete. The present verse needs no reinterpretation; it refers directly to the period when Jesus' presence among the disciples in the Paraclete is not visible.

11. *has been condemned. Krinein;* see *krisis* in 8. The thesis that in the very act of Jesus' death Satan's domination came to an end seems to have been common in NT times. Hebrews ii 14 speaks of Jesus' death nullifying the power of death (a power of the devil). The ending of Mark in the Freer ms. reads: "The limit of the years of Satan's authority has been fulfilled." Yet I John raises a difficulty: while Christians are praised for having overcome the Evil One (ii 13) and the world is said to be passing away (ii 17), the whole world is still said to be in the power of the Evil One (v 19). Thus, while defeated, the Prince of this world keeps power over his own domain (see Eph ii 2, vi 12). One may also reflect on Rev xx 2–3 where the devil or Satan is bound for a thousand years before he will be released on the world once more. It is clear, however, that Satan has no dominant power over the believer.

12. *much more.* Literally "still many things"; the "still" is omitted by Tatian, OS[sin], and some of the Patristic witnesses.

bear. Barrett, p. 407, remarks that this use of *bastazein* is not overly common in Greek, and it may reflect Semitic usage (Heb. *nāśā'*, or rabbinic *sābal*). While the basic idea is that they cannot *understand* now, there is also a question of endurance because persecution by the world is involved.

it. The pronominal object is not expressed but is supplied by some Western witnesses.

now. This is omitted in Codex Sinaiticus and some of the minor versional witnesses. SB suggests that a shorter form of this verse may have been original: "I have much to tell you, but you cannot bear it."

13. *Spirit of Truth.* This title appeared in the first Paraclete passage (xiv 17), as well as in xv 26. Bultmann regards it as the evangelist's addition to the material taken from the Revelatory Discourse Source. See App. V.

guide you along the way. The verb *hodēgein* is related to *hodos*, "way" (xiv 6: "I am the way"); the verb is used in Rev vii 17 to describe how the Lamb leads the saints to living water. Some of the Greek Fathers (Cyril of Jerusalem, Eusebius) read another verb here, namely, *diēgeisthai*, "to tell about"; and this verb may lie behind the Vulg. translation: "he will teach you"— a translation which makes the second Paraclete passage in xvi echo the second Paraclete passage in xiv (26: "will teach you everything"). The textual witnesses are rather evenly divided on what preposition should be read with *hodēgein*. Vaticanus and Alexandrinus read *eis*, "into," while Sinaiticus, Bezae, and OL read *en*, "in." Among the modern commentators Westcott, Lagrange, Bernard, Bultmann, Braun, Leal, and Mollat prefer *eis*, while Barrett, Dodd, Grundmann, and Michaelis prefer *en*. Some object to *eis* on the grounds that truth is not the goal of the Paraclete's guidance, for the guidance itself is truth; consequently they prefer *en* which indicates that truth is the sphere of the Paraclete's action. Yet De la Potterie, "Le paraclet," p. 45[1], responds that *eis* has a wider meaning than direction alone: it can signify also that the movement will terminate in the interior of the place toward which it is directed and thus can fittingly express how the Paraclete's guidance is related to truth. Probably too much is made of shades of difference in prepositions that were used quite vaguely at this time (BDF, §218; but De la Potterie would not agree).

of all truth. "All" is omitted by Sinaiticus* and Boh.; its position varies in other witnesses.

For. This conjunction shows that the Paraclete's function of guiding along the way of all truth is related to his speaking about what he has heard from Jesus.

not speak on his own. This has also been said of the Son (xii 49; xiv 10).

will speak only what he hears. Codices Vaticanus and Bezae (a strong combination) have the future tense of "hear"; Sinaiticus has the present; the Byzantine tradition, by way of grammatical improvement, reads the subjunctive with *an* ("whatever he may hear"). The choice between the future and the present is a difficult one. The suggestion that the present tense represents an adaptation to Trinitarian theology (the Spirit goes on hearing) is dubious. Elsewhere the work of the Paraclete is described both in future tenses ("will teach" in xiv 26; "will prove" in xvi 8; "will guide" in xvi 13) and in present tenses (often proleptic: "remains" and "is within" in xiv 17—see NOTE there). Note the meaningless variation between "will receive" and "receives" in the one saying recorded in 14 and 15 below. The principle of preferring the more difficult reading inclines toward acceptance of the present tense here, for all the verbs in the immediate context are future, and a scribe would be tempted to make this verb conform. In any case it should be noted that the tense used of the Paraclete differs from the aorist used of Jesus in viii 26: "The only things I say to this world are what I have heard from Him" (also xii 49). Westcott, p. 230, maintains that the tense difference implies that the message that the Son had to deliver was complete and definite, while the message of the Paraclete is continuous or extended. We doubt the validity of this distinction: since John considers the Paraclete's message to be that of Jesus, the Paraclete's message is also complete. (Moreover, present tenses are used also of what Jesus receives from the Father in v 19, vii 17, xiv 10.) If there is a tension between the completeness of the message and the need for continual application, that tension runs through the work both of Jesus and of the Paraclete, for they have the same task of revelation. In concluding we note that John does not specify from whom the Paraclete hears what he speaks. But it is not a meaningful question to ask whether the Paraclete hears from Jesus or from the Father. If the implication is that he hears from Jesus (see 14), all that Jesus has is from the Father (15).

declare. The verb *anangellein,* "announce, disclose, declare," appears three times in 13–15. P. Joüon, RSR 28 (1938), 234–35, finds the classical meaning of the verb most appropriate throughout the Johannine literature (six uses), namely, saying over again what has already been said; the only possible exception is John iv 25. In this interpretation the prefix *ana-* has the force of English "re-", thus "re-announce, re-proclaim." If we use the LXX use of *anangellein* as our guide to the meaning in John, the results are partially similar. The verb is very common in Isaiah (fifty-seven times; cf. F. W. Young, "A Study of the Relation of Isaiah to the Fourth Gospel," ZNW 46 [1955], 224–26). That book makes clear that the declaring of things to come is a privilege of Yahweh that false gods do not possess (xlviii 14). Almost the same expression that John uses is found in the LXX of Isa xliv 7 where Yahweh challenges anyone else to declare the things that are to come (see also xlii 9, xlvi 10). In xlv 19 we find Yahweh declaring truth—an expression that combines two of John's descriptions of the Paraclete's role in xvi 13. Thus, the statement that the Paraclete will declare to the disciples the things that are to come is perfectly consonant with the contention that the Paraclete is given or sent by the Father, for in so declaring the Paraclete is performing a function peculiar to God alone. De la Potterie, "Le paraclet," p. 46, has made a study of *anangellein* in the apocalyptic literature, for example, in the Theodotion version of Dan ii 2, 4, 7, 9, etc. There the verb is used to describe the interpretation of mysteries *already communicated* in dreams or visions. The declarative interpretation deals with the future by seeking a deeper meaning in what has already happened (see the same idea in Acts xx 27). We may note that the cognate words *apangellein* ("proclaim" in I John i 2, 3) and *angelia* ("message" in I John i 5, iii 11) clearly involve interpretation of what has been already revealed in Jesus Christ.

14. *He will glorify me.* There is a passage in the *Gospel of Truth* (see vol. 29, p. LIII) that has a superficial resemblance to this: "His spirit rejoices within him and glorifies him in whom he came to be" (xliii 17–18). However, the Gnostic document may be speaking of the believer's inner self rather than of the Holy Spirit; so K. Grobel, *The Gospel of Truth* (Nashville: Abingdon, 1960), p. 201.

from me. Literally "from what is mine." It has been suggested that John meant to stress the partitive in the sense that the whole of divine truth implicit in Jesus would not be revealed to men and that the Paraclete would choose from it only what is appropriate. The universalism of xiv 26 ("teach you everything and remind you of all") and of xvi 13 ("all truth") makes this emphasis unlikely.

15. The whole verse is omitted in P66* by homoioteleuton (14 and 15 have the same ending).

Everything that the Father has is mine. In Trinitarian theology this has been used to show that the Son has the same nature as the Father, but John is thinking about revelation to be communicated to men.

that is why. It is sometimes hard to determine whether the expression *dia touto,* "because of this," refers to what precedes or to what follows; here it clearly refers to what precedes.

he receives. A present is read here by the best Greek witnesses as contrasted with the future in 14. The witnesses that read a future in 15 are harmonizing with 14. There is no apparent significance to the change in tenses.

COMMENT

Verse 4b seems to have been constructed to serve as a transition between two subdivisions of the Last Discourse, namely, the originally independent material on persecution now found in xv 18 – xvi 4a, and the material in xvi 5–33, which, as we have seen in Chart I (pp. 589–91 above), is very closely parallel to xiii 31 – xiv 31. We broke down xiii 31 – xiv 31 (Division One) into an introduction and three units. The breakdown in xvi 4b–33 is more problematic, for the material here is less organized than in Division One. Because the Paraclete passages come to an end in xvi 15, it has seemed logical to most scholars (Loisy, Buchsel, Hoskyns, Strathmann, Barrett, Dodd) to acknowledge a break between 15 and 16. But Bultmann finds a break between 11 and 12. This latter division has the advantage of joining the second Paraclete passage in xvi (13–15) with a passage mentioning that the disciples will see Jesus again (16–22) and a passage mentioning the Father (23–28). Thus, one might uncover a triadic motif in xvi 12–28, matching Unit Two in Division One (xiv 15–24) which spoke of the coming of the Paraclete, of Jesus and of the Father to dwell with men. Yet this similarity would be artificial, for there is no mention of an indwelling of the Father in xvi. The parallels between xvi 4b–33 and Division One are in the matter treated rather than in the construction of the discourse.

For convenience, then, we shall treat xvi 4b–15 as a unit. Within it we may distinguish three groupings of verses: an introductory passage in 5–7 (concerned with Jesus' departure and the sadness of the disciples) leading into the two Paraclete passages of 8–11 and 13–15. We speak of *two* Paraclete passages although they are placed closer together than are the other three Paraclete passages in the Last Discourse, and it is not implausible that by the insertion of the transitional vs. 12 the author intended 8–15 to be read as one long treatment of the Paraclete.

Verses 5–7: Jesus' departure and the sadness of the disciples

The theme of Jesus' impending departure has not been heard since ch. xiv; its return in vss. 4b–5 shows that we are once more dealing with material that is totally at home in the setting of the Last Discourse. The opening verses of this subdivision have close parallels in the first unit of xiv. We pointed out in discussing xiv 1 that the troubling of the disciples' hearts in the face of Jesus' departure was more than mere sentiment and reflected the dualistic struggle between Jesus and the Prince of this world. This is even clearer in xvi 6 when we reflect that the sadness of the disciples is consequent upon Jesus' frightening description of the persecution that they shall suffer in the world.

This sorrow is so pervasive that not one of the disciples asks Jesus, "Where are you going?" (5). Here we encounter a famous crux in the Last Discourse since there actually have been requests about where Jesus is going, made by Simon Peter (xiii 36) and by Thomas (xiv 5). We have already mentioned theories of rearrangement that seek to do away with the difficulty by putting xvi 5 before the other two passages (pp. 583–84 above). Others like Wellhausen see a contradiction here and a proof that the various parts of the Last Discourse are not by the same hand. Still others seek to explain away the seeming contradiction. Barrett, p. 405, emphasizes the present tense in xvi 5: the disciples are so sorrowful that, while they have asked before where Jesus is going, no one asks *now*. Lagrange, pp. 417–18, has a similar view: they do not ask him *any more;* and Schwank, "Es ist gut," p. 341, points to Amos vi 10 for proof that in Hebrew speech pattern there is not always a sharp distinction between "not" and "no more." Perhaps these latter observations can be used to explain the meaning of the passage as it stands in the final, edited form of the Gospel when we are seeking to make sense of the Last Discourse as it now stands. But, as to the origins of the difficulty, we have already indicated our belief that xvi 5 is a duplication of the incident basic to xiii 36 and xiv 5. In one form of the account the question is posed by the disciples to Jesus and the context indicates that they do not understand where he is going. In the other form the question is not even posed because the disciples do not sufficiently understand the import of his going away.

The statement in the first part of vs. 7 that it is good for the disciples that Jesus goes away has its parallel in xiv 28: "If you loved me, you would rejoice that I am going to the Father." However, there the implication is that it is better for Jesus himself that he is going away, while the idea in xvi 7 is that it is better for the disciples. Lagrange, p. 418, wonders why mankind could not have had the privilege of the continued presence both of the glorified Son and of the Paraclete. If our understanding of the Paraclete (App. V) is correct, however, this would be a contradiction. The Paraclete is the Spirit understood as the presence of the absent Jesus, and by definition the Paraclete and Jesus cannot be on earth together. We recall vii 39: "For there was as yet no Spirit, since Jesus had not been glorified." This implies not only that it is the glorified Jesus who gives the Spirit, but also that the role of the Paraclete/Spirit is to take the place on earth of the glorified Jesus. But one may still ask why John says that this exchange of place between Jesus and the Paraclete is for the good of the disciples—why would they not be just as well off if Jesus remained? The answer is that only through the internal presence of the Paraclete do the disciples come to understand Jesus fully. Or, if we call upon other passages where John describes the Spirit, only the communication of the Spirit begets men as God's children (iii 5, i 12–13); and in God's plan it is the Spirit that is the principle of life from above. The promise of vs. 7 is fulfilled in xx 22 where the first action of the risen Jesus who has ascended to his Father (xx 17) is to breathe on his disciples and say, "Receive a holy Spirit."

Verses 8–11: The Paraclete Against the World

The first Paraclete passage in xiv (15–17) also concerned the relationship between the Paraclete and the world. In xiv 17 it was said that the world cannot accept the Paraclete since it neither sees nor recognizes him. In xvi it becomes clear that this failure to see the Paraclete does not result in indifference but in hostility, the same type of hostility that marked the relationship of the world to Jesus.

Commentators have not found the detailed exposition of 8–11 easy. Augustine avoided the passage as very difficult; Thomas Aquinas cited opinions but gave none of his own; Maldonatus found it among the most obscure in the Gospel. Loisy, p. 430, remarks that the pattern of mentioning the three charges (8) and then explaining each (9–11)—"a methodical explanation that has not much clarity"—is more characteristic of the subtlety of I John than of the Gospel (cf. I John ii 12–13, v 6–8). Part of the problem concerns the verb *elenchein* which we have rendered as "prove wrong" (see NOTE). Who is to be the recipient of this proof? Some have thought that the Paraclete's task is to prove to the world its own error, and thus *elenchein* means "convince." But Mowinckel, p. 105, has argued persuasively that *elenchein* does not necessarily imply the conversion or reform of the party involved in the conviction. Rather it is a question of bringing the merciless light of truth to bear on guilt: the one certainty is that the party who is the object of *elenchein* is guilty. Moreover, the idea that the world is to be convinced by the Paraclete contradicts the statement of xiv 17 that the world cannot accept the Paraclete. The world cannot be convinced by the Spirit of Truth because its rejection of the truth is deliberate (iii 20).

What then? Is John thinking of something like a trial conducted before God where the guilt of the world will be publicly demonstrated to the disciples? Certainly the proof of the world's guilt is directed to the disciples, but the forum is internal. In Johannine realized eschatology elements of world judgment are incorporated here; yet the courtroom is not in some apocalyptic Valley of Jehoshaphat (Joel iii 2, 12) but in the mind and understanding of the disciples. (This has been shown by Berrouard, *art. cit.*) Moreover, the trial is only indirectly a trial of the world. It is properly a rerun of the trial of Jesus in which the Paraclete makes the truth emerge for the disciples to see. Its effect on the world stems from the fact that, having been assured by the Paraclete of the victory of Jesus in that trial, the disciples go forth to bear witness (xv 27) and thus challenge the world and its interpretation of the trial. In being the moving force behind this the Paraclete is simply continuing the work of Jesus who himself bore evidence against the world that what it does is evil (vii 7).

The first element (vs. 9) in the Paraclete's forensic activity is to prove to the disciples that the world is guilty of sin—the basic sin which consists in refusing to believe in Jesus. This has been a theme of the Gospel description of the ministry of Jesus, a ministry that has been presented throughout in the legal atmosphere of a trial (vol. 29, p. 45). In Jesus' first discourse he summed up the effect of his coming: "The light has come into the world, but men have preferred darkness to light because their deeds were evil" (iii 19). At the end of the public ministry the Johannine writer gave this evaluation: "Even though Jesus had performed so many of his signs before them, they refused to believe in him" (xii 37). All other individual sins find expression in or are related to this basic sin of disbelief. It is an entirely culpable sin (xv 22–24) and one that represents a permanent choice of evil (ix 41) which merits God's enduring wrath (iii 36). The Paraclete will focus on the expression of disbelief that culminated in putting Jesus to death, but those who are guilty are a much wider group than the participants in the historical trial of Jesus. Those participants are only the forebears of men in every generation who will be hostile to Jesus. Perhaps the attitude found in John strikes Christians of today as puzzling, accustomed as they are to a pluralistic society where disbelief in Jesus need represent no particular hostility toward him or toward God. But John was not really considering subjective, individual guilt; and his dualistic attitude was conditioned by the polemic context in which he lived.

The second element (vs. 10) in the Paraclete's forensic activity is to prove the world wrong about justice by showing that Jesus, whom it adjudged guilty, was really innocent and just. Influenced by Paul's debate about justice (*dikaiosynē*), some of the Church Fathers, including Augustine, and some of the reformers thought that vs. 10 refers to the justice *of the Christian* by faith. Yet the "I am going to the Father" shows that the theme is the vindication of Jesus, the manifestation of God's justice in Jesus' exaltation. (In these verses John is dealing with very basic notions, and the justice of the Christian is derivative from the justice of his master.) "The Jews" had regarded Jesus' claim of oneness with the Father as arrogant and had accused him of being a deceiver, a sinner, and a blasphemer (v 18, vii 12, ix 24, x 33). The purpose of the trial and of sentencing him to death was to show that he was guilty and was not God's Son (xix 7). Yet the Paraclete will demonstrate to the disciples that this same death sentence really showed that Jesus was what he claimed, for after his death he is with the Father; and by glorifying Jesus (xvii 5), the Father has certified him. "The return to the Father is God's imprimatur upon the righteousness [justice] manifested in the life and death of His Son" (Hoskyns, p. 485). The idea that Jesus' exaltation is a manifestation of God's justice is seen also in the hymn of I Tim iii 16 which contrasts incarnation and exaltation in these words: "He was manifested in the flesh, *justified* in the Spirit." It has interesting OT roots, as seen in Isa v 15–16: "The eyes of the haughty are humbled, but the Lord of Hosts is exalted in justice." Being exalted to the Father's presence, Jesus is in the sphere of divine justice. How will the Paraclete show to the disciples that Jesus is with the Father? To explain this some have called upon Acts vii 55 where Stephen, *full of the Spirit,* bears witness to Jesus at the right hand of the Father— in other words the Spirit gives the insight to see the victory of Jesus. Others have made a logical deduction from John vii 39 where it is stated that there would be no giving of the the Spirit before Jesus' glorification. But if we reason from the very nature of the Paraclete, the argument is more forceful: that in himself the Paraclete is the spiritual presence in the world of that Jesus who is with the Father (App. V). The whole idea of the Paraclete is meaningless and self-contradictory if Jesus has not over-come death; and so once the disciples recognize the Paraclete (xiv 17), they recognize that Jesus is with the Father.

The last clause of 10, "You can see me no longer," is almost a paradox. How can the fact that the disciples cannot see Jesus prove to them the justice of Jesus' claims? This is probably to be interpreted in terms of the Paraclete's presence, especially if we think of these words being addressed not primarily to the disciples at the Last Supper but to the Christians of the Johannine church (Loisy, p. 429). Until Jesus returns to take them with him to his heavenly dwelling place (xiv 2–3, xvii 24), believers shall not see him physically but only in and through his Spirit, the Paraclete. They come under the rubric of those fortunate ones "who have not seen and yet have believed" (xx 29). During his ministry Jesus warned that soon men would lose the opportunity of seeing him (vii 33–34, viii 21); after his death there is the Paraclete whom only believers can see and accept. Thus, in putting Jesus to death, the world has condemned itself.

This leads us to the last element (vs. 11) in the Paraclete's forensic activity, namely, to prove that in condemning Jesus the world itself was judged. In Jesus' death on the cross the trial that endured throughout his ministry seemed to end with the victory of his enemies. But in the Paraclete Jesus is still present after his death, and so the trial had a surprising outcome. If the hour of passion and death represented the confrontation of Jesus and the Prince of this world (xii 31, xiv 30), then in being victorious over death, Jesus was victorious over the Prince of this world. The very fact that Jesus stands justified before the Father means that Satan has been condemned and has lost his power over the world (see NOTE). We have here in realized form some of what the Book of Revelation describes in terms of final eschatology. While Rev xii 5, 7–12 pictures simultaneously the exaltation of the Messiah and the ejection of Satan from heaven, the binding of Satan (xx 2) and his final condemnation to fiery torment (xx 10) are yet to come. The thought in I John is close to that of John, and there it is made clear that those who believe participate in Jesus' victory over the Evil One (ii 13–14, iv 4, v 4–5). In bearing witness to this victory the Paraclete is truly, then, an antidote to the sorrow that seizes the heart of the disciples in face of Jesus' departure and of the onslaught of persecution in the world.

Verses 12–15: The Paraclete, Guide of the Disciples in the Things of Jesus

The second Paraclete passage in xvi, like its counterpart in xiv 26, concerns the role of the Paraclete as teacher of the disciples. Verse 12 offers a transition to this aspect of the Paraclete's work. What does Jesus mean when he says he has much more to tell that the disciples cannot bear now? Does this imply that there will be new revelations after his death? Some have thought so, and a certain mystique has been built on the basis of this statement. Augustine thought it temerarious to investigate what these things might be. Systematic theologians have used this verse to support the thesis that revelation continued after Jesus' death until the death of the last apostle. Roman Catholic theologians have seen in it a reference to continued unfolding of dogma during the period of the Church's existence. Yet we should be made cautious by comparing it to xv 15 which seems to exclude further revelations: "I revealed to you everything I heard from the Father." (Loisy, p. 432, treats these as contradictory, somewhat along the line of the supposed contradiction between xvi 5 and xiii 36 mentioned above.) More likely vs. 12 means that only after Jesus' resurrection will there be full understanding of what happened and was said during the ministry, a theme that is familiar in John (ii 22, xii 16, xiii 7). This promise of deeper understanding may be phrased in terms of "I have more to tell you" because, acting in and through the Paraclete, Jesus will communicate that understanding. It is unlikely that in Johannine thought there was any concept of further revelation after the ministry of Jesus, for Jesus is *the* revelation of the Father, the Word of God.

And so we are led to vs. 13 and to the Paraclete as the one who guides the disciples to the full truth of what Jesus has said. Some would trace this picture of the Paraclete as a guide to the role of the guide in the pagan mystery religions, but there is also OT background. We recall Pss cxliii 10: "Your good *spirit* will guide me along a level path" and xxv 4–5 "O Lord, teach me your paths; guide me in your *truth*." In LXX of Isa lxiii 14 we read: "The spirit came down from the Lord and guided them along the way." Sometimes it is objected that these OT passages deal with a moral guidance and not with a deeper understanding of revelation and that therefore John's portrayal of the Paraclete as a guide is quite different. Obviously "spirit," "way," and "truth" have a meaning in Johannine thought that goes beyond the OT; but we are asking a question only of background and at least this writer presupposes that the originality of John's Christian message would demand a transformation and adaptation of whatever came to the evangelist from his background. But more to the point, the Paraclete's guidance along the way of all truth involves more than a deeper intellectual understanding of what Jesus has said—it involves a way of life in conformity with Jesus' teaching, and thus is not so far removed from the OT notion of guidance as might first seem. We may also mention that the role of guiding men was attributed to Lady Wisdom (Wis ix 11, x 10); just as the figure of the Johannine Jesus is patterned upon personified divine Wisdom, so also is the figure of the Paraclete (see App. V).

The Paraclete is to guide men *along the way of all truth*. In viii 31–32 Jesus had promised: "If you abide in my word, you are truly my disciples; and you will know the truth." This is fulfilled in and through the Paraclete. We have an interesting example of how it is accomplished in Acts viii 31 where the eunuch cannot understand that the Suffering Servant passage in Isa liii refers to Jesus until he is *guided* by Philip who in turn is under the influence of the Spirit (viii 29). Guidance along the way of truth is guidance to the mystery of Jesus who is the truth (John xiv 6). The mention of *all* truth in 13 (cf. "all that I told you [myself]" in xiv 26) and the stress that the Paraclete will not speak on his own but only what he hears seem to confirm the suggestion that no new revelation is involved.

But the last line of 13 presents a difficulty. Does not the promise "He will declare to you the things to come" imply new revelation? Wikenhauser, p. 295, and Bernard, II, 511, are among the many who see here a reference to the existence of a prophetic office or charism in the Johannine (or pre-Johannine—Windisch) church, similar to the Spirit-guided prophecy of I Thess v 19–20; I Cor xii 29, xiv 21–33; Eph iv 11. Loisy, p. 433, thinks of Spirit-guided apocalyptic prophecy about things to come (Rev ii 7, xiv 13, xix 10, xxii 17). Bultmann, p. 443, for whom the line has been added by the evangelist to the Revelatory Discourse Source, thinks that, while in itself the line may reflect community belief in the spirit of prophecy, in its present context it loses its apocalyptic overtones. This last view seems most reasonable since it would fit in within the Johannine emphasis on realized eschatology. The word studies of *anangellein*, "declare," that we have reported in the NOTE suggest that the declaration of the things to come consists in interpreting in relation to each coming generation the contemporary significance of what Jesus has said and done. The best Christian preparation for what is coming to pass is not an exact foreknowledge of the future but a deep understanding of what Jesus means for one's own time. In his role of prophetic declaration the Paraclete continues the work of Jesus who identified himself to the Samaritan woman as the Messiah who announces or declares (*anangellein*) all things to men (iv 25–26). We saw in the NOTE on iv 25 that for the Samaritans this meant that Jesus was the expected Prophet-like-Moses, that is, a prophet who would interpret the Mosaic Law, given long before, so as to solve the present legal problems of the community. Vis-à-vis Jesus, the Paraclete has the same function of announcing or declaring all things.

Barrett, p. 408, sees a special nuance in the Paraclete's declaration of the things to come; he thinks that this is the unveiling of sin, justice, and judgment as narrated in 8–11. Although the trial of Jesus is past, the implications of the death of Jesus and his glorification must be worked out for the disciples and for the world in each generation. The Paraclete would then be telling the disciples the import of the message of Jesus that they cannot bear now (12).

Verse 14 reinforces the impression that the Paraclete brings no new revelation because he receives from Jesus what he is to declare to the disciples. Jesus glorified the Father (xvii 4) by revealing the Father to men; the Paraclete glorifies Jesus by revealing him to men. Glory involves visible manifestation (vol. 29, p. 503); and by making witnesses of men (xv 26–27), the Paraclete publicizes the risen Jesus who shares his Father's glory (xvii 5). (Elsewhere in John we learn that the Spirit glorifies Jesus by begetting children of God who thus reflect God's glory in a way similar to that in which Jesus reflects God's glory—see NOTE on xvii 22). We note one more element of realized eschatology in this reference to glory. For the Synoptic Gospels the Son of Man will come in glory on the Last Day (Mark xiii 26), but for John there is already glory in Jesus' presence in and through the Paraclete.

Verse 15 touches obliquely on the Paraclete's relation to the Father as well as to the Son. We have observed that ch. xvi emphasizes the agency of Jesus with regard to the Paraclete (vs. 7: "I shall send him") as contrasted with ch. xiv 16, 26, where the Father is the agent. But vs. 15 shows that the author of xvi knew also that ultimately the Paraclete, like Jesus himself, was the emissary of the Father. In declaring or interpreting what belongs to Jesus, the Paraclete is really interpreting the Father to men; for the Father and Jesus possess all things in common. Later the theologians of East and West would dispute in Trinitarian theology whether the

Spirit proceeds from the Father alone or from the Father and the Son. In Johannine thought it would be unintelligible that the Paraclete have anything from Jesus that is not from the Father, but all that he has (for men) is from Jesus.

[The Bibliography for this section is included in the Bibliography for ch. xvi, at the end of §56.]

56. THE LAST DISCOURSE:
—DIVISION TWO (SUBDIVISION THREE)
Unit Two (xvi 16–33)

Jesus' return will bring the disciples joy and understanding

XVI

16 "In a little while you will not see me any more,
   and then again in a little while you will see me."

17 At this some of his disciples remarked to one another, "What does this mean? He tells us, 'In a little while you will not see me, and then again in a little while you will see me'; he also says, 'Because I am going to the Father.'" 18 So they kept wondering, "What is this 'little while' [of which he speaks]? We don't understand [what he is talking about]." 19 Knowing that they wanted to question him, Jesus spoke to them, "You are asking yourselves about my saying, 'In a little while you will not see me, and then again in a little while you will see me.'

20 Truly I assure you,
   you will weep and go into mourning
   while the world will rejoice;
   you will be sad
   but your sadness will be turned into joy.
21 When a woman is in labor, she is sad
   that her hour has come.
   But once the baby is born,
   her joy makes her forget the suffering,
   because a child has been born into the world!
22 So it is with you too—you are sad now;
   but I shall see you again,
   and your hearts will rejoice
   with a joy that no one can take from you.
23 And on that day you will have no more questions to put to me.

Truly I assure you,
if you ask anything of the Father,
He will give it to you in my name.
24 Until now you have asked nothing in my name.
Ask and you shall receive
that your joy may be full.
25 I have said this to you in figures of speech.
An hour is coming
when I shall no longer speak to you in figures
but shall tell you about the Father in plain words.
26 On that day you will ask in my name,
and I do not say that I shall have to petition the Father for you.
27 For the Father loves you Himself
because you have loved me
and have believed that I came forth from God.
28 [I came forth from the Father]
and I have come into the world.
Now I am leaving the world
and I am going back to the Father."

29 "There," his disciples exclaimed, "at last you are speaking plainly,
without figures of speech! 30 Now we know that you know everything—
you do not even need that a person ask you questions. Because of this
we believe that you came forth from God." 31 Jesus answered them,

"So now you believe?
32 Why, an hour is coming—indeed has already come—
for you to be scattered, each on his own,
leaving me all alone.
Yet I am never alone
because the Father is with me.
33 I have said this to you
so that in me you may find peace.
In the world you find suffering,
but have courage:
I have conquered the world."

29: *exclaimed*. In the historical present tense.

NOTES

xvi 16. *a little while. Mikron;* see NOTE on xiii 33. In the similar statements in vii 33, xii 35, and xiii 33, when Jesus says he is going to be with his hearers a little (while) longer, he follows this with a threat that he will depart to where he cannot be seen. A closer parallel for the more benevolent verse under consideration is xiv 19: "In just a little while the world will not see me any more; but you will see me."

not see me any more. The negative is *ouketi.* The verb is *theōrein;* in the next line it is *horan (opsesthai).* The latter is thought by some to refer to deeper spiritual insight (so Bernard, II, 513), but see our comments in vol. 29, p. 502.

again in a little while. The idea that there will be only a little while before finding happiness with God appears in an apocalyptic context in Isa xxvi 20: "Hide yourself for a little while until the anger of the Lord shall have passed away." This is interesting, for Isa xxvi 17 is part of the background of vs. 21 (see COMMENT).

you will see me. The Byzantine Greek tradition, along with the Latin and Syriac versions, adds a line: "because I go to the Father." This clause (which in vii 33 does follow a statement about seeing Jesus no longer) has been introduced to justify the second citation in the next verse (17). A scribe must have thought that both citations in 17 came from 16.

17. *his disciples remarked.* This intervention marks the first time they have spoken since Judas gave voice to his confusion in xiv 22; thus ends the longest monologue in the Gospel. The interventions in Division One of the Last Discourse were by individual disciples; the interventions in xvi are by the disciples as a group.

What does this mean? He tells us . . . This is similar to a frequent rabbinic formula (Schlatter, p. 314).

'In a little. . . '. This first citation in 17 is taken verbatim from 16 with the exception of the use of a shorter negative (*ou* for *ouketi*).

he also says. The Greek has simply "and"; the verb of saying that precedes the first citation is understood to cover the second as well.

'Because I am. . . '. The second citation begins with *hoti,* presumably with the meaning "in that, because" that it has in 10 from which the citation is taken verbatim, although with a variance of word order. However, it is possible that the *hoti* in 17 is simply the "that" used to introduce (indirect) discourse. Many favor the latter because it gives a smoother translation: "he also says that I am going to the Father." Yet the discourse is really direct, not indirect, and so the narrative *hoti* would be otiose; moreover there is no narrative *hoti* before the first citation and so we would not expect one before the second citation.

18. *So they kept wondering.* Literally "saying" (to themselves). This is omitted by many Western textual witnesses. As we shall see, there are many scribal variants in the text of this verse, perhaps because of its repetitious character. Such repetition is typical of simple narrative, especially in the Near East.

'little while.' In most witnesses *mikron* is preceded by an article (omitted

in P⁵, Vaticanus, Sinaiticus corrector, and seemingly in P⁶⁶). Lagrange, p. 426, argues that even without the article the sense is: Will his absence really last only a *little while?*

[*of which he speaks*]. This is omitted by P⁶⁶ and some important Western witnesses.

[*what he is talking about*]. Most witnesses read the verb *lalein*, while Bezae and Koridethi read *legein*. Vaticanus omits the clause. It could have been added by scribes in an attempt to clarify.

19. *Knowing*. John frequently attributes to Jesus the power to read men's minds (ii 24–25, iv 17–18). In the other Gospels it is often difficult to be sure whether the evangelist wishes us to think that this knowledge was supernatural or simply an instance of shrewd insight: cf. Luke vii 39–40; Matt ix 22 with Mark v 30; Mark iii 23 with the "Q" tradition of Matt xii 25 and Luke xi 17. In John the special knowledge attributed to Jesus seems to be consistently presented as supernatural; and certainly in the present instance the enthusiasm that his knowledge evokes (30) indicates that more than natural knowledge is meant.

they wanted to. Some witnesses, including Sinaiticus and P⁶⁶ᶜ, read "they were going to." P⁶⁶* had both verbs—this is interesting, for usually it is a later witness that conflates two different readings.

You are asking. This could be a question: "Are you asking . . . ?"

you will not see. The negative is *ou* as in 17, not *ouketi* as in 16.

20. *weep . . . mourning*. The reference is to the loud wailing and lamentation that is the customary reaction to death in the Near East. For these verbs used in the context of death see Jer xxii 10; Mark xvi 10 ("weep"); Luke xxiii 27 ("mourn").

sad. The *lypē* theme of xvi 6 returns in 20–22. In the NT *lypē* describes primarily an anguish of mind or spirit. Loisy, p. 435, comments that a word for physical pain would have been more appropriate, for example, *ōdin*, the technical term for birth pains (and for the messianic woes). But the vocabulary of the allegorical parable is governed by the situation of the disciples where "sadness" is more appropriate.

turned into. Probably a Hebraism (*hyh l*); cf. MTGS, p. 253. We shall see in the COMMENT that John is using ancient Hebrew symbolism here.

21. *a woman*. Literally "the woman." This is parabolic speech, as vs. 25 makes clear; and the definite article is frequent in introducing nouns that are the subjects of parables (cf. xii 24).

in labor. *Tiktein*, "to bear, give birth to."

sad. *Lypē;* see NOTE on xvi 6. Feuillet, "L'heure," pp. 178–79, calls attention to Gen iii 16: "In sadness [*lypē*] you shall bring forth [*tiktein*] children." This is important because the narrative of Adam and Eve is sometimes suggested as possible background for the symbolism used by John.

her hour. Codex Bezae, P⁶⁶, OL, and OS read "day," but we have followed the majority of textual witnesses. Good arguments can be advanced on both sides why scribes might have changed one word to the other. One may argue that "hour" was inserted to favor Johannine theology whereby the passion and resurrection constitute "the hour" of Jesus; note also the use of "hour" in 25 and 32. Yet "day" may have been inserted to establish a reference to "the day of the Lord" with its expected tribulations and sufferings; note the use of "day" in 23 and 26.

suffering. Thlipsis; see COMMENT. The theme returns in 33.

a child has been born into the world. The literal expression, "a human being has been born into the world," is somewhat tautological, for in rabbinic language "one born into the world" is a description of a human being; see NOTE on i 9. However, the idea may be that her joy is not simply because she has a child but also because she has contributed to mankind or the world. Feuillet, "L'heure," pp. 175–77, thinks that the use of "human being" (*anthrōpos*) rather than "son" is another echo of the Genesis background mentioned above. In particular, he cites Gen iv 1: "Eve conceived and bore Cain, saying. 'With the help of the Lord I have begotten *a man*'" (Philo *De Cherubim* XVI–XVII;※53–57, calls attention to the use of "man" here). On pp. 366–69, Feuillet suggests that the phrase *"into* the world" is meant by John to be evocative of the career of Jesus who came into the world by his incarnation and will return into the world after his passion and resurrection as a New Adam (an interpretation offered in times past by Chrysostom, Aquinas, Cornelius a Lapide, and others).

22. *are sad.* Literally "have sadness." A strong combination of textual witnesses (P66, Bezae, Alexandrinus) supports a future tense, but the difference in meaning is not significant.

I shall see you again, and your hearts will rejoice. This echoes LXX of Isa lxvi 14: "You shall see, and your hearts will rejoice." Barrett, p. 411, observes that John's change of "You shall see" to "I shall see" can scarcely be accidental. Others, comparing the "I shall see you" of this verse with the "you will see me" of 16, remark that there has been a progression because it is better to be seen by God than to see Him. However, one may suspect that "you shall see me" and "I shall see you" are simply the two sides of a coin, much as the "you in me and I in you" indwelling of which we have several examples.

hearts. Literally singular, as in vs. 6; see NOTE on xiv 1.

can take. Literally "takes" or "will take"; Vaticanus and Bezae* support a future tense, but the present (P66) is probably original, being used to express the certainty of the future.

23. *on that day.* The phrase appears here and in 26; see NOTE on xiv 20.

no more questions to put to me. The verb of interrogation is *erōtan.* Commentators are divided on whether this line refers to what has preceded or to what follows. If it refers to what has preceded (Westcott, Loisy, Lagrange, Bultmann, Hoskyns, Barrett), the reference is to the type of question that was the subject of 17–19: a question that betrays a lack of understanding. Jesus is promising that "on that day" they will understand. This would agree with our thesis in the COMMENT that this passage refers to Jesus' presence through the Paraclete. The Paraclete will bring understanding since he will teach the disciples everything (xiv 26) and guide them along the way of all truth (xvi 13). One finds a similar idea in I John ii 27: "The anointing that you received abides within you; so you have no need for anyone to teach you."

If it refers to what follows (Chrysostom, Bernard), the questioning is the same as asking (*aitein*) things of the Father: a request or petition for something that one wants. Jesus is promising that "on the day" they will no longer put their requests to him but will be able to ask the Father directly. The fact that two different verbs of interrogation (*erōtan* and *aitein*) are used in lines 1 and 3 does not favor this solution, although often these verbs are interchangeable (in 26 below *erōtan* is used for a petition). The fact that lines 1 and 3 are separated by the solemn double "Amen" ("Truly I assure you") also suggests a change of subject and thus favors the first interpretation. But in our mind the conclusive argument for the first interpretation is the context. Our NOTES on 26 and 30 below give reason for thinking that the "questions" of vs. 23, line 1, concern understanding and are not petitions.

Truly I assure you. Jesus began his response to his disciples in 20 with these words, and now that response takes a new turn. Bernard's dictum (I, 67) that the double "Amen" never introduces a new saying unrelated to what precedes is true only if one inserts a "totally" before "unrelated." This phrase often marks the beginning of a new thought or a new phase in the discourse, as in x 1.

if. A rare use of *an* for *ean* (BDF, §107); cf. xiv 14: "If [*ean*] you ask anything of me in my name, I will do it."

of the Father. As the citation from xiv just given indicates, ch. xiv favors petitions made to Jesus, while xvi favors petitions to the Father. See discussion on pp. 634–35 above.

give it to you in my name. In Vaticanus, Sinaiticus, and the Coptic versions, the phrase "in my name" comes after the verb "to give" and must be interpreted thus. But in Bezae, Alexandrinus, and the Byzantine tradition, "in my name" is placed before the verb "to give" and so *may* be translated with the preceding line: "If you ask anything of the Father in my name, He will give it to you." This translation, supported by OL and OS, agrees with xv 16 ("The Father will give you whatever you ask Him in my name") and also, in sentence pattern, with xiv 14 cited above. The textual witnesses are evenly divided, but we prefer the former rendering because it is more difficult and unusual. Nowhere else in John or in the NT is it said that things will be given in Jesus' name, and scribes may have conformed this statement to the more usual pattern of asking in that name. That the idea of the Father's giving in Jesus' name would be at home in Johannine thought is seen in xiv 26: "The Paraclete . . . that the Father will send in my name."

24. *Ask.* The present imperative ("keep on asking") puts emphasis on the persistence of the request. For the format of this saying and its Synoptic parallels see pp. 634–35 above.

joy may be full. Literally "may be fulfilled"; the construction is periphrastic; and often, but not always, this is a sign of translation from Semitic.

25. *this.* Literally "these things."

figures of speech. Paroimia, like *māšāl* which it translates in LXX, covers a wide range of parabolic and allegorical speech (See NOTE on x 6; also A. J. Simonis, *Die Hirtenrede im Johannes-Evangelium* [Analecta biblica 29; Rome: Pontifical Biblical Institute, 1967], pp. 75–79). Often in such speech there is an element of the difficult, the obscure, or the enigmatic; for instance, in Sir xxxix 3 we find in parallelism "the secrets of *paroimiai*" and "the enigmas of *parabolai.*" There has been figurative language both in Division One of the Last Discourse (the symbolism of the washing in xiii 8–11; the servant and the messenger in xiii 16) and in the present Division (the vine and the branches in xv 1–17; the woman in labor in xvi 21). In recalling Jesus' custom of speaking in figures of speech, John is in agreement with Mark iv 34: "He did not speak to them without a parable [*parabolē,* synonym of *paroimia*], but explained everything privately to his own disciples" (also Mark iv 11). Yet for John the full explanation did not come until the era of the Spirit.

An hour is coming. See vol. 29, p. 518.

tell. This verb, *apangellein,* is used in I John i 2, 3 to describe the apostolic proclamation of what had been heard from Jesus. In the COMMENT we shall develop the thesis that Jesus' promise to tell the disciples about the Father in plain words is accomplished through the Paraclete. An association of this verse with the work of the Paraclete is suggested by the Byzantine textual tradition which (incorrectly) reads *anangellein,* "to declare," the verb used in the Paraclete passage of xvi 13–15.

plain words. Parrēsia can also mean "openness, confidence, boldness." If we are correct in interpreting the promise to speak "in plain words" as a task of enlightenment accomplished in and through the disciples (COMMENT), then John's thought is somewhat similar to that of Acts where speaking with boldness (*parrēsia*) is a special gift of the Spirit (see Acts ii 29, iv 13, 29, 31, xxviii 31).

26. *On that day.* This means: when the hour mentioned in 25 has come to its fulfillment. In 23 it was said: "On that day you will have no more questions to put to me." We argued that these were questions for information and understanding and not petitions; we see here that "on that day" there will still be petitions.

you will ask in my name. The verb is *aitein.* In xiv 13 ("Whatever you ask in my name I will do") there was an explicit promise that the petition would be granted; here it is implicit.

petition. The verb is *erōtan;* see NOTE on "no more questions" in 23. Lagrange, p. 430, suggests that the idea is that Jesus will not have to call attention to someone in need (the use of *erōtan* in Luke iv 38).

27. *Father . . . Himself.* Bernard, II, 520, cites Field as to the "elegant Greek use" of the pronoun *autos* here, meaning "the Father on His own" (*proprio motu*); he says it is evidence that much of John's Greek is not a translation from Semitic. However, *autos* may represent a proleptic pronoun used to anticipate a following noun for emphasis, a grammatical construction which Black, pp. 70–74, characterizes as a pure Aramaism. MTGS, pp. 258–59, cites this as an instance where "It is not easy to decide, but probably the pronoun has some emphasis."

loves . . . loved. Philein; the same thing was said with *agapan* in xiv 21, 23 (see vol. 29, p. 498).

have believed. Here faith is the second condition for gaining the Father's love; in xiv 21, 23 the second condition was keeping Jesus' commandments and word. For John, love, faith, and obedience are all parts of the complexus of Christian life, and one supposes the other. Note the perfect tense in the verbs "have loved" and "have believed"; a continuous attitude of life is implied.

came forth. This is the aorist of *exerchesthai* as in viii 42 (see NOTE there); also xvii 8. In xv 26 we heard that the Spirit of Truth *comes forth* (present of *ekporeuesthai*) from the Father.

from God. Vaticanus, Bezae, Tatian, and the Coptic versions read "from the Father"—a strong combination. The witnesses that read "God" are divided on whether or not to read the article before *theos.* With the article *theos* refers to the Father (NOTE on i 1), and the reading "the Father" may be a clarification of this. Or else "the Father" may represent the cross influence of the first line of the next verse and of xv 26 (yet see viii 42 which has "God").

28. [*I came forth from the Father*]. This clause is found in the best witnesses, including Sinaiticus and Vaticanus, but is omitted in some of the Western witnesses, perhaps by homoioteleuton. The confusion at the end of the

preceding verse about whether to read "from God" or "from the Father" may have caused some scribe to conflate and to include both readings by repeating the verb. But it is hard to believe that the perfect chiastic pattern now found in 28 was created by a scribe's haphazard addition: lines 1 and 4 treat the incarnation and resurrection from the viewpoint of the Father; lines 2 and 3 treat them from the viewpoint of the world. This argument tips the scales in favor of the authenticity of the first line.

came forth . . . have come. Respectively the aorist and the perfect tenses. The first tense acknowledges that the incarnation took place at a particular moment in time; the second acknowledges its enduring effect. A similar contrast appears in viii 42: "From God I came forth and am here" (an aorist and a present with a perfect meaning).

from the Father. The witnesses that have this bracketed first line are divided on whether to read *para* or *ek* ("from"). There is no real difference in meaning; indeed, a third preposition, *apo*, appears in 30. *Ek* cannot be interpreted theologically in reference to the intra-Trinitarian relationship of Father and Son ("came out of the Father"), for this line refers to the incarnation, not to what later theology would call the procession of the Son. (Moreover, in viii 47 the phrase *ek tou theou* is used to describe an ordinary believer: "The man who *belongs to God*.")

Now. Palin, "again," is used here to mark what is next in sequence; yet it also has the connotation of a return to a previous condition, whence our addition of "back" in the next line. Cf. BAG, p. 611, and the usage in xi 7.

leaving . . . going. The verbs are *aphienai* and *poreuesthai;* for other vocabulary see NOTE on xvi 5.

29. *at last.* Literally "now"; *nyn* appears again at the beginning of 30. Bultmann, p. 454, proposes this meaning: now, in the Last Discourse, you are speaking plainly, as contrasted with the way you spoke in the public ministry. But if one does not accept Bultmann's rearrangement whereby ch. xvi comes earlier in the Last Discourse, then it becomes less likely that the disciples are contrasting what is said in the Last Discourse (which they have frequently misunderstood) with what was said in the ministry. They may be pictured as thinking that, as Jesus' departure becomes more imminent, he has begun to speak more clearly than was true earlier in the Discourse, and that the hour has now come that was promised in 25, an hour when he would no longer speak in figures.

30. *we know . . . we believe.* There was also a combination of a verb of knowing with the verb of believing when Peter voiced the disciples' convictions in vi 69: "We have come to believe and are convinced [*ginōskein*] that you are God's Holy One."

you do not even need that a person ask you questions. The verb is *erōtan.* The present verse, which must refer to questions of information, is important for the understanding of the promise in 23a: "On that day you will have no more questions [*erōtan*] to put to me"; apparently the disciples think that the promise has been fulfilled. Some exegetes have not made a connection with 23a and think that the statement in the first part of 30 that Jesus knows everything should be followed logically by a statement that *Jesus* (not "a person") has no need to ask questions, thus, the OS: "You do not need to ask a person questions" (cf. also Augustine *In Jo.* CIII 2; PL 35:1900). However, not only is there little textual support for such a reinterpretation, but also it neglects the Jewish idea that the ability to anticipate questions and not to need *to be asked* is a mark of the divine. In Josephus, *Ant.* VI.xi.8;※230, Jonathan swears to David by "This God . . . who, before I have expressed my thought in words, already knows what it is." The same idea is found in Matt vi 8: "Your Father knows what you need before you ask Him."

More precisely, in the present sequence in John, why do the disciples conclude that Jesus does not need that a person ask him questions, and why does this conclusion lead the disciples to affirm their belief that he came forth from God? (H. N. Bream has devoted an important article to these questions, and we but summarize briefly here.) Many commentators consciously or unconsciously betray the awkwardness of the sequence by shifting the negated need from Jesus to the disciples and explaining why the disciples no longer need to ask Jesus questions (so Luther, Spitta, Strachan, Lightfoot). However, this destroys the parallelism between the first and second parts of vs. 30: "You know everything—you do not even need. . . ." Other scholars, working with the disciples' statement as we have translated it, explain that the disciples have been impressed by Jesus' ability to know and answer their unspoken questions, e.g., in 19, and perhaps in 20–28 (so Chrysostom, B. Weiss, Westcott, Lagrange, Bernard, Bultmann, Barrett). But we must note that the statement affirms more than that Jesus does not need that *the disciples* ask him questions; it affirms that he does not need that anyone ask him questions. Bream suggests that this affirmation may be related to the custom of seeking answers from oracles, a practice which Christian thought equated with false prophecy. In the *Shepherd of Hermas,* Mandate xi 2–5, there is an attack upon the false prophet who has to be asked questions: "For every spirit which is given from God is not asked questions [*erōtan*], but has the power of the Godhead and speaks all things of itself, because it is from above" (xi 5). In Johannine thought Jesus would have this power because he is the only true revealer of God. When the disciples recognize that he knows questions before they are asked, they recognize automatically that he came forth from God.

Because of this. Literally "in this" (=the reason why; BDF §219²). The "this" is Jesus' ability to anticipate questions and his knowing everything.

you came forth from God. The preposition is *apo* here, as contrasted with *ek* in 28; but certainly (*pace* Lagrange, p. 432) the Johannine writer does not insinuate by this change of vocabulary that the disciples are making a lesser affirmation than what Jesus claimed in 28. They are accepting what Jesus said of himself to the extent that they can understand it, and the change of preposition is meaningless.

31. *So now you believe?* Grammatically it is difficult to decide whether this is a question or a declaration; BDF, §440, speaks of ambiguity. The similar instance in xiii 38 suggests a question. Even if it is a declaration ("Now you believe"—namely, for the moment), it casts doubt on the adequacy of the disciples' faith. Theirs is a faith that is not complete; it will waver (32). This interpretation runs contrary to an exegesis (e.g., Lagrange) whereby Jesus exclaims that the disciples have come to believe at last—and none too soon, for he is about to be arrested.

32. *Why. Idou,* literally "behold," is adversative as in iv 35.

an hour is coming . . . for. Often *hōra* is combined with *hote,* "when" (iv 21, 23, v 25, xvi 25), but here and in three other instances (xii 23, xiii 1, xvi 2) it is constructed with *hina.* BDF, §382¹, and Zerwick, §428, deny any final nuance to the *hina,* so that they see no difference of meaning in the two constructions. Yet it is tempting here to see in *hina* an implication that what happened was *in order to* fulfill the prophecy of Zechariah about the sheep being scattered.

scattered. John uses *skorpizein;* in the COMMENT we shall point out the parallel with Mark xiv 27 which uses *diaskorpizein* in citing Zech xiii 7. Codex Alexandrinus of Zechariah also uses *diaskorpizein;* yet almost certainly the original LXX reading of Zechariah was *ekspān,* found in Vaticanus and Sinaiticus. Although the Johannine and Marcan verbs are slightly different, some have suggested that John is dependent on Mark's form of the Zechariah citation. However, it is possible that both John and Mark are dependent here on a tradition of testimonies or texts collected for their christological reference (so Dodd) in which there was a variant form of the Greek text of Zechariah. Also it is not inconceivable that John and Mark represent independent attempts to render the Hebrew of Zechariah more faithfully into Greek.

on his own. Literally "to his own." The meaning "to his own occupation" is possible, but the meaning "to his own home" is more likely (see usage in Esther v 10; III Macc vi 27; John xix 27). Does this refer to the disciples' temporary dwellings in Jerusalem or to their home towns in Galilee? The *Gospel of Peter,* 59, specifically mentions that the disciples went to their homes.

leaving me all alone. This is somewhat evocative of Isa lxiii 3: "I have trodden the wine press alone, and there was not one of my people with me."

I am never alone. The same claim was made in viii 16 ("I am not alone—I have at my side the One who sent me") and in viii 29 ("The One who sent me is with me. He has not left me alone.").

33. *said this.* Literally "these things"; note the inclusion with 25. The "these things" must refer to more than the dire threat in 32, for that would scarcely give the disciples peace. Probably the reference is to the promises in 26 and 27 and perhaps to some of the earlier promises of the chapter. The fact that 33 does not agree easily with 32 has led some (E. Hirsch, Dibelius) to suggest that originally 33 followed 28 and that 29–32 is a redactor's addition (from Synoptic tradition). Wellhausen proposed that 33 belongs best with 24; Lagrange thought that it would fit well after xvi 3. It is probably wise simply to recognize the composite character of the material here without attempting to reconstruct the original sequence.

find suffering. A few witnesses support a future tense. The word for "suffering" is *thlipsis;* see COMMENT on 21.

I have conquered. In the NT, particularly in Revelation (v 5, vi 2, xvii 14), Jesus is described as the one who conquers. Also I Cor xv 57: "Thanks be to God who gives us victory through our Lord Jesus Christ."

COMMENT

As ch. xvi now stands, there can be little doubt that the final Johannine editor thought of xvi 4b–33 as a whole and that, therefore, in distinguishing between the units 4b–15 and 16–33, we are distinguishing between two parts within a whole rather than between two really independent subdivisions. The over-all unity is illustrated by the reference in 17 to something said in 10. Of course, this does not mean that such unity is original.

Indeed, the fact that the specific mention of the Paraclete theme is confined to 4b–15 suggests that we are dealing with a unity imposed on what were once independent blocks of material. We note also that 16–33 has the style of a dialogue between Jesus and his disciples, while 4b–15 does not. The theme of sadness that we saw in 6 reappears in 20–22; yet in these verses the answer to the sadness is not a promise of the coming of the Paraclete but a promise that the disciples will see Jesus again (16; cf. 22). Considerable reinterpretation by the Johannine writer was required in order to give unity to such diverse expectations, as we shall see below.

Within 16–33 is there any recognizable structure? Many scholars (Lagrange, Hoskyns, Barrett, Bultmann) propose a twofold grouping of verses: 16–24 and 25–33. They point out that 25 can serve as the beginning of a new group of verses since it has an air of finality, as if the Discourse were now drawing to its close. Moreover, one can find an inclusion in the refrain, "I have said this to you," that appears in 25 and 33. However, there are also arguments against such a division; for instance, the theme of 23b–24 (asking and receiving) is very much like the theme of 26–27, and it seems odd to separate these verses into different groupings.

We suggest that the material should be divided into 16–23a and 23b–33 and that these two groups of verses are related to each other in a typical Johannine chiastic pattern, thus:

	16 – 23a		23b – 33
Prediction of trial and of subsequent consolation	16	–	31 – 33
Intervening remarks of the disciples	17 – 19	–	29 – 30
Promise of blessings to be enjoyed by disciples	20 – 23a	–	23b – 28

We are conscious of the danger that we are reading more structure into the unit than the Johannine writer intended, but there are specific points that lend plausibility to the thesis that this strucure was intended. The warning of trial in 16 ("In a little while you will not see me any more") is matched by one in 32 ("Why an hour is coming—indeed has already come—for you to be scattered"). The accompanying note of consolation in 16 ("again in a little while you will see me") is matched by one in 33 ("so that in me you may find peace"). The interventions by the disciples in 17–19 and 29–30 are explicitly connected by the reference in 30 to Jesus' knowing what was in their minds before it was put as a question— a faculty that was exemplified in 19. Finally, the two large groups of discourse (20–23a, 23b–28) are almost of equal length, and each is introduced by "Truly, I assure you." Each concerns what will happen to the disciples "on that day" (23a, 26) when "the hour" has fully come (21,

25). The first (20–23a) promises the disciples lasting joy (20–22) and knowledge (23a); the second (23b–28) promises the granting of their petitions (23–24, 26) and knowledge (25).

Verses 16–23a: The Disciples Will See Jesus Again and Rejoice

Verse 16, the key to this group of verses and, indeed, to the whole unit, illustrates the great difficulty of determining what is meant in the Last Discourse by the return of Jesus, a difficulty already mentioned on pp. 602–3 above. If we treat 16 as a saying uttered in the context of the Last Supper, the first impulse is to understand it thus: Jesus will die shortly, and so in a little while the disciples will not see him; but then in a little while they will see him again, because after his entombment he will rise and appear to them. This was the view of most of the Greek Fathers. (Obviously such an interpretation presupposes that Jesus knew in detail what would happen after his death, a presupposition that many scholars, Protestant and Catholic, would no longer make.) Yet there are certain elements in John's description of the state of the disciples after they see Jesus that do not fit in well with a reference to post-resurrectional appearances. It is true that in John's view the promises of joy and peace (xvi 20–22, 24, 33) were to some extent fulfilled in the post-resurrectional appearances of the risen Jesus (xx 20, 21, 26), but do those appearances really grant "a joy that no one can take from you"? Much of what John reports in xvi 16 ff. anticipates a more permanent union with Jesus than that afforded by transitory post-resurrectional appearances. Verse 23a promises the disciples plenary understanding so that they will have no more questions to pose. Such a depth of understanding was scarcely achieved in the brief post-resurrectional era within which Jesus appeared to them. The theme of making petitions and having them granted (23b–24, 26) seems to imply a long period of time when this would be a customary procedure.

Another solution has been proposed. Augustine (*In Jo.* CI 6; PL 35: 1895) understands the second "little while" in 16 as the period before the parousia and suggests that the disciples (Christians) will see Jesus again when he comes at the end of time. The Roman Liturgy seems to follow this interpretation, for it reads this passage on a Sunday *after* the Feast of the Resurrection. That the expression "you will see me" could refer to the parousia is shown by Synoptic passages that speak of seeing the Son of Man coming on the clouds in power and glory (Mark xiii 26, xiv 62). The figure of birth pains (21) is employed in the OT to describe the eschatological day of the Lord, a day that is also echoed in the phrase "on that day" of 23 and 26. Yet we cannot confine the promise of 16 solely to the parousia, for that would imply that nothing Jesus had promised would have yet been fulfilled.

If we are to interpret the saying in the historical context of the Last Supper, perhaps we can combine what is best in both of the views given above. Jesus may have promised to his disciples blessings that would be theirs after his victory over death and evil, but his expectation of what that victory would consist in may not have been clearly defined. It may have been an expectation that was phrased in the traditional language both of resurrection and of parousia. (We suggested in vol. 29, p. 146, that the vague Johannine statements about Jesus' being lifted up may be more original in their outlook than the detailed Synoptic predictions of resurrection.) Thus a distinction between seeing Jesus at the time of his post-resurrectional appearances and seeing him at the time of his parousia may well have been a distinction formulated by the early Church precisely when it came to realize that all Jesus' promises had not been fulfilled in his appearances after the resurrection. Such a distinction would not be original in sayings stemming from the ministry.

As we turn from what the saying may have meant if it was uttered at the Last Supper to what it came to mean in the total Gospel context, we find that in Johannine thought "seeing" Jesus and the joy and knowledge that are consequent upon this experience are considered as privileges of Christian existence after the resurrection. Jesus' promises have been fulfilled (at least to a significant extent) in what has been granted to all Christians, for the Last Discourse is addressed to all who believe in Jesus and not only to those who were actually present. "Seeing" Jesus has been reinterpreted to mean the continued experience of his presence in the Christian, and this can only mean the presence of the Paraclete/Spirit. Such a reinterpretation is legitimate in Johannine thought because the Paraclete is given by the risen Jesus precisely as a way to make permanent his glorified presence among his disciples, now that his place is with the Father. While the saying in 16 may have originally referred to physical sight, it now refers to a spiritual insight; and thus there is no real contradiction between "you will see me" in 16 and "you can see me no longer" in 10; cf. also xx 29. As the parallels with the Synoptic Gospels in 23–24, 25, 26, and 32 suggest, the Johannine writer was dealing here with sayings that had their roots in early tradition. Rather than completely rewrite these sayings in terms of seeing Jesus in and through the Paraclete, he accomplished his reinterpretation by placing them side by side with the Paraclete sayings of xvi 8–15. (In treating xiv 2–3 [pp. 625–27 above] we saw a similar technique of reinterpretation through context.) Division One of the Last Discourse has a parallel to xvi 16 in the saying of xiv 19: "In just a little while the world will not see me any more, but you will see me because I have life and you will have life." As we pointed out on pp. 645–46, this saying was also reinterpreted to refer to a more abiding presence of Jesus than was possible in the post-resurrectional period; following shortly after the Paraclete passage in xiv 15–17, it too is best interpreted in terms of the coming of the Paraclete/Spirit.

Moving on to the dialogue in xvi 17–19, we find that, if we have had difficulty in determining the meaning of what Jesus said in 16, the disciples were also confused. The promise of Jesus that they would see him again in a little while (16) seems to conflict with his claim that he was going to the Father (10: "I am going to the Father and you can see me no longer"). We have pointed out above that the Johannine writer has solved the apparent contradiction by reinterpreting the meaning of "see"; but without the advantage of that later reinterpretation, the disciples had every right to be confused. We are told that Jesus read their mind and antici-pated their question, but the answer that he gave never really tells them or us how to resolve the difficulty within the historical context of the Last Supper—despite the fact that the disciples later (29–30) became en-thusiastic over the fact that Jesus had anticipated their question and was now speaking plainly.

The Johannine Jesus has a habit of answering questions obliquely, and his reply in 20 ff. is really a description of the privileges that the disciples will enjoy after "the little while," namely, "on that day" (23, 26), when "the hour" has fully come (21, 25). In 20–23a two privileges are described, joy and understanding.

The enduring joy of the disciples (20–22) is contrasted with the false and cruel joy that seizes the world when Jesus dies. The joy of the disciples is also related to his death, but it is a joy that emerges triumphant from suffering. In describing this phenomenon Jesus resorts to a parable drawn for the ordinary experience of human birth. Yet the figurative language that he employs also has roots in the OT portrayal of the birth pangs that Israel will have to endure before the day of the Lord comes or before the Messiah comes. In Isa xxvi 17–18 (LXX) we read: "Like a woman with child who cries out in her pangs in her time of labor, so were we. . . . We have brought forth the spirit of your salvation." This is followed by a promise that the dead shall live and by an appeal to those who lie in the dust to *rejoice* (*euphrainein;* not the *chairein* of John), for the anger of the Lord lasts only *a little while* (*mikron*). Isa lxvi 7–10 describes the labor pains of Zion in bringing forth her children and then encourages all who love her to rejoice (*euphrainein*) with her. This passage may have been in mind in John xvi 21, for 22 cites Isa lxvi 14 (see NOTE). See also Hos xiii 13; Mic iv 9–10, v 2(3). The figure of birth pangs continued to be employed in the post-OT period of Jewish thought. In the Dead Sea Scrolls, 1QH iii 8 ff. describes a woman pregnant with her first child, a male. After terrible pains she gives birth to the "marvelous counselor" (the description of the promised king in Isa ix 5[6]). The import of this Qumran hymn is obscure, but it *may* describe figuratively the birth of the Messiah.

The imagery is also found in Rev xii 2–5 where the woman clothed with the sun, having cried out in the pangs of her labor, gives birth to a male child who is to rule all the nations with a rod of iron (the description of the anointed [messiah] king in Ps ii 9). In discussing the first miracle at Cana and Mary's role there (vol. 29, pp. 107–9), we had occasion to comment on this scene in Revelation. We pointed to its background in Gen iii 15–16 where it is said that woman will bring forth her children in pain and that her offspring will bruise the head of the evil serpent. (See the NOTES for striking parallels to the Genesis story in John xvi 21 too.) We suggested that the woman of Revelation is a symbol of the people of God, for whom Mary, the mother of Jesus, is a personification. In the article that we cited, A. Feuillet has argued persuasively that Rev xii, in alluding to the painful birth of the Messiah, is referring to the death and resurrection of Jesus. This is hinted at in Rev xii 5 where the moment the child is born, he is caught up to heaven. The equation of resurrection and birth is made at the beginning of Revelation (i 5), for there Jesus is called "the firstborn of the dead." The idea that the resurrection-ascension brought forth the Messiah is in accord with Acts ii 34–36; there Peter proclaims that, in elevating Jesus to His right hand, God made him Messiah.

In light of this background, Feuillet suggests that the little parable in John xvi 21 is also an allegory. (For the Johannine mixture of parable and allegory see vol. 29, pp. 390–91.) Not only are the present sadness and future joy of the disciples compared to the sadness and joy that a woman normally has in the birth of her child, but also there is reference to a familiar symbolic pattern wherein Jesus' death and victory are portrayed as the woman's birth pangs and subsequent bearing of the messianic child. How far can one press this allegory? Loisy (1903 ed.), p. 788, held that the woman of vs. 21 appears to represent the Synagogue converted to Christianity—a view rejected by Hoskyns, p. 488, and by Bultmann, p. 446[5] ("absurd"). By the time of his 1921 edition, Loisy, p. 436, was more cautious about identifying allegorical details. A. Kerrigan, *Antonianum* 35 (1960), 380–87, sees a particular reference to Mary; he supports this by calling on John xix 25–27 where at *the death* of Jesus, Mary is addressed as "Woman" and made the mother of the Beloved Disciple (symbolizing the Christian). W. H. Brownlee, NTS 3 (1956–57), 29, sees a particular reference to the apostles who are compared to a woman in labor whose infant is the risen Jesus. Perhaps it is best to say simply that John ii 4, xvi 21, xix 25–27, and Rev xii all echo in one way or another the allegory of the woman's role in the emergence of the Messiah as victor, without attempting to be more specific about the details of xvi 21.

One detail, however, can very plausibly be seen to have allegorical significance, the "suffering" or *thlipsis* of the woman. This is a word that is used almost technically to describe the tribulation that will precede God's eschatological action, for example, in the Greek of Dan xii 1: "There shall be a time of *suffering,* such suffering as there has never been before; but at that time your people shall be delivered." In Zeph i 14–15 we hear: "The great day of the Lord is near. . . . That day is a day of great wrath, a day of *suffering* and anguish." See also Hab iii 16. In the NT *thlipsis* is used by Jesus to describe the suffering or tribulation that will precede the coming of the Son of Man (Mark xiii 19, 24; cf. Rom ii 9).

By a type of realized eschatology the afflictions of the Church in her time on earth came to be regarded as *thlipsis* (Mark iv 17; Acts xi 19). In harmony with the symbolism wherein the combined death and resurrection of Jesus is represented by the messianic birth of a child, John sees the disciples' suffering at the death of Jesus as *thlipsis* which precedes the emergence of the definitive divine dispensation. The second mention of *thlipsis* in 33 extends the notion of suffering to include the continued affliction of the disciples under persecution from the world (this agrees with the usage in Rev vii 14). Just as the suffering has a double focus, so does the joy that follows it. The joy of the Christian disciple is not only the joy of recognizing that Jesus has conquered death in his resurrection (xx 20); it is an abiding joy resulting from Jesus' presence in the Paraclete. The first joy follows the sadness and suffering of Jesus' departure in death; the second joy (which is the continuation of the first) exists alongside suffering imposed by the world.

The second privilege that the disciples will enjoy after the "little while" is mentioned in 23a: a plenary understanding that obviates further questions. In the post-resurrectional period the disciples will come to understand what Jesus had said and done in his ministry (ii 22, xii 16, xiii 7). This understanding may have begun with the appearances of the Lord (xx 9, 24–28, xxi 4–7; cf. Luke xxiv 27), but its perfection and continuance are the work of the Paraclete (xvi 13–15). The two privileges of joy (through Jesus' presence in the Paraclete) and understanding (afforded by the Paraclete) are not really distinct, for the joy flows from the fact that the Christian has come to know and understand Jesus. The connection between understanding and joy is made in I John i 4 where the author says he is writing about what he had seen and heard of Jesus in order "to bring to fullness our common joy."

Verses 23b–33: The Disciples Will Have Their Requests Granted and Understand Jesus Plainly

The words of Jesus in 23b–28, which are somewhat parallel to those in 20–23a (p. 728 above), also promise two privileges that the disciples will enjoy after the "little while": the privilege of being so intimate with God that their requests will be granted (23b–24, 26), and, once again, the privilege of understanding Jesus as the revelation of the Father (25). The privilege of having requests granted really flows from "seeing" Jesus (16). Since the Christian will experience Jesus in the internal dwelling of the Paraclete, he will remain united to Jesus; and, as was promised in xv 7: "If you remain in me . . . ask for whatever you want and it will be done for you." Precisely because the Christians will have the intimate presence of Jesus in the Paraclete, they will also be close to the Father who is one with Jesus. This fact enables us to understand the peculiar stress of xvi 23b–24 that not only are things to be asked for in Jesus' name, but also they will be given in Jesus' name. Since Jesus dwells in the Christians, their petitions are in Jesus' name; since the Father is one with Jesus, the petitions He grants are granted in Jesus' name. Verse 24 is more profound than appears at first glance. The statement that up to now (the Last Supper) the disciples have not asked anything *in Jesus' name* really implies that the disciples cannot be completely united to Jesus (and thus act in his name) until after the hour of passion, death, resurrection, and giving of the Spirit. Only then, as Eph ii 18 phrases it, will they "have access in one Spirit to the Father."

What type of requests does John have in mind in recording these sayings about asking and receiving? We have suggested in discussing xiv 13–14 and 15–17 (pp. 636 and 644 above) that it is not primarily a question of the ordinary needs of life but of whatever will deepen eternal life and make fruitful the work of the Paraclete. In xvi, the context of the saying in 23b–24 confirms this, for both 23a and 25 concern a deeper understanding of Jesus (through the Paraclete). We may also compare the saying in 24, "Ask and you shall receive that your joy may be full," with what was said in xv 11: "I have said this to you that my joy may be yours and your joy may be fulfilled." The fullness of Christian joy comes through the understanding of what Jesus has revealed, an understanding that leavens the Christian's way of living.

With vs. 25 it becomes obvious that Jesus' remarks are drawing to a close. The promise of deeper understanding in 23a was in terms of the disciples' not needing to put more questions to Jesus; now the promise is in terms of Jesus' speaking more clearly. (Actually vs. 25 seems intrusive between 24 and 26, both of which deal with the theme of asking. *Parrēsia,* "in plain words," is found associated with the theme of asking and receiving in I John iii 21–22 and v 14–15, where it refers to the "confidence" with which one can be sure that the request will be answered.) What does the contrast between "figures of speech" and "plain words" imply? During the ministry "the Jews" challenged Jesus to speak in plain words (x 24), but he claimed that the real problem was that they obstinately refused to believe what he said; this answer seems to imply that he was speaking in plain words during the ministry. The use of *parrēsia* in xi 14 is more helpful: there Jesus had been speaking in figurative language of Lazarus' being asleep, but the disciples did not understand and so Jesus had to tell them plainly that Lazarus was dead. In the present instance the disciples have not understood the figure of the woman in labor that Jesus uses to illustrate his departure, and so Jesus promises that the time will come when such figures will no longer be necessary. Perhaps we should go beyond the literal meaning of "figures of speech" in the immediate context and think of the expression as referring to the element of the mysterious that characterizes all the words of Jesus in the Gospel—the inevitable mystery presented by one from above when he speaks to those who are on earth (in short, the Johannine form of what the Synoptics speak of as the mystery of the kingdom hidden *in parables:* see NOTE). This mystery can be dispelled only when they have been begotten from above (iii 3–6, 31–32). In promising to speak plainly, then, Jesus is doing more than promising an interpretation of the allegorical parables he has used at the Last Discourse; he is referring to a general enlightenment about his whole revelation. Once again in reference to vs. 25, systematic theologians have thought of a new revelation after the resurrection, but John probably has the work of the Paraclete in mind. We may compare vs. 25 to xiv 25–26: "I have said this to you while I am still with you. But the Paraclete . . . will teach you everything and remind you of all that I told you [myself]." In particular, according to xvi 25, Jesus (through the Paraclete) will tell the disciples *about the Father.* This is because the Paraclete/Spirit comes from the Father and begets the disciples as the Father's own children, so that their knowledge of the Father is almost connatural.

Verses 26–27 develop the note of intimacy with the Father and apply it to the theme of asking and receiving (resumed from 23b–24). Previous sayings about this subject (p. 635 above) have emphasized either the asking or the granting *in Jesus' name;* vs. 26 is new in seeming to exclude intercession on Jesus' part. Yet there are other statements in the Johannine writings that take for granted Jesus' intercession on behalf of the Christians in the post-resurrectional period. In xiv 16 the Paraclete is given at Jesus' request, and I John ii 1 describes Jesus himself as a Paraclete ("intercessor") in the Father's presence, helping Christians who have sinned. Perhaps then the real import of xvi 26 is not to exclude intercession but to explain that in interceding Jesus will not be a *tertium quid* between the Father and His children. Rather, Jesus' necessary role in bringing men to the Father and the Father to men (xiv 6–11) will set up so intimate a relationship of love *in and through Jesus* that Jesus cannot be considered as intervening. The Father will love the disciples with the same love with which He has loved Jesus (xvii 23–26); and the Father, Jesus, and the disciples will be one (xvii 21–23). Jesus will not have to ask the Father on behalf of the Christian, for the Christian's prayer will be Jesus' prayer. Loisy, p. 438, phrases John's thought thus: "In his glorified state Christ will not pray for his own; he will pray with them and through them in his Church. Here one comes to the deepest point of Christian mysticism. The Father sees in the Christians Christ himself, who is at the same time the object of their faith and love."

In a magnificent saying (vs. 28) that brings to a conclusion this great Discourse (or, at least, what is now Division Two of the Last Discourse), Jesus explains how he is one with men and one with the Father. Coming into the world, he has established a bond of union with his fellow men; leaving the world, he returns to reestablish in its fullness his union with the Father (Schlatter, p. 316). Only when that has been done will "the hour" be complete wherein the disciples will share the joy, the understanding, and the confidence in making petitions that he has promised. Schwank,

"Sieg und Friede," p. 398, points out that vs. 28 is a christological parallel to Deutero-Isaiah's (lv 10–11) beautiful description of the word of God: "Just as from the heavens the rain and snow come down . . . so shall my word be that goes forth from my mouth. It shall not return to me empty but shall do my will, achieving the end for which I sent it."

Despite the majesty and conciseness of vs. 28, all that it says has been said before. Therefore, when in 29 the disciples greet this saying or what has immediately preceded it as an instance of speaking in plain words, they are being impetuous. Hitherto they have not understood Jesus when he said these things, but now they boast: "We know . . . we believe that you came forth from God" (30). Yet they are not much closer to true understanding than they were when they asked naïve questions earlier in the Discourse. They have an incipient faith, of course; they have had that since the early days of the ministry (i 41, 45, 49, ii 11). (Dodd, *Interpretation*, p. 392, points out that the affirmation of the disciples in vs. 30 is almost a doublet of Peter's confession in vi 69: "We have come to believe and are convinced that you are God's Holy One.") And since they are now in the atmosphere of "the hour," this incipient faith may have grown considerably. But full faith is impossible without the gift of the Spirit that will come in the post-resurrectional period. Jesus promised that when the hour had fully come, he would speak in plain words (25). The disciples think that this has happened because, as described in 19, Jesus has anticipated their question before it was put into words—a sign that he has come from God (see NOTE on the ability to anticipate questions as a mark of the divine). This evaluation shows that their understanding and their faith are not complete (31). The hour can come only through suffering and death, and they must share in this if they are to understand and to believe (32).

In the reference in 32 to the disciples' being scattered now that the hour has already come, we seem to have a Johannine parallel to what is found in Mark xiv 27 (Matt xxvi 31) where after the Last Supper on the way to the Mount of Olives Jesus predicts that all the disciples will fall away and thus fulfill the prophecy of Zech xiii 7: "I will strike the shepherd, and the sheep will be scattered." In the Synoptic tradition this prediction comes true in the Gethsemane scene (which Mark xiv 35 describes as "the hour" of Jesus), for there all the disciples forsake him and flee (Mark xiv 50; Matt xxvi 56). In the *Gospel of Peter* we are told that the disciples hid themselves from their pursuers (26); each returned to his own home, while Simon Peter and Andrew went back to fishing (59–60). But in John there is no mention of such a desertion in the Gethsemane scene, and indeed the Fourth Gospel stresses the fidelity of one of the disciples, the Beloved Disciple, during the crucifixion (xix 26–27). Moreover, the scene in xx 19 where the disciples are gathered together on the evening of the day of the resurrection scarcely gives the impression of their having been scattered. (John xxi, with its picture of the disciples back in

Galilee at their ordinary work, is more amenable to the prediction of their being scattered.) Fascher, *art. cit.,* has exhaustively examined attempts to solve this difficulty, including the rearrangement of the passage so that it precedes the prediction of Peter's denial in xiii 36–38 (a rearrangement that is made on the basis of the union of the two predictions in Mark xiv 26–31; Matt xxvi 30–35). But it seems best to regard John xvi 32 as an example of early tradition preserved in the Last Discourse, even though it does not correspond perfectly with the development of the subsequent narrative. On the level of meaning intended by the Johannine writer, the passage lost its reference to the disciples in Gethsemane and became a prediction of the suffering to be endured by the Christians scattered in the hostile world.

At the end of vs. 32 Jesus' sovereignty reasserts itself. His control of his own destiny was implicit in 28, but now he reasserts the source of his confidence as he lays his life down (see x 18). He is serene in the assurance that his Father will not desert him even if his chosen disciples do. Some have suggested that in 32 the Johannine writer is correcting a misunderstanding of what Jesus is reported to have said on the cross: "My God, my God, why have you forsaken me?" (Mark xv 34; Matt xxvii 46) —a misunderstanding because some may not have realized that he was citing Ps xxii. Hoskyns, p. 492, maintains that the Johannine saying presumes and interprets the correct meaning of the earlier tradition. However, we cannot be certain that the Johannine writer knew of this Marcan–Matthean saying. We may be safer in suggesting that xvi 32 indicates that the Johannine conception of Jesus' relation to the Father would militate against John's attributing to Jesus the words just cited from Mark and Matthew, no matter how innocently those words were meant. See p. 930 below.

The section ends on a triumphant tone in vs. 33. Division One of the Last Discourse (xiv 30) closed with Jesus' assertion of power in relation to the Prince of this world; Division Two closes with a victory proclamation over the world. (The alternation between conquering Satan and conquering the world is found in I John ii 13, 14, v 4. J. E. Bruns, JBL 86 [1967], 451–53, is quite right in insisting that victory over the world and over its Prince includes victory over death; however, we find little real evidence to support his contention that John's description of Jesus as victor echoes the pagan myth of Herakles, the conqueror of death and evil. The thought pattern is closer to that of late Jewish dualism [see vol. 29, p. LXII].) The contrast between "in me" and "in the world" shows that the writer is thinking of post-resurrectional Christian existence. The suffering (*thlipsis*) is the persecution predicted in xv 18 – xvi 4a (also Matt xxiv 9–10). The theme of peace, which appeared at the end of Division One (xiv 27), appears here too; and once again (see p. 653 above) we stress that it is a salvific gift. The fact that it exists alongside suffering shows that it is not peace in the ordinary sense of the word. In xiv 29

Jesus said, "I have told you this . . . so that . . . you may believe." Here he says, "I have said this to you so that in me you may find peace." Peace flows from belief in Jesus and consists of union with him. Peace is not acquired effortlessly, for it comes only from victory over the world. If Jesus conquers the world, the individual Christian must also conquer the world (Rev iii 21); and this is done through faith (I John v 4–5). Thus the command, "Have courage," in 33 is very necessary. It reminds the Christian of the never-ending task of choosing between Jesus and the world.

BIBLIOGRAPHY
(xv 18 – xvi 33)

See the general bibliography on the Last Discourse at the end of §48 and the Bibliography on the Paraclete in App. V.

Bream, H. N., "No Need to Be Asked Questions: A Study of Jn. 16:30," *Search the Scriptures—New Testament Studies in Honor of Raymond T. Stamm* (Gettysburg Theological Series 3; Leiden: Brill, 1969), pp. 49–74.

Fascher, E., "Johannes 16, 32," ZNW 39 (1940), 171–230.

Feuillet, A., "L'heure de la femme (Jn 16, 21) et l'heure de la Mère de Jésus (Jn 19, 25–27)," *Biblica* 47 (1966), 169–84, 361–80, 557–73.

Schwank, B., " 'Da sie mich verfolgt haben, werden sie auch euch verfolgen' (15, 18–16, 4a)," SeinSend 28 (1963), 292–301.

——— " 'Es ist gut für euch, dass ich fortgehe' (16, 4b–15)," SeinSend 28 (1963), 340–51.

——— "Sieg und Friede in Christus (16, 16–33)," SeinSend 28 (1963), 388–400.

Zerwick, M., "Vom Wirken des Heiligen Geistes in uns (Jo 16, 5–15)," GeistLeb 38 (1965), 224–30.

57. THE LAST DISCOURSE:
—DIVISION THREE (UNIT ONE)
(xvii 1–8)

Jesus, having completed his work, prays for glory

XVII 1 After these words Jesus looked up to heaven and said:

"Father, the hour has come:
glorify your Son
that the Son may glorify you—
2 inasmuch as you granted him power over all men
that he might grant eternal life to all that you have given him."

3 And eternal life consists in this: that they know you, the one true
God, and Jesus Christ, the one whom you sent.

4 "I glorified you on earth
by completing the work you have given me to do;
5 so now glorify me, Father, in your presence
with that glory which I had with you before the world existed.

6 I revealed your name to the men
whom you gave me out of the world.
They were yours and you gave them to me,
and they have kept your word.
7 Now they have come to know
that from you comes all that you have given to me.
8 For the words that you gave to me
I have given to them,
and they accepted them.
And they knew in truth
that I came forth from you,
and they believed
that you sent me."

NOTES

xvii 1. *these words.* Literally "these things."

looked up to heaven. A similar action is recorded before the prayer of xi 41; see NOTE there.

Father. This characteristic, abrupt address is found in xi 41, xii 27; for its special meaning see vol. 29, p. 436. The Father is very much the operative agent in this prayer; and the address "Father" is frequent throughout, being used alone in 1, 5, 21, and 24, and with modifiers in 11 and 25. The textual witnesses are not agreed on whether to read a vocative (*pater*) or a nominative (*patēr*) that functions as a vocative (BDF, §147). The variation may be explained if, as in P[66], the manuscript from which the scribes were copying used an abbreviation ($\overline{pr}$).

the hour has come. We have heard this already in xii 23 and xiii 1; obviously "the hour" is a long perod of time, beginning with the first indication that the process which would lead to Jesus' death had been set in motion, and terminating with his return to his Father. In the Book of Glory, the only previous unmodified use of "the hour" at the Last Supper was in xiii 1, whence the rationale behind Bultmann's rearrangement (see COMMENT) that puts xvii 1 immediately after xiii 1. He thinks that "Jesus was aware that the hour had come for him to pass from this world to the Father" makes an excellent introduction to the prayer that Jesus addresses to the Father about the hour. But even without the rearrangement, the atmosphere of "the hour" in which Jesus returns to his Father dominates the Last Supper and provides a setting for the prayer.

glorify your Son. The process of glorification has already begun with the commencement of "the hour," but it is not yet complete. Cf. xiii 31–32: "Now has the Son of Man been glorified, and God has been glorified in him. . . . God will, in turn, glorify him in Himself and will glorify him immediately."

that the Son. Some important witnesses, both Western and Byzantine, read "your Son." This is the first of two subordinate clauses introduced by *hina;* the second one is in 2b: "that he might grant. . . ." They are separated by the *kathōs* ("inasmuch as") clause of 2a. The same construction appears below in 21 (also xiii 34).

may glorify you. Bernard, II, 560, remarks that the whole passion is under the rubric *"ad maiorem Dei gloriam."*

2. *you granted him.* The aorist tense implies a past action: the power was granted as a part of the earthly ministry. Nevertheless, this power to grant life would not become fully effective until Jesus' exaltation.

power. Or "authority" (*exousia;* see vol. 29, pp. 10–11).

over all men. Literally "all flesh," a Semitism (cf. viii 15). The usual Johannine dualism between flesh and Spirit does not seem to be in mind here. Perhaps the power over all men is the power of judgment (v 27), for the next line makes clear that Jesus has the power to give life only to a select group, i.e., those whom the Father has given to him.

that he might grant. This is the second *hina* clause (see "that the Son" in 1). Upon what is it dependent? Is it dependent on "glorify your Son" in 1, so that it is parallel to the first *hina* clause? (Then the *kathōs*, "inasmuch as," clause must be treated as parenthetical; so Bernard.) Or is it dependent on "granted him power" in the *kathōs* clause of 2a? (So Lagrange and Barrett.) It is probably better to recognize that the interpretations are not exclusive, and that to some extent the second *hina* clause elaborates both antecedents. The granting of eternal life is the goal of the power over all men that has been granted to the Son (second interpretation); yet the granting of eternal life also constitutes the purpose for which the Son asks to be glorified (first interpretation)—it is the way by which the Son glorifies the Father. Bultmann, p. 376[1], treats the whole of vs. 2 as the evangelist's prose addition to the Revelatory Discourse Source.

eternal life. Here and the next verse are the only times that *"eternal* life" is mentioned in the Book of Glory, as contrasted with the frequent use of the expression in the Book of Signs. Perhaps a stress on the different kind of life that Jesus offers was more important in the earlier period when men were just coming to Jesus, while in this Discourse, addressed to "his own" (xiii 1), the qualificatory clarification is no longer necessary. Elsewhere in John (vi 63, vii 38–39) it is apparent that the gift of the Spirit is Jesus' way of granting eternal life; but the Spirit is not mentioned in xvii, not even under the title of Paraclete.

all that. A neuter instead of a masculine as in vi 37 (see NOTE there), 39; also neuter below in 7 and 24. Here (see vs. 6) the writer is clearly referring to men, and the use of a neuter may give a certain unity to the group—they are "his own."

you have given him. The perfect tense is fitting because the men are still in Jesus' possession (vs. 12). This chapter stresses what the Father has *given* to Jesus, namely, men (2, 6, 9, 24); all things (7); words (8); the divine name (11, 12); and glory (22, 24). The idea that Jesus gives eternal life to a select group is found in x 27–28 (to the sheep who hear his voice); in I John ii 23–25 (to those who confess the Son and the Father); etc.

3. *consists in this.* Literally "Now this is eternal life." The explanatory style is a Johannine trait, for example, iii 19, "Now this is judgment."

they know you. Although some witnesses have a future indicative, the best witnesses have a present subjunctive; this implies that the knowledge is a continuing action.

one true God. "One" (or "only") and "true" are traditional attributes of God: *monos* in Isa xxxvii 20; John v 44; *alēthinos* in Exod xxxiv 6; Rev vi 10. Generally such attributes were stressed in opposition to the polytheism of the Gentile world; cf. "You turned from idols . . . to serve a living and true God" (I Thess i 9). We note that the "one true God" and "Jesus Christ" are not identified. This verse runs somewhat contrary to other verses in John that call Jesus "God" (i 1, 18, xx 28); see vol. 29, p. 24.

Jesus Christ. Although John has Jesus speak of himself in the third person, for example, as "the Son," it is anomalous that Jesus should call himself "Jesus Christ." Elsewhere in the Gospel the name occurs in the Prologue (i 17), a Christian hymn. This verse is clearly an insertion into the text of Jesus' prayer, an insertion probably reflecting a confessional or liturgical formula of the Johannine church (see I John iv 2). There are similar explanatory insertions in the Prologue.

4. *glorified.* This verb is in the aorist (also the verb in 6: "made known"), as if the action were completed. Some think that Jesus is referring to his past glorification of God in his ministry; yet the glorification of the Father was

scarcely completed before the hour of death, resurrection, and ascension. The vantage point in time of these statements does not seem to be the Last Discourse but the period after "the hour" and after the exaltation of Jesus.

on earth. This is contrasted with "in your presence" in 5; cf. "from above . . . of the earth" (iii 31); "earthly things . . . heavenly things" (iii 12).

by completing the work. There are only three active uses of the verb *teleioun* in John, and all are connected with the work(s) of the Father (for a passive use see 23). In iv 34 Jesus said that his food was: "Doing the will of Him who sent me and bringing His work to completion." In v 36 he cited as one of his witnesses: "The works the Father has given me to complete." Now the work is completed. Obviously, however, completion comes only in the whole complex of "the hour" stretching from xiii to xx. The "end" (*telos*) is mentioned in xiii 1, and the passive of *teleioun* (xix 28: "bring to complete fulfillment") is employed as Jesus hangs on the cross.

given me to do. The "to do" is a *hina* clause. Vanhoye, *art. cit.*, discusses at length whether this clause (and the one in v 36) expresses purpose (=the work has been given to Jesus with the intention that *he* should do it) or is simply complementary (=the work given to Jesus consists in the doing, i.e., in the carrying out of the Father's will; see BDF, §392). We doubt that the distinction should be pressed to the point where one connotation excludes the other.

5. *so now.* Laurentin, *art. cit.*, has thoroughly studied this phrase *kai nyn.* Frequent in Acts (ten times) and in the Johannine writings (nine times), it is often a Semitism, rendering *we'attāh*, a Hebrew phrase that is both a conjunction and an interjection. In the OT it appears in juridical formulas, especially those related to covenant demands (for the theme of the covenant in John xvii see pp. 753, 781 below), and in liturgical petitions (xvii is a prayer). Often followed by an imperative, the Hebrew expression can mark the transition from the summary of a situation to the demand for some result that should follow. Good examples are in Exod xix 5; Josh ix 6, xxiv 14; Judg xiii 4; II Sam vii 25. In particular, Laurentin, p. 425, points out that *kai nyn* can introduce a more decisive repetition of a request already made; and this seems to be the function in the present instance, if we compare 5 and 1. In Johannine thought the "now" is the "now" of "the hour" ("an hour is coming and is now here": iv 23, v 25).

in your presence . . . with you. The preposition *para* is used in both these phrases; contrast i 1: "The Word was in God's presence [*pros* with the accusative]"; i 18: "The only Son, ever at the Father's side [*eis ton kolpon*]." There is a tendency among the textual witnesses to omit or to move to a different position one or other of these two phrases. Boismard, RB 57 (1950), 394–95, 398–99, presents the arguments for a shorter form of the text that would omit both "in your presence" and "so now" from 5a; yet the latter expression is almost certainly original if Laurentin's investigation is valid. The position of the second phrase, "with you," would, if taken literally, permit another translation: "with that glory which I had before the world existed beside you." J. M. Ballard, ET 47 (1935–36), 284, argues for this translation, but the difference in meaning does not seem crucial. Both translations refer to pre-creational glory in the fellowship of the Father and the Son. The two prepositional phrases we have been discussing are the Johannine way of expressing the picture of Jesus at the right hand of God (Acts ii 33, vii 55).

that glory. Does this imply that the glory that Jesus has after his exaltation in the flesh will be the same as the glory he had before the incarnation? If so, the "flesh" of Jesus does not seem to play a profound role in John's view of his exaltation. Difficulties like these have led Käsemann, p. 21, to insist that John's eschatology is really a "protology," for the goal is a restoration of all things as they were "in the beginning."

which I had with you. Seemingly some of the Greek textual witnesses once read *ēn*, a form of the verb "to be," in place of *eichon*, a form of the verb "to have." Among the Latin Fathers and in some Ethiopic mss. there is support for the reading: "that glory which *was* with you" or "that glory by which *I was* with you." Boismard, RB 57 (1950), 396[1], followed by Mollat in SB, suggests the originality of a text without any connecting verb ("that glory with you"), a reading for which there is some evidence in other Ethiopic mss. and in the *Diatessaron*.

before the world existed. Instead of "existed" (*einai*), some Western witnesses read "came into existence" (*ginesthai*). This may be under the influence of viii 58, "Before Abraham even came into existence [*ginesthai*], I AM." If *einai* is the correct reading, this is the only example in the NT of the preposition *pro* with a present infinitive (BDF, §403). The verb "to be" is characteristically used of the Son in this Gospel; he *is,* while all other things come into existence. Bultmann, p. 378, treats this phrase as a gloss of the evangelist on the Revelatory Discourse Source.

6. *I revealed your name.* The verb is *phaneroun.* This is another way of phrasing what was said in 4: "I glorified you."

out of the world. This echoes the theme of xv 19: "I chose you out of the world."

have kept your word. The chronological standpoint from which the statement is made seems to be that of the writer's time rather than that of the Last Supper, for the idea that the disciples had kept God's word in the past and were still keeping it (perfect tense) is out of place at the Last Supper. Elsewhere in John (viii 51, xiv 23) it is *Jesus'* word that men are asked to keep, but Jesus' word came from the Father (vii 16).

7. *Now they have come to know.* A perfect tense of the verb "to know." Codex Sinaiticus and some of the versions have "I have come to know," perhaps on the pattern of the verbs in the first person singular that open vss. 4 and 6. With its initial *nyn* this verse is similar to xvi 30: "Now we know that you know everything." The disciples who have only partially understood during the ministry are thought of as coming to fuller knowledge during "the hour" (see also xiii 17). Yet once again "the hour" must be understood to encompass the exaltation of Jesus and the giving of the Paraclete who will teach the disciples everything (xiv 26, xvi 12–13). At the Last Supper the disciples show clearly that they do not fully understand (xiv 7, 9, xvi 5, 18), and Jesus casts doubt on their claim to believe (xvi 31).

from you comes all that you have given to me. The tautology emphasizes Jesus' dependence upon the Father.

8. *For.* It is possible, but not plausible, that the introductory *hoti* continues the indirect discourse of the previous verse: "Now they have come to know . . . that the words that you gave to me I have given to them."

words. This is the plural *rēmata,* as contrasted with the singular *logos* in 6 and 14. Barrett, p. 421, thinks that the singular refers to the divine message as a whole, while the plural more nearly means "precepts." The distinction is tenuous when we compare 8 and 14; see NOTE on xiv 23.

that you gave to me. The best reading seems to be the aorist, although some witnesses have the perfect. In xv 15 Jesus spoke similarly: "I revealed to you everything I heard from the Father."

they accepted them. Aorist tense; contrast the perfect in 6: "they have kept your word." No object is expressed in most textual witnesses but is demanded by the sense of the line.

And they knew in truth. Some important textual witnesses, East and West, omit this clause and make the verb "accepted" in the previous line govern the following noun clause, thus: "and they accepted that I came forth from you." If "they knew in truth" is the correct reading, it should probably be understood in terms of their finding knowledge and learning the truth (Barrett, p. 422). "In truth" translates the adverb "truly," but here the adverb must mean more than that they really knew. The verb "knew" in this line and the verb "believed," two lines below, are in the aorist tense; contrast the perfect tense of "have come to know" in 7. Bultmann, p. 381[13], says that the perfect tenses of 6 and 7 describe the essence of faith, while the aorist tenses in 8 describe how faith came about. We cannot be sure that the Johannine writer was so precise, however, and both tenses are from the viewpoint of a time later than the Last Supper; yet see xvi 30. The parallelism of "knew" and "believed" in 8 illustrates the fact that in John these two verbs are almost interchangeable (vol. 29, p. 513). In xvi 27, 30 the coming forth of Jesus from the Father is the object of the verb "to believe"; here it is the object of "to know."

I came forth from you. That this refers to the earthly mission of the Son rather than to an intra-Trinitarian procession is seen from the parallelism of this line with the last line of the verse: "you sent me." See NOTES on viii 42 and on xvi 28 ("from the Father").

you sent me. This clause is almost a refrain throughout the prayer of xvii (Bernard, II, 565); it occurs four more times (18, 21, 23, 25).

COMMENT: GENERAL

The Role and Literary Genre of xvii

We now come to one of the most majestic moments in the Fourth Gospel, the climax of the Last Discourse where Jesus turns to his Father in prayer. We have already identified the literary genre of the Last Discourse as a whole (pp. 598–601 above): it is a farewell speech. And we have pointed out that it is not unusual for a speaker to close a farewell address with a prayer for his children or for the people he is leaving behind. The Book of Deuteronomy is particularly instructive here. As a collection of Moses' last discourses to his people, it offers an interesting parallel to the Johannine Last Discourse. In particular it is noteworthy that near the end of Deuteronomy there are two canticles of Moses, one in xxxii where Moses turns from the people to address the heavens, the other in xxxiii where Moses blesses the tribes for the future. So also in John xvii Jesus turns to heaven and addresses the Father, but much of what he says concerns the future of his disciples. Thus, in placing the prayer of xvii at the end of the Last Discourse, the Johannine writer has remained faithful to the literary genre of farewell address that he has adopted. On the other hand, in rearranging the Discourse so that xvii now stands at the beginning, Bultmann makes a blunder against good literary sense: this prayer is certainly better as a climax than as an introduction. Bultmann is correct in seeing that xiii (the beginning of the Last Supper scene) and xvii are closely related, only it is by way of inclusion rather than by way of direct sequence. We may note the following parallels between the two chapters: the reference to the coming of "the hour" (xiii 1, xvii 1); God's glorifying the Son (xiii 31–32, xvii 1, 4–5); *telos* and *teleioun* (xiii 1, xvii 4—see NOTE); the disciples' being in the world (xiii 1, xvii 11, 15); all things and power given to Jesus (xiii 3, xvii 2); Judas, the instrument of Satan and the son of perdition (xiii 2, 27, xvii 12); the fulfillment of Scripture about the betrayer (xiii 18, xvii 12).

We shall see that various sayings in xvii have Synoptic parallels; and the chapter was probably constructed, much as the rest of the Discourse, by elaborating upon traditional sayings of Jesus, some of which were original in the setting of the Last Supper. Certainly it more directly evokes the atmosphere of departure characteristic of the Last Supper than does the material in xv 1–6 or in xv 18–xvi 4a. According to the theory of composition we have followed (pp. 585–87 above), the prayer of xvii was not part of the Last Discourse in the first edition of the Gospel where xiv 31 was followed directly by xviii 1. Nor was this prayer part of the independently formed discourse that now stands as xv–xvi (Division Two of the final Last Discourse). The prayer seems to have been an independent composition that the redactor added at the same time that he added xv–xvi. Perhaps the prayer came from the same circle within the Johannine church that produced the Prologue, for the two works have interesting similarities in their poetic quality, careful structure (including explanatory prose comments), and theme (see xvii 5).

The comparisons with the canticles of Moses in Deuteronomy and with the Prologue suggest that xvii has a hymnic quality. Dodd, *Interpretation*, pp. 420–23, points out that several times in the Hermetic writings (see vol. 29, pp. LVIII–LIX) a dialogue is concluded with a prayer or hymn, and that the language of these hymns has some interesting parallels in xvii. The definition of eternal life as knowledge in xvii 3 has given encouragement to those who stress the Gnostic affinities of the Gospel. Bultmann, p. 374, finds a parallel for xvii in the Gnostic Mandean literature which records prayers uttered by those sent into the world on the occasion of their leaving it. The evaluation of these parallels, of course, will be influenced by one's general position on the influences that have shaped Johannine thought.

Others think more of a hymn within a liturgical context. Functionally xvii has a role in John's account similar to that played by the hymn which Mark xiv 26 reports as having been sung at the end of the Last Supper (presumably a Hallel hymn terminating the Passover meal). It has been suggested that xvii was recited or sung in Christian eucharistic celebrations, and Poelman, *art. cit.*, theorizes that vs. 3 may be a remnant of antiphonal answering by the congregation! Hoskyns, who thinks that the whole Last Discourse reflects the order of Christian worship, proposes (p. 495) that the teaching part of the service (xiv–xvi) was followed by a comprehensive eucharistic prayer. Bultmann, who has placed xvii at the beginning of the Discourse, suggests that this prayer has actually taken the place of the eucharistic action! Roman Catholic liturgists have often compared John xvii to the Preface hymn that precedes the sacrificial part of the Roman Mass, a hymn that is always addressed to God the Father. Analogously, they point out, Jesus speaks to his Father before he sets out on the path to his historical sacrifice. Westcott, p. 236, speaks of xvii as a prayer of consecration whereby the Son offers himself as a perfect oblation. J. Schneider, IMEL, pp. 139–42, thinks that xvii may have been composed somewhat in the manner of vi (where, as we saw, there is a eucharistic theme and where liturgical practice may have had a formative role: vol. 29, p. 290).

It should be obvious that some of these hypotheses (and they are but a selection) are highly romantic and quite incapable of proof. Although there may be an allusion to self-oblation in xvii 19, there is no major or clear emphasis on the theme of sacrificial offering in xvii: Jesus does not say that he is laying down his life but that he is coming to the Father. As for the eucharistic interpretation of xvii (favored by Loisy, Cullmann, Wilkens, and others), the best argument is based on parallels with the eucharistic prayer of the early Church as found in *Didache* ix–x (see also vol. 29, p. 248, and p. 673 above). The prayer in *Didache* x 2 begins, "We give thanks [*eucharistein*] to you, O Father most holy"; John xvii 1 begins with the address "Father" and in vs. 11 we find "O Father most holy." Just as the theme of glory runs through John xvii (1, 5, 22), the theme of glory to the Father through Jesus Christ appears frequently in the *Didache* (ix 2, 3, 4, x 2, 4, 5). Parenthetically it is worth noting that some of the Greek Church Fathers, like Cyril of Alexandria and John Chrysostom, relate the glory of John xvii to the Eucharist. John xvii mentions the divine name which is given to Jesus (11, 12) and which he in turn reveals to the disciples (6, 26); *Didache* ix 5 says that no one can receive the Eucharist who has not been baptized in the Lord's name, and x 2 gives thanks to the Father for "your holy name which you made to dwell in our hearts." The next verse in the *Didache* says that the Lord created all things for the sake of His name. Knowledge and what Jesus has made known is a theme of John xvii (3, 6, 7, 8, 23, 25, 26); *Didache* ix 3 and x 2 thank God for knowledge and what was made known by Jesus. There is a petition in *Didache* x 5 that God will deliver the Church "from all evil" (*ponēros* as in John xvii 15), bring it to completion in love (*teleioun;* cf. John xvii 23), and gather it together in holiness (or consecration; cf. John xvii 17, 19) into the kingdom which God has prepared for it (cf.

John xvii 24). Yet, despite these parallels, *Didache* ix–x mentions the eucharistic bread and wine, while John xvii does not. The theme of unity in John xvii is a theme often associated with the Eucharist, but one must admit that such a reference to the Eucharist is far less obvious than what we found in John vi 51–58. And so we would qualify that eucharistic interpretation of the prayer in xvii as no more than possible. The thesis of the liturgical usage of xvii as a hymn is also possible, but this thesis can play no great part in our interpretation of the thought of the chapter.

The prayer of xvii has been traditionally designated as priestly prayer. Already in the early 5th century Cyril of Alexandria (*In Jo.* xi 8; PG 74:505) speaks of Jesus in xvii as a high priest making intercession on our behalf. The Lutheran theologian David Chyträus (1531–1600) entitled xvii "the high-priestly prayer" (*precatio summi sacerdotis*). But if Jesus is a high priest here, it is not primarily in the sense of one about to offer sacrifice, but more along the lines of the high priest described in Hebrews and in Rom viii 34—one who stands before the throne of God making intercession for us. It is true, of course, that in the prayer of John xvii Jesus still speaks in the context of the Last Supper; but from the tone of what he says and from the tenses of the verbs, one feels that Jesus has crossed the threshold from time to eternity and is already on the way to the Father or, at least, halfway between this world and the Father's presence. Lagrange, p. 437, gives voice to the ambiguity when he says that the prayer is written *sub specie aeternitatis* and yet it truly represents Jesus' own words. How can the Jesus of xvii say both, "I am no longer in the world" (11), and "While still in the world, I say all this" (13)? We have maintained that the Jesus of the Last Discourse transcends time and space, for from heaven and beyond the grave he is already speaking to the disciples of all time. Nowhere is this more evident than in xvii where Jesus already assumes the role of heavenly intercessor that I John ii 1 ascribes to him after the resurrection. Dodd, *Interpretation*, p. 419, has phrased it well: in some way the prayer itself is the ascension of Jesus to the Father; it is truly the prayer of "the hour."

But we must investigate more thoroughly the qualified sense in which xvii is intercession and a prayer. It has many of the characteristics of Jesus' prayers, for example, his looking up to heaven and his use of "Father" (see NOTES). There are definite parallels to the petitions of the Lord's Prayer: compare the petition "May your name be glorified [hallowed]" to the themes of glorification of the Father and the use of the divine name in xvii 1, 11–12; the petition "May your will be done" to the theme of completing the work that the Father gave Jesus to do in xvii 4; the petition "Deliver us from the Evil One" to the theme expressed almost in the same words in xvii 15. Yet the prayer of xvii is a special prayer, and Jesus is no ordinary suppliant. The frequency of the word "Father" in the prayer gives it a note of unique intimacy. The disciple and the reader are party to a heavenly family conversation. Jesus puts his

"I wish" (24) to his Father with the assurance of the divine Son. There can be no doubt that what he asks for will be granted, for his will and the Father's will are one. The Synoptic Gospels too know of a last prayer of Jesus uttered after the Last Supper and just before he was taken prisoner, namely, his prayer to his Father in Gethsemane (Mark xiv 34–36). But how different are the Synoptic and Johannine prayers! In Gethsemane a sorrowful and troubled Jesus, prostrate on the ground, begs to have the chalice of suffering pass him by—a prayer that cannot be granted. That is a human prayer occupied with the present time (George, p. 395). But divinity and timelessness are the mark of the Johannine prayer. The Johannine Jesus does not ask anything for himself. (It is true that in 1 and 5 he asks for glory, but this glory is really for the sake of his disciples that he may grant life to them [2].) He does not ask to be delivered from suffering, but only that he leave a world in which he has been a stranger (Käsemann, pp. 5, 65). This is more a prayer of the union or communion of the Son and the Father than it is a prayer of petition.

This prayer is said aloud before the disciples precisely so that they may share this union (21–23). Because there is an audience, the prayer is just as much revelation as it is intercession. The "you" addressed is God, but Jesus is speaking to the disciples as much here as in the rest of the Discourse. (We note that the other Johannine prayers in xi 41–42 and xii 27–28 also envisage an audience; Morrison, pp. 259–60, points out that this technique would not have seemed so strange to the ancients as it does to us. We find the same phenomenon in Luke x 21–22.) And "disciples" means not only those at the Last Discourse but, and even primarily, the Christians of later generations (pace Agourides, p. 141, who stresses one main subject, the Twelve). This interest in future generations is made more specific in vss. 20 ff. than it is anywhere else before the resurrection. Chapter xvii has been compared to a personal message that a dead man has recorded and left behind him for those whom he loved, but the comparison limps for such a message would soon become dated. Rather in xvii, in the intention of the Johannine writer, we have Jesus speaking in the familiar accents of his earthly career but reinterpreted (by the working of the Paraclete) so that what he says is always a living message.

The Structure of xvii

Even many of the scholars who do not find a poetic format in the Johannine discourses in general recognize the poetic style of xvii. This prayer stands intermediary between the poetry of the Prologue and the looser quasi-poetry of the other discourses. A careful structure might be anticipated, but different divisions have been defended. With assurance Loisy, p. 441, asserts: "It can be broken down without difficulty into seven strophes of eight lines each." Adapted to our translation, the strophes he recognizes are 1–2, 4–5/ 6–8/ 9–11c/ 11d–12c, 13–14/ 15–19/ 20–23/

24–26; both vs. 3 and the last lines of 12 are treated as prose additions. The system whereby he finds eight lines in each strophe is quite debatable, however. With no less assurance ("everyone agrees," even Thomas Aquinas), Lagrange, p. 436, accepts a fourfold division: 1–5, 6–19, 20–23, 24–26. Dodd, *Interpretation*, p. 417, favors another fourfold division: 1–5, 6–8, 9–19, 20–26; and this is a frequently accepted schema. One difficulty that faces both of the fourfold divisions is the unequal length of the units. A threefold division into 1–8, 9–19, 20–26, which is followed below, is about as common as the fourfold division. (For a careful survey of the variety of divisions proposed for ch. xvii, see Becker, pp. 56–61.)

Before we go into our reasons for accepting the threefold division, we should mention a division defended by Laurentin, pp. 427–31, on the grounds that it is less subjective and less Western in its outlook than the systems proposed above. He divides xvii thus:

1–4:   Introduction: a unit that begins and ends with the theme of glory. In the use of "Father" and "I glorified you" there is an inclusion with 25–26 below.

5–6:   Transition: *kai nyn* verse (see NOTE on 5). "Before the world existed" is an inclusion with 24.

7–12:   First Part: begins with *nyn:* there is a pattern of pronouncement (7–8), petition (9), and a reference both to glory (10) and to unity (11).

13–23: Second Part: begins with *nyn:* there is a pattern of pronouncement (13–14), petition (15), and a reference both to glory (22) and to unity (21–23).

24:     Transition: "before the creation of the world."

25–26: Conclusion: "O Father most just"; "I revealed your name."

There is much that is attractive in Laurentin's division, and we shall use some of his observations in our comments. However, because his division rejects what seem to us clear dividing marks in 9 and 20, we cannot accept it as a whole.

Another elaborate structure of xvii has been propounded by Becker, p. 69. He finds the principal petition of the prayer in vss. 1–2, and this in turn is developed in four individual petitions consisting of vss. 4–5, 6–13, 14–19, and 22–26. In each of these four Becker detects rather consistent patterns: (a) a statement about what Jesus has done; (b) sometimes a preliminary statement that he is praying or asking for something; (c) the petition itself; (d) the grounds for the petition. Such an isolation of patterns is of importance, even if one prefers to follow a more traditional division of ch. xvii.

The key to the organization of xvii is found in Jesus' three indications of whom he is praying for: he prays for his own glorification in 1, for the disciples whom the Father has given him in 9, and for those who will believe through the preaching of the disciples in 20. Feuillet (*art. cit.* in Bibliography of §56), p. 375, points to a similar threefold division in

Aaron's prayer in Lev xvi 11–17: the high priest prays for himself, for his
house or priestly family, and for the whole people (this is interesting
when we remember that xvii is called Jesus' high priestly prayer). The
chief point of difference between the frequently held fourfold and threefold divisions concerns 6–8 where the disciples are mentioned. Should these
verses be treated as a separate unit, or should they be joined to 1–5, or
should they be joined to 9–18 (Bultmann, Giblet)? By putting them with
1–5, one arrives at a division of three units roughly the same in length
(1–8, 9–19, 20–26). It will be objected that 1–5 treat of Jesus' glorification
while 6–8 treat of the disciples. But when in 1–5 Jesus prays for
glorification, the basis of his prayer is the work that he has already
done among those whom God has given him, and the purpose of his
glorification is so that he may grant them eternal life. In other words, the
disciples are already mentioned in 1–5 in relation to Jesus' glory. Verses
6–8 are merely an expansion of the theme in 4: they tell in detail how
Jesus did do God's work among the disciples. Nevertheless, if 6–8 belong
to 1–5, these verses prepare the way for the second unit (9–19) where
Jesus prays more directly for the disciples. We find at the end of the
second unit exactly the same phenomenon of concluding verses that serve
as a transition: in 18 Jesus mentions the sending of the disciples, and this
prepares for the third unit where Jesus prays for those who are brought
to belief by that mission.

There are some interesting features that relate the three units to each
other and illustrate the careful structuring that has gone into this chapter:

- each unit begins with what Jesus is asking or praying for (1, 9, 20)
- each has the theme of glory (1–5, 10, 22)
- each has an address to the Father part way through the unit (5, 11, 21)
- each mentions the men given to Jesus by the Father (2, 9, 24)
- each has the theme of Jesus' revelation of the Father to men (6 "your
  name"; 14 "your word"; 26 "your name")

There are also common features shared by two of the three units. There
is similarity by inclusion between the first and the third units, that is, between the beginning and the end of the prayer. If the three units use the
unmodified address "Father," this occurs with more frequency in the first
and third units (1, 5, 24, 25). These two units share the theme of Jesus'
relationship with the Father before the world existed (5, 24) and also the
theme of making known God's name (6, 26). If we compare the first and
second units, both contrast what has been done on earth and what will be
done (4–5, 12–13) and both mention that Jesus has given to the disciples
the word(s) given him by the Father (8, 14). If we compare the second
and third units, both begin with "I pray" (9, 20); both have the theme of
unity (11, 21–23); both use an adjectival qualifier in addressing the Father
(11, "O Father most holy"; 25, "O Father most just"). Within the second
unit, there may be an inclusion between 9 and 19 (9, "on their behalf"

[*peri autōn*]; 19, "for them" [*hyper autōn*]). Within the third unit, there is an inclusion between 21 and 26 in the theme of indwelling.

COMMENT: DETAILED

Verses 1–5: Jesus Asks for Glory

If we leave aside for a moment the parenthetical prose comment in 3, the theme of glory dominates these verses. In 1–2 we hear why the Son should be glorified in light of what the glorified Son will do—glorify God; grant life to the disciples. In 4–5 we hear why Jesus should be glorified in light of what he has already done—completed the work given him by the Father. (We note the switch from the third person ["the Son"] in 1–2 to the first person ["I"] in 4–5; it is not impossible that we are dealing with originally independent sayings.) We pointed out in vol. 29, p. 503, that "glory" has two aspects: it is a *visible* manifestation of majesty through *acts of power*. The glory that Jesus asks for is not distinct from the glory of the Father, for the sayings in viii 50 and xii 43 rule out ambition for any glory except the glory of God. "The hour" will bring Jesus back to the Father, and then the fact that he and the Father possess the same divine glory will be visible to all believers. The particular act of power that will make visible the unity of Jesus and the Father will be the gift of eternal life to believers (vs. 2, "to all that you have given him"). The giving of eternal life is intimately related to the work that Jesus has been doing on earth (vs. 4) and brings that work to a completion, for his works on earth were signs of his power to give eternal life (vol. 29, App. III). Bultmann, p. 376, phrases the idea well when he says, "His work does not come to an end with his earthly life but in a real sense only begins with the end of that life." In his glorification Jesus will glorify the Father (vs. 1) by the gift of eternal life, for this gift will beget for God new children who will honor Him as Father (see i 12). Thus, in his request to return to his heavenly home, Jesus does not seek anything for himself; he is interested in the recognition of his Father and the welfare of his disciples.

Jesus' request for glory may seem strange since John has made it clear that Jesus possessed and manifested glory throughout his ministry. The "We have seen his glory" of the Prologue immediately follows the reference to the Word's becoming flesh (i 14). At Cana (ii 11) Jesus revealed his glory to his disciples; see also xi 4, 40, xii 28. Yet the glory of Jesus during the ministry was seen by way of sign, even as his life-giving power was exercised by way of sign. In "the hour" we have passed from sign to reality, so that "the hour" is the time for "the Son of Man to be glorified" (xii 23). When "the hour" is complete, eternal life can truly be granted in the gift of the Spirit (xx 22). The idea that in the ministry Jesus already possessed glory appears in the Synoptic Gospels in the account of the Transfiguration (especially Luke ix 32); but it is clear that the full recognition of Jesus as the Son of God stems from his death (Mark xv 39), resurrection, and ascension (Acts ii 36, v 31). John's thought about Jesus' glorification through his return to the Father has some features in common with the thought of the early hymn cited by Paul in Philip ii 9: "Therefore God has highly exalted him and bestowed upon him the name that is above every name" (see the theme of the name in John xvii 11–12). Yet there is a difference; Käsemann, p. 10, is correct in insisting that the evaluation of Jesus' ministry in Philip ii 7 as a kenosis is not found in John. If "the Word became flesh," he did not empty himself, for in the incarnation he was granted power over all other flesh (xvii 2; also v 27). To the earthly ministry of Jesus, John attributes a universal power that is attributed only to the risen Christ in Matt xxviii 18; contrast also Rev xii 10 where only after the defeat of Satan by the elevation of the messianic child are the kingdom of God and the *power* of Christ proclaimed.

The parenthetical, explanatory comment in vs. 3 requires special attention. As we have mentioned, this verse has been cited as an example of Johannine Gnosticism, for here the salvific gift of life is defined in terms of knowing. For John, of course, knowing God is not a purely intellectual matter but involves a life of obedience to God's commandments and of loving communion with fellow Christians (I John i 3, iv 8, v 3). This is in agreement with the Hebrew use of the verb "to know" with its connotation of immediate experience and intimacy. Yet we cannot deny that xvii 3 does relate eternal life to a correct appreciation of the Father and of Jesus. If in Johannine thought faith is a way of life in commitment to Jesus, this does not mean that faith is without intellectual content. Käsemann, p. 25, rightly stresses that the idea of faith as the acceptance of orthodox doctrine is already present inchoatively in John. To receive eternal life one must accept as a creedal doctrine that Jesus is the Son of God (I John ii 22–23). Elsewhere in the Bible the adjectives "one" and "true" may be applied to God to distinguish Him from the pagan gods; but for John the "one true God" has a special connotation—he is the God who is known through and in His Son, Jesus Christ, so that a person who does not confess the Son does not confess the "one true God."

By way of comparing John xvii 3 with Gnosticism we may make two observations. First, for John the knowledge of God in which eternal life consists has been mediated by something that happened in history (the death and resurrection of Christ) and this knowledge is salvific in that it frees men from sin (viii 32). Second, the eternal life is granted to men on this earth. While the Johannine Jesus wishes to isolate his followers so that they are not really part of the world (xvii 14, 16) and ultimately to draw them to him in heaven (24), they receive eternal life while they are in the world. In these points John differs from a Gnosticism that is really independent of history and where life is gained by leaving the world and the flesh.

Although the concept that eternal life consists in knowledge has a peculiar modality in John, we should recognize that there is background material for the idea in the OT. Jeremiah promises as one of the fruits of the renewed covenant an intimate knowledge of God: "I will give them a heart to know me, that I am the Lord; and they shall be my people and I will be their God" (xxiv 7, xxxi 33–34). This parallel is important because several of the most important ideas of the Last Discourse are related to the covenant setting of the Last Supper and the Passion Narrative (see pp. 614, 653). The knowledge of God was also looked on as characteristic of the eschatological period: "The earth will be filled with the knowledge of the glory of God" (Hab ii 14), and John's Last Discourse has some of the characteristics of an eschatological discourse. We see the expectation of the life-giving knowledge of God translated into Jewish Hellenistic vocabulary in Wis xv 3: "To know you is perfect justice and to know your power is the root of immortality." (R. E. Murphy, CBQ 25 [1963], 88–93, suggests that "power" in this citation is the power to destroy death and finds a real parallel to Johannine thought.) At Qumran the author of the hymn that concludes the Community Rule speaks of his being justified because he has been granted the knowledge of God: "For my light has sprung from the source of His knowledge; my eyes have beheld His marvelous deeds; and the light of my heart is in the mystery to come" (1QS xi 3–4). It is true that the sectarian idea of the knowledge of God consisted for the most part in a special understanding of the Law; but we have already seen that for John, Jesus takes the place of the Law (vol. 29, p. 523).

In the NT it is not only in John that eschatological happiness is said to consist in knowing. Paul writes in I Cor xiii 12: "I know now in part; but then I shall know even as I am known." For Paul this knowledge is something still future; John puts more emphasis on its realization in the present. A parallel for John's thought may also be found in the saying from the ancient "Q" source preserved in Matt xi 27; Luke x 22; this saying emphasizes the importance of knowing the Father through the revelation given by the Son. The next verse in Matthew promises eschatological rest to all those who come to the Son. By the end of the 2nd century Irenaeus gives the idea a more formal theological expression: "He who is incomprehensible, intangible, and invisible has made Himself seen and grasped and understood by men so that those who understand and see Him may live. . . . The only life is participation in God, and we do this by knowing God and enjoying His goodness" (*Adv. Haer.* iv 20:5; SC 100:640–42).

In xvii 5 the glory that Jesus requests is identified with the glory that Jesus had with the Father before the world existed. Later in 24 this glory will be said to stem from the love that the Father had for Jesus before the creation of the world. Bultmann, p. 379, characterizes this as the thought pattern of the Gnostic myth. It is similar to the theological outlook of the Prologue (i 1), and we suggest the same background that we suggested for the Logos, namely, Jewish speculation about personified Wisdom. Wisdom existed *before the earth was created* (Prov viii 23); during creation she was *with God* who took *delight* in her (viii 30); she was a pure effusion of His *glory* (Wis vii 25). Jesus who speaks as divine Wisdom had the same origins. The relation that xvii 5 established between the ultimate glory of Jesus and his pre-creational glory helps to explain why the first action of the glorified Jesus is that of a new creation in imitation of Genesis (see p. 1037 below).

Verses 6–8: Jesus' Work of Revelation Among the Disciples

Verse 2 mentioned the men that God had given to Jesus; vs. 4 said that Jesus had glorified God on earth by completing the work that God had given him to do. Verses 6–8 bring these two themes together: the work of Jesus that glorified God was his revelation of God to those whom God had given him. In 6 the task of revelation is phrased in terms of making God's name known. (This chapter is the only place in John where Jesus is explicitly said to have revealed God's name to men.) The background and meaning of this idea deserve careful discussion.

In the OT the author of Ps xxii 23(22) says "I will proclaim your name to my brethren." By this the psalmist means that he will praise God, but the psalm may have taken on a deeper meaning when it was applied by the Christians to Jesus (Heb ii 12). In the OT knowledge of God's name implied a commitment of life ("Those who know your name put their trust in you," Ps ix 11[10]), and the same is true in John, for those to whom Jesus has revealed the name keep God's word (xvii 6). Passages in Deutero-Isaiah seem to speak of a special name (of God?) that will be given to God's servants in the eschatological era (see Young, ZNW 46 [1955], 223–23). For instance, LXX of Isa lv 13: "The Lord shall be for a name, for an everlasting sign"; lxii 2: "You shall be called by a new name which the Lord shall give"; lxv 15–16: "The Lord God . . . will call His servants by a different name, so that he who blesses himself in the land shall bless himself by the God of truth." This is quite like Rev ii 17, iii 12 where the Christian alone knows a new name and has the name of God written on him; in xix 12–13 we are told that Jesus bears a name which no one knows but himself, namely, "The Word of God." Another significant OT usage would be the Deuteronomic custom of speaking of the central site of Israel's worship (where the Tabernacle or the Temple was) as the place where God has put His name (Deut xii 5, 21, etc.). For John, Jesus replaces the Tabernacle (see vol. 29, pp. 32–33) and the Temple (pp. 124–25), and so is now the place where God has put His name.

In the Judaism of Jesus' time there were undoubtedly speculations about the divine name. G. Scholem (*Major Trends in Jewish Mysticism* [3rd ed.; New York: Schocken paperback, 1961], pp. 68 ff.) thinks that the emphasis on the name in later Jewish mystical writings had earlier origins. In particular there was speculation about the angel of the Lord mentioned in Exod xxiii 20–21: "Behold I send an angel before you to guard you on the way and to bring you to the place which I have prepared . . . *my name is upon him.*" This description could well fit the Jesus of John xvii. The speculations on the divine name that appear in early Gnostic works may also have had Jewish roots; see G. Quispel in *The Jung Codex* (London: Mowbray, 1955), pp. 68 ff.; and J. E. Ménard, *L'Evangile de Vérité* (Paris: Letouzey, 1962), pp. 183–84, who cites wider Eastern background. Two passages from the recently discovered Chenoboskion works are worth noting:

> The name of the Father is the Son. It is He who in the beginning gave a name to him who came forth from Him—that one being Himself—and whom He begot as a Son. He gave to him His name which belonged to Him. . . . The Son can be seen, but the name is invisible. . . . The Father's name is not spoken but is revealed by the Son. (*Gospel of Truth* xxxviii 6 ff.)

> One single name they do not utter in the world, the name which the Father gave to the Son, which is above all things, which is the name of the Father. For the Son would not become the Father except he clothe himself with the name of the Father. Those who have this name know it indeed but do not speak of it. But those who do not have it do not know it. (*Gospel of Philip* xii; see R. McL. Wilson, *The Gospel of Philip* [New York: Harper, 1962], p. 30.)

The thoughts of these Gnostic works have a certain similarity to John but go beyond John in identifying the Son and the Father and in stressing the unspeakable character of the name. Finally we note that the Jewish anti-Christian legends of the *Toledoth Jeshu* trace Jesus' (magical) power to the fact that he had gained possession of the divine name.

What was the name of God that Jesus revealed? It is well attested that in Judaism the use of the expression "the name" was a way of avoiding the tetragrammaton (YHWH), so that it is possible that John has in mind a special divine name. On the other hand, since for the Semite a name is an expression of one's personality and power, the revealing of God's name may simply be a Semitic description of divine revelation in general (Bultmann, p. 385[1]). We are inclined to the former and less abstract interpretation of the Johannine theology of the name. In an interesting article, Bonsirven points out that the Church Fathers, like Cyril of Alexandria and Augustine, were more inclined to emphasize the personal relationship of the name, while later commentators spoke of the name as an abstraction. (The latter tendency is still found in modern translations; in xvii 11 in the NEB and in the 1966 American Bible Society's "Today's English Version" we find "the power of your name" instead of "your name.")

In particular we tentatively suggest that the divine name that the

Johannine Jesus made known to men was "I AM." In xvii 11–12 Jesus says that God has given him the divine name; obviously this gift would not become totally apparent until the glorification of Jesus. This corresponds with what Jesus has said about "I AM." "When you lift up the Son of Man, then you will realize that I AM" (viii 28). In vol. 29, App. IV, we discussed the OT background for Jesus' peculiar absolute use of "I AM." Particularly pertinent for John xvii 6 is God's promise in LXX of Isa lii 6: "On that day my people shall know my name, that I am (egō eimi) He who speaks." Another significant passage would be Exod iii 13–15. When Moses asked God's name so that he might go to the people with proper credentials, God replied, "Say this to the people of Israel, 'I AM has sent me to you.'" (In vol. 29, p. 536, we acknowledged that this may not have been the original meaning of the passage containing the tetragrammaton, but this seems to be the meaning given to it in later times.) So also the Johannine Jesus has come among men, not only knowing the name of God as "I AM," but even bearing it, because he is the revelation of God to His people. In vss. 6, 11, and 12 the name is mentioned in relation to those whom Jesus is leaving behind and who have been sent into the world (18). Much as in the instance of Moses, the fact that those sent by Jesus know his divine name and are committed to all that it implies authenticates their mission.

Once again Johannine thought has certain similarities to the thought expressed in the hymn of Philip ii 9 which says that "the name which is above every other name" was bestowed on the exalted Jesus. The name of which Paul speaks is kyrios, "Lord," the Greek translation of YHWH; the name of which John speaks, "I AM," is indirectly related to YHWH (vol. 29, p. 536). But for Paul the name is given only after the resurrection; for John, Jesus bears the divine name during the ministry. In another strain of Johannine thought, however, in Rev xix 12–13 Jesus has inscribed on him the divine name, "The Word of God," at a moment still in the future when he descends from heaven to defeat the evil hordes.

Verses 7 and 8 in xvii draw out the implications of the fact that the disciples have been given knowledge of the divine name that Jesus bears. This has made them realize that all that Jesus has comes from the Father (7), especially his words (8). Since Jesus bears the name of God, they know, as with Moses, that he has been sent by God (8). The description of Jesus in the first lines of 8 echoes the description of the Prophet-like-Moses in Deut xviii 18: God puts His words in the mouth of the prophet who then speaks as God has commanded. It is interesting that this prayer where the glory and divinity of Jesus are so prominent also stresses emphatically his dependence on the Father.

[The Bibliography for this section is included in the Bibliography for ch. xvii, at the end of §59.]

58. THE LAST DISCOURSE:
—DIVISION THREE (UNIT TWO)
(xvii 9–19)

Jesus prays for those whom the Father has given him

XVII
9 "It is on their behalf that I pray.
I do not pray for the world
but for those whom you have given me,
since they really belong to you
10 (just as all that is mine is yours
and all that is yours is mine),
and it is in them that I have been glorified.
11 I am no longer in the world;
but while I am coming to you,
they are still in the world.
O Father most holy,
keep them safe with your name which you have given to me
[that they may be one, just as we].
12 As long as I was with them,
I kept them safe with your name which you have given to me.
I kept watch and not one of them perished,
except the one destined to perish—
in order to have the Scripture fulfilled.
13 But now I am coming to you.
Yet, while still in the world, I say all this
that they may share my joy to the full.
14 I have given to them your word,
and the world has hated them
because they do not belong to the world
[any more than I belong to the world].
15 I am not asking you to take them out of the world
but to keep them safe from the Evil One.
16 They do not belong to the world,
any more than I belong to the world.

17 Consecrate them in the truth—
'Your word is truth';
18 for as you sent me into the world,
so I sent them into the world.
19 And it is for them that I consecrate myself,
in order that they too may be consecrated in truth."

NOTES

xvii. 9. *I pray.* Literally "I ask." In vss. 9, 15, and 20 the verb *erōtan* is used absolutely without a direct personal object; the Father is understood as the addressee of the request. In earlier uses of this verb for prayer in the Last Discourse (xiv 16, xvi 26), "the Father" is the expressed object. Schwank, "Für sie," p. 487, makes the point that the Johannine Jesus speaks of his own prayer in terms of *erōtan* and does not use *aitein*, the verb most frequently used of his disciples' prayer. See xvi 26 where the verbs seem synonymous and xiv 23 where they seem not to be synonymous.

those whom you have given me. In the context of the Last Supper this is a reference to the immediate disciples of Jesus, presumably the Twelve (see NOTE on xiii 5). Later on (vs. 20) the prayer will switch from these disciples to future converts. Nevertheless, since the historical disciples are a model for all Christians, both in 9–19 and 20–26 the Christians of a future time are envisaged.

since they really belong to you. This clause is explicative both of why Jesus is praying for them and of why Jesus can say that it was the Father who gave them to him. Bultmann, p. 382[7], emphasizes only the former relationship, but that the latter is also in mind is seen in the parenthetical opening lines of the next verse. The last two lines of 9 (you have given them to me—they really belong to you) reverse the third line of 6 ("They were yours and you gave them to me").

10. (*just as all that is mine is yours* . . .). This parenthetical sentence is similar to xvi 15. We note that there has been a switch from masculine pronouns in 9 ("those whom") to neuter pronouns in 10 ("all that"); the neuter has the effect of broadening the already remarkable claim. The equivalence between those who belong to Jesus and those who belong to the Father means that in Johannine thought it is not the creation of a man that makes him belong to God but his reaction to Jesus. A man cannot accept Jesus unless he belongs to God, and a man cannot belong to God unless he accepts Jesus.

in them . . . I have been glorified. In reference to his immediate disciples, Jesus' glory was first revealed at Cana (ii 11). However, from the author's standpoint in time, Jesus has been glorified in the Christian believers who came to faith after the resurrection. Codex Bezae reads "You glorified me," perhaps on the analogy of vs. 1 where the Father is the agent of glorification.

11. *I am no longer in the world.* Contrast with 13 below: "While still in the world, I say all this"; yet in both verses Jesus says, "I am coming to you." The three lines of 10 and the first three lines of 11 all begin with *kai*, "and"; it is difficult to decide what to coordinate and what to subordinate in English translation.

coming. Elsewhere in the Last Discourse Jesus is said to be *going* to God

(NOTES on xiv 2, xvi 5), but here he is speaking directly to the Father and "coming" is more appropriate. After this clause Codex Bezae and some OL witnesses add: "I am no longer in the world; yet I am in the world." The addition seems to unite the statement in 11 that precedes "I am coming to you" with the statement in 13 that follows "I am coming to you."

O Father most holy. Literally "holy Father." God is called "the Holy One" (of Israel) in the OT and is addressed as holy in Jewish prayers: "O holy Lord of all holiness" (II Macc xiv 36); "O Holy One among the holy" (III Macc ii 2). We mentioned above (p. 746) the usage in *Didache* x 2.

keep them safe. Literally "keep them"; the disciples kept the Father's word (6), so Jesus asks the Father to keep them. Keeping them safe means keeping them from the contamination of the world (I John ii 15–17).

with your name. Literally "in your name"; the "in" is both local and instrumental: they are to be both marked with and protected by the divine name that has been given to Jesus. P66* has "in *my* name" both here and in 12.

which you have given. The perfect tense of the verb is to be preferred to the aorist that appears in some mss.; the name was given in the past and is still possessed. A more important problem concerns the antecedent of the relative pronoun "which." The best witnesses, including P66, have the dative neuter singular relative, and this means that "your name" is the antecedent. A large number of later and less reliable textual witnesses have a masculine plural relative, the antecedent of which must be "them," namely, the disciples. We have accepted the first reading, while SB and NEB accept the second (RSV is ambiguous). The second reading probably represents a scribal harmonization with vss. 2, 6, and 9 which speak of men being given by God to Jesus. The reading that we have followed makes 11 and 12 the only instances in John where God is said to have given the (divine) name to Jesus. There have been several attempts to solve the diversity of reading. Burney suggested that an ambiguous Aramaic relative has been understood in two different ways. Huby, *art. cit.,* has argued that the original reading was the accusative neuter singular pronoun (found in Bezae*) but that it referred to the disciples (an instance of John's tendency to use a neuter collective for a masculine plural idea).

[*that they may be one, just as we*]. The whole clause is omitted in P66*, OSsin, OL, Coptic, and perhaps Tatian—an important combination of textual witnesses. The theme of unity is more at home in the third unit of the prayer (see 21–23) than it is here. Codex Vaticanus and some minor witnesses add "also" to "as we." John uses the neuter *hēn* for "one"; and Barrett, p. 424, interprets this to mean that the disciples are not to be kept as units but as a unity. It is interesting that John does not use the abstract noun for "unity," *henotēs*, found in Eph iv 3, 13, and frequently in Ignatius of Antioch.

12. *kept safe . . . kept watch.* The verbs are *tērein* and *phylassein.* Here Jesus has done for his disciples what Lady Wisdom did for Abraham according to Wis x 5: "She found the just man and kept [*tērein*] him blameless before God and preserved [*phylassein*] him resolute. . . ."

name which you have given to me. The textual witnesses are divided over the relative pronoun in much the same way as they were divided in 11. Codex Sinaiticus* and OSsin omit the clause altogether; so does P66* (K. Aland, NTS 10 [1963–64], 67). Bultmann omits the clause in his reconstruction of the poetry of the Revelatory Discourse Source.

not one of them perished. In iii 16 it was stated that God gave the Son "that everyone who believes in him may not perish"; in x 28 Jesus said of his sheep: "They shall never perish. No one will snatch them from my hand"; in vi 39 he said: "It is the will of Him who sent me that I should lose nothing of what He has given me."

except the one destined to perish. Literally "the son of perdition"; the word "perdition" is of the same Greek root as "perish." In the NT "perdition" frequently means damnation (Matt vii 13; Rev xvii 8); and so "the son of perdition" refers to one who belongs to the realm of damnation and is destined to final destruction. Although, as F. W. Danker, NTS 7 (1960–61), 94, has pointed out, this type of phrase can be found in classical Greek, we are almost certainly dealing with a Semitism. R. E. Murphy, *Biblica* 39 (1958), 66[4], suggests that John's Greek phrase translates *ben šaḥat;* for while *šaḥat* can refer to the pit of Sheol, in Qumran Hebrew it means "corruption" and is a synonym for *'āwel,* "wickedness," a term used in Qumran dualism to describe the realm opposed to good (vol. 29, p. LXII). The phrase "the son of perdition" is used in II Thess ii 3 to describe the antichrist who comes before the parousia. It is interesting that in Johannine realized eschatology "the son of perdition" appears during the ministry of Jesus before his return to the Father. Whether this is an intentional modification of the apocalyptic expectation is hard to say; see vol. 30 of the Anchor Bible for our discussion of the Johannine approach to the antichrist in relation to I John ii 18, 20. Clearly in the Gospel the reference is to Judas as the tool of Satan. Judas is described as a devil in vi 70; and in xiii 2, 27, and 30 we are told that Satan entered Judas' heart and that he went out into the realm of darkness to betray Jesus.

in order to. The mentality whereby it was thought that things happened in Jesus' ministry in order to fulfill what had been predicted in Scripture is described in vol. 29, pp. 484–85. It is not clear whether this last line of 12 is presented by the Johannine writer as Jesus' own words or as an observation by the writer himself. Instances of both practices are found in John; contrast xiii 18 with xii 14–15.

the Scripture. Presumably a particular passage is meant. Evidently the early Christians quickly sought out OT passages to explain the betrayal by Judas, for the varying accounts of Judas' demise give prominence to OT background. Acts i 16–20 claims that the Holy Spirit had spoken beforehand about Judas and explicitly cites Pss lxix 26(25), cix 8. Matt xxvii 3–10 implicitly cites a legal principle about not using tainted money in the house of the Lord (cf. Deut xxiii 19[18]), then explicitly but freely cites Zech xi 12–13 about the thirty pieces of silver, perhaps combining it with a passage from Jeremiah (xxxii 6–15?). Our only clue to the passage that John has in mind is that the description of Judas' treachery in xiii 18 explicitly cites Ps xli 10(9). If this last line of John xvii 12 with its reference to "the Scripture" is an explanatory prose addition to the hymn of ch. xvii (as was vs. 3), then the redactor who added it may have recalled xiii 18. Freed, OTQ, p. 97, points to the possibility that the OT passage in mind is not one that predicts treachery but one that uses the expression "the son of perdition," hence LXX of Prov xxiv 22a (the only OT occurrence— "children of perdition" appears in Isa lvii 4). Freed's own view that "the Scripture" is not the OT but the words of Jesus in vi 70–71 is implausible in this writer's opinion.

13. *But now.* Laurentin, *art. cit.,* points out that with its initial *nyn* vs. 13 resembles 7 and uses this observation as the key to his division of the chapter

(p. 749 above). In thought content, however, 13 (first two lines) is much closer to 11.

all this. Literally "these things"; presumably the earlier part of the prayer is meant rather than the whole Last Discourse.

may share my joy to the full. Cf. xv 11: "I have said this to you that my joy may be yours and your joy may be fulfilled"; xvi 24: "Ask and you shall receive that your joy may be full." Currently their hearts are *filled* with sorrow (xvi 6). *Full* joy is an eschatological concept in the rabbinic writings (Bultmann, p. 388).

14. *your word.* Here the singular *logos;* see NOTE on "words" in 8.

the world has hated them. We have softened the awkward aorist tense; this statement is certainly written from the author's standpoint in time. Almost the same thought and expression is found in xv 18–19; notice the present tense there.

do not belong to the world. Literally "are not of the world." In Johannine thought the Christian is begotten from above and is of God (iii 3–6, i 13). The disciples have been chosen out of the world (xv 19). The *Letter to Diognetus* (vi 3), from the late 2nd century, seems to draw on John: "Christians dwell in the world but do not belong to the world."

[*any more than I belong to the world*]. This is omitted by P66* and important Western witnesses. Was it omitted because it seemed redundant in view of vs. 16? Or was it added in imitation of 16? The latter seems more plausible.

15. *to take them out of the world.* Schlatter, p. 323, shows good rabbinic parallels for the expressions used in both lines of this verse.

to keep them safe from the Evil One. The word *poneros,* "Evil One," is capable of being translated as an abstract noun, "evil"; but on the analogy of I John ii 13–14, iii 12, v 18–19, a personal application to the devil is probably intended. The Evil One is the Prince of this world, for I John v 19 states: "The whole world is under the Evil One." This line is the Johannine parallel to the petition in the Matthean version of the Lord's Prayer: "Free us from the Evil One" (Matt vi 13—customarily but less accurately rendered as "Deliver us from evil"). The preceding petition in Matthew which deals with the final trial ("temptation") shows that a deliverance at the end of days is envisaged. John's petition is in terms of realized eschatology; it asks for protection while the disciples are in the world. Rev iii 10, on the other hand, is in terms of final eschatology: "Because you have kept my word . . . I shall keep you safe from the hour of trial which is to come upon the whole world." I John ii 13–14 illustrates the granting of the petition spoken by Jesus in the present verse, for there young Christians are told that they have conquered the Evil One.

16. Except for a slight change in word order this verse is the same as the last two lines of 14. Along with a few other witnesses P66 (corrector) expunges the whole verse.

17. *Consecrate.* Literally "make holy"; there is an echo of "Father most holy" in 11.

in the truth. The article (missing when the phrase is repeated in 19) means that the expression is not simply abverbial: "truly consecrate them." "Truth" has power to act; cf. viii 32: "Truth will set you free." Here "truth" is both the agency of the consecration and the realm into which they are consecrated; the "in" means both "by" and "for."

'Your word is truth.' Codex Vaticanus and some witnesses to Tatian's text

read an article before "truth"; the Byzantine tradition has a clarifying "your" before "truth." The passage is identical with LXX form of Ps cxix 142 as found in Codex Sinaiticus; but MT and the other witnesses of LXX read the psalm verse as "Your law is truth." Is John citing a variant form of the psalm known in the 1st century and still preserved in Sinaiticus? Or does the Sinaiticus tradition adapt the OT to conform with John? We may mention that being consecrated in a truth which consists of the divine word resembles the idea of being cleansed by Jesus' word (xv 3).

18. *for as you sent.* On the assumption that the citation (?) in the last line of 17 is parenthetical, we have not begun a new sentence in 18 but have supplied a "for" to relate this *kathōs* clause to the first line of 17. (Compare the *kathōs* clause in 2 which is related to the Son's glorifying the Father in 1.) The consecration in truth is not simply a purification from sin (see xv 3) but is a consecration to a mission; they are being consecrated inasmuch as they are being sent.

so. The "as . . . so" construction sets up a parallelism between what the Father has done for Jesus and what Jesus does for the disciples. Elsewhere in the Gospel this parallelism is found in relation to life (vi 57), knowledge (x 14–15), love (xv 9, xvii 23), and unity (xvii 22).

I sent them. The Ferrar family of minuscule mss. read a present tense here, but this is a scribal attempt to smooth over the difficulty caused by the aorist. From the viewpoint of the Last Supper, when in the past had Jesus sent the disciples? It is risky to point to incidents in the Synoptics (Matt x 5; Luke x 1) not recorded by John (unless one supposes that we are dealing with an ancient saying that has been preserved in John even though the incident to which it originally referred has not been preserved). Is this the same mission that was mentioned in the past tense in iv 38 (vol. 29, p. 183) in reference to the spiritual harvest among the Samaritans? More likely the tense is from the viewpoint of the evangelist and refers to the true mission of the disciples that came after the resurrection (xx 21–22).

19. *I consecrate myself.* A number of important witnesses, including P66, omit the emphatic pronoun "I"; but the context gives an emphatic cast in any case. In x 36 it was said that the Father consecrated (past) Jesus; here Jesus does the consecrating himself—another example of the same power possessed by the Father and by Jesus (vol. 29, p. 407).

in truth. The phrase occurs after the participle "consecrated" in most witnesses but seemingly before it in P66. The use of "truth" without the article after the preposition "in" is common in Johannine style (I John iii 18; II John 1, 3, etc.; see BDF, §258). The meaning here is not really distinct from the meaning of the phrase with the article in 17, but here "truth" is more the realm of the disciples' consecration than the agency of that consecration— Jesus' consecration of himself is the agent in consecrating the disciples (cf. J. Reid, ET 24 [1912–13], 459–60).

Comment

Verses 9–16: The Disciples and the World

As background for his request that the Father glorify him, Jesus has mentioned his work among the men given him by the Father: he showed God's glory among them (vs. 4); he revealed God's name to them (6); and he gave them God's words (8). Now in his prayer he turns to include these men directly in his request to his Father. By way of parallel we note that in Luke's account of the Last Supper Jesus prays for one of the disciples, Simon Peter, and shows a concern for the others that they may be armed to face struggle (Luke xxii 32, 36).

The prayer on behalf of his disciples (9) is an extension of the prayer for his own glorification (1); for it is in the perseverance and mission of these disciples that the name of God, given to Jesus, will be glorified on earth. As Jesus says in 10, "It is in them that I have been glorified." The theme of opposition between the disciples and the world, prominent in Division Two of the Last Discourse (especially in xv 18 – xvi 4a), now appears in the final prayer of Jesus. The disciples are to be left in the world (11); but they do not belong to the world (14, 16), any more than their master's kingdom belongs to this world (xviii 36). Because they are aliens in the world, their very presence provokes trouble. Jesus has given them God's word (14) and has sent them into the world (18), but the world reacts with hatred (14).

How can one reconcile the idea that Jesus sends the disciples into the world with his refusal to pray for the world (9)? Some would soften the harshness of "I do not pray for the world" by understanding this to mean that at the Last Supper Jesus is concerned only with his disciples, leaving aside (but not rejecting) the world for the moment (Schwank, "Für sie," p. 488). The attitude of the Johannine Jesus is often interpreted through the Synoptic tradition where Jesus urges prayer for enemies (Matt v 44; also Luke xxiii 34) and through the Pauline command to pray for all men (I Tim ii 1). But this attempt to tone down John xvii 9 does not do justice to Johannine dualism. At the beginning of the ministry Jesus said that God so loved the world that He gave His only Son (iii 16). However, the coming of the Son provoked judgment (iii 18–19), so that "the world" came to represent those who have turned away from Jesus and are under the power of Satan (I John v 19), the world's Prince or leader (xii 31, xiv 30). The world has been condemned in the person of its Prince (xvi 11); and so the world is not to be prayed for but proved wrong (xvi 8–11) and conquered (I John v 4–5). Barrett, p. 422, phrases the Johannine outlook well:

". . . the only hope for the *kosmos* is precisely that it should cease to be the *kosmos*." The world must pass away (I John ii 17).

If the disciples are *sent* by Jesus into the world, it is for the same purpose for which Jesus was sent into the world—not to change the world but to challenge the world. In each generation there is on earth a group of men given by God to Jesus, and the task of the disciples is to separate these sons of light from the sons of darkness who surround them. Those given to Jesus will recognize his voice in and through the mission of the disciples and will band together into one (end of 11).

This community of Christians will be hated by the world, but Jesus does not wish to have them spared this hostility. So that the depth of his love might become apparent, Jesus himself could not leave the world without facing the hostility of its Prince (xiv 30–31). Similarly each of his followers must face the Evil One (xvii 15; cf. I John ii 15–17 on the allurements of the world) if eventually he is to be with Jesus (xvii 24). Jesus knows that his followers need help in this eschatological warfare, a warfare waged not at Armageddon (Rev xvi 16) but in each man's soul. Consequently Jesus asks God to keep the disciples safe with the divine name that has been given to him (xvii 11). The protective power of God's name is a Jewish theme already attested in Prov xviii 10: "The name of the Lord is a strong tower; the just man runs into it and is safe." If we are right in our contention that for John the name is *egō eimi*, "I AM," we have an example of how this name protects the disciples in John xviii 5–8; for when Jesus says *egō eimi*, those who have come to arrest him fall down powerless, and Jesus demands that they allow his disciples to leave unharmed.

This attitude toward the world strikes many modern Christians as strange and even as a distortion of the true Christian apostolate. In an age of involvement where men are considering the role of the Church in the modern world, the refusal of the Johannine Jesus to pray for the world is a scandal. And yet hostility to the world is not peculiar in the NT to John. James iv 4 tells the Christian: "To be a friend of the world is to be an enemy of God." In Gal i 4 Paul says that Christ gave himself to deliver men from the present evil age. Distrust for a world that is looked on as evil is, of course, not the whole NT message, and there are many passages that inculcate involvement in the world. But if Christians believe that Scripture has a certain power to judge and correct, then the latter passages are more meaningful in eras when the Church tends to be sequestered from the world, while passages such as those we have found in John have a message for an era that becomes naïvely optimistic about changing the world or even about affirming its values without change. (On the Johannine concept of the world see vol. 29, pp. 508–10.)

In conclusion we may note that the certitude of encountering hostility in the world is not meant to make the disciples sad. Jesus' promise of divine protection will offset sadness and bring the disciples' joy to fullness (13). The theme of joy amid the hostility of the world appeared two times in the Second Division of the Last Discourse (see pp. 681, 733 above). Evidently this paradoxical combination was a common Christian motif; for instance, Matt v 11: "Happy are you when men revile you and persecute you . . . on my account"; I Thess i 6: "You received the word in much affliction, with joy inspired by the Holy Spirit."

Verses 17–19: The Consecration of the Disciples and of Jesus

In 11 Jesus addresses his Father as "holy." To the Jewish mind this would suggest something about the holiness to be expected of the disciples for whom Jesus is praying, for the principle of Leviticus (xi 44, xix 2, xx 26) is that men must make themselves holy because God is holy. The fact that the disciples belong to God (9) is the reason for their keeping themselves separate from the world, since in the OT mentality the holiness of God is opposed to what is secular and profane. The theme of the holiness of the disciples becomes explicit in 17 where the Father is asked to consecrate them (make them holy) in truth. In earlier passages we have been told that the Father who is holy Himself consecrated Jesus and sent him into the world (x 36). Now Jesus, the Holy One of God (vi 69), wants the disciples consecrated and sent into the world (18). As we have emphasized in the NOTES, the consecration of the disciples is directed toward their mission (Morrison, *art. cit.*, stresses this). This is in harmony with the OT understanding of consecration; for example, Moses, who himself has been consecrated by God (Greek of Sir xlv 4), is told in Exod xxviii 41 to consecrate others so that they *may serve* God as priests. The disciples are to be consecrated so that they may serve as apostles, that is, as ones sent.

In particular, the disciples are to be consecrated in the truth that is God's word. In common Jewish prayer (StB, II, 566), it was proclaimed that God sanctifies (consecrates) men through His commandments—an idea that is partially similar to John's thought, since for John "word" and "commandment" are virtually interchangeable (NOTE on xiv 23). A Jewish prayer for New Year's, cited by Westcott, p. 245, is also interesting: "Purify our hearts to serve you in truth. You, O God, are truth [Jer x 10], and your word is truth and stands forever." We must remember that in Johannine theology Jesus is both the Word and the truth (xiv 6), so that consecration in a truth that is the word of God is simply an aspect of belonging to Jesus (and, of course, belonging to Jesus is belonging to God [xvii 10] who is holy). The disciples have accepted and kept the word that Jesus brought them from God (xvii 6, 14); this word has cleansed them (xv 3); now it sets them aside for a mission of conveying it to others (xvii 20).

It is curious that in the prayer of xvii which concerns the future of the disciples there is no mention of the Paraclete/Spirit who will be the most important factor in that future. Yet, especially in Eastern Orthodox theology, the prayer has been interpreted in terms of the role of the Holy Spirit (P. Evdokimov, *Verbum Caro* 14 [1960], 250–64). In particular, some exegetes would see an implicit reference to the Spirit in the theme of consecration in the truth that is the word of God. Frequently in the Gospel we have seen a similarity between the work of Jesus' revelatory word and the work of the Spirit (vol. 29, pp. 178–79, 327–28). Perhaps "truth" in xvii 17 is meant to be identified not only with God's word but also with the Paraclete who is the Spirit of Truth. If the disciples are to be made holy in the truth, then this is the realm of the *Holy* Spirit or the Paraclete (xiv 26) who makes Jesus' word intelligible. The association of these ideas is found in II Thess ii 13: "God chose you from the beginning to be saved through *sanctification* by the *Spirit* and belief in the *truth*."

In the last verse of the unit (19) we find that Jesus is not only asking the Father to consecrate the disciples in truth but also consecrating himself for that purpose. What does this self-consecration of Jesus consist in? In the OT both men and animals are consecrated. In particular, prophets and priests are consecrated for a special task. An example of prophetic consecration is found in the words of God to Jeremiah (i 5): "Before you came forth from the womb I consecrated you; I appointed you a prophet to the nations" (also Sir xlix 7). The prophet had to be made holy because he was the bearer of God's word. References to the consecration of priests are found in Exod xl 13; Lev viii 30; II Chron v 11. These examples of prophetic and priestly consecration are good background for John x 36 where the Father is said to have consecrated Jesus and sent him into the world; they are less appropriate for the interpretation of xvii 19 where Jesus consecrates himself. Here we may be closer to the idea of consecrating sacrificial victims (Deut xv 19).

Is Jesus thinking of his offering himself in death for the disciples when he says, "It is for them that I consecrate myself"? The phrase "for [*hyper*] them" may suggest death, as we see from the use of *hyper* throughout the Gospel. In xi 51 Jesus is to die *for* the nation; in x 11 the model shepherd lays down his life *for* his sheep; in xv 13 Jesus speaks of laying down one's life *for* those whom one loves. (Also elsewhere in the NT, for example, Rom viii 32: "He did not spare His own Son but delivered him up *for* us.") The solemn authority of the "I consecrate myself" may be compared to the tone of x 17–18: "I lay down my life . . . I lay it down of my own accord." If Jesus' self-consecration is related to the consecration and sending of the apostles, the sending does not take place until after Jesus' death and resurrection (xx 21). And if the consecration in truth of the disciples involves the Holy Spirit, that Spirit is not given until after Jesus' death and resurrection (xx 22). Thus it is plausible that, when in xvii 19 Jesus speaks of self-consecration, we

are to think of him not only as the incarnation of God's word consecrated by the Father but also as a priest offering himself as a victim
for those whom God has given him. The priestly theme seemingly reappears
in xix (see pp. 920–21 below).

We have mentioned that the high-priestly prayer of John xvii has an
atmosphere not unlike that of the Epistle to the Hebrews where Jesus
is portrayed as a high priest in heaven, making intercession for men. In
Heb ix 12–14 we find that Jesus offered himself as a sacrificial victim, a
thought that may correspond to John xvii 19. We may also mention the
parallel to xvii in Heb ii 10–11. There the author speaks of Jesus being
made perfect through suffering, and this resembles John's idea of Jesus
being glorified through his return to the Father. The author of Hebrews
describes Jesus as the one who consecrates (or sanctifies), while the Christians are Jesus' brothers whom he has consecrated. The idea is reiterated in
Heb x 10: "We have been consecrated through the offering of the body
of Jesus Christ once for all." John xvii 19 has Jesus consecrating himself,
seemingly as a victim, so that his disciples may be consecrated—disciples
who are one with him (11, 21–23). See also vol. 29, p. 411.

[The Bibliography for this section is included in the Bibliography
for ch. xvii, at the end of §59.]

59. THE LAST DISCOURSE:
—DIVISION THREE (UNIT THREE)
(xvii 20–26)

Jesus prays for those who believe through the disciples' word

XVII
20 "Yet it is not for these alone that I pray
    but also for those who believe in me through their word,
21 that they all may be one,
    just as you, Father, in me and I in you,
    that they also may be [one] in us.
    Thus the world may believe that you sent me.
22 I have even given to them the glory which you have given me,
    that they may be one,
    just as we are one, 23 I in them and you in me,
    that they may be brought to completion as one.
    Thus the world may come to know that you sent me
    and that you loved them even as you loved me.
24 Father, they are your gift to me;
    and where I am, I wish
    them also to be with me,
    that they may see my glory which you have given me
    because you loved me before the creation of the world.
25 O Father most just,
    while the world did not know you
    (though I knew you),
    these men came to know that you sent me.
26 And to them I made known your name;
    and I will continue to make it known
    so that the love you had for me may be in them
    and I may be in them."

NOTES

xvii 20. *I pray.* The verb *erōtan* appears at the beginning of this section just as it did at the beginning of the last section (vs. 9).

those who believe. If the viewpoint is that of the Last Supper, this present participle is proleptic, having the force of a future (BDF, §339²ᵇ; ZGB, §283), a usage that may reflect a Semitism. If the viewpoint is that of the time of the Johannine writer, the believers are a present reality.

in me through their word. In the Greek word order the first of these two phrases follows the second; thus it would be possible to translate as: "believe through their word about me." The idea is not too far from that of Rom x 14; Heb ii 3–4.

21. There is a remarkable grammatical parallelism between the six lines of 20–21 and the six lines of 22–23. In particular, note the following:

21a	[*hina*]	that they all may be one
21b	[*kathōs*]	just as you, Father, in me and I in you
21c	[*hina*]	that they also may be [one] in us
21d	[*hina*]	Thus the world may believe that you sent me

22b	[*hina*]	that they may be one
22c–23	[*kathōs*]	just as we are one, I in them and you in me
23b	[*hina*]	that they may be brought to completion as one
23c	[*hina*]	Thus the world may come to know that you sent me

Each of these blocks of four lines consists of three *hina* clauses with a *kathōs* clause separating the first and the second. The first and second *hina* clause in each involves the oneness of the believers, while the third involves the effect on the world. The second *hina* clause does not merely repeat the first but develops the notion of unity. The *kathōs* clause in each block holds up for the believers the model of the unity of Jesus and the Father. Randall, p. 141, is excellent on this parallelism.

just as you. Kathōs has both a comparative and causative force here (BDF, §453²): heavenly unity is both the model and source of the unity of believers. In the 4th century the Orthodox tended to use John x 30 ("The Father and I are one") as an argument against the Arians. The Arians replied by using this verse to prove that the unity of the Father and the Son is the same type of unity that exists among believers, namely moral unity. However, as Pollard, *art. cit.*, points out, John does not model heavenly unity on earthly unity but vice versa.

you, Father, in me and I in you. In the last line of 11 the comparison offered for the unity of the disciples was simply "just as we." Here the comparison is spelled out in detail, and we find that the model of unity is the mutual indwelling of Father and Son. There is no reason to think that the unity proposed in 11 ("that they may be one, just as we") is a different type of unity from that proposed here, despite the attempt of some to distinguish between a unity in faith and a unity in God. Ignatius, *Ephesians* v 1, is rather close to Johannine language: "I count you blessed who are so united with him [your bishop] as the Church is with Jesus Christ, and as Jesus Christ is with the Father, that all things may be harmonious in unison."

may be [one] in us. On purely textual grounds, the evidence for the omission of "one" (Vaticanus, Bezae, OL, OSsin, seemingly P66) is stronger than the evidence for its inclusion (Sinaiticus, Byzantine tradition, Vulgate, Peshitta). If "one" is an addition, it is probably a scribal attempt to conform the second *hina* clause to the first. On the other hand, the *hen* could have been accidentally omitted by a scribe through a type of homoioteleuton (*en hēmin hen ōsin*). The parallelism of these *hina* clauses with those in 22–23 favors inclusion, for the latter have "one" in both lines. With or without the "one," the second *hina* clause in 21 is a development over the first, since it asks not only for unity (first clause) but also for divine indwelling.

It should be noted that for the first three lines of 21 (the *hina, kathōs, hina* clauses) Origen on ten occasions reads a much shorter text: "As I and you are one, that they may be one in us." It is tempting to dismiss this reading as a free summary of what is said in vss. 11, 21, 22, and 23; but the same reading occurs in many of the Fathers, including Jerome (ten times). Boismard, RB 57 (1950), 396–97, cites this as an example where the Fathers preserve an older and shorter reading that may be original. Yet the careful parallelism of the clauses in 21 to those of 22–23 militates against the acceptance of the shorter reading, in our judgment.

Thus the world may believe. Literally "in order that the world. . . ." It is quite clear that the first and second *hina* clauses of 21 constitute the content of Jesus' prayer: he is praying for unity and indwelling. Is the third *hina* clause also part of the prayer ("I pray . . . that the world may believe that you sent me")? J. C. Earwaker, ET 75 (1963–64), 316–17, argues that it is; but Bultmann, p. 394¹, thinks that the third clause is not related to "I pray" —rather it supplies the goal of the indwelling mentioned in the second *hina* clause (p. 394⁴). Bultmann's view fits better with the rest of Johannine theology where Jesus does not pray directly for the world. The unity and indwelling visible among his followers challenges the world to believe in Jesus' mission, and thus indirectly the world is included in Jesus' prayer.

may believe. The best witnesses, including P66, read a present subjunctive, while the Byzantine tradition has an aorist, which is easier to understand. Bultmann, p. 394⁶, sees no real difference of meaning. However, Abbott, JG, §§2524–26, 2511, points out that John is very strict in observing the distinction between the present and aorist tenses in *hina* clauses; see x 38 where in one line the present and aorist of the same verb are used with different meanings. In §2528 Abbott maintains that the present of *pisteuein* in this construction would imply continuous faith, while the aorist would refer to belief at its beginning or first formation. In §2554 Abbott contrasts the clause in 21d (="that the world may grow in belief") with the parallel clause in 23c which employs the aorist (="that knowledge may dawn on the world"). If one follows Abbott, 21d implies that the world is already believing and that Jesus is praying that it may continue to believe. Such an attitude would contradict many of the other statements of the Johannine Jesus about the world (xvi 33, xvii 9). See COMMENT. On the whole question consult H. Riesenfeld, "Zu den johanneischen *hina*-Sätzen," ST 19 (1965), 213–20.

that you sent me. This theme was involved in the prayer of xi 42.

22. *I have even given . . . you have given me.* According to the best textual witnesses, both these verbs are in the perfect tense, not the aorist. Jesus continues to possess the glory given him by the Father, and the disciples

continue to possess the glory given them by Jesus. When did Jesus give them this glory? The prayer in vs. 1, "Glorify your Son that the Son may glorify you," suggests that glory will be given after the exaltation of Jesus, since the Son glorifies the Father through the disciples. Consequently the tenses in 22 seem to be from the standpoint of the time in which the Johannine writer is living. Rom viii 30 makes the glorification of the Christian consequent upon his justification. We note that the theme of glory occurs in all three units of John xvii (1 and 5, 10, 22).

just as we are one. The comparison for unity in the last line of 11 was "just as we"; in 21b it was "just as you, Father, in me and I in you." The present line almost combines the two previous comparisons.

23. *that they may be brought to completion as one.* The last phrase is literally "into one." The verb is the passive of *teleioun*, a verb that was used actively in 4 (see NOTE there) when Jesus spoke of bringing to completion the work given him by the Father to do. The passive is particularly common in I John (ii 5, iv 12, 17, 18) where it is mentioned that God's love is brought to completion or perfection; note that the theme of love appears in the last line of the present verse. Apparently in Johannine thought the believers are to be brought to completion as one *in this life,* for this completion is to have an effect on the world. By way of comparison, we note that Paul confesses that he is not yet made perfect or complete, but he presses on because Christ Jesus has taken possession of him (Philip iii 12).

Thus the world. We may raise the same question about the third *hina* clause in 22–23 that we raised about the third *hina* clause in 21 (see NOTE there). Does it explain why Jesus gives glory to the believers or does it modify the idea in the second *hina* clause, so that it is the complete unity of the believers that challenges the world to knowledge? The latter appears to be the dominant idea, despite the objections of Earwaker. There is a chain of ideas: the gift of glory leads to the unity of the believers, and this in turn challenges the world to recognize Jesus as the emissary of the Father from whom all glory comes.

may come to know. An aorist tense; see NOTE on "may believe" in 21. During Jesus' ministry the world did not know Jesus (i 10), but through the ministry of the disciples the world will get another chance, for their message will again provoke the world to self-judgment.

that you sent me. The chain of ideas in this verse has an interesting parallel in Zech ii 12–13(8–9): The avenging angelic messenger has been sent *by the glory* of God *to the* wicked *nations* as a lesson for Israel so that *they may know* that the Lord of Hosts *has sent him.*

that you loved them. Bernard, II, 579, interprets this to mean that the world will understand that God has loved *it,* but more likely it means that the world will understand that God has loved the Christian believers. The love of God for the world is mentioned only as a preparation for the incarnation of the Son in iii 16; contrast xv 19. Codex Bezae and some Latin witnesses read, "*I* love them," and Barrett, p. 429, thinks that this was possibly the original reading. A reading that would have Jesus loving the disciples as the Father has loved him would be thoroughly Johannine (see 26 below; also xv 9). Yet one of the themes of this prayer is the involvement of the Father in Christian life, and "you loved them" is in harmony with this. This verse states that the unity of the believers will prove to the world that God has loved them.

Part of that unity is the love the believers have for each other, and xiii 35 gives that a probative force: "By this will all identify you as my disciples— by the love you have for one another."

even as you loved me. The standard of comparison is breathtaking but logical; since the Christians are God's children and endowed with the life that Jesus has from the Father (vi 57), God loves these children as He loves His Son. There is only one love of God; cf. Spicq, p. 210.

24. *Father.* The prayer now draws to a conclusion; and to signal this, several inclusions have been inserted, echoing features of the opening in 1–5. The address "Father" appears in 1; and the present verse rephrases the request for glorification made in 1.

they are your gift to me. Literally "that which you have given me," or, as in many later Greek witnesses, "those whom you have given me." For the use of a neuter instead of a masculine see NOTE on "all that" in 2. This noun clause is in a *pendens* construction, anticipating the pronoun "them" in the third line of the verse. Since such a construction is designed to give emphasis, we have turned the subordinate clause into a main clause.

I am. Some would translate the form *eimi* as representing another verb: "I am going"; see NOTE on vii 34.

I wish. No longer does Jesus say "I pray"; now he majestically expresses his will. (Compare Mark xiv 36: "Not what I wish but what you wish.") In Johannine theology this "I wish" is not presumptive, for Jesus' will is really that of the Father (iv 34, v 30, vi 38). In v 21 we heard: "The Son grants life to those whom he wishes"; there, as here, the will of the Son is expressed in terms of gifts for men.

to be with me. Jesus has made it clear that those who do not believe cannot come with him to where he is going (vii 34, viii 21); nor can the disciples who are with him at the Last Supper come with him. But eventually those who serve and follow Jesus will be with him (xii 26, xiv 3). A similar hope is found in II Tim ii 11: "If we have died with him, we shall also live with him," while Rom viii 17 speaks of the Christian's being glorified with Christ. We may have here the Johannine equivalent of the words that Jesus speaks in Luke's account of the Last Supper: "You shall eat and drink at my table in my kingdom" (Luke xxii 30).

see my glory. This usage of *theōrein* is difficult for those who think that the verb involves sight that is accompanied by only limited understanding; see vol. 29, p. 502.

which you have given me. Once more the perfect, not the aorist, is probably the correct reading, although Codex Vaticanus has the aorist.

because you loved me. Aorist tense. The love of the Father for the Son from before creation is the basis of the glory which the Son possessed before creation (xvii 5). This love is also the basis of the earthly mission of Jesus (iii 35).

before the creation of the world. Literally "foundation" or "beginning." This is not LXX phrasing, although it occurs in the apocryphal *Assumption of Moses* (i 13–14), a work of the early 1st century A.D. Evidently it was well known in the NT period, for it occurs nine times in the NT; see especially Eph i 4; I Pet i 20.

25. *O Father most just.* Literally "O just Father"; this is parallel to "O Father most holy" in 11. Rather romantically Hoskyns, p. 495, sees a

progression in the titles "Father," "Father most holy," "Father most just," reflecting the movement of the prayer from the death of Christ to the glorification of the Church. So also Schwank, "Damit," p. 544, who thinks of the appellation "just" as an advance over the appellation "holy" and cites I Cor vi 11: "You were washed, you were *sanctified,* you were *justified*." This is very doubtful; in our opinion "holy" and "just" are not significant variants, but "just" was thought more appropriate in 25 because the rest of the verse describes a judgment (see COMMENT). That God is just or righteous is a common OT belief (Jer xii 1; Pss cxvi 5, cxix 137), echoed in the NT (Rom iii 26; Rev xvi 5). In the NT the justice of God is thought to have both positive effects (He will save the innocent) and negative effects (He will punish the wicked). The former emphasis appears in I John i 9: "But if we acknowledge our sins, *He is just* and can be trusted to forgive our sins and cleanse us from all that is not right"; also ii 1–2 which describes Jesus as just when he intercedes before the Father for our sins.

while the world . . . these men. Literally "and the world . . . and these men"—an awkward coordination of the two clauses. The writer is describing the two groups that stand before the justice of the Father, namely, the world that did not know and the men who have come to know.

(though I knew you). The clause is parenthetical, interrupting the *kai . . . kai* coordination of the second and fourth lines. It explains in what sense the world has not known God: it has not known Jesus who alone knows God (i 10, x 14–15, xiv 7, xvi 3). A close parallel is viii 55: "You do not know Him. But I do know Him"; there the perfect tense of *eidenai (oida)* has a present value. All three uses of "know" in the present verse are aorist.

these men came to know. In I John ii 14(13) the writer addresses the Christians as children "for you have known the Father."

26. *I made known.* The verb *gnōrizein* is related to *ginōskein,* "to know," used three times in the previous verse. Men came to know Jesus because Jesus made it possible for them to know. This line is little more than a rephrasing of 6a.

will continue to make it known. Revelation has taken place during the ministry and will take place after the ministry; the same thing was true of Jesus' glorifying his Father (1, 4).

the love you had for me. Literally "the love (with) which you loved me"; a similar construction is found in Eph ii 4. The tautology may be a Semitism. The Father loved the Son before creation (24); this love now becomes a creative force making possible God's indwelling in men.

love . . . may be in them. In Greek the copula is not expressed either in this line or in the next. The closeness of the love of God to the Christian is proclaimed in Rom viii 39: nothing "will be able to separate us from the love of God in Christ Jesus our Lord."

COMMENT

In this third unit in the prayer of xvii Jesus turns his attention directly to the future, foreseeing the success of the mission of the disciples mentioned in 18. The prayer for the disciples in the second unit (9–19) also had in mind future Christians, since the disciples are symbols of what believers should be; but now the future orientation is more direct, perhaps because unity is to be the main theme. Not only does Jesus foresee a community on earth confessing his name (21–23); he also yearns for the eschatological deliverance of that community so that its members will be with him in heaven (24–26).

Verses 20–23: The Oneness of Those Who Believe in Jesus

Two features are important in the description of the future Christians in vs. 20. First, they believe in Jesus. While this belief involves personal commitment and love, in Johannine thought belief is more than adherence to Jesus, for it entails an appreciation of who Jesus is. Only the man who believes that Jesus bears the divine name, only the man who confesses that Jesus is the Christ, only the man who confesses that Jesus is the Son of God (xx 31)—only this man fulfills the Johannine requirement of believing in Jesus. Käsemann, p. 25, has correctly emphasized that for John Christians must adhere to at least one christological dogma, namely, the relationship of the Son to the Father; see R. E. Brown, Interp 21 (1967), 397–98. This agrees with I John iv 2–3 where a christological criterion is offered for distinguishing between those who have the spirit of God and those who have the spirit of the antichrist.

Second, Christians have come to faith through the word of Jesus' disciples. Lucan theology emphasizes the chain of tradition from the disciples to the believer much more than does Johannine theology; indeed, the concept of the Paraclete (see App. V), who is given directly to each believer, militates against overdependence on human tradition. Yet, even in Johannine thought, it is taken for granted that the disciples who were with Jesus were commissioned to preach to men and that faith came through hearing them. If the Paraclete bears witness to Jesus, he has done this through the disciples and not in a purely spiritual way (xv 26–27). See the role given to the Beloved Disciple in xix 35.

As for the constituency of the group of those who will come to believe in Jesus through the word of the disciples, we may recall x 16 and xi 52 where the call is extended to Gentiles ("other sheep . . . that do not belong to this fold"; "the dispersed children of God"), as well as to Jews. For John there is a divine selection, but this is not on an ethnic basis. Jesus has come to call those scattered throughout the world whom his Father has given him, those whose deeds are done in God (iii 21). The "word" of Jesus preached by the disciples is a dynamic force that is heard by those who are the sheep of Jesus' flock (x 3). To those who hear it this word is spirit and life (vi 63), but for those who refuse to listen the word is a judge (xii 48).

In the last line of 11 Jesus asked his Father that his disciples might be one; now in 21–23 he prays that those who come to believe in him through the word of the disciples may also be one. In each instance the model offered for this oneness is the unity of the Father and the Son. What does this oneness consist in?

John xvii 21–23 has been used frequently in ecumenical discussions with the presumption that it refers to *church* unity. For Roman Catholics, in particular, "That they all may be one" is *the* ecumenical slogan. However, T. E. Pollard, *art. cit.*, has used xvii 21 to argue against church union. Since the unity of the believers is modeled on the unity of the Father and Son, this unity should allow for diversity, for the Father and the Son remain distinct persons despite their unity. Accordingly, Pollard contends, the unity among Christians should recognize and preserve a distinction of denominational identity. His argument has been answered by E. L. Wenger who maintains that Pollard does not do justice to the description of the unity desired by the Johannine Jesus, especially to the ideas that this unity is to offer the world an opportunity to believe and to come to know that Jesus was sent by the Father (21, 23) and that this unity brings the Christians to completion (23). In Wenger's view no mere intercommunion of denominations corresponds to these features; only organic church unity does that. While this discussion of the ecumenical implications of xvii 21–23 certainly is important, let us be clear that such problems were scarcely in the author's mind. The Johannine outlook is not overly ecumenical; II John 10, for example, forbids the Christian to say welcome to anyone whose doctrine is not orthodox!

These verses in John have also been used to bolster theories of how the Church should be organized. B. Häring, *This Time of Salvation* (New York: Herder & Herder, 1966), pp. 12 ff., calls upon John xvii as a model for the post-Vatican II Roman Catholic Church, especially in the question of the collegiality of the bishops. This is but one example of various approaches to John xvii that consciously or unconsciously interpret the thought in light of the Pauline doctrine of the body with its different members.

Other scholars have maintained that there is no real evidence that ch. xvii envisages church unity and that in the verses we are discussing there is nothing about organization or community. Randall, pp. 12–16, 40–41, cites many opinions. Is the unity a question of united purpose expressing itself in a common Christian mission and message (Strachan)? Is it a question of Christians harmoniously working together without dissidence (Schlatter)? Is the union of Christians with each other and with Christ patterned on the union that exists between persons, especially between husband and wife (Strathmann)? Is unity achieved through the unique character of God's image in the consciousness of every believer (Holtzmann)? Is it a mystical union (B. Weiss, Bernard)? Is it a unity founded upon the unity of each Christian with the Father and the Son (Behler)? Is this unity to be related to the eucharistic mystery (A. Hamman)? Is it a unity that manifests itself in the power to work miracles (W. Bauer; cf. xiv 11–12)? Is it a unity under the "word" that founded the community—

a unity that has nothing to do with personal feeling or common purpose and is not simply brotherly harmony, nor organization, nor dogma, even though these can bear witness to unity (Bultmann)? Sooner or later most authors say that it is a union of love. It is that; but Käsemann, p. 59, has a point when he says: "We usually bypass the question at this point with edifying language by reducing unity to what we call love."

Instead of taking up these theories one by one, let us point out features that seem clear in John's statements about unity. Any approach that places the essence of unity in the solidarity of human endeavor is not really faithful to John's insistence that unity has its origins in divine action. The very fact that Jesus prays to the Father for this unity indicates that the key to it lies within God's power. In 22 Jesus implies that the oneness of the believers flows from his giving to the believers the glory that the Father has given to him, and so unity comes down from the Father and the Son to the believers. None of this need imply passivity on the part of the believers in the question of unity, but their action is not the primary source of unity.

The Johannine statements about unity imply both a horizontal and a vertical dimension. The unity involves the relation of the believers to the Father and the Son (vertical) and the relation of the believers among themselves (horizontal). The latter dimension is found in all the statements stressing love of one another that we have heard in the Last Discourse (xiii 34–35, xv 12, 17); see also the theme of fellowship with one another in I John i 7. Thus unity for John is not reducible to a mystical relationship with God. On the other hand, the vertical dimension, apparent in the frequent statements about immanence in the Last Discourse (especially vs. 21: "that they also may be [one] in us"; vs. 23: "I in them and you in me"), means that unity is not simply human fellowship or the harmonious interaction of Christians. (We should note that in introducing the Father as well as the Son into the unity, John goes beyond the unity envisaged in the Pauline imagery of the body of Christ.)

Some type of vital, organic unity seems to be demanded by the fact that the relationship of Father and Son is held up as the model of unity. The Father-Son relationship involves more than moral union; the two are related because the Father gives life to the Son (vi 57). Similarly the Christians are one with one another and with the Father and the Son because they have received of this life.

The fact that the unity has to be visible enough to challenge the world to believe in Jesus (21, 23) seems to militate against a purely spiritual union. If we interpret xvii 21–23 in the light of x 16 with its stress on one sheep herd, one shepherd, then it becomes plausible that unity involves community, even though the latter idea is not explicit in xvii. Certainly in the *mashal* of the vine and the branches, which has the same Last Discourse context as the prayer of xvii, the notion of unity with Jesus involves community (xv 5–6). The *koinōnia* or "communion" of I

John i 3, 6, 7 may be an expression of the idea of oneness found in the Gospel.

The impression that John is presupposing a Christian community is now greatly strengthened by the evidence of the Dead Sea Scrolls. The Johannine statements have hitherto sounded somewhat strange with their emphasis on being "one" (neuter *hen*) especially 23b: ". . . that they may be brought to completion as [into] one." In the search for the background of the idea some have turned to Pythagoras and the Stoics for whom "the one" (*hen*) was an important philosophical and religious concept. The ideal of union with "the one" also played a role in Gnosticism. But now we have a better parallel in the religious vocabulary of Qumran; cf. F. M. Cross, *The Ancient Library of Qumran* (New York: Doubleday Anchor ed., 1961), p. 209. The sectarians spoke of themselves as the *yaḥad* or "unity"; the term occurs some seventy times in 1QS alone. There have been a number of articles dedicated to analyzing the precise meaning of the term: S. Talmon, VT 3 (1953), 133–40; A. Neher, in *Les manuscrits de la Mer Morte, colloque de Strasbourg* (Paris: Presses Universitaires, 1957), pp. 44–60; J. C. de Moor, VT 7 (1957), 350–55; J. Maier, ZAW 72 (1960), 148–66; E. Koffmahn, *Biblica* 42 (1961), 433–42; B. W. Dombrowski, HTR 59 (1966), 293–307—summary in Randall, pp. 188–206. It seems clear that the Qumran usage of *yaḥad* does not stem directly from the OT, although such a usage may have become common in post-testamental Judaism, as we see from the interesting examples that Neher has discovered in the early sections of the Talmud. Maier stresses that *yaḥad* at Qumran does not center on organizational unity; rather the term is a *nomen actionis* with ritual and covenantal overtones. Koffmahn sees the feasibility of interpreting the *yaḥad* as a moral person. The root meaning of the word gives it the possible connotations both of "together" and "alone."

It is difficult to combine all these observations. From the Qumran documents we get the impression that the *yaḥad* is a communion of men living the same way of life, united by their common acceptance and observance of a particular interpretation of the Law. The organization of the community flows from the union of the members, not vice versa. Their union has an eschatological dimension: they have already a certain communion with the angels, but they anticipate the day when God will gather them to Himself. They are alone, bound by love to one another and united in their opposition to a hostile world. It is not impossible that the Johannine *hen*, "one," literally translates the concept of *yaḥad*. Cross points out several Qumran expressions that resemble the language of John, for example, *lhywt lyḥd*, "to be a unity" (1QS v 2; compare John's "that they may *be one*"); *bh'spm lyḥd*, "on their being gathered into the unity" (1QS v 7; compare John xi 52: "to *gather together into one* the dispersed children of God"). In any case the Johannine picture of Christian unity, with its eschatological and vertical elements and its opposition to the world, has much in common with the Qumran *yaḥad*.

That the Johannine notion involves community is suggested also when we probe for the situation in the life of early Christianity that may have provoked the stress on unity in xvii 21–23. Käsemann, pp. 56–57, points out that the situation underlying John xvii resembles what we find in Ephesians (this is significant if the epistle was really addressed to Ephesus, the site usually favored for the composition of the Fourth Gospel) and in the Pastorals (the two letters to Timothy envisage him as the apostolic delegate to Ephesus; *if* these letters are post-Pauline, their date of composition may not be far distant from that of the Fourth Gospel). We may add to the comparison the situation underlying I John. There is a stress on unity in Ephesians (iv 3–6) and on sound doctrine in the Pastorals (I Tim i 10, vi 3; II Tim i 13, iv 3) and in I John (ii 22–24, iv 2–3, 15, v 10). The visible Church is the pillar and bulwark of truth (I Tim iii 15), and those who teach different doctrines are castigated (I Tim i 3–7, 18–20, vi 3–5; II Tim iv 3–5; I John ii 19). In I Tim i 3 and I John iv 6 the importance of the authoritative teacher is underlined. Only some of these elements come to the fore in John. The authoritative teacher for John is Jesus, who acts through the Paraclete, and there is little stress on human teachers. (Yet if John xxi 15–17 is admitted as a witness to Johannine thought, Jesus, the one shepherd, may have been thought to have had human representatives.) But there is a doctrinal stress in John not unlike the stress in the other NT works we have cited, for only those who confess Jesus as the Son of God are eligible to be part of the unity of the believers. And if Johannine unity is opposed to the world that surrounds the Christians, part of that world consists of dissident Christians who have been cast off (xv 6; cf. I John ii 19). An ideal of unity that evolved against such a background would almost of necessity be an ideal of community.

Before we conclude our treatment of unity in 21–23, we should briefly discuss the desired effect that this unity is to have on the world. We have referred in the NOTES on 21 and 23 to the theory of those who understand in a very optimistic manner the two clauses: "Thus the world may believe that you sent me" and "Thus the world may come to know that you sent me." But we contend that these statements do not mean that the world will accept Jesus; rather the Christian believers will offer to the world the same type of challenge that Jesus offered—a challenge to recognize God in Jesus (cf. M. Bouttier, RHPR 44 [1964], 179–90). Those whom God has given to Jesus will come to believe and know; for the rest of men, that is, those who constitute the world, this challenge will be the occasion of self-condemnation, for they will turn away. How does Christian *unity* present such a challenge? Jesus presented a challenge because he claimed to be one with the Father; now the Christians are part of this unity ("that they may be [one] in us") and so present the same challenge. Jesus presented a challenge because he claimed to be the revelation of God's glory; now Jesus has given this glory to the Christians (22) and so the challenge comes through them. (From the viewpoint of a later and more precise theology, one might like to have a sharper differentiation than John provides between God's incarnation in Jesus and God's indwelling in the Christian—in other words between natural Sonship and general Christian sonship. That such a distinction was not strange to Johannine thought *may* be indicated by John's custom of referring to Jesus as the *huios* or "Son" of God, while the Christians are designated as *tekna* or "children"; but no sharp differentiation is apparent in the verses we are considering.)

Verses 24–26: Jesus' Wish That the Believers Be with Him

If the unity of the Christians is to challenge the world and bring it to the moment of judgment, we find the outcome of the judgment implicitly described in 24–26. In 25 we see two groups of men placed before the "Father most just": those who constitute a world that did not know Jesus and hence did not know God (NOTE on 25), and those who come to know Jesus as the representative of God. The fate of the world is not mentioned, but we are told that the fate of the Christian is to be with Jesus where he is (namely, with the Father) and to see his eternal glory (24). We have heard that the disciples saw the glory of Jesus during the ministry (ii 11; cf. i 14) and that a fuller manifestation of his glory was to be realized in the post-resurrectional period (xvii 10, 22). But evidently there is a final manifestation of Jesus' glory that awaits the Christian when he joins his master in heaven. The thought is not unlike I John iii 2: "We are God's children right now; what we shall be has not yet been revealed. We know that at this revelation we shall be like Him, for we shall see Him as He is." (I John, however, seems to be speaking of seeing God, while John is concerned with seeing the glory that God has given to Jesus.) Rom viii 18 distinguishes between the present time with its suffering and "the glory that is to be revealed to us." II Cor iii 18 speaks of the present time when, "Beholding the glory of the Lord, we are being changed into his likeness from one degree of glory to another."

It is the final wish of Jesus that his followers be with him. Since the verb *thelein* in 24 means both "to wish" and "to will," we may speak of the Last Will of Jesus, provided that we recognize that it is not the will of a dead man but the continuing will of the living Jesus who is with the Father. Jesus has recognized that his followers cannot be taken out of the world without first struggling with the Evil One (15), but it is his will that after this struggle they will ultimately be delivered from the world that is below and brought to heaven which is now their home (xiv 2–3) since they have been begotten from above (iii 3). Käsemann, p. 72, points out that in John's description of the destiny of the believer some of the old motifs of Jewish apocalyptic have been spiritualized. The prophets spoke of the gathering of the dispersed children of Israel to Jerusalem to share the blessings of the Lord and of His anointed; but in John those who are foreordained to be God's children are gathered together to be with God's Son in the Father's presence. In Qumran apocalyptic and in the NT Book of Revelation it is thought that God will intervene in battle to deliver His community from their evil opponents in the world, but in John the community is taken out of the evil world to be with Jesus. The goal of world history is not a new heaven and a new earth (Rev xxi 1) but the gathering of souls into their heavenly home. The Son of Man is not pictured as coming on the clouds of heaven to help his followers, but his followers are drawn up to him in heaven (John xii 32). Therefore Käsemann sees Johannine thought as markedly different from that of most of the NT, and he characterizes it as Gnostic in orientation since it holds up an ideal of withdrawal from the world. While many of Käsemann's insights are valid, he overemphasizes the isolation and peculiarity of Johannine thought. Paul, for instance, expresses a desire to leave the world and be with Jesus (II Cor v 8: "We would rather be away from the body and at home with the Lord"; Philip i 23: "My desire is to depart and be with Christ, for that is far better"); and, like the theme of distrust for the world, this may have been a common Christian view.

To what extent the hope of joining Jesus in heaven excluded apocalyptic expectations is debatable. Apocalyptic is found in Revelation, a work of the Johannine school, and in the Gospel itself (vol. 29, p. cxviii). Undoubtedly the Gospel stresses realized eschatology, but it does not preclude future eschatology. For instance, xvii 24 does not explain how the Christians will join Jesus in heaven. Will the Son of Man come down to call them forth from the tomb (v 28–29)? Perhaps the original understanding of xvii 24 involved such an apocalyptic scene; and then when the expectations of futuristic eschatology became less vivid, the wish of Jesus was thought to be fulfilled in the death of the Christian. (On pp. 625–27 above we suggested exactly this development of meaning in xiv 2–3.) This would harmonize with xi 25 which promises eternal life after physical death. Since for John the Christian children of God are closely conformed to Jesus the Son of God, the idea that Jesus entered his glory through death may have led to the realization that after death the Christian would see Jesus in his glory. Of course, the idea that death leads to union with Jesus need not have excluded the expectation of an ultimate deliverance of the whole Christian community in the parousia—compare the Pauline citations given above with Paul's apocalyptic expectations in I Thess iv 13–17; I Cor xv 51–57. Thus, while Johannine thought about the future has its own modality (a modality that later Gnosticism would find sympathetic in its theology of deliverance from the world), we must not allow the dialectic method to make us attribute to John attitudes more developed than the evidence warrants.

The last verse of xvii explains why the believers should ultimately be united to Jesus, namely, because they have been intimately united to Jesus during their stay on earth. Jesus has already made God's name known to them and will continue to make it known. When we remember that supposedly Jesus is speaking at the Last Supper and referring to future believers who will be converted by his disciples, the statement "To them I made known your name" is a bit odd. Presumably this past revelation is the work of the ministry that his disciples will communicate to the believers. The second statement, "I will continue to make it known," may refer to the work of the Paraclete (xiv 26, xvi 13). This continued deepening of the understanding of the revelation of God in Jesus has as its purpose and goal the indwelling of Jesus in the Christian (26d). Jesus can dwell only in those who understand and appreciate his revelation. If the last two lines of 26 are compared, it will be noted that the presence of Jesus in the Christian stands in parallelism with the presence of the love of God in the Christian. This means that Jesus' presence is dynamic, expressive of love and expressed in love. The medieval scholar Rupert of Deutz (PL 169:764; see Schwank, "Damit," p. 541) identifies the indwelling love described in 26c ("the love you had for me") as the Holy Spirit—clearly a reflection of later Trinitarian theology where the Spirit is the love between the Father and the Son. Yet he may not be far wrong in seeing that only through the Spirit can the promises of Jesus in 26 be fulfilled. The implication in John may not be unlike what is specifically said by Paul (Rom v 5): "God's love has been poured into our hearts through the Holy Spirit which has been given to us."

It is fitting that this beautiful prayer, which is the majestic conclusion of the Last Discourse, is itself terminated on the note of the indwelling of Jesus in the believers—a theme bolstered by Jesus' claim to have given glory to the believers (22) and to have made known to them God's name. We have contended that the motif of the new covenant runs through the Johannine account of the Last Supper even though there is no explicit mention of the eucharistic body and blood of Christ. We saw (p. 614 above) that the commandment of love, mentioned in the first lines of the Last Discourse (xiii 34), is "new" because it is the essential stipulation of the new covenant. So also the closing note of indwelling is an echo of covenant theology. After the Sinai covenant the glory of God that dwelt on the mountain (Exod xxiv 16) came to dwell in the Tabernacle in the midst of Israel (xl 34). In Johannine thought Jesus during his lifetime was the tabernacle of God embodying divine glory (John i 14), and now in a covenantal setting he promises to give to his followers the glory that God gave to him. In the language of Deuteronomy the Tabernacle (or the site that housed the Ark) was the place where the God of the covenant had set His name. So now the name of God given to Jesus has been entrusted to his followers. The Lord God who spoke on Sinai assured His people that He was in their midst (Exod xxix 45; Num xi 20; Deut vii 21, xxiii 14). Jesus, who will be acclaimed by his followers as Lord and God (xx 28), in the last words that he speaks to them during his mortal life prays that after death he *may be in them.*

BIBLIOGRAPHY
(xvii)

See the general bibliography on the Last Discourse at the end of §48.

Agourides, S., "The 'High Priestly Prayer' of Jesus," StEv, IV, 137–45.

Becker, J., "Aufbau, Schichtung und theologiegeschichtliche Stellung des Gebetes in Johannes 17," ZNW 60 (1969), 56–83.

Bonsirven, J., "Pour une intelligence plus profonde de Saint Jean," RSR 39 (1951), 176–96. (A history of the exegesis of xvii 11, 12, 26.)

Bornkamm, G., "Zur Interpretation des Johannes-Evangeliums," EvTh 28 (1968), 8–25. Reprinted in *Geschichte und Glaube I* (Gesammelte Aufsätze III; Munich: Kaiser, 1968), pp. 104–21. A critique of Käsemann's work on John xvii cited below.

Braun, F.-M., "La Seigneurie du Christ dans le monde selon saint Jean," RThom 67 (1967), 357–86, especially 359–66 on xvii 1–3.

D'Aragon, J.-L., "La notion johannique de l'unité," ScEccl 11 (1959), 111–19.

George, A., "L'heure de Jean xvii," RB 61 (1954), 392–97.

Giblet, J., " 'Sanctifie-les dans la vérité' (Jean 17, 1–26)," BVC 19 (1957), 58–73.

Huby, J., "Un double problème de critique textuelle et d'interprétation: Saint Jean xvii 11–12," RSR 27 (1937), 408–21.

Käsemann, E., *The Testament of Jesus According to John 17* (Philadelphia: Fortress, 1968).

Laurentin, A., *"We'attah—Kai nyn.* Formule charactéristique des textes juridiques et liturgiques (à propos de Jean 17, 5)," Biblica 45 (1964), 168–97, 413–32.

Morrison, C. D., "Mission and Ethic: An Interpretation of John 17," Interp 19 (1965), 259–73.

Poelman, R., "The Sacerdotal Prayer: John xvii," *Lumen Vitae* 20 (1965), 43–66.

Pollard, T. E., " 'That They All May Be One' (John xvii 21)—and the Unity of the Church," ET 70 (1958–59), 149–50.

Randall, J. F., *The Theme of Unity in John xvii 20–23* (Louvain University, 1962). All our references are to this dissertation, but there is also a summary article in ETL 41 (1965), 373–94.

Schwank, B., " 'Vater, verherrliche deinen Sohn' (17, 1–5)," SeinSend 28 (1963), 436–49.

———— " 'Für sie heilige ich mich, die du mir gegeben hast' (17, 6–19)," SeinSend 28 (1963), 484–97.

———— " 'Damit alle eins seien' (17, 20–26)," SeinSend 28 (1963), 531–46.

Spicq, C., *Agapè* (Paris: Gabalda, 1959), III, 204–18. Citations are from the French, but there is an abbreviated Eng. form in *Agape in the New Testament* (St. Louis: Herder, 1966), III, 74–85.

Thüsing, W., *Herrlichkeit und Einheit. Eine Auslegung des Hohepriesterlichen Gebetes Jesu (Joh. 17)* (Düsseldorf: Patmos, 1962).

Vanhoye, A., "L'oeuvre du Christ, don du Père (Jn 5, 36 et 17, 4)," RSR 48 (1960), 377–419.

Wenger, E. L., " 'That They All May Be One,' " ET 70 (1958–59), 333.

THE BOOK OF GLORY

Part Two: The Passion Narrative

OUTLINE

Part Two: The Passion Narrative
(chs. XVIII–XIX)

A.   xviii 1–27   *Division 1:* The Arrest and Interrogation of Jesus. (§§61–62)

        (1–11)   *Unit 1:* The arrest of Jesus. (§61)
            1–3: Setting of the scene in the garden.
            4–8: Jesus meets the arresting party and shows his power.
            (9): Parenthetical explanatory addition.
            10–11: Peter reacts to the arrest by striking at the servant.

        (12–13)   Change of scene, closing the first unit and opening the second, as Jesus is taken from the garden to Annas.

        (14–27)   *Unit 2:* The interrogation of Jesus. (§62)
            (14): Parenthetical explanatory addition.
            15–18: Introduction of Peter into high priest's palace; first denial.
            19–23: Annas interrogates Jesus who protests his innocence.
            (24): Insertion to prepare for Pilate trial: Jesus sent to Caiaphas.
            25–27: Peter's second and third denials.

B.   xviii 28 – xix 16a   *Division 2:* The Trial of Jesus before Pilate. (§§63–64)

      xviii (28–32)   *Episode 1:* The Jewish authorities ask Pilate to condemn Jesus. (§63)
        (33–38a)   *Episode 2:* Pilate questions Jesus about kingship.
        (38b–40)   *Episode 3:* Pilate seeks to release Jesus; "the Jews" prefer Barabbas.
      xix (1–3)   *Episode 4* (intermediary): The Roman soldiers scourge and mock Jesus. (§64)
        (4–8)   *Episode 5:* Pilate presents Jesus to his people; "the Jews" shout for crucifixion.
        (9–11)   *Episode 6:* Pilate talks with Jesus about power.
        (12–16a)   *Episode 7:* Pilate yields to the Jewish demand for Jesus' crucifixion.

C.   xix 16b–42 *Division 3:* THE EXECUTION OF JESUS ON THE CROSS AND
                              HIS BURIAL. (§§65–66)

  (16b–18) *Introduction:* The way of the cross and the cruci-
             fixion. (§65)
  (19–22)   *Episode 1:* Pilate and the royal inscription.
  (23–24)   *Episode 2:* The executioners divide Jesus' clothes;
             the seamless tunic.
  (25–27)   *Episode 3:* Jesus gives his mother to the Beloved
             Disciple.
  (28–30)   *Episode 4:* Jesus' cry of thirst; the executioners offer
             him wine; he hands over the spirit.
  (31–37)   *Episode 5:* Pilate and the breaking of Jesus' legs;
             flow of blood and water. (§66)
  (38–42)   *Conclusion:* The burial of Jesus by Joseph and
             Nicodemus.

60. THE PASSION NARRATIVE:
GENERAL REMARKS

In his *The Gospel of the Hellenists* (New York: Holt, 1933), pp. 226–27, B. W. Bacon puts under three headings the peculiarities of the Johannine Passion Narrative. First, there is an apologetic tendency: "the Jews" emerge as the sole villains of the plot. The real charges against Jesus are exclusively religious, and Pilate becomes a sympathetic figure, earnestly interested in Jesus' welfare. Second, there is a precise doctrinal orientation: Jesus goes through the passion not as a victim, but as a sovereign and superhuman Being who at any moment could bring the process to a halt. Third, there is a strong dramatic element that Bacon traces to the addition of imaginative details. These are unhistorical improvements upon the Synoptic narratives.

In underlining the apologetic, the doctrinal, and the dramatic, Bacon has certainly caught the spirit of the Johannine Passion Narrative. If we were to evaluate Bacon's attitude toward each, however, we should have minor qualifications about the first and the second and a major qualification about the third. These general remarks will be directed to all three points. We shall begin with the relations of John's Passion to the Synoptic accounts, and then turn to an over-all evaluation of what is historical in all the Gospel accounts. Lastly, by treating the structure of the Johannine Passion Narrative, we shall bring out the element of the dramatic.

John and the Synoptics

The Passion Narrative supplies the best material for a study of the relationship of the Fourth Gospel to the Synoptic Gospels, for it is the longest narrative of the same action that the two traditions have in common. Since most scholars study this relationship in terms of reconstructed earlier traditions underlying the Gospels, the passion is again uniquely important; for it is generally agreed that the stories of the passion were the first large sections of Gospel material to be formed into consecutive narrative. For detailed tables comparing the different Gospels see Léon-Dufour, cols. 1439–54.

We may begin with the relationship of John to **Mark.** Critical scholars of diverse tendencies (Bultmann, Jeremias, and Taylor, to name a few) agree that the Marcan Passion Narrative is composite and that one of

TAYLOR'S ANALYSIS OF THE MARCAN PASSION NARRATIVE

A=Primitive Account	B=Marcan Additions
xiv 26–31: Jesus goes out to the Mount of Olives; *he predicts Peter's denial*	
	xiv 32–42: Agony in Gethsemane
43–46: Arrest of Jesus	
	47–52: Cutting off servant's ear; Jesus claims he taught daily in Temple; young man runs away naked
(53, 55–64: *Jesus before the Sanhedrin [at night]*)	
	54, 65, 66–72: Abuse of Jesus by the Sanhedrin; Peter's denials
xv 1: Jesus before the Sanhedrin in the morning	
3–5: Chief priests accuse Jesus before Pilate	xv 2: Pilate asks Jesus, "Are you 'the King of the Jews'?" 6–14: Barabbas incident
15: Pilate delivers Jesus to be crucified	
	16–20: Mockery of Jesus by Roman soldiers
21–24: Simon carries cross; arrival at Golgotha; drink of wine; crucifixion of Jesus; division of garments	25: Crucifixion of Jesus at third hour
26: Inscription: "The King of the Jews"	27: Crucifixion of two bandits
29–30: *Mockery by passers-by*	31–32: Mockery by chief priests and the two bandits
34–37: *Jesus cries out at the ninth hour; guard offers sponge of common wine;* Jesus cries out and breathes his last	33: Darkness from sixth to ninth hours 38: Tearing of the veil of the Temple
39: *Centurion's exclamation* 42–46: *Joseph asks Pilate for body; Pilate has centurion check; body given to Joseph who wraps it and buries it in a tomb*	40–41: Women look on from afar 47: Two Marys see where Jesus is buried

Mark's chief sources was an earlier consecutive account of the passion. This account seemingly began with the arrest of Jesus and continued with a presentation of Jesus before the Sanhedrin, a trial by Pilate, the condemnation of Jesus, his being led out to Golgotha, his crucifixion and death. (The predictions in viii 31, ix 31, and x 33–34, which contain pre-Marcan material, give the same picture; and the phrasing is partially independent of the Marcan Passion Narrative.) Jeremias deduces the existence of this primitive account from a comparison of Mark and John and from the information in Mark x 33–34. Bultmann deduces its existence from literary criticism of the Marcan Narrative, comparing it with the other Synoptic Passion Narratives. Taylor's deductions are based on the presence and absence of Semitisms in the different parts of the Marcan Passion. In general, Bultmann and Jeremias attribute less material to the primitive account than does Taylor, but the over-all consensus flowing from three different methods is impressive. (It should be made clear that this "primitive" account is not straight, factual reporting; already theological reflection has left its marks.) Now to this primitive account Mark added other material. Bultmann would look on this added material as legendary or doctrinal accretions. Taylor, however, points to the strong Semitic flavor of the added material: it is not consecutive, but it consists of vivid self-contained narratives and of supplementary details. Taylor thinks that Mark has added the reminiscences of Peter to the primitive account that he found in circulation in Rome. Because we shall have many occasions to refer to the two types of Marcan material, we present a summary schema of Taylor's view (*Mark*, p. 658). Taylor is not sure if the passage in parentheses (xiv 53, 55–64) belongs in A. Within the A column we italicize scenes that Bultmann, HST, pp. 268 ff., does *not* accept as primitive.

In the question of the relations between John and Mark, it is becoming more common to study the resemblance of John to one of the Marcan sources, A or B, rather than to the Marcan Passion Narrative as a whole. Since Jeremias, EWJ, p. 94, bases his reconstruction of the primitive consecutive account on a comparison of Mark and John, logically he should find many similarities between John's Passion and A. However, Buse, in a study based precisely on Taylor's theory, finds impressive similarities between John and B, on which, he suggests, John drew and which is posited to have circulated separately. S. Temple, *art. cit.*, has restudied the A and B traditions of Mark xiv, suggesting corrections to be made in Taylor's allotment of material. For example, in the account of the arrest, Temple's reconstructed B (Mark xiv 32–42, 43a, 44–46) has no Johannine parallels. We shall have to examine the similarities to Mark as we discuss each scene in John, but by way of anticipation we may state that we find that John has elements in common with both A and B. On the other hand, some of the scenes in B are missing in John: agony in Gethsemane; *protracted* abuse by Sanhedrin; crucifixion at the third hour; darkness; tearing of Temple veil; women at a distance; the two Marys seeing where

Jesus is buried. (The list would be longer if one follows Bultmann in classifying more material as non-A.) Many of the scenes in A are also missing in John: Sanhedrin night session; Simon of Cyrene; mockery by passers-by; Jesus' cry *"Eloi";* centurion's exclamation. (If one accepts the shorter A of Bultmann, only a few episodes would be found in A that do not appear in John.) Even in the scenes shared by John and either A or B there are important differences; and, of course, John has much material, some of it quite plausible, that is not found in either Marcan source. Thus, our anticipated conclusion is that the primitive tradition of the passion underlying John (Stage 1—vol. 29, p. xxxiv) was similar in some points to both the Marcan sources, A and B, but was independent of them.

The comparison of John and **Matthew** is complicated by the failure of Synoptic criticism to reach a consensus on whether Matthew drew on an independent pre-Gospel tradition for the passion or simply modified Mark. All agree that some of the scenes and details peculiar to Matthew reflect theological elaboration and popular embellishments. In general the German critics tend to think that Matthew depended on Mark and had no important primitive source, while the French and Belgians think that Matthew had a more primitive source than Mark in many instances (see Léon-Dufour, cols. 1448–53). Personally we accept Matthean dependence on Mark for most episodes, but we shall keep the other possibility in mind as we comment on John's relation to the Synoptic tradition in each episode. P. Borgen, who admits that no direct literary relationship can be posited between John and the Synoptics, suggests that in John units of Synoptic provenance have been added to a once independent Johannine tradition. He concentrates particularly on parallels to Matthew; but Buse's critique of Borgen's position is persuasive, namely, that the Johannine parallels with Matthew are not particularly decisive or clear. For instance, in the episode where Jesus is arrested, only John and Matthew have Jesus instruct the disciple to put away his sword, but both the words used to phrase the instruction and the reason given for it are quite different.

The comparison between the Passion Narratives of John and **Luke** is in some ways the most interesting. Luke seems to have used Mark as a source for some sections of the passion (about one-quarter of the Lucan account may be claimed to reproduce Mark), but for much of the passion Luke differs noticeably from Mark. Loisy, Holtzmann, Lietzmann, Dibelius, and Bultmann are among those who hesitate to attribute to Luke the use of a primitive source truly independent of Mark and the Marcan sources— these scholars tend to attribute most of the differences between Luke and Mark to imaginative Lucan editing of Mark or of an earlier form of Mark's sources. But here, much more than in the case of Matthew, we think that a solid defense can be made for the thesis that Luke drew on a truly independent, non-Marcan source, a thesis ably presented by A. M. Perry, *The Sources of Luke's Passion Narrative* (University of Chicago, 1920) and supported by B. Weiss, Spitta, Burkitt, Easton, Streeter, Taylor, Jeremias, Benoit, Winter and others. Osty, *art. cit.*, has pointed out more than forty instances where Luke and John alone have something in common in the Passion Narrative, some of the instances too precise to be accidental. Osty has suggested that a disciple of Luke or one who knew Luke's Gospel was involved in the editing of John; Boismard has identified the Johannine editor as Luke himself. (This goes far beyond our position—vol. 29, p. xxxviii—that *possibly* the final editor of John added some details to the finished Gospel from the Synoptic tradition, especially from Mark.) We think that the parallels can be explained in terms of John's dependence on an earlier tradition that in many instances was close to the special tradition used by Luke. It is not impossible that Luke knew an early form of the developing Johannine tradition (a thesis which Osty also embraces in his effort to explain the Johannisms of Luke).

Thus our general conclusion about the Passion Narrative, to be substantiated in detail by the comments on the individual sections, is the same conclusion dictated by our study of the rest of the Fourth Gospel, namely, that John does not draw to any extent on the existing Synoptic Gospels or on their sources as reconstructed by scholars. The Johannine Passion Narrative is based on an independent tradition that has similarities to the Synoptic sources. Where the various pre-Gospel sources agree, we are in the presence of a tradition that had wide acceptance at a very early stage in the history of the Christian Church and, therefore, a tradition that is very important in questions of historicity. However, the historical value of details peculiar to one or the other pre-Gospel tradition is not to be discounted quickly, although there is greater possibility that such details stem from the theological or apologetic concern of the respective tradition.

Certainly in the Johannine Passion Narrative the underlying pre-Gospel tradition has been drastically reshaped by doctrinal, apologetic, and dramatic concerns, as Bacon has insisted. For instance, John's story of Jesus on the cross consists of episodes selected for their symbolic import and scarcely a detail has been included that is not theologically oriented. The Johannine trial of Jesus before Pilate has been given a dramatic scenario and become a vehicle explaining the nature of Jesus' kingdom and the guilt of "the Jews" in Jesus' death. Yet the acceptance of the thesis of an independent, early tradition underlying John should make us cautious about assuming too quickly that the doctrine, apologetics, and drama *created* the raw material basic to the scenes involved. In our opinion, John's genius here as elsewhere consisted in reinterpreting rather than in inventing.

Historical Reconstruction of the Arrest and Trial of Jesus

While in some ways this discussion might better follow our commentary on the scenes involved, it will prevent repetition and confusion if we give an over-all view before we start the commentary. Moreover, since The Anchor Bible is directed to a mixed audience for some of whom this may be a sensitive question, we think it wise to clarify from the beginning our line of approach. One historical fact is lucidly clear: Jesus of Nazareth was sentenced by a Roman prefect to be crucified on the political charge that he claimed to be "the King of the Jews." On this Christian, Jewish, and Roman sources agree. The real problem concerns whether and to what degree the Sanhedrin or the Jewish authorities of Jerusalem played a role in bringing about the crucifixion of Jesus.

True, there is another problem raised by the NT itself as to whether responsibility for the crucifixion of Jesus is to be placed on the whole Jewish nation of his time and even on subsequent generations of Jews. Embarrassing as this second problem is to many Christians today, one must honestly recognize that it has its origins in NT generalizations about the Jews (vol. 29, pp. LXXI–LXXII) and in passages like Matt xxvii 25; John vii 19, viii 44; and I Thess ii 14–16. (While the hostility in these statements sprang from a polemic between Synagogue and Church, often the Christians hoped to arouse in Jews a guilt about the rejection of Jesus and thus to effect conversion.) This problem is not solved either by pretending that the respective NT authors did not mean what they said or by excising the offending passages (for example, as done by Dagobert Runes, *The Gospel According to Saint John . . . edited in conformity with the true ecumenical spirit of His Holiness, Pope John XXIII* [New York: Philosophical Library, 1967]). The solution lies in the acknowledgment that the books of both Testaments can serve as meaningful guides only when allowance is made for the spirit of the times in which they were written. Nevertheless, this is obviously more a theological than a historical problem.

Confining ourselves to the primary problem and the only one that offers hope of historical solution, namely, the problem of the involvement of the Jewish authorities, we may distinguish at least four views:

(1) The classical Christian position that the Jewish authorities were the prime movers in Jesus' arrest, trial, and sentencing. They plotted against him because they disbelieved his messianic claims; the Sanhedrin tried him on a charge of blasphemy and sentenced him. However, either because the Romans alone could execute criminals or because the Jewish authorities wished to pass on to the Romans the public responsibility for killing Jesus, the Sanhedrin handed him over to Pilate on a political charge and blackmailed Pilate into passing sentence. (Some would even say that Pilate only ratified the Jewish death sentence.) In this view the Romans were little more than executioners. With variations this is the interpretation of Mommsen, Schürer, Von Dobschütz, W. Bauer, Billerbeck, Dibelius, and Blinzler.

(2) A modification of the previous view calls into question the formal character of the Sanhedrin trial and suggests that no Jewish sentence on Jesus was actually passed. Although the Jewish authorities were

deeply involved, all the main legal formalities were carried out by the Romans. Today many Christian scholars adopt a form of this view.
(3) The Romans were the prime movers. They had heard of Jesus as a possible troublemaker and forced Jewish cooperation. Many Jewish scholars have suggested that only a small clique within the Sanhedrin (the adherents of the high priest or the Sadducean leaders, but not the Pharisees) were involved in the apprehension and investigation of Jesus. P. Winter thinks that the Sanhedrin reluctantly acceded to Roman pressure as a gesture of political expediency, but there was no real religious antagonism to Jesus. A. Büchler (1902) suggests that there were two Sanhedrins, one involved with religious matters, the other with civil matters (also, with variations, Lauterbach, Abrahams, Zeitlin). It is theorized that the religious Sanhedrin, the real governing body of Judaism, had nothing to do with Jesus' death, but only the political Sanhedrin which was a Roman rubber stamp.
(4) No Jewish authorities were involved in any way, not even as a tool of the Romans. All the references to them or to the Sanhedrin in the NT represent an apologetic falsification of history.
(For further details on the holders of these positions and for modifications see Blinzler, *Trial*, pp. 10–20; Léon-Dufour, cols. 1488–89.)

One may sympathize with the last mentioned thesis as a reaction to centuries of anti-Jewish persecution, often waged as a revenge for supposed Jewish responsibility for the crucifixion. Nevertheless, it has little claim to be recognized as scientifically respectable. It is a relatively modern claim, for the oldest Jewish references to the subject frankly accept Jewish involvement in Jesus' death. This is true of the *baraitha* in TalBab, *Sanhedrin*, 43a, a passage whose value and antiquity (before 220) is defended by M. Goldstein, *Jesus in the Jewish Tradition* (New York: Macmillan, 1950), pp. 22 ff. The *Testimonium Flavianum*, or the reference to Jesus in Josephus, *Ant.* XVIII.iii.3;※64, says that Jesus was indicted by the first men among the Jews. (An increasing number of scholars are willing to recognize that this reference to Jesus belongs substantially to the 1st-century text of Josephus; cf. L. H. Feldman, vol. IX in the Loeb Classical Library edition [Harvard, 1965], p. 49; Winter, "Josephus.") Neither in the Jewish apologetics against Christianity reflected in Justin's *Dialogue with Trypho*, and in Origen's *Celsus*, nor in the various versions of the bitterly anti-Christian legends of the *Toledoth Jeshu* is there evidence of an early attempt to put the sole responsibility for Jesus' death on the Romans (E. Bammel, NTS 13 [1966–67], 328).

If we turn from the Jewish evidence to that of the NT, one can trace back into the 40s the claim of Jewish involvement. It is true that the Gospels tend to magnify Jewish responsibility; but one cannot maintain that the evangelists invented the thesis that the Jewish authorities were involved, for it appears before the time of the written Gospels. H. E. Tödt, *The Son of Man in the Synoptic Tradition* (Philadelphia:

Westminster, 1965), pp. 155 ff., has plausibly argued that the predictions attributed to Jesus concerning his passion, death, and resurrection in Mark viii 31, ix 31, and x 33–34 were of pre-Marcan and, for the most part, of Palestinian origin; and these predictions suppose Jewish involvement. (G. Strecker, Interp 22 [1968], 421–42, agrees that the basic prediction is pre-Marcan, coming from the early post-Easter community.) Furthermore, the primitive pre-Marcan passion account discussed above seems to have included a presentation of Jesus to the Sanhedrin or high priest. According to many, the sermons attributed to Peter in Acts contain very early material; and these sermons (iii 14–15, iv 10, v 30; cf. xiii 27–28) also give the Jewish authorities a role in Jesus' death. In the earliest preserved Christian writing (A.D. 51) Paul speaks of "the Jews who killed the Lord Jesus" (I Thess ii 14–15). This is a polemic passage that generalizes and exaggerates; but one cannot reasonably suppose that Paul, who knew well the Palestine of the 30s, voiced a complete fabrication.

If we reject the fourth view mentioned above and suppose some involvement of the Jewish authorities, we must also recognize the weaknesses of the first view that makes the Jewish authorities almost totally responsible for the death of Jesus whom they hated for religious reasons alone. It was obviously in the interest of the Christian Church, seeking tolerance from the Roman authorities under whom it had to live, to avoid blaming the Romans for the death of Jesus. (We do not find particularly persuasive the objection that by the end of the NT period the Church had turned against Rome, as witnessed in Revelation, and would not care about Roman opinion. The Church would still not want it said that there was any justification in the claim that its Master was a political revolutionary against Rome.) The effects of this exculpating tendency on the Gospel narratives is clear as we move from the earliest to the latest. In Mark xv 6–15 Pilate attempts to have Jesus released but makes no great issue of his reluctance to sentence Jesus. In Matt xxvii 19, 24–25 Pilate's reluctance is much more noticeable; not only does his wife tell him of her dream that Jesus is an innocent man, but Pilate publicly washes his hands of the business, proclaiming, "I am innocent of this man's blood." In Luke xxiii 4, 14, and 22 Pilate solemnly states three times that he finds Jesus not guilty. He sends Jesus to Herod in an attempt to avoid passing sentence on Jesus, and even offers the Jewish leaders the compromise of having Jesus whipped rather than put to death (xxiii 16, 22). In John xviii 28 – xix 16 Pilate makes a determined effort to pardon Jesus and actually does have Jesus scourged and presented to the people in an effort to win their sympathy. Pilate stands in awe of Jesus' self-possession and seems to fear that he is dealing with someone divine (xix 7–8). The process of bettering Pilate's image continues beyond the NT period until the time of Eusebius. For instance, the *Gospel of Peter*, 2, makes Herod, not Pilate, the one who pronounces the death sentence. In the Syriac tradition (OS[sin]) the

Passion Narrative of Matthew is rewritten to make it appear that the Jews alone ill-treated and crucified Jesus. The *Didascalia Apostolorum* (v 19:4; Funk ed., p. 290) from 3rd-century Syria states that Pilate did not consent to the wicked Jewish deeds. Tertullian, *Apologeticum* XXI 24; PL 1:403, thinks of Pilate as a Christian at heart, and later legends tell of his conversion. In Coptic and Ethiopic hagiography Pilate and his wife Procla have qualified as saints whose feast is celebrated on June 25th. If this process of exculpating Pilate and the Romans can be traced from A.D. 60 on, we may well suspect that it was at work in the pre-Gospel era as well and that to some extent Mark's Gospel had already toned down Roman involvement.

If the Romans were more responsible than may seem from a first reading of the Gospels, were the Jewish authorities correspondingly less involved? According to Mark and Matthew the case of Jesus was formally tried by the Sanhedrin, witnesses were called, and a death sentence was passed. The sentence is clearer in Mark xiv 64 than in Matt xxvi 66; but both Gospels (Mark x 33; Matt xx 18) report a version of Jesus' third prediction of his death wherein it is said that the chief priests and scribes will *condemn* him to death. This latter evidence means that the idea of a Jewish death sentence was known to the pre-Marcan Palestinian community; it also rules out benevolent interpretations (Lagrange, Bickermann) of the trial scene wherein the Sanhedrin is said merely to have expressed an opinion that Jesus was deserving of death. Following the lead of Hans Lietzmann, many scholars with quite different biblical outlooks (e.g., Goguel, Bickermann, Benoit, Winter) have in varying degrees called into question both the Marcan and pre-Marcan picture of a formal trial and a sentence. One may doubt that such a scene was found in the primitive passion account (Marcan A account); and Luke and John seem to agree independently on a version of the Jewish involvement that does not include a trial with witnesses or a death sentence. Let us consider briefly these two Gospels. In John xviii the arrest of Jesus is effected by the temple police force with the aid of Roman soldiers. Brought to Annas for interrogation, Jesus demands that proof be offered that he has done anything wrong. Then he is sent to Caiaphas who takes him to Pilate. Thus there is but a meager description of the Jewish legal action against Jesus. In Luke xxii 66–70 the high priest interrogates Jesus before the Sanhedrin but no witnesses are brought forward and no sentence is delivered. It is difficult to evaluate Luke's omission of witnesses against their presence in Mark/Matthew. The Lucan lack of witnesses is cast into doubt by Luke xxii 71 where the question "Why do we still need testimony?" *may* imply that there has been testimony other than Jesus' own. On the other hand, the presence of witnesses in Mark/Matthew may reflect the influence of the OT on the story of the passion: "False witnesses have risen against me" (Ps xxvii 12). The omission of a judicial sentence in Luke is scarcely accidental, for in the Lucan form of the third prediction of the passion (Luke xviii 31–33) there is nothing reported about Jesus' being delivered to the chief priests and their condemning him to death, as in the Marcan/Matthean form. Luke's tradition about the Jewish legal action against Jesus seems to be summed up in Acts xiii 28: "Though they [those who lived in Jerusalem and their rulers] could charge him with nothing deserving death, they asked Pilate to have him killed."

From comparing the Gospels, then, we are left with an impression of possible exaggeration in Mark's tradition of a formal trial. This impression is strengthened when we consider the unlikelihood of some of the events narrated in Mark/Matthew. After recording a night session of the Sanhedrin that passes a death sentence on Jesus, Mark (xv 1) and Matthew (xxvii 1) describe a second session of the Sanhedrin in the morning! There is no clear purpose for this second session, and it probably results from the fusion of two accounts of the same scene. A question has often been raised about how the followers of Jesus could have learned the contents of the Sanhedrin session. The difficulty is not too serious, for some of those present may subsequently have commented on the proceedings. Nevertheless, the standard reply that some of the Sanhedrin were followers of Jesus (Joseph of Arimathea? Those mentioned in John xii 42?) is not of much help here, for Mark xiv 55 speaks of the whole Sanhedrin being present and xiv 64 contends that *all* of them condemned him. At most the highly placed friends of Jesus may have used their influence to find out what happened.

How do the legal details of the trial of Jesus, as narrated in the Gospels, compare with what we know of the contemporary jurisprudence? Many Jewish scholars have pointed out the total irregularity of the proceedings of the Sanhedrin if they are judged in the light of the criminal code found in the Mishnah *Sanhedrin* which dates from the century after Jesus' death but which may contain earlier material. Altogether the legal procedure described in the Gospels violates the Mishnaic code in twenty-seven details! For example, a night session of the Sanhedrin on the Feast of Passover (Synoptic chronology) or on the eve of Passover (Johannine chronology) would have been irregular both in its lateness of hour and in its proximity to the holyday. According to the Mishnah, two sessions were required for a death penalty, and neither should have been held on a feast or on the eve of a feast. We do not know, however, whether these laws of the Mishnaic period were applicable in Jesus' time. H. Danby, JTS 21 (1920), 51–76, has argued that they were not, while I. Abrahams, *Studies in Pharisaism and the Gospel* (New York: KTAV reprint, 1968), II, 129–37, has argued that they were. One reason why they might not have been applicable is that the Mishnah codifies Pharisaic tradition, and in Jesus' time the Sanhedrin was dominated by Sadducees (StB, II, 818 ff.; J. Blinzler, ZNW 52 [1961], 54–65). There is a counterargument that, in order to have Pharisee support, the Sadducees had to yield in some legal procedure to the Pharisees. Blinzler denies this and contends that Jesus was judged by an entirely Sadducean code, for every detail in the later Mishnah code that has OT backing and thus would have been accepted by the Sadducees (who accepted the written Law of the OT but not the oral law of the Pharisees) was observed in the procedure against Jesus. (Blinzler continues to defend his views against recent objections in his "Zum Prozess Jesu," *Lebendiges Zeugnis* 1 [1966], 15–17.) Winter, *Trial*, p. 71, takes another tack: he maintains that the 1st-century rules were different from the juridical rules of the later Mishnah because in the 1st century the Sanhedrin was not only a juridical body but also a legislative and executive one (yet see NOTE on xviii 31). Jeremias, EWJ, p. 78, argues that even were the Mishnaic law applicable, the trial of Jesus as described in the Gospels was still possible; for the OT itself permitted truly serious crimes to be dealt with in festival times (Jeremias thinks that Jesus was accused of the very serious crime of false prophecy). We may summarize by acknowledging that we simply do not know enough about the customs of the Sanhedrin in Jesus' time to be certain that the actions of that body described in Mark/Matthew were possible, but the intrinsic unlikelihood of there having been two sessions so close together (one of them held at night) subjects the narrative to doubt.

The question might be conclusively settled if we knew the exact competence of the Sanhedrin in capital punishment. Despite the affirmation of John xviii 31 (see NOTE) that the Sanhedrin could not execute a death sentence, some scholars have maintained that the Jewish authorities did have the power of execution, even for political crimes. If that were so, then the very fact that Jesus was handed over to the Romans would be proof that Jesus was not sentenced by the Sanhedrin; for the Sanhedrin sentence could have been carried out without Roman intervention. But, as we shall see, the evidence behind this theory is far from conclusive, and John's information may be correct, at least as regards political crimes. Leaving aside the question of capital punishment, some have thought it unlikely that there would be two trials, a Jewish and a Roman one; but experts in Roman provincial jurisprudence find nothing peculiar in two such trials (Verdam, p. 286).

Despite the fact that we cannot obtain certainty, it does seem, then, that the *prima facie* Gospel position of almost total Jewish responsibility for the death of Jesus (the first of the four views we enumerated) is exaggerated and that the second or third view may be more accurate. The role of the Jewish authorities on the night or morning before Jesus died, whether of Annas acting alone or of the Sanhedrin, is better interpreted in terms of a *preliminary investigation*. Since the results of this investigation were to be placed at the disposal of Pilate, the analogy of a grand jury action on the part of the Sanhedrin is not too inappropriate. (We shall use this term "grand jury" action, even though we are quite aware of the peril of modernizing and even Americanizing the situation. It is no more than a convenient way to describe what we envision to have been the procedure: the Sanhedrin was empowered to question someone who had been arrested, to hear the deposition of witnesses, and then to determine whether there was sufficient evidence to send the prisoner to trial before the Roman prefect.) In light of this evaluation, how do we decide between the second and third views? They differ in two aspects: the degree of Jewish involvement (were the chief priests anxious to destroy Jesus or were they unwilling tools of the Romans?) and the motive behind this involvement (religious or political?). Perhaps the human situation was too entangled for us to unravel the exact degree and motive, but let us see the evidence.

According to non-Christian tradition (Jewish and Roman) neither Pilate nor the Jewish priests of the house of Annas were admirable figures. (For a more favorable outlook on Pilate, see H. Wansbrough, *Scripture* 18 [1966], 84–93.) That there was collusion between Caiaphas and the Romans is suggested by the fact that he was able to hold office for eighteen years—the longest pontificate in the one hundred years from the accession of Herod the Great to the fall of Jerusalem! And ten of these years were under Pontius Pilate, so that the two men must have been able to work together when it served their purposes. (It is noteworthy that as soon as Pilate was removed from office, Caiaphas was deposed as well.) Pilate's term as prefect was marked by outbursts of Jewish nationalism, and he would have had every reason to be sensitive about someone who was hailed as "the King of the Jews." According to Josephus, *Ant.* XVII.x.8;⁂285, Judea was alive with guerrilla bandits (*lēstēs*); and anyone might make himself king at the head of a band of rebels and then press on to the destruction of the community. (For the long list of 1st-century revolutionaries, see E. E. Jensen, "The First Century Controversy over Jesus as a Revolutionary Figure," JBL 60 [1941], 261–62.) Jesus was a Galilean, and Pilate had already had trouble with Galileans (Luke xiii 1). Jesus' apocalyptic prophecies contained references to impending wars. Among Jesus' closest followers was a Zealot or revolutionary (Luke vi 15). His entry into Jerusalem before Passover had produced a wild reception in which many hailed him as king. As the Passover drew near, Jesus was a possible source of disturbance in the crowded city which had recently seen an insurrection and where the jails were filled with guerrilla bandits (Mark xv 7; Luke xxiii 19). Jesus' followers were bearing weapons in case of trouble (Luke xxii 38; Matt xxvi 51; John xviii 10). While all these Gospel details may not be historical, even a selection of them would make it understandable why Pilate might have decided to take no chances and to put pressure upon the Jewish authorities to arrest Jesus before the feast. This need not mean that Pilate intended to crucify Jesus, but only that he wanted to acquire information about Jesus' intentions and claims and wanted to get Jesus out of the way during an explosive period.

As for the motivation of the Jewish authorities, John xi 47–53 gives a description of a session of the Sanhedrin that may contain more history than scholars generally admit (vol. 29, p. 441). It shows the Sanhedrin fearful of the attraction that Jesus had for the masses and apprehensive lest such a movement cause the Romans to interfere against the Temple, and Jerusalem, and the whole nation. We may suppose that such political motives played a role in causing the chief priests to work with the Romans in apprehending Jesus. Christian writers often assume that all the Jewish leaders were aware that Jesus was not a potential revolutionary and so used the political charge as a smoke screen for their religious antipathy to Jesus. The situation was not so simple. Acts v 33–39 presents Gamaliel, one of the leading members of the Sanhedrin, as an honest man of sound judgment who is interested in serving God's will. Yet Gamaliel thinks it possible that the Christians are another revolutionary movement similar to that of Theudas and of Judas the Galilean. (The speech in Acts is not necessarily historical, but it may correctly reflect the doubts that many had about Jesus.) In any case, at Roman bidding and perhaps with the aid of Roman troops, the priest-leaders of the Sanhedrin may have had Jesus arrested in a solitary spot lest he cause an uprising among the crowds present in Jerusalem for the feast. Seemingly the party sent to perform the arrest was well armed and expecting trouble, but only one of his followers fought back. Jesus recognized that he was being arrested as a revolutionary and protested that there had been nothing in his actions to warrant their treating him as a guerrilla bandit (*lēstēs:* Mark xiv 48 and par.).

We cannot be certain to what extent the Gospel accounts of the Jewish interrogations of Jesus are historical, but they all consist of religious questions that have a political overtone, probing Jesus' revolutionary status. In John xviii 19 Annas asks him about his followers and his teaching, perhaps with the insinuation that he is subversive. In Mark xiv 58 and Matt xxvi 61 the question arises about Jesus' intention to destroy the Temple—certainly a revolutionary gesture. (Whether this was part of the interrogation or not, there is wide agreement that Jesus did make statements against the Temple and indeed may have recently taken violent action in the temple court. See vol. 29, pp. 116–20.) In the three Synoptic accounts Jesus is asked by the high priest whether he considers himself to be the Messiah, i.e., the Davidic king who was to liberate Israel. Once more Christian writers sometimes presuppose that the Jewish authorities understood that Jesus was speaking in a figurative way about destroying the Temple and that his Messiahship was non-political. This is most unlikely, for the NT itself betrays that it took his own followers years to come to these understandings. In handing Jesus over to the Romans as the would-be "King of the Jews," these authorities may sincerely have thought that Jesus and his movement were politically dangerous.

If the interpretation that we have presented thus far brings out the strong political motives that seemingly bound together the Roman and

Jewish authorities in arresting, interrogating, and trying Jesus, we must beware of several oversimplifications. First, the fact that some of Jesus' opponents and followers interpreted his career in political terms does not mean that Jesus was a political revolutionary. Between the lines of the Gospels we find evidence that his preaching of the kingdom disappointed many, often precisely because it did not fit into political expectations. His uneasiness about accepting the title Messiah (Mark viii 29–31) and being acclaimed as king (vol. 29, pp. 249–50, 462–63) betray that his concept of his own role was not the standard political one. We do not deny the possibility that the Gospels may have deemphasized some of the political coloring of Jesus' ministry; yet we respect the solid strain of Gospel tradition to the effect that those who interpreted Jesus primarily in political terms misunderstood him. And so, in affirming the presence of a strong political motif in the legal action against Jesus, we would emphatically dissociate our view from theories like that of S. G. F. Brandon, *The Trial of Jesus of Nazareth* (New York: Stein & Day, 1968), pp. 146–47, who infers that Jesus went up to Jerusalem to stage a Messianic *coup d'état* against the sacerdotal aristocracy, possibly as part of a concerted attack with Barabbas on the Temple and on Roman positions.

A second oversimplification that we caution against is the exclusion of all religious motivation from the minds of the Jewish authorities who handed Jesus over to the Romans. In the history of Israel from Moses to the present day the destiny of the nation has never been a purely political question in the Israelite or Jewish mind. If the authorities feared that Jesus would catalyze a revolutionary movement that might precipitate Roman action against the Temple, the priesthood, or the city, the danger was religious as well as political. It seems clear that at some time in his life Jesus acted prophetically against the Temple (or against abuses in the Temple) by word or by deed or by both. Could this have been any less a religious problem than the prophet Jeremiah's outbursts against the Temple? If the priests wanted to get rid of Jesus because of their fear of Rome, this does not exclude a desire to get rid of him because he had attacked what was sacred in their eyes. There was a similar reaction to Jeremiah: "The man deserves the sentence of death because he has prophesied against this city" (cf. Jer xxvi 6, 11, 20–23—the example of Uriah who was put to death is also cited). Only some 150 years before Jesus' time, the opposition of the Qumran Teacher of Righteousness to the Jerusalem Temple and to its priesthood caused the high priest to seek to kill him on a feast day (cf. 1QpHab ix 4–5, xi 4–7).

The question of Jesus as the Messiah would also have had strong religious overtones. Again, whether or not this question was raised in the Sanhedrin's interrogation of Jesus is not crucial; it certainly came up during his ministry and would have been known to the authorities. (The point is not whether Jesus identified himself as the Messiah—there are reasons for thinking that he did not do so explicitly—but whether his followers so proclaimed him.) Some have argued that the identification of Jesus as the Messiah would not have caused religious antagonism on the part of the Jewish authorities, for there were many would-be messiahs in the 1st century who were not condemned by the Sanhedrin. In fact, in the 2nd century Simon Bar-Kochba (Ben Kosiba) received religious support for his messianic claims from some of the highest Jewish religious authorities. Yet these other would-be messiahs were nationalistic, and their success would have meant political independence for the Sanhedrin and the glorification of Jerusalem and the Temple. A messiah who at the same time threatened to overthrow the Temple could well have provoked religious opposition. But perhaps we are not getting to the core of the religious problem when we discuss Jesus as the Messiah (especially if he did not unreservedly accept the title himself). There is reason to believe that the real religious charge against Jesus was that he was a false prophet. R. H. Fuller, *The Foundations of New Testament Christology* (New York: Scribner, 1965), pp. 125–29, in a critical analysis of Jesus' self-understanding, maintains that Jesus did not claim to be the Messiah, the Son of Man, or the Son of God; rather Jesus interpreted his mission in terms of eschatological prophecy. Be this as it may, it is significant that the ancient Jewish reference to Jesus in TalBab, *Sanhedrin*, 43a, says that he was executed for practicing sorcery and enticing Israel to apostasy—in short, because he was a false prophet coming under the death sentence of Deut xiii 5, xviii 20. This clearly religious charge is echoed in the Synoptic accounts of the Jewish mockery of Jesus (Mark xiv 65 and par.) and perhaps in Annas' interrogation of Jesus (see p. 835 below; also compare John vii 15–19 with Deut xviii 20). P. E. Davies, BiRes 2 (1957), 19–30, gathers abundant NT evidence showing that the early Christians conceived of Jesus' suffering and death in terms of the fate of a martyr prophet.

We must mention, too, that many of Jesus' actions during his ministry had deep religious implications, as those who interrogated him would have been well aware. Could Jesus' opposition to the Pharisees (certainly a historical feature of his ministry) have been forgotten by the scribes who were part of the Sanhedrin? May not his prophetic attitude toward wealth and his appeal to the poorer classes have upset the monied aristocracy from among whom some of the elders in the Sanhedrin came? We cannot be certain if the explicit charge of blasphemy was hurled against Jesus, even though it appears independently in the different Gospel traditions (see vol. 29, p. 408). Perhaps the Gospel description of what constituted the blasphemy, namely, the claim to be God's Son, has been read back into the ministry of Jesus from the later Synagogue condemnations of the theology of Jesus' followers (vol. 29, p. LXXIV). But the uncertainty about the formulation should not blind us to the reality involved, arising from the ministry of Jesus. Would not Jesus' bold proclamation of the advent of God's kingdom and the authority with which he preached and acted have been offensive to those who held the established religious views, Pharisee and Sadducee alike? O. Linton, NTS 7 (1960–61), 261, may well be correct in insisting that whether or not the authorities would have denounced Jesus for blasphemy in the technical sense, they would have objected to him as implicitly intruding upon God's special privileges and thus making an attack on the confession that there is one God besides whom there is none else. To think that religious motives did not enter into the condemnation of such a figure as Jesus is to go against all that we know from the long history of conflict between prophets and authority.

The Sanhedrin (whole or part) that was involved with Jesus would have been the most unique religious body in history if it did not contain a mixture of ecclesiastical politicians, righteous men of burning zeal, and pious men of mercy and justice. In turning Jesus over to the Romans with the recommendation that he be tried as a potential revolutionary with monarchical claims, some were undoubtedly acting selfishly and without much probing of conscience, in order to protect their vested interests in the *status quo*. Others were also acting out of political motivation but had long since decided that their interests coincided with what was best both temporally and spiritually for the nation. Still others may have despised Roman intervention and have acted solely out of righteous anger against one who had struck out against the Temple of God and who was behaving and speaking contrary to sacred religious customs. There is scarcely a Christian church that cannot find in its history condemnations of good men leveled by religious assemblies with a similar variety of motives.

The Structure of the Johannine Passion Narrative

With relative ease one may discern the general lines of the structure of the two chapters involved in the Johannine Passion Narrative (pp. 785–86 above). There are three principal divisions of approximately the same length, containing respectively 27, 29, and 26 verses. The first division (xviii 1–27) consists of the arrest of Jesus and of his interrogation by the Jewish authorities. The arrest leads directly into the interrogation (vss. 12–13). The second division (xviii 28 – xix 16a) consists of the trial of Jesus by Pilate, a highly dramatic and well-staged encounter. The third division (xix 16b–42) consists of the episodes surrounding the crucifixion, death, and burial of Jesus.

Within the major divisions there are signs of careful arrangement and subdivision. In each of the two units of the first division (arrest, interrogation) there is a subsidiary incident involving Peter (cutting off Malchus' ear, denying Jesus). In the second division the Pilate trial consists of seven episodes, each of three to six verses in length. They are alternately located outside and inside the praetorium and arranged in the manner of an inclusion (diagram p. 859 below). The third division has an introduction (the crucifixion), five episodes on the cross, and a conclusion (the burial), also arranged somewhat in the manner of an inclusion.

Janssens de Varebeke, *art. cit.*, has made a detailed study of the structure of these chapters, using the method that scholars like Vanhoye and Laurentin have been applying to other NT books. He rightly recognizes the seven episodes of the second division, and on this basis has tried to find seven episodes or subsections in the other two divisions. We shall challenge his conclusions as we discuss the structure of the first and third divisions below. On the whole we find that he forces upon the Passion Narrative a pattern and a consistency that lie beyond the demonstrable intention of the evangelist.

BIBLIOGRAPHY

GENERAL TREATMENTS OF THE PASSION

Benoit, P., "Le procès de Jésus," *La Vie Intellectuelle*, February 1940, pp. 200–13; March 1940, pp. 372–78; April 1940, pp. 54–64. Reprinted in *Exégèse et théologie* (Paris: Cerf, 1961), I, 265–89.

———— "Jésus devant le Sanhédrin," *Angelicum* 20 (1943), 143–65. Reprinted in *Exégèse et théologie*, I, 290–311.

———— *The Passion and Resurrection of Jesus Christ* (New York: Herder & Herder, 1969).

Blinzler, J., *The Trial of Jesus* (Westminster, Md.: Newman, 1959).

Dalman, G., *Sacred Sites and Ways* (New York: Macmillan, 1935), especially pp. 346–81, ch. xxi on "Golgotha and the Sepulchre."

Jeremias, J., *Golgotha* (Leipzig: Pfeiffer, 1926).

Kilpatrick, G. D., *The Trial of Jesus* (Oxford, 1953).

Léon-Dufour, X., "Passion (Récits de la)," DBS 6 (1960), cols. 1419–92.

Lietzmann, H., "Der Prozess Jesu," *Kleine Schriften* (Berlin: Akademie, 1958), II, 251–63. Originally published in *Sitzungsberichte der Preussischen Akademie der Wissenschaften*, phil.-hist. Klasse 1931, 14 (1934), 313–22.

Lohse, E., *History of the Suffering and Death of Jesus Christ* (Philadelphia: Fortress, 1967).

Sherwin-White, A. N., *Roman Society and Roman Law in the New Testament* (Oxford: Clarendon, 1963), especially pp. 1–47.

———— "The Trial of Christ," in *Historicity and Chronology in the New Testament* (Theological Collections 6; London: SPCK, 1965), pp. 97–116.

Verdam, P. J., "Sanhedrin and Gabbatha," *Free University Quarterly* 7 (1960–61), 259–87.

Wilson, W. R., "The Trial of Jesus" (Duke University, Religion Department dissertation, 1960).

Winter, P., *On the Trial of Jesus* (Studia Judaica 1; Berlin: de Gruyter, 1961).

———— "Josephus on Jesus," *Journal of Historical Studies* 1 (1968), 289–302.

The Johannine Passion Narrative

Borgen, P., "John and the Synoptics in the Passion Narrative," NTS 5 (1958–59), 246–59.

Braun, F.-M., "La passion de Notre Seigneur Jésus Christ d'après saint Jean," NRT 60 (1933), 289–302, 385–400, 481–99.

Buse, I., "St. John and the Marcan Passion Narrative," NTS 4 (1957–58), 215–19.

——— "St. John and the Passion Narratives of St. Matthew and St. Luke," NTS 7 (1960–61), 65–76.

de la Potterie, I., "Passio et mors Christi apud Johannem" (mimeographed; Rome: Pontifical Biblical Institute, 1962–63).

Dibelius, M., "Die alttestamentlichen Motive in der Leidensgeschichte des Petrus- und des Johannes-Evangeliums," BZAW 33 (1918), 125–50. Reprinted in Botschaft und Geschichte (Tübingen: Mohr, 1953), I, 221–47.

Dodd, Tradition, pp. 21–151.

Fenton, J. C., The Passion According to John (London: SPCK, 1961).

Haenchen, E., "Historie und Geschichte in den johanneischen Passionsberichten," in Zur Bedeutung des Todes Jesu (Gütersloh: Mohn, 1967), pp. 55–78.

Janssens de Varebeke, A., "La structure des scènes du récit de la passion en Joh., xviii–xix," ETL 38 (1962), 504–22.

Jeremias, J., "A Comparison of the Marcan Passion Narrative with the Johannine," EWJ, pp. 89–96.

Meeks, W. A., The Prophet-King: Moses Traditions and the Johannine Christology (SNT XIV, 1967), especially pp. 55–80.

Osty, E., "Les points de contact entre le récit de la passion dans saint Luc et dans saint Jean," Mélanges J. Lebreton (RSR 39 [1951]), 146–54.

Riaud, J., "La gloire et la royauté de Jésus dans la Passion selon saint Jean," BVC 56 (1964), 28–44.

Summers, R., "The Death and Resurrection of Jesus: John 18–21," RExp 62 (1965), 473–81.

Temple, S., "The Two Traditions of the Last Supper, Betrayal, and Arrest," NTS 7 (1960–61), 77–85.

61. THE PASSION NARRATIVE:
—DIVISION ONE (UNIT ONE)
(xviii 1–12)

The Arrest of Jesus

XVIII 1 After this discourse Jesus went out with his disciples across the Kidron valley to where there was a garden, which they entered together. 2 This place was also familiar to Judas, his betrayer, for Jesus had often gone there with his disciples. 3 So Judas took a detachment of soldiers, together with police supplied by the chief priests and the Pharisees, and went there equipped with lanterns and torches and weapons.

4 Knowing fully what was to happen to him, Jesus came out to them and asked, "Whom are you looking for?" 5 "Jesus the Nazorean," they replied. He told them, "I am he." (Now Judas, his betrayer, was also there with them.) 6 When Jesus said to them, "I am he," they stepped back and fell to the ground. 7 So he asked them again, "Whom are you looking for?" "Jesus the Nazorean," they repeated. 8 "I told you that I am he," Jesus answered. "And if I am the one you want, let these men go." (9 This was to fulfill what he had said, "I have not lost even one of those whom you have given me.")

10 Then Simon Peter, who had a sword, pulled it out and struck at the servant of the high priest, cutting off his right earlobe. (The servant's name was Malchus.) 11 But Jesus told Peter, "Put back that sword. Am I not to drink the cup the Father has given me?"

12 At that the soldiers with their tribune and the Jewish police arrested Jesus and bound him.

3: *went;* 4: *asked;* 5: *told.* In the historical present tense.

NOTES

xviii 1. *After this discourse.* Literally "Having said these things." De la Potterie and others see the connotation of purpose or preparation in this phrase, so that the Passion Narrative that follows represents the culmination of Jesus' words. For instance, the crucifixion would be the glorification spoken of in xvii 1–5. The connection is possible, but elsewhere in John the phrase is purely sequential (xiii 21, xx 20).

went out with his disciples. Virtually the same words appear in the Synoptic accounts of the end of the supper. Mark xiv 26 (Matt xxvi 30) has: "They went out"; Luke xxii 39: "And going out, he went . . . and his disciples followed him." All the Gospel accounts imply that Jesus intended to spend the night in the environs of the city rather than in the city itself. This would agree with what we know of the crowded conditions of the city at Passover time (see NOTE on xi 55). Jewish custom demanded that Passover night (Synoptic chronology) be spent in Jerusalem—this was the contemporary exegesis of Deut xvi 7. But to solve the problem of accommodations, the city district had been enlarged for Passover purposes to include the environs as far as Bethphage on the Mount of Olives. Bethany, Jesus' usual place of residence in the Jerusalem area (NOTE on xi 1), lay outside the legal limit. See Jeremias, EWJ, p. 55.

As for the designation of those with Jesus as "his disciples," Jeremias, EWJ, p. 95, points out that in the primitive, pre-Marcan passion account the word "disciples" is not used in the scene of the arrest, but only the vaguer designation "those who stood by."

across the Kidron valley. Literally "the winter-flowing Kidron" (or Kedron if one follows the Greek spelling). The Kidron, not mentioned by the Synoptics, is a wadi that has flowing water only in the rainy or winter season. John's use of the correct terminology for the Kidron is not necessarily a proof that the Gospel is drawing on an authentic Palestinian tradition (vol. 29, p. XLII), for "winter-flowing" is the usual designation of the Kidron in LXX (II Sam xv 23; I Kings xv 13). Loisy, Lagrange, and others think that John is subtly alluding here to the story of David's flight before Absalom in II Sam xv (14: "Arise and let us flee" [John xiv 31]; 23: "And the king crossed the Kidron valley"). Guilding, p. 165, relates the Johannine narrative to I Kings ii, read as a *haphtarah* two months before Passover in the first year of the triennial cycle of synagogue readings (vol. 29, pp. 278–80). In particular she points to the warning of Solomon to Shimei: "On the day you go out across the Kidron valley, know for certain you shall die" (I Kings ii 37; also see NOTE on Malchus in vs. 10 below). The fact that the waste blood of the temple sacrifices was disposed into the Kidron is mentioned by StB, II, 567. However, the reference to the Kidron is not obviously symbolic.

to where there was a garden. Some detect here a note of finality: because there was a garden there. The word *kēpos* refers to a plot of land where vegetables or flowers are planted, and sometimes trees as well. Only John gives the site this name. D. M. Stanley and B. P. Robinson (*art. cit.*), following an ancient tradition (Cyril of Alexandria, Aquinas), think that in setting the struggle between Judas (the tool of Satan) and Jesus in a garden, John is alluding to the theme of the Garden of Paradise in Gen ii–iii. Some of the proposed Paradise motifs (Tree of Life) emerge from combining this garden with the garden mentioned in xix 41–42, where Jesus was crucified, buried and rose; but nothing in John suggests that the same garden is involved in both episodes. Moreover, John does not use the word *paradeisos* found in the Genesis story, even though that word is known elsewhere in the Johannine writings (Rev ii 7). Thus the symbolic exegesis is hard to justify. Mark xiv 32 and Matt xxvi 36 mention "a piece of land [*chōrion*] with the name

Gethsemane." This name, which comes from the B source of Mark (see p. 788 above), is not found in Luke (who speaks simply of "the place") or in John. It means "oil valley" or "oil press," and was not an inappropriate designation for a site on the Mount of Olives. (Note that while *the Mount of Olives* appears in the A source of Mark and in all three Synoptics, even this general identification of the locale is absent from John.) One may combine the Gospel information and think of the site as an olive grove on the lower slopes of the Mount of Olives, just across the Kidron valley from Jerusalem; and this is where Christian tradition has localized the site since the 4th century. In Zech xiv 4 (one of the two explicit references to the Mount of Olives in the OT) the Lord stands on this Mount for the final battle against the nations and after this battle come the blessings of the day of the Lord. By placing the agonized struggle of Jesus on the Mount of Olives, the Synoptic Gospels may be exploiting the theological symbolism of Zechariah (cf. also Mark xiii 3–4), a symbolism that John does not draw upon. Finally we may note that the customary title "Jesus' agony in the garden" is a mélange: the "agony" is described in the Synoptics (Luke xxii 44, alone, has the word *agōnia*); only John mentions the "garden."

entered. The verb *eiserchesthai* (=*erchesthai* . . . *eis* of Mark xiv 32; Matt xxvi 36) evokes the image of an enclosed area; so also "came out" in vs. 4.

together. Literally "he and his disciples."

2. *his betrayer.* Literally here and in 5: "the one who was handing him over"; see NOTES on vi 64, 71. In the Book of Glory John has already identified Judas as the betrayer three times (xiii 2, 11, 21), and the instances here and in 5 are usually thought to reflect the hand of the editor. Caution is necessary, however, in judging the present verse—in the primitive pre-Gospel passion account there may well have been a need to identify Judas in the scene of the arrest of Jesus, for this would have been the first time he appeared. In the story of the arrest in Mark xiv 42, 44 and Matt xxvi 46, 48, Judas is called "the betrayer"; cf. Luke xxii 48: "Would you *betray* the Son of Man with a kiss?"

often gone there with his disciples. Or "stayed there with"; the verb *synagesthai* normally means "meet together" (cf. Acts xi 26). In the present instance, however, and perhaps previously, Jesus' disciples went with him to the garden, rather than meeting him there (Reynen, *art. cit.*). John's information that Jesus frequented the garden may be compared to Luke's information (xxi 37) that Jesus used to spend the night on the Mount of Olives; but John alone draws the logical inference that Jesus' habit enabled Judas to know where to find him.

3. *Judas took.* Here the participle "taking" implies little more than accompaniment as a guide (BAG, p. 465¹ᵃ; cf. BDF, §418⁵); no particular authority is necessarily attributed to Judas. Thus, we do not find convincing Winter's contention (*Trial,* pp. 44–45) that here John erroneously implies that Judas was in charge of Roman soldiers and thus contradicts vs. 12 which mentions a Roman military officer. We are hesitant in supposing that the final editor overlooked such a discrepancy within a few verses.

a detachment of soldiers. Literally "the cohort." That soldiers (as distinguished from police) were involved in the arrest of Jesus is mentioned only in John. In the NT "cohort" always refers to Roman soldiers, describing either the cohort of 600 men or the maniple of 200. Perhaps the mention here of a cohort instead of a smaller detachment came by way of confusion with the cohort mentioned in the crucifixion accounts. (Mark xv 16 mentions the calling together of "the whole cohort" for the mockery of Jesus, and some scribes have copied that reading into this verse in John.) The reference to a tribune in vs. 12 confirms the impression that John is thinking of Roman soldiers (*pace* Blinzler, *Trial*, pp. 64–70; Benoit, *Passion*, p. 46). An appeal to LXX where Roman military terms were used anachronistically for non-Roman troops does not throw light on the present situation. A writer living under Roman domination would scarcely use a technical Roman military term for a Jewish force when he intends to mention alongside the cohort and distinct from it "the police supplied by the chief priests and the Pharisees." If the mention of Roman troops is historical, then we must assume that they were placed at the disposal of the priests or the Sanhedrin by Pilate, perhaps because he feared the danger of another insurrection (cf. Mark xv 7; Luke xxiii 19). This may also explain the difficulty of the large number of soldiers, if we are to take "cohort" literally. From a few years after Jesus' time (Acts x 1) until mid-2nd century the Roman prefect or procurator in Palestine had at his disposal troops of a cohort (*Cohors Secunda Italica*) consisting of troops mustered in Italy and complemented by recruits from Samaria and Caesarea (Josephus *Ant.* XIX.ix.2;※365). While the Synoptic account of the arrest of Jesus does not mention Romans, some see a reference to them in Mark xiv 41 (Matt xxvi 45): "The Son of Man is betrayed into the hands of *sinners* [i.e., Gentiles?]."

police supplied by the chief priests and the Pharisees. For these temple police (*hypēretai*) see NOTE on vii 32. Literally they are the police "*of* the chief priests"; and in 12 they are called "the Jewish police" in distinction from the (Roman) cohort with its tribune. The Synoptic descriptions of the group involved in the arrest of Jesus are more general, with Luke being the closest to John. Mark xiv 43 (Matt xxvi 47) speaks of "a (great) crowd . . . from the chief priests, the scribes, and the elders (of the people)"; Luke xxii 52 places the chief priests and the elders themselves in the scene along with "the officers of the Temple" (from Acts v 22–24, 26 we may conclude that Luke's *stratēgoi* are the officers over the *hypēretai* of the Temple).

Turning to John's expression "the chief priests and the Pharisees," we note that it has occurred four times before (vii 32, 45, xi 47, 57). In itself, the combination offers no great difficulty (it occurs in Josephus *Life* 5;※21), but some would see here an amalgamation of the priests of Jesus' time and the Pharisees of the evangelist's time. Let us consider each term. The plural usage "high priests" occurs some ten times in John (five times in the Passion Narrative) and is very frequent in the Synoptics and Acts. It does not necessarily indicate that the NT writers did not know that there was only one official high priest at a time, for the plural is an accepted idiom found in Josephus and the Mishnah. Under the rubric of chief or high priests were included the incumbent high priest (John and Matthew mention Caiaphas in the Passion Narratives), former high priests who had been deposed but were still living (e.g., Annas), and members of the privileged families from whom the high priests were chosen. See Schürer, II, i, 203–6. Perhaps the rubric also covered holders of priestly offices (so Jeremias, as cited in BAG, p. 112). All the Gospels give the chief priests the most prominent role in the action against Jesus. Mark and Matthew frequently mention the elders, while Luke (xxiii 13, 35, xxiv 20) mentions the rulers as well as the elders (xxii 52; cf. 66).

In the Passion Narratives proper John alone mentions the Pharisees, and then only in the present instance (Matt xxvii 62 involves them in the setting of the guard at the tomb—certainly a late addition to the narrative). However, John probably means to include them elsewhere in the Passion Narrative under the rubric of "the Jews," as do the Synoptists when they refer to the whole Sanhedrin (Mark xv 1) and to the scribes (all three Gospels). Some scholars think John guilty of error here in speaking of the temple police supplied by the Pharisees who actually had no authority over such police. However, John may mean no more than that the police were sent by the Sanhedrin in which priests, Pharisee scribes, and elders had a voice (Mark xiv 43). Historically, it is impossible to determine just how involved in the action against Jesus were the Pharisees or the *whole* Sanhedrin (seemingly twenty-three of the seventy councilors were enough to form a quorum); but one may plausibly surmise both that the Pharisees were too important to have been ignored by the priests and that they had no love for Jesus after his public statements about them.

Lanterns and torches. Mentioned only by John, this detail may have been included in the narrative to emphasize the theological theme that it was night (see COMMENT). This does not rule out the possibility that the detail is factual. The objection that lanterns would not have been needed for this was the time of the nearly full paschal moon is weak: common sense indicates that an olive grove would have had dark corners in which a man might hide. Haenchen, "Historie," p. 59[9], thinks it unrealistic that 600 or even 200 men would have come carrying lanterns and torches, but one need not interpret John to mean that *all* carried these.

weapons. Mark xiv 43 and Matt xxvi 47 mention swords and clubs. P. Winter, "The Trial of Jesus" (mimeographed lecture, February 19, 1964, p. 10), contends that the Jewish police carried batons (clubs) and the Roman soldiers carried swords; implicitly, then, for him the Marcan/Matthean account would acknowledge the presence of the two groups.

4. *Knowing.* There is weaker textual support for "seeing," a reading that is less theological. Jesus' foreknowledge is a strong Johannine theme (vi 6, xiii 1). In Mark xiv 42 (Matt xxvi 46) Jesus knows that his betrayer is at hand before Judas appears on the scene.

came out. Only in John does Jesus take the initiative in going to meet Judas; for John, Jesus remains in full control of all that happens.

5. *Nazorean.* We may distinguish three designations of Jesus: (a) *apo Nazareth,* "from Nazareth": Matt xxi 11; Mark i 9; John i 45; Acts x 38. (b) *Nazarēnos,* "Nazarene": four times in Mark; twice in Luke; a Western textual variant in this verse of John. (c) *Nazōraios,* "Nazorean": twice in Matthew; eight times in Luke-Acts; three times in John's Passion Narrative (here, xviii 7, xix 19). This third term has been the subject of scholarly discussion. By the time Matthew's Gospel was written, *Nazōraios* was interpreted as a reference to Jesus' coming from Nazareth (Matt ii 23). In the story of Peter's denial after the arrest of Jesus, Mark xiv 67 mentions Jesus the Nazarene while Matt xxvi 71 speaks of Jesus the Nazorean. It is true that M. Black, p. 144, and others have questioned the derivation of *Nazōraios* as a gentilic from *Nazareth,* but most scholars still support this derivation as

plausible and it remains the best working hypothesis. (See G. F. Moore in *The Beginnings of Christianity*, ed. by K. Lake and F. J. Foakes-Jackson [London: Macmillan, 1920], I, i, 426–32; W. F. Albright, JBL 65 [1946], 397–401.) It is perfectly logical that a party sent to arrest a man would wish to identify him fully by name and locale. There is no reason here to think that a reference to Nazareth as Jesus' hometown would contain a note of contempt as in i 45–46 (cf. vii 41, 52). Some of the other hypotheses for explaining *Nazōraios* include: (a) The name designates a pre-Christian Jewish sect ("Observants" from the root *nṣr*), perhaps the followers of John the Baptist. The Mandeans, who claim descent from the Baptist's movement, occasionally call themselves *naṣorayya*. Church Fathers, like Theodoret and Epiphanius, knew of a heretical Jewish-Christian sect called Nazōraioi, but Epiphanius (*Haer.* xviii, xxix; GCS 25:215, 321) distinguishes between them and the pre-Christian Nasaraioi. (b) The name is to be related to the ancient Nazirites (Heb. *nāzîr*) who were consecrated to Yahweh by a vow; see Judg xiii 5, and the argument of E. Schweizer in *Judentum, Urchristentum, Kirche* (J. Jeremias Festschrift; Berlin: Töpelmann, 1960), pp. 90–93. (c) The name designates Jesus as the "messianic branch" (Heb. *nēṣer*) of Isa xi 1. (d) The name is related to the passive of the verb *naṣar*, "to preserve," thus *nāṣūr*, "the preserved," with connotations of the messianic remnant—Jesus is the one who has been set aside and kept for the messianic task; his followers are the remnant. B. Gärtner, *Die rätselhaften Termini Nazoräer und Iskariot* (Horae Soederblomianae 4; Uppsala: Gleerup, 1957), p. 14, thinks that the passages Isa xlii 6 and xlix 6, which contain this verb, are the prophecies referred to in Matt ii 23 as the basis for calling Jesus a Nazorean. Gärtner also brings into his explanation the cognate Isaian noun *nēṣer* mentioned above. For a survey of views, see H. H. Schaeder, TWNTE, IV, 874–79.

"*I am he.*" Literally "I am" (*egō eimi*). Codex Vaticanus, which reads "I am Jesus," preserves a scribal attempt to clarify. An *egō eimi* occurs in the Marcan Passion Narrative (xiv 62) as Jesus' answer to the high priest's question about his being the Messiah. Moreover, in Mark xiv 44, in the arrest of Jesus, Judas says, "Whomever I shall kiss, it is he [*autos estin*]."

(*Now Judas . . .*). This seems to be a very awkward editorial insertion: not only has Judas' presence already been mentioned, but he has no further role that would warrant his being mentioned again. Bultmann, p. 493, thinks that this was the first reference to Judas in the garden scene of the passion account used by the evangelist, while the reference to Judas in vs. 3 represents an introductory addition composed by the evangelist. Winter, *Trial*, p. 45, thinks that all references to Judas in this scene are secondary. Is the second mention of Judas an echo of the Synoptic tradition where Judas has a more important role? For the possibility of minor additions from the Synoptic tradition see vol. 29, p. xxxviii.

6. *they stepped back.* The Synoptic accounts do not report any hesitancy in arresting Jesus. However, elsewhere in John there are reports of difficulty in arresting or harming Jesus (vii 30, 44, viii 20, 59, x 39, xii 36; also Luke iv 29–30). J. H. Hingston, ET 32 (1920–21), 232, has made an attempt to solve the difficulty by interpreting the words to mean: "they went behind [him]," an interpretation that requires the omission of the next phrase.

and fell to the ground. Mein, *art. cit.*, is perfectly correct in rejecting Bernard's interpretation (II, 586–87) that the words imply no more than that the men who came to make the arrest were overcome by Jesus' moral ascendancy and so were "floored." But Mein's own thesis is not convincing either, namely, that this is an echo of LXX of Isa xxviii 13b: ". . . that they may go and fall back and be crushed and be in danger and be destroyed." Mein combines this with the mention of the chosen cornerstone three verses later in Isaiah, so that in John's imagery Jesus the cornerstone becomes a stone of stumbling, as in I Pet ii 6–8. But there is nothing else in the Fourth Gospel to suggest that this cornerstone symbolism played a role in Johannine thought. Lagrange, p. 457, who takes the Johannine account literally, says that one must not exaggerate the miracle, for relatively few soldiers would have heard the words and fallen down! S. Bartina, *art. cit.,* who also takes the scene literally, thinks that the Jews out of habit prostrated themselves on the ground when Jesus spoke the divine name "I AM." The latter theme is involved (see COMMENT), but we have here a Johannine theological construction rather than a historical reminiscence. Haenchen, "Historie," p. 59, makes the suggestion that the Psalms, which played such an important role in the reflection of the early Church on the passion, also entered Johannine thought in this scene, for example: Pss xxvii 2: "When evildoers come at me to devour my flesh, my foes and my enemies themselves stumble and *fall";* xxxv 4: "Let those be *turned back* and confounded who plot evil against me." See COMMENT for even more pertinent Psalms.

9. *This was to fulfill what he had said.* As often in John (NOTE on xv 25), this is simply a *hina* purpose clause, and we have had to supply the governing verb "This was" (MTGS, p. 304). Other interpreters offer the less plausible solution of an imperatival *hina:* "What he had said must be fulfilled" (MTGS, p. 95—"doubtful"). Elsewhere (Matthew, John, and Acts especially) the verb *plēroun* is used to describe the NT fulfillment of OT passages: to fulfill "what was said by the Lord"; "what was said through the prophet"; or simply "the Scripture." Only here and in xviii 32 do we have the verb used for fulfilling the words of Jesus (yet see Freed's theory in the NOTE on xvii 12). Such usage implicitly puts Jesus' words on a level with the words of the Jewish Scriptures and is the beginning of an attitude that would lead toward the recognition of canonical Christian writings alongside the Jewish ones. The basis in John for this usage is that Jesus' words have been given to him by God (xvii 8) and that Jesus' revelation surpasses the Torah given through Moses (i 17). We note that in the Gethsemane scene of Matt xxvi 54 there is a reference to the fulfilling of Scripture but in a different context.

"I have not lost even one of those whom you have given me." In fact, however, Jesus has not said this verbatim previously in John. Is this a free citation of the import of xvii 12: "I kept them safe with your name which you have given to me. I kept watch and not one of them was lost"? (The resemblance is closer if we take the alternative reading of that verse: "I kept safe with your name those whom you have given to me"—see NOTES on xvii 11 and 12.) Bultmann, p. 495, thinks of vi 39: "It is the will of Him who sent me that I should lose nothing of what He has given me" and maintains that the present verse was added by a redactor who misunderstood the passage in vi. In any case the final editor seems to be the one who supplied the parenthetical comment, and he may be citing Jesus' words as freely as the other NT authors cite the OT. Notice the implication that Judas, who was lost, was not really given

by the Father to Jesus. Judas is explicitly listed as an exception to the general rule in xvii 12 but not in vi 39.

10. *Simon Peter . . . Malchus.* All four evangelists mention the incident of the servant's ear, but only John gives the names of those involved. For the assailant Mark xiv 47 has "one of those who stood by"; Matt xxvi 51 has "one of those with Jesus"; Luke xxii 50 has "one of them." All four evangelists describe the victim as a servant of the high priest (thus not one of the temple police, for the servants and the police are distinct in vs. 18). Some scholars think that the presence of the names in John reflects the evangelist's imaginative attempt to lend plausibility to his narrative. However, since the tendency of legend-makers is to identify anonymous figures with *better known* ones, this explanation will work for Peter's name but not for that of Malchus. The latter name is not uncommon in the era; it is found five times in Josephus and is known from Palmyrene and Nabatean inscriptions (whence the suggestion that Malchus was an Arab). Some have tried to discover a symbolism behind John's use of the name. Guilding, p. 165, sees a reference to Zech xi 6, read as a *haphtarah* some months before Passover in the first year of a triennial cycle (vol. 29, pp. 278–80): "I will deliver . . . each into the hand of *his king* [*malkô*]." Krieger, *art. cit.*, suggests that Judas was the servant of the high priest struck by Jesus' disciple. Such imaginative explanations are not less demanding on one's credulity than the possibility that John's tradition preserved accurate information. (Also see NOTE on 26 below.) As for Peter, the action fits his impetuous character (John xiii 37). Lagrange and Taylor, in discussing the Marcan description of the disciple who assailed the servant, find a hint that this disciple was known to Mark. This would not be unfavorable to John's identification, for tradition associates Mark with Peter.

sword. The group possessed two swords according to Luke xxii 38. The unforeseen action of Peter suggests a weapon about the size of a dagger that could be concealed.

pulled it out. John uses *elkein;* Mark xiv 47 and Matt xxvi 51 also mention the drawing (*[apo]span*) of the sword.

cutting off. John uses *apokoptein;* the Synoptics use *aphairein.*

right earlobe. Mark and the best textual witnesses of John use *ōtarion,* a double diminutive, hence our "earlobe." Matthew, Luke xxii 51, and John xviii 26 use *ōtion* (read in the present verse of John by P[66], Alexandrinus, and the Byzantine tradition), also a diminutive. Luke xxii 50 uses *ous,* "ear," an Atticization according to BDF, §111[3]. Benoit, *Passion*, p. 371[1], understands the diminutive as designating the external part of the ear.

Only John and Luke designate the *right* ear, and this detail seems to be supplied independently, for the two Gospels use different words for "ear." Benoit, *Passion*, p. 43, thinks that Peter deliberately chose the right organ, the more valuable according to the indemnity laws of the time, as a mark of defiance. Some ingenious interpreters, observing that a right-handed man will normally strike at the left ear of an opponent who is facing him, have drawn from this episode the vital information that Peter was left-handed—unless Peter was a cowardly right-hander who struck at a man whose back was turned!

11. *Put back that sword.* Literally "Put into the scabbard." Among the Synoptics Matthew alone mentions this command, but the wording is different.

Am I not . . . ? Abbott, JG, §2232, thinks that literally this is a negative exclamation: "I am, of course, not to drink it [according to your desire]." Most interpret the phrase as a rhetorical question with an affirmative implication (BDF, §365⁴).

cup. Or "chalice." The symbolism is of a cup of suffering, also mentioned by the Synoptics in the Gethsemane scene (Mark xiv 36 and par.: "Remove this cup from me").

12. *the soldiers.* Literally "the cohort" as in 3.

tribune. The Gr. *chiliarchos* is literally a captain or officer over 1,000 men, but the term was used to translate the Roman *tribunus militum*, a commander of a cohort of 600. Winter, *Trial*, p. 29, suggests that John's account has upgraded the officer and that he was more likely a *decurio* or corporal over ten men.

arrested Jesus and bound him. According to Mark xiv 46 and Matt xxvi 50, they had seized (*kratein*) Jesus before the incident of the servant's ear; John and Luke xxii 54 describe the arrest (*syllambein*) as taking place after the incident. The latter is the more logical order. Mark xiv 48 and Matt xxvi 55 use the verb *syllambein* when Jesus asks, "Have you come out to arrest me as if I were a bandit?" Only John mentions that Jesus was bound at this time.

COMMENT

The Structure of Division One of the Passion Narrative

The passion begins with the account of the arrest of Jesus in the garden across the Kidron. A transition to the Passion Narrative from the Last Discourse is made in xviii 1. We have seen that there is an ending of a more original form of the Last Discourse in xiv 31 where Jesus says, "Let us leave here and be on our way," and that the present arrangement where this ending is followed by three chapters of discourse is a product of editing (pp. 586–87 above). Thus many would suggest that once xiv 31 immediately preceded xviii 1. This is possible but the history of these chapters is probably more complicated than we can reconstruct today. And we must remember that the Passion Narrative may well have been an entity before it was joined to any form of Last Supper Discourse.

The first division of the Passion Narrative covers xviii 1–27. As we have mentioned (p. 803 above), Janssens de Varebeke would impose here a pattern of seven subdivisions. For instance, he makes xviii 1 a subdivision by itself, separated from 2–3. More plausibly in our judgment vss. 1–3 belong together as a setting for the two episodes in 4–8 and 10–11. Again Janssens de Varebeke treats 12–16a as a subdivision, but we would consider 12–13 a transitional passage between the scene in the garden and the scene in the palace of the high priest. To split 15–18 at 16a also seems to upset the structure. The Johannine writer surrounds the interrogation of Jesus with two halves of a scene where Peter denies Jesus (15–18 and 25–27). Part of Janssens de Varebeke's argument is based on what we judge to be accidental assonances between words (e.g., *hestōs* in 18 and 25 and *parestēkōs* in 22). Part of it is based on the numerical usage of certain words (*erchesthai*) in the various divisions. He also invokes some inclusions that we can only characterize as farfetched, for example, an inclusion between Peter's blow in cutting off the servant's earlobe in Division One and the blow the soldier struck with a lance at Jesus' side in Division Three. As is evident in the outline we have given on p. 785 above, we detect a less complicated structure in Division One. It consists of two units: the arrest of Jesus in the garden (vss. 1–11), and the interrogation of Jesus by Annas in the high priest's palace (vss. 14–27). The transition between the two units is smoothly effected in vss. 12–13. (By putting 12 with the first unit and 13 with the second, we are subdividing for practical convenience; the author meant the two to go together.)

Notice how well the two units balance each other: in each Peter's behavior is implicitly contrasted with that of Jesus. Jesus shows that he can thwart the arrest with divine power (vs. 6), but he allows himself to be arrested and bound. Peter tries to resist the arrest with human power (the sword), but this is ineffectual. Jesus bravely defends himself before Annas by appealing to the forthright character of his teaching. Meanwhile, Peter, who has heard that teaching, denies that he knows Jesus. In the first verses of each unit we find Jesus' disciples loyally following him; but at the end of each unit we find Peter, a representative disciple, incapable of handling the situation in which Jesus has proved himself. Here is exhibited the Johannine sense of dramatic organization at its best.

The Historicity and Independence of the Johannine Account of the Arrest

In even a very critical evaluation of the Gospel evidence there can be little doubt that Jesus was arrested somewhere on the Mount of Olives shortly before his crucifixion and brought back to the city for trial. This basic fact has undergone theological interpretation in all the Gospels; as we shall see below, the Johannine orientation is different from that of the Synoptics and fits in with the peculiar theological interests found elsewhere in the Fourth Gospel. If we leave aside for a moment the theology of the scene, we note that two major points of difference from the Synoptic accounts require attention, namely, that John omits the scene of the agony in Gethsemane and that John attributes a role to Roman troops in the arrest of Jesus.

First, the absence of an agony scene. This is often dismissed as an obvious effect of Johannine theology. Bultmann, p. 493, says that John had to omit this scene because Jesus had already been described as "glorified." However, we note that in ch. xii, after Jesus had proclaimed that the hour of glorification had come (xii 23), he went through a troubling of soul (27) similar to that of the Synoptic agony scene. Thus it is not certain that glory and anguish are mutually exclusive. Nevertheless, one may theorize that in the flow of Johannine thought the note of anguish was best put as a prelude to the hour (xii) rather than halfway through it (xviii).

But even then the question is not so easily settled. Most critics agree that the scene of the agony in Gethsemane was missing from the primitive consecutive passion account (the Marcan A source—p. 788 above). Therefore its absence in John may not be the result of an editorial omission or rearrangement but may stem from the fact that in this detail the Johannine pre-Gospel tradition was similar to the Marcan A source. The historicity of the agony scene is a problem for Synoptic study and does not concern us here. (The present Marcan account may well be a conflation of two forms of the story, only one of which is preserved in Luke [cf. K. G. Kuhn, EvTh 12 (1952–53), 260–85].) Its most difficult feature is what Jesus is supposed to have said in his agony, sayings for which there were no witnesses (the three disciples were asleep). Have the Marcan B tradition and the Lucan tradition (if independent) filled out the agony scene with sayings that once had another setting in Jesus' ministry? This would perhaps explain why John contains scattered sayings similar to the sayings of the Synoptic agony scene; see vol. 29, pp. 470–71 and p. 656 above; also T. Boman, "Der Gebetskampf Jesu," NTS 10 (1963–64), 261–73.

Second, the presence of Roman soldiers in the garden. We have mentioned in the NOTE on vs. 3 some of the objections of detail against John's information and have shown that these objections are not unanswerable. The real problem concerns the likelihood of Pilate's involvement with Sanhedrin in the arrest of Jesus. Such cooperation could have been mutually beneficial if Pilate wanted Jesus temporarily out of the way (see p. 798 above) and if the Sanhedrin wanted Roman support in the event that Jesus' followers caused an uproar over his arrest. There is no clear Synoptic evidence for Pilate's deep involvement from the beginning, as implied in John. H. Conzelmann (*The Theology of St. Luke* [New York: Harper, 1960], pp. 90–91) thinks that in Acts iii 13–14, iv 27, and xiii 28 we have evidence of pre-Lucan formulae that attributed to Pilate great responsibility in the death of Jesus. He suggests that in his own Gospel Luke failed through misunderstanding to reproduce this theme. In Mark xv 2 and Matt xxvii 11, Pilate, without having been informed, knows what Jesus is accused of. However, this does not necessarily mean that Pilate played a role in the arrest; abbreviation of a longer account or common knowledge about Jesus would be sufficient explanation. In the pre-Marcan tradition of passion predictions (Mark viii 31, ix 31, x 33–34) there is no hint of Roman involvement in the arrest.

Many critics suggest that John introduced Roman soldiers into the garden scene for theological purposes (so Loisy, Bultmann, Barrett, Lohse). The presence of Roman troops alongside the Jewish police might be symbolic of the whole "world" being lined up against Jesus. Barrett reminds us of the opposition between Rome and Christianity in the Book of Revelation. Some suggest that the participation of Roman authority in the arrest is meant to prepare the way for the dramatic confrontation of Jesus and Pilate which dominates the Johannine account of the passion. One must admit, however, that the Gospel itself does not draw any attention to the symbolic value of the Roman soldiers as representative of "the world"; in fact, the presence of the soldiers is not emphasized even as constituting the presence of Rome—it is only by deduction that we realize that Pilate and thus the Roman authority must have been consulted. Nor does the arrest scene really prepare the way for the confrontation of Jesus and Pilate. The information that Pilate had a part in the arrest of Jesus runs contrary to the picture of Pilate in the trial where he is sympathetic to Jesus and thinks that the Jewish case against Jesus is not convincing. Now if one of these two contrary pictures (Pilate plotting to have Jesus arrested; Pilate plotting to have Jesus released) is true and the other has been reshaped by theological motives, the Pilate of the trial is more likely the theological creation. It is not easy to write off a picture of Roman involvement in Jesus' arrest as the evangelist's invention; and Goguel, Cullmann, Winter, and others may well be right in thinking that here John has preserved a historical detail suppressed in the other Gospel accounts. (Cf. NOTE on "weapons" in vs. 3.)

We find, then, that in the two major points where John differs from the Synoptic Gospels in the account of the arrest, John's information or approach has considerable plausibility as representing older tradition. Let us turn to an incident that John shares with the Synoptics but where there are peculiar Johannine details. In the NOTES on vss. 10–11 we have pointed out the similarities and dissimilarities between the Johannine and Synoptic accounts of the cutting off of the servant's ear. Of course, no one can establish the veracity of the details narrated by John alone (Peter, Malchus, right earlobe [Luke also has *right* ear]); but they are not implausible, and the theories of the invention of these details are not altogether convincing.

This leads us to the question of the extent to which the Johannine Passion Narrative is dependent on the Synoptic Gospels or their sources. We discussed this in general above (pp. 787–91), but promised to back up our conclusions by individual studies. The scene of the arrest gives us a chance to test Buse's theory that John is related to the Marcan B source. John lacks almost all the material found in B: the agony in Gethsemane and the incidents of Mark xiv 49–51. (Mark xiv 49 has some similarity to John xviii 20, but there can be no question of dependency.) In fact, John shares with B only the incident of the cutting off of the servant's ear; and except for words like "strike" and "earlobe" the two accounts are not at all close. In the incidents narrated John is somewhat closer to the Marcan A source (the primitive passion account). Benoit thinks that Matthew has an independent account of the arrest; many think that Luke has an independent source. It is worth noting, however, how much

John differs from all three (Mark A, Matthew, Luke): John's description
of the arresting forces is different; John includes the detail of the lanterns
and torches; John omits Judas' kiss; John does not mention the Mount of
Olives and describes the locale differently. In face of these differences,
Borgen's theory that details from several Synoptic accounts have been
fused and added to John seems unlikely. If John agrees with Luke against
Mark and Matthew in placing the disciple's attack on the high priest's
servant before the arrest of Jesus, John has virtually none of the other
details in which Luke differs from Mark and Matthew (the question by
the disciples in Luke xxii 49; the healing of the servant's ear in 51; the
presence of the chief priests in the arresting party in 52). Nor does John
have the details in which Matthew differs from Mark and Luke (e.g., the
sayings of Matt xxvi 52–54—see NOTE on vs. 11). Differences such as
these cause us to favor the theory of Johannine independence.

The Meaning Given to the Scene in Johannine Thought

If John does draw on older independent tradition, the material
from that tradition has been reworked in the interests of Johannine
theology. In a recent article Richter has argued that the Johannine
account of the arrest is simply a theological elaboration of the Synoptic
or pre-Synoptic account, but he draws his main arguments from the type
of material that we are going to discuss below and not from the details
we treated above. In our judgment, in order to do justice to all the
complexities of the Johannine account, one must allow for both a reliable
independent tradition and a highly theological elaboration.

Verse 2 implies that Judas' treason consisted in telling the authorities
where Jesus could be arrested secretly at night without danger of riots.
But John may be more interested in the symbolic value of Judas' presence.
In xiii 27, 30, when we last saw Judas, he had become the tool of Satan
and had gone off into the night. This was the evil night of which Jesus
had warned in xi 10 and xii 35, the night in which men stumble because
they have no light. Perhaps this is why Judas and his companions come
bearing lanterns and torches. They have not accepted the light of the
world, and so they must have artificial light. This moment of darkness
may be contrasted with the final triumph of Jesus in the heavenly Jerusalem
(Rev xxii 5) where the blessed will need no lamps for the Lord God will
be their light. There is an echo of this same type of symbolism in the
Lucan scene of the arrest (xxii 53) where Jesus says to his captors: "This
is your hour and the power of darkness." (If John were drawing from the
Lucan account, the omission of such an appropriate saying would be
inexplicable.)

The direct confrontation of Jesus and the forces of darkness is
narrated with dramatic instinct. Jesus knows what is going to happen and
goes out to meet his opponents. We have heard him say: "No one has

taken it [my life] away from me; rather, I lay it down of my own accord" (x 18). Jesus had given Judas permission to leave the Last Supper to betray him (xiii 27); now he will permit Judas and his forces to arrest him. For John the passion is not an inevitable fate that overtakes Jesus; he is master of his own fate. (Richter, *art. cit.*, may well be right in arguing that this Johannine picture of Jesus is meant to answer the type of Jewish objections encountered later in Origen *Celsus* II 9; GCS 2: 135: If Jesus were divine, how could men have taken him prisoner and killed him?) In John there is to be no physical contact between Judas and Jesus, no kiss as in the Synoptic account. (Is the kiss a symbolic addition to the original story?) The two sides are divided in warfare. Jesus asks of the forces led by the renegade disciple a question similar to that which he had posed to his first disciples ("What are you looking for?" [i 38]). Those disciples had followed him looking for life; Judas' party has come looking for Jesus' death.

On the level of ordinary conversation the phrase by which Jesus answers, "I am (he)," serves simply to identify Jesus as the one sought, the function played by the kiss of Judas in the Synoptic tradition. But the reaction of falling back in confusion at Jesus' answer is not simply spontaneous astonishment. The adversaries of Jesus are prostrate on their face before his majesty (Bartina, *art. cit.*), and so there can be little doubt that John intends "I AM" as a divine name (see vol. 29, App. IV). Falling down is a reaction to divine revelation in Dan ii 46, viii 18; Rev i 17. Perhaps Ps lvi 10(9) may have entered the formation of the scene: "My enemies will be turned back . . . behold I know that you are my God." Even better background would have been available if the legend was already in circulation that when Moses uttered before Pharaoh the secret name of God, Pharaoh fell speechless to the ground (Eusebius, *Praeparatio evangelica* IX. xxvii. 24–26; GCS 43[1]:522, attributes it to Artapanus, a writer who lived before the 1st century B.C.; see R. D. Bury, ET 24 [1912–13], 232–33). The Johannine scene illustrates that Jesus has God's power over the forces of darkness because he has the divine name. It reinforces the impression that Jesus could not have been arrested unless he permitted it. The attitude will be put into words before Pilate in xix 11: "You would have no power over me at all were it not given to you from above."

But this time Jesus does not choose to leave his enemies powerless. In the agony scene in the Synoptics it is clear that Jesus does not wish to resist his Father's will; so in John, Jesus permits himself to be arrested provided that his followers are not harmed. Jesus does not use the protection of the divine name for himself but for those whom he loves. The sparing of the disciples fulfills the theme of xvii 12 which had proclaimed the protective power of the divine name.

[The Bibliography for this section is included in the Bibliography at the end of §62.]

62. THE PASSION NARRATIVE:
—DIVISION ONE (UNIT TWO)
(xviii 13–27)

The Interrogation of Jesus

XVIII 13 First they took Jesus to Annas, for he was the father-in-law of Caiaphas who was high priest that year. (14 Remember, it was Caiaphas who had advised the Jews that "it was more advantageous to have one man die for the people.")

15 Now Simon Peter was following Jesus, along with another disciple. This disciple, who was known to the high priest, accompanied Jesus into the high priest's palace, 16 while Peter was left standing outside at the gate. So the [other] disciple (the one known to the high priest) came out and spoke to the girl at the gate and brought Peter in. 17 This servant girl who kept the gate said to Peter, "Are you too one of this man's disciples?" "No, I am not," he replied. 18 Since it was cold, the servants and police had made a charcoal fire and were standing around warming themselves; so Peter too stood with them and warmed himself.

19 The high priest questioned Jesus about his disciples and about his teaching. 20 Jesus answered,

"I have spoken openly to all the world.
I always taught in a synagogue or in the temple precincts
where all the Jews come together.
There was nothing secret about what I said.

21 Why do you question me? Question those who heard me when I spoke. Obviously, they should know what I said." 22 At this reply one of the police in attendance gave Jesus a slap in the face, exclaiming, "Is that any way to answer the high priest?" 23 Jesus replied, "If I've said anything wrong, produce some evidence of it. But if I was right, why do you hit me?" 24 Then Annas sent him bound to Caiaphas, the high priest.

17: *said, replied.* In the historical present tense.

25 In the meantime Simon Peter had been standing there, warming himself. So they said to him, "Are you too one of his disciples?" "No, I am not," he said, denying it. 26 "Didn't I see you with him in the garden?" insisted one of the high priest's servants, a relative of the man whose ear Peter had cut off. 27 Peter denied it again, and just then a cock began to crow.

26: *insisted*. In the historical present tense.

NOTES

xviii 13. *took*. Literally "led," *agagein*, as in Luke xxii 54. Many later witnesses read "led away," *apagagein*, harmonizing with Mark xiv 53; Matt xxvi 57.

Annas. According to Josephus (*Ant.* XVIII.ii.1;※26) the high priest Ananus (Gr. *Ananos*, from Heb. *Hᵃnanyāh;* the NT form *Annas* is a shortening) was appointed by the Roman prefect Quirinius in A.D. 6 and deposed by Valerius Gratus in 15 (XVIII.ii.2;※34). He remained powerful, for his five sons eventually became high priests (XX.ix.1;※198). The family of Ananus is mentioned several times in later Jewish writings; it was noted for its greed, as well as for its wealth and power. Luke is the only other evangelist who associates Annas with the general period of Jesus' ministry. Luke iii 2 dates to the high priesthood of Annas and Caiaphas the coming of the word of God to John the Baptist in the desert; Acts iv 6 says that Peter was brought before "Annas the high priest, and Caiaphas, and John [perhaps Jonathan, son of Ananus who ruled in 36–37, after Caiaphas], and Alexander [otherwise unknown]." Most critics assume that Luke mistakenly thought that Annas was still high priest or at least co-high priest with Caiaphas. Winter, *Trial*, p. 33, thinks Luke was guilty of the even more egregious error of antedating to the 30s Ananus II who reigned in A.D. 62 and had James the brother of Jesus stoned. Apparently (p. 35) Winter thinks the same mistake was made by the author of John xviii 12–27! At least in the instance of Luke iii 2 this minimalist approach to Lucan accuracy may be hypercritical; for it is not impossible that in calling Annas "high priest," Luke is preserving a title of courtesy given to former high priests. We have evidence of such a usage both in the Mishnah (*Horayoth* 3:1–2, 4—the high priest retained his sanctity and obligations even after he was no longer in office) and in Josephus (*War* II.xii.6;※243— Jonathan is referred to as a high priest fifteen years after his deposition). It may even have been that ultra-orthodox Jews refused to recognize the Roman deposition of high priests and considered Annas the legitimate high priest since high priesthood was supposed to be a lifetime office (Num xxxv 25). And perhaps in the *de facto* situation the shrewd, old Annas was the effective high priest, wielding the power behind the scenes while his relatives held the title.

John is our only source for two details: that Annas played a role in the interrogation of Jesus and that Annas was Caiaphas' father-in-law. From what we have said neither detail is implausible, despite the tendency of many critics to dismiss them. The serious problem is that John calls Annas "the high priest" in 15, 16, 19, and 22. We would interpret this in light of the suggestions made above about the Lucan use of that title. (The Johannine writer clearly knew that Caiaphas was the official high priest at the time of Jesus' death [vs. 14; xi 49], and we can scarcely think that he was so ignorant of the Palestinian situation that he thought there could be two official high priests at the same time. Critics who make this suggestion cannot explain how an author who knew the OT so well could make such an elementary mistake.) Others have tried to solve the problem by literary criticism. We find in the OS[sin], the Philoxenian Syriac, the margin of the Evangeliarium Hierosolymitanum, the Greek Cursive 225, and Cyril of Alexandria support for a rearrangement whereby vs. 24 is read immediately after 13. This would mean that after Jesus was led to Annas, he was quickly sent from Annas on to Caiaphas; and thus the interrogation took place before Caiaphas who is designated throughout as "the high priest." While this rearrangement has appealed to different scholars (Luther, Calmes, Lagrange, Streeter, Durand, Joüon, Vosté, Sutcliffe) and continues to receive modern support and improvement (articles of Church and Schneider), it is probably an ancient scribal attempt to improve the sequence rather than a genuine echo of the original order. OS[sin], which is the basic witness for the rearrangement, tends to make such "improvements" in order; for instance, it places 19–23 after 14–15. If in the original vs. 24 followed 13, there is no reasonable explanation how the order now found in most witnesses came about; but one can explain easily that a copyist would move 24 and place it after 13 to make John harmonize with the Matthean tradition wherein Jesus was interrogated by Caiaphas. Moreover, the rearrangement makes the mention of Annas superfluous.

Finally some have objected that Roman soldiers (vs. 12) would never have delivered a prisoner to Jewish authorities. But this objection presumes that Pilate was not working in cooperation with the leaders of the Sanhedrin. It should be noted that the evangelist does not suggest that the Roman troops entered the courtyard of the high priest; only the temple police and the servants are placed there (vs. 18).

Caiaphas. Among the Synoptic Gospels only Matthew identifies the high priest who interrogated Jesus: "Then those who had seized Jesus led him away to Caiaphas the high priest" (Matt xxvi 57). Mark and Luke simply speak of the high priest; and Winter, *Trial*, p. 33, thinks that Christian tradition did not preserve the high priest's name. Unless one thinks that John copied from Matthew, one would have to suppose that independently the two evangelists sought out Jewish information about the high priest who would have been in office at the time of Jesus' death. Rather the omission of the name in Mark and Luke may reflect the Gentile origins and destination of those two Gospels; and Matthew and John in this instance may be closer to the Palestinian tradition.

high priest that year. See NOTE on xi 49. Bultmann, p. 497, like Wellhausen before him, treats the entire reference to Caiaphas in 13 and 14 as a gloss by the evangelist on his source. Verse 14 does seem to be a parenthetical addition and is probably to be related to that stage of Johannine editing responsible for the introduction of chs. xi–xii into the outline of the Gospel (vol. 29, pp. 414–15, 427–30). But this addition may have been suggested by the fact that the account of the interrogation identified Annas as the father-in-law of Caiaphas, and so it is not clear that the last part of 13 is also an addition.

14. *Remember*. The writer refers back to xi 50: "Don't you realize that it is more to your advantage to have one man die [for the people] than to have the whole nation destroyed."

die. Apothanein; the later witnesses read *apolesthai,* "perish, be destroyed." Both verbs appear in xi 50. It is tempting to theorize that the original of the present verse had "one man perish" and that scribes inserted "die" to make the citation match the original.

15. *Simon Peter*. Throughout the denials the simple name "Peter" will be used (16, 17, 18, 27); but when the disciple is first mentioned, here and again in 25 after the Annas inquiry, John uses the favored full name (NOTE on i 40). The three Synoptic Gospels agree that Peter *followed* Jesus.

another disciple. Is this unnamed disciple to be identified with "the other disciple" of xx 2 who is the Beloved Disciple? See vol. 29, pp. XCIII–XCIV. Some ancient scribes made this identification, for they wrote *"the* other disciple" in the present verse. Bultmann, p. 499⁶, rejects the identification, but there are arguments in its favor. This "another disciple" is associated with Peter, a hallmark of the Beloved Disciple (xiii 23–26, xx 2–10, xxi 7, 20–23). The Beloved Disciple must also have followed Jesus during the passion because he appears at the foot of the cross in xix 25–27. Moreover, the fact that this "another disciple" accompanied Jesus into the high priest's palace suggests the deep attachment to Jesus characteristic of the Beloved Disciple. We shall see the difficulties about the identification in the NOTES that follow.

known to the high priest. Schlatter, p. 332, argues that *gnōstos* does not necessarily imply friendship but only that one was not unknown. Yet, Barrett, p. 439, points out that in LXX *gnōstos* refers to a close friend. This description raises two problems. First, if this "another disciple" was known to the high priest, can he be the Beloved Disciple? Would it not be also known that he was the favorite of Jesus and how then could he be admitted to the high priest's palace without question when Peter was interrogated? We get the impression that if Peter confessed to being Jesus' disciple, he would not have been admitted or would have been arrested; but this "another disciple" moves about freely. This difficulty leads Bultmann to suggest that the disciple was not one of the Twelve and was not known to be a follower of Jesus. E. A. Abbott (cf. ET 25 [1913–14], 149–50) has made the ingenious proposal that the disciple was Judas, the one member of the Twelve whom we know to have had dealings with the high priest and whose presence in the palace would not have raised questions. Matt xxvii 3–4 has a tradition that Judas followed the interrogation of Jesus closely. But there is no evidence that the Fourth Evangelist is thinking of the disciple as Judas in the description in 15–16. Another proposal, made by E. A. Tindall, ET 28 (1916–17), 283–84, is that the disciple was Nicodemus, a Jerusalem inhabitant (John ii 23–iii 1) who was involved in the events of the passion (xix 39) and who, as a member of the Sanhedrin, would have had an entrée to the high priest.

The second problem stems from the possibility of an affirmative answer to the first: if the disciple is the Beloved Disciple, can the Beloved Disciple be John son of Zebedee? How would a poor, uneducated Galilean fisherman be known to the high priest? Yet while a relationship to the high priest might be easier if the disciple were a Judean rather than a Galilean (Dodd, *Tradition*, pp. 88–89), John son of Zebedee is not so easily excluded. W. Wuellner, *The Meaning of "Fishers of Men"* (Philadelphia: Westminster, 1967) has

exposed the weak foundation underlying the common attitude toward the ignorance and poverty of the Galilean disciples. The fact that a man was a fisherman
tells us little of his social class or education. Mark i 20 presents Zebedee,
the father of John, as a man with hired servants, and either John or his
mother had ambition for prestige (Mark x 35–45; Matt xx 20–28). Nor does
the remark in Acts iv 13 that John was unlettered tell us much about his
education, for this remark is polemic and may be a vilification. In one of
our oldest comments on the identity of this "another disciple," Nonnus (mid-5th
century) in his metrical paraphrase of the Gospel thinks of him as a young
man, a fisher by trade (cf. W. Drum, ET 25 [1913–14], 381–82). For other
comments on this verse see vol. 29, p. xcvii. Obviously no certain solution
is possible for either problem.

  into the high priest's palace. The word *aulē* can refer to a palace building
or to an open courtyard. The latter meaning is apparently intended by all
three Synoptists when they use the term for the site of Peter's denials. (The
"aulē of the high priest" is mentioned in Mark xiv 54 and Matt xxvi 58, while
Luke xxii 54–55 speaks of "the house [*oikia*] of the high priest" and refers to an
aulē in that house.) They have Peter sitting in the *aulē* with the police,
and Mark and Luke mention a fire burning in the *aulē* for warmth. In
Mark xiv 66 the *aulē* is downstairs while the trial is held in an upstairs
room; in Matt xxvi 58 the *aulē* is outside; in Luke xxii 54–55 it is only
part of the high priest's "house." But in the Johannine account the question
is more complicated. Here too Peter is undoubtedly pictured as outside in
the courtyard near the gate, while seemingly Jesus is interrogated elsewhere.
But John does not use *aulē* for the place where Peter is waiting and warming
himself. The one use of *aulē* in this episode is better rendered "palace," for
normally one does not speak of having access to a courtyard.

  Where was the high priest's palace? Caiaphas was the official high priest;
presumably he lived in the Hasmonean palace on the West Hill of the city,
overlooking the Tyropoeon valley and facing the Temple. (Since the 4th
century the "house of Caiaphas" has been localized on the southern part
of the West Hill, just outside the Zion gate and near the Cenacle; but the
historicity of this tradition is quite dubious. See Kopp, HPG, pp. 352–57.)
However, in John's account the reference is to Annas' palace, *from* which
Jesus was subsequently sent to Caiaphas. Did Annas have a palace of his
own? (In the 13th century the local tradition of Jerusalem began to distinguish
between the "house of Annas" and the "house of Caiaphas"; previously no
attention was paid to Annas' residence—Lagrange, p. 460.) Had Annas gone
to the official high priest's palace from which Jesus would be sent to Caiaphas
who was at the place where the Sanhedrin met? This suggestion would agree
with Luke xxii 54, 66 in which Jesus is led from "the high priest's house" to
"the Sanhedrin." Many scholars (Augustine, Zahn, Plummer, Dalman, Blinzler)
suggest that Annas and Caiaphas lived in different wings of the same palace,
wings bound together by a common courtyard through which Jesus passed
as he went from one priest to the other. Much of this is pure speculation.

  16. *Peter was left standing outside.* None of the Synoptics indicate that
Peter had trouble entering the court.

  the [other] disciple. Some minor witnesses read "that disciple"; P66 has
neither "other" nor "that."

  known to the high priest. In 15 *gnōstos* governed a dative; here it governs a genitive. There is no apparent difference of meaning, but perhaps a different hand (the redactor) added the parenthetical clarification here.

girl at the gate. The noun *thyrōros* can be masculine or feminine according to the sex of the gatekeeper; here the article indicates that a woman is meant. (For women gatekeepers see LXX of II Sam iv 6; Acts xii 13.) A masculine reading is reflected in OSsin, the Ethiopic, and one witness to Tatian's text; Benoit, *Passion*, p. 68, thinks this may have been the original reading. See next NOTE.

17. *servant girl who kept the gate.* A *paidiskē* or maid servant appears in all the Gospel accounts of Peter's first denial, but John alone specifies her work. Mark, who has the girl serve as the interrogator in the second denial as well, places that denial in the forecourt (xiv 68: *proaulion*—in Matt xxvi 71 this is a gateway or *pylōn*); thus there may be a hint in the Synoptic tradition that associates the maid with the gate into the courtyard. Many scholars (Bultmann, p. 499[7]) have expressed doubt that a woman would be allowed to tend the gate of the high priest's palace, especially at night. Some propose that the Johannine editor turned the originally undefined or masculine gatekeeper of 16 into a girl to harmonize with the Synoptic tradition of a maid servant, and so the clause under consideration represents an editorial combination of the two ideas. Here the OSsin and the Ethiopic read "the girl servant of the man who kept the gate"; this reading implies that a male gatekeeper let Peter in, but his servant girl questioned Peter. This is attractive, but we remember that OSsin has betrayed a penchant for ironing out the difficulties of this scene.

said. Tatian and OSsin add that she stared at Peter, a borrowing from Luke xxii 56.

"Are you too one . . . ?" A question with *mē* normally anticipates a negative answer. The normal meaning would be possible in the present context if we theorize that the servant might be loath to think of Peter as a troublemaker since he was being sponsored by one known to the household. But in 25 the same question with *mē* reappears, and there it is more difficult to explain how a negative answer might be anticipated. It is simpler to suppose that sometimes *mē* has lost its force in Johannine questions (see John iv 29 and MTGS, p. 283). Nevertheless, the third question asked of Peter (26) employs an *ouk* (sign of anticipating an affirmative answer), and so there is some contrast intended between the two types of questions.

What is the force of the "too" here? Some (Lagrange, Westcott) think that she knew the other disciple was one of Jesus' followers. But then why was the other disciple admitted and why was he not in danger, as Peter seemingly would have been if he had told the truth? "You too" and "this man too" appear in the Synoptic accounts of the accusation of Peter (Mark xiv 67 and par.) where there is no question of a comparison with another disciple; the "too" implicitly refers to the disciples who were with Jesus when he was arrested. Thus, in John as well the idea may be: "Are you, like those others, a disciple?"

I am not. Grundmann, NovT 3 (1959), 65[1], suggests that the *ouk eimi* of Peter here and in 25 are the negative counterparts of the *egō eimi* of Jesus in 5 and 8. Thus Grundmann arrives at an interesting contrast between Jesus' confession of who he is in defense of the disciples and Peter's denial that he is a disciple.

18. *cold.* Only John gives this detail, but it is an obvious implication in Mark and Luke which mention a fire in the courtyard. Jerusalem, a half-mile above sea level, can be cold on spring nights.

servants and police. Along with Roman troops, there were servants and police in the garden for the arrest of Jesus (servant in vs. 10; police in 3 and 12). Mark xiv 54 and Matt xxvi 58 mention police in the high priest's courtyard, although they did not mention them in the scene of the arrest.

had made a charcoal fire. Of the Synoptics Luke (xxii 55) alone mentions the kindling of the fire (*pyr;* in 56 *phōs,* "light") as soon as the arresting party arrived at the high priest's house. Mark xiv 54 speaks of a blaze (*phōs*) but omits the kindling; Matthew omits all mention of a fire. John speaks of *anthrakia* or charcoal (fire).

warming themselves. The verb appears in a different form in Tatian and some Syriac witnesses; it is missing in a few Greek mss. Since it occurs twice in this verse, one occurrence may represent a scribal addition.

stood. In the three Synoptic accounts Peter sits down with the police or those present. However, "stood" need not be taken too literally if we judge by Semitic usage. ZGB, §365: "*Estōs* occasionally means no more than mere presence in a place."

warmed himself. Only Mark (xiv 54 and 67) mentions this; John too has it twice (here and 25). Buse, "Marcan," p. 217, sees a literary connection between this verse in John and Mark xiv 54; however, note the differences we have been pointing out.

19. *high priest.* See NOTE on Annas in 13. Verse 24 implies that Caiaphas was not present.

20. *Jesus answered.* Only with hesitancy have we put Jesus' answer in verse format; Bultmann and SB do not. Although the third line is rather prosaic, the first two are in parallelism, and along with the last line they may echo the motif of Wisdom speaking in public to men (Prov viii 2–3, ix 3; Wis vi 14, 16; Bar iii 37[38]).

I have spoken openly. The tense is perfect while the subsequent verbs ("I taught"; "I said") are in the aorist. MTGS, pp. 69–70, points to this as an example of a verb in the perfect tense functioning in an aoristic sense. Is Jesus claiming that his doctrine is not esoteric or that it is not subversive? Historically the latter may have been the problem if he was arrested as a revolutionary. In Mark xiv 48–49 Jesus complains that they have come out armed to arrest him as if he were a guerrilla bandit; yet, "I was with you daily, teaching in the temple precincts, and you did not seize me." The parallel to John is closer if Winter, *Trial,* p. 49, is right in claiming that Mark's *kath hēmeran,* "daily," means "by day, in the hours of daylight" and thus has the same import as John's "openly." Jesus' statement here agrees with some previous passages in John, for example, vii 26 where the people of Jerusalem acknowledged that Jesus was speaking in public and wondered whether the fact that the authorities failed to check him did not mean that they had accepted him as Messiah. See also xi 54 which implies that moving about "openly among the Jews" was Jesus' normal policy until just before the end of the ministry. Yet in x 24 "the Jews" challenged Jesus: "If you are really the Messiah, tell us so in plain words [*parrēsia*="openly, publicly"]." Thus, for John, in a certain sense Jesus did speak openly and plainly, but in another sense his words were obscure. Sometimes the obscurity arose from the unwillingness of the audience to believe; yet the evangelist also recognizes a depth in Jesus' words that only the Paraclete can clarify (xvi 12–13). It is interesting to compare Jesus' answer to the high priest with Socrates' answer to his judges: "If anyone says that he has ever learned or heard anything from me in private that all others could not have heard, then know that he does not speak the truth" (Plato *Apology* 33B).

always. This is not to be taken too literally; obviously Jesus spoke in private to Nicodemus and to the Samaritan woman.

in a synagogue. Only one instance of this is recorded in John (vi 59).

in the temple precincts. See ii 14, vii 14, 28, viii 20, x 23. A Synoptic parallel was given above; yet the picture of frequent teaching in the temple precincts does not accord with the Synoptic outline where Jesus comes to Jerusalem only once.

where all the Jews come together. Jesus would scarcely have to tell this to the high priest. If this verse preserves an original saying of Jesus, it has been expanded so that it could be addressed to the Gentile readers of the Gospel. Yet the second and third lines of this verse are the ones that Bultmann, p. 500, judges to have come from an earlier passion source, while the first and fourth represent the evangelist's expansion (for they are the more theological).

There was nothing secret about what I said. This echoes Yahweh's words in Isa xlv 19: "I have not said anything in secret" (also xlviii 16).

21. *Why do you question me?* The principle that it is improper to have an accused person convict himself is explicit in the Jewish law of later times (e.g., Maimonides) and may have already been in effect at this time. The Byzantine tradition reads a stronger verb ("interrogate") for "question."

Question those who heard me. Jesus is demanding a trial with witnesses—a good indication that the hearing before Annas was not a formal trial. Such self-assurance before authority was probably startling; for Josephus, *Ant.* XIV.ix.4; ⅜172, tells us that the normal attitude before a judge was one of humility, timidity, and mercy-seeking.

22. *One of the police . . . gave Jesus a slap in the face.* The Synoptic Gospels describe more elaborately the indignities to which Jesus was subjected. According to Matt xxvi 67, at the conclusion of Jesus' nighttime trial before the high priest and the Sanhedrin, they (seemingly the Sanhedrin members) spat at, struck, and *slapped* him, challenging him to prophesy. The Matthean account is probably a simplification of the composite form in Mark xiv 65 where two groups are involved: first, some (of the Sanhedrin) spat in Jesus' face, struck him, and challenged him to prophesy; then, the police took him and slapped him (see P. Benoit, "Les outrages à Jésus prophète," in NTPat, pp. 92–110). The account in Luke xxii 63–64 is appreciably different: in the high priest's house or courtyard after Peter had denied Jesus three times, the men who were holding Jesus mocked and hit him, blindfolding him and challenging him to prophesy. Then they spoke against him, reviling him. John's account is somewhat closer to the last line of Mark and to Luke in the question of those who committed the indignities, but closer to Mark and Matthew in the question of what was done (Luke does not mention a slapping). The slap was more an insult than a physically damaging blow.

"Is that any way to answer the high priest?" An attitude of propriety was demanded by Exod xxii 28: "You shall not revile God nor curse [say something wrong of] a ruler of your people." It is not unheard of that an attendant at a

trial might be carried away to act against a prisoner; cf. the story of the trial before Rabbi Papa in TalBab *Shebuoth* 30b.

23. *Jesus replied.* Only in John does Jesus answer the indignities.

If I've said anything wrong. Jesus implicitly cites the law of Exod xxii 28 mentioned above and denies that he has violated it.

produce some evidence of it. Jesus exhibited the same confidence in his innocence in viii 46: "Can any one of you convict me of sin? If I am telling the truth, why do you not believe me?" See also xv 25: "They hated me without cause."

hit. Among the Synoptic accounts of the indignities, Luke (xxii 63) alone uses this verb *derein*.

24. *Then.* Or "so"; perhaps because Jesus was demanding a formal hearing and the interrogation was getting nowhere.

sent. We mentioned above (NOTE on Annas in 13) the attempts to move this verse to a position immediately after vs. 13 and thus to make Caiaphas the interrogator in 19. Another proposal with the same goal is to understand the aorist verb as a pluperfect (Grotius, D. F. Strauss, Edersheim), turning this into a parenthetical remark that Annas *had sent* Jesus to Caiaphas, namely, before the interrogation of 19–23.

bound. Jesus had been brought to Annas bound (12). Had he been unbound during the interrogation, or is Lagrange right in suggesting that this means "still bound"? (Compare Acts xxii 30 where Paul was unbound when he was brought before the chief priests and the Sanhedrin, but this privilege may have been accorded to him because he was a Roman citizen.) In still another attempt to solve the problem of an interrogation of Jesus before Annas, A. Mahoney, *art. cit.,* resorts to textual emendation: in place of *dedemenon,* "bound," he reads *de menōn:* "But Annas *remaining* (after the departure of Caiaphas) sent him to Caiaphas." This emendation supposes unmentioned details: Caiaphas was with Annas when Jesus was interrogated, but after the interrogation he went on to where the Sanhedrin was assembling.

In the Marcan/Matthean tradition the first mention of Jesus' being bound is when he is sent forth from the Sanhedrin to Pilate (Mark xv 1; Matt xxvii 2). Luke has no reference to binding.

to Caiaphas. To the palace of the official high priest, or (if Annas was already there) to another wing of the palace, or to wherever the Sanhedrin met (see NOTE on "palace" in 15). Of course, John does not mention the Sanhedrin but only Caiaphas; yet the "they" of 28 (NOTE there) may well imply the leaders of the Sanhedrin. We do not know where the Sanhedrin met at this time. See Blinzler, *Trial,* pp. 112–14. Mishnah *Middoth,* 5:4, speaks of the Hall of Hewn Stone on the south side of the temple court; but according to TalBab, *Abodah Zarah,* 8b, the Sanhedrin left this hall forty years (round number?) before the Temple was destroyed (A.D. 70) and moved to the market place (see vol. 29, p. 119)—thus seemingly always about Jesus' time.

25. *In the meantime.* This is a free rendition of *de;* seemingly John is turning back to tell us what happened while Jesus was being interrogated. Mark and Matthew make it clear that Peter was outside or downstairs while Jesus was being interrogated inside or upstairs. In John we get the impression (but no clear statement) of a shift of scene from one part of the building to another.

Simon Peter . . . warming himself. This is a repetition of vs. 18 so that the first two denials are connected. John agrees with Luke on the localization of the second denial; see chart on p. 838 below.

they said. Presumably the servants and police mentioned in 18.

"Are you too . . . ?" "No, I am not." John has the same question and answer as in the first denial.

he said, denying it. Literally "he denied it and said"—a Hebraism; cf. MTGS, p. 156.

26. *a relative.* The author betrays a detailed knowledge of the high priest's household; he knew of Malchus in 10, and here he knows of Malchus' relative. Some would explain this on the grounds that the Beloved Disciple who is the source of the Fourth Gospel's tradition was the "another disciple" known to the high priest (15). If the name in 10 is fictional, the author has gone to pains to carry on the fiction.

27. *a cock began to crow.* Cockcrow is associated with Peter's denials in all the Gospels. John does not have the Marcan detail that this was the second time the cock crowed, nor the Lucan detail that when the cock crowed, the Lord turned and looked at Peter. The three Synoptics recall Jesus' warning that Peter would deny his master; John does not. Some have questioned whether there would be cocks in Jerusalem; for the Mishnah, *Baba Kamma,* 7:7, forbids the raising of fowl in Jerusalem (cf. StB, I, 992–93). But we are not sure that this was strictly observed; see J. Jeremias, *Jerusalem in the Time of Jesus* (Philadelphia: Fortress, 1969), pp. 47–48[44]. Bernard, II, 604, endorses the suggestion that what was involved was not the bird's cry but the signal on the trumpet given at the close of the third watch named "cockcrow" (12 P.M. to 3 A.M.). This would mean that the interrogation by Annas and Peter's denials had come to an end at 3 A.M. Père Lagrange's self-sacrificing study of the question has produced the information that natural cockcrow at Jerusalem in March–April occurs most frequently between 3 and 5 A.M., with the earliest recorded at 2:30. H. Kosmala, *Annual of the Swedish Theological Institute* 2 (1963), 118–20; 6 (1967–68), 132–34, reports consistent evidence for three distinct nocturnal cockcrows throughout the year in Palestine, about 12:30, 1:30, and 2:30, with the second as traditionally the most important. Consult also C. Lattey, *Scripture* 6 (1953–54), 53–55.

COMMENT

In the outline of this unit given on p. 785 above, we pointed out that basically it consists of a central episode, the interrogation of Jesus by Annas, surrounded on both sides by Peter's denial of Jesus. The central episode has only remote parallels in the Synoptic accounts; the episode of the denials of Peter has close parallels. Let us study each episode in detail.

The Interrogation of Jesus by Annas (vss. 13–14; 19–23)

Scholars find great difficulty in their attempts to establish a historical sequence from the diverse Gospel presentations of the interrogations of Jesus by the Jewish authorities. On an accompanying chart we have schematized the evidence. We may begin our study by listing what seems factual or plausible in the Synoptic accounts (remembering the problem of whether Luke's presentation is independent of Mark's—p. 790 above): (1) A session of the Sanhedrin (whole or part) was convened to deal with Jesus and to determine whether he should be handed over to the Romans for trial. The three Synoptics testify to this (also see NOTE on "to Caiaphas" in John xviii 24); it seems to have been part of the pre-Marcan primitive account (Taylor's A source, xv 1—p. 788 above); and it is mentioned in two of the three predictions of the passion (Mark viii 31, x 33), which are, in part at least, pre-Marcan in origin.

(2) The morning session described in Luke is a doublet of the night session described in Mark/Matthew. The Lucan form, wherein there are no witnesses and no death sentence, gives the impression of an interrogation rather than of a trial and may be more original. See pp. 795–96 above.

(3) The Lucan tradition of only one Sanhedrin session is preferable to the tradition of two sessions (night and morning) in Mark/Matthew. The idea of two sessions probably results from the combination of sources. The pre-Marcan primitive passion account (Mark's A source) seems simply to have mentioned a session (Mark xv 1) without giving its content. The more detailed account now appearing in Mark/Matthew as the night session probably stems from Mark's B source (so Bultmann, while Taylor hesitates). We judge unsuccessful the many attempts to explain as reasonable the Marcan/Matthean sequence, for example: that a morning session was needed to determine how to get the Romans to carry out the death sentence passed at night; or that Matt xxvii 1 does not report a new session but summarizes the preceding session ("When morning came, . . . they had taken counsel against Jesus to put him to death").

(4) The one session probably took place very early in the morning (Luke; primitive account). Court trials held in the middle of the night are avoided in the jurisprudence of almost every country, and a night session would have cast doubt on the good faith of the Sanhedrin. If the Sanhedrin still met in the temple precincts (NOTE on "to Caiaphas" in 24), the temple area would have been locked at night. The early hour of the session would have been dictated by the knowledge that Jesus might have to be brought to the Roman prefect who would normally be available for official matters at dawn (see NOTE on xviii 28). This factor, plus the realization that all the legal processes would have to be terminated by sundown (beginning of Passover), encouraged brevity.

(5) The narrative of the abuse of Jesus must be taken seriously since it exists in independent accounts (Mark/Matthew; Luke; also John). All four Gospels agree that it took place at night after Jesus' arrest; but since it was not in the primitive passion account (A source), its localization is uncertain. The attempt of Mark/Matthew to attach it to a formal trial and to

JESUS BEFORE THE JEWISH AUTHORITIES

	MATTHEW	MARK	LUKE	JOHN
	xxvi 57, 59–68	xiv 53, 55–65	xxii 54, 63–65	xviii 13–15, 19–24
Night	Trial before Caiaphas and Sanhedrin; witnesses; Temple saying; "Are you the Messiah, Son of God?"; blasphemy charge; deserving of death.	Trial before high priest and Sanhedrin; witnesses; Temple saying; "Are you the Messiah, Son of the Blessed?"; blasphemy charge; all condemn him as deserving of death.	Brought to high priest's house (no trial reported).	Interrogation by Annas about his disciples and his teaching; Jesus says he has taught openly and they should question those who heard.
	They (the Sanhedrin) spit at him, strike and slap him, challenging him to prophesy.	Some (of the Sanhedrin) spit at him, covering his face, strike him, challenging him to prophesy. Police take him with slaps.	Those who hold him mock and beat him, blindfolding him, challenging him to prophesy. They revile him with words.	Policeman gives Jesus a slap, accusing him of impropriety toward high priest. Jesus demands evidence he has done evil.
				Jesus is sent bound to Caiaphas (no trial reported).

	xxvii 1–2	xv 1	xxii 66–71, xxiii 1	xviii 28
Early Morning	A consultation by Sanhedrin against him to put him to death.	A consultation by whole Sanhedrin.	Led from high priest's house to Sanhedrin meeting. (No witnesses); Two questions: "If you are the Messiah, tell us"; "Are you the Son of God?" They need no further witnesses. (No condemnation)	They lead Jesus from Caiaphas to the praetorium.
	They bind and lead Jesus away, delivering him to Pilate.	They bind and lead Jesus away, delivering him to Pilate.	Whole Sanhedrin rise and lead Jesus to Pilate.	

831

have the indignities committed by the Sanhedrin members is implausible and probably stems from anti-Jewish apologetic.

These brief observations do not solve all the problems. For instance, if Mark combined two accounts of a Sanhedrin session, why did he not use the fuller account from the B source to expand the reference to a session found in A? Why did he put the account of the B source as a night session held before the early morning session of the A account? Was there a vague remembrance of two hearings, one held at night and one in the morning? This thesis receives support from the curious arrangement in John. John reports in detail the interrogation of Jesus at night by Annas and then mentions without detail that Jesus was sent to Caiaphas and kept there until daybreak when he was taken from Caiaphas to Pilate. Thus, like Mark/Matthew, John presents a narrative in which Jesus appears twice before the Jewish authorities; one of these appearances John describes, the other he simply mentions.

The harmonization of John and the Synoptic accounts does not overly concern us; but before we treat the properly Johannine questions, it may be useful to present a *modified* summary based on Benoit's harmonization in order to illustrate the method involved. Benoit suggests that there were two legal procedures that brought Jesus before the Jewish authorities. At night, as John relates, there was a preparatory investigation by Annas, the former high priest. Since the chief priests were in authority over the temple police who brought Jesus in, we may compare this to the interrogation at police headquarters of a newly arrested prisoner (a procedure that, unlike a court trial, often takes place at night immediately after the prisoner has been apprehended). The interrogation accordingly took place at the high priest's palace (Luke xxii 54) rather than at the court building of the Sanhedrin (xxii 66). While John is the main source for this interrogation, Luke xxii 52 may preserve an echo of it by picturing the chief priests as part of the group that arrested Jesus. Mark/Matthew may preserve a confused memory of the interrogation in having Jesus brought before the high priest *at night* (although what they actually describe took place in the morning). Actually the official high priest was not present lest he compromise the role he would have to play in the morning at the (one and only) Sanhedrin investigation. But naturally Caiaphas appreciated whatever information his father-in-law was able to get the night before. Caiaphas may have been anxious to see what type of defense Jesus would present in order to know how to present the charges against him. He was probably also interested in any preparatory steps that would expedite the morning session.

At the end of the preliminary night investigation, Jesus was abused by the police who held him (Luke xxii 63–65; John xviii 22). This was not done by the Sanhedrin members (Mark/Matthew) and perhaps not even in Annas' presence (John); it may have been done in the courtyard as his captors were waiting for daylight to lead him to Caiaphas and the Sanhedrin. The three Synoptics are right in describing a morning Sanhedrin session; but the details of the night session found in Mark/Matthew belong in the morning (as in Luke). Caiaphas presided (Matthew, John). Pilate had cooperated with Caiaphas in arranging the arrest of Jesus, but now it was the Sanhedrin's task to determine if the case against Jesus was such that he should be brought to trial before the governor for the capital offense of treason against the emperor (e.g., was he a revolutionary [lēstēs] who pretended to be "the King of the Jews"?). In this "grand jury" procedure the Sanhedrin decided affirmatively and delivered Jesus to Pilate with a resumé of the proceedings and a recommendation that Pilate find him guilty.

Such a harmonization is plausible if one accepts most of the Gospel tradition as historical and tries to preserve it with a minimum of modification. More critical scholars, however, would doubt that the historical memory of the early Christian community was so trustworthy.

If we turn from harmonization, three problems in John's account deserve further attention: the omission of the Sanhedrin procedure before Caiaphas; the value of the information about the interrogation by Annas; and the value of John's description of the abuse of Jesus.

First, how do we account for John's omission of the Sanhedrin session? The most obvious explanation is that the pertinent information was not in the pre-Gospel Johannine tradition. Despite Taylor's hesitation we should probably assign to the Marcan B source the information about the session, namely: the calling of witnesses; the reference to Jesus' statement about destroying the Temple; the question of whether Jesus was the Messiah; the charge of blasphemy; and the condemnation to death. We have already seen the problem of certain details (the calling of witnesses, the death sentence) that are lacking in Luke's form of the narrative. Many scholars (e.g., Bultmann, Dibelius) would reject the account completely; others (Benoit, Kümmel) posit at least a partial historicity. We should note that an evaluation of the historicity of the account is affected not only by the inclusion of later theology but also by the abbreviation of what must have been a longer discussion.

For our purposes it is interesting that while John omits the session, most of the details found in the Synoptic accounts appear elsewhere in John:

- In xi 47–53 there is a session of the Sanhedrin under Caiaphas where it is recommended that Jesus should die. A fear is expressed that he may provoke the Romans to destroy "the place," that is, the Temple (see vol. 29, pp. 441–42).
- In ii 19 we find a statement by Jesus about the destruction of the Temple similar to Mark xiv 58 (see vol. 29, pp. 118–20).
- In x 24–25, 33, 36 the questions, accusations, and answers are similar to

the questions and answers in the Sanhedrin session, especially as it appears in Luke xxii 67, 70 (see vol. 29, pp. 405–6, 408–9).

■ In i 51 Jesus makes a promise about a future vision of the Son of Man that has some similarity to the answer he gives to the high priest in Matt xxvi 64 (see vol. 29, pp. 84, 89).

Thus the themes of the Sanhedrin session as recorded by the Synoptic Gospels are, according to the independent witness of John, truly themes preserved in the community's tradition of the ministry of Jesus. But we must ask whether, in an effort to fill in the account of the Sanhedrin session, the traditions behind Mark and Luke have gathered together charges made about Jesus during his ministry on the presumption that these must have formed the substance of the Sanhedrin's investigation. Or has John's tradition dispersed the contents of the Sanhedrin session so that Christians would understand that these charges against Jesus did not suddenly arise at the end of his ministry? (If so, then presumably there was no need for the evangelist to repeat the incidents in the Passion Narrative. We find too subjective the suggestions that the evangelist deliberately abbreviated the Jewish legal procedures because he was primarily interested in Jesus' confrontation with Rome or because he wished to eliminate the apocalyptic reference to the Son of Man found in Mark xiv 62 [Bultmann, p. 498].) Perhaps both the Synoptic and the Johannine traditions preserve a historical element: the charges were made during the ministry (John) and they were taken up again to form the substance of the Sanhedrin investigations of Jesus (Synoptics). While this last suggestion is a type of harmonization, one must admit that it is not implausible.

Second, what value is to be attributed to the questioning of Jesus by Annas, the sole Jewish legal action described in the Johannine Passion? We find strange the confident contention of Bultmann, p. 500 (followed by Jeremias, EWJ, p. 78[4]), that John thinks of this as a Sanhedrin session and a regular trial. Annas alone is mentioned. Verse 24 makes it clear that Caiaphas was not present; and from xi 45–53 we may conclude that the Johannine writer knew perfectly well that, if there were a Sanhedrin session, Caiaphas would have presided. Twice in the interrogation (vss. 21, 23) Jesus demands of Annas that witnesses and evidence be produced—in short, a demand for a trial or hearing. Thus, *pace* Bultmann, we are in the atmosphere of a police interrogation of a newly arrested criminal before any formal trial procedures are begun.

We would also have to disagree with Bultmann, p. 497, that the interrogation by Annas reproduces a tradition similar to that behind the Synoptic Sanhedrin interrogation but shaped in a different way. There is really no similarity between the two, and we think that the two traditions stem from two different hearings. If the interrogation by Annas is historical, we may be certain that John's tradition has preserved only an abridgement; but Bultmann has no evidence for assuming that at one time it contained more material closely parallel to the Synoptic versions of the Sanhedrin session. Plausibly such material would pertain, not to the interrogation by Annas, but to the scene in vs. 24 where Jesus is brought before Caiaphas and yet we are told nothing of what Caiaphas did.

The two questions that Annas asks Jesus about his disciples and about his teaching are more general than the two points raised in the Synoptic reports of the Sanhedrin session (destruction of the Temple, Messiahship). Yet the questions are susceptible of religious and political implications consonant with the Synoptic picture of what the authorities feared about Jesus. On the religious or theological level, they may reflect the charge that Jesus was a false prophet—a charge seen in the Synoptic account of the nighttime mockery of Jesus after his arrest (cf. below) and in the first accusation of Luke xxiii 2. Meeks, pp. 60–61, points to the two marks of the false prophet given in Deut xiii 2–6, xviii 20: he leads others astray (the question about Jesus' disciples) and he falsely presumes to speak in God's name (the question about Jesus' teaching). We have mentioned that Jeremias, EWJ, p. 79, thinks that historically the charge of being a false prophet was the basis of the Jewish action against Jesus.

On the political level, the question about Jesus' disciples may have concerned the likelihood of their causing an uprising and the danger presented by their growing numbers (xi 48, xii 19). Unless the evangelist was controlled by his tradition, it is hard to explain why he records no response to this question. Elsewhere it has been made clear that the Johannine Jesus did not welcome followers who interpreted his movement in political terms (vi 15, xii 14–see vol. 29, pp. 461–63), and so Jesus could have refuted honestly the political implications of Annas' query about his disciples. As for the question about Jesus' teaching, there may have been a concern not only about his orthodoxy and training (vii 15) but also about the possibilities of subversion (see NOTE on "I have spoken openly" in xviii 20).

Thus the interrogation before Annas may have had a very practical purpose. It may have reflected the real concern of the religious leaders about whether Jesus was a false prophet; and it may have been meant to gain information for the "grand jury" proceedings before the Sanhedrin the next morning which would determine whether or not there was a political charge on which Jesus should be handed over to the Romans for trial. Haenchen, "Historie," p. 63, states: "We should not expect to find here historical information beyond that found in the Synoptics." Personally we are not convinced of this. There are difficulties about some details, as we have mentioned in the NOTES, but they are not so grave as to make us disbelieve the whole account. More important, we find no clear Johannine theological motive that would explain the invention of the Annas narrative. Haenchen contends that the scene was fashioned so that the Jewish procedures in the Passion Narrative would lose all importance and the Pilate trial become decisive. But then why bother inserting a narrative of a nighttime interrogation at all? Luke's Passion Narrative got along without one. Another suggestion, namely, that the scene was created to illustrate Jesus' independence before his captors fits in better with attested Johannine thought, and undoubtedly the Johannine writer has made Jesus majestic in delivering his dignified rebuttal. But we cannot put this scene on a par with the "I AM" incident in the garden where the narrative is truly implausible. There is nothing unlikely in the basic idea that Jesus accused his captors of having made up their minds without evidence and without asking those who heard him frequently. This motif appears in the Synoptic accounts as well (Mark xiv 49). Of course, since the Annas interrogation appears in John alone, one cannot verify it with certitude; but neither should one be swayed by an *a priori* attitude that where John is our sole source, the information is of little value.

Lastly, what value is to be attributed to John's account of the abuse of Jesus? We have already insisted that John, Luke, and the last part of Mark xiv 65 are more credible in attributing the abuse to the police (Luke xxii 63: "the men who were holding Jesus") rather than to the Sanhedrin members (Matthew and the first part of Mark xiv 65). In Luke the scene is not set in the course of any legal procedure, but then Luke does not record any nighttime interrogation. John sets the abuse in the course of Annas' interrogation; but this is not incredible since John speaks only of a policeman's slapping Jesus and not of the full-scale mockery reported in the Synoptic tradition (or traditions—here Luke may be independent of Mark/Matthew and more primitive). Those who think of John as dependent on the Synoptics explain that the fourth evangelist omitted the mockery because he found it inconsistent with his theme of Jesus' majesty. But then why did he not also omit the Roman mocking of Jesus (xix 1–3)? Without discussing whether the Synoptic accounts of the mockery are historical, we would simply point out that they are more theologically oriented than John's account. If the slapping of Jesus reported by John and by Mark/Matthew fits in with the theme that Jesus died as the Suffering Servant (LXX of Isa l 6: "I gave my cheeks to slaps"), this theme is carried on in the Marcan/Matthean mention of his being spit at (the other half of Isa l 6: "I did not turn away my face from the shame of spitting"). The Synoptic report of the scoffing at Jesus' ability to prophesy agrees with Isa liii 3: "He was dishonored and not esteemed"; and the silence of Jesus under this treatment agrees with liii 7: "in his affliction he did not open his mouth." Thus, as regards this incident, one may claim with justice that John's account is the simplest, the least theologically oriented, and (along with Luke) has the more likely details as to setting and agent.

Peter's Denials of Jesus (vss. 15–18, 25–27)

All four Gospels place Peter's denials during the night in which Jesus was arrested. In all, the incident consists of an introduction that brings

Peter on the scene and of three denials. Only Luke (xxii 54–62) makes a continuous narrative of the introduction and the denials. Mark/Matthew separate the introduction (Mark xiv 54; Matt xxvi 58) from the three denials (Mark xiv 66–72; Matt xxvi 69–75) by the intervening scene of the night trial of Jesus before the high priest and the Sanhedrin. John places the introduction and the first denial together (xviii 15–18) and this combination is separated from the second and third denial (25–27) by the intervening scene of the interrogation of Jesus before Annas. It seems clear that at one time the introduction and the three denials were a unit, and that in this matter Luke is more original. The different ways of breaking up the scene in Mark/Matthew and in John have the same purpose, namely, to indicate simultaneity with the nighttime legal procedure against Jesus. (A recognition of the primitive unity of the scene gives no support to the ancient or modern attempts to rearrange John's narrative to restore the "original" Johannine order wherein the introduction and denials would form a unit—so Spitta, Moffatt, and Church. The present breaking up of the scene was, in our judgment, the deliberate work of the evangelist. On rearrangements see vol. 29, pp. xxvi–xxvii.) With this stress on simultaneity Mark/Matthew and John express their understanding that Jesus was not present when Peter denied him; Luke (xxii 61) seems to think that he was present.

While the general pattern of the denials is the same in the four Gospels, the details vary greatly as can be seen from the accompanying chart. Some of the variations undoubtedly represent deliberate rearrangement; for instance, as regards the replies of Peter, Luke's first and third reply seem to have reversed Mark's, so that Luke's first is similar to Mark's third, and Luke's third is similar to Mark's first. Nevertheless, a glance at ⌗⌗1, 6, 7, 8, 10, 11, and 13 suggests that within the Synoptic Gospels Luke preserves an independent tradition (Bultmann, HST, p. 269; yet Taylor disagrees, *Behind the Third Gospel* [Oxford: Clarendon, 1926], pp. 48–49). Only in ⌗⌗3, part of 10, 11, and 12 is John close to Mark/Matthew; in ⌗⌗3, 7, the other part of 10, and 12 John is close to Luke (cf. also ⌗⌗9 and 13). Thus John seems to preserve still a third independent tradition (see Dodd, *Tradition*, p. 85). We recall with amusement some of the attempts of the past to deal with the divergent details of the three traditions (Mark/Matthew, Luke, John); some literal-minded interpreters have concluded that there must have been three sets of three denials, thus making Peter guilty nine times! Rather the three traditions stand at a distance from an original account, and the intervening transmission has had its effect on the details. It has been suggested that the earliest form of the story was much simpler than any of the three and involved only one denial by Peter. C. Masson, RHPR 37 (1957), 24–35, proposes the attractive hypothesis that Mark's threefold denial stems from combining doublets of the incident, one with a single denial and one with a double denial. But then, if Luke and John preserve independent versions, how

COMPARATIVE CHART OF THE THREE DENIALS OF JESUS BY PETER

First Denial:

	Matt xxvi 69–70	Mark xiv 66–68	Luke xxii 56–57	John xviii 17–18
1. Sequence	after trial of Jesus	after trial of Jesus	no trial or interrogation	before interrogation of Jesus
2. Place	in the *aulē*	in the *aulē*	in the middle of the *aulē* (55) at the fire	at the gate (*thyra*) while entering
3. Questioner	servant girl	one of the servant girls	servant girl	servant girl who kept gate
4. Question or Accusation	"You too were with [*meta*] Jesus the Galilean"	"You too were with [*meta*] the Nazarene Jesus"	"This one too was with [*syn*] him"	"Are you too one of this man's disciples?"
5. Reply	He denied it before all: "I don't know what you are talking about"	He denied it: "I don't know or understand what you are talking about"	He denied it: "Woman, I don't know him"	"No, I am not"

Second Denial:

	Matt xxvii 71–72	Mark xiv 69–70a	Luke xxii 58	John xviii 25
6. Sequence	after Peter had moved outside	after Peter had moved outside	after a short time	after interrogation of Jesus
7. Place	outside the *aulē* in gateway (*pylōn*)	outside the *aulē* in forecourt (*proaulion*)	in the middle of the *aulē* (55) by the fire	in the *aulē* by the fire
8. Questioner	another servant girl	same servant girl	another (a man)	"they"=servants and police (18)
9. Question or Accusation	"This man was with Jesus of Nazareth"	"This man is one of them"	"You too are one of them"	"Are you too one of his disciples?"
10. Reply	He denied it again with an oath: "I don't know the man"	He denied it again	"Man, I am not"	He denied it: "No, I am not"

Third Denial:

	Matt xxvi 73-75	Mark xiv 70b-72	Luke xxii 59-62	John xviii 26-27
11. Sequence	after a little while	after a little while	after about an hour's interval	immediately?
12. Place	no change	no change	no change	no change
13. Questioner	the bystanders	the bystanders	another (a man)	servant of high priest, relative of man Peter hit
14. Question or Accusation	"Truly you too are one of them, for your accent betrays you"	"Truly you are one of them, for you are a Galilean"	"In truth, this one too was with him, for he is a Galilean"	"Didn't I see you with him in the garden?"
15. Reply	He began to curse and swear: "I don't know the man"	He began to curse and swear: "I don't know this man you are talking about"	"I don't know what you are talking about"	He denied it again
16. Cockcrow	Immediately a cock crowed and	Immediately a cock crowed a second time and	At that moment a cock crowed while he was speaking	Just then a cock crowed
	Peter remembered what Jesus had said	Peter remembered what Jesus had said	Peter recalled the word of the Lord after the Lord looked at him	
	Peter wept bitterly	Peter wept	Peter wept bitterly	

did they also hit upon a threefold denial? (Benoit, *Passion*, pp. 71–72, actually finds some confirmation of Masson's hypothesis in the way John has divided the denials: one denial before the Annas scene, and two after it. But more likely this reflects a literary technique and is not the result of joining doublets of different provenance.) G. Klein, ZTK 58 (1961), 309–10, is probably right in insisting that as far back as we can trace, we have no evidence for simplifying the narrative to fewer than three denials (even though *a priori* we may suspect that the pattern of three is an elaboration).

The story of Peter's denials was not part of the primitive passion account (it stems from Mark's B source in the Marcan outline). What historical value should we attach to it? Many think that the Marcan form of the story came from the reminiscences of Peter and is basically reliable (Loisy, E. Meyer, J. Weiss, Schniewind, Taylor). But others have doubts. Goguel thinks that the threefold denial was invented to fulfill the prediction of Jesus that Peter would deny him. Bultmann dismisses the narrative as legendary. E. Linnemann, ZTK 63 (1966), 1–32, thinks that historically all the disciples denied Jesus and that the story about Peter is simply an imaginative concretizing of the general denial. G. Klein, ZTK 58 (1961), 285–328, and ZNW 58 (1967), 39–44, also denies historicity but for a different reason. He and others before him have stressed that Peter's denials form a unity with the prediction of the denials in Mark xiv 29–31 and par. In the context of this prediction Luke xxii 31–32 has another prediction about Peter: "Simon, Simon, behold Satan asked for all of you [plural] that he might sift you like wheat; but I have prayed for you [singular] that your faith may not fail, and *when you have turned, you must give strength to your brothers.*" This second prediction is accepted by Klein as very old (but not the words of Jesus). The italicized words, however, are a gloss to make the original prediction, which said that Peter would not fail, conform to the later and contradictory idea that he denied Jesus. Moreover, the story of the denials presupposes that Peter followed Jesus after the arrest, and this is seen as contradictory to Mark xiv 27 which foretells that the disciples would be scattered. As for the common-sense objection that the primitive community would scarcely invent a story that casts shame on Peter, a leading Christian figure, we are told that such invention reflects an anti-Petrine movement in the history of the Gospel tradition (cf. Mark viii 32–33; Matt xiv 31; the "suppression" of the appearance to Peter mentioned in I Cor xv 5).

In evaluating this argumentation, one may well wonder if reconcilable sayings have not been hardened into contradictions. Is it not more reasonable to accept Mark's own judgment that there is no contradiction between the general flight of the disciples (xiv 27, 50) and the fact that Peter later followed to see what was happening to Jesus? The contention that Luke added the italicized clause in xxii 32 is not certain at all. But even without that clause, does Luke xxii 31–32 necessarily rule out Peter's denial of Jesus? May not Luke's addition of the clause, if it was an addition, have interpreted the saying correctly? The idea may have been that the real test of Peter's faith where he would need special divine help was after he had denied Jesus, so that he might not follow the course of Judas but might repent and thus set an example to the others who had implicitly denied Jesus by fleeing. Obviously the question of the historicity of Peter's denials needs more detailed study than space permits here, but some of these complicated theories about how a fictional story evolved tax one's credibility more than the acceptance of the narrative as based on history.

Our particular interest concerns the value or plausibility of the peculiarly Johannine details. The most notable is the statement that Peter was not alone but was introduced into the palace grounds of the high priest by another disciple of Jesus. Some would see this as an even more flagrant violation of the tradition that all the disciples fled, as predicted in Mark xiv 27 and stated in xiv 50. True, John does not state that all the disciples fled, but there is a prediction to that effect (see pp. 736–37 above) in John xvi 32: "An hour is coming . . . for you to be scattered, each on his own, leaving me all alone." (The seeming contradiction is more noteworthy if the unnamed disciple who accompanied Peter was not the Beloved Disciple; for then the Beloved Disciple, present at the foot of the cross, is still a third follower of Jesus who did not desert his master!) In the NOTES we have pointed out the many problems that surround this "another disciple," and they are not easily answered. One would be inclined to dismiss the incident as imaginative if one could find an intelligible reason for its invention or inclusion. Certainly the disciple plays no role of theological significance in the scene. Bultmann suggests that the disciple may owe his existence to the need for explaining how Peter got into the palace of the high priest. But how much need was there to explain this? The other three Gospels have Peter present in the courtyard without offering any explanation of how he got by the gate. If the Johannine writer had simply joined the beginning of 15 to 17 ("Now Simon Peter was following Jesus . . . into the high priest's palace . . . but the servant girl who kept the gate said to Peter etc."), who would have had difficulty with the narrative? To invent a disciple of Jesus who inexplicably was acceptable at the palace of the high priest is to create a difficulty where there was none. There is much truth in Dodd's judgment (*Tradition*, p. 86) about John's scene: "This vivid narrative . . . is either the product of a remarkable dramatic flair, or it rests on superior information."

As for the many minor details in which John differs from Mark/Matthew and from Luke, it is dangerous to make an over-all evaluation. It may well be that one account is closer to the original in one detail while another account is closer in another detail. In Mark, Peter's third answer is climactic, being a true denial rather than a claim that he did not understand. John lacks this drama, for Peter denies Jesus from the start. If John is more elaborate than either Mark/Matthew or Luke in identifying the questioners, John is more sober than both in describing Peter's reaction to cockcrow. It is difficult then to justify the contention that the Johannine account is consistently secondary.

Nevertheless, John makes unique theological use of the scene of Peter's denials. By making Peter's denials simultaneous with Jesus' defense before Annas, John has constructed a dramatic contrast wherein Jesus stands up to his questioners and denies nothing, while Peter cowers before his questioners and denies everything. In no real sense is Peter's coming after Jesus to the high priest's palace a contradiction of Jesus' prediction (xvi 32) that the disciples would leave him all alone. Jesus was never more alone, humanly speaking, than when Peter said three times that he was not Jesus' disciple. The Johannine tradition represented by John xxi found still another theological motif in the denials of Peter, namely, that these denials could be atoned for only by a triple confession of Peter's love for Jesus (xxi 15–17)—a theological nicety not found in the Synoptic Gospels.

BIBLIOGRAPHY
(xviii 1–27)

See the general bibliography on the Passion Narrative at the end of §60.

Bartina, S., " 'Yo soy Yahweh'—Nota exegética a Jn. 18, 4–8," in *XVIII Semana bíblica española* (Madrid: Consejo superior de investigaciones, 1959), pp. 393–416.

Brown, R. E., "Incidents that are Units in the Synoptic Gospels but Dispersed in St. John," CBQ 23 (1961), 143–52 on the Agony in Gethsemane and on the Caiaphas trial. Also in NTE, pp. 192–203, or 246–59.

Church, W. R., "The Dislocations in the Eighteenth Chapter of John," JBL 49 (1930), 375–83.

Krieger, N., "Der Knecht des Hohenpriesters," NovT 2 (1957), 73–74.

Mahoney, A., "A New Look at an Old Problem (John 18, 12–14, 19–24)," CBQ 27 (1965), 137–44.

Mein, P., "A Note on John xviii. 6," ET 65 (1953–54), 286–87.

Reynen, H., *"Synagesthai,* Joh 18, 2," BZ 5 (1961), 86–90.

Richter, G., "Die Gefangennahme Jesu nach dem Johannesevangelium (18, 1–12)," BiLeb 10 (1969), 26–39.

Robinson, B. P., "Gethsemane: The Synoptic and Johannine Viewpoints," ChQR 167 (1966), 4–11.

Schneider, J., "Zur Komposition von Joh 18, 12–27. Kaiphas und Hannas," ZNW 48 (1957), 111–119.

Schwank, B., "Jesus überschreitet den Kidron (18, 1–11)," SeinSend 29 (1964), 3–15.

——— "Petrus verleugnet Jesus (18, 12–27)," SeinSend 29 (1964), 51–65.

63. THE PASSION NARRATIVE:
—DIVISION TWO (EPISODES 1–3)
(xviii 28–40)

The Trial of Jesus before Pilate

EPISODE 1

XVIII 28 Now, at daybreak, they took Jesus from Caiaphas to the praetorium. They did not enter the praetorium themselves, for they had to avoid ritual impurity in order to be able to eat the Passover supper. 29 So Pilate came out to them. "What accusation are you bringing against this man?" he demanded. 30 "If this fellow were not a criminal," they retorted, "we would certainly not have handed him over to you." 31 At this Pilate told them, "Take him yourselves then and pass judgment on him according to your own law." But the Jews answered, "We are not permitted to put anyone to death." (32 This was to fulfill what Jesus had said, indicating the sort of death he was to die.)

EPISODE 2

33 Then Pilate went [back] into the praetorium and summoned Jesus. "Are you 'the King of the Jews'?" he asked him. 34 Jesus answered, "Do you ask this on your own, or have others been telling you about me?" 35 "Surely you don't think that I am a Jew?" Pilate exclaimed. "It is your own nation and the chief priests who handed you over to me. What have you done?" 36 Jesus answered,

> "My kingdom does not belong to this world.
> If my kingdom belonged to this world,
> my subjects would be fighting
> to save me from being handed over to the Jews.
> But, as it is, my kingdom does not belong here."

28: *took;* 29: *demanded.* In the historical present tense.

37 "So then, you are a king?" said Pilate. Jesus replied,

"You say that I am a king.
The reason why I have been born,
the reason I have come into the world,
is to testify to the truth.
Everyone who belongs to the truth listens to my voice."

38 "Truth?" retorted Pilate. "And what is that?"

EPISODE 3

After this remark Pilate went out again to the Jews and told them, "For my part, I find no case against this man. 39 Remember, you have a custom that I release someone for you at Passover. Do you want me, then, to release for you 'the King of the Jews'?" 40 At this they shouted back, "We want Barabbas, not this fellow." (Barabbas was a bandit.)

38: *retorted, told.* In the historical present tense.

NOTES

xviii 28. *at daybreak. Prōi*, literally "the early hour," was the last Roman division of the night (coming after "cockcrow"), from 3–6 A.M. One can interpret John to mean that the interrogation by Annas and the simultaneous denials by Peter came to an end about 3 A.M. (NOTE on 27), that during the next three-hour period Jesus was with Caiaphas, and that finally toward 6 A.M. Jesus was led to Pilate where the trial lasted until about noon when he was sentenced (xix 14). According to Mark xv 1 and Matt xxvii 1 the second Sanhedrin session took place at "the early hour" and immediately afterward Jesus was taken away to Pilate. Luke xxii 66 speaks of the gathering of the Sanhedrin "when it had become day." Sherwin-White, "Trial," p. 114, points out that the working day of a Roman official began at the earliest hour of daylight and that, for instance, the Emperor Vespasian finished his desk-work before dawn. (Sherwin-White uses this as an argument for the validity of a night session of the Sanhedrin, but Roman custom can be reconciled also with a very early morning Sanhedrin session.)

they. Who? The last sentence in reference to Jesus was in 24: "Annas sent him bound to Caiaphas." John has not mentioned a Sanhedrin session while Jesus was with Caiaphas; but the "they" may well include some of the authorities of the Sanhedrin if we judge from what John tells us of Jesus' accusers during the Roman trial. In 35 Pilate identifies the chief priests as being among those who have handed Jesus over to him; cf., also "the Jews" (31, 38, etc.) and "the chief priests and the temple police" (xix 6).

took. In the instances of bringing Jesus from the garden to the high priest's palace or house and of bringing him from Caiaphas to Pilate, John (xviii 13, 28) and Luke (xxii 54, xxiii 1) use the verb *agagein*, "to take, lead"; Mark (xiv 53, xv 1), followed by Matthew, uses *apagagein*, "to take away." The latter verb appears in Luke xxii 66 for the conducting of Jesus from the high priest's house to the Sanhedrin.

from Caiaphas. From the high priest's palace or from the meeting place of the Sanhedrin (NOTE on 24)? A few OL mss. mistakenly read "to Caiaphas" under the influence of 24.

to the praetorium. Originally this term designated that tent within a military camp where the Roman praetor set up his headquarters. It came to denote the place of residence of the chief official in subjugated Roman territory. In Palestine the Roman governor's permanent residence was at Caesarea (see Acts xxiii 33–35 which places the Roman governor in the praetorium of Herod, i.e., in an adapted Herodian palace). Here we are concerned with the governor's residence in Jerusalem, occupied during festivals or in times of trouble. Mark xv 16 (cf. Matt xxvii 27) places "praetorium" in apposition to the *aulē*, "palace, court"; and it seems clear that the three Gospels that use the term "praetorium" (Luke does not) envisage a large building with an outside court where the Jewish crowd could assemble. There would have been inside rooms, including bedchambers (Matt xxvii 19 mentions the presence of Pilate's wife) and barracks for the soldiers. Mark xv 8 has the crowd "come up" to Pilate, perhaps reflecting a tradition that the praetorium was in the upper section of town. Of course, we cannot be sure whether such information reflects the evangelist's imagination or a historical remembrance.

The location of the Jerusalem praetorium is uncertain, but among the Herodian strongholds of the city there are two likely candidates, both mentioned by Josephus, *Ant.* XV.viii.5;※292. (1) The fortress Antonia, a Hasmonean castle converted by Herod the Great ca. 35 B.C. and used by him both as a castle and a palace for twelve years. This stood on the East Hill just north of the temple precincts, and the praetorian cohort garrisoned it during festival times precisely because of its proximity to the place where trouble was most likely to break out. Christian tradition has honored this site as the praetorium since the 12th century. In 1870 the tradition received support from the discovery in the area of a pavement of massive stone slabs. Subsequent excavation has led Père Vincent to identify this as the *Lithostrotos* or "Stone Pavement" mentioned in xix 13 (see NOTE there). For details see Mother Aline de Sion's Sorbonne thesis *La forteresse Antonia et la question du Prétoire* (Jerusalem, 1955). (2) The Herodian Palace on the West Hill (today near the Jaffa gate) dominating the whole city. Herod the Great built this as a more grandiose dwelling and moved here from the Antonia in 23 B.C. From the evidence in Josephus and Philo this served as the usual Jerusalem residence for the Roman procurators (Kopp, HPG, pp. 368–69). According to Philo, *Ad Gaium* 38;※299, Pilate set up some gilded tablets there, perhaps as a refurbishing of the governor's residence. The word *aulē* which Mark xv 16 uses to describe the praetorium appears frequently in Josephus' references to the Herodian Palace, but never in reference to the Antonia. In a discussion with Vincent, P. Benoit, RB 59 (1952), 513–50, argues that the ancient evidence conclusively favors this site as the praetorium. So also E. Lohse, ZDPV 74 (1958), 69–78.

to avoid ritual impurity. Acts x 28 says that it was unlawful for Jews to associate with or visit anyone of another nation, and some scholars have interpreted this to mean that in the 1st century A.D. the Palestinian Jews thought all Gentiles to be levitically impure (Schürer, II.i, p. 54). In a careful study in the *Jewish Quarterly Review* 17 (1926–27), 1–81, A. Büchler has shown that this is not true. Although the stricter attitudes of the Pharisees had a certain dominance, even the Pharisees did not consider the Gentiles automatically impure. About the beginning of the century Gentile women were judged to be impure because they ignored the laws of Lev xv 19–24 involving impurity after menstruation (the Hillelites were stricter than the Shammaites in this question), and it was judged that this impurity was communicated to Gentile husbands. Somewhat later the Hillelites, against Shammaite opposition, wanted to declare Gentiles liable to defilement by a corpse (Num xix 16, xxxi 19); and this would have meant almost a permanent state of defilement since Gentiles often buried beneath their houses. The Qumran "Temple Scroll" from the 1st century B.C. expresses disgust for the Gentile custom of burying "the dead everywhere, even in their houses" (Y. Yadin, BA 30 [1967], 137). What cause of impurity did the evangelist have in mind in the present instance? Was Pilate impure because of his wife? Normally the governor's wife would not have come with him to Jerusalem from Caesarea, but Matt xxvii 19 (of dubious historical value) records her presence. Was the praetorium unclean on the general grounds of Gentile burial customs? Yet both the possible sites for the praetorium, mentioned above, were built or rebuilt by Herod the Great, so that any burials there would have had to come after the Gentiles took possession. Or was the impurity based on the presumed presence of leaven in a Gentile's house? In Passover time (the Feast of the Unleavened Bread) the Israelite was to have no contact with leaven (Deut xvi 4) beginning from noon on the 14th of Nisan.

to be able to eat the Passover supper. If a Jew contracted impurity and could not eat the Passover meal at the regular time, he had to postpone the celebration for a month (Num ix 6–12). Büchler, p. 80, points out that contamination by the levitical impurity of the Gentile, where it existed, was a practical danger only to the priest on temple duty and to the ordinary Jew who had been purified for participation in a sacrificial meal. The circumstances envisaged in John come precisely in the area where contraction of impurity had to be avoided: the priests would normally take part in the slaughtering of the paschal lambs in the afternoon (see NOTE on xix 14) and in the meal after sunset. Yet if they had become impure by entering the praetorium, why could the temporary impurity not have been removed before the meal by a bath at sunset (Num xix 7)? Perhaps this could be answered if we knew the evangelist's mind about the cause of the impurity. Impurity from contact with a corpse was a seven-day contamination (Num xix 11). It is interesting that according to Josephus, *Ant.* XVIII.iv.3;⧣93–94, the Jews who went to get the vestments of the high priest from Roman custody were careful to do this seven days before the festival. (But in XV.xi.4;⧣408, Josephus speaks of only one day before the festival.)

The reference to the coming Passover supper makes it clear that for John, Jesus was tried by Pilate and crucified on the day before Passover. Jeremias, EWJ, pp. 80–82, tries to explain away several other Johannine passages that support this chronology, but he admits that here John is unambiguous. In describing the meal that would take place that night, John uses the same Greek expression, *phagein to pascha*, that the Synoptics use to describe the Last Supper of the previous night (Mark xiv 12; Matt xxvi 17; Luke xxii 15).

29. *Pilate.* Although this is the first mention of the man's name in John, he is not identified for the reader as the governor (contrast Matt xxvii 2).

Probably Christians knew Pilate's name from the first time they heard the kerygma. He is mentioned in the sermons of Acts (iii 13, iv 27, xiii 28), and he has found a place in the creed (already in the Roman creeds from ca. 200: DB §§10, 11). Mark, Matthew (but see variant in xxvii 2), and John refer to him by his cognomen alone; Luke (iii 1; Acts iv 27) uses the nomen-cognomen pattern, Pontius Pilate, and he is introduced thus by Josephus, *Ant.* XVIII.II.2; ⚹35. His praenomen is unknown. He was of equestrian rank, that is, of the lower nobility, as contrasted with senatorial rank. He ruled Judea from A.D. 26 to 36. Judea was a lesser imperial province: from the time of Claudius (41–54) the title given to the ruling officials of such provinces was *procuratores Caesaris pro legato*. (Legions could be commanded only by legates who were senators; the appointment *pro legato* was a way of giving a lesser noble the power to deploy the legionaries.) Thus Pilate is usually identified as a procurator (so Tacitus); but the inscription of Pilate discovered in 1961 at Caesarea refers to him as a prefect, *praefectus Iudaeae* (JBL 81 [1962], p. 70). This seems to confirm the thesis held by some scholars that before Claudius' time a province like Judea had a prefect rather than a procurator. See D. Hirschfeld, *Die kaiserlichen Verwaltungsbeamten* (Berlin, 1905) and A. M. Jones, "Procurators and Prefects in the Early Principate," *Studies in Roman Government and Law* (Oxford, 1960), pp. 115–25.

A reasonable amount about Pilate is known from Jewish writing, and the picture is not favorable. Philo, *Ad Gaium* 38;⚹302, attributes to Pilate robbery, murder, and inhumanity. (The accuracy of Philo's report has been questioned by P. L. Maier, HTR 62 [1969], 109–21, who thinks that the more sympathetic NT portrayal may be truer than hitherto suspected.) Josephus, *Ant.* XVIII.III.1–2 and IV.1–2;⚹55–62, 85–89, writes vividly of his blunders and atrocities (cf. also the slaughter of the Galileans mentioned in Luke xiii 1). His action against Jesus is one of the few Gospel details that have ancient non-Christian attestation, for Tacitus, *Annals* XV 44, reports: "Christ had been executed in Tiberius' reign by the procurator of Judea, Pontius Pilate." As we have mentioned (pp. 794–95 above), a tendentiously favorable portrait of Pilate has been painted in Christian tradition.

came out to them. Only John mentions this, and indeed the picture of movement in and out of the building throughout the trial is Johannine. The Synoptics seem to suppose that the whole trial took place in public, for the crowds come up and shout their views (see Mark xv 8). Only after Jesus is sentenced do Mark xv 16 and Matt xxvii 27 report that he was brought into the praetorium. From this verse in John one might get the impression that Pilate was expecting the delegation (an attitude quite explicable if Roman soldiers were involved in the arrest).

What accusation? In Luke xxiii 2 the Sanhedrin members begin to accuse Jesus before Pilate says anything; in Mark xv 2 and Matt xxvii 11 Pilate needs no briefing but immediately raises the question of kingship. If we are right in suggesting that the Jewish authorities had conducted "grand jury" proceedings against Jesus (p. 797 above), Pilate would have expected to be given the results of their investigation. However, Verdam, p. 285, points out that Pilate's question fits in also with the idea of a formal Jewish trial of Jesus. If they had tried him, they would have come to Pilate expecting to obtain a license to prosecute the sentence (an *exsequatur*); but Pilate treats their decision merely as an accusation (*katēgoria*) and plans to try Jesus himself.

30. *this fellow*. This seems to be a contemptuous use of *houtos* (BAG, p. 601).

were . . . a criminal. Literally "were . . . one doing evil," a periphrastic construction consisting of the verb "to be" and a present participle governing a noun. The awkwardness of this Semitism provoked scribal attempts to improve, as attested in the variant readings. It is not made clear what precise evil or crime the authorities are thought to have had in mind. On the historical level it was a political crime, probably that of being a revolutionary (he was arrested as a *lēstēs:* Mark xiv 48); but the evangelist thinks that the real motive was theological (xix 7; cf. x 32).

handed him over. The verb *paradidonai* (also "to betray") has been used eight times previously in the Gospel to identify Judas; now the onus of handing Jesus over has passed to the Jewish authorities.

to you. Is there a tone of insolence here?

31. *pass judgment*. This statement supposes that there was no formal Jewish judgment on Jesus; the opposite is found in Mark xiv 64 and to a lesser extent in Matt xxvi 66. See pp. 795–97 above. Some understand Pilate to be speaking ironically: he knows that the Jewish authorities want to put Jesus to death and he knows they have no power to do so; and so he is sarcastically reminding them of their impotence. Others think the evangelist guilty of a somewhat stupid mistake: he presents Pilate as not knowing that the Jewish authorities had no power to execute. Still others take Pilate's statement seriously: he does not know what the Jewish authorities have decided about Jesus; he has asked them for the results of their deliberations and they have not given them to him; and so he tells them he cannot conduct a trial under these circumstances and they will have to do so themselves.

Leaving until another NOTE the problem of whether the Sanhedrin had the power to execute a *death sentence*, we ask here what legal competence did the Sanhedrin have under the Roman governors? On the evidence of Josephus and of the Mishnaic statements of a later period many scholars think that the Sanhedrin had broad competence in both civil and religious matters, so that only very serious political offenses warranting a capital sentence were reserved to the governor. Others, drawing on the research of R. W. Husband (*The Prosecution of Jesus* [Princeton, 1916]), argue that in Roman provincial administration a local court, such as the Sanhedrin, would have been entrusted only with minor cases and that a civil or criminal case of any import would have had to be submitted to the Romans. Uncertainty about the broad competence of the Sanhedrin is echoed by Danby, JTS 21 (1920) 56–57. The recent studies of the question by A. N. Sherwin-White are based on the more detailed investigations of Roman provincial administration that have been possible in the interim since Theodor Mommsen's classic treatise on the Roman judicial system, published in 1899. Sherwin-White points out that an equestrian prefect in a minor province like Judea had no Roman assistants of high rank who could share with him the important duties of administration and jurisdiction. The Roman presence was of a military nature, and the overburdened governor had to depend on local officials for civic matters. But the "governors kept in their own hands the essential powers on which the maintenance of order depended, and left lesser things to the municipalities. All crimes for which the penalty was hard labor in mines, exile, or death, were reserved for the governors" ("Trial," p. 99). In handling criminal trials, the prefect was not bound by the law of Rome which applied only to Roman citizens and to Roman cities. Thus, there was no universal criminal code for provincial trials, which were known as *extra ordinem* or "trials outside the system." Although he followed a customary pattern in conducting the trials, the prefect was free to make his own rules about what charges he would accept for consideration or reject. Granting this situation, we see how difficult it is to reconstruct with any certainty Pilate's motives in offering to give the case back to the Jewish authorities (if John preserves a historical remembrance here). On the theological level John may be making it clear from the start that Pilate did not wish to be involved and thus that the full responsibility rested on "the Jews."

on him. This is omitted in some important witnesses, including Codex Sinaiticus* and P66. It may be a scribal clarification.

the Jews. Here the term undoubtedly has its special Johannine reference to the authorities, especially those at Jerusalem, who were hostile to Jesus (vol. 29, pp. LXXI–LXXII); and we remember that usually it covers the Pharisees as well as the priests.

"We are not permitted to put anyone to death." In Mark/Matthew it is not clear why the Jewish authorities bring Jesus to Pilate instead of executing him themselves, especially since they have found him guilty of blasphemy, a religious crime punishable by death. Only John offers a reasonable explanation: the Sanhedrin cannot execute a capital sentence. If Jesus is to die, he will have to be sentenced and executed by the Romans. This also clarifies why a non-religious or political charge must be brought to the fore. (We have suggested above [pp. 799–802] that, even if we agree that there was real religious opposition to Jesus in the Sanhedrin, the political charge may have been made sincerely—a possibility glossed over in the Gospels.) Is John's reasonable explanation an imaginative invention of the evangelist in order to solve a difficulty, or has John alone preserved a vitally important reminiscence of the judicial procedures in pre-70 Palestine? A work by Jean Juster, *Les juifs dans l'Empire romain* (Paris, 1914), has had much influence in establishing the view that the Sanhedrin's power was not limited in regard to capital sentences, so that scholars like Goguel, Lietzmann, Burkill, and Winter think that John is mistaken. Others, however, like Büchsel, Blinzler, Benoit, and Jeremias contend that John is correct.

There is no doubt, of course, that the Roman governor had the power of capital punishment (Josephus *War* II.VIII.1;⨳117) or that he may have given the Sanhedrin this power for specific offenses, especially of a religious nature (the automatic death penalty for Gentiles caught trespassing in the inner parts of the temple precincts is attested by an inscription). But did the Sanhedrin have general competence to execute prisoners found guilty in serious religious, civil, and criminal cases? Those who think so point to a number of executions carried out by the Jewish authorities, some precisely affecting Christians. Stephen was stoned in the 30s (Acts vii 58–60); James, the leader of the Jerusalem church, was stoned in the 60s (Josephus *Ant.* XX.IX.1;⨳200). Paul's reluctance to be tried by the Sanhedrin in Jerusalem (Acts xxv 9–11) is more intelligible if that court had the power to pass capital sentence (see also Acts xxii 30, xxiii 20). The story of the adulteress in John viii 3–5 may be interpreted as an indication that Jewish authorities could execute culprits (vol. 29, p. 337). However, those who think that the Sanhedrin did not have the general competence to execute offer another explanation for each instance. For example, they suggest that Stephen's case was "lynch law," and that, as Josephus indicates, James was executed in the interim between the terms of two Roman governors, with the result that the high priest involved was subsequently punished. There is a Jewish tradition of uncertain reliability that jurisdiction over life was taken from Israel forty years (round number?) before the Temple was destroyed (TalJer, *Sanhedrin*, I 18a, 34; VII 24b, 41; see Barrett, p. 445). For detailed discussion of this material and for differing conclusions, one may consult Blinzler, *Trial*, pp. 157–63, and Winter, *Trial*, pp. 11–15, 76–90. Although no firm decision is possible on the present state of the evidence, there is impressive cogency in the arguments that Sherwin-White has brought forward in support of John's over-all accuracy. From his detailed study of Roman provincial structure, he concludes that the Romans zealously kept control of capital punishment; for in local hands the power of a death sentence could be used to eliminate pro-Roman factions. Turbulent Judea was the last place where the Romans would have been likely to make an exception (*Roman Society*, pp. 36–37). Verdam, pp. 279–81, takes a similar stand, pointing out that even such an authoritarian as Herod the Great refused to take steps against his sons without Roman authorization.

There have been some attempts, not particularly successful, to circumvent the difficulty by interpreting John's statement in a limited way. Augustine (*In Jo.* cxiv 4; PL 35:1937), followed by Belser, understands John to mean that the Jews were not permitted by their own law to stone someone *on a feast day*. This interpretation might be more plausible if the day involved in John's account were Passover, whereas it is only Passover Eve; moreover, Jeremias, EWJ, p. 78, shows that in fact certain serious crimes could be punished with the death penalty on feast days. Hoskyns, p. 616, suggests that there is an implicit limitation concerning the *manner of execution:* John means that the Jews could not shed blood, although they could stone. In support, it is pointed out that vs. 32 sees in the statement an implication about the type of death Jesus was to die. Döllinger thinks that the limitation concerns *the crime involved:* John means that the Jewish authorities were not permitted to execute for political crimes, and Jesus was accused of a political crime. However, the Johannine text gives no hint of limitation or qualification as regards time, manner, or crime.

32. *This was.* We have supplied these words; the Greek has simply an elliptic *hina* construction. (See NOTES on xv 25, xviii 9.)

to fulfill. Once again (NOTE on xviii 9) John uses the term in reference to previous words of Jesus. The passage in mind is xii 32: "When I am lifted up from the earth . . . ," for the editorial remark in xii 33 makes clear that this statement indicated what sort of death he was going to die.

indicating. See NOTE on xii 33.

the sort of death. We have explained that the Jewish answer in 31 clarifies *for us* why the Jewish authorities brought Jesus to Pilate. But notice that the evangelist is not interested in the answer as a clarification of history; he is interested in its theological implication. If the Jewish authorities could not execute Jesus, then he would die at the hands of the Romans by way of crucifixion, and so he would be *lifted up* from the earth on a cross (see COMMENT). Evidently the evangelist thinks of crucifixion as a Roman and not as a normal Jewish penalty. E. Stauffer, *Jerusalem und Rom* (Bern: Francke, 1957), pp. 123–27, maintains that the Jews frequently practiced crucifixion, but Winter, *Trial*, pp. 62–66, is almost certainly correct in refuting Stauffer's arguments. Incidents where crucifixion was practiced were looked on with horror, for instance, when Alexander Jannaeus crucified the Pharisees (Josephus *War* I.iv.6;⚹97; 4QpNahum 1:7). In Jewish eyes the execution of Jesus on a cross would bring him into disrepute. It was considered the same as hanging (Acts v 30, x 39), and Deut xxi 23 enunciates the principle: "A hanged man is accursed by God" (see Gal iii 13). As for how the Sanhedrin itself would have executed Jesus, we are not totally certain of what *the Sadducees* would have regarded as acceptable forms of capital punishment. Of the four forms mentioned in the later Pharisaic law (Mishnah *Sanhedrin* 7:1), namely, stoning, burning, beheading, and strangling, the first three were recognized in the OT and should have been acceptable to the Sadducees (see NOTE on viii 5). In the Gospels the most common Jewish charge against Jesus is blasphemy for which execution by stoning is the penalty specified in the OT (Lev xxiv 16), in the NT (John x 33; Acts vii 57–58), and in the Mishnah (*Sanhedrin* 7:4, 9:3).

33. [*back*]. The best witnesses are divided on where to localize this word (*palin*), and some minor witnesses omit it.

summoned Jesus. It is not clear whether Jesus was already inside the praetorium.

"Are you 'the King of the Jews'?" In all the Gospel accounts these are Pilate's first words to Jesus. On Pilate's lips the expression "the Jews" does not have its special Johannine sense as a designation of the hostile Jewish authorities (as in vs. 31) but refers to the Jewish nation. (The same was true when another foreigner, the Samaritan woman, spoke of the Jews in iv 9, 22.) "The King of the Jews" may have been a specific title first used by the Hasmonean priest kings, the last truly independent rulers of Judea before Rome's appearance in Palestine. Josephus, *Ant*. XIV.iii.1;⚹36, cites a passage from Strabo (not otherwise preserved) that a golden vine was given to Pompey by Alexander, son of Alexander Jannaeus, and that it was later put in the temple of Jupiter Capitolinus at Rome; it bore the inscription: "From Alexander, the King of the Jews." Later Josephus applies the title to Herod the Great (*Ant*. XVI.x.2;⚹311). Perhaps the title was kept alive during the Roman governorship as a designation for the expected liberator. (We saw that some of the imagery used to greet Jesus at his entry into Jerusalem was evocative of Maccabean/Hasmonean panoply: vol. 29, p. 461.) In the question that Pilate asks, it is possible that the "you" is emphatic (so Bernard, II, 609, but MTGS, p. 37, doubts this), expressing incredulity. Pilate, having heard of the expected appearance of the national liberator, "the King of the Jews," may have been amazed at the mien of Jesus who has been accused of claiming the title. The more ancient title, "the King of Israel," was also used of Jesus (see vol. 29, p. 87).

34. *Jesus answered*. In the Synoptic Gospels Jesus' answer to Pilate's question about being the King of the Jews is "You say so [*legein*]"; see NOTE on 37 below. According to the Synoptics that is all that Jesus says in the whole trial before Pilate!

Do you ask this on your own. Schlier, "Jesus," p. 61, thinks that if Pilate had said this on his own, he would have been delivering an unconscious prophecy much as Caiaphas in xi 49–52.

35. *"Surely you don't think that I am a Jew?"* Literally "Am I a Jew?", a

question introduced by *mēti* and expecting a negative answer. Many commentators see here an undertone of Roman contempt for the Jews. This may well be; but Haenchen, "Historie," p. 68, is correct in insisting that the only clear import of Pilate's remark is that he claims no real knowledge of Jesus other than what the Jewish authorities have reported to him.

nation and the chief priests. Compare Luke xxiii 13: *"the chief priests, and the rulers, and the people."* Since neither John nor Luke explicitly brings a Jewish crowd on the scene (Mark and Matthew do), these references to "the nation" and "the people" are their only indication of the participation of a wider group than the Sanhedrin authorities.

36. *My kingdom.* Jesus does not answer the last question of Pilate, "What have you done?", but the question asked in 33: "Are you 'the King of the Jews'?" Even then his answer is in terms of kingdom rather than of kingly title.

does not belong to this world. Literally "is not of this world." This somewhat resembles the answer that the grandsons of Jude, the "brother" of the Lord, are supposed to have given to Domitian's question about Christ's kingdom: "They said that it was not worldly or on earth, but heavenly and angelic, and that it would be established at the end of the world" (Eusebius *Hist.* III 20:4; GCS 9[1]:234). One version of the apocryphal *Acts of Pilate* states that Jesus' kingdom is not *in* this world, but most commentators interpret John's thought in the light of xvii 11, 16: Jesus' kingdom, like his disciple, is in the world but not of it. For instance, Schlier, "Jesus," pp. 61–62, cites with approval Augustine's interpretation: "His kingdom *is here* till the end of time . . . but it does not belong here because it is in the world only as a pilgrim" (*In Jo.* cxv 2; PL 35:1939). Nevertheless, we must not forget that in Johannine thought the ultimate goal of the disciples is to be withdrawn from the world (cf. xiv 2–3, xvii 24).

If my kingdom belonged to this world. The first and second lines of this verse are in a type of staircase parallelism (vol. 29, p. 19) where the second line takes up an expression from the first. But Schlier, "Jesus," p. 61[1], exaggerates in comparing the format of this verse to the more consistently careful poetry of John i 1.

my subjects. The word is *hypēretēs* which John has been using for temple police, and perhaps there is a deliberate contrast with those who arrested Jesus. In LXX the term can refer to the minister or officer of a king (Prov xiv 35; Isa xxxii 5; Dan iii 46; Wis vi 4). Most commentators understand Jesus as affirming that his kingdom has subjects. Some take as a parallel Matt xxvi 53: "Do you think that I cannot appeal to my Father who would send me more than twelve legions of angels?"; and Bernard thinks that the reference in John is to angels. However, John is a Gospel that gives little stress to the angels; and since the hypothesis concerns a kingdom of this world, one would more logically expect the subjects to be of this world. Schlier, "Jesus," p. 64, identifies the subjects as those who listen to Jesus' voice (vs. 37). We should note, however, that "subjects" are mentioned only in the contrary-to-fact part of Jesus' statement—if his kingdom were of this world, he would have subjects. We are not explicitly told that a kingdom that is not of this world has subjects. Jesus would not think of his disciples as subjects in the sense of their being his servants, for in xv 15 he refused to call them servants. If the word "subject" is applicable within Jesus' kingdom, it has undergone as much reinterpretation as the notion of kingdom itself.

would be fighting. There is an ambiguity in the imperfect tense used here; BDF, §360[3], offers this translation: "would have fought and continued to fight." Actually Peter had fought, but Jesus ordered him to put away his sword (xviii 10–11).

from being handed over to the Jews. Jesus has now been handed over to the Romans (Pilate's words in 35), but he serenely ignores the importance of the Romans. The real enemies are "the Jews."

as it is. Literally "now"—the real situation as opposed to the contrary-to-fact condition that has preceded.

my kingdom does not belong here. The phrase "to be of" ("belong") indicates not only the origin but also the nature of what is involved.

37. *So then.* Oukoun occurs only here in the NT; like *oun*, it has the force of returning the conversation to the main theme after a parenthesis (BDF, §451[1]), and so Pilate is getting back to his question of 33. MTGS, p. 337, states, "The interrogative *oukoun* may be Pilate's *ipsissimum verbum.*" The present writer is not sure what that means but would resist any thesis that Pilate spoke to Jesus in a Greek that has been preserved verbatim.

you are a king. Pilate does not repeat "the King of the Jews"; perhaps he has understood that this title is not accepted by Jesus who speaks of "the Jews" as his enemies. The repetition of the question is not unusual; for by Roman usage, when the defendant made no real attempt to defend himself, the direct question was put to him three times before his case was allowed to go by default (Sherwin-White, "Trial," p. 105).

You say that I am a king. This is a variant of the "you say so" by which Jesus answers Pilate in the Synoptic accounts (first NOTE on 34 above). Most often (Bultmann, p. 506[7]) it is treated as an affirmative answer: "Yes, you have said it correctly, I am a king." Dodd, *Tradition*, p. 99[1], points out that there is little support for this interpretation in rabbinical usage; he finds valid only one of the examples presented by StB. Evidence is sometimes sought in Matt xxvi 64 where, in response to the high priest's question as to whether he is the Messiah, Jesus answers: *"You have said so* but I tell you, you will see. . . ."* The parallel in Mark xiv 62 reads: *"I am* and you will see. . . ."* The idea that Mark's "I am" is equivalent to Matthew's "You have said so" is based on the dangerous assumption that the two evangelists understood the answer in the same way, an assumption made questionable by the fact that Matthew follows it by an adversative "but," while Mark follows it by "and." In conformity with the Christian tendency to identify Jesus as the Messiah, Mark may be simplifying a more nuanced understanding of Jesus' attitude in which he did not wholeheartedly accept that designation. In John too, the statement that follows "You say that I am a king" may be adversative in tone: the reason that Jesus has come into the world is not to be a king but to bear witness to the truth. O. Merlier, *Revue des Études Grecques* 46 (1933), 204–9, is probably right in interpreting John's phrase not as an affirmative but as a qualified answer: "It is you who say it, not I"; so also BDF, §§277[2], 441[3]; MTGS, p. 37; Benoit, *Passion*, p. 106 ("In Aramaic, as in Greek, this is an evasive reply"). Jesus does not deny that he is a king, but it is not a title that he would spontaneously choose to describe his role. For this attitude toward kingship see vi 15; also COMMENT on xii 12–16 in vol. 29, pp. 461–62.

There is little to recommend the suggestions that the saying should be read as a question ("Do you say . . . ?"—Westcott-Hort Greek NT, marginal) or that it should be punctuated differently ("You say it. Because I am a king, I have been born. . . .").

I have been born . . . I have come into the world. Lagrange, p. 477, correctly denies any suggestion that the first verb refers to Jesus' birth while the second refers to his public ministry. Rather they are in parallelism and both refer to the same thing. John does not elsewhere use the verb *gennan*, "to be begotten, be born," of Jesus (vol. 29, pp. 11–12), and in the present instance he uses parallelism to make it clear that Jesus' birth was the coming into the world of divine truth.

to testify to the truth. In ix 39 Jesus said, "I came into this world for judgment"; since the revelation of truth has the effect of judgment, there is nothing contradictory in the purposes enunciated for Jesus' coming into the world. In v 33 (see Qumran parallel in NOTE there) we heard that John the Baptist had testified to the truth; now the same language is used by Jesus of himself. Jesus can testify to the truth because he belongs to what is above (viii 23) and is the only one who has come down from heaven (iii 13); thus he has seen what the Father does (v 19) and has heard what the Father has said (viii 26). Indeed he is the embodiment of truth (xiv 6), so that the deeds and words of his ministry constitute testimony to the truth. Schlier, "Jesus," p. 64, sees here a hint that Jesus' death will be the supreme testimony.

Everyone who belongs to the truth listens to my voice. The verb *akouein,* "to hear," is constructed with the genitive here and refers to listening with understanding and acceptance; contrast the construction with the accusative (NOTE on viii 43; ZGB, §69). In x 3 we were told that the sheep hear or listen to the voice of the shepherd. (This parallel is interesting because, as we saw in vol. 29, p. 397, the shepherd motif has its background in the OT portrait of the king, and here Jesus is answering a question about his kingship.) Thus those who belong to the truth are the sheep given to Jesus by the Father; but those who do not hear or listen do not belong to God (viii 47). I John iii 18–19 gives a practical way of testing who belong to the truth, namely, if men show by deeds that their love is genuine instead of merely talking with words. Obviously Jesus is speaking in dualistic language and is not referring simply to a moral disposition (putting one's life in harmony with revealed truth) but to the status of being called by God to accept His Son. See M. Zerwick, VD 18 (1938), 375. Meeks, p. 67, sees in the theme of listening to Jesus' voice another echo of the Prophet-like-Moses motif: "The Lord will raise up for you a prophet like me . . . you shall listen to him" (Deut xviii 15).

38. *I find no case against this man.* This "not guilty" judgment will be given twice more (xix 4, 6); a very similar judgment is also found three times in Luke (xxiii 4, 14, 22). The first occurrence in both Gospels comes right after the question on kingship. For "case" Luke uses *aition* while John uses the cognate *aitia* (=the crime of which a prisoner is accused).

39. *you have a custom that I release someone . . . at Passover.* There is no extra-biblical confirmation for this custom to which the Gospels bear

witness (Luke alone is ambiguous since xxiii 17 may be a scribal addition); and the historical correctness of the Gospel reports is hotly debated (see Blinzler, *Trial*, pp. 218–21, versus Winter, *Trial*, pp. 91–94). What type of custom or practice did the evangelists have in mind? The Synoptics describe this as a practice of Pilate (Mark xv 6; [Luke xxiii 17]) or of the governor (Matt xxvii 15); John describes it as a Jewish custom. For John it is a Passover custom (whence the name *privilegium paschale*), and presumably this is what the Synoptics mean also when they use the expression "at the feast." (It is not impossible that the custom existed at the other pilgrimage feasts as well; but amnesty fits the general theme of release from Egypt that characterizes Passover.) Are we then to think of an annual amnesty peculiar to Palestine and acknowledged by all the Roman governors; or are we to think of a practice peculiar to Pilate's reign, meant to better his relation with his Jewish subjects? From the Gospels we get the impression that the amnesty is not limited to a certain class of crimes, for Barabbas who is released is described as a murderer and a revolutionary! R. W. Husband, *American Journal of Theology* 21 (1917), 110–16, has tried to narrow down the implausible scope of the amnesty by suggesting that Barabbas had not been found guilty but was accused and awaiting trial—thus he and Jesus, the two candidates for the amnesty, would have been at the same stage of legal proceedings. Yet the fact that two revolutionary bandits were executed together with Jesus suggests that the fate of those involved in the recent insurrection (Mark xv 7; Luke xxiii 19) had been decided. The frenzied interest in having Barabbas released would be more explicable if he were on his way to death.

C. B. Chavel, JBL 60 (1941), 273–78, and others have sought to substantiate the existence of an amnesty by the reference in Mishnah *Pesahim* 8:6, that speaks of the need of slaughtering a paschal lamb for one whom "they promised to release from prison" (on Passover Eve). Chavel argues that the reference is to political prisoners in the time of Roman rule and that the Romans may have taken over the custom from the Hasmoneans (the priest-rulers of Palestine in the 2nd and 1st centuries B.C.). But obviously this passage is capable of explanations that have nothing to do with a *privilegium paschale*. Some have found an analogy in Livy's report (*History* V 13) of the *lectisternium*, an eight-day religious feast, one feature of which was a release of prisoners. A more likely analogy is the incident that took place in Egypt in A.D. 85 when the governor released a prisoner to the people (Deissmann, LFAE, p. 269). However, many would agree with H. A. Riggs, JBL 64 (1945), 419–28, in the negative judgment he passes on the value of the proposed parallels. While there is considerable evidence in antiquity for occasional amnesties, the evidence of an amnesty for serious crimes at an annual feast is lacking.

to release for you. The "for you" is omitted in Tatian and appears as a genitive, not as a dative, in some witnesses. It may not be original.

'the King of the Jews'. See NOTE on vs. 33. Pilate now understands that Jesus claims no political kingship, for he has found Jesus innocent. Why then, *as conceived by the evangelist*, does Pilate persist in giving Jesus this title? Some have suggested that he is being sarcastic, but he would scarcely choose to be offensive if he is sincerely trying to have Jesus released. (Even though the evangelist is not interested in writing a psychological study of the

prefect, we must suppose that Pilate is presented as acting rationally.) Others have thought that Pilate is using the title to appeal to the nationalistic sense of the crowd—the crowd was interested in revolutionaries like Barabbas, and Pilate is pointing out that Jesus too is a hero. This explanation may fit Mark xv 9 where Pilate addresses himself to a crowd that has come up seeking the release of a prisoner jailed for insurrection; but it does not fit John where Pilate has declared that Jesus is innocent of political crime and where he is addressing himself not to a crowd that could be swayed but to "the Jews" who are Jesus' enemies. Perhaps Pilate foresees that they will not opt for the release of Jesus and he wants to make "the Jews" implicitly renounce their expectation of "the King of the Jews." This motive is certainly involved in xix 15. In any case the present episode puts more emphasis on what "the Jews" are forced to do than on Pilate's motivation: "the Jews" are forced to prefer a bandit to their king.

40. *shouted back.* Shouting fits better into the Marcan/Matthean account where there is a crowd than in John where "the Jews" (the Jewish authorities) are involved—a clear proof that the Johannine evangelist rewrote the tradition in light of his hostility to the Jews (the Synagogue) of a later period. Some later mss. read "they all shouted," perhaps a scribal attempt to turn the audience into a crowd; also see xix 6 where John has the chief priests and the temple police shouting. The word *palin* means "back" or "again." The latter meaning in the present instance would imply that they had shouted before, and some think that John is condensing and selecting from a longer account that pictured a crowd shouting earlier in the trial. Blinzler, *Trial,* p. 212[20], raises the question of whether the shout was a genuine oral vote.

Barabbas. In Matthew (xxvii 17) it is Pilate who first mentions Barabbas, while in the other three Gospels Barabbas is suggested by the Jews (the authorities or the crowd) in place of Jesus. We know nothing of him beyond the Gospel evidence. "Barabbas" is not a personal name but an identifying patronymic (like Simon *Barjonah*) that occurs also in the Talmud. Presumably it means "son of *abba,*" that is, "of the father." But if one accepts the variant spelling Barrabbas found in some witnesses, it may mean "son of *rabban,*" that is, "of our teacher" (so Jerome). Some of the textual witnesses to Matthew present the man's name as Jesus Barabbas, a reading already ancient in Origen's time. In this case Pilate would have been dealing with two men named Jesus at the same time. Winter, *Trial,* p. 99, advances the conjecture that Pilate did not know which Jesus he was to prosecute and was asking this of the crowd. Accordingly, when he found out that Barabbas was not the one, he released him. In this conjecture, the *privilegium paschale* becomes an erroneous explanation advanced by the evangelists who had forgotten why Barabbas was released. Others have thought of Barabbas as a fictional creation. Riggs, JBL 64 (1945), 417–56, thinks that originally Jesus Barabbas ("Son of the Father") was another designation of Jesus the Messiah and that the two names express the religious and political charges against Jesus. Loisy is one of those who have resorted to Philo's information (*In Flaccum* VI; ⚹36–39) that, when the Jewish king Agrippa I visited Alexandria at Passover time, the mob dressed up an imbecile as king, paid mock homage to him, and then beat him. The actor was called *Karabas,* and Loisy takes Barabbas as another form of the title for such a role. Recently, Bajsić, *art. cit.,* has argued that Barabbas was a notorious troublemaker whom Pilate feared and that Pilate was using

Jesus as a ploy to prevent the amnesty from being extended to the dangerous Barabbas.

bandit. Cf. J. J. Twomey, *Scripture* 8 (1956), 115–19, on this remark. *Lēstēs* can refer to a simple robber or highwayman, as distinct from a thief (*kleptēs*) who relies on stealth rather than on violence. Frequently (e.g., *War* II.xiii.2–3;⁂253–54) Josephus uses *lēstēs* to describe the revolutionary banditti or guerrilla warriors who, from mixed motives of plunder and of nationalism, kept the countryside in constant insurrection. K. H. Rengstorf, TWNTE, IV, 258, observes: "It is constantly used for the Zealots who . . . make armed conflict against Roman rule the content of their life and are prepared to risk everything, even life itself, to achieve national liberty." We are not certain how John understood the word, but the Synoptic tradition clearly understood Barabbas as a revolutionary. Mark xv 7 says that he was one of those imprisoned for having committed murder in an insurrection; Luke xxiii 19 describes him as a man who had been thrown into prison because of an insurrection in the city and for murder. The fact that he is the only one of the revolutionaries whom the crowd nominates for the amnesty suggests that he may have been the leader and well-known. Matt xxvii 16 characterizes him as *episēmos* or "notorious," a word used by Josephus (*War* II.xxi.1;⁂585) to describe the Zealot leaders; and a few minor textual witnesses of this verse in John read *archilēstēs* or "bandit chieftain." If he had committed murder, then according to Israelite law no pardon should have been permitted (Num xxxv 31), and the fact that the authorities and the people want him released indicates that they regarded his killing more in terms of patriotism than of crime.

COMMENT: GENERAL

Throughout this commentary we have been compelled to recognize two conflicting aspects of the Gospel: on the one hand, it preserves a nucleus of historical tradition that commands more respect than has been given it in recent years; on the other hand, the evangelist radically re-shapes all his traditional material for reasons theological and dramatic. Nowhere does the interplay between historical tradition and the interests of theology and drama become more apparent than in the scene of the trial before Pilate that constitutes Division Two of the Passion Narrative. Blank and Haenchen have recently insisted on the dominance of theological motifs here. Boismard, Janssens de Varebeke, and others have commented on the careful dramatic organization of the material. Dodd has stressed the presence of a plausible historical tradition. Let us begin by studying the interplay of these factors.

The Dramatic Arrangement of the Scene

The careful scenario of the Johannine account of the trial raises acutely the question of historicity. The Marcan/Matthean account of the trial is very simple in outline and consists of three episodes: (a) Jesus is brought to Pilate to be questioned about his claiming to be a king, but he refuses to answer; (b) when a crowd gathers to ask for the release of Barabbas, Pilate offers Jesus to them but they refuse; (c) at their insistence Pilate hands Jesus over to be crucified. The whole scene takes place in one outdoor setting, and only after Jesus is handed over to be crucified is he brought inside the praetorium to be mocked. The Lucan scene is almost the same, although it is interrupted by an interlude wherein Jesus is sent to Herod (xxiii 6–12), and there is no final episode of mocking inside the praetorium. Throughout the Synoptic versions of the trial Jesus remains silent.

The Johannine scenario is far more complicated and dramatic. There are two stage settings: the outside court of the praetorium where "the Jews" are gathered; the inside room of the praetorium where Jesus is held prisoner. Pilate goes back and forth from one to the other in seven carefully balanced episodes. The atmosphere inside is one of calm and reason in which the innocence of Jesus is made clear to Pilate; outside there are frenzied shouts of hate as "the Jews" put pressure on Pilate to find Jesus guilty. Pilate's constant passing from one setting to the other gives external expression to the struggle taking place within his soul, for his certainty of Jesus' innocence increases at the same rate as does the political pressure forcing him to condemn Jesus. Several episodes in the Johannine narrative have touches worthy of great drama, for example, the *ecce homo* incident, and the climax where "the Jews" are forced to proclaim that they accept the Emperor as their king.

Different schemes for dividing the scene have been proposed. Bultmann, p. 501, would recognize six episodes to be apportioned into two groups, the first group (xviii 28 – xix 7) consisting of four episodes, the second group (xix 8–16) consisting of two episodes. We agree in general with his delineation of the episodes, although we find seven rather than six, for we divide xix 1–7 into two episodes (see p. 889 below). But we do not find convincing his unbalanced grouping of the episodes nor the argument that the first group draws to an end with "Behold the man" (xix 5) and the second group with "Here is your king" (xix 14). Rather, like many other scholars, we find here another example of a chiastic Johannine pattern seen several times before (vol. 29, p. 276; above pp. 667 and 728).

The arrangement is not perfect; for instance, some of the movements outside and inside are not expressly indicated even though they are clearly implied (NOTES on xix 4, 9, 12). But there is a very careful balancing of the episodes, 1 and 7, 2 and 6, 3 and 5—a balance in setting, content, and even in length (1=7; 2+3=5+6). The only episode in which Pilate does not figure prominently is 4, the middle episode. Obviously the hand of a meticulous planner has been at work here, and in this instance we find justified the sevenfold division that Janssens de Varebeke would impose on all three divisions of the Passion Narrative (p. 803 above).

To achieve this arrangement the evangelist undoubtedly had to effect

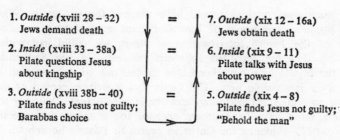

1. *Outside* (xviii 28 – 32)   =   7. *Outside* (xix 12 – 16a)
   Jews demand death   Jews obtain death

2. *Inside* (xviii 33 – 38a)   =   6. *Inside* (xix 9 – 11)
   Pilate questions Jesus   Pilate talks with Jesus
   about kingship   about power

3. *Outside* (xviii 38b – 40)   =   5. *Outside* (xix 4 – 8)
   Pilate finds Jesus not guilty;   Pilate finds Jesus not guilty;
   Barabbas choice   "Behold the man"

4. *Inside* (xix 1 – 3)
Soldiers scourge Jesus

considerable change in the traditional material that came down to him within the Johannine school. For instance, he took the liberty of moving the scourging from the end of the trial to the middle. He expanded episodes by adding dialogue and may have abbreviated longer episodes (NOTES on xviii 40, xix 8). Haenchen, "Jesus," p. 96, objects that John implausibly presents Pilate as if he were a private citizen going in and out of his house. But one may suppose that a more complicated picture has been simplified and that some of the intermediaries and messengers have been removed lest they distract from the confrontation between Pilate and the two contending parties. However, since, as Sherwin-White has pointed out (see NOTE on xviii 31: "pass judgment"), there was a dearth of administrative assistance in Roman provincial government, John may be perfectly correct in describing Pilate as personally conducting the interrogation.

The Question of Historicity

Was the dramatic rewriting on such a scale that little historical material remains? No simple answer to this question is possible. Too much trust should not be placed in confident affirmations that the Johannine picture is impossible on psychological grounds; for example, Haenchen, "Historie," p. 64, argues that a Roman governor would never have lowered himself to go out to the Jewish authorities if they refused to enter the praetorium. How can one be so sure? Were there never moments when Pilate, like other politicians, had to swallow his pride in order to avert worse trouble? But even if we leave aside the objections that are incapable of proof, there remain well-founded difficulties about John's account.

According to the Synoptic Gospels the trial seems to have been held in public (and this was Roman custom); yet these Gospels report virtually nothing of the content of the trial. John gives much more detail from conversations that were conducted in private inside the praetorium! Barrett, p. 443, judges it highly improbable that reliable information concerning such conversations should have reached the evangelist. When the similar problem was posed of how Christians got information about the content of the Jewish interrogation of Jesus, we could say with some plausibility that the recorded followers of Jesus in the Sanhedrin and among the priests may have been able to find out what happened; but no such answer is possible here. The thesis that a written record of the trial was later consulted in the Roman archives is pure fiction. One may theorize that there must have been others present, for instance, interpreters; but there is no NT evidence for Christian access to Pilate's household. To the difficulty of how the conversation could have become known one must add the problem of the notable Johannine character of the dialogue between Pilate and Jesus. Jesus speaks in the semipoetic style of the Johannine discourses. His words sound very much like what must have been the standard Church apologetic in face of Roman suspicion of treason in the latter part of the 1st century (NOTE on "does not belong to this world" in xviii 36). We saw that in the Johannine account of the public ministry some of the debates between Jesus and "the Jews" reflected the later arguments between Church and Synagogue. Here the answers of Jesus to the Roman governor reflect the later answers of the Christians to the authorities of the Roman Empire.

If we have reason to think that the dialogue between Jesus and Pilate is not historical, what are we to say of John's general portrait of Pilate? We have already pointed out the Christian tendency to "whitewash" Pilate that appears in all the Gospel accounts (pp. 794–95 above); but John, more than the other Gospels, dwells on Pilate's desire to do what was right in regard to Jesus. If we may believe Josephus and Philo, John is almost certainly romantic in attributing to Pilate such moral sensitivity. Yet John and the other Gospels may have been correct in their remembrance that Pilate sought to release Jesus. Bajsić, art. cit., has suggested that Pilate made this effort, not for justice' sake but because he did not want to release Barabbas, a notorious and dangerous insurrectionist. Bajsić conjectures that Pilate shrewdly judged Jesus to be politically harmless and he hoped that the populace might be swayed to accept Jesus' release. This political motivation, which agrees with implications in the biblical data, would have befitted the callous despot described in the Jewish sources. While such a theory cannot be proved, it warns us to consider the possibility that John may be preserving historical remembrances to which a new direction has been given.

Many of the details of the trial peculiar to John's account cannot be verified but are not implausible. It is not unlikely that Pilate might wish to interrogate privately a potentially dangerous political prisoner while the Jewish authorities remained outside. Even if Pilate cooperated with the Sanhedrin or indeed supplied the impetus in the arrest of Jesus, he may not have been overly trusting of the Sanhedrin's report on Jesus and may have wanted to find out for himself about the man. Some of the information that John gives about the praetorium has a good chance of being accurate (NOTE on "Stone Pavement" in xix 13). While we acknowledge the Johannine recasting of the dialogue between Jesus and Pilate, John may be historical in remembering that Jesus did answer Pilate during the trial. One suspects that in picturing Jesus as silent during the trial, the Synoptics reflect the theology of the Suffering Servant (NOTE on xix 9). Some have thought that in I Tim vi 13 we have an independent confirmation of the more loquacious Johannine Jesus. This passage, which probably echoes a primitive baptismal creed, mentions Jesus "who bore witness to the same noble confession before Pilate [or: in the time of Pilate]." Does the epistle refer to verbal witness? The context is not unfavorable to this, for it refers to Timothy's noble confession in the presence of many witnesses, seemingly a verbal confession at baptism or before a magistrate. Nevertheless, the epistle may mean simply that Jesus bore witness *by dying* under Pontius Pilate.

Moreover, John's account of the trial is not easily dismissed as a secondhand reshuffling of Synoptic material (Dodd, *Tradition*, p. 120). Substantial parallels to the Synoptic accounts are found only in Episodes 3 and 4, and even then there are considerable divergencies (see charts on pp. 870–71, 887 below). In Episode 2 only the question "Are you 'the King of the Jews'?" and part of the answer *"You* say . . ." in xviii 37 are similar to what is found in the Synoptics. The other episodes consist largely of properly Johannine material. We note that in some of this material John runs close to a tradition reflected in Luke (who, *pace* Bultmann, seems to have had an independent source for the Pilate trial). For instance, John and Luke have the following in common: Pilate says three times that he finds Jesus not guilty, and the sequence in which the three statements appear is much the same (NOTES on xviii 38, xix 4, 6); the mockery of Jesus takes place midway through the trial and not at the end; Jesus is handed over to the Jews to be crucified and not specifically to Roman soldiers. The similarities are not so close verbally that we think one evangelist copied from the other, and we may posit that such details came to both evangelists from earlier traditions. This does not necessarily make the details historical, but it cautions against assuming too facilely that material for the most part peculiar to John represents the evangelist's creation.

With all its drama and its theology, John's account of the trial is the most consistent and intelligible we have. Only John makes it clear why Jesus was brought to Pilate in the first place and why Pilate gave in and had Jesus crucified. John's chronology, where the judicial process takes place on the 14th of Nisan, is more credible than that of the Synoptics, where it takes place on the feast of Passover. John makes it lucidly clear that at the outset Pilate is asking Jesus about a *political* charge that has been made against him, a charge that would make him a threat to the Emperor. The portrait of Pilate yielding to the subtle interplay of political forces carries a certain conviction. Sherwin-White, *Roman Society*, p. 47, after carefully reviewing Roman provincial practices, concludes that the legal and administrative details peculiar to John are by no means implausible. Dodd, *Tradition*, p. 120, argues that a writer late in the 1st century and in a Hellenistic environment could not have invented such a persuasive account of a trial conducted under conditions that had long passed away. He thinks that the author had a lively sense for the situation in Palestine before the extinction of local Judean autonomy. Dodd's summary judgment is stated as follows: "While there is evidence of some degree of elaboration by the author, the most probable conclusion is that in substance it represents an independent strain of tradition, which must have been formed in a period much nearer the events than the period when the Fourth Gospel was written, and in some respects seems to be better informed than the tradition behind the Synoptics, whose confused account it clarifies." Personally we would emphasize more strongly the elaborative efforts of the Johannine writer, but over-all we prefer Dodd's evaluation to Winter's sweeping statement (*Trial*, p. 89): "From John 18, 29 onward the Fourth Gospel contains nothing of any value for the assessment of historical facts."

If we think that in John we have details from an early tradition reworked into a theological and dramatic whole, nevertheless we eschew an attempt to determine with certainty or great precision what comes from the tradition and what represents elaboration by the evangelist. (Even Bultmann, pp. 502–3, who usually writes with assurance in such matters, finds this section difficult to analyze; he detects John's Passion Source particularly in xviii 39 – xix 6 [see Smith, p. 49].) Some elaborations are more or less obvious, but we are always limited in detecting the evangelist's hand by our contention that the source of tradition was not extraneous to the Johannine school. We have proposed (vol. 29, pp. xxiv ff.) that the molding of the tradition into a Gospel took place over a period of years and in a living context of preaching and teaching. Theories that picture the evangelist making additions to a fixed written document that had recently been placed at his disposal are inevitably more optimistic about the modern scholar's ability to distinguish between the evangelist and the tradition.

The Roman Trial as a Vehicle of Johannine Theology

John omits an account of the interrogation of Jesus before the Sanhedrin under Caiaphas. Even if details from that procedure are scattered throughout the Fourth Gospel, the effect of the omission gives a peculiar orientation to the Johannine Passion Narrative. The Jewish legal proceedings have been reduced to a question asked of Jesus by Annas, and thus the Roman judicial process becomes *the* trial of Jesus. Is there a theological reason for John's stress on the Roman trial?

Perhaps the secular atmosphere of the trial permitted the Johannine writer to use it more effectively than he could have used the Jewish proceedings for expounding the kingship of Jesus. Blank, p. 62, is correct in insisting that kingship is the theological motif that dominates the episodes of the trial. Episode 2 discusses the nature of Jesus' kingship, a kingship that Pilate proclaims twice (Episodes 3 and 7). Episode 4 describes the mock enthronement of Jesus as king, and in Episode 5 Jesus is brought forward and presented to his subjects who acclaim him with cries of crucifixion. Note that John ties in the theme of suffering with that of kingship. The addition of the *ecce homo* incident makes the ordeal of Jesus during the trial more apparent in John than it is in the Synoptic Gospels. Thus there is no need to think that in stressing kingship John has glossed over entirely the picture of the Suffering Servant. Additional motifs of the trial that we may mention include the innocence of Jesus and Jesus as the true judge who puts his adversaries on trial.

Other interpreters have found the key to the theological importance of the Roman trial for John in the stress on Pilate. Some point to Ps ii 2 (cited in Acts iv 25–26) as a guiding motif: "The kings of the earth set themselves in array, and the rulers were gathered together against the Lord and His anointed." However, the Synoptic accounts of the Pilate trial would fulfill this text just as much as John's account does. If John were enlarging the scope of the Roman trial in light of this text, we would expect him to have cited it explicitly or implicitly. Another suggestion is that the evangelist highlighted the Pilate trial because he wished to portray Jesus in direct confrontation with Rome. In the ministry Jesus had faced the opposition of "the Jews"; now he stands before the Roman incarnation of worldly power. It is possible to see here a duel between the religious and secular realms wherein the secular has brute power over the religious, but the religious dominates by force of its integrity. Yet on close examination we find the theme of power brought to the fore only in Episode 6 (xix 10–11) and perhaps to some extent in Episode 2; so that a clash between the religious and the secular is scarcely a dominant motif. The variation of this thesis in which Pilate becomes a personification of a Rome that is hostile to Christianity reflects the Book of Revelation rather than the Fourth Gospel. We grant that in John a Roman cohort is part of the party that arrests Jesus and that Roman soldiers mock Jesus during the trial; but Pilate himself is presented as favorable to Jesus. The malevolence of "the Jews" remains the dominant note, and Jesus is handed over to the Jews for crucifixion.

In still another theological interpretation of Pilate's role, he becomes representative of the State being asked to decide between the world and truth. John is using Pilate to show that the State cannot remain neutral to truth, for neutrality will force the State to temporize even in the most elementary questions of justice and to act against its real self-interests. By not deciding against the world, the State is soon subjected to the world.

This interpretation has been popular among German writers (Schlier, Bultmann) and understandably reflects the theological agonizing about the role of the State prompted by the Nazi experience. But Von Campenhausen, Haenchen, and others have wisely asked if this is not a reinterpretation of John in light of a modern theological problem rather than an exposition of the evangelist's own viewpoint. True, the struggle between Jesus and "the Jews" is a struggle between truth incarnate and the world, but the abstraction "the State" is a later concept.

While John has painted "the Jews" as dualistically opposed to Jesus and utterly refusing to believe in him, he has also given us examples of other reactions to Jesus where men neither refuse to believe nor fully accept Jesus for what he really is (vol. 29, pp. 530–31). Nicodemus, the Samaritan woman, the man healed at the Pool of Bethesda come to mind. We would look on the Johannine Pilate not as a personification of the State but as another representative of a reaction to Jesus that is neither faith nor rejection. Pilate is typical, not of the State that would remain neutral, but of the many honest, well-disposed men who would try to adopt a middle position in a struggle that is total. In studying the story of the Samaritan woman (vol. 29, pp. 176–78), we saw how artistically John described a person who, despite attempts to escape decisions, might be led to believe in Jesus. Pilate's story gives us the other side of the coin, for it illustrates how a person who refuses decisions is led to tragedy. In a few words Jesus dispels Pilate's original fear of political danger (xviii 36); but Jesus is not content to stop there: he must challenge Pilate to recognize the truth (xviii 37). Pilate will not face the challenge of deciding for Jesus and against "the Jews"; he thinks he can persuade the Jews to accept a solution that will make it unnecessary for him to decide in favor of Jesus. First, Pilate offers them a choice between prisoners: Jesus or Barabbas (xviii 39–40). When that fails, he begins to yield to the world by having Jesus scourged and mocked, hoping that this will be sufficient (xix 1–6). When that fails, he offers to hand Jesus over to the will of "the Jews" under what he considers an impossible condition. If they want Jesus crucified, he will make them ask in such a way that they have to deny all their messianic hopes and proclaim that the Emperor is their only king (xix 14–15). But "the Jews" will not balk even at this blasphemy; for they know that this is a struggle to the death, and that if Jesus does not die, the world will be vanquished by truth. And so Pilate, the would-be neutral man, is frustrated by the intensity of the participants. Having failed to listen to the truth and decide in its favor, he and all who would imitate him inevitably finish in the service of the world. In our judgment this is the profound Johannine theological understanding of Pilate. If the dramatization of such an understanding required skill and effort on the evangelist's part, one must admit that the result is worthy of his conception: many are those who can find mirrored in Pilate their own tragic history of temporizing and indecision.

Thus there were theological reasons for John to emphasize the Roman trial of Jesus, but we must not naïvely suppose that theological reasons explain every facet of the Roman trial. It is not inconceivable that John emphasized the Roman trial also because his tradition preserved a correct historical reminiscence wherein it was the most important of the legal procedures against Jesus and indeed the only real trial. Pilate may really have had a dominant role in the passion of Jesus (see pp. 798–99 above). The speeches of Peter and Paul in Acts, which may contain early tradition, proportionately *emphasize* Roman involvement (Acts ii 23: "killed by the hands of lawless men"; iii 13: "in the presence of Pilate"; xiii 28: "they asked Pilate to have him killed"). And so we close the discussion on the note with which we began it: the delicate Johannine blending of history and theology.

COMMENT: DETAILED

Episode One: The Jewish Authorities Ask Pilate to Condemn Jesus (xviii 28–32)

We shall first compare this episode to the Synoptic narrative. The opening of the Roman trial in Mark (xv 2–5) is composite, drawing on the two Marcan sources (p. 788 above). From the Marcan B source comes xv 2 which we shall discuss in relation to Episode 2 in John. From the Marcan A source or primitive consecutive account comes xv 3–5: the chief priests accused Jesus of many things; Pilate was surprised at the number of charges and asked Jesus about them; Jesus remained silent. The Marcan sequence is awkward, for vss. 3–5 would make a better beginning than vs. 2. Luke has only a partial parallel to the Marcan A material. In xxiii 2, perhaps reflecting an independent source, Luke records that the members of the Sanhedrin listed three charges against Jesus: misleading the nation; forbidding that taxes be paid to the Emperor; claiming to be the Messiah-King. Luke does not record that Pilate asked Jesus about the three charges or that Jesus remained silent. The present episode in John discusses the accusation brought against Jesus by "the Jews"; the silence of Jesus is mentioned in another context in Episode 6 (xix 9). It is difficult to believe that John has taken the Marcan A material and totally rewritten it; the differences are far more prominent than the similarities. Moreover, some of the material that is found only in John is of major import, for example, the explanation that the Jewish courts could not execute death sentences. If that information is correct (NOTE on xviii 31), then John is clearly drawing on a historical tradition independent of Mark and the Marcan sources.

In the NOTES we have discussed the detailed historical problems. Here we shall concern ourselves with the logical sequence of the narrative *as the evangelist presents it* and with the theological implication the evangelist draws from what he describes.

The scene opens at daybreak—a chronological indication common to the Gospel traditions about the Roman trial. But exegetes like Bultmann and Blank find a theological overtone in John's usage: the night of evil mentioned in xiii 30 was passing, and the day was dawning when the light of the world would conquer the darkness (i 5). Actually John does not mention light here and there is no clear indication he intended symbolism, but it would fit in with Johannine theology.

The opening confrontation of Pilate and "the Jews" is described with subtle irony. Having cynically decided on the death of Jesus because it was more advantageous that one man die than that the whole nation be destroyed (xi 50), the Jewish authorities are, nevertheless, scrupulously correct in their observance of ritual purity. They do not hesitate to make use of the Gentile to destroy their adversary, but they will not enter the Gentile's house. Implicitly there may be another element of irony: they fear that ritual impurity will prevent their eating the Passover lamb, but unwittingly they are delivering up to death him who is the Lamb of God (i 29) and thus they are making possible the true Passover.

Pilate's opening remark presents a problem in the logic of the Johannine narrative. If Roman troops had been sent to arrest Jesus and thus Pilate was cooperating with Caiaphas, why the charade of Pilate's asking what accusation was being brought against Jesus? Yet the question is intelligible as part of the provincial system of administering justice through the personal *cognitio* of the Roman governor (see Sherwin-White, *Roman Society*, p. 17). While charges and penalties were freely formulated, eventually a proper, formal accusation had to be made to the holder of the *imperium*, so that he could investigate and acquire personal knowledge (*cognitio*). Pilate may have cooperated with the Sanhedrin in putting a possible troublemaker under temporary arrest during a dangerous festival period; indeed, he may have been the moving spirit behind the arrest of a man who he had heard was a revolutionary, and he may have intended the Sanhedrin to investigate whether the man should undergo trial. But now the Sanhedrin authorities were turning over a prisoner for an official trial, and Pilate had to follow legal format. A record would be kept of this trial, and Pilate could not afford to give his enemies evidence of legal irregularities. In this light Pilate's opening question is the expected legal formality: he wishes to know the results of the "grand jury" proceedings against Jesus.

Even though Haenchen, "Historie," p. 65, thinks that the answer of the Jewish authorities should not be interpreted psychologically, we find it difficult not to see a tone of insolence here. And insolence would not be too unexpected if the Sanhedrin had been acting on Pilate's orders, and consequently the authorities felt sure that Pilate would have to accept their decision. But Pilate answers the insolence by insisting on correct procedure.

If he has ordered or allowed them to conduct an inquiry, he has not ceded his right to judge. The Jewish authorities would be capable of judging Jesus guilty on religious grounds and according to their own laws, and Pilate invites them to do so. Only in response to his rebuff do "the Jews" indicate to Pilate that they are accusing Jesus of a capital civil offense, implicitly the offense that Pilate had suspected: Jesus is a revolutionary with monarchical pretensions. The rumors that had reached Pilate and had caused him to send Roman troops to arrest Jesus had proved correct: Jesus is claiming to be "the King of the Jews." We have given a reconstruction that seems to make sense of John's narrative, a reconstruction whereby Pilate takes a judicial stance similar to that of the Roman officials described in Acts xviii 14–15, xxiii 28–29. Naturally we cannot be sure that the reconstruction correctly interprets the evangelist's intention. As in other Johannine narratives (vol. 29, p. 103) we have to surmise and to read between the lines to fill out the sequence. In the long run, however, such reconstruction seems less implausible than the assumption that in this carefully thought out trial scene the evangelist makes naïve errors, for instance, the error of thinking that Pilate would not know that the Jewish courts could not execute a capital sentence and would have to be reminded of this by his subjects.

The Jewish answer, "We are not permitted to put anyone to death," serves several theological purposes. Since John has not described a Sanhedrin proceeding in the previous night, we have not hitherto been told that the decision of xi 53 ("they planned to kill him") is still in effect. Clearly it is: the enemies of Jesus have not only turned away from the light but are determined to extinguish it. The irony is that through death the victory of the light will be seen. Moreover, his enemies have determined that Jesus is to die in a particular Roman way, namely, on a cross; for in their eyes this will disgrace him. But they do not know that Jesus is master over his own life and death (x 17–18) and that, if he is to die on a cross, this is the form of death he himself has predicted and chosen (xii 32–33). His elevation on the cross will not be a disgrace but will be a step upward in his return to his Father. "The Jews" are putting Jesus to death on a cross to prevent all men from coming to believe in him (xi 48), but ironically they are lifting him up so that he can draw all men to himself.

Episode Two: Pilate Questions Jesus about Kingship (xviii 33–38a)

We saw that Episode 1 vaguely resembled the material in Mark xv 3–5 from the A source or primitive passion account. The material in Episode 2 is built around Pilate's question, "Are you 'the King of the Jews'?", which appears in Mark xv 2 from the B source (also in Luke xxiii 3). Bultmann, who distrusts the Marcan B material, looks on this as an addition expressing the Christian viewpoint that Jesus was executed for his messianic claims (HST, p. 272). However, Lohse, *History*, p. 89, correctly points out we do not find "the King of the Jews" as a Christian messianic formulation. It does not appear in Christian preaching, and we suggest in the NOTE that it had a nationalist political connotation and thus would have fitted plausibly into the historical trial. However, while we regard the basic question found in all four Gospels as historical, we recognize that the expansion of this question in Episode 2 is largely a construction of the Johannine writer or his forebears (p. 860 above).

If there was more than one political accusation made against Jesus (Mark xv 3; Luke xxiii 2), only one is recorded to have occupied Pilate's attention, the charge that Jesus claimed to be "the King of the Jews." John alone takes the trouble to answer the charge and to explain that Jesus' kingship was not political. Between vss. 33 and 37a (the two verses that have Synoptic parallels) there is a block of peculiarly Johannine material (34–36) which Benoit, *Passion*, p. 147, characterizes as "a theological exposition in which John puts words into Pilate's mouth that he could not have uttered as they stand and, above all, makes Jesus say things that Pilate could not have understood." Yet if we agree that this dialogue reflects the Church's apologia to the Empire in the 70s and 80s, we cannot rule out the possibility of a vague remembrance of a historical fact, namely, that Pilate did look into the claim that Jesus was a pretentious revolutionary and that one of the negative signs was that his followers made no armed resistance when he was arrested (vs. 36—we discount Peter's striking a slave, for that is scarcely a revolt).

Be this as it may, John gives us a splendid theological exposition of Jesus' kingship, all the more welcome because John has not explicitly dwelt on the theme of the kingdom of God so prominent in the Synoptic Gospels (vol. 29, p. cx). The Johannine Jesus first distinguishes between "king" used in a political sense which the Romans would understand and "king" in the Jewish sense with religious implications (vs. 34). Note that the accused criminal asks questions as if he were the judge, and from the first words of Jesus it is the prefect who is on trial! Pilate is a man who is facing the light and who must decide whether he will prefer light or darkness (iii 19–21). Pilate answers that he is simply repeating what has been told to him, and with Roman bluntness asks what Jesus has done. (The question, "What evil has he done?", appears on Pilate's lips later in the trial in Mark xv 14; Luke xxiii 22.) This will tell Pilate whether the "King" is any threat to Roman hegemony.

Jesus' answer is phrased in solemn and poetic diction. In the five lines of 36, the absolute statement of the first line is rephrased and repeated in the last line, while the intermediary lines 2–4 offer an explanation. Jesus does not talk about himself but about his kingdom. We note that for John it is a question of *Jesus'* kingdom, while the Synoptics generally prefer to speak of the kingdom *of God* (also John iii 3). But this is not a significant difference, for in Johannine thought what belongs to God belongs to Jesus and vice versa (xvii 10). Jesus does not deny that his kingdom or kingship affects this world, for the world will be conquered by those who believe in him (I John v 4). But he denies that his kingdom belongs to this world; like himself it comes from above. It belongs to the realm of the Spirit rather than to the realm of the flesh. Blank, p. 69, stresses the openness with which Jesus proclaims his kingdom here; in face of death there is to be no misunderstanding. (However, one can scarcely compare the situation in John to that in Mark where in the Jewish and Roman trials the veil of messianic secrecy is lifted—the Johannine Jesus has been more open in his proclamations during the ministry.)

Pilate seems to miss the import of Jesus' remarks; he has heard the word "kingdom" and for him this is a political entity; and so he presses for a confession (37). Jesus will not categorically refuse to be known as a king (see NOTE), but he indicates that he prefers to describe his role in terms of testifying to the truth. John has not portrayed Jesus as a preacher of the kingdom but as the unique revealer who alone can speak and show the truth about God. Jesus has no real subjects as would be true if his kingdom were like other kingdoms; rather he has followers who hear his voice as truth. Only those who belong to the truth can understand in what sense Jesus has a kingdom and is a king. The real reason that Jesus has been handed over to Pilate is precisely because he has borne witness to the truth: "The world . . . hates me because of the evidence I bring against it" (vii 7).

In one way Jesus' statement allows Pilate to relax: Jesus' kingship presents no danger to the genuine political interests of Rome. Yet in another way Jesus' statement makes Pilate uncomfortable, for Jesus has implicitly challenged Pilate to recognize the truth. Everyone who belongs to the truth listens to Jesus—does Pilate belong to the truth? From this moment on, the subject of the trial is no longer whether Jesus is innocent or guilty; Pilate admits this by immediately proclaiming Jesus not guilty (vs. 38b). The subject of the trial is now whether or not Pilate will respond to truth. We see a hint of the direction Pilate will take in his retort, "Truth? And what is that?" This question has been interpreted in many ways, for instance, as an expression of worldly skepticism or even as philosophical pondering. Even John is not likely to have painted a venal politician as a philosopher. On the level of the progression of the trial the evangelist may have meant the question to vocalize Pilate's failure to understand or perhaps the politician's impatience with Jewish theological jargon. But on the theological level the evangelist uses the question to show that Pilate is turning away from the truth. He does not accept the charges of "the Jews" but neither will he listen to the voice of Jesus. He does not recognize the truth.

Episode Three: Pilate Seeks to Release Jesus; "the Jews" Prefer Barabbas
(xviii 38b–40)

In this episode a detailed comparison of John and the Synoptics is necessary; see the accompanying chart. The Marcan account is drawn from the B source. It is not certain that Luke has an independent tradition, for the differences from Mark may be the result of editing.

COMPARATIVE CHART FOR THE BARABBAS INCIDENT

(Mark xv 6–11; Matt xxvii 15–21; Luke xxiii 18–19; John xviii 38a–40)

(a) *Sequence*

Mark, Matt, John: Immediately after the question of whether Jesus is "the King of the Jews."

Luke: After Pilate had sent Jesus to Herod and Herod had sent him back.

(b) *The group addressed by Pilate*

Mark, Matt: A crowd that has come up for the release of the prisoner (Matt xxvii 20: "crowds"). Among the crowd are chief priests (and elders—Matt).

Luke: The chief priests, the rulers, and the people* (cf. Acts iii 13 where Peter tells *the people* that they denied Jesus in the presence of Pilate).

John: "The Jews," i.e., the hostile authorities.

(c) *The privilegium paschale*

Mark, Matt: Described by the evangelist as a practice or custom of the governor.

Luke: Described by the evangelist as an obligation of the governor, but xxiii 17 is missing in many mss. and is probably unauthentic.

John: Described by Pilate as a Jewish custom.

(d) *The initiative*

Mark: The crowd asks Pilate to release a prisoner.

Matt: While the crowd is there to seek a prisoner's release, no specific request is made, so that Pilate mentions the release first, asking whether the crowd wants Barabbas or Jesus.

Luke: The chief priests, the rulers, and the people demand the release of Barabbas.

John: Pilate reminds the Jews of their custom that he release someone.

---

* This verse (Luke xxiii 13) is the only instance in the Lucan Passion Narrative where the evangelist presents "the people" as hostile to Jesus. Elsewhere Luke contrasts "[all] the people," who are favorable to Jesus, with the authorities, who hate him (Luke xix 47 – xx 1, xx 6, 19, 26, 45, xxi 38, xxiii 27, 35, 48, xxiv 19–20). G. Rau, ZNW 56 (1965), 41–51, argues for Winter's thesis that xxiii 13 should read "the rulers of the people." In any case Luke knows of a crowd hostile to Jesus (xxii 47, xxiii 4).

(e) *Pilate's question*

Mark, John: "Do you want [Mark: *thelein;* John: *boulein*] me to release for you 'the King of the Jews'?"

Matt: "Do you want me to release for you (Jesus) Barabbas or Jesus called Messiah?"

Luke: none

(f) *The response*

Mark, Matt: The chief priests (and elders) get the crowd(s) to ask for the release of Barabbas (and death of Jesus—Matt).

Luke: The chief priests, the rulers, and the people cry out together (*anakrazein*): "Take this fellow and release for us Barabbas!"

John: "The Jews" shout (*kraugazein*) back: "We want Barabbas, not this fellow."

(g) *Aftermath*

Mark: Pilate asks what he should do with "the King of the Jews," and the crowd cries out to crucify him. Barabbas released when Jesus is sentenced.

Matt: The governor asks again, "Which of the two do you want me to release for you?" They say, "Barabbas." The rest as in Mark.

Luke: Pilate addresses them once more, desiring to release Jesus, but they shout to crucify him. Barabbas released when Jesus is sentenced.

John: Different sequence: Barabbas never mentioned again.

While Matthew is close to Mark, there is a higher than usual percentage of differences. When we compare John to the Synoptics, we find that although John agrees with Luke (xxiii 14) in the "Not guilty" statement that introduces the episode, otherwise John agrees with Luke only in (b) and (f). Where Matthew is different from Mark, John agrees with Matthew only in (d), and even that similarity is only partial. John agrees with Mark in (a) and especially in (e). John's account of the episode is the shortest. Since a certain dramatic effect is achieved by the brevity (see below), John may well have abbreviated an earlier account, closer to Mark's present account.

The Barabbas episode appears in the B source of Mark, and so we are not surprised to find that Bultmann (HST, p. 272) characterizes it as legendary. Yet, since the Johannine account and perhaps the Lucan account may stem from a tradition independent of Mark's, caution seems to be demanded. There is legitimate reason for uncertainty about the *privilegium paschale* (NOTE on 39), and thus one may question whether there was a choice between Jesus and Barabbas. But we think that the evidence points, at least, to the historicity of the release of a guerrilla warrior named Barabbas at the time when Jesus was condemned. Otherwise it is too difficult to explain why the story was invented and how it found its way independently into diverse pre-Gospel traditions.

We have mentioned the thesis of Bajsić that, once Pilate discovered that Jesus was politically harmless, he sought until the end of the trial to have the people choose Jesus rather than Barabbas because he knew that the latter was a dangerous revolutionary. If there should be truth in that theory (which obviously depends on the historicity of the *privilegium paschale*), then John's account is not so close to what happened as is Mark's account. The Marcan/Matthean picture of a crowd coming up to ask the release of a prisoner fits such a thesis. Also Pilate would have had a better chance of swaying the choice of a crowd than that of the hostile Jewish authorities who figure in John's account. It is crucial for Bajsić's thesis that the decision to release Barabbas not have come till the end of the trial (so all three Synoptics). Thus, by omitting any further mention of Barabbas after xviii 40 (see NOTE on "took" in xix 1), John may have obscured the motivation for Pilate's continued efforts on Jesus' behalf.

If John's account of the Barabbas incident leaves something to be desired from the aspect of completeness, its brevity is, nevertheless, dramatic. "The Jews" have presented Jesus to Pilate as a revolutionary, a would-be king; but now the sham becomes evident. Even though Pilate finds Jesus innocent, "the Jews" would prefer the release of one who is truly a revolutionary. John captures the irony of the situation with the caustic remark: "Barabbas was a bandit." (John seems to evoke implicitly the contrast that x 1–10 made between the model shepherd whose sheep hear his voice [notice the end of xviii 37] and the bandit who enters the sheepfold surreptitiously.)

At the same time we see the futility of Pilate's attempt to avoid a decision between the truth and the world. The world represented by "the Jews" is not interested in a compromise: truth must be exterminated. Ironically, by failing to give Jesus justice and to release him after declaring his innocence, Pilate is forced to make a travesty of justice by releasing one who is guilty. By not protecting Jesus' interests, Pilate now finds himself compelled to act against his own interests. Pilate did not accept the challenge to listen to the voice of Jesus (vs. 37; see NOTE); now he must listen to the voice of "the Jews" as they demand the release of a bandit. Weakened by his failure to decide, Pilate is reduced from a position where he could have commanded the freeing of Jesus to a position where he must bargain for it.

[The Bibliography for this section is included in the Bibliography at the end of §64.]

64. THE PASSION NARRATIVE:
—DIVISION TWO (EPISODES 4–7)
(xix 1–16a)

The Trial of Jesus before Pilate (continued)

EPISODE 4

XIX 1 Then Pilate took Jesus and had him scourged. 2 And the soldiers wove a crown out of thorns and fixed it on Jesus' head, and they threw around him a cloak of royal purple. 3 Time and again they came up to him, saying, "All hail, 'King of the Jews'!" And they would slap him in the face.

EPISODE 5

4 Once more Pilate went out and said to them, "Look here, I am going to bring him out to you to make you understand that I find no case [against him]." 5 When Jesus came out wearing the thorny crown and the purple cloak, Pilate said to them, "Behold the man!" 6 As soon as the chief priests and the temple police saw him, they shouted, "Crucify him! Crucify him!" Pilate told them, "Take him yourselves and crucify him; I find no case against him." 7 "We have our own law," the Jews replied, "and according to that law he must die because he pretended to be God's Son." 8 When Pilate heard this kind of talk, he was more afraid than ever.

EPISODE 6

9 Going back into the praetorium, Pilate said to Jesus, "Where do you come from?" But Jesus would give him no answer. 10 "Do you refuse to speak to me?" Pilate demanded. "Don't you know that I have power to release you and power to crucify you?" 11 Jesus answered,

> "You would have no power over me at all
> were it not given to you from above.

4: *said;* 5: *said;* 6: *told;* 9: *said;* 10: *demanded.* In the historical present tense.

For that reason, he who handed me over to you
is guilty of a greater sin."

EPISODE 7

12 After this Pilate was eager to release him; but the Jews shouted,
"If you free this fellow, you are no 'Friend of Caesar.' Any man who
pretends to be a king becomes the Emperor's rival." 13 Once he heard
what they were saying, Pilate brought Jesus out and sat down on a
judge's bench in the place called "Stone Pavement" (*Gabbatha* being
its Hebrew name). (14 Remember, it was the Day of Preparation for
Passover, and the hour was about noon.) Then he said to the Jews,
"Look, here is your king!" 15 At this they shouted, "Away with him!
Away with him! Crucify him!" "What!" Pilate exclaimed. "Shall I
crucify your king?" The chief priests replied, "We have no king other
than the Emperor." 16a Then, at last, Pilate handed Jesus over to
them to be crucified.

14: *said;* 15: *exclaimed.* In the historical present tense.

NOTES

xix 1. *Then.* This is not an exact indication of time but sets up a contrast
with the preceding episode (BDF, §459²).

took. Barabbas' release has not been mentioned (and in the Synoptic
accounts he is not released until Jesus is sentenced), but some would interpret
this verb to imply that Pilate kept Jesus while at the same time he released
Barabbas (A. Mahoney, CBQ 28 [1966], 297²⁶).

had him scourged. Literally the Greek says that Pilate scourged Jesus,
but vs. 2 makes it clear that this was done by others at his order. See
the similar usage in xix 19. Mark xv 15 and Matt xxvii 26 use the Latinized
verb *fragelloun* ("flog"), while John uses *mastigoun.* (According to Luke xxiii
16, 22, Pilate offered to have Jesus beaten [*paideuein*].) John's word choice
here and in vs. 3 ("slap") may reflect the vocabulary of Isa 1 6: "I gave my
back to scourges and my cheek to slaps"; see p. 836 above.

The Romans used three forms of bodily chastisement with sticks or whips:
fustigatio (beating), *flagellatio* (flogging), and *verberatio* (scourging)—in ascending gradation. Beating was used as a corrective punishment in itself, but
severer punishment was part of the capital sentence.

2. *the soldiers.* John leaves the number indefinite, but Mark xv 16 and
Matt xxvii 27 speak of "the whole cohort" (600 soldiers!). Nothing is said
in John about where the mockery took place; but since in vs. 5 Jesus is
brought outside after the mockery, we may presume that it took place inside.
This is specifically stated in Mark and Matthew.

a crown out of thorns. The mockery is probably based on the crown
as generally representative of kingship, although some have thought more

specifically of a mockery of the laurel wreath worn by the Emperor. The type of crown was probably the radiant corona that serves as a ruler's adornment on many of the coins of Jesus' time (see Campbell Bonner, HTR 46 [1953], 47–48). Several types of trees could have furnished the thorns. In RB 42 (1933), 230–34, E. Ha-Reubeni suggests the common bush *Poterium spinosum L.* (Heb. *sīrāh*, "thorn bush"—Isa xxxiv 13; for interwoven thorns see Nah i 10). In JTS N.S. 3 (1952), 66–75, H. St. John Hart suggests the date palm which has thorns near the base; and we remember that palm branches were mentioned in the scene of Jesus' entry into Jerusalem just five days before (yet see NOTE on xii 13). E. R. Goodenough and C. B. Welles, HTR 46 (1953), 241–42, suggest that the crown may have been of acanthus rather than of thorns.

a cloak of royal purple. In this scene only John and Matthew specifically name a garment. Matt xxvii 28 mentions a red *chlamys* or outer cloak; this was worn by the Emperor, by minor officials, and by soldiers. John uses the word *himation*, "clothing" in general, or more precisely, "outer clothing, robe." John and Mark (xv 17) give the color as purple, the imperial color (see Rev xvii 4, xviii 16). A genuine purple cloak would not have been as easily obtainable as a red cloak, for purple dye obtained from shellfish was expensive.

3. *Time and again they came up to him.* The imperfect tense is used to indicate repetition. MTGS, p. 66, lists this among the instances of an imperfect used to make the narrative continuous and interesting. The clause is omitted in some important witnesses, seemingly by homoioteleuton, for there are two short "and" clauses in a row.

All hail. The soldiers mimic the *"Ave Caesar"* greeting given the Emperor.

King. The nominative with the article is used by John (a usage classified as semitizing by BDF, §147[3]), while Mark and Matthew use the more classical vocative. Barrett, p. 449, agrees with Moulton that the nominative has a fitting nuance here: "Hail, you 'King'!"

4. *went out.* Pilate had come outside in xviii 38. We have not been told that he went inside again but are obviously meant to presume that he did so during the scourging.

I find no case. P[66] and Codex Sinaiticus read: "I do not find a case." The second "not guilty" judgment (NOTE on xviii 38) occurs in John after Jesus had been mocked by the Romans; the second one in Luke (xxiii 14) occurs just after Jesus has been mocked by Herod's soldiers.

[against him]. This is omitted in Sinaiticus, and is found in a different sequence in another group of witnesses.

5. *wearing the thorny crown and the purple cloak.* In vs. 2 John wrote of "a crown of thorns," which is the same Greek expression employed in Matt xxvii 29; here John uses the Greek expression found in Mark xv 17. Mark and Matthew indicate that, at the end of the mocking, the soldiers took off the garment they had put on Jesus and restored his own clothes; of course, in these Gospels the mockery takes place just before the crucifixion and after the death sentence. John indicates that the crown and cloak were kept on during the latter part of the trial and, indeed, never mentions that Jesus was allowed to put on his own clothes again. It is because of John's evidence that in popular art the crucified Jesus is portrayed as still wearing a crown of thorns.

Pilate said to them, "Behold the man!" This is omitted by P[66], OL, and the sub-Achmimic Coptic—an important combination. "Behold" is *idou;* contrast "Look, here is your king!" in vs. 14 below, which employs *ide*. John uses *ide* fifteen times and *idou* only four times; in particular, *ide* is common (six times) when a nominal object follows—this is the one instance of *idou* in such a construction. G. D. Kilpatrick, JTS 18 (1967), 426, would read *ide*. In itself there is nothing particularly significant about the use of "the man" (*ho anthrōpos*; cf. Peter's "I do not know the man" in Matt xxvi 72, 74), but the dramatic context lends importance. Seeking the intelligibility of this statement as reported on the lips of Pilate, some commentators interpret the *ecce homo* to be equivalent to "Look at the poor fellow!", either by way of eliciting pity (Bernard), or by way of emphasizing the ridiculousness of taking seriously a figure so hapless (Bultmann), or by way of contempt designed to goad the crowd into demanding Jesus' release (Bajsić). Lohse, *History*, p. 93, takes it as an indication of the strong impression that Jesus has made on Pilate: "Here is a *man!*" Other commentators are interested in the theological implications of the pronouncement. The thesis that the evangelist means to stress the incarnation is unlikely. Barrett, p. 450, thinks of the Jewish and Hellenistic myths of the primal Man; he sees also a contrast between the title "the man" used here and the title "God's Son" which Jesus is said to have claimed (vs. 7). An equation with the "Son of Man" or with the "man of sorrows" (the Servant in Isa liii 3) has been proposed. More plausible is Meeks' contention (pp. 70–71) that "Man" was an eschatological title in Hellenistic Judaism. As a possible background for John's usage, Meeks points to Zech vi 12: *"Behold a man* [LXX: *anēr*] whose name is the Branch . . . he shall build the Temple of the Lord."* "The Branch" came to be understood messianically; and in the MT of Zechariah the second part of the verse recalls the oracle of Nathan to David: "He shall build a house for my name" (II Sam vii 13). In LXX the word for "Branch" is *anatolē* (from the verb "to rise, spring up," thus "sprout"), and this is reminiscent of the LXX form of the "messianic" oracle of Balaam (Num xxiv 17): "A star shall rise [*anatelein*] from Jacob, and *the man* [*ho anthrōpos*] shall arise from Israel." Thus, in John's thought Pilate may be presenting Jesus to the people under a messianic title. (We note that in the Marcan/Matthean accounts of the Sanhedrin session the question whether Jesus is the Messiah is related to the question of his building the Temple—a theme also found in Zech vi 12).

6. *the chief priests and the temple police*. The repetition of the definite article before the second noun preserves the separation of the two groups (MTGS, p. 182); together they constitute "the Jews" mentioned in the next verse. The cry to crucify comes from the crowd in Mark/Matthew and from "the chief priests and the rulers and the people" in Luke.

shouted. Kraugazein (NOTE on xi 43); Mark/Matthew use *krazein;* Luke uses *epiphonein*.

"Crucify him! Crucify him!" Literally "Crucify! Crucify!"; contrast vs. 15 where the "him" is expressed. Here too some witnesses have supplied "him," while others read only one "Crucify!". These are scribal assimilations to the Synoptic forms of the shout: Mark xv 13: "Crucify him!"; Matt xxvii 22: "Let him be crucified"; Luke xxiii 21: "Crucify, crucify him!". The double cry reflects intensity; and the two Gospels that have the double cry in this first instance of a shout for crucifixion (cf. NOTE on 15 below) present Jesus' enemies as persistently hostile (see Luke xxiii 23; John xix 12–15). In the Synoptic Passion Accounts this cry is the first indication that Jesus is

to be crucified; John has prepared the way in xviii 32. In the three Synoptic Gospels the cry follows closely upon the choice between Jesus and Barabbas.

Take him yourselves and crucify him. Some commentators understand Pilate as seriously offering an alternative to the priests. Schlier, "Jesus," p. 68, thinks that Pilate's control is so far gone that he is willing to let the Jews crucify Jesus even though he finds Jesus innocent. In this vein the statement would be either an exception to or a direct contradiction of the statement in xviii 31 that the Jews did not have power to put anyone to death. That the Johannine editor would not have seen such a blatant contradiction seems incredible, and so it seems more likely to think that Pilate is not serious. (Moreover, John could scarcely mean that Pilate thought the Jewish leaders would carry out a *crucifixion,* for this form of punishment was not acceptable among the Jews—see NOTE on xviii 32.) The statement is simply an expression of Pilate's exasperation; Pilate is rebuffing "the Jews" and refusing to have anything to do with crucifying Jesus by telling them to do what both parties knew was impossible. We note that "the Jews" understood that he was not serious, for they did not hasten to seize Jesus and execute him themselves. Rather they continued to press Pilate to order the execution because that was the only way it could be effected.

I find no case against him. This is the third and final "not guilty" judgment in John (xviii 38, xix 4). The corresponding third judgment in Luke (xxiii 22) also immediately follows the shout for crucifixion.

7. *according to that law he must die.* Origen (*In Jo.* XXVIII 25[20]; GCS 10:423) points out that this reasoning illustrates John xvi 2: "The hour is coming when the man who puts you to death will think that he is serving God." The law invoked is Lev xxiv 16 which imposes a death sentence for blasphemy; cf. John x 36 which associates the claim to be God's Son with blasphemy. For our uncertainty about the laws of blasphemy in Jesus' time see vol. 29, p. 408.

he pretended to be God's Son. Literally "made himself"; see v 18, viii 53. In all three Synoptic accounts of the trial before the Sanhedrin, the question was asked whether Jesus was the Son of God (in Mark xiv 61 and Matt xxvi 63 this title stands in apposition to "Messiah"), and in Mark/Matthew Jesus' answer brings a charge of blasphemy and a death sentence. Even though the Fourth Gospel does not report this trial (but see vol. 29, pp. 408–9), the evangelist reflects the common Christian tradition that Jesus' claim of relationship to God was the decisive factor in the hostility of the authorities toward him. Here "God's Son" is anarthrous, a factor that leads Dodd, *Tradition,* p. 114, to deny that John has borrowed directly from the Synoptic accounts of the trial, for in these the article appears before "Son." (Mark xiv 61 has literally "the Son of the Blessed One.")

8. *more afraid than ever.* It has not hitherto been reported that Pilate was afraid, and some find here proof that a longer account has been abbreviated (NOTE on xviii 40, "shouted back"). This theorizing is not really necessary, however; Bultmann, p. 511[5], is perfectly correct in observing a hint of fear in the hesitancy already exhibited by Pilate. Moreover, the comparative here may have the force of an elative and indicate no more than that he was very afraid. The root of Pilate's intensified fear is not clear (see P. P. Flourney, BS 82 [1925], 314–20). It may be superstitious; for to a Hellenistic mind "God's Son" would be translated in terms of a *theios anēr,* a divine man

with magical powers of occult origin (Dodd, *Tradition*, pp. 113–14; Bultmann, p. 512[1]—there is a note of superstition in the reaction of Pilate's wife in Matt xxvii 19). Or the root of the fear may be political if we understand "the Jews" to be accusing him of something that could be reported to Rome, namely, that he was violating the established custom whereby Roman provincial administrators respected local religious practices. Still another possibility is that, having now realized that "the Jews" were determined on Jesus' death for a religious reason and knowing that he would never shake their fanatical determination, Pilate became afraid that he would not be successful in his plan to prevent the release of Barabbas by applying the amnesty to Jesus.

9. *Going back into the praetorium.* Pilate had brought Jesus outside in vs. 4, but there has been no mention of his sending Jesus back inside. Presumably we are to think that he did so in face of the frenzied shouting.

"Where do you come from?" The evangelist may well mean this question to be interpreted in light of Jesus' claim to be God's Son; thus it would be tantamount to asking whether Jesus comes from heaven or is human. Jesus' silence would then be intelligible: if Nicodemus and the Jews could not understand how he had come from above, he could scarcely expect a Roman to understand. However, at an earlier stage of the tradition (or at another level of the narrative) the question may have represented Pilate's search for a legal loophole. In Luke xxiii 6 we find Pilate asking whether Jesus was a Galilean and using this information to send Jesus to Herod under whose jurisdiction Jesus would come. There is an interesting parallel to this episode in Josephus *War* VI.v.3;≹305, in the interrogation of the prophet Jesus, son of Ananias, by the Roman procurator Albinus. Because the prophet has been proclaiming the destruction of Jerusalem and of the Temple, the procurator had him brought in and asked him who he was and *where he came from.*

Jesus would give him no answer. We find a similar reference to Jesus' silence in Mark xv 5 and Matt xxvii 14 but not in Luke. (Jesus' silence is mentioned by the Synoptics also in the interrogations before the Sanhedrin [Mark xiv 61; Matt xxvi 63] and before Herod [Luke xxiii 9].) In John the silence is momentary for Jesus will speak again in 11; in the three Synoptics Jesus remains silent during the whole trial except for an answer to Pilate's question about his being king. The motif of silence echoes the theme of the Suffering Servant in Isa liii 7: "Just as a sheep is mute before its shearers, he did not open his mouth." This motif is elaborated in relation to Jesus' death in I Pet ii 22–23.

10. *power.* Or "authority"; see NOTE on i 12.

11. *from above. Anōthen;* see NOTE on iii 3. Obviously this does not mean from the Emperor Tiberius but from God; cf. iii 27: "No one can take anything unless heaven gives it to him." (Acts iv 27–28 treats Pontius Pilate as a tool of God.) Any power over Jesus must come from God, for only the Father is greater than Jesus (xiv 28). The logic of this verse is difficult (cf. R. Thibaut, NRT 54 [1927], 208–11). Some have even argued that the last two lines make sense only if here Jesus is saying that Pilate has been given power over him by "the Jews" who delivered him into Pilate's hands (xviii 35). See references in Bultmann, p. 513[1].

he who handed me over to you. Or "betrayed me"; the present tense, instead of the aorist, appears in many mss., a variation that occurs in other Johannine passages where this expression describes Judas (NOTES on vi 64,

71, xviii 2). There is no reference to Judas here, however, even though he did betray Jesus to Roman soldiers. John attributes to the Jewish nation and the chief priests or to "the Jews" the handing over of Jesus to Pilate (xviii 35–36). It is not certain whether the singular "he who" is to be taken as a reference to Caiaphas (as representative of "the Jews") or as a generalizing reference to "the Jews" (Bultmann, p. 513[2]). Von Campenhausen, col. 390, cites Luke xvii 1 where *"he* through *whom* scandal comes" is generic.

guilty of a greater sin. We have mentioned the difficult logic: because Pilate has no power over Jesus except that which comes from God, the one who handed Jesus over is guilty of a greater sin. The implication seems to be that, since Pilate has been given a role in the passion by God, he is acting against Jesus unwittingly or unwillingly, but the one who handed Jesus over is acting deliberately. Bultmann, p. 511, interprets the verse in terms of the State and the World: the State may misuse its power but it does so without the personal hatred of truth that characterizes the World. In putting Jesus to death the State (Pilate) is serving the World ("the Jews"), and the greater guilt rests on the World. In a similar vein Schlier, "Jesus," p. 71, writes: "When political power acts against the truth, it is always less guilty than the intellectual and spiritual forces of the world." Such interpretations, however, are really theological applications of John's idea rather than literal exegesis.

12. *After this.* Literally "from this." The meaning seems to be temporal but may be causal ("for this reason"). Pilate is implicitly pictured as having gone outside again, for he speaks to "the Jews."

Pilate was eager to release him. Or "was striving"; the conative imperfect implies a series of attempts which "the Jews" shout down. There is a parallel in Luke xxiii 20 (occurring after the Barabbas episode but before "Crucify, crucify him!"): ". . . desiring to release him." Note also Acts iii 13: ". . . Jesus whom you delivered up and denied in the presence of Pilate, when he had decided to release him."

shouted. Some mss. have the imperfect: "kept shouting."

this fellow. The contemptuous use of *houtos* as in xviii 30.

'Friend of Caesar.' Is this a title that had been granted to Pilate or simply a general expression meaning "loyal to the Emperor"? In later Roman usage "friend of Caesar" was an honorific title bestowed in recognition of service, but Bernard, II, 621, says that the official title is not found before the time of Vespasian (A.D. 69–79). Others argue for a much earlier usage and think that the reference here is to the title (so BAG, p. 396; Deissmann, LFAE, p. 378). E. Bammel, TLZ 77 (1952), 205–10, has marshaled the arguments for the latter view, and they are impressive. In Hellenistic times the "friends of the king" were a special group honored by the king for loyalty and often entrusted by him with authority (I Macc ii 18, iii 38, x 65; III Macc vi 23; Josephus *Ant.* XII.vii.3;⁂298). In the early Empire the "friends of Augustus" were a well-known society. The coins of Herod Agrippa I (A.D. 37–44) frequently bear the inscription PHILOKAISAR, "friend of Caesar," a designation that Philo (*In Flaccum* vi;⁂40) also gives him. Sherwin-White, *Roman Society,* p. 471[1], maintains that during the Principate or early imperial times the term "friend" is often used for the official representative of the Emperor, and he compares John's use of the term to Philo's use. Thus the objection that the title was not used in Pilate's time is rather weak. As for

the likelihood that the title would have been granted to Pilate, he was of equestrian order and thus eligible for such an honor. Moreover, the all-powerful Aelius Sejanus seems to have been his patron at Rome; and Tacitus (*Annals* VI 8) says, "Whoever was close to Sejanus had a claim on *the friendship of Caesar.*"

Any man. The introductory "For" that is found in some witnesses of the Western tradition gives expression to the implicit logic of the sentence.

a king. In the East the Emperor was often referred to as a king.

the Emperor's. Literally "Caesar's." The latter was the cognomen of Julius (Gaius Julius Caesar) and the adopted name of Augustus (a great-nephew by marriage of Julius) and of Augustus' successors. When did "Caesar" shift in connotation from a proper name to a title equivalent to "Emperor"? There can be no doubt that the shift had occurred by the time of Vespasian and the Flavian emperors who had no family relationship to Julius, but probably it came earlier. For instance, while through adoption Tiberius and Caligula were legal descendants of Augustus and could claim the name Caesar, Claudius was not so adopted and thus in his case "Caesar" was more an element in the titulature than a family name. And indeed an ambivalent use of "Caesar" may go as far back as Augustus' time. The procurator (or prefect) coinage of Judea under Augustus already bore only the name KAISAROS and a date—possibly a reflection of an attitude wherein "Caesar" was looked on as the ruler's title.

13. *heard.* Here the verb *akouein* is followed by the genitive (NOTE on "listens" in xviii 38), a construction that implies Pilate's understanding and accepting the thrust of the remarks of "the Jews." In xix 8 *akouein* was followed by the accusative: he heard them but was still willing to oppose them. But now his opposition has been broken.

sat down. The Greek verb *kathizein* is sometimes transitive (cause to sit down) and sometimes intransitive; and there has been a vigorous debate whether John means that Pilate caused Jesus to sit down on the bench or that Pilate sat down himself. Such scholars as Von Harnack, Loisy, Macgregor, and Bonsirven have argued for the transitive translation, a position now eloquently defended by I. de la Potterie, *art. cit.* There is some ancient support for the transitive translation in the *Gospel of Peter*, 7, and in Justin, *Apology* I.xxxv.6, where the Jews (note: not Pilate) set Jesus upon a judgment seat and mock him. But the strongest argument for this translation stems from its suitability in the framework of Johannine theology. For John, Jesus is the real judge of men, for in condemning him they are judging themselves; therefore, it is fitting for him to be on the judgment seat.

Nevertheless, there are difficulties (see J. Blinzler, MüTZ 5 [1954], especially 175–82). Although *kathizein* may be transitive, we would expect it to be followed by a pronominal object if it meant "sat *him* down." (De la Potterie, pp. 223–25, counters this objection by insisting that the noun "Jesus," which comes between the two verbs "brought out" and "sat down," is the object of both.) More important, the intransitive use of *kathizein* with "judge's bench, tribunal" is well attested. For instance, the same expression that appears in John (aorist active of *kathizein* with *epi bēmatos*) is used in Josephus' description of Pilate where it clearly means "he sat down on the tribunal" (*War* II.ix.3;⚹172). Finally, we must ask ourselves whether John is continuing to present his theology in terms of a plausible historical narrative. It is most difficult to believe that the Roman governor put a prisoner on the judge's bench—the seriousness of Roman law militates against such buffoonery. And so if John's statement means that Pilate set Jesus upon the judge's bench, the evangelist has abandoned the guise of history. We cannot discount this difficulty so easily as Meeks, p. 75, who thinks that there is no evidence that the Johannine account seeks to relate factual occurrences as such. While John's primary interest is undoubtedly in the theological implications of the narrative, we have had reason to believe that the evangelist respected the historical tradition that had come down to him. Some have sought to escape the difficulty in this verse by theorizing that the verb *kathizein* is meant to have a double meaning: intransitive on the historical level, transitive on the theological level. However, in previous Johannine instances of double meaning (vol. 29, p. cxxxv), the phenomenon has not been based on syntactical ambiguity, nor is it usual for the second meaning to be the opposite of the first.

on a judge's bench. De la Potterie, who holds the transitive interpretation of the verb, suggests that here the anarthrous *bēma* is not the judgment bench but another seat on the magistrate's platform (yet see the Josephus reference above). *Bēma* does mean "platform," but in the context of a trial it usually refers to the judge's bench, as in Matt xxvii 19. The *bēma* or *sella curilis* would normally have stood in the forecourt of the procurator's residence, elevated with steps leading to it so that the judge could look over the spectators. The *bēma* of the procurator Florus is thus described by Josephus, *War* II.xiv.8;※301. In Matthew's account the whole trial seems to have taken place with Pilate seated on the judgment bench and Jesus standing before him. Such a procedure would have been normal as we may see from accounts of trials before the governors Festus (Acts xxv 6, 17) and Florus (Josephus, *loc. cit.*). However, it was not absolutely necessary for the governor to sit on the judge's bench when passing sentence except in the case of capital sentences. Thus, John's account is not necessarily inexact, and Matthew may be giving us a generalization.

in the place. Literally "into [*eis*] the place." If this phrase is thought to continue the verb "brought out," there is no problem; in fact, however, the phrase follows the verb of sitting. J. O'Rourke, CBQ 25 (1963), 124–26, discusses the problem, pointing out that in a series of two verbs, when a phrase follows the second verb, it is usually to be construed with the second verb. That a phrase indicating motion would follow the intransitive verb "to sit" is awkward, and some scholars call upon the use of *eis* here as an argument for the transitive interpretation of the verb, an argument particularly persuasive to De la Potterie who believes that *eis* always has the sense of motion in John (a belief that, in our opinion, requires extraordinary translations— see NOTE on i 18). The problem disappears if we recognize that *eis* sometimes means no more than *en*, "in, at" (BDF, §205). Meeks, p. 75, who is otherwise favorable to De la Potterie's thesis, characterizes this as the weakest argument for the thesis, "since *kathizein* is frequently used pregnantly with *eis* and the accusative not only in Hellenistic Greek but already in classical poetry."

"Stone Pavement." Benoit, RB 59 (1952), 547, says that *lithostrotos* is a generic term applicable to different types of stone pavements, ranging from simple ones of uniform stone slabs to ones of fine mosaic. A few scholars have thought that a mosaic pavement is meant here, although it is difficult

to visualize an artistic pavement in the forecourt of a palace where there was frequent and heavy traffic. J. A. Steele, ET 34 (1922–23), 562–63, argues that the *bēma* of a Roman official was often set up on a transportable pavement of tesselae or colored cubes, inserted in a design portraying the gods. (He thus sees the scene as a confrontation between Jesus and Jupiter!) More often scholars have visualized a pavement of large stones. For instance, in LXX of II Chron vii 3 *lithostrotos* describes the pavement of Solomon's Temple, a monumental construction. On the lower levels of the fortress Antonia, one of the two candidates for identification as the praetorium (NOTE on xviii 28), there has been excavated a paved court, the central area of which measures about 2,300 square yards. The massive paving blocks of this court are more than a yard square and a foot thick. Such a floor may well have been famous as "Stone Pavement." However, we are not certain whether the excavated pavement was part of the Antonia in Jesus' time—Kopp, HPG, pp. 372–73, gives the archaeological reasons for thinking that it was not laid until about A.D. 135.

Gabbatha. This is not the Aramaic ("Hebrew"=Aramaic; NOTE on v 2) equivalent of *lithostrotos,* and we note that John gives the two names without saying that one is a translation of the other. Many interpretations of *Gabbatha* have been suggested, but the most likely involve derivations from the root *gbh* or *gbʿ,* "to be high, protrude." A designation as "elevated place, ridge, hump" (the meaning given for Gabath by Josephus, *War* V.ii.1;⚡51) could fit either localization suggested for the praetorium. Vincent has demonstrated that the fortress Antonia stood on a rocky elevation, and Herod's Palace was upon the heights of the upper town. The term might also have referred to the elevation of the *bēma* on a stepped platform.

14. *Day of Preparation.* This is the sense of the Greek word *paraskeuē,* although the Semitic word that it probably represents (Heb. *ʿereb;* Aram. *ʿarubâ*) has the narrower connotation of "vigil, day before." The term, which appears in all the Gospels, was associated in the tradition with the day on which Jesus died. It was applicable to Friday, the day before the Sabbath (Josephus *Ant.* XVI.vi.2;⚡163), and this is the way in which the Synoptics understood it (Mark xv 42; Matt xxvii 62; Luke xxiii 54). But for John this is not only the day before Sabbath but also the day before Passover, and John's "Day of Preparation for Passover" reflects the Hebrew expression *ʿereb pesah* (StB, II, 834 ff.). Torrey's theory (JBL 50 [1931], 227–41) that Passover should be understood as the festival period of seven days and that John is speaking of Friday within Passover week has been refuted by S. Zeitlin, JBL 51 (1932), 263–71.

noon. Literally "the sixth hour." Some witnesses, including the corrector of Sinaiticus, read "the third hour" (9 A.M.). Ammonius (early 3rd century) has this reading; and S. Bartina, VD 36 (1958), 16–37, upholds it on the grounds that when letters were used for numbers, an original old digamma (=3) may have been confused with the open sigma or *episēmon* (=6). Although such confusion is possible (and, indeed, other explanations for the confusion have been advanced), we think it more likely that the reading "9 A.M." was a scribal harmonization with the statement of Mark xv 25 that Jesus was crucified at 9 A.M. In all of this we suppose that John was reckoning hours from daylight rather than from midnight (NOTE on i 39), so that the sixth hour was noon rather than 6 A.M. Some have favored the latter as a means for reconciling John's information with Mark's horarium for the crucifixion. But Jesus can scarcely have been brought to Pilate at the daybreak hour (close to 6 A.M.—NOTE on xviii 28), have undergone an extended trial, including scourging and mocking, and still have received his sentence at 6 A.M. (For a recent defense of our understanding of John's reckoning of time see J. E. Bruns, NTS 13 [1966–67], 285–90.)

Only Mark fixes the crucifixion at 9 A.M. Since John's reference to noon has theological significance (see COMMENT), some scholars have rejected the idea that the trial took the whole morning and have accepted Mark's horarium as historically correct. But Mark's horarium means an incredibly crowded morning since the (second) session of the Sanhedrin is not supposed to have begun until about 6 A.M. Moreover, the three Synoptic Gospels (Mark xv 33; Matt xxvii 45; Luke xxiii 44) state that there was darkness over the whole land from noon until 3 P.M., a statement that would seem to designate the period when Jesus was on the cross. (Has Mark unwittingly combined two sources with contradictory time indications?) A. Mahoney, CBQ 27 (1965), 292–99, has tried to get around the difficulty by explaining that the reference to 9 A.M. in Mark applies only to the casting of lots for Jesus' clothes which took place when Jesus was stripped to be scourged—obviously a hypothesis that cannot be proved. Some have thought that Mark was counting in three-hour periods, so that "the third hour" could mean the period beginning with the third hour, i.e., 9–12 A.M. E. Lipinski (see NTA 4 [1959–60], ⌗54) observes that Mark xv 21 describes Simon of Cyrene as coming in from the fields— a detail that would favor noon as the time of the crucifixion, for all work stopped about noon on Passover Eve (except that for Mark the day is Passover itself!).

The hour of noon on the Preparation Day for the Passover was the hour for beginning the slaughter of the paschal lambs. The ancient law of Exod xii 6 required that the paschal lamb be kept alive until the 14th of Nisan and then slaughtered in the evening (literally, "between the two evenings," a phrase sometimes interpreted as meaning between sunset and darkness). By Jesus' time the slaughtering was no longer done at home by the heads of the families but in the temple precincts by the priests. A great number of lambs had to be slaughtered for the more than 100,000 Passover participants in Jerusalem (NOTE on xi 55), and so the slaughtering could no longer be done in the evening, in the technical sense of after sunset. By casuistry "evening" was interpreted to begin at noon when the sun began to decline, and thus the priests had the whole afternoon of the 14th to accomplish their task. See Bonsirven, art. cit., for the rabbinical citations—he points out that the rule whereby only unleavened bread could be eaten also went into effect at noon. The parenthetical Johannine reference to noon is probably meant to indicate the time for the whole action described in vss. 13–16, including the death sentence.

"Look, here is your king!" This translates ide; see NOTE on "Behold the man" in 5. Some would relate this mock proclamation to the transitive interpretation of vs. 13, so that Pilate, having seated Jesus, points to him enthroned as king (although a bēma is scarcely a throne). However, the proclamation is perfectly intelligible without this interpretation; for we are probably to think of Jesus as still wearing the pseudo-regalia of the thorny crown and purple cloak (vs. 5) and thus presenting a pathetic picture of royalty. We find implausible the contention of E. E. Jensen, JBL 60 (1941), 270–71, that the Johannine Pilate is not speaking in mockery but has recognized the reasonableness of Jesus' claim to be a king in a spiritual sense and is asking for Jewish approbation of this. Yet the evangelist may have seen in Pilate's mockery an unconscious proclamation of truth.

15. *shouted.* There are a few important textual witnesses that read "said," and it is possible that this less dramatic reading was original.

Away with him! The "him" is not expressed in Greek. A similar cry, "Away with this man," occurs once in Luke xxiii 18 at the beginning of the Barabbas incident; also see Acts xxi 36.

Crucify him! Here the "him" is expressed, unlike vs. 6 where the cry of crucifixion was raised for the first time. In having a second cry for crucifixion John agrees with Mark and Matthew. Although Luke xxiii 23 states that they shouted for crucifixion a second time, it does not give the words of the cry as do the other Gospels. John's phraseology is the same as that of Mark xv 14, while Matt xxvii 23 has "Let him be crucified."

"We have no king other than the Emperor." J. W. Doeve, *Vox Theologica* 32 (1961), 69–83, argues that this cry could have fitted in with the attitude of some Jews who were tired of nationalistic movements and uprisings and preferred Roman rule to the vicious struggles of the Hasmonean times when the Jews had a king.

16a. *handed Jesus over.* All four Gospels use this verb to describe Pilate's final action. The verb is meant to have the juridical value of a condemnation, and this is made clearer in the later Gospels. For instance, both Matthew and John have Pilate on the judgment seat when he does this, and Luke xxiii 24 specifies that Pilate passed sentence (*epikrinein*). The usual form of the death sentence was: *Ibis in crucem* (You shall go to the cross—Petronius *Saturae* 137); the indirect description of it in Latin literature is usually: *Iussit duci* (He ordered him to be led off—Sherwin-White, *Roman Society*, p. 27). According to a resolution passed in A.D. 21 there was to be an interval of ten days between a death sentence by the Senate and its execution (Tacitus *Annals* III 51; Suetonius *Tiberius* 75), but this did not affect a governor's court where immediate execution was frequent.

to them. The last antecedent is "the chief priests." Mark xv 15–20 and Matt xxvii 26–31 have Jesus handed over to Roman soldiers who flog and mock him before the crucifixion, but neither John nor Luke has such a scene at this moment. Luke xxiii 25 reports that Pilate "delivered up Jesus to their will," with the last antecedent being "the chief priests and the rulers and the people" (vs. 13). Later on, both Gospels speak of the Roman soldiers who take part in the crucifixion (Luke xxiii 36; John xix 23); nevertheless, they have given the initial impression that Jesus was given over to the Jewish authorities to be crucified. This could be an oversight or careless writing, but more likely it reflects the later tendency to exculpate the Romans and inculpate the Jews (pp. 794–96 above). We find the theme that *the Jews* crucified Jesus in Acts ii 36, iii 15, x 39; and it is continued in Justin, *Apology* I.xxxv.6; PG 6:384B. We are told by Tertullian, *Apology* xxi 18; CSEL 69:57, that the Jews extorted from Pilate a sentence giving Jesus "up *to them* to be crucified."

to be crucified. The Gospels are plausible when they describe Pilate not only as finding Jesus guilty but also as fixing his exact punishment. In trials in Rome where the legal *ordo* prevailed, there were fixed penalties for specific crimes; but in the provinces the trials were *extra ordinem*, and the penalty was at the governor's discretion. Lietzmann contends that if Pilate had accepted the Jewish religious charge against Jesus, he would have sentenced Jesus to be executed in the Jewish fashion, by stoning. Sherwin-White, *Roman Society*, p. 35, however, maintains that from what we know of the Roman *cognitio* procedure, it would have been most unusual for a Roman governor to assign a non-Roman punishment.

COMMENT

As we have insisted (p. 859 above), the seven episodes of the trial before Pilate are a close dramatic unity—our breaking the scene into two parts has really been a question of convenience, so that we would not have too long a section upon which to comment. Nevertheless, the tone does change in Episodes 4–7. The political charge against Jesus quickly fades into the background. Pilate now knows that Jesus is not a dangerous revolutionary, and "the Jews" no longer seriously try to persuade him to the contrary. In xix 7 they confess that the real charge against Jesus is a religious one. Despairing of winning Pilate over, they resort to a type of blackmail that forces him to act against his better judgment. Pilate must deal with "the Jews" not as humble plaintiffs in a case which he is free to decide but as adversaries who have the power to destroy him. He tries stratagem after stratagem to defeat them, but in the end he is vanquished and must hand Jesus over to them.

Episode Four: The Roman Soldiers Scourge and Mock Jesus (xix 1–3)

The Gospels are at variance in the setting they give the incident(s). According to Mark and Matthew there was a flogging and mocking of Jesus at the end of the trial: Pilate handed Jesus over to be flogged and crucified, and the Roman soldiers took him into the praetorium to mock him. The sentence that Jesus should be flogged (Mark xv 15) comes from the Marcan A source or primitive passion account (p. 788 above), while the description of the mockery (xv 16–20) comes from the Marcan B source. Are two incidents involved? Bultmann, HST, p. 272, regards the mocking as a secondary elaboration of the flogging. Taylor, p. 584, rejects this as unproved and argues that two different actions are described. The latter view gets some support from Luke. According to Luke xxiii 11 the mockery of Jesus took place midway through the Roman trial but was the work of Herod and his soldiers. After Jesus had been returned from Herod, Pilate twice (16, 22) said that he would have Jesus beaten and released, but we are never told that this took place. (In Luke the only action taken against Jesus by the Roman soldiers was their mockery of him as he hung on the cross [36–37].) Like Mark and Matthew, John has both a scourging and a mocking by Roman soldiers; like Luke, John places the episode in mid-trial.

The accompanying chart enables us to study the mockery in detail. The Lucan account seems to be independent of the others, and John has no particular affinity to Luke here. Although we have not been able to indicate it on the chart, some of the details in Matthew are in different order from those in Mark (Matthew puts all the non-violent actions before the violent), but otherwise the two accounts are quite similar. Is John dependent on either or both? Buse, "Marcan," p. 218, in harmony with his thesis that John drew on the Marcan B source, sees a great similarity between John and Mark. However, if we take ※3 in the chart for an example, John's wording differs from Mark's and is almost verbatim the same as Matthew's (although Matthew places the crowning with thorns after the putting on of the robe, while John has it precede). John differs from Mark in ※※7, 10, and 11; John is similar to Mark but not totally the same in ※※1, 2, 3, 6, and 8. Thus it is not easy to establish a case for Johannine dependence on Mark or the Marcan B source. Borgen, p. 252, suggests that here John "consists almost only of combinations and agreements with Matthew and Mark" and that the omission of details in John reflects editorial reworking. It is true that of the seven episodes in the Pilate trial, this one lends itself best to such a theory of Johannine dependence. Yet except for details ※※3 and 8 John shows enough divergency that one may argue with equal plausibility for an independent Johannine tradition.

Passing on now from a discussion of the details, how plausible are the incidents of the scourging and the mocking of Jesus by the soldiers? First we shall consider the question of motivation and then the question of sequence. For Mark and Matthew the flogging and the mocking are part of the crucifixion punishment. For Luke the mocking is an expression of Herod's contempt. It is John who raises the problem, for here the scourging and the mocking seem to be part of Pilate's benevolent plan for Jesus' release! Before and after this episode Pilate affirms that Jesus is not guilty; therefore we must suppose that Pilate is having Jesus reduced to a bloody and battered figure in order to placate "the Jews" and to persuade them that Jesus is too helpless to be a threat. Haenchen, "Historie," p. 71, suggests that John has taken what was originally a hostile action against Jesus and awkwardly worked it into his picture of a Pilate who is personally interested in Jesus. Yet we must recognize that in part Luke's presentation of Pilate's motivation is close to John's: Pilate offers to have Jesus beaten before he is released (cf. the same treatment of the apostles in Acts v 40). In fact, Sherwin-White, *Roman Society,* p. 27, points out that the Lucan picture may be perfectly correct, since *beating* (as distinct from the more serious scourging mentioned by John—see NOTE on xix 1) was used as a punishment in itself; he cites an instance from Callistratus where those

COMPARATIVE CHART OF THE SOLDIERS' MOCKERY OF JESUS

	Matt xxvii 27–31	Mark xv 16–20	Luke xxiii 11	John xix 1–3
⁑1	Roman soldiers; whole cohort	Roman soldiers; whole cohort	Herod and his soldiers	Roman soldiers; see xviii 3
⁑2	in the praetorium	inside the court [or palace], i.e., the praetorium	Herod's residence	presumably inside the praetorium
⁑3	having woven a crown out of thorns, they fixed it on his head	they fixed on him a thorny crown they had woven		having woven a crown out of thorns, they fixed it on his head (thorny crown: xix 5)
⁑4	put a reed in his right hand			
⁑5	stripped him			
⁑6	fixed a scarlet robe about him	clothed him with purple	threw splendid garments about him	threw a purple cloak around him
⁑7	kneeling before him, they mocked him	bending their knees, they gave him homage	they treated him with contempt and mocked him	time and again they came up to him
⁑8	"Hail, 'King [vocative] of the Jews'"	"Hail, 'King [vocative] of the Jews'"	see xxiii 37 when Jesus is on the cross	"Hail, 'King [nominative] of the Jews'"
⁑9	they spat on him	they spat on him		
⁑10	took the reed and hit him on the head	hit him on the head with a reed		they were slapping him in the face
⁑11	stripped him of the robe and put on his clothes	stripped him of the purple and put on his clothes		Jesus continued to wear thorny crown and purple cloak (xix 5)

who stirred up the populace were beaten and dismissed. Therefore, this benevolent interpretation, implausible as it may be, is not an original creation of the fourth evangelist but had a wider circulation in Christian circles. If there is any truth in Bajsić's theory that Pilate was anxious to have Jesus released only to avoid releasing Barabbas, then one could give another interpretation to the physical violence or outrage done to Jesus: Pilate was making him an example of Roman brutality in order to anger the people and arouse them to ask for his release. But this remains sheer speculation, and one would have to suppose that John or his pre-Gospel tradition confused beating with scourging.

If we find John's interpretation of Pilate's motivation unlikely, how do we solve the problem of the sequence in which the scourging and mocking occurred? The scourging is best placed with the sentence of crucifixion as in Mark/Matthew. Crucifixion damaged no vital part of the body, and so the death of the victim came slowly (from suffocation, exposure, fatigue, hunger, thirst), often after many days. To speed up the process—in the present instance, perhaps, because Passover or the Sabbath was approaching—the prisoner was often severely scourged. Josephus, *War* II.xiv.9;※306, cites an example of scourging before crucifixion under the procurator Florus.

The mockery presents a greater problem. Some have doubted the Marcan/Matthean evidence, pointing out that there was pressure to have the prisoners executed and the bodies off the crosses before sunset, so that the soldiers would scarcely have been allowed to waste time playing games with Jesus. Benoit thinks the mockery more typical of Herod's soldiers and favors the theory that, while the scourging took place at the conclusion of the trial (Mark/Matthew), the mockery took place in mid-trial (Luke, John) at Herod's court (Luke). It would, then, have been a tendency to join and confuse similar actions that caused Mark/Matthew mistakenly to place the mockery at the end of the trial and John mistakenly to place the scourging in the middle of the trial. Again we are in the realm of conjecture.

Still others have dismissed the mocking of Jesus by the soldiers as a doublet of the mocking of Jesus before the Jewish authorities. Winter, *Trial*, p. 105, thinks that the influence was the other way around: the mockery in the high priest's court or palace was a secondary tradition. However, in our judgment the details of the two scenes are quite different, and we think that the tradition from early times preserved the story of two different mockeries of Jesus. (We note that both mockeries are in the Marcan B source, so that we cannot posit a duplication resulting from the combination of sources.) The temple police mocked Jesus primarily as a prophet; the soldiers (Herodian or Roman) mocked him as a king. The parallelism between the two is heightened in the *Gospel of Peter*, 7, where the soldiers say: "Judge righteously, O King of Israel"—compare Matt xxvi 68: "Prophesy for us, O Messiah."

In mocking Jesus as king the soldiers seem to follow an established ritual, and some customary actions are involved. We find similar details in Philo's report of the mob's mocking of Karabas in Alexandria (NOTE on "Barabbas" in xviii 40): the man was dressed in royal style with a diadem of papyrus on his head and a reed in his hand as a scepter; he received homage as some saluted him as king. Philo points out that this was in imitation of familiar pantomimes. Similarly, in mocking Jesus the soldiers were probably copying practices frequently seen on stage and in the Roman circuses (Winter, *Trial*, p. 103). Many scholars make allusion to the game of "mock king" played by soldiers during the Roman Saturnalia, and it is interesting that on the stone pavement of the fortress Antonia

(NOTE on xix 13) there are scratchings pertinent to this game made by the Roman legionaries quartered there. None of these parallels is perfect, but they do indicate that the mockery described in the Gospels would not have been strange.

Finally we may turn to the particular role that the episode plays in the development of the Johannine account of the Roman trial. Faced with the failure of his first ploy to get Jesus released (Episode 3), Pilate now turns to action. While his intentions are good, Pilate's sense of justice becomes more and more warped. In the preceding episode he failed to release Jesus even though he found him not guilty. Now he has the innocent Jesus scourged. The weakness exhibited in Pilate's concession will be recognized instinctively by Jesus' enemies when Pilate brings Jesus to them in the next episode. On a theological level John's abbreviated account and localization of the mockery makes the motif of the kingship of Jesus more central than do the Synoptic accounts. In Episode 3 Pilate had mocked the proceedings by speaking of Jesus as "the King of the Jews"; now the Roman soldiers take up the mockery. Jesus has been proclaimed as king; they will crown him. Perhaps, granted John's liking for a type of irony where the protagonists speak the truth unbeknown to themselves, we may see here a sign that the Gentiles will ultimately confess the kingship of Jesus.

Episode Five: Pilate Presents Jesus to His People; "the Jews" Shout for Crucifixion (xix 4–8)

Bultmann, p. 510[2], regards vss. 1–7 as a continuous episode, and certainly there is a close continuity between the mockery of Jesus and his presentation to his people. However, we believe that xix 4 ("Once more Pilate went out and said to them") is meant by the evangelist to start a new episode, so that the beginning of Episode 5 is the same as the beginning of Episode 3 (xviii 38b: "Pilate went out again to the Jews and told them"). Similarly Pilate's first words are the same in both episodes: "I find no case against the man." This parallelism is lost unless xix 1–3 is treated as a separate episode—the mid-point of the trial (diagram p. 859 above). As to whether Episode 5 should end with vs. 7 (Bultmann) or vs. 8, we are not certain. Yet since Episode 3 ends with the evangelist's comment about Barabbas, the evangelist's comment about Pilate in vs. 8 may have been meant to conclude Episode 5. Moreover, if vs. 9 begins Episode 6, then the opening lines of Episodes 2 and 6 (xviii 33, xix 9) are parallel.

The only feature that this episode shares with the general Synoptic account of the Roman trial is the cry to crucify Jesus. Between John and Luke, however, there is a similarity; for the incident in vs. 4 where Pilate brings Jesus out to "the Jews" and says that he is not guilty resembles the incident in Luke xxiii 13–16 where, when Jesus has been brought back from Herod, Pilate calls together the chief priests, the rulers, and the people to tell them that Jesus is not guilty. Both incidents follow immediately after Jesus has been mocked by soldiers.

In John the episode develops the motif of Jesus' kingship. Acknowledged by Pilate as "the King of the Jews" (Episode 3), crowned and invested by the soldiers (Episode 4), Jesus now undergoes another ceremony in the coronation ritual: he is brought out, royally bedecked and empurpled, to be presented to his people for acclamation. In John's eyes Israel's long wait for its messianic king thus comes to ironic fulfillment.

The dramatic scenario of the presentation of Jesus to "the Jews" is typically Johannine, but we may wonder whether the evangelist's creative sense has not been controlled by some details that he found in his tradition. If he were inventing with complete freedom, this would have been the perfect moment to have had Pilate say, "Behold the king!" (as in vs. 14). Instead we find the enigmatic "Behold the man!" While this designation is capable of being understood as a messianic title (see NOTE for possible meanings), it is too ambiguous to be the obvious choice of an inventive evangelist. It is more likely that he has taken an expression of contempt that came in the tradition and has reinterpreted it as an exalted title.

Whatever Pilate intended by his designation of Jesus, his ploy of presenting him to "the Jews" fails. They have sensed Pilate's weakness in this second attempt to compromise, and so they hail their king with a strange acclamation: "Crucify him!" Perhaps in using the verb "to shout," the evangelist wishes us to recall by way of contrast that only five days before another crowd had shouted to Jesus: "Hosanna! . . . Blessed is the King of Israel!" (xii 13). We may note that in Bajsić's theory the cry for the crucifixion of Jesus is not an expression of the popular feeling against Jesus but a rejection of Pilate's stratagem.

Pilate's irritated response, "Take him yourselves and crucify him" (see NOTE), causes "the Jews" to begin psychological warfare against him. If Pilate will not yield to their expressed desire, they will wear him down by a type of blackmail: they will imply that his conduct in this case will bring him into disfavor at Rome. The Synoptic Gospels never adequately explain why Pilate yielded to the importunings of the crowd and the priests. Mark xv 15 says that Pilate wished to satisfy the crowd; Matt xxvii 24 says that Pilate saw he was gaining nothing and that a riot was breaking out; Luke xxiii 23 simply underlines the urgency of the demand for crucifixion. But these descriptions scarcely fit the Pilate familiar to us in Josephus' accounts: a Pilate who broke up riots and was stubborn in the face of Jewish demands. John's picture of a Pilate worried about what might be said at Rome has a very good chance of being historical. According to Philo, *Ad Gaium* xxxviii;※301–02, Pilate was naturally inflexible and stubbornly resisted when the Jews clamored against him until they mentioned that the Emperor Tiberius would not approve his violating their customs. "It was this final point that particularly struck home, for he feared that if they actually sent an embassy, they would also expose the rest of his conduct as governor." (Note, however, that the historicity of Philo's report has been questioned by P. L. Maier, HTR 62 [1969], 109–21.) Moreover, at the very moment when Jesus stood before Pilate, the governor may have been vulnerable in Rome as never before. Many theorize that Pilate owed his appointment in Palestine to Aelius Sejanus; and it was in the year 31 that Sejanus lost favor with Tiberius. Perhaps the tremors that presaged the fall of Sejanus were already felt by sensitive political observers, and Pilate feared that soon he would have no protector at court. A shrewd ecclesiastical politician like Caiaphas would have been quite aware of the prefect's vulnerability and prompt to probe it. (This suggestion is uncertain, for we do not know the exact year of Jesus' crucifixion; it occurred between A.D. 27 and 33. See P. L. Maier, "Sejanus, Pilate, and the Date of the Crucifixion," *Church History* 37 [1968], 3–13.)

In any case it is precisely on the question of Pilate's not respecting local customs that "the Jews" open their attack. Pilate has found Jesus not guilty and refuses to continue the civil trial against Jesus, but he has ignored the fact that Jesus, whether or not a revolutionary, has violated the Jewish religious laws. Beneath this assertion is the reminder that Roman provincial administrators characteristically respected regional religious practices. As soon as this point is made Pilate retreats in fear (see NOTE on "more afraid" in 8). It is ironic that the representative of mighty Rome has now been reduced to a state of apprehension about Jesus similar to that which characterized the head of the Sanhedrin in xi 47–53. In John's thought no leader, secular or religious, can withstand the power of Jesus. Pilate tried to be neutral to the truth, the truth that sets men free (viii 32); and now he is enslaved by his own fears.

The last lines of this episode have theological as well as political import for the understanding of the narrative. At last the real motive of "the Jews" in wanting Jesus killed has been brought out: they resent his "making himself" God's Son. Sherwin-White, *Roman Society,* pp. 46–47, comments that it is perfectly possible "in Roman usage that, when Pilate refused a verdict on the political charge, they fell back on the religious charge which Pilate finally accepted under . . . political pressure." For John this charge is false only in the sense that Jesus did not *make himself* God's Son— he was God's Son. We have stated our belief (pp. 798–802 above) that the Jewish opposition to Jesus was not only political but also religious. John has simply given this religious opposition a later form of expression more appropriate to the time and substance of the acrimonious struggles between the Synagogue and the Church. We saw that at the beginning of the ministry, in i 35–51, titles were given to Jesus as the faith of the disciples grew (vol. 29, pp. 77–78); these included Son of God, King of Israel, and Son of Man. At the end of his life, in a crescendo of disbelief, Jesus is mockingly or incredulously called "the King of the Jews" (xviii 39), "the man" (xix 5), and "God's Son" (xix 7).

Episode Six: Pilate Talks with Jesus about Power (xix 9–11)

We have pointed out that this episode is remarkably parallel to Episode 2. They both begin with Pilate's going back into the praetorium to question Jesus—about the political and the religious charges respectively. They are the only two episodes in which Jesus speaks. In each, Pilate's first question gets him nowhere, and only his excited second question elicits an explanation from Jesus. The explanation in each instance is in solemn didactic style and emphasizes that Jesus' interests are with what is above and not with this world. Pilate is questioning on one level; Jesus is answering on another—a technique akin to "misunderstanding" (vol. 29, p. cxxxv). These are the two episodes in the Roman trial where Johannine elaboration is the most obvious and probably the most extensive. Episode 6 shares with the Synoptic tradition only the motif of Jesus' silence (NOTE on vs. 9), and obviously this motif means less for John than it does for the Synoptics. Barrett, p. 451, observes: "By provoking the next question the silence continues the conversation as effectively as a reply."

Presumably the interrogation to which Pilate now subjects Jesus is another desperate effort to effect Jesus' release, but Pilate's intentions are less transparent here (NOTE on "Where do you come from?"). One gets the impression that exasperation has left the prefect grasping for straws and that he himself does not know how to proceed. He is now dealing with a religious charge beyond his understanding. Ironically fear causes him to bluster about his power, and it is evident that Pilate has lost patience with the uncooperativeness of the man he is trying to protect. (Notice John's dramatic characterization of Pilate.) Pilate's previous efforts to find a middle way in the struggle between the truth and the world have been frustrated by the intransigence of the world; now he finds the truth no more accommodating. He is speaking to a Jesus who has consistently rebuffed even more serious overtures of friendship or approval when they fell short of faith (ii 23–25, iii 2–3, iv 45–48).

The core of the episode is Jesus' statement about power or authority. Pilate has spoken of his physical power over Jesus—he can take Jesus' life away. Jesus speaks to him on another level, the level of truth and of "genuine" power. What genuine power from above does Pilate possess over Jesus? Most commentators interpret John in the light of Rom xiii 1 where Paul insists that civil governors have their authority from God. Some who think that Pilate stands for the State (p. 863 above) see this as a key verse in interpreting the relation between the legitimate powers of the State and the demands of truth. However, we agree with Von Campenhausen, *art. cit.*, that the Johannine Jesus is not lecturing Pilate on the God-given rights of the prefect's office, nor, *a fortiori*, on the relations of Church and State. (The interpretation of John in the light of Paul's idea came later in the Donatist period and was developed by Augustine.) Rather we must understand Jesus' saying in the light of x 17–18: no one can take Jesus' life from him; he alone has power to lay it down. However, now Jesus has voluntarily entered "the hour" appointed by his Father (xii 27) when he will lay down his life. In the context of "the hour," therefore, the Father has permitted men to have power over Jesus' life. Although Pilate does not realize it, the reason that he has the power he boasts of is not simply because he has legionaries at his disposal. The power is his because God has assigned him a role in "the hour." John stated that Caiaphas could prophesy that Jesus was to die for the nation because Caiaphas was high priest "that year" (xi 51—see vol. 29, pp. 439–40); so too Pilate has power over Jesus because he is prefect of Judea "that year."

Pilate has tried to use this power over Jesus to free him. He will not be successful because he has not totally committed himself to the truth and has sought in vain to be neutral; yet he did not instinctively hate the truth, and so his sin is less than that of Caiaphas and "the Jews" who want to kill Jesus. The real interest of the Johannine Jesus is not in explaining Pilate's lesser guilt but in accusing those who are really responsible. Matthew's scene (xxvii 24–25) where Pilate washes his hands of Jesus' blood has much the same import.

Episode Seven: Pilate Yields to the Jewish Demand for Jesus' Crucifixion (xix 12–16a)

John's final episode parallels the Synoptic accounts only in the repeated cry for crucifixion and in the outcome whereby Jesus is handed over for crucifixion. On the whole John's account of the condemnation is more detailed, more dramatic, and more theological. The meticulous setting of the episode on the "Stone Pavement" at noon not only gives a dramatic touch but also is indicative of the author's interest in the climax of the trial. Since the place name has no obvious symbolism, it may be historical; the time is a greater problem (see NOTE). The evangelist may also be historically accurate in the motivation given for Pilate's decision, but his real interest is theological: he has turned the decision into a drama of the Jewish rejection of the Davidic covenant.

As the episode opens, Pilate has been moved by Jesus' charge that he is guilty of misusing his God-given power; and so he tries again to effect Jesus' release. This prompts "the Jews" to renew their political blackmail by implicitly raising again the threat of denouncing him to Rome. In Episode 5 we saw Pilate's terrified reaction to the implication that he was open to blame for not respecting local Jewish customs; now his loyalty to the Emperor is pointedly questioned. If those are right who suggest that Pilate bore the privileged title "Friend of Caesar," then "the Jews" may be hinting that his title will be taken away from him. This would entail severe punishment, for the Emperor was harsh in dealing with the disloyalty of those whom he had favored. It would be understandable that

Pilate might feel his position as "Friend of Caesar" jeopardized if, as mentioned above, there were signs of the fall of his patron Sejanus. (Haenchen, "Historie," p. 74, dismisses with assurance any tie-in of the Gospel with well-known history on the grounds that the evangelist had certainly not probed into the details of Roman politics and that this political background would not have been of concern to John's readers. While this may be true, there remains the question of whether the historical tradition elaborated by the evangelist retained valid memories of the political situation in Palestine ca. A.D. 30, even if the evangelist did not investigate the implications.) But if we do not wish to depend overly on "Friend of Caesar" as a title of which Pilate might be deprived, the threat of being accused of benevolence toward a rival of the Emperor still has verisimilitude in the reign of Tiberius. A suspicious old recluse on Capri, this Emperor was hypersensitive to crimes of lese majesty; and Suetonius, *Tiberius* LVIII, tells us that he enforced the law against them savagely. According to Blinzler, *Trial,* p. 213, it was precisely of such a crime that Jesus would be declared guilty—a violation of the *lex Iulia maiestatis* decreed by Augustus. Independently of John, we have in Acts xvii 7 an indication that even in less danger Roman officials would react strongly to a claim of kingship. There we read that the Jews of Thessalonica dragged some of the Christians before the city authorities charging that they had acted against the decrees of the Emperor, "saying that there is another king, Jesus"; and this disturbed the authorities.

Pilate remains convinced that Jesus is harmless, but "the Jews" are forcing his hand. The prefect who had just boasted to Jesus that he had the power to release and the power to crucify is now deprived of a truly free exercise of that power. If a charge of lese majesty is filed in Rome against Pilate for having released a king who is a potential threat to the Emperor, Pilate will be thoroughly examined, and all his shortcomings as governor will come to light. Possible disgrace is too great a price to pay for defending the truth. Pilate yields to "the Jews" and sets the scene for passing judgment. Seated on the judgment seat, with a final gesture of defiance and perhaps still with a half-hearted hope he can obtain clemency, Pilate shows Jesus to "the Jews" as their king. When they persist in demanding crucifixion, Pilate takes his revenge by humbling their nationalistic spirit. In their quest to have Jesus condemned, "the Jews" have shown a touching loyalty to the Emperor—does this mean that they have given up their hope in the expected king? No price is too great to pay in the world's struggle against the truth: "the Jews" utter the fateful words: "We have no king other than the Emperor." The real trial is over, for in the presence of Jesus "the Jews" have judged themselves; they have spoken their own sentence.

Israel had proudly claimed Yahweh as its king (Judg viii 23; I Sam viii 7). From the time of Nathan's promise to David (II Sam vii 11–16), according to the theology of Jerusalem, God's kingship was made visible in the rule of the Davidic king whom He took as His son (Ps ii 7). In post-exilic times a mystique had grown up around the unique anointed king of the House of David, the future Messiah, who was to come and establish God's rule on earth. Only one raised up by God could be the true king of God's people—not the Persian, nor Ptolemaic, nor Syrian, nor Roman overlords whose troops marched across the land. "O Lord our God, other lords besides you have ruled over us, but your name alone we acknowledge" (Isa xxvi 13). But now hundreds of years of waiting had been cast aside: "the Jews" had proclaimed the half-mad exile of Capri to be their king. Throughout the ministry John described Jesus as replacing Jewish institutions, feasts, and customs. Now in the breaking of the covenant whereby God or his Messiah was Israel's king, the movement of replacement comes to a climax, for "the Jews" have renounced their status as God's people. John's scene has an impact similar to that of Matt xxvii 25 where all the people say, "His blood be on us and on our children." Obviously here both Gospels are reflecting apologetic theology rather than history—they are having the audience of the trial give voice to a late 1st-century Christian interpretation of salvation history. The tragedy of Jesus' death is compounded as it is seen through the veil of hostility between the Church and the Synagogue in the 80s or 90s (see vol. 29, p. LXXIV). And the tragedy will be compounded still further through the centuries as the Matthean and Johannine theological presentations of the crucifixion, wrenched from their historical perspectives and absolutized, will serve both as a goad to and an excuse for anti-Jewish hatred.

The time when this fatal renunciation of the Messiah takes place is noon on Passover Eve, the very hour when the priests have begun to slaughter the paschal lambs in the temple precincts. It is an ironical touch of the Johannine writer to have "the Jews" renounce the covenant at the moment when their priests are beginning the preparations for the feast that annually recalls God's deliverance of His people. By the blood of the lamb He marked them off to be spared as His own, and now they know no king but the Roman Emperor. As they recite the Passover Haggadah, how hollow will ring the frequent praise of the kingly reign of God! They think of Passover as a traditional time for God's judgment of the world (Mishnah Rosh Hashanah 1:2), and on Passover Eve they have judged themselves by condemning the one whom God has sent into the world, not to judge it but to save it (iii 17—for other possible references to Passover motifs in this scene, see Meeks, p. 77).

At the beginning of the Gospel John the Baptist had pointed Jesus out as the Lamb of God who takes away the world's sin (i 29). By way of inclusion this prophecy is now fulfilled; for at the moment when the Passover lambs are being slaughtered, Jesus' trial comes to an end, and he sets out for Golgotha to pour forth the blood that will cleanse men from sin (I John i 7). Truly, as John sees it, God has planned "the hour" carefully.

BIBLIOGRAPHY
(xviii 28 – xix 16a)

See the general bibliography on the Passion Narrative at the end of §60.

Bajsić, A., "Pilatus, Jesus und Barabbas," *Biblica* 48 (1967), 7–28.

Blank, J., "Die Verhandlung vor Pilatus: Joh 18, 28 – 19, 16 im Lichte johanneischer Theologie," BZ 3 (1959), 60–81.

Bonsirven, J., "Hora Talmudica: La notion chronologique de Jean 19, 14, aurait-elle un sens symbolique?" *Biblica* 33 (1952), 511–15.

de la Potterie, I., "Jésus, roi et juge d'après Jn 19, 13: *ekathisen epi bēmatos,*" *Biblica* 41 (1960), 217–47. Abbreviated Eng. trans. in *Scripture* 13 (1961), 97–111. English digest in TD 11 (1963), 21–26.

Haenchen, E., "Jesus vor Pilatus (Joh 18, 28–19, 15)," TLZ 85 (1960), cols. 93–102. Reprinted in *Gott und Mensch* (Tübingen: Mohr, 1965), pp. 144–56.

Mollat, D., "Jésus devant Pilate (Jean 18, 28–38)," BVC 39 (1961), 23–31.

Schlier, H., "Jesus und Pilatus nach dem Johannesevangelium," in *Die Zeit der Kirche* (Freiburg im Breisgau: Herder, 1956), pp. 56–74.

————— "The State according to the New Testament," in *The Relevance of the New Testament* (New York: Herder & Herder, 1968), pp. 215–38.

Schwank, B., "Pilatus begegnet dem Christus (18, 28–38a)," SeinSend 29 (1964), 100–12.

————— "Der Dornengekrönte (18, 38b–19, 7)," SeinSend 29 (1964), 148–60.

————— "Der königliche Richter (19, 8–16a)," SeinSend 29 (1964), 196–208.

von Campenhausen, H., "Zum Verständnis von Joh. 19, 11," TLZ 73 (1948), cols. 387–92.

65. THE PASSION NARRATIVE:
—DIVISION THREE (INTRODUCTION; EPISODES 1–4)
(xix 16b–30)

The Execution of Jesus on the Cross

INTRODUCTION

XIX 16b So they took custody of Jesus; 17 and, carrying the cross by himself, he went out to what is called "The Place of the Skull" (*Golgotha* being its Hebrew name). 18 There they crucified him along with two others—one on either side and Jesus in the middle.

EPISODE 1

19 Now Pilate also had a notice written and placed on the cross; it bore the words:

JESUS THE NAZOREAN
THE KING OF THE JEWS

20 This notice, which was in Hebrew, Latin, and Greek, was read by many Jews, for the place where Jesus was crucified was quite near the city. 21 And so the chief priests of the Jews tried to tell Pilate, "Do not leave it written: 'The King of the Jews'; instead write: This man claimed to be 'The King of the Jews.' " 22 Pilate answered, "What I have written, I have written."

EPISODE 2

23 When the soldiers had crucified Jesus, they took his clothes and separated them into four parts, one for each soldier. There was also his tunic; but this tunic was woven in one piece from top to bottom and had no seam. 24 So they said to one another, "Instead of tearing it up, let's toss to see who gets it." (The purpose of this was to have the Scripture fulfilled:

> "They divided up my clothes among them,
> and they rolled dice for my clothing.")

So that is what the soldiers did.

EPISODE 3

25 Meanwhile, standing near the cross of Jesus were his mother, and his mother's sister, Mary the wife of Clopas, and Mary Magdalene. 26 When Jesus saw his mother there with the disciple whom he loved, he said to his mother, "Woman, here is your son." 27 In turn he said to the disciple, "Here is your mother." And from that hour the disciple took her into his care.

EPISODE 4

28 After this, aware that all was now finished, in order to bring the Scripture to its complete fulfillment, Jesus said, "I am thirsty." 29 There was at hand a jar full of common wine; so they stuck a sponge soaked in this wine on some hyssop and raised it to his lips. 30 When Jesus took the wine, he exclaimed, "It is finished"; and bowing his head, he handed over the spirit.

26: *said;* 27: *said;* 28: *said.* In the historical present tense.

NOTES

xix 16b. *they took custody of Jesus.* By strict sequence the "they" here and in vs. 18 ("they crucified him") should refer to the last mentioned plural subject, namely, the chief priests (vs. 15). However, in 23 it becomes clear that the soldiers (Romans, under Pilate's jurisdiction: vss. 31–32) were the ones who crucified Jesus. For an explanation see the NOTE on "to them" in xix 16a. The abruptness of the phrasing here has caused some scribal attempts to improve by means of additions: "and they put the cross on him"; "and they led him away" (the latter is in imitation of the Synoptics, particularly of Matt xxvii 31; Luke xxiii 26).

17. *carrying the cross by himself.* The pronoun *heautō* is usually understood as a dative of advantage ("for himself": BDF, §188²); but D. Tabachovitz, *Eranos* 44 (1946), 301–5, argues that it is an instrumental dative, equivalent to *di' heautou* ("by himself"). The verb is *bastazein;* presumably "the cross" means just the crosspiece or transverse beam (*patibulum*), since the upright beam, about nine feet high, was usually left standing as a permanent feature at the place of execution. That the criminal should carry the *patibulum* to the place of execution was quite normal, and Bultmann, p. 517⁴, sees nothing emphatic or symbolic in "by himself" (see COMMENT). Mark xv 21 and Matt xxvii 32 report that the soldiers compelled Simon to take (*airein*) the cross; Luke xxiii 26 reports that the cross was laid on Simon that it might be borne (*pherein*) behind Jesus. (While Luke may have had independent tradition about some of the incidents that took place on the road to Calvary, V. Taylor, NTS 8 [1962], 333–34, regards this particular description as an adaptation of Mark.) The popular representation of Jesus carrying the front part of the cross and Simon carrying the back part uses Luke's wording as a guide in combin-

ing the Johannine picture and that of Mark/Matthew. Another harmonization supposes that Jesus carried the cross as long as he was able and then the soldiers compelled Simon to help him. Serious scholars of the caliber of Dodd and Taylor judge the latter solution a perfectly reasonable interpretation of the evidence.

he went out. That the place of Jesus' crucifixion was, in fact, outside the city is stated explicitly in vs. 20; it is implied in the adverbial prefixes of the verbs used by the four Gospels in describing the process of leading Jesus to Calvary (*apagein, exagein, exerchesthai*—see also Matt xxi 39; Heb xiii 12). According to Israelite custom stonings took place outside the camp or city (Num xv 35; Acts vii 58) and apparently this custom was observed for crucifixion as well. Certainly a place for Jewish burials (John xix 41) would not have been in the city. Mark and Luke mention that Simon was coming in from the fields or from the country when he met the crucifixion procession; this agrees with the information in vs. 20 below that the place of execution was near where the road entered the city. Jeremias, *Golgotha,* p. 3, thinks that the site was close enough to the city to be seen by people standing on the city walls.

The Church of the Holy Sepulcher, containing the sites traditionally venerated as the place of crucifixion and the tomb, is within the present city walls. This has led some to reject the identification, for they think that the northern line of the present city walls coincides closely with the line of the walls in Jesus' time (the second of the three city walls in Josephus' enumeration of the defenses constructed throughout Jerusalem's history: *War* V.iv.2; ※142ff.). Others theorize that the Second North Wall ran considerably south of the present city walls, so that Calvary could have been outside the walls in Jesus' time and yet within the present city walls. The latter theory is strongly supported by Miss K. Kenyon's recent excavation of Jerusalem (PEQ 96 [1964], 14–16; see R. H. Smith, BA 30 [1967], 74–90; E. W. Hamrick, BASOR 192 [1968], 21–25). Despite the biblical evidence, Melito of Sardis in his paschal homily (72, 94) states that Jesus was killed in the midst of Jerusalem, perhaps because by his time (ca. 170) the traditional site of Calvary stood within the walls of Aelia Capitolina, the city that Hadrian built over Jerusalem (see A. E. Harvey, JTS 17 [1966], 401–4).

to what is called "The Place of the Skull" (Golgotha *being its Hebrew name*). There is no definite article before "Skull," so that one can translate "Place of a skull," as does the NEB in Matt xxvii 33 and Mark xv 22, but not here. There are minor textual variants, e.g., Codex Vaticanus and the Sahidic read *Golgoth*. The Aramaic word *Gulgoltâ* and the Heb. *Gulgōlet* mean "skull, cranium"; *calvaria* is the Latin equivalent. Mark/Matthew speak of "a place called *Golgotha* which means 'The Place of the Skull,' " giving the Aramaic and Greek words in an order that is the inverse of John's— note also the twofold use of "place." Luke does not give the Aramaic form of the name, but speaks of "the place that is called 'The Skull.' " Jeremias, *Golgotha,* p. 1[1], argues that John's phrasing should also be translated "to the place that is called 'The Skull,' " for he thinks of the genitive as appositive (BDF, §167). This is possible, and indeed is favored by the word order in P[66] where "place" precedes "called."

It is usually conjectured that the name comes from the topology of the place, namely that it was a hill with a rough resemblance to a skull—

perhaps an abandoned quarry where man-made caverns were used for burial. (The Arabs will often call a hill *rās,* "head," even if there is no resemblance to a skull.) Actually the Gospels do not mention a hill; but pilgrims in the 4th century spoke of a *monticulus* or "small hill" (the site venerated as Golgotha in the Church of the Holy Sepulcher is about sixteen feet high). Jeremias, *Golgotha,* p. 2, argues that the topography of the area has changed too much for us to make any judgment; but he admits that sometimes hills were used, for the executions were meant to be seen. Another explanation of the name resorts to the pious tradition attested by Origen (*In Matt.* XXVII 33; GCS 38:265 and 411:226) that Adam was buried here. A century later Pseudo-Basil mentions the *skull* of Adam (*In Isa.* v 1, 14; PG 30:348C), and so we get the imagery of Jesus' cross having been erected over Adam's skull. Although some have argued that this legend may be pre-Christian, it is highly unlikely that Pilate would have crucified a criminal in a site venerated by the Jews. (A rival tradition that Adam's body was buried in the temple area or in the cave of Machpelah has a better chance of being authentically Jewish.) Still another explanation of the name is that "Skull Hill" was a place of public execution where skulls could be found on or near the surface. The proximity of Joseph's tomb (xix 41) and the Jewish abhorrence of exposed remains renders this theory unlikely also.

18. *they crucified him.* All the Gospels are content with this laconic description without entering into gruesome details. The condemned prisoner was nailed or tied to the crossbar with his arms spread out; the bar was lifted into place on the vertical beam; the feet were fastened with nails or rope; the body rested on a peg (*sedile*) that jutted out from the post. Josephus, *War* VII.vi.4;⚹203, calls crucifixion "the most wretched of deaths"; and Cicero, *In Verrem* II.v.64;⚹165, speaks of it as a "most cruel and terrible penalty."

two others. Mark/Matthew identify these as bandits (*lēstai*); Luke calls them criminals (*kakourgoi*). We should probably think of them as prisoners taken in the same insurrection in which Barabbas was arrested (Mark xv 7). Perhaps Isa liii 12, describing the Suffering Servant as "numbered among transgressors [*anomoi*]," had an influence on preserving the memory of these fellow prisoners of Jesus. (The Isaian passage is cited in Luke's Last Supper account [xxii 37].) Only Luke xxiii 39–43 reports that Jesus dealt kindly with one of the two who showed signs of repentance and of noble sentiments. From later times at least four different sets of names have been given to the two; for example, Dismas or Titus for "the Good Thief," and Gestas or Dumachus for the other. A later Jewish law forbade the condemning of two men on the same day (StB, I, 1039), but we do not know that this law was in effect in Jesus' time or that it would have been honored by the Romans. The Jewish high priest Alexander Jannaeus (88 B.C.) crucified eight hundred persons at the same time (Josephus *War* I.iv.6;⚹97).

one on either side. All the Gospels agree on the relative position of the three crucified men, although the Synoptic tradition uses different words: "one on the right side and one on the left" (Mark xv 27 and par.). John's expression seems to be Semitic (see Num xxii 24). The Gospels may be recalling Ps xxii 17(16): "a company of evildoers [*ponēreuomenoi*] encircle me."

19. *Pilate also had a notice written.* While all the Gospels mention the

inscription, only John attributes it to Pilate's order. We have understood John's Greek (literally "Pilate wrote") in a causative sense, i.e., that he caused others to prepare the notice (cf. NOTE on "scourged" in xix 1). But some scholars think that John attributes the writing directly to Pilate, so that having vigorously affirmed during the trial that Jesus was not guilty, ironically Pilate now writes out with his own hand the crime of which Jesus is guilty. John's term for "notice" is *titlos*, a Latinism reflecting *titulus* (or vulgar Latin *titlus:* BDF, §51), the technical Roman designation for the board bearing the name of the condemned or his crime, or both. Seemingly *titulus* could also refer to *the inscription* placed on the board—see F. R. Montgomery Hitchcock, JTS 31 (1930), 272–73. Only John (also vs. 20) uses this technical term; Mark xv 26 speaks of an "inscription [*epigraphē*; also Luke xxiii 38] inscribed with his crime"; Matt xxvii 37 speaks simply of the written charge. Suetonius, *Caligula* 32, mentions the public exposition of the title indicating the culprit's crime. However, while we have evidence of the criminal's carrying the title hung around his neck or having it carried in front of him to the place of execution, we have no evidence of the custom of affixing it to the cross.

on the cross. Mark xv 26 does not mention where the inscription was placed; Matt xxvii 37 says that it was placed over Jesus' head (Luke xxiii 38: "over him")—it is to the latter information that we owe the common pictorial representation of a cross where the crossbeam is inserted in the length of the upright beam (*crux immissa*) rather than being placed on top of the upright beam (*crux commissa*). The *crux immissa* seems to have been the more common style.

bore the words. Literally "was written," a perfect passive participle employed by Matthew as well.

JESUS THE NAZOREAN, THE KING OF THE JEWS. The wording of this inscription varies in the four Gospels—an interesting attestation to the freedom of evangelical reporting, even when supposedly all are drawing on the memory of something written. (We judge fanciful the thesis of P.-F. Regard, *Revue Archéologique* 28 [1928], 95–105, that Matthew preserves in literal translation the Hebrew form of the inscription, that Luke preserves the Greek form, and John, the Latin form.) The wording is as follows:

Matt xxvii 37: This is Jesus, the King of the Jews
Mark xv 26 (cf. John xix 21 below): The King of the Jews
Luke xxiii 38: This is the King of the Jews

Matthew and John share the peculiarity of mentioning the person as well as the charge. Mark's form is the shortest, and the fact that it appears in John's second reference to the title may mean that it is the original form. Loisy, p. 484, for instance, thinks that the Johannine author added "Nazorean" here as an ironical touch: the Jewish leaders had mocked the fact that Jesus was from Galilee (equivalently Nazareth: John vii 41), and yet the man from Nazareth is their king. However, if "Nazorean" does mean "from Nazareth" (NOTE on xviii 5), John may simply be giving us the full legal identification of Jesus, something that would be appropriate in the statement of a criminal charge.

20. *Hebrew, Latin, and Greek.* Some Western witnesses read "Greek" before "Latin," an order that gives the language of the Roman conquerors the place of dignity at the end. Only John mentions the languages of the inscription, although this information is found in a slightly different form in an addition to Luke xxiii 38 that appears in many textual witnesses. Polyglot inscriptions

were not infrequent in antiquity (Barrett, p. 457), and Jewish tombstones in Rome were sometimes inscribed in these three languages. Gordian III's tomb, erected by Roman soldiers, was inscribed in Greek, Latin, Persian, Hebrew, and Egyptian in order that it might be read by all.

near the city. See NOTE on "went out" in 17.

21. *the chief priests of the Jews.* This is almost tautological since for John "the Jews" normally means the hostile authorities at Jerusalem. Is "of the Jews" added to heighten the irony that Jesus has been entitled "The King of the Jews"?

tried to tell. The imperfect tense seems to have conative force (BDF, §326).

Do not leave it written. The present imperative with *mē* has the sense of forbidding the continuity of an act (ZGB, §246). MTGS, p. 76, suggests the translation: "Alter what you have written."

This man. Perhaps a contemptuous use of *ekeinos* (MTGS, p. 46).

claimed to be 'The King of the Jews.' This is the only time that the title appears in John without the definite article before "King," but the difference is not significant. Following E. C. Colwell's investigation of the use of the article with determinate nouns, ZGB, §175, maintains that the absence of the article here is quite normal because the noun "King" precedes the verb.

22. *"What I have written, I have written."* The verbal forms are both perfect in tense; the first perfect is the equivalent of an aorist; the second connotes a lasting effect (BDF, §342[4]). We find in I Macc xiii 38 a similar expression used by the Seleucid king Demetrius, "The things we have guaranteed to you have been guaranteed" (see also StB, II, 573). Bernard, II, 628-29, stresses the Roman respect for a written document—the Jewish request touched upon a legal decision that could not be altered.

23. *the soldiers.* See NOTE on "to them" in xix 16a. These are soldiers under Pilate's jurisdiction (xix 31-32).

had crucified Jesus. While this may be understood as having resumptive force, it is somewhat tautological after the "they crucified him" of vs. 18. (The English translation of SB avoids the tautology by an addition: "When the soldiers had *finished* crucifying Jesus.") Bultmann, p. 515, detects here a sign that vss. 20-22 are the evangelist's addition to his source to which he is now returning in continuation of vs. 19.

they took his clothes. Himatia refers to outer garments. This stripping may have left Jesus naked, as was normal in Roman treatment of the crucified; but many theorize that in Palestine the Romans would have respected the Jewish dislike for public nudity and would have left the prisoner's underclothing. (The Mishnah, *Sanhedrin* 6:3, records a dispute about whether a man who is to be stoned should be completely stripped.) Yet either a tunic or a breechcloth was the usual undergarment, and we are told that Jesus wore a tunic which was taken from him. In Roman practice the soldiers had a right to the prisoner's clothes as their perquisites. Mark/Matthew agree with John in joining the incidents of the inscription on the cross and the stripping, but their ordering of the two incidents is the inverse of John's.

separated them into four parts. John gives details not mentioned by the Synoptic Gospels which report simply: "They divided his clothes, rolling dice for them" (Mark xv 24 and par.). Some ingenious scholars have tried to identify the clothing on the principle that each part consists of one item. For example, A. Edersheim, *The Life and Times of Jesus the Messiah* (New York: Longmans, 1897), I, 625, and A. R. S. Kennedy, ET 24 (1912–13), 90–91, agree that three of the pieces had to be (a) a head gear or turban; (b) a *tallith,* an outer cloak or robe (see John xiii 4); and (c) a cincture or girdle. They disagree on whether Jesus would have worn sandals (Edersheim) or would have gone to the crucifixion barefoot, so that the fourth garment could have been an undershirt (*ḥālūq*) worn beneath the tunic (Kennedy).

one for each soldier. Only John specifies that the executionary squad was a quaternion; and actually allotments of four seem to have been customary, for Acts xii 4 speaks of four squads of four. We do not know if other quaternions were occupied with the crucifixion of the two bandits: Mark xv 27 seems to attribute the other crucifixions to the same soldiers, while Matt xxvii 38 is vaguer. The Synoptic Gospels mention a centurion (Mark xv 39 and par.).

tunic. The *chitōn* was a long garment worn next to the skin (Colonel Repond, "Le costume du Christ," *Biblica* 3 [1922], 3–14).

woven in one piece . . . and had no seam. A seamless cloth precluded any danger that two materials had been joined together, something that was forbidden. For a discussion of the weaving technique used in making a seamless garment, see H.-Th. Braun, *Fleur bleue, Revue des industries du lin* (1951), pp. 21–28, 45–53. Such a garment was not necessarily a luxury item, for it could be woven by a craftsman who had no exceptional skill.

24. *Instead of tearing it up.* Literally "Let us not tear it." It is interesting that Lev xxi 10 forbids the priest to rend his garments.

let's toss. A colloquialism is justified by the situation envisaged in the passage. The Greek word *lagchanein,* normally meaning "to obtain by lot," must in this instance mean "to cast lots." The Synoptics use the more normal expression for this: *ballein klēron* (appearing in John's OT citation). The *Gospel of Peter,* 12, and Justin, *Trypho* xcvii; PG 6:705A, have *ballein lachmon* which is a cross between the Johannine and Synoptic expressions.

The purpose of this was. See initial NOTE on xviii 9. The same grammatical formation appears in the Marcan Passion Narrative in xiv 49.

the Scripture. Ps xxii 19(18) is cited by John according to LXX. Although the Synoptics do not explicitly cite the psalm in reference to this incident (a few textual witnesses have a citation in Matt xxvii 36), their wording of the incident is influenced by the psalm. It has been suggested that John's explicit citation is an attempt to improve on the implicit citation in the Synoptics. Dodd, *Tradition,* p. 40, however, thinks that we have exemplified two independent ways of using Psalm xxii, which, along with Isa lii–liii, constituted the principal source from which OT coloring was given to the Passion Narrative. (For a similar difference between explicit and implicit citation, see John xiii 18 and Mark xiv 18—p. 571 above.) Some witnesses to the text of John add the explanatory clause "that says" after "Scripture."

So that is what the soldiers did. For the resumptive use of *men oun,* see MTGS, p. 337. The wording of this summation has suggested to some that John intended to contrast what the soldiers did with what Jesus' friends were doing, to be described in vss. 25–27. We think this quite unlikely, for there is no evidence that John thinks of the soldiers' action of dividing the clothes as particularly hostile. Dauer, p. 225, goes considerably beyond the evidence when he holds that the contrast between the soldiers and the women is an instance of the dualistic reaction produced by the Johannine Jesus. This sentence may simply be meant to conclude "Let's toss to see who gets it" after the parenthetical citation of Scripture. Or if it refers to the Scripture, it emphasizes that the soldiers unwittingly did exactly as prophesied.

25. *standing near the cross.* Only after reporting Jesus' death (and therefore more in relation to the burial) do the three Synoptics (Mark xv 40 and par.) mention the presence of the Galilean women. They clearly state that the women had seen the proceedings from a distance; in fact, Luke xxiii 49, "They stood at a distance," is almost a direct contradiction of John. (The Synoptic writers do not explain how, under these conditions, they envisage that the words of Jesus on the cross were heard and preserved.) One can harmonize by claiming that during the crucifixion the women had stood close to the cross (John), but as death approached they were forced to move away (Synoptics). P. Gaechter, *Maria im Erdenleben* (Innsbruck, 1954), p. 210, theorizes that the friends of Jesus were able to approach the cross (John) during the darkness that came over the earth (Synoptics). Others reject the historicity of the Johannine account. Barrett, p. 458, doubts that the Romans would have allowed Jesus' friends to approach the cross; but E. Stauffer, *Jesus and His Story* (London: SCM, 1960), pp. 111, 179[1], cites evidence to the effect that the crucified was often surrounded by relatives, friends, and enemies during the long hours of this agonizing penalty. It is worth noting that the Synoptic picture has an orientation toward fulfilling Ps xxxviii 12(11): "My kinsmen stand at a distance from me" (also Ps lxxxviii 9[8]). Kerrigan, p. 375, suggests that for John the women at the cross are witnesses, seeing and hearing what happened; but actually only Jesus' mother has a role in the episode, and the witness of the Beloved Disciple suffices (xix 35).

his mother, and his mother's sister, Mary the wife of Clopas, and Mary Magdalene. How many women are meant, two, three, or four? The thesis that two women are involved would mean that we read: "his mother and his mother's sister, namely, Mary of Clopas and Mary Magdalene." The unlikelihood that John identifies the mother of Jesus as Mary of Clopas makes this interpretation of the verse the least plausible of all. The thesis that three women are involved would mean that we read: "his mother, and his mother's sister (Mary of Clopas), and Mary Magdalene." Although grammatically this is possible, there is some unlikelihood that Mary, Jesus' mother, would have a sister also named Mary. The Syriac Peshitta and Tatian definitely think of four women, for they insert "and" between the second and third designations: "his mother's sister and Mary the wife of Clopas." Even without this clarification, the sentence structure would seem to favor four women: "A and B, C and D." (While, then, we think four women are meant, we doubt that there was a deliberate attempt by the evangelist to contrast them to the four soldiers, *pace* Hoskyns, p. 530; for in each instance the fact that there are four is only obliquely indicated.) Evidently the evangelist leaves the first two women unnamed, while he names the second two. One explanation may be that Jesus' mother was well known among Christians and would not have to be named, while the last two women both bore the name Mary and so had to be distinguished more clearly ("of Clopas"; "Magdalene"). But why is Jesus' mother's sister not named? Perhaps her name was not given in the tradition, or perhaps she was well known to the circle for whom the evangelist wrote (see below for the suggestion that she was Salome, mother of John the son of Zebedee). In any case, the fact that the Gospel will concern itself in the subsequent verses only with Jesus' mother makes it unlikely that the mention of the other three women is the creation of the evangelist—their presence was mentioned in his tradition, even as it was part of the tradition(s) behind the Synoptic Gospels. (The fact that each of the Synoptic Gospels names three women without mentioning Mary the mother of Jesus may be used as an argument that John refers to four women including Mary.)

Let us compare the three women mentioned in John (besides Jesus' mother) to the women mentioned in the Synoptics. Mark xv 40 (see xv 47, xvi 1) and Matt xxvii 56 give the names of three women who stood at a distance from the cross; Luke xxiv 10 (see xxiii 49, 55) mentions three women who visited the tomb. The table below follows the Marcan/Matthean order of listing the women.

	Matthew	Mark	Luke
1	Mary Magdalene	Mary Magdalene	Mary Magdalene
2	Mary mother of James and Joseph	Mary mother of James and Joses	Mary (mother?) of James
3	The mother of the sons of Zebedee	Salome	
			Joanna

There is no problem about the name in the *first* position, for all four Gospels associate Magdalene with Calvary and the empty tomb. For her name "Mary," see NOTE on xx 16. There is a small problem about the name in the *second* position. Obviously Mark and Matthew are referring to the same woman; she may have been the mother of two of the "brothers" of the Lord, for the variation that occurs between "Joseph" and "Joses" appears also in the respective listing of the "brothers": Matt xiii 55 has *"James and Joseph and Simon and Judas,"* while Mark vi 3 has *"James and Joses and Judas and Simon."* (Since the Mary who is their mother is certainly not Mary the mother of Jesus, there is an internal biblical reason for questioning the thesis that these "brothers" were uterine brothers of Jesus—see NOTE on "brothers" in ii 12. Hence Barrett's objection, p. 459, that Jesus would not have entrusted his mother to the care of the Beloved Disciple when one of his own brothers was available as a more obvious custodian is not too persuasive.) It seems very likely that Luke's "Mary of James" is the same woman as the Mary mentioned in Mark/Matthew.

As for the name in the *third* position, granted the closeness of Matthew to Mark, it is not improbable that Salome is the mother of the sons of Zebedee (James and John). But Salome is not the same as Joanna, for Joanna, mentioned only in Luke's Gospel, is the wife of Chuza, Herod's steward (viii 3).

Is "Mary of Clopas," mentioned by John, the same as the Mary (mother of James and Joses/Joseph) mentioned in the second position on our Synoptic table? (Many of the versions read Cleopas, seemingly identifying Clopas with the Cleopas of Luke xxiv 18, one of the two disciples of Jesus who were on the road to Emmaus. Actually the two names are different: "Clopas" seems to have been a Semitic name, but it may have served as an equivalent for the genuine Greek name "Cleopas" [Cleopatros—BDF, §125²].) If the two Marys are the same, then perhaps two of the "brothers" of the Lord were the sons of Clopas (and thus we have another good argument against the already weak case for identifying James the "brother" of Jesus with James the son of Alphaeus, one of the Twelve). Hegesippus (ca. A.D. 150) says that Clopas was the brother of Joseph, the putative father of Jesus (Eusebius *Hist.* III 11 and 32:1–5; GCS 9¹:228, 266–68); this would make the two "brothers" cousins of Jesus on his father's side of the family. We have assumed that John's phrase "Mary of Clopas" refers to the wife of Clopas (BDF, §162⁴); but E. F. Bishop, ET 73 (1961–62), 339, contends that it means "daughter of Clopas" (BDF, §162¹); it could even mean "mother of Clopas" (BDF, §162³).

Is Jesus' mother's sister, mentioned by John, the same as Salome the mother of the sons of Zebedee (a combination of the Marcan and Matthean information)? This would mean that James and John, Zebedee's two sons, were cousins of Jesus (see NOTE on "was there" in ii 1), a relationship that would better explain why the dying Jesus entrusted his mother to the Beloved Disciple (presumably John son of Zebedee). Thus, one set of Jesus' relatives, his "brothers" would not have believed in him (John vii 5), while another set would have been members of the Twelve disciples! The close relationship of the sons of Zebedee to Jesus would also explain why their mother or the sons themselves expected special favors (Matt xx 20; Mark x 35). If John's mother was Mary's sister, then the Fourth Gospel's failure to give the personal name of Jesus' "mother's sister" would be consonant with this Gospel's reticence about naming the members of the family of Zebedee. On the other hand, some scholars would identify Jesus' "mother's sister," mentioned by John, with the woman mentioned in the second position on the Synoptic table, "Mary the mother of James and Joses/Joseph," for then it would be clear in what way James and Joses/Joseph were "brothers" of Jesus, namely, that they were cousins on his mother's side of the family.

Obviously, while such speculation about Jesus' family and friends is interesting, it is most uncertain. However, our very difficulty in deciding whether the women mentioned by John are the same as the women mentioned by the Synoptics is eloquent argument against the thesis that John's list of the women was borrowed from the Synoptic lists.

26. *the disciple whom he loved.* For his identity, see vol. 29, pp. XCII–XCVIII. This is the only time that he does not appear in Peter's company. Luke (xxiii 49) is the only Synoptic to indicate the presence at Calvary of male companions of Jesus: "all his acquaintances [masculine] with the women." The agreement of John and Luke on this point should be evaluated in light of the fact that these are the two Gospels that mention appearances to the disciples in Jerusalem on the Sunday immediately after the Friday of the crucifixion. Mark xiv 50 and Matt xxvi 56 report that all the disciples fled when Jesus was arrested; correspondingly Mark and Matthew indicate that the first appearance of the risen Jesus to the disciples would or did take place in Galilee (see pp. 969–72 below).

Woman. This address is omitted by the Coptic versions and one OL ms. See NOTE on ii 4.

here is your son. Ide appears in the best Greek witnesses, but there is strong support for *idou* (see NOTE on "Behold the man" in xix 5). Barrett, p. 459, and Dauer, p. 81, point out the similarity to an adoption formula; yet seemingly there is no precise parallel where the mother is addressed first. In fact, the adoption formulas we find in Scripture generally have a "you are" pattern, unlike John's "here is" (Ps ii 7: "You are my son; today I have begotten you"; I Sam xviii 21: "Today you will be my son-in-law"; Tob vii 12 [Sinaiticus]: "Henceforth you are her brother, and she is your sister"; for the Code of Hammurabi, see R. de Vaux, *Ancient Israel* [New York: McGraw-Hill, 1961], pp. 112–13). Lagrange, p. 494, comments that ordinarily in antiquity a dying person commended his mother to another with a direct commission or charge: "I leave to you my mother to be taken care of."

27. *from that hour the disciple took her.* A few minor textual witnesses read "day" for "hour." Are we to understand that Jesus' mother and the Beloved Disciple left Calvary immediately, before Jesus died? One can find grammatical support for such an interpretation in the contention of Joüon (Black, p. 252) that the expression "from that hour" is an Aramaism frequent in the rabbinic writings, meaning "at that very moment." However, if in the light of John's theology we understand "that hour" as the hour of Jesus' return to the Father, we need posit no such precise time indication for the Disciple's departure. Later, in vs. 35, the Beloved Disciple seems to be still present. Ceroke, pp. 132–33, takes the phrase "from that hour" as implying the perpetuity of the Disciple's care for Mary; but this is again to read too much into it. What is true is that in this half verse the writer turns our attention from Calvary to something future (Dodd, *Tradition*, p. 127)—only Matthew among the Synoptics similarly interrupts sequence in the Passion to carry to its conclusion a story about some of the characters involved (death of Judas in xxvii 3–10; also xxvii 52–53).

into his care. Literally "to his own [neuter]," a phrase used elsewhere by John (i 11: "to his own [country]"; xvi 32: "scattered, each on his own"). Here it has the connotation "to his own home," as in Esther v 10; III Macc vi 27; Acts xxi 6. Yet the phrase implies care as well. In harmony with the broad meaning we suggested above for "from that hour," we need not think that the Beloved Disciple had a home *in Jerusalem* to which he took Mary from Calvary. Hoskyns, p. 530, sees a possible contrast between the Beloved Disciple who takes Mary "to his own" and the disciples who were scattered "each on his own."

28. *After this.* For the problem of whether *meta touto* is chronologically precise, as distinct from *meta tauta*, see NOTE on ii 12. For instance, Kerrigan, p. 373, takes *meta touto* as an indication that this incident immediately followed the previous incident.

aware. For the same phraseology, see xiii 1. Some minor witnesses read "seeing"; P66 supports the reading of the major witnesses.

all was now finished. "Now" is omitted in many of the versions, or another word ("behold") is read. The "all" means all that the Father had given the Son to do: "God had handed over all things to him" (xiii 3; also iii 35, xv 15). Here and in vs. 30 the verb employed is *telein*, "to bring to an end." It has the connotation of completion as well as that of simple ending. Occasionally it has sacrificial overtones; and Dodd, *Interpretation*, p. 437, suggests a connection with the use of "consecrate" in xvii 19: namely, if in that verse (p. 766 above) Jesus appears as a priest offering himself as a

victim for those whom God had given him, here we see that his death is a
completion of the sacrifice. However, the sacrificial connotation of *telein* is
a fragile base to serve as sole support for this interesting hypothesis (which
would fit very well with our interpretation of the priestly symbolism of the
tunic in Episode 2—see COMMENT). We are surely to relate *telein* to the
telos of xiii 1: "He now showed his love for them *to the very end*." In the
remainder of the crucifixion scene we shall see that John relates the finishing
of Jesus' work and life to the completion of God's preordained plan given
in Scripture. It is interesting that Acts xiii 29 uses the verb *telein* for
the accomplishment of Scripture through the death of Jesus: "They asked
Pilate to have him killed; and when they had *accomplished* all that was
written of him, . . ." *Telein* appears also in the Lucan account of the Last
Supper in reference to the disciples' possessing a sword: "I tell you that
the Scripture must be *accomplished* in me, . . . for what is written about
me has its accomplishment [*telos*]" (Luke xxii 37; see also xviii 31; Rev
xvii 17). P. Ricca, *Die Eschatologie des Vierten Evangeliums* (Zürich:
Gotthelf, 1966), pp. 63 ff., sees here an attempt to relate the crucifixion to
"the beginning" mentioned in the Prologue: in between the beginning (John i 1)
and the end (xix 28, 30) took place the career of the Word become flesh.
Ricca also suggests a connection with v 17 where Jesus says, "My Father is
at work even till now, and so I am at work too." The work is now finished,
and the Sabbath that begins after Jesus' death (xix 31) is the Sabbath of
eternal rest (see vol. 29, p. 217). Finally, because of the frequent parallelism
between Jesus and Moses in the Fourth Gospel, we may call attention to
Exod xl 33: "So Moses completed the work"—a reference to the completion
of the Tabernacle (see vol. 29, pp. 32–33).

in order to. Normally a final clause is related to a governing verb
that precedes it; this would mean that the all that "was now finished in
order to bring the Scripture to its complete fulfillment" would include the
previous incident (Episode 3) where Jesus gives his mother to the Beloved
Disciple. O. M. Norlie, *Simplified New Testament* (Grand Rapids: Zondervan,
1961), translates thus: "Jesus, knowing that everything had been done to fulfill
the Scriptures, said. . . ." Bampfylde, p. 253, has a similar translation: "Jesus,
knowing that all was now finished in order for the Scripture to be brought to
fruition, said. . . ." However, most grammarians (BDF, §478; MTGS, p.
344) cite this verse as an example where the final clause precedes the main
clause, so that the fulfillment of Scripture is related to Jesus' saying "I am
thirsty" (Episode 4). Perhaps the two possibilities should not be sharply
separated, and we have deliberately made our translation somewhat ambiguous.
We shall point out in the COMMENT possible Scripture background for both
Episode 3 and Episode 4.

bring the Scripture to its complete fulfillment. The normal NT verb for
the fulfillment of Scripture is *plēroun*, used in vss. 24 and 36. Here John
employs *teleioun*, a verb not otherwise used in the NT in reference to Scripture
(however, we noted above such a use of *telein*, a related verb). C. F. D.
Moule, NTS 14 (1967–68), 318, suggests that the Johannine employment of
teleioun for *plēroun* is simply stylistic variation. In xvii 4, 23 John uses
teleioun for the completion of Jesus' work (see NOTE on xvii 4); its use
in the present verse presumably implies that the fulfillment of Scripture is

brought to completion as Jesus passes from this life on the way to his Father. Actually, this is *not* the last Johannine reference to the fulfilling of Scripture in Jesus' career (see vss. 36, 37).

"I am thirsty." These words are found only in John. The last time we heard of Jesus' thirst was in iv 6 (see NOTE there) as he sat by the well of Samaria at noon (cf. xix 14).

29. *a jar.* Mentioned only by John.

common wine. The *oxos*, mentioned also in the Synoptic accounts of the second drink offered to Jesus (see COMMENT), was *posca*, a diluted, vinegary wine drunk by soldiers and laborers. Its only purpose could have been to quench thirst, and it is not to be confused with the narcotic (?) mixture of wine (*oinos*) and myrrh or gall, spoken of in the Marcan/Matthean account of the first drink offered to Jesus. A confused combination of the two is echoed by the *Gospel of Peter*, 16, and the *Epistle of Barnabas* VII 3. Curiously, Hoskyns, p. 531, sees here a gesture of cruelty to aggravate thirst, while the *Gospel of Peter* seems to think of the mixture of gall and common wine as a poison to hasten Jesus' death.

they. The agents are not identified, but probably we are to think of the soldiers last mentioned in 24. In Luke xxiii 36 the agents are soldiers; Matt xxvii 47–48 speaks of one of the bystanders; Mark xv 36 speaks of "someone," perhaps one of the bystanders if 36a is to be related to 35 (Taylor, *Mark*, pp. 594–95, denies the relationship and suggests that Mark is referring to a soldier). Of course, only one individual would have held up the wine to Jesus, so that the Johannine plural includes those who suggested the idea and helped.

a sponge soaked in this wine. Luke mentions no sponge; Mark xv 36 has someone "filling a sponge with wine"; Matt xxvii 48 has "a sponge full of wine." Some witnesses to John's text have variants influenced by the Marcan and Matthean wording.

on some hyssop. Mark/Matthew speak of a reed, presumably a long, strong stalk. What does John mean by "hyssop"? Usually biblical hyssop (Heb. *'ēzōb;* Gr. *hyssōpos*) is a small bushy plant that can grow out of cracks in walls, a plant that I Kings iv 33 classifies as the humblest of shrubs (=*Origanum Maru L.;* Syrian marjoram; a plant of the labial family, related to mint and thyme). While the Palestinian variety of hyssop has a relatively large stem, the branches are suited for sprinkling (Lev xiv 4–7; Num xix 18) but scarcely for bearing the weight of a wet sponge. Some have suggested that in this instance "hyssop" refers to *Sorgum Vulgare L.* (the reed of Mark/Matthew); and while such harmonization is forced, we must admit that the identification of hyssop is not certain, for at least eighteen different plants have been suggested as answering its description, and the biblical term may cover several species (J. Wilkinson, ScotJT 17 [1964], 77).

An 11th-century cursive ms. (476) reads *hyssos,* "javelin," for *hyssōpos.* It is interesting that, without knowing this ms., J. Camerarius (d. 1574) suggested the emendation. It has been accepted by Lagrange, Bernard, and the NEB editors. Hoskyns, p. 531, proposes the possibility that the evangelist himself, finding *hyssos* in the tradition that came to him, was reminded of *hyssōpos* and introduced that word for symbolic purposes. In our judgment the textual support for *hyssos* is forbiddingly weak, and we are almost certainly dealing with a scribe's ingenious attempt to improve a difficult reading. (When

John does speak of a spear-like weapon, he uses *logchē* [vs. 34] not *hyssos*.) In speaking of hyssop, John altered the historical scene in favor of symbolism (see COMMENT).

raised it. Luke and John use *prospherein* to describe the action.

to his lips. Literally "mouth"; mentioned only in John.

30. *took the wine*. Only John tells us that Jesus accepted the proferred drink.

"It is finished." See NOTE on "all was now finished" in 28. Mark/Matthew report that before Jesus died, he uttered a loud cry, but they do not specify the content. Luke xxiii 46 reports Jesus' last words as "Father, into your hands I commit [*paratithenai*] my spirit" (from Ps xxxi 6[5]).

bowing his head. Only John mentions this detail. Several modern authors (e.g., Loisy, Braun) have followed Augustine, *In Jo*. CXIX 6; PL 35:1952, in commenting that this is the action of a man who is going to sleep rather than that of a man who is in a death agony—the action thus symbolizes Jesus' mastery over his death. This is a rather imaginative interpretation of the evidence.

he handed over the spirit. The same verb *paradidonai* ("deliver, entrust") is used in 16a: "Pilate handed Jesus over to them to be crucified." We may compare John's wording to that of the Synoptics: Mark xv 37: "He breathed his last [*ekpnein*]"; Matt xxvii 50: "He yielded [*aphienai*] the spirit"; Luke xxiii 46 is the same as Mark, but see the saying that Luke attributes to Jesus, cited two notes above. There were two traditional ways of describing the death of Jesus: (a) He breathed his last—Mark, Luke; (b) He yielded/committed/handed over his spirit—Matt, Luke, and John. In John's use of *paradidonai*, Bernard, II, 641, sees an element of voluntary giving. It is the verb used by Isa liii 12 to describe the death of the Suffering Servant: "His soul was handed over to death . . . and he was handed over because of their sins." It will be noted that, unlike Luke who specifies that it was into his Father's hands that Jesus committed his spirit, John does not identify a recipient (see COMMENT). In the 2nd-century *Acts of John*, the death of John is described in terms resembling John's description of the death of Jesus.

COMMENT: GENERAL

The Structure of the Scene

While the scene of Jesus on the cross is not as precisely or dramatically arranged as the scene of Jesus before Pilate, we detect a chiastic pattern here as well, as indicated in the accompanying diagram.

The structure we have proposed implicitly rejects two current views about the arrangement of this scene. Meeks, p. 62, treats xix 17–22 as an eighth episode of the relations between Pilate and Jesus and thus as belonging to the previous Division of the Passion Narrative. It is true that Pilate figures strongly in these verses and that one might even get the impression that Pilate was at Calvary (p. 918 below). However, the

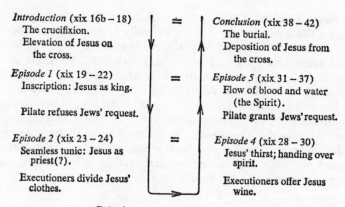

Introduction (xix 16b – 18)
The crucifixion.
Elevation of Jesus on
the cross.

≒

Conclusion (xix 38 – 42)
The burial.
Deposition of Jesus from
the cross.

Episode 1 (xix 19 – 22)
Inscription: Jesus as king.

Pilate refuses Jews' request.

=

Episode 5 (xix 31 – 37)
Flow of blood and water
(the Spirit).
Pilate grants Jews' request.

Episode 2 (xix 23 – 24)
Seamless tunic: Jesus as
priest(?).

Executioners divide Jesus'
clothes.

=

Episode 4 (xix 28 – 30)
Jesus' thirst; handing over
spirit.

Executioners offer Jesus
wine.

Episode 3 (xix 25 – 27)
Jesus' mother and the Beloved Disciple.
Jesus' provision for the future.

previous scene had its own chiastic concord, keyed to the movement of Pilate outside and inside the praetorium. The introduction and addition of an episode that took place at Calvary would disrupt the whole arrangement. Moreover, the presence of Pilate in what we consider the first episode of the crucifixion has importance for the arrangement of the present Division of the Passion Narrative, since it is matched by Pilate's presence in the fifth or last episode of the crucifixion. The other view that we have rejected is that of Janssens de Varebeke (p. 803 above) who would once more introduce a pattern of seven episodes (he joins our Introduction to Episode 1, and his Episodes 6 and 7 are gained by dividing up what we call the Conclusion into vss. 38–40 and 41–42). It is true that in our own arrangement there is something like a sevenfold pattern if we add the Introduction and Conclusion to the five episodes, but we have a reason for speaking of five rather than seven episodes. The episodes are centered around theological symbolism; the Introduction and the Conclusion do not have this symbolism, at least to the same extent, for they serve more to set the scene (in each, the place where Jesus was crucified is described—vss. 17–18a and 41).

The diagram we have given highlights the more obvious parallels of the chiastic structure; note also that there is a certain parallelism in the vertical columns between Episodes 1 and 2 (concerning the role of Jesus) and Episodes 4 and 5 (concerning the Spirit). Episode 3, in which Jesus himself speaks at greater length than in the other episodes, is the central episode. Some have suggested an alternation of good and bad treatment of Jesus throughout the scene (good in 1, 3, and the Conclusion; bad in the Introduction, 2, and 5). However, it is difficult to decide whether Episode

4 (and even Episode 2) is bad treatment. In our judgment, John does not categorize the action of the soldiers as really hostile to Jesus—"the Jews" are his enemies. Finally, we may observe that some of the episodes have internal inclusions: Episode 1 begins and ends with the theme of Pilate's writing; Episode 2 begins and ends with a reference to the soldiers; Episode 4 begins and ends with the theme of all being finished. There is a certain unity between Episode 5 and the Conclusion, for both describe what took place after Jesus' death; the theme of the Day of Preparation that begins Episode 5 ends the Conclusion. Nevertheless, our decision to treat the Introduction and Episodes 1–4 in the present section, while we reserve Episode 5 and the Conclusion to the next section, is primarily a matter of convenience determined by length.

Dominant Johannine Motifs in the Crucifixion Scene

We saw that the motif of Jesus' kingship was pervasive in the trial of Jesus before Pilate. Since a false claim to kingship was the charge on which Jesus was tried and condemned, this motif naturally dominated the interrogation. But, more than this, the motif of kingship affected what was done to Jesus: he was attired as a king and hailed in mockery by the soldiers; he was presented to the people as a king by Pilate. It is not surprising then to find a certain continuity of the motif into the crucifixion scene. The crucifixion itself, described in the Introduction, is an enthronement of Jesus, as Episode 1 makes clear when his royal title is proclaimed trilingually and thus internationally. Moreover, the burial of Jesus, described in the Conclusion, has features suggestive of royalty (p. 960 below). B. Schwank may well be correct in stressing that the principal episodes of the crucifixion are concerned with the gifts that the enthroned king gives to those who accept his kingdom, for certainly these episodes have as a motif what Jesus does for the believer. The Johannine crucifixion scene is, in a certain way, less concerned with the fate of Jesus than with the significance of that fate for his followers. The crucifixion is the fulfillment of Jesus' promise in xiii 1 that in "the hour" he would show to the very end his love for his own. Jesus dies as the model shepherd who lays down his life for his sheep (x 11, 14–15), i.e., for those who hear his voice and know him.

Perhaps it would be useful to summarize here our understanding of the principal ideas found in the episodes of the crucifixion scene, for many of them are proposed through symbolism and would not be immediately apparent. (In the DETAILED COMMENT we shall indicate the varying degrees of probability with which these interpretations can be proposed.) Episode 1 proclaims to the whole civilized world the kingship of Jesus. "The Jews" reject this claim, but the Gentile governor insists on its multilingual proclamation. Episode 2 is concerned with the symbolism of the seamless tunic, a priestly garment. Jesus is not only a king but also a priest whose death is an action offered for others. In Jesus' own words: "It is for them that I consecrate myself" (xvii 19). Episode 3 is centered on Jesus' lasting concern for the community of those whom he leaves behind (see also xvii 9–19). His mother, the symbol of the New Israel, was denied a role at Cana because his hour had not yet come. Now that his hour has come, she is given a role as the mother of the Beloved Disciple, i.e., of the Christian. We are being told figuratively that Jesus was concerned for the community of believers who would be drawn to him now that he is lifted up from the earth on the cross (xii 32). Episode 4 shows the death of Jesus as the completion of all that the Father had given him to do, a task described beforehand in the Scriptures. This episode ends by describing Jesus' death as his handing over the spirit—seemingly a symbolic way of indicating that Jesus' own Spirit will now take up the work of Jesus. "If I do not go away, the Paraclete will never come to you" (xvi 7). Episode 5 continues the proleptic symbolism of the giving of the Spirit; for the flow of water colored with Jesus' dying blood fulfills the promise of vii 38–39: "As the Scripture says, 'From within him shall flow rivers of living water.' (Here he was referring to the Spirit . . .)." On a secondary level the flow of blood and water symbolizes the origin of the sacraments of the Eucharist and Baptism through which the life of Jesus is communicated to the Christian. It is important to remember that during this episode Jesus is already dead. In Johannine thought the drama of the cross does not end in death but in a flow of life that comes from death: the death of Jesus is the beginning of Christian life.

The motif of the fulfillment of Scripture is also very prominent in the crucifixion scene. Specific passages are cited in Episodes 2 and 5; and it is stated that Episode 4 occurred that the Scripture might be brought to its complete fulfillment. The Messiah-king motif of Episode 1 and the Mother Zion and New Eve symbolism of Episode 3 are also thoroughly scriptural. In this preoccupation with the OT background for the passion, John is probably reflecting the general early Christian concern to show the Jews that the crucifixion did not eliminate the possibility that Jesus was the promised Messiah but rather fulfilled God's words in Scripture. Nevertheless, the selection of the specific OT passages and themes as background for the crucifixion seems to have been done in the light of Johannine theological interest.

Comparison with the Synoptic Accounts of the Crucifixion

It is difficult to detect any organization or theological pattern in the sequence of the Synoptic scenario of Calvary. Only in the mockery hurled at Jesus do we discern any planning, for both in Mark/Matthew and in Luke there is a sequence in the mockeries by the various groups (bystanders, authorities, soldiers [Luke], and crucified criminals). Some of the details that are narrated seem to be purely factual and without obvious theological import. Therefore, John is unique both in the chiastic arrangement of the episodes and in the exclusive concentration on episodes of theological import. Each of the Johannine vignettes is carefully drawn, and the narrative is stripped of all that could distract. It is interesting to make a list of the details of the Synoptic narratives *not* found in John:

Simon of Cyrene (all three)
Wailing women on the way to Calvary (Luke)
Offering of drugged potion (Mark/Matthew)
Jesus' prayer for the forgiveness of his executioners (Luke)
Time indications, e.g., 9 A.M. (Mark); noon to 3 P.M. (all three)
Various mockeries (all three)
Repentance of the "good thief" (Luke)
Darkness over the land (all three)
The cry *"Eloi, Eloi, lama sabachthani"* (Mark/Matthew)
The suggestion that he seeks deliverance by Elijah (Mark/Matthew)
Jesus' final loud cry (all three)
The words "Father, into your hands I commit my spirit" (Luke)
The rending of the temple curtain (all three)
The earthquake and the opening of the tombs (Matthew)
Reaction of the centurion (all three)
Repentance of the multitudes going home (Luke)
Pilate's investigation to affirm the death of Jesus (Mark)
The wrapping of the body in a linen shroud (all three)
The presence of the women at the tomb (all three)
Purchase of spices by the women (Luke)

All these Johannine omissions can scarcely be explained as deliberate excisions, for such details as the mockery by the priests, the darkness over the land, and the rending of the temple curtain would have served as admirable vehicles for Johannine theology. The fact that the seemingly independent Lucan passion tradition omits details found in Mark/Matthew suggests the possibility that at least some of the Johannine omissions can be explained on the grounds that the independent tradition on which the Fourth Gospel is based was lacking in details found in the pre-Synoptic traditions. We may note that John omits details both of the Marcan A account and of the Marcan B account, although in what he includes, John may be somewhat close to the Marcan A account [as understood by Bultmann, rather than by Taylor]. John shows little knowledge of the peculiarly Lucan material.

When we turn to consider the incidents that John includes, there is a partial Synoptic parallel for the Introduction, the Conclusion, and four of the five episodes; only Episode 5 has no echo in the Synoptic traditions. Yet in virtually all of these instances, the aspect that John emphasizes is the very part of the incident that has no Synoptic counterpart. In the Introduction John agrees with the Synoptics about the place of crucifixion and the relative position of Jesus and the two other crucified men; but the

only element here that lends itself to Johannine theological interest is that
Jesus carried his own cross, and this is the one point in which John's
Introduction differs from the Synoptic accounts. In Episode 1 John agrees
with the Synoptics about the fact and substantial content of the title
on the cross; but John's interest is in the international character of the
proclamation and in Pilate's role in making and keeping the proclamation
—points on which the Synoptics are silent. In Episode 2 John agrees
with the Synoptics on the detail of the soldiers' dividing Jesus' clothes by
gambling; but the symbolism of the Johannine episode seems to be
centered on the seamless tunic, a garment not mentioned by the Synoptics.
In Episode 3 John agrees with the Synoptics about the presence of Galilean
women at Calvary; but John is particularly interested in Jesus' words to his
mother and the Beloved Disciple, neither of whom is mentioned in the
Synoptic accounts. In Episode 4 John agrees with the Synoptics that wine
was offered to the crucified Jesus; but John stresses that Jesus' thirst fulfilled
the Scriptures and brought his work to completion, and this element is
totally missing from the Synoptic descriptions of the incident. Nor do the
Synoptics describe Jesus' death in a way that would favor John's insight
that in dying Jesus handed over his Spirit to his followers. In the Conclusion John agrees with the Synoptics about the urgency of burial, about
the role of Joseph of Arimathea, and about the use of a new tomb;
but, if there is any Johannine theological emphasis here, it centers on the
large amount of myrrh and aloes brought by Nicodemus—again a detail on
which the Synoptics are silent. Thus, even in the incidents they have in
common, the differences between John and the Synoptics are quite substantial.

One solution would be that John drew some basic facts from the
Synoptic Gospels or from the pre-Synoptic traditions and then expanded
these by adding details that lent themselves to Johannine theologizing.
Substantially this is Barrett's evaluation (p. 455): "John is probably dependent on Mark, but either he, or intermediate tradition, has modified the
source markedly." However, there are two objections to this theory. First,
when John has material in common with the Synoptics, the parallel
descriptions often show notable differences in vocabulary; for example, see
the NOTE on xix 25 concerning the names of the women present on
Calvary. Moreover, in this common material, the sequence is not the
same. The Marcan order is: (1) the crucifixion, (2) the division of garments,
(3) the inscription, (4) the mention of the two bandits; the Lucan order
of the same events is 1, 4, 2, and, after an interim, 3; the Johannine order
is 1, 4, 3, 2. The second objection is that it is very difficult to tell whether
the properly Johannine details are imaginative additions or are traditional.
If plausibility is any guide, at times these Johannine details give just as
plausible a picture as do the contradictory or different details of the
Synoptic tradition. What is implausible about Jesus' possessing a seamless
tunic or his crying out in thirst? The most peculiar of the properly

Johannine incidents, the flow of the blood and water, is one for which the author emphatically claims eyewitness support! From a total consideration, then, both of the Johannine omissions and of the problem of the partial Synoptic parallels in the crucifixion incidents that John narrates, we would agree with Dodd (*Tradition*, pp. 124–39) in positing the existence of an independent Johannine tradition, leaving open the possibility that the evangelist has supplemented that tradition by creative imagination.

COMMENT: DETAILED

Introduction: The Way of the Cross and the Crucifixion (xix 16b–18)

These verses serve as a transition from the episodes where Jesus is judged by Pilate to the episodes that occur while Jesus is on the cross. While we have rejected the suggestion that this Introduction would better be classified as part of the judgment of Jesus by Pilate, we recognize that John has bound the crucifixion to the trial more tightly than any other evangelist. The way of the cross is described laconically; and no scene of commiseration, such as that found in Luke xxiii 27–31, is allowed to distract the reader. A bare minimum of detail is given—just enough to set the scene for Episode 1 where Pilate speaks once more.

It is most notable that John preserves no reminiscence of the role of Simon of Cyrene in carrying the crossbeam, as recorded in the three Synoptic Gospels. In particular, Mark (xv 21) betrays special knowledge of Simon, namely that he was the father of Alexander and Rufus, two men who may have been known to the Christian community at Rome for whom Mark was writing (Rom xvi 13?). Although some scholars (e.g., S. Reinach) have proposed that the role of Simon was an imaginative dramatization of the saying in Mark viii 34, "If anyone wishes to come after me, let him deny himself, take up his cross, and follow me," there is every reason to think that here the Synoptics have a reliable tradition. Admittedly it was normal for the criminal to carry the crossbeam himself, but perhaps the very departure from the normal pattern reinforces the historical likelihood. If Simon's role is not historical, why would his name have been remembered or introduced; he serves no obvious theological purpose.

What judgment, then, should we pass on John's statement that Jesus carried the cross by himself? Whether or not we accept an ingenious harmonization with the Synoptic accounts (see NOTE), we must still decide whether John's omission of Simon was through deliberate excision or through ignorance. The suggestion that it was through ignorance, because the tradition that came down to the evangelist did not mention Simon, runs up against the objection that the Johannine Passion Narrative is professedly dependent on the testimony of an eyewitness who was at

Calvary (xix 35). Of course, one can always answer that the eyewitness did not necessarily see what happened on the way to Calvary or that he did not regard Simon's role important enough to warrant inclusion; but neither of these answers is truly satisfactory.

Most scholars think that there was a deliberate excision of the memory of Simon. Some have found a theological reason for such an excision in an anti-Gnostic apologetic. Irenaeus (*Adv. Haer.* I.24:4; PG 7:677) reports that the 2nd-century Gnostics, especially Basilides, as part of their docetic christology, proposed that Simon of Cyrene and not Jesus was crucified. However, we are uncertain about just how strong a factor anti-Docetism was in the Fourth Gospel (vol. 29, p. LXXVI), and we are far from positive that such an interpretation of Simon's role was in circulation at the time when the Gospel was written.

A much more likely reason for the omission of Simon is John's desire to continue the theme that Jesus went to his death as sole master of his own destiny. Previously we have heard that Jesus would lay down his own life and that no one would take it from him (x 18). Jesus permissively instructed Judas to be quick about the business of betrayal (xiii 27). Jesus showed that he could have resisted arrest by rendering his enemies powerless (xviii 6), and he stood unafraid before Annas (xviii 20–23) and before Pilate (xix 9–11). So now he goes to Calvary without human assistance.

Another possible theological reason for the Johannine stress that Jesus carried his own cross may have been a desire to introduce the typology of Isaac who carried the wood for his own sacrifice (Gen xxii 6). This interpretation was frequent among the Church Fathers, e.g., John Chrysostom, *In Jo. Hom.* LXXXV 1; PG 59:459. Certainly OT allusions in the Gospel accounts of the crucifixion are frequent, and the Isaac motif was a popular one in Jewish circles and seemingly in Christian circles as well (Glasson, p. 98, thinks that Rom viii 32 alludes to LXX of Gen xxii 12; see also Heb xi 17–19; and note J. E. Wood, "Isaac Typology in the New Testament," NTS 14 [1967–68], 583–89.) Detailed study of the early development of the Isaac motif has been made by G. Vermes, *Scripture and Tradition in Judaism* (Leiden: Brill, 1961), pp. 193–227, and by R. Le Déaut, *La nuit pascale* (Analecta biblica 22; Rome: Pontifical Biblical Institute, 1963), especially pp. 198–207. In the 1st century A.D. Isaac was depicted as an adult who voluntarily accepted death (a combination of the story in Gen xxii with the theme of the Suffering Servant in Isa liii). Moreover, a relation was established between the Passover lamb (a Johannine theme in the Passion Narrative) and the sacrifice of Isaac, since that sacrifice was dated to the 15th of Nisan. Vermes, *op. cit.*, p. 216, cites a text from the Mekilta of Rabbi Ishmael: "And when I see the blood, I shall pass over you [Exod xii 13]—I see the blood of the binding of Isaac." In relation to the Johannine passage we are now considering, the comment on Isaac's carrying the wood in Midrash Rabbah LVI 3 (a late work) is most interesting: ". . . as one bears *the cross* [or stake of execution] on one's shoulder."

Parenthetically we may note that the Isaac symbolism is only one factor in leading us to think that John looked upon Jesus as a sacrificial victim who died at the same hour that the paschal lambs were being slaughtered in the Temple (see pp. 951, 953 below; also I John ii 2; Rev i 5). Nevertheless, we reject the thesis of Miguens, pp. 9–10, that Jesus was a victim *offered by Caiaphas* who was "high priest that year" (John xi 51, xviii 14). In Johannine theology Jesus lays down his own life (x 18) and consecrates himself (xvii 19). We shall see in the COMMENT on xix 23 that Jesus goes to his death clothed in a symbolically priestly garment—a seamless tunic reminiscent of the garment of the high priest. Like Isaac in popular Jewish thought, he is a victim who offers himself.

Still another suggestion for why John insists that Jesus carried his own cross has been made by Dodd, *Tradition*, pp. 124–25. He points out the similarity between Jesus' action as described in John and the saying recorded in Luke xiv 27: "Whoever does not carry his own cross and come after me cannot be my disciple." However, it is difficult to think that John's scene is described so as to fulfill this saying, for the Synoptic picture where Simon carries the cross behind Jesus fulfills it more literally. Moreover, the Johannine form of the saying (xii 26; see vol. 29, p. 475) does not mention carrying the cross.

As we pass on from the Johannine description of the way of the cross to the crucifixion itself, we note that the evangelist mentions but shows no interest in the two men who were crucified with Jesus. He will not report that they reviled Jesus (Mark xv 32; and, differently, Luke xxiii 39–43); he mentions them only because they will figure in the later episode of the breaking of the legs (John xix 32).

Episode One: Pilate and the Royal Inscription (xix 19–22)

The first real incident in the crucifixion of Jesus stands in a certain continuity with what happened in the praetorium; for the antagonists in the trial, the Jewish leaders and Pilate, clash once more over Jesus. By way of drama, this confrontation restores dignity to Pilate and fits in with the evangelist's sympathetic portrayal of the prefect. Pilate has been weak but he will cower no longer. If Pilate has been forced to yield to "the Jews" in the matter of crucifixion, his final words in the Gospel are words of defiance. Could any playwright have given Pilate a more effective or impressive final line?

When one tries to evaluate the episode as history, there are difficulties. Some make the difficulties almost insurmountable by supposing that John means that Pilate wrote the inscription with his own hand (see NOTE on vs. 19) and actually came to Calvary to witness the crucifixion. The latter thesis is based on the fact that none of the delegations that speak to Pilate are said to go to him (vss. 20, 31, 38), and so he must have been on hand. This is probably to base too much on an argument from silence. John may well be employing again the front and back stage technique (vol. 29, pp. 176, 181) to show what is happening simultaneously in two different places. A more serious objection against John's narrative is centered on the mentality of "the chief priests of the Jews." In Mark xv 32 and Matt xxvii 42 the chief priests themselves call Jesus "King of Israel." They are mocking him, to be sure; but this tradition militates against their being so disturbed about the use of the term "The King of the Jews" in an official statement of his crime. Dodd, *Tradition*, p. 122, footnote, says that the Synoptic and Johannine presentations of this matter reflect the tendencies of different channels of tradition, for they set in relief the ambivalent reaction of official Judaism before the fall of Jerusalem to popular messianic claims: some Jewish authorities speak of messianic claims mockingly, while others feel that national honor forbids entirely the use of messianic titles by criminal revolutionaries. Be this as it may, we can scarcely imagine that the priests thought they could force the Roman prefect to change an official inscription that many had already seen. Bultmann and others solve the problem by regarding only vs. 19 as coming to the evangelist from his tradition, while vss. 20–22 represent the evangelist's imaginative expansion.

In any case the evangelist's primary motive in this episode is theological. The complaint of the priests reintroduces the theme of kingship so prominent at the trial. All the Gospels agree that the charge of being a royal pretender was inscribed against Jesus; Matthew and Luke agree with John that the charge was placed on the cross; but only John turns the charge into a world-wide proclamation of enthronement. In discussing the trial before Pilate we rejected the thesis that in xix 13 John describes Jesus as being placed on the judgment seat as part of the enthronement ritual (see NOTE there on "sat down"). The real enthronement comes now on the cross when the kingship of Jesus is acknowledged by heraldic proc- lamation ordered by a representative of the greatest political power on earth and phrased in the sacred and secular languages of the time. The confrontation between Pilate and the priests brings out the depth and seriousness of the proclamation (even as the confrontation between Jesus and Pilate during the trial brought out the real meaning of Jesus' king- ship—an adaptation of the Johannine use of dialogue to solve misunder- standing). Pilate's refusal to change the title means that Jesus' kingship is affirmed despite all the attempts of "the Jews" to eradicate it. In fact, Pilate's insistence may be an ironic way of hinting that eventually the Gentiles will acknowledge the kingship that "the Jews" deny (a suggestion we have previously made in reference to the Roman soldiers' acclamation of Jesus as king during the trial). This may be the first instance of a theme we shall encounter several times in the crucifixion narrative: now that Jesus has been lifted up from the earth, he is beginning to draw all men to himself (xii 32). As Dodd, *Interpretation,* p. 437, remarks, John's portrayal of the crucified Jesus is harmonious with the famous Christian interpolation in Ps xcvi 10: "The Lord reigns *from the wood* [of the cross]" (a reading not found in MT or LXX but known to Justin, Tertullian, and the Latin tradition).

Episode Two: The Executioners Divide Jesus' Clothes; the Seamless Tunic (xix 23–24)

Although the other evangelists mention the rolling of dice to divide up Jesus' garments, only John makes a distinction between the (outer) clothes and the seamless tunic that was not to be divided. The distinction is seen as fulfilling Ps xxii 19(18). Actually the two lines of the psalm verse are in poetic synonymous parallelism whereby the same thing is said twice in different words; for the psalmist "dividing up the clothes [MT: *beged;* LXX: *himatia*]" and "rolling dice for the clothing [*lābūš; himatismos*]" constituted one action pertaining to one set of apparel. But John thinks of two distinct actions (dividing up; tossing dice in order not to divide) pertaining to separate items of apparel (outer garments; inner tunic). This splitting of synonymous OT parallelism seems also to be attested in Matt xxi 2–5 (see NOTE on xii 14). There is a very slight possibility that an Aramaic targum of the psalm offered more justification for John's interpretation than does the Hebrew text (in reference to this phenomenon, see vol. 29, pp. 133, 322); for the later targum tradition gives the two words for apparel as *lᵉbūšâ*, "clothes," and *pᵉtāgâ*, "cloak."

Many scholars have proposed that the incident of the tunic is the product of the evangelist's fanciful or erroneous interpretation of the psalm, a reference to which came to him in his tradition. However, it seems more likely that the interpretation of the psalm is stretched to cover an incident that the evangelist found in his tradition rather than vice versa. For instance, if the evangelist were inventing on the basis of the psalm, why would he not have used the same verbal expression as in the psalm, namely, "to roll dice" instead of the difficult "toss" (see NOTE). Moreover, how would the second word for apparel in the psalm (*lābūš* or *himatismos*) have suggested the tunic (*chitōn,* which does not translate *lābūš* but *kᵉtonet*)?

No matter where the idea of the tunic came from, this item is the center of the theological symbolism in the episode. One popular suggestion is that the seamless tunic woven in one piece is meant to remind the reader of the clothing of the (high) priest, and thus to proclaim that Jesus died not only as a king but also as a priest. Exod xxviii 4 and Lev xvi 4 use *chitōn* (Heb. *kᵉtonet*) in reference to one of the garments of the high priest. The word seamless (*arraphos*) is not found in LXX; but Josephus, *Ant.* III.vii.4;⋕161, describes the ankle-length tunic of the high priest as one long woven cloth, not composed of two pieces. Exod xxxix 27 (LXX:

xxxvi 35) speaks of the linen tunic of the priest as "a woven piece." The
theme that Jesus was priest and king seems to appear in Rev i 13 where
he wears the garments of the two offices. In that passage *podērēs* is used
to portray the long robe reaching to his feet; and this word is found
adjectivally with *chitōn* in a description of the high priest's ankle-length
tunic in Exod xxix 5. Certainly the idea of Jesus' going to his death as a
priest was known in NT times. It is particularly prominent in Hebrews,
a work with many Johannine affinities (see C. Spicq, *L'Épître aux Hébreux*
[Paris: Gabalda, 1952], I, 109–38; also "L'origine johannique de la conception du Christ-prêtre dans l'Épître aux Hébreux," in *Aux sources de
la tradition chrétienne* [Goguel volume; Neuchatel, 1950], pp. 258–69).
That the seamless tunic of the high priest would be of importance in the
minds of the people is suggested by the care that both Herod and the
Romans exercised in keeping control of the priestly vestments. That it
would not be unusual to see a theological symbolism in the tunic is
suggested by the allegory that Philo, *De fuga* xx;※110–12, builds around
the fact that the priest does not rend his garments: the priestly clothing
reminds one of the clothing that the *logos* makes for itself out of the
contexture of the universe (vol. 29, p. 520).

While the priestly symbolism of the tunic is plausible, some scholars
have felt that it does not explain the Johannine scene fully, for it offers
no explanation of why the soldiers did not divide the tunic. Therefore,
either as a substitute for the priestly symbolism or in addition to it, some
wish to see a symbolic reference to the unity of Jesus and his followers.
For instance, Cyprian, *On the Unity of the Catholic Church* vii; CSEL
3[1]:215, sees in the garments that were divided into four parts a symbol
of the four corners of the earth, while the seamless tunic represents the
undivided Church. Drawing on a reading of vs. 23 wherein the tunic "was
woven from the upper part throughout without seam," Cyprian interprets
"from the upper part" to mean that the unity of the Church comes from
God and must not be destroyed or cut up by men. If Cyprian indulges in
theologizing that goes beyond the obvious meaning of the text, nevertheless,
the theme of unity would not be out of place in John (x 15–16, xi 51–52,
xvii 11, 21–23). Hoskyns, p. 529, points out that the Greek verb "to tear,"
used in the soldiers' conversation, appears elsewhere in John in reference to
the division of people into factions (vii 43, ix 16, x 19, etc.—see also the
symbolic import of the tearing of the garment in I Kings xi 29–31). In
evaluating this interpretation of John, it is very difficult to draw the line
between exegesis and eisegesis. Bultmann, p. 519[10], points out even further
symbolic possibilities in light of the rabbinic idea that both Adam and
Moses received a seamless tunic from God. B. Murmelstein, *Angelos*
4 (1932), 55, recalling that in popular Jewish thought the patriarch Joseph
was a salvific figure, points to the long (?) tunic of Joseph in Gen xxxvii
3, 23, of which he was stripped and for which lots were cast (Midrash

Rabbah LXXXIV 8). Of course, we have no way of knowing whether such references were in the evangelist's mind.

Episode Three: Jesus Gives His Mother to the Beloved Disciple (xix 25–27)

We have already pointed out in the NOTES that not only in mentioning Jesus' mother and the Beloved Disciple (vss. 26–27) but also in listing the women in vs. 25, John differs significantly from the Synoptic reports. Because the Synoptics do not mention the women until the end of the crucifixion scene, after Jesus' death, both Bultmann, pp. 515, 520, and Dauer, pp. 224–25, suggest that originally the mention of the women came later in John, and that it was shifted to before Jesus' death only when Jesus' remarks to his mother and the Beloved Disciple were added. Of course, there is no real way of determining this, and its plausibility depends on how close a connection we make between vs. 25 and vss. 26–27. For instance, was the reference to "his mother" inserted into the list of women in 25 in order to facilitate the addition of vss. 26–27, or was it part of the original list? If the evangelist were simply expanding 25 to prepare the way for 26–27, why did he not add the Beloved Disciple as well? While vss. 26–27 are certainly Johannine in style and lend themselves to Johannine theologizing, not all scholars would regard them as an invention of the evangelist. Barrett, p. 455, thinks that the theological interest of the scene is too slight for the presence of Mary and of the Beloved Disciple to have been inserted by the evangelist—it was part of his tradition even though in this case the tradition was incorrect. Loisy, p. 487, thinks that the presence of Mary and of the Beloved Disciple was part of the original Johannine tradition, while the names of the other women were added by a redactor to bring John in harmony with the Synoptics (despite the fact that the names differ from the Synoptic names!). Our own view is that Mary was specifically mentioned in the tradition that came to the evangelist, as seen in vs. 25, but that the reference to the Beloved Disciple, here as elsewhere, is a supplement to the tradition. (If the Johannine community draws on a tradition that has come down from the Beloved Disciple, his role in various scenes may well have been part of the general knowledge of the community, even though by a type of reticence, he was not mentioned in the preached, and later written, official pre-Gospel tradition—in other words, if the presence of the Beloved Disciple is added by the evangelist to a traditional scene in which he was not mentioned, that addition is not necessarily unhistorical.) All those who deny Peter's presence in the high priest's courtyard as contradictory to Mark xiv 27 (see pp. 840–41 above) will *a fortiori* deny the possibility that a disciple of Jesus was present at Golgotha. As we indicated in the NOTES, it is not certain that the Synoptic picture of the women at a distance is to be preferred to the Johannine picture.

While the historical question is probably insoluble, we are much more concerned with the import that the episode has for John. Recently, Dauer, *art. cit.*, has argued that the evangelist's main purpose was to highlight the importance of the Beloved Disciple, the witness behind the Gospel. He was so important that Jesus raised him to the rank of his own brother. This may have been a subsidiary motif in the evangelist's mind, but we doubt that it was primary. Some of Dauer's presuppositions are open to question, e.g., to what extent "Here is your son" is an adoption formula (see NOTE); as we shall indicate below, we think of this much more emphatically as a revelatory formula. Also we question Dauer's contention that the Beloved Disciple is more important in this episode than the mother of Jesus. After all, the mother of Jesus is addressed first; and her future, and not that of the Beloved Disciple, is considered at the end of vs. 27. Moreover, Dauer's interpretation divorces this scene from that of the first sign at Cana where the mother of Jesus appeared previously; we shall stress that the similarities between the two scenes are too strong to be ignored.

Another explanation of the evangelist's intent in this episode has the advantage of simplicity: the evangelist is interested only in relating the fact that the dying Jesus provided for the care of his mother after his death. Many of the Church Fathers (Athanasius, Epiphanius, Hilary) so interpreted the episode, using this interpretation as an argument to prove Mary's perpetual virginity: if she had other sons, Jesus would not have entrusted her to John son of Zebedee, the Beloved Disciple. Indeed, a tradition still recalled on the hilltop of Panaya Kapulu in modern Turkey, some five miles from Selçuk (Ephesus), maintains that Mary subsequently resided with John, even when he moved to Ephesus. Setting aside the apologetic and popular developments, we doubt that Jesus' filial solicitude is the main import of the Johannine scene. Such a non-theological interpretation would make this episode a misfit amid the highly symbolic episodes that surround it in the crucifixion narrative. Moreover, the Gospel gives several indications that something more profound is in mind. The wording "Here is your son" and "Here is your mother" is another instance of the revelatory formula that De Goedt has detected elsewhere in John (vol. 29, p. 58). In this formula the one who speaks is revealing the mystery of the special salvific mission that the one referred to will undertake; thus, the sonship and motherhood proclaimed from the cross are of value for God's plan and are related to what is being accomplished in the elevation of Jesus on the cross. A deeper meaning is also suggested by the verse that follows this episode in John: "After this, [Jesus was] aware that all was now finished." The action of Jesus in relation to his mother and the Beloved Disciple completes the work that the Father has given Jesus to do and fulfills the Scripture (see NOTE on "in order to" in xix 28). All this implies something more profound than filial care (although, if the scene is historical, filial care may have been its original import).

Most commentators find a theological import by interpreting Jesus' mother and the Beloved Disciple as figures representative or symbolic of a larger group. R. H. Strachan, *The Fourth Gospel* (3rd ed.; London: SCM, 1941), p. 319, thinks that Mary represents the heritage of Israel that is now being entrusted to the Christians (the Beloved Disciple). E. Meyer, *art. cit.*, points out that, just as the unbelieving brothers of Jesus (vii 5) have now given place to a new brother (the Beloved Disciple), so Jewish Christianity is being replaced by Gentile Christianity. Bultmann, p. 521, thinks of Mary as Jewish Christendom and the Beloved Disciple as Gentile Christendom: the Jewish Christians find a home among the Gentile Christians. Origen, *In Jo.* I 4(6); GCS 10:9, sees in the scene a lesson for the perfect Christian: "Every man who becomes perfect no longer lives his own life, but Christ lives in him. And because Christ lives in him, it was said to Mary concerning him, 'Here is your son, Christ.'" Obviously we cannot seriously discuss such a wealth of figurative possibilities. We shall present below the interpretation we think most plausible, drawing upon the articles of Koehler and Langkammer for historical information, and upon the works of Braun, Gaechter, and Feuillet for suggestions about the symbolism.

There is little doubt that in Johannine thought the Beloved Disciple can symbolize the Christian; Origen is a witness to the antiquity of this interpretation. The real problem concerns the symbolic value of Jesus' mother. There is evidence in the 4th century that Mary at the foot of the cross was taken as a figure of the Church. Ephraem the Syrian states that, just as Moses appointed Joshua in his stead to take care of the people, so Jesus appointed John in his stead to take care of Mary, the Church (Koehler, p. 124). In the West, about the same time, Ambrose maintained that in Mary we have the mystery of the Church and that to each Christian Jesus may say in reference to the Church: "Here is your mother"—in seeing Christ victorious on the cross, the Christian becomes a son of the Church (*In Luc.* vii 5; PL 15:1700C). This 4th-century interpretation of Mary at the foot of the cross as the Church may be related to the 2nd-century (and earlier) understanding of Mary as the New Eve (vol. 29, p. 108). We must now ask ourselves how well such an interpretation fits into the Johannine mentality.

Parenthetically, before we go further, we should make two observations for the sake of clarity. First, we do not pretend that the interpretation which sees Mary at the foot of the cross as the Church is the predominant exegesis of the 4th century or even of subsequent centuries. Second, this symbolic interpretation of Mary's role is quite distinct from the theory that Mary *as an individual* becomes the mother of all Christians. As with the Cana incident, there is a large body of Roman Catholic literature that has concerned itself with the scene at the foot of the cross, often seeking in this episode the basis for the theology of the spiritual motherhood of Mary. The articles of Ceroke and Kerrigan, cited in the Bibliography, are examples of serious studies in this vein (as distinct from purely pious and meditative writing). On the grounds that papal citations of the passage constitute an authoritative interpretation, D. Unger, *art. cit.*, would maintain that the spiritual motherhood is Roman Catholic Marian *doctrine*. However, many Catholic exegetes, for example, Tillmann, Wikenhauser, see such an interpretation as the fruit of later theologizing upon the text, a theologizing that goes considerably beyond any provable intention of the evangelist; and certainly that would be the view of the present writer. (Protestant commentators, perhaps in reaction to Catholic thought, have been somewhat wary about giving importance to the figure of Mary in this Johannine passage; Hoskyns and Thurian are notable exceptions.) While the interpretation of Mary as a symbol of the Church is quite ancient, the concept of the personal spiritual motherhood of Mary makes its appearance in relation to the scene at the foot of the cross in the 9th century in the East with George of Nicomedia (Jesus made Mary the mother not only of John but also of the other disciples) and in the 11th century in the West with Pope Gregory VII (Koehler, *art. cit.*, pp. 141–45; Langkammer, *art. cit.*).

Returning now to our quest for John's motif in the episode, we think that it is clear that whatever symbolism is involved must be centered on Jesus' mother's becoming the mother of the Beloved Disciple. (Perhaps also the address "Woman" is important; see NOTE on ii 4.) We ask the reader to recall what we said about the symbolism of the mother of Jesus at Cana (vol. 29, pp. 107–9) and of the woman about to give birth in xvi 21 (pp. 731–33 above). The episode at the foot of the cross has these details in common with the Cana scene: the two scenes are the only places in the Gospel that the mother of Jesus appears; in each she is addressed as "Woman"; at Cana her intervention is rejected on the grounds that Jesus' hour had not yet come, but here we are in the context of Jesus' hour (the "hour" is mentioned in vs. 27—the only time the word occurs in its theological sense in chs. xviii–xix); in both scenes the disciples of Jesus figure prominently. The scene at the foot of the cross has these details in common with xvi 21: the use of the words "woman" and "hour"; the theme of maternity; and the theme of Jesus' death. We suggested in vol. 29, p. 109, that if Mary was refused a role during the ministry of Jesus as it began at Cana, she finally received her role in the hour of Jesus' passion, death, and resurrection. In this climactic hour men are to be recreated as God's children when the Spirit is breathed forth (pp. 931, 1037 below). The sorrowful scene at the foot of the cross represents the birth pangs by which the spirit of salvation is brought forth (Isa xxvi 17–18) and handed over (John xix 30). In becoming the mother of the Beloved Disciple (the Christian), Mary is symbolically evocative of Lady Zion who, after the birth pangs, brings forth a new people in joy (John xvi 21; Isa xlix 20–22, liv 1, lxvi 7–11)—see Feuillet, "Les adieux," pp. 477–80; "L'heure," pp. 361–80. Her natural son is the firstborn of the dead (Col i 18), the one who has the keys of death (Rev i 18); and those who believe in him are born anew in his image. As his brothers, they have her as mother.

Jesus' mother is the New Eve who, in imitation of her prototype, the "woman" of Gen ii–iv, can say: "With the help of the Lord I have begotten a man" (cf. Gen iv 1—Feuillet, "Les adieux," pp. 474–77). Perhaps we may also relate Mary the New Eve to Gen iii 15, a passage that describes a struggle between the offspring of Eve and the offspring of the serpent, for "the hour" of Jesus is the hour of the fall of the Prince of this world (John xii 23, 31). The symbolism of the Fourth Gospel has a certain resemblance to that of Rev xii 5, 17 where a woman gives birth to the Messiah in the presence of the Satanic dragon or ancient serpent of Genesis, and yet also has other offspring who are the targets of Satan's wrath after the Messiah has been taken to heaven. It is interesting that the offspring of the woman of Revelation are described as "those who keep the commandments of God"; for in John xiv 21–23 we are told that those who keep the commandments are loved by Father and Son, so that a beloved disciple is one who keeps the commandments.

By way of summary, then, we may say that the Johannine picture of Jesus' mother becoming the mother of the Beloved Disciple seems to evoke the OT themes of Lady Zion's giving birth to a new people in the messianic age, and of Eve and her offspring. This imagery flows over into the imagery of the Church who brings forth children modeled after Jesus, and the relationship of loving care that must bind the children to their mother. We do not wish to press the details of this symbolism or to pretend that it is without obscurity. But there are enough confirmations to give reasonable assurance that we are on the right track. Such a symbolism makes intelligible John's evaluation (xix 28) that this episode at the foot of the cross is the completion of the work that the Father has given Jesus to do, in the context of the fulfillment of Scripture. Certainly the symbolism we have proposed is scriptural (and thus this episode of the crucifixion falls into line with the other episodes that emphasize Scripture so strongly). And since the symbolism is centered on Jesus' provision for the future of those who believe in him, in many ways it does complete his work. He shows to the very end his love for his own (xiii 1), for symbolically he now provides a communal context of mutual love in which they shall live after he is gone. The revelatory formula "Here is . . . ," on which we have commented, is truly appropriate in this scene, since Jesus' mother and the Beloved Disciple are being established in a new relationship representative of that which will bind the Church and the Christian.

By way of appended observations, we note that those scholars who interpret the preceding Johannine episode of the seamless tunic as symbolic of the undivided Church find this theme reinforced in the symbolism of the close relationship between Mary and the Beloved Disciple. We do not find persuasive Bultmann's objection, p. 521[6], that the mother of Jesus cannot represent the Church, for (in the Book of Revelation) the Church is the bride of Jesus. Symbolism is very plastic, especially in different contexts: in Hos ii 18(16) Israel is the wife of Yahweh, while in xi 1 Israel is the son of Yahweh. Loisy, p. 488, has captured an element of truth in comparing the Johannine episode at the foot of the cross to the incident in Mark iii 31–35 where Jesus says that his true mother and his true brothers are those who do the will of God. Mary was denied a role at Cana when she intervened simply as Jesus' physical mother; she is most truly his mother in this "hour" of God's plan when she brings forth Christian children in the image of her son. Less satisfactory is the Synoptic parallel suggested by Barrett, p. 459, namely the fulfillment of the promise that Christians who have left house and mother are to receive them in the age to come (Mark x 29–30).

Episode Four: Jesus' Cry of Thirst; the Executioners Offer Him Wine; He Hands Over the Spirit (xix 28–30)

We may begin with a study of the complicated relationship of this episode to two incidents involving wine found in the Synoptic narrative of the crucifixion.

(1) The Marcan Account A and Matthew, but not Luke, report that a drink was offered to Jesus as soon as he arrived at Golgotha and before he was crucified. Mark xv 23 describes it as wine (*oinos*) with myrrh in it and says that Jesus did not take it. The context suggests that the drink was meant as an anaesthetic to help the condemned to endure the pain of being nailed to the cross (cf. StB, I, 1037, for the custom of giving a narcotic to alleviate suffering). However, neither in fact nor in what we know of ancient pharmacology does myrrh serve as an anodyne or narcotic. Perhaps the myrrh was only a flavoring and the wine itself was thought to numb (see Prov xxxi 6–7). Matt xxvii 34 describes the wine as mixed with gall (*cholē*) and reports that Jesus tasted it before refusing it, thus seeming to imply that Jesus did not know what was being offered to him. Although the different readings "myrrh" and "gall" may have arisen from a confusion (the Hebrew terms are respectively *mōr* and *mārāh;* the Aramaic terms are *mūrâ/mōrâ* and *mārâ*), more likely Matthew chose his description to show the reference to LXX of Ps lxix 22(21):

> For my food they gave me *gall* (*cholē*—something bitter)
> and for my thirst they gave me *vinegar* (*oxos*—sour wine)

The parallelism means that the psalmist is describing the same hostile action under two aspects; but Matthew evidently thinks of two incidents, neither really hostile: in this incident he mentions *cholē*, and in the incident to be described below he mentions *oxos*.

(2) Mark (A Account according to Taylor; B Account according to Bultmann) and Matthew report that a second drink was offered to Jesus on the cross as his death approached. After Jesus had uttered his last words

in Hebrew or Aramaic, one of the bystanders ran and filled a sponge full
of common wine (*oxos*), put it on a reed (*kalamos*), and offered it to
Jesus to drink (Mark xv 36; Matt xxvii 48). We are not told whether in
fact Jesus did drink. Luke mentions only one episode involving wine, an
episode that occurs in the middle of the crucifixion narrative, before Jesus'
last words. Luke xxiii 36 reports: "The soldiers also mocked him, coming
up and offering common wine [*oxos*], and saying, 'If you are the King of
the Jews, save yourself.'" The motive is clearly mockery, a motive that is
not clear in the Marcan/Matthean description where the action could be a
sympathetic gesture (cf. Blinzler, *Trial*, p. 255[37]). Although different agents
are involved (soldiers vs. bystanders—see NOTE on "they" in vs. 29) and
although Luke does not mention a sponge, we are surely dealing with two
Synoptic versions of the same incident.

The Johannine narrative gives us a third version of this second incident. Oddly, Freed, OTQ, p. 105, seems to relate it to the first Synoptic
incident and characterizes it as "one of the clearest examples of the
[Johannine] writer's creative use of his Synoptic sources." Moreover, Freed
thinks that John may have invented the whole scene by being the "first
interpreter of the Synoptics to see in Mk 15:23 and parallels an allusion
to OT Scripture" and by putting this allusion on Jesus' lips. We judge
this thesis doubly improbable. First, such a process of composition should
have produced a clearer Scripture reference than we now find in John (see
our difficulty below in identifying the passage). Second, the theory does not
explain the differences between John's version and those of the Synoptics. In
the NOTES we make a detailed comparison, but here we may summarize.
John agrees with the second incident in Mark/Matthew against the Lucan
version in situating the incident just before Jesus' death, in mentioning the
sponge, and perhaps in not seeing the gesture as mockery. On the other
hand, John agrees with Luke against Mark/Matthew in describing only one
incident involving a drink offered to Jesus, in having soldiers (seemingly)
make the gesture, and in not associating it with a saying about Elijah.
John is alone in mentioning the cry of thirst, the jar, the hyssop, and the
fact that Jesus drank. It really defies imagination to detect a pattern or
motivation in such a selection and addition of details (only the thirst and
the hyssop have discernible symbolism). The variations are more convincingly explicable if we posit a non-Synoptic tradition behind the Fourth
Gospel.

As we turn to the theological import of the episode, we recall Loisy's
observation (p. 489): "We may suppose that Jesus really is thirsty; but he
is thirsty only by his own volition, because of his awareness that there is
a prophecy to be realized." The prefatory statement of this episode in
John is that "[Jesus was] aware that all was now finished," a statement
evocative of xiii 1, the opening line of the Book of Glory: "Jesus was
aware that the hour had come for him to pass from this world to the
Father." Thus Jesus' cry of thirst and the offering of the wine are to be

related to the finishing of the great work of "the hour." They are to be
related to his death which is the final act of the work committed to him
by the Father, as iii 16 makes clear: "God loved the world so much that
He gave [i.e., to death] the only Son." In this context of thought John so
describes Jesus' thirst and the drinking of the wine as to leave the impression that Jesus was not to die until he had done this. The apparent
reason is that in his thirst and the response to it Jesus fulfills the Scripture
that had predicted his death (see NOTE on "in order to" in vs. 28). The
act that finishes (*telein*) his work brings the Scripture to complete fulfillment (*teleioun*), for both his work and the plan of Scripture come from his
Father.

What Scripture is involved? Perhaps it is a question of the total witness
of the OT to the suffering Messiah (as understood by the primitive
Christian community, and not as understood by modern critical standards).
Luke xxiv 25–27 maintains that Scripture had foretold that the Messiah
must die (also Acts xiii 29). Paul has the same idea in I Cor xv 3: "Christ
died for our sins in accordance with the Scriptures." On the other hand, it
is possible that John has in mind a specific text. In this case, Ps lxix
22(21), cited above in relation to the first Marcan/Matthean incident, is
the most likely candidate. (It is worth noting that this passage is also
cited by the Qumran psalmist in 1QH iv 11.) An objection to this identification is that the offering of vinegar or sour wine is, for the psalmist, a
hostile gesture expressive of the hatred of the psalmist's enemies; and this
does not seem to be John's understanding of the soldiers' motive in offering
Jesus common wine. Yet the NT often uses the OT in a non-literal way.
Favorable to this identification is the fact that Psalm lxix is cited twice
elsewhere in the Fourth Gospel: John ii 17 cites vs. 10(9) of the psalm
and John xv 25 cites vs. 5(4). Although John does not become entangled
in Matthew's strange double fulfillment of Ps lxix 22(21—as discussed
above), in its own way the Johannine narrative fulfills the verse exactly; for
only John mentions the thirst as well as the common wine: "For *my thirst*
they gave me *sour wine*."

Another noteworthy candidate for identification as the Scripture passage meant by John is Ps xxii 16(15), a verse from the best known OT
source for the Passion Narrative: "My tongue cleaves to my jaws; you
have brought me down to the dust of death." While here the thirst is
expressed only by the circumlocution of the parched tongue, the thirst is
closely juxtaposed with death, as in John. Hoskyns, p. 531, suggests a
number of other passages from the psalter (Pss xlii 3[2], lxiii 2[1]).
Bampfylde, *art. cit.*, argues that the Scripture in John xix 28 is the one
cited previously in vii 37, namely Zech xiv 8 (in conjunction with Ezek
xlvii), and he relates its fulfillment to Jesus' handing over the Spirit in
John xix 30 (see below).

Is it enough to maintain that Jesus' cry "I am thirsty" fulfills the
Scripture, or does John attribute to the phrase its own symbolism? Loisy,

p. 489, sees in it an expression of Jesus' desire to go to God and to assure the salvation of the world. Others see here an expression of Johannine irony: Jesus who is the source of living water (vii 38) cries out in thirst—he thus signifies that he must die before the living water can be given, and in the next episode water will pour forth from his corpse (xix 34). Perhaps the most plausible symbolism is to connect the episode with xviii 11: "Am I not to drink the cup the Father has given me?" The cup was one of suffering and death; and now having finished his work, Jesus thirsts to drink that cup to the last drop, for only when he has tasted the bitter wine of death will his Father's will be fulfilled.

The mention of hyssop (see NOTE on vs. 29) should probably be explained in terms of theological symbolism. Exod xii 22 specified that hyssop was to be used to sprinkle the blood of the paschal lamb on the doorposts of the Israelite homes. In describing how the death of Jesus ratified a new covenant, Heb ix 18–20 recalls that Moses used hyssop to sprinkle the blood of animals in order to seal the earlier covenant. (We recall that this Epistle's conception of Jesus as priest offered a parallel to the symbolism in John's second episode of the crucifixion.) In discussing John xix 14, we noted that Jesus was sentenced to death at the very hour when the slaughter of the paschal lambs began in the temple precincts, and we shall encounter more paschal lamb symbolism below in Episode 5 of the crucifixion. Thus, in the context of Johannine thought, the mention of hyssop may well be symbolically evocative of Jesus' dying as the paschal lamb of the new covenant. In Egypt the blood of the lamb sprinkled by means of hyssop spared the Israelites from destruction; Jesus dies as "the Lamb of God who takes away the world's sin" (vol. 29, pp. 61–63). Of course, there is a difference between using hyssop to sprinkle blood and using hyssop to support a sponge full of wine, but John shows considerable imagination in the adaptation of symbols. (In a way it is just as imaginative to see a reference to the paschal lamb in the fact that Jesus' bones were not broken, but John xix 36 does not hesitate to make the connection.) It is difficult to apply rigorous logic to symbolism.

The cry "It is finished" (vs. 30), which constitutes Jesus' last words in John, has often been contrasted with the agonized "My God, my God, why have you forsaken me?" which constitutes Jesus' last words in Mark/Matthew. (John is closer in tone, at least, to the last words reported by Luke: "Father, into your hands I commit my Spirit.") Loisy, pp. 489–90, emphasizes that the Johannine Jesus deliberately accepts death because it is the completion of God's plan, and death does not come until he signifies his readiness (see x 17–18). "The death of the Johannine Christ is not a scene of suffering, of ignominy, of universal desolation [as in the Synoptics] —it is the beginning of a great triumph." Thus, for Loisy and others, "It is finished" is a victory cry replacing the cry of apparent defeat in Mark/Matthew. Such an approach, however, demarcates the differences too sharply, not doing justice to the implicit note of agony in the Johannine Jesus' cry of thirst (Spurrell, *art. cit.*, sees this as part of the theme of the suffering Messiah), and perhaps exaggerating the element of defeat in the Synoptic scene. Hoskyns, p. 531, rebuts this approach, albeit a bit romantically, by relating both the Marcan/Matthean cry and the Johannine cry to Ps xxii and by seeing an element of triumph in both. He maintains that if Mark/ Matthew cite the first words of the psalm, John's "It is finished" sums up the meaning of the whole psalm; for at the end of the psalm (vs. 28[27]) we hear that all the ends of the earth turn toward the Lord. In John's theology, now that Jesus has finished his work and is lifted up from the earth on the cross in death, he will draw all men to him (xii 32). If "It is finished" is a victory cry, the victory it heralds is that of obediently fulfilling the Father's will. It is similar to the "It is done" of Rev xvi 17, uttered from the throne of God and of the Lamb when the seventh angel pours out the final bowl of God's wrath. What God has decreed has been accomplished.

The very last words of vs. 30 are so phrased as to suggest another theme in Johannine theology. Although Matthew and Luke also describe Jesus' death in terms of his yielding up his life spirit (see NOTE), John seems to play upon the idea that Jesus handed over the (Holy) Spirit to those at the foot of the cross, in particular, to his mother who symbolizes the Church or new people of God and to the Beloved Disciple who symbolizes the Christian. In vii 39 John affirmed that those who believed in Jesus were to receive the Spirit once Jesus had been glorified, and so it would not be inappropriate that at this climactic moment in the hour of glorification there would be a symbolic reference to the giving of the Spirit. If such an interpretation of "he handed over the spirit" has any plausibility, we would stress that this symbolic reference is evocative and *proleptic*, reminding the reader of the *ultimate* purpose for which Jesus has been lifted up on the cross. In Johannine thought the actual giving of the Spirit does not come now but in xx 22 after the resurrection.

[The Bibliography for this section is included in the Bibliography for the whole of xix 16b–42, at the end of §66.]

66. THE PASSION NARRATIVE:
—DIVISION THREE (EPISODE 5; CONCLUSION)
(xix 31–42)

The Removal and Burial of Jesus' Body

EPISODE 5

XIX 31 Since it was the Day of Preparation, the Jews did not want to have the bodies left on the cross during the Sabbath, for that Sabbath was a solemn feast day. So they asked Pilate to have the legs broken and the bodies taken away. 32 Accordingly, the soldiers came and broke the legs of the men crucified with Jesus, first of one, then of the other. 33 But when they came to Jesus and saw that he was already dead, they did not break his legs. 34 However, one of the soldiers stabbed at Jesus' side with a lance, and immediately blood and water flowed out. (35 This testimony has been given by an eyewitness, and his testimony is true. He is telling what he knows to be true that you too may have faith.) 36 These events took place in order to have the Scripture fulfilled:

"Not a bone is to be broken."

37 And still another Scripture passage says:

"They shall look on him whom they have pierced."

CONCLUSION

38 Afterwards, Joseph of Arimathea, since he was a disciple of Jesus (although a secret one for fear of the Jews), asked Pilate's permission to remove Jesus' body. Pilate granted it, and so he came and took the body away. 39 Nicodemus (the man who had first come to Jesus at night) also came and brought a mixture of myrrh and aloes, weighing about a hundred pounds. 40 So they took Jesus' body; and, in accordance with Jewish burial custom, they bound it up in cloth wrappings with aromatic oils. 41 Now in the place where Jesus had been crucified there was a garden, and in the garden a new tomb in which no one

had ever been buried. 42 And so, because of the Jewish Day of Preparation, they buried Jesus in this nearby tomb.

NOTES

xix 31. *Since it was the Day of Preparation.* Here the term seems primarily to refer to the vigil of the Sabbath (thus ca. 6 P.M. Thursday to ca. 6 P.M. Friday) rather than to the vigil of Passover. This is unlike the occurrence of the term in xix 14 (see NOTE there). Bultmann, p. 524[5], thinks that this verse reflects a tradition where Jesus died on the 15th of Nisan (the Synoptic position—see pp. 555–56 above), so that the next day, a Sabbath, would have been the 16th of Nisan, a particularly solemn day, for in the Pharisaic tradition it was the day for offering sheaves (cf. Lev xxiii 6–14). We can make no decision about a single verse; but we observe that in vs. 36 there is a comparison of Jesus' death to the condition of the paschal lamb, so that plausibly this scene can be held to have occurred on the 14th of Nisan, the day when the lambs were slaughtered. Perhaps the phraseology of the clause under discussion is dependent on Mark xv 42 (which introduces the incident of Joseph's asking for the body): *"Since it was the Day of Preparation,* that is, the day before the Sabbath." Despite the difference of context, this clause constitutes one of the rare verbatim agreements between the Johannine and Marcan narratives of the crucifixion. In the different witnesses to the text of John the clause appears in different places in the verse—sometimes a sign of scribal addition.

the Jews. In vs. 21, immediately after Jesus had been crucified, "the chief priests of the Jews" came to Pilate to protest about the title on the cross; evidently the same group is involved here. Only John has a confrontation between Pilate and the Jewish leaders on this Friday after the morning trial. Matt xxvii 62 has the chief priests and the Pharisees gathering before Pilate *on the next day* in reference to the guarding of the tomb. The *Gospel of Peter* seems to have a confused echo of this episode in John or of some of the elements that went into it. In that account, even before Jesus is crucified, Joseph asks Pilate for the body of the Lord; and Herod acknowledges the propriety of burying Jesus with haste "since the Sabbath is drawing on" (3–5; yet see 27 where this gospel may imply a longer period between the crucifixion and the Sabbath). When "the Jews" crucify Jesus between two malefactors, one of the malefactors speaks on Jesus' behalf, calling him the "savior of men." This angers the Jews who order the legs of this man *not* to be broken so that he may die in torment (10–14); the implication seems to be that the legs of Jesus and the other malefactor would be broken. Then about noon, when darkness comes over the land, they begin to fear that the sun has set while Jesus is still on the cross, so they give Jesus gall with vinegar to drink (15–16). Later, after the Lord has been "taken up" (19), they take the nails from his hands and lay the body on the earth. The sun shines again, and they are happy to find that it is only 3 P.M. They give the body to Joseph for burial (21–23).

did not want to have the bodies left on the cross. The Roman practice was to leave the corpse on the cross as a warning to would-be criminals;

but Philo, *In Flaccum* x;⁂83, mentions that at times, especially at festivals, the bodies were taken down and given to the relatives. The Jewish attitude was governed by Deut xxi 22–23 (Josh viii 29) which ruled that bodies of hanged criminals should not remain overnight on a tree. (The *Gospel of Peter*, 5, cites this law of Deuteronomy.) Josephus, *War* IV.v.2;⁂317, tells us that the Jews had extended the practice of Deuteronomy to cover the crucified whose bodies they took down before sunset. It is interesting that Gal iii 13 also regards the law about the hanged criminal as applicable to Jesus on the cross.

for that Sabbath was a solemn feast day. The 15th of Nisan, the first day of Passover, was a *holy* day (LXX of Exod xii 16), and the fact that in this particular year it fell on a Sabbath would make it even more solemn. However, we have no early Jewish attestation of the word "solemn" (literally "great") being used to designate a Sabbath that is also a feast day (I. Abrahams, *Studies in Pharisaism and the Gospel* [New York: KTAV reprint, 1968], II, 68). The designation "great Sabbath" for a Sabbath in February appears in the 2nd-century *Martyrdom of Polycarp* VIII 1, but perhaps in dependence on John. Barrett, p. 461, suggests that John may have misunderstood the prohibition about leaving the bodies on the cross overnight and have thought that the law applied only because the next day was the Sabbath. It is simpler to interpret John to mean that the imminence of a doubly holy feast day increased the ordinary desire to have the bodies removed before nightfall (when the feast day would begin) and offered a motive that the Romans might respect. The danger of violating the sacrosanct Sabbath ordinance against work may also have been part of the concern.

they asked Pilate. It is not said that they *went* to Pilate, an omission emphasized by those who think that, according to John, Pilate was at Golgotha.

to have the legs broken. Among the canonical Gospels only John mentions this; his expression *katagnynai ta skelē* contrasts with the *skelokopein* of the *Gospel of Peter*, 14, raising the question whether the confused account in the apocryphal gospel has an independent source. The *crurifragium* was done with a heavy mallet; usually only the legs were broken, but occasionally other bones as well. Originally a cruel capital punishment in itself, the *crurifragium*, despite its brutality, was a mercy when it accompanied the crucifixion, for it hastened death. It is noteworthy that in the instance of the recently discovered skeletal remains of a man crucified in Palestine in the 1st century (see first NOTE on xx 20), both his legs were broken. Since the request of "the Jews" applies to the three bodies, apparently they thought that Jesus was still alive; perhaps we are to think that while Jesus was still dying, they left Golgotha to go to Pilate and make the request.

and the bodies taken away. Literally these clauses read: "that their legs be broken and that they be taken away." The grammar is awkward, for syntactically the subject of the second verb is "their legs," although obviously John means the bodies. The verb is *airein*, not the more technical *kathairein*, "to take down," found in Mark xv 46 and Luke xxiii 53. Nowhere does John explicitly describe the taking down of Jesus' body from the cross.

32. *Accordingly.* Pilate's acquiescence is implied.

first of one, then of the other. Why was Jesus passed over and the criminals on either side dealt with first? Perhaps Jesus appeared to be dead, and the soldiers wanted to deal first with the criminals who were obviously alive. Or, more likely, we have a literary arrangement to highlight Jesus.

33. *saw.* Codex Sinaiticus, the Coptic and OL versions have "found," and SB accepts this reading.

already dead. Ēdē tethnēkota—the position of ēdē varies in the textual witnesses. In the Marcan account (xv 44) of Joseph's request for the body of Jesus, Pilate wonders if Jesus has already died (*palai apethanen*) and summons the centurion who assures him that Jesus is dead. Among the Synoptics only Mark has a soldier verify the death of Jesus (Marcan A account according to Taylor; B addition according to Bultmann). Often a crucified person hung on the cross for several days before death came.

34. This verse appears at the end of Matt xxvii 49 in Sinaiticus, Vaticanus, and some important versional witnesses, probably copied from John by an early scribe in the Alexandrian textual tradition (see Bernard, II, 644). Curiously this localization of the verse in Matthew means that the lance thrust comes before Jesus' death, at the same time that the bystander puts the sponge on a spear to offer wine to Jesus! It is either a *coup de grâce* or a final act of hostility.

one of the soldiers. The name Longinus has been given to him because of the *logchē* (Latin *lancea,* "lance, long slender spear") that he used. Already in various mss. of the *Acts of Pilate* (copies made in the 5th and 6th centuries) John's lancer is identified with the centurion of the Synoptic tradition who proclaimed Jesus as innocent (Luke xxiii 47) and as Son of God (Mark xv 39). Michaels, *art. cit.,* takes this identification seriously.

stabbed at. The verb *nyssein* has the connotation of pricking or prodding, sometimes lightly (so as to waken a sleeping man), sometimes deeply (so as to inflict a mortal wound). The common English translation "pierce" more accurately represents the verb *ekkentein* of vs 37. The sequence of the narrative suggests that the soldier gave an exploratory jab to see if the apparently dead body would react and thus be still alive; there is no intelligible reason why he should want to inflict a wound if he was positive Jesus was dead. The Vulgate and the Peshitta have "opened" instead of "stabbed at," probably reflecting a misreading of the Greek (*ēnoixen* for *enyxen*); this translation facilitated an interpretation whereby Baptism and the Eucharist, and even the Church are seen as coming forth from Jesus' pierced side. Augustine, *In Jo.* cxx 2; PL 35:1953, comments: "He did not say 'pierced through,' or 'wounded,' or something else, but 'opened,' in order that the gate of life might be stretched wide whence the sacraments of the Church flow."

Jesus' side. The Ethiopic specifies that it was the right side, a specification that appears also in the apocryphal works (*Acts of Pilate*) and has guided artistic reproduction of the scene. Lagrange, p. 499, thinks of a deep wound aimed as a mortal blow at the heart, but this understanding of the lance thrust would favor locating the wound on the left side, nearer the heart. The word for side, *pleura,* used in the singular here, is more normal in the plural. Some, including Feuillet, "Le Nouveau," p. 328[33], have suggested that John is recalling the use (singular) in Gen ii 21–22 where God takes a *pleura* from Adam and forms it into a woman.

immediately. The position in which this word is found varies in the textual witnesses.

blood and water. The order "water and blood," as in I John v 6, 8, appears in a few textual witnesses (mostly versional or Patristic; only one Greek ms.), as well as in the addition to Matt xxvii 49 mentioned above. Boismard, RB 60 (1953), 348–50, argues that it may have been original, having later been conformed by scribes to the more customary order "blood and water."

35. Although some Latin witnesses omit the verse, there is no serious question about its genuineness, despite the implication in BDF, §291[6]. The verse is parenthetical, probably editorial, but completely Johannine.

eyewitness. There can be little doubt that in the writer's mind this witness was the Beloved Disciple mentioned in vss. 26–27. In xxi 24, which may be a clarification of this verse, the Beloved Disciple is identified as an eyewitness whose testimony is true. Michaels, p. 103[8], argues that the similarity between xix 35 and xxi 24 is not conclusive, because the Johannine literature speaks of other true witnesses beside the Beloved Disciple, for example, the writer of III John 12 says, "You know that our witness is true." However, in a question such as this we must argue from within the Gospel. The Beloved Disciple is the only male follower of Jesus mentioned as present at the foot of the cross; he is a true eyewitness on whom the writer depends (xxi 24). Are we to think that at the foot of the cross there was another disciple, otherwise unmentioned, who was also a true witness on whom the Johannine writer depends in a special way?

his testimony is true. He is telling what he knows to be true. The "his" is *autou*, whereas the "he" that begins the next sentence is *ekeinos,* "that one" (literally "That one knows that he tells the truth"). Grammatically, many have found it odd that *ekeinos* would refer to the eyewitness about whom the writer has already been talking; for instance, Bultmann, p. 526, says that *ekeinos* must refer to someone other than the eyewitness. Among the possible suggestions are: **(a)** *ekeinos* is the Johannine writer (whether the evangelist or the redactor): "The writer knows that the eyewitness is telling the truth." This translation is favored by many who wish to distinguish between the Johannine writer and the Beloved Disciple. We have instances in Greek where a writer refers to himself as *ekeinos,* for example, Josephus *War* III.vii.16;⁂202: "All this they did, I cannot help thinking, not because they begrudged him [*ekeinos*=Josephus] a chance of safety, but because they thought of their own interests." (For Hebrew examples in a similar vein, see Schlatter, p. 353.) Of course, in most of these instances the context helps to clarify the peculiar meaning of *ekeinos*—something that is not true in John. A variant of this theory is Torrey's contention that *ekeinos* reflects Aram. *hāhū gabrâ,* "that man, a certain man," which serves as a circumlocution for "I." An important objection against the interpretation of *ekeinos* as a reference to the writer is that in xxi 24 one can see how a Johannine writer actually wrote of himself as distinct from the eyewitness—he did not use "that one" (*ekeinos*) but "we": "It is he [the Beloved Disciple] who wrote these things; and his testimony, *we* know, is true." **(b)** *ekeinos* is Jesus Christ: "Jesus knows that the eyewitness is telling the truth." Erasmus, Sanday, Abbott, Lagrange, Strachan, Hoskyns, and Braun are among those who follow this interpretation (see E. Nestle, ET 24 [1912–13], 92). The use of *ekeinos* for Jesus is well attested in John (iii 28, 30, vii 11, ix 28), but usually in a context where the reference is clear. **(c)** *ekeinos* is God: "God knows that the eyewitness is telling the truth. The use of *ekeinos* for God is also well attested in John (v 19, vi 29, viii 42), but again in instances clarified by context.

Probably the best explanation is that, despite objections, *ekeinos* refers to the eyewitness. (To facilitate this, some have tried to recast the sentence, e.g., Nonnus of Panopolis [mid-5th century], followed by Bultmann, p. 526: "We know him [*ekeinon* instead of *ekeinos*], that he tells the truth"; but such recasting is not necessary.) Both BDF, §291⁶, and MTGS, p. 46, acknowledge the anaphorical use of *ekeinos*, meaning simply "he." We would add that if *ekeinos* is the eyewitness and consequently the Johannine writer is speaking of the eyewitness/Beloved Disciple in the third person, this does not necessarily mean that the writer and the Beloved Disciple are *not* the same person, although that they are not is certainly implied in xxi 24. In vol. 29, pp. XCVIII–CI we have defended the thesis that in fact they are not the same, and that the Beloved Disciple is the source of the tradition that came down to the Johannine writer(s).

that you too may have faith. The final clause probably modifies the whole idea in the verse rather than simply the nearest verb—the eyewitness is not only *telling the truth* that you may have faith; more important he is giving testimony of what he has seen that you may have faith. The "too," omitted in the Byzantine textual tradition, means that the eyewitness himself is a believer and wishes by his testimony to ensure that the readers of the Gospel are also believers. Although the aorist subjunctive of the verb "to have faith" appears in some witnesses, the present subjunctive has the best attestation (see also xx 31); this tense implies a continuation and deepening of faith rather than a conversion. The immediate object of the faith involves the death of Jesus on the cross and its effects—a truth in which is subsumed the whole revelation of Jesus. The readers are asked to have faith not only in what the eyewitness saw, but also in its theological implications (see COMMENT).

36. *These events.* Logically, this refers to two incidents: that Jesus' legs were not broken (vs. 33), and that his side was jabbed by a lance (vs. 34). The Scripture citation in 36 refers to the former; the citation in 37 to the latter.

"Not a bone is to be broken." Literally "Its [or his] bone shall not be broken"; in order to preserve the ambiguity of the Greek, we have used neither possessive. There are several candidates for identification as the Scripture passage that John has in mind, candidates that are not mutually exclusive: **(a)** one of the descriptions of the paschal lamb: "A bone of it shall not be broken" (LXX, Codex Vaticanus, of Exod xii 10); "You shall not break a bone of it" (Exod xii 46); "They shall not break a bone of it" (Num ix 12). John is closest to the first form of this Passover provision (Freed, OTQ, p. 113). Of the various Scripture passages directly cited in the Johannine Passion Account, this would be the only one taken from the Pentateuch. **(b)** Ps xxxiv 21(20): "He [the Lord] watches over all his bones [i.e., the just man's]; not one of them will be broken." Here the passive verb is close to John's wording, but "the bones" (note plural) are not directly the subject of the verb "to break." While psalm citations are common in the Passion Accounts, this psalm is not elsewhere cited in relation to the passion (cf. I Pet ii 3, iii 10–12). B. Weiss, Torrey, and Dodd are among those who have argued for the psalm as the more plausible source of John's citation. Bultmann,

p. 524[8], thinks that in John's source the citation was from the psalm, but the evangelist saw in it a reference to Exod xii 46. Barton, *art. cit.*, cites some Egyptian parallels for the prohibition against breaking the bones of a corpse.

37. *And still another Scripture passage says.* Schlatter, p. 355, points out that this is a fixed rabbinic formula for introducing another citation.

"They shall look on him whom they have pierced." John's citation of Zech xii 10 does not follow verbatim either the MT or the most common LXX reading. The MT is: "They shall look upon me whom they have pierced." In the context the "me" is Yahweh; the implication is strange and the text may well be corrupt, perhaps accounting for early translators' attempts to improve. Since all the following sentences refer to "him," both scribes (forty-five of the Hebrew mss. collated by Kennicott and De Rossi) and commentators have read "him" for "me." Codex Vaticanus and most other LXX witnesses read: "They shall look upon me because they have danced insultingly [=mocked]," reflecting a verbal form from the Hebrew root *dqr*, "to pierce," misread as a form from *rqd*, "to skip about." Yet there is a Greek reading in the 5th- or 6th-century Vienna Codex (L) that is much closer to a literal rendering of the MT. Almost certainly the Vienna reading stems from an early (proto-Theodotionic) recension, conforming the LXX to what was then (1st century A.D.) becoming the standard Hebrew text. We can be reasonably certain that John's citation stems from such an early Greek recension, perhaps in the short form, "They shall look upon whom they have pierced." (Actually there is no "him" in John's text, but it is required by sense; compare the citation of Zechariah in Rev i 7: "Every eye will see him, everyone who pierced him.") See S. Jellicoe, *The Septuagint and Modern Study* (Oxford, 1968), p. 87.

38. *Afterwards.* This connective (*meta tauta*) is so vague that Bernard, II, 653, prefers the explanation that Joseph's petition to Pilate was presented at the same time as the petition of "the Jews." The more obvious interpretation is that one episode followed the other. We are probably dealing with an editorial link between two independent items of tradition (see COMMENT).

Joseph of Arimathea. He is mentioned in all four Gospels in connection with the burial of Jesus, but nowhere else in the NT. There is every reason to think that the reminiscence of his role in the burial is historical, since there was no reason for inventing him. (Without information to the contrary, it would have been natural to have assumed that Jesus' relatives buried him, especially since, according to John, his mother was present.) Arimathea, which Luke xxiii 50 calls "a town of the Jews," was his birthplace or former residence; but his role in the Sanhedrin and the information that he owned a tomb just outside Jerusalem (Matthew) suggest that he was now a resident of the Holy City. Arimathea has been thought to be Ramathaim-zophim of I Sam i 1. Eusebius fixes the site at Remphthis or Rentis, nine miles northeast of Lydda (I Macc xi 34 associates Ramathaim and Lydda as districts); but W. F. Albright, AASOR 4 (1922–23), 112–23, objects that this site is too far from Shiloh, the destination of Samuel's family in the narrative of I Samuel. He proposes identification with Ramallah. Another suggestion is Beit Rimeh, five miles east of Rentis and twelve miles northwest of Bethel. None of these locations is in Galilee, so that Joseph would have been one of the Judean disciples of Jesus (John vii 1; see NOTE on "Judas" in vi 71).

a disciple of Jesus. A similar designation of Joseph, but in different Greek, is found in Matt xxvii 57, while Mark xv 43 and Luke xxiii 51 describe him as expecting the kingdom of God. The additional information about Joseph's background supplied by the Synoptics is of interest: (a) he is a rich man, according to Matt xxvii 57; (b) he is a respected member of the council (Sanhedrin), according to Mark xv 43 and Luke xxiii 50; (c) he is a good and holy man who did not consent to what was being done to Jesus, according to Luke xxiii 50–51. John has none of this information, although he does associate Joseph with Nicodemus who was a member of the Sanhedrin, perhaps in implicit agreement with (b). The *Gospel of Peter,* 3, has Joseph come to Pilate before the crucifixion to ask for Jesus' body and identifies Joseph as a friend of Pilate; but this is almost certainly a deduction from the tradition that Pilate granted Joseph's request. The fact that John does not identify Joseph as a rich man, as in (a), militates against Loisy's suggestion, p. 497, that the burial may be another allusion to the theme of the Suffering Servant (Isa liii 9: "They made his grave . . . with a rich man").

a secret one. Clandestine disciples were judged harshly and with contempt in xii 42, but evidently Joseph's coming forward to ask for Jesus' body has won the Johannine writer's esteem. (Mark xv 43 specifies that this was a daring act.) Or else, more simply, John mentions the detail only to explain why Pilate granted the request: the Roman prefect would scarcely have granted favors to an acknowledged follower of a man executed as a revolutionary.

asked Pilate's permission to remove Jesus' body. The Synoptic Gospels (Mark xv 43 and par.) describe Joseph as *going* to Pilate to ask for the body of Jesus. Once again (see NOTE on "they asked Pilate" in vs. 31) John's omission of a verb of motion has been cited to prove that John pictures Pilate as present on Golgotha. We note the different vocabulary of John and of the Synoptics: the verb "to ask" in the Synoptics is *aitein,* while both here and in vs. 31 above John uses *erōtan.*

Pilate granted it. Again there is a difference of vocabulary: Mark uses *dōrein,* "to give"; Matthew has "he ordered it to be given" [*apodidonai*]; John uses *epitrepein.* John is closest to Matthew in the sequence of asking and granting, for Mark xv 44–45 interrupts this sequence by a description of Pilate's attempt to find out if Jesus was really dead (an apologetic theme, seemingly). Luke does not give any response on Pilate's part.

so he came and took the body away. Neither of these verbs (*erchesthai, airein*) is used in the parallel Synoptic accounts; Mark and Luke refer to Joseph's "taking it down" (*kathairein*); Matthew to his "taking [*lambanein*] the body" (see vs. 40a below for a Johannine parallel to Matthew). In the text of John plural verbs ("they came"; "they took away") are read by Sinaiticus, Tatian, and some OL, Sahidic, Syriac, and Armenian witnesses. On the grounds of preferring the more difficult reading, one may favor the plural as original, as do SB and Bultmann. However, there are several possible explanations of how a plural could have been introduced into the text: for example, a contamination from the plural verb used in vs. 40; or a reflection of vs. 31 where the soldiers are to take away the body. If the plural is accepted, who would the "they" be? Perhaps Joseph and Nicodemus—the latter is first mentioned in the following verse. Perhaps there is an echo of the tradition in Mark xv 47 and par. that the Galilean women were present at the burial.

Perhaps there is an implicit indication that Joseph did not undertake the task singlehandedly but called on servants or friends. Gaechter, "Begräbnis," p. 222, argues that Joseph and Nicodemus had to use slaves; for if they handled the body themselves, they would have been ritually impure for seven days (Num xix 11) and thus unable to celebrate the Passover feast (cf. John xviii 28)—a difficulty John does not envisage. "The body" is literally "his body"; some textual witnesses have "Jesus' body," probably in imitation of the occurrence of this phrase earlier in the verse; other witnesses simply have "it."

39. *Nicodemus.* He is mentioned only in John (iii 1, vii 50). There is no apparent reason why John should have invented a role for him here, unless the tradition preserved the memory that a Sanhedrin member was involved and the only Sanhedrin member favorable to Jesus known to the writer was Nicodemus. It has been suggested that, since Nicodemus was a Pharisee, his presence would guarantee the correctness of the burial ritual.

(*the man who had first come to Jesus at night*). An identifying reminder is typical Johannine style. Such a reminder is supplied most frequently for those figures who are peculiar to the Johannine tradition or who have a special role in that tradition, e.g., Mary of Bethany (xi 2), Lazarus (xii 1), Philip (xii 21), Nathanael (xxi 2), the Beloved Disciple (xxi 20)—an exception would be Judas Iscariot (xii 4). In general, these reminders are more common in passages that we have regarded as inserted during later stages of Gospel editing or redaction (xi–xii, xxi). The previous reminder about Nicodemus in vii 50 was simply: "the man who had come to Jesus."

came and brought. Literally "came bringing"; a few witnesses, including Sinaiticus*, have "came having." Does John want us to think that Nicodemus bought this mixture on short notice or that he already had such an immense amount? Bernard, II, 654, favors the former, while Lagrange, p. 503, thinks that Joseph and Nicodemus divided the tasks: one went to Pilate, while the other went shopping for burial materials. Gaechter, "Begräbnis," pp. 221–22, proposes that the purchases were made while Jesus was on the cross—Joseph bought the cloth wrappings, while Nicodemus bought the spices. However, the problem should probably be dealt with by considering vs. 39 a different tradition that has been added here.

a mixture. We read *migma* with the majority of mss., although several important witnesses, including Vaticanus and Sinaiticus*, read *heligma*, "packet, roll." The latter is the more difficult reading and might well be favored if it were really meaningful. Bernard, II, 653, offers an explanation of how confusion could have occurred in copying an original *smigma*, a reading found in two cursive mss.

of myrrh and aloes. Smyrna or "myrrh" is a fragrant resin used by the Egyptians in embalming (see vol. 29, p. 448); *aloē* is a powdered aromatic sandalwood used for perfuming bedding or clothes, but not normally for burial. (For this reason some think John meant the bitter aloe plant used by the Egyptians for embalming.) The purpose of the aloes was probably to counteract unpleasant odor and slow down corruption. (We find somewhat far-fetched Hoskyns' suggestion, p. 536, that this spice has the symbolism of making Jesus' sacrifice a sweet-smelling odor.) The combination of myrrh and aloes appears in the Song of Sol iv 14. None of the Synoptic Gospels mentions that embalming spices were put into the tomb on Friday; and while Mark and Luke (but not Matthew) mentions spices in another context, the vocabulary is not the same. Mark xvi 1 says that on Easter morning the women brought aromatic oils (*arōma*) to anoint Jesus. Luke xxiii 56 says that Friday *after* the burial the women prepared aromatic oils (*arōma*) and perfumes (*myron*); and Luke xxiv 1 says that on Easter morning the women came bearing the aromatic oils they had prepared. The *Gospel of Peter*, 24, says that Joseph washed the body before burial.

about a hundred pounds. The Roman pound was about twelve ounces, so that this would be the equivalent of about seventy-five of our pounds; but the amount is still extraordinary. Without textual evidence, Lagrange, p. 503, raises the possibility of scribal error. Barrett, p. 465, recalls the immense amount of wine at Cana (ii 6); and Dodd, *Tradition,* p. 139[2], points to the 153 fish in xxi 11. This Johannine penchant for extravagant numbers is explained in the other instances in terms of symbolism, and that may be true here as well (see COMMENT).

40. *They took Jesus' body.* This seems to duplicate the end of vs. 38, even though the verbs are different (*lambanein* is used here, as in Matt xxvii 59).

in accordance with Jewish burial custom. Literally "custom for burying." It is true that the verb *entaphiazein* means "to prepare for burial," but the author scarcely means that they were preparing now for a burial three days later, as those contend who think that John describes only a provisionary burial and that the women were coming on Sunday to complete what had been begun. In burying, the Jews did not eviscerate the cadaver, as did the Egyptians in mummification. Rather the Jews simply washed the body, anointed it with oil, and clothed it. II Chron xvi 14 describes the burial of King Asa: "They laid him on a bed which had been filled with all kinds of aromatic oils and perfumes." See also John xi 44 where we read of the hands and feet being bound with linen strips, and the face wrapped in cloths.

they bound it up. John uses *dein;* Mark xv 46 uses *eneilein* ("wrap or tie up"); Matt xxvii 59 and Luke xxiii 53 uses *entylissein* ("roll up, swaddle"). The latter verb appears in John xx 7 (see NOTE there) to describe the cloth that had been wound around Jesus' head. The *Gospel of Peter*, 24, says that Joseph wrapped (*eilein*) the body of Jesus.

in cloth wrappings. If we leave aside Luke xxiv 12 (a verse about which there is some textual doubt; see pp. 1000–1 below), only John uses *othonion* (in the plural) in describing the burial dress of Jesus. *Othonion* is frequently said to be a diminutive of *othonē*, "linen cloth, sheet"; and the use of the plural is thought to indicate that strips of cloth or bandages were involved (BAG, p. 558, col. 1). This understanding, however, creates a twofold problem. First, it does not harmonize with the Synoptic description (and that of the *Gospel of Peter*) where Jesus is said to have been wrapped in a *sindōn* that Joseph had bought. A *sindōn* is a large piece of linen; in Mark xiv 51 the youth who runs away in the garden is wearing a *sindōn* as his entire clothing. Second, the interpretation of *othonia* as linen strips presents a difficulty to many Roman Catholic scholars who accept the authenticity of the Holy Shroud of Turin as the burial dress of Jesus. The shroud is about fourteen feet in length and less than four feet wide. Stains on the cloth possess the quality of a photographic negative; and when photographed, they yield a positive image of a human form. A medical analysis has led some to conclude that for a few days only the Shroud was folded lengthwise over a body that had been buried with aloes—a body that had been scourged, crowned with thorns, pierced with nails as in crucifixion, and had the heart opened after death. The lineage of the Shroud can be traced back to 1353 and the church of Lirey in Troyes, France, but we hear of a similar shroud a century earlier in Constantinople. Because the Shroud made its appearance in recorded history at a time when the crusades had flooded Europe with fraudulent relics from the East, it is *a priori* suspect, especially since Pope (or Antipope) Clement VII allowed it to be exposed to the public in 1389 only on the condition that one clearly state that it was *not* the real shroud of Christ. (For a readable account, see John Walsh, *The Shroud* [New York: Doubleday Echo, 1965]; for the objections of modern biblical criticism, see J. Michl, *Theologische Quartalschrift* 136 [1956], 129–73, especially 142 ff.— like Braun, Blinzler, Gaechter, and other contemporary Catholic exegetes, Michl rejects the authenticity of the Shroud; for a discussion of the Shroud in the light of the Johannine evidence, see F.-M. Braun, NRT 66 [1939], 900–35, 1025–46.)

A very careful lexicographical study of the meaning of *othonion* has been done by A. Vaccari, *"Edēsan auto othoniois* (Joh. 19, 40)," in *Miscellanea biblica B. Ubach* (Montserrat, 1953), pp. 375–86, as well as by C. Lavergne in *Sindon* 3, nos. 5/6 (1961), 1–58. The result is that, even though we feel no compulsion to harmonize John with the Synoptics and have not the least interest in defending the Shroud of Turin, we cannot jump to the conclusion that John meant "bandages." Frequently, in koine Greek, diminutive forms do not have a truly diminutive force (BDF, §111³); and it is even questionable that *othonion* is a diminutive, for *othonē* may designate the material and *othonion* may denote an article made of that material. The plural may be a plural of category designating no more than one object, or a plural of extension indicating the size of a piece (see BDF, §141). The translation of *othonia* as "linen strips" or "bandages" is relatively modern (ca. 1879 on); previously the word was understood generically as "linen cloths." There is really no ancient papyrus support for understanding the term to refer to strips of cloth, and there is no evidence that the Jews wrapped their corpses with bands or strips similar to those used for Egyptian mummies. Some common Talmudic terms for burial clothes are *sādīn* ("linen sheet") and *takrīkīm* (plural, "shroud"). There is a 4th-century A.D. papyrus in the Rylands collection (vol. IV, n. 627) where *othonion* seems to be a general classification under which *sindōn* is a species. Granted the obscurity of the term, we had best translate it vaguely as "cloth wrappings."

with aromatic oils. Here John uses *arōma*, a word found in the Marcan and Lucan narratives of the attempt of the women to anoint Jesus (NOTE on vs. 39 above). The word can mean "spices," in which case it is probably another way of describing the previously mentioned myrrh and aloes. However, it was customary for the Jews to use oil, so that a third element in burial preparation may be being introduced.

How does John envisage the use of the spices and the oil? Were they used separately, for instance, the myrrh and aloes sprinkled among the wrappings, while the oil was rubbed on the body or poured over the already wrapped corpse? Or were they combined, so that the powdered myrrh and aloes were mixed into neutral vegetable oil to create a liquid ointment? The latter agrees better with the insistence on anointing in the Jewish burial procedures.

41. *in the place where Jesus had been crucified.* Only John specifies that the tomb was so near Golgotha. In the Church of the Holy Sepulcher (see NOTE on "he went out" in vs. 17), the site of the tomb is only about 125 feet from Calvary. It would have been an obvious convenience to maintain a burial place near the site of execution (Mishnah *Sanhedrin* 6:5 specifies that there be two burial places for different types of executed criminals), and not too difficult if caves in a quarry were used for tombs. However, the Gospels make it clear that Jesus was not buried in a common tomb; and, of course, we are not certain that Golgotha was an habitual place for execution. In the nearness of the tomb, Loisy, p. 498, sees another possible echo of the paschal lamb motif, for Exod xii 46 stresses that the lamb must be eaten on the spot and none of the flesh carried away—this is very tenuous.

there was a garden. This term (*kēpos*) was used in xviii 1 for the orchard (olive grove?) where Jesus was arrested; and here as there some would see a symbolic play on the Garden of Eden, even though Gen ii 15 uses *paradeisos*, not *kēpos*. The Synoptic Gospels do not designate the place of burial as a "garden"; but this description is found in the *Gospel of Peter*, 24, where we are told that Joseph brought the body "into his own tomb, called 'the garden of Joseph' "—one of the few instances where this apocryphal gospel agrees with information found only in John. We are not certain what type of garden John envisages, for later Jewish law discouraged the planting of fruit trees near a site of burial. The mention of the garden here must be related to Mary Magdalene's mistaking Jesus as the gardener in xx 15, and it is interesting that in 2nd-century Jewish apologetic against the resurrection this gardener is supposed to be a cabbage farmer (see NOTE there).

The information that the tomb was near Golgotha and in a garden agrees with the speculation that the place of execution was just (perhaps 100–125 yards) outside the Second North Wall of the city (NOTE on xix 17, "he went out"); for one of the four gates in the North Wall was the Garden Gate ("Gennath": Josephus *War* V.IV.2; ※ 147). The tombs of the Hasmonean high priests John Hyrcanus and Alexander Jannaeus were in this northern area (*War* V.VI.2 and VII.3; ※ ※ 259, 304), so that it may have been a prestigious place for burial. Cyril of Jerusalem (ca. A.D. 350) reports in *Catechesis* XIV 5; PG 33:829B that in his time the remains of a garden were still visible adjacent to the Church of the Holy Sepulcher that Constantine had recently built over the traditional site of Jesus' tomb.

a new tomb in which no one had ever been buried. The verb is *tithenai*, "to put, lay." For "tomb" John uses *mnēmeion*, employed by the three Synoptic Gospels as well (Mark and Luke also speak of a *mnēma*). Mark makes no reference to the hitherto pristine character of the tomb; Matt xxvii 60 calls it "a new tomb"; Luke xxiii 53 refers to it as a tomb "where no one had yet been placed [*keimai*]." The three Synoptics supply the additional information that the tomb was hewn out of the rock. Only Matthew, followed by the *Gospel of Peter*, draws the inference that it was Joseph's own tomb.

42. *Jewish.* Omitted by the OL and some Syriac witnesses.

Day of Preparation. Here it is not clear whether the term refers primarily to the day before the Sabbath or to the day before Passover (NOTE on vs. 31 above). Tatian and some Syriac witnesses clarify the situation by reading: "because Saturday had begun." Burial on the Sabbath would not have been permitted, although the body could have been washed and anointed (Mishnah

Sabbath 23:4–5). Mark xv 42 mentions the Day of Preparation at the beginning of the burial narrative; Luke xxiii 54 makes reference to it at about the same point in the narrative where John's reference is found.

COMMENT

Episode Five: Pilate and the Breaking of Jesus' Legs; Flow of Blood and Water (xix 31–37)

As we have pointed out, this last episode in the crucifixion narrative corresponds to the first. In both "the Jews" make a request of Pilate concerning Jesus on the cross; whereas Pilate refused their first request to change the title, Pilate tacitly grants this request to have the bodies taken away. Despite the fact that the episode begins with this request, the episode does not concern itself with the taking away of the body, but rather with the soldier's observation that it was not necessary to break Jesus' legs because he was already dead and with the soldier's probing lance thrust that brought forth blood and water.

This is the only part of the crucifixion narrative that apparently has no parallel, even partial, in the Synoptic Gospels. Nevertheless, some commentators do detect an equivalence; for in describing the interlude between Jesus' death and the time that his body was taken down from the cross for burial, all the Gospels narrate incidents illustrating a faith that has its origins in Jesus' death. In the Synoptic tradition (Mark xv 38–39 and par.) the setting is clearly miraculous: the temple curtain is torn from top to bottom (Mark/Matthew; cf. Luke xxiii 45); there is an earthquake that opens tombs and releases the bodies of the saints (Matthew only). The expression of faith comes from a Roman centurion (and from "those who were with him": Matt xxvii 54) who proclaims that Jesus was a Son of God (Mark/Matthew) or that he was innocent (Luke). As a result the multitudes are repentant as they leave Golgotha (Luke). The Johannine episode is quite different. Bultmann, pp. 516, 523, characterizes it as relatively late, in part because it is so centered on the fulfillment of Scripture. Yet the element of the obviously miraculous is absent (although some deem the flow of blood and water miraculous, as we shall see); and there is no implausible confession of faith by Roman soldiers. The soldiers have the more logical task of finishing the execution by hastening the death of the criminals through *crurifragium*, an attested practice. The faith that is strengthened by or born of the Johannine episode is the faith of the Beloved Disciple (NOTE on "eyewitness" in 35) and of John's readers who accept the Disciple's testimony.

The idea that John replaced the Synoptic episode with a dramatization that better suited his theological purpose is not only beyond proof but implausible, for such features as the rending of the temple curtain at

Jesus' death and a confession of faith by a Roman would have been quite at home in Johannine theology. A more nuanced thesis is that of Michaels, *art. cit.*, who thinks that Mark and John are offering different interpretations of the one set of historical events that gave rise to both traditions. He thinks that John's lancer is the same as the Marcan centurion (NOTE on "one of the soldiers" in 34); and by combining John xix 35 and i 34, Michaels relates the true testimony of the eyewitness to a confession that Jesus is the Son of God. Since Jesus' body is the Temple for John (ii 21), a figurative interpretation of the Marcan rending of the temple curtain can be related to the opening of Jesus' side. Such relationships, however, are highly speculative, and more likely the product of the interpreter's ingenuity than of the evangelist's plan. The Synoptic and Johannine episodes that follow the death of Jesus have a certain similarity of theological function; but there is no real evidence that one has been substituted for the other, or that they are two refractions of the one happening.

The Johannine narrative presents the following problems: the question of editorial additions in vss. 34–35; the historicity and meaning of the flow of blood and water; the reason for appealing to testimony in vs. 35; and the theological intent of the writer in citing two passages of Scripture in vss. 36–37.

Let us begin with the question of *editorial additions.* Bultmann thinks that, in general, 31–37 came to the evangelist shaped by a community tradition, for there are no peculiarly Johannine theological themes and the dominating motive is the fulfillment of Scripture. (On the contrary, we shall treat the episode as one dominated by Johannine theological themes!) He proposes that 34b ("and immediately blood and water flowed out") and 35 are a contribution of the Ecclesiastical Redactor. (Wellhausen and Loisy treat also 34a and 37 as redactional.) Bultmann points out that the theme of the flow of blood and water is not taken up in the Scripture citations of 36–37, for those citations relate to the themes of 33 (the breaking of the legs) and 34a (the lance thrust)—thus at one time 36–37 followed 33–34a immediately. The addition of 34b is attributed to the Ecclesiastical Redactor rather than to a reediting by the evangelist because the blood and water is a reference to the sacraments of the Eucharist and Baptism; and the evangelist was not interested in sacramentalism. The addition of vs. 35 is attributed to the Ecclesiastical Redactor because it resembles xxi 24, and the latter is part of a chapter added by the redactor. In vol. 29, pp. XXX–XXXI, we indicated our uneasiness about Bultmann's understanding of redaction; in our opinion, nowhere is his theory more open to question than here. Obviously vs. 35 is a parenthetical addition. However, as Smith, p. 233, points out, xxi 24 is clearer than xix 35, so that in xxi 24 we may well have an improvement by the redactor on a remark made by the evangelist in xix 35. Bultmann's analysis of 34b is even more problematical. If the mention of blood and water has sacramental reference, in our judgment this is no infallible indicator that the redactor has been at work, for we see a secondary strain of sacramentalism in the work of the evangelist (vol. 29, pp. cxii–cxiv). And in regard to 34b, as we shall see below, any sacramental reference is secondary to a theological symbolism that is in perfect harmony with Johannine thought. Moreover, we think that the scriptural citation in 37 is a reference to the whole of 34 (p. 955 below), and so 34b is an integral part of the episode.

This leads us to our second problem: *the historicity and meaning of the flow of blood and water.* We have no confirmation for this detail from the Synoptic tradition; even Luke xxiv 39, which mentions wounds in Jesus' hands and feet, is silent about a wound in the side. Nevertheless, there is nothing intrinsically improbable in either the *crurifragium* or in the probing of an apparent corpse to see if death has really come, especially if the death is premature. The surprising detail is the insistence that blood and water flowed from the dead body of Jesus. It is common knowledge that dead bodies do not bleed since the heart is no longer pumping blood through the system. Capitalizing on this, Hultkvist, *op. cit.,* has sought to show that Jesus was not dead but only in a coma resulting from severe hemorrhage. (He goes on to theorize that Jesus revived in the tomb, but that his body was still sore from the wound two days later— that is why [xx 17] he told Mary Magdalene not to touch him!) Most physicians who have studied the question (see the discussions of Barbet and Sava) do not find the bleeding so great a difficulty, for a flow of pent-up blood through a wound received *shortly* after death is not unheard of, especially from a corpse that is in a vertical position. The real difficulty centers on the flow of water from the corpse. Even if we accept the common suggestion that "water" is the writer's popular description of a colorless or nearly colorless bodily fluid, for example, serum, it is hard to conceive why the blood and this fluid were so sharply separated.

We may begin with explanations that assume John to be describing something that really happened, whether naturally or miraculously. Doctors have offered several theories explaining the flow of blood and "water" as a natural phenomenon. In 1847 J. C. Stroud, M.D., published *The Physical Cause of the Death of Christ* (rev. ed., 1871), proposing what has become the classical thesis of a violent rupture of Jesus' heart—a convenient thesis that gives preachers the opportunity to stress that literally the Lord died of a broken heart. Stroud theorized that after a hemorrhage had taken place through the heart wall into the pericardial sac, there was a clotting of blood, separating it from serum. The lance thrust opened the pericardial sac, releasing the two substances. The theory is held by few today; it runs afoul of the subsequently gained experience that such cardiac ruptures do not occur spontaneously or under the pressure of mental agony, but are the result of a previous, diseased condition of the heart muscle. Moreover, the coagulation of blood in the pericardium would have required more time after death than the Gospel allots. Some recent medical investigators of the Gospel prefer to speak of the flow of blood from the heart itself (rather than from the pericardial sac) and the flow of watery fluid from the pericardial sac (Barbet) or even from the stomach dilated by shock. In this thesis the lance thrust would have had to open two organs at the same time, and the two liquids would have had to pass through a relatively large space separating those organs from the body surface and still come out separately. Sava, *art. cit.*, has proposed a simpler theory. He cites good evidence for the thesis that the scourging of Jesus could have produced, several hours before his death, a hemorrhage in the pleural cavity between the ribs and the lungs. This hemorrhagic fluid, which in some cases is of considerable volume, could have separated into light serous fluid above and dark red fluid below, a separation fostered by the rigid position in which Jesus' body was held on the cross (so rigid that some think he died of suffocation related to circulatory failure—see V. Marcozzi, *Gregorianum* 39 [1958], 440–62). Since the pleural cavity is just inside the rib cage, even a shallow lance thrust could have opened it and the two parts of the blood have come out relatively unmixed. However, seemingly the most that can be gleaned from such medical discussions is that John's description of the flow of blood and water is not impossible, and so a natural phenomenon cannot be ruled out.

A more common view in times past was that John thought of the flow of blood and water as a miracle and that is why the testimony of the eyewitness to the event is underlined. Origen, Thomas Aquinas, Cajetan, Cornelius a Lapide, and Lagrange are among those who have upheld this interpretation. However, there is nothing in the narrative of the flow of blood and water that hints at the miraculous; and, as we shall see, the emphasis on the eyewitness' testimony may be more related to the theological import of the scene than to its being a miracle.

Before we discuss the possibility that the episode is a fictional creation, we may mention an intermediary solution, namely, that John is describing something that really happened, but is using imaginative language to do so. Some suggest that he is speaking in light of the medical lore of his time; for instance, a later work, the Midrash Rabbah xv 2 on Lev xiii 2 ff., says: "Man is evenly balanced, half of him is water, and the other half is blood." Greek thought from Heraclitus to Galen stressed that the proper proportions of blood and water in man guaranteed health. In describing the death of the eldest of seven sons, IV Macc ix 20 reports that his *blood* smeared the wheel while the *fluids* of his body quenched the burning coals. Still another theory is that by describing the blood and water John is stressing Jesus' divine origins. There was an old Homeric legend that the gods did not have blood in their veins but a type of blood mixed with water; for example, we are told that Aphrodite bled lymph blood diluted with water (see P. Haupt, *American Journal of Philology* 45 [1924], 53–55; E. Schweizer, EvTh 12 [1952–53], 350–51). It is interesting to note that this possibility was brought forward as early as Celsus' time (ca. A.D. 178); for he mockingly asked if Jesus had the divine liquid that was the blood of the gods, and Origen answered that the incident was a miracle (*Celsus* II 36; GCS 2:161–62). The main objection to such theories is the parenthetical vs. 35: whoever added that verse would scarcely have emphasized the importance of eyewitness testimony if he knew that what had happened was not being described as it occurred.

The appeal to eyewitness testimony remains a serious argument also against the thesis of many scholars that John simply invented the incident of the blood and water for theological purposes. Of course, if one accepts the contention that the parenthetical vs. 35 does not stem from the evangelist but from a redactor who did not know that the evangelist had invented the scene, the objection is overcome. Some have even argued that the very necessity of an appeal to eyewitness testimony is indicative that the incident of the blood and water is something new about which the hearers of the Gospel message might have some doubts—a highly debatable understanding of the function of 35, as we shall see below. These suggestions imply a conception of the method of the evangelist and/or of the redactor that we find hard to verify elsewhere in the Gospel.

To conclude the discussion of the historicity of xix 34b, while we recognize the difficulty of taking John's description at face value, we wonder if it is not more plausible to do so than to judge that the description is a fiction deliberately supported by citing false testimony or testimony that the writer did not know to be true, even though he stated otherwise. Barrett, p. 461, phrases the problem well: "It seems, if we may judge from the character of the gospel as a whole, unlikely that John is simply manufacturing an event for the sake of its allegorical significance" (also Dodd, *Tradition*, p. 135).

We must now turn to the meaning that John attaches to the incident. Is it simply a dramatic way of showing that beyond doubt Jesus was dead when his body was taken down from the cross—possibly against a theory that would explain the resurrection in terms of the revival from a coma? Another apologetic interpretation is suggested by D. Daube, *The New Testament and Rabbinic Judaism* (London University, 1956), pp. 325–29: in Jewish thought disfiguration was an obstacle to resurrection, and that is why John is careful to stress that no bone was broken. An anti-docetic apologetic has been proposed (already by Irenaeus, *Adv. Haer.* III 22:2 and IV 33:2; SC 34:376; 100:806). The Docetists who denied that Christ was truly human regarded the crucifixion as an illusion. In the 2nd-century *Acts of John*, 101, Jesus is represented as denying that blood came from his body. Against such theorizing John's statement in 34b would be a rebuttal. However, 1st-century Docetism is not well known, and we must admit that I John v 6 is more clearly anti-docetic than John xix 34b (see also vol. 29, p. LXXVI). After all, the peculiarity of the Gospel incident is not so much that blood came forth from Jesus (for blood is associated with death) but that water came forth; and the flow of water not only has no discernible anti-docetic motif but could even obscure Jesus' humanity.

In any case, John's purpose is not purely apologetic, for vs. 35 stresses that the incident is being reported in order to deepen existing Christian faith (NOTE on "that you too may have faith" in 35). The reference to the testimony concerning the blood and water as "true" (*alēthinos*) indicates that the real significance of the scene is not on the visible, material level but in what it tells us of the world of spirit (see vol. 29, pp. 500–1). If the eyewitness of vs. 35 is the Beloved Disciple of 26–27, as we think, then we should not forget that in the earlier episode he was identified with the revelatory formula "Here is your son." He speaks here as a witness to a revelation that is important for all the Christians whom he symbolizes. Thus we have every reason to search for a profound theological symbolism in the flow of blood and water.

Much OT background has been suggested as a guide to possible symbolism. In Isa liii 12 we are told that the Suffering Servant *poured out* his soul unto death (if that is the imagery meant in the hiphil of '*rh*). Many Church Fathers (see Hoskyns, pp. 534–35) relate the Johannine incident to Gen ii 21 where Eve is taken from the side of Adam and see here the emergence of the New Eve, the Church. This interpretation, which is as old as the 4th century (Braun, JeanThéol, III, 168[2]), received the approval of the Council of Vienne (1312—the fifteenth ecumenical council by Roman Catholic reckoning) where, against the errors of Peter John Olivi, it was affirmed that Christ "bore a lance wound in his side so that, with the waves of water and blood that flowed out, there might be formed one, immaculate and virginal holy Mother Church, the spouse of Christ, just as from the side of the first man, while he slept, Eve was formed as a matrimonial partner" (DB, §901; this exegesis was aimed at the contention that the true Church was coming into being only in the Middle Ages with the advent of the spiritualists). In modern times this interpretation has been espoused by Loisy, p. 492. While it would harmonize well with some of the symbolism we suggested for vss. 26–27 (see pp. 925–26 above), we find little evidence that the Genesis story was in John's mind here (see NOTES on "stabbed" and "side" in vs. 34).

A better key to the meaning of the symbolism lies within the Johannine works themselves. In John vii 38–39 Jesus cited a Scripture passage: "From within him shall flow rivers of living water." (In vol. 29, p. 322, we suggested that the probable Scripture background was the scene where Moses struck the rock and water flowed forth [Num xx 11]. It is interesting that in later Jewish thought, as exemplified in Midrash Rabbah III 13 on Exod iv 9, it was held that he struck the rock twice because he first brought forth blood and then water.) The evangelist interrupted to remark that by water Jesus was referring to the Spirit which those who believed in Jesus were to receive, for as of yet there was no Spirit since Jesus had not been glorified. We think it most probable that in this flow of water

from the side of Jesus (from within him) John sees the fulfillment of Jesus'
own prophecy, taking place in the hour of Jesus' glorification (cf. xii 23).
The parenthetical vs. 35 triumphantly insists that this really happened just
as Jesus had predicted and that there was an eyewitness to affirm it. Thus,
for John the flowing of the water is another proleptic symbol of the giving
of the Spirit, carrying on the theme of vs. 30: "He handed over the spirit."
That is why vs. 35 says that testimony is given to the incident "that you
too may have faith"—the incident is not merely a demonstration of the
accuracy of Jesus' foreknowledge, but also it assures the Christian that
Jesus truly gave the Spirit who is the source of faith. (It is worth noting
that this interpretation of the water from Jesus' side *seemingly* goes back
to the 2nd century: Irenaeus, *Adv. Haer.* IV 14:2; SC 100:544, says that
in many passages water represents the Spirit of God; see also III 24:1;
SC 34:400.)

To understand why the blood is also mentioned, we should probably
turn to I John v 6–8: "Jesus Christ is the one who came through water
and blood—not in water only, but in water and blood. And it is the Spirit
that testifies to this, for the Spirit is truth. Thus there are three who
testify: the Spirit and the water and the blood; and these three are of one
accord." Some scholars, like Bultmann, object to the use of I John to
interpret John; and it is true that the two works do not always have the
same theological stress. But we do seem to have here two closely related
passages from the same school of writing: they share in common the
themes of water and blood, the Spirit, and testimony. When we treat the
Johannine Epistles in vol. 30, we shall discuss in detail the meaning of
I John v 6–8, but one frequent interpretation would see therein a contrast
between the baptism of Jesus by John the Baptist and the crucifixion.
Baptism by the Baptist did not convey the Spirit, for he baptized only in
water (i 31); the real begetting by water and Spirit (iii 5) was something
that would not come until Jesus had been glorified (vii 39). The Spirit
would not be able to come until Jesus had departed (xvi 7), that is, until
he had shed his blood. In the poetic phrasing of the First Epistle the water
had to be mingled with Jesus' blood before the Spirit could give testimony:
"not in water only, but in water and blood. And it is the Spirit that testifies
to this." Thus, it would seem that in the Gospel picture of a flow of blood
and water from the side of Jesus, John is saying that now the Spirit can be
given because Jesus is obviously dead and through death has regained
the glory that was his before the world existed (xvii 5). The Spirit is the
principle of life that comes from above, and now Jesus is on his way to
dwell with the Father on high. The soldier's lance thrust was meant to
demonstrate that Jesus was truly dead; but this affirmation of death is
paradoxically the beginning of life, for from the dead man there flows living
water that will be a source of life for all who believe in him in imitation
of the Beloved Disciple. Well has Origen observed that this is a new
type of dead man (*Celsus* II 69; GCS 2:191). The fact that through the

Disciple the effects of the flow of blood and water reach out to touch all those who have faith means that there is an ecclesiastical dimension to the passage, even without depending on the dubious allusion to Eve being taken from Adam's side in Genesis. ("We were all made to drink of one Spirit," says Paul in I Cor xii 13.) Once again, as in evaluating xix 30, we do not think that in this scene John is referring to the actual giving of the Spirit, for that is specifically described in xx 22. The symbolism here is proleptic and serves to clarify that, while only the risen Jesus gives the Spirit, that gift flows from the whole process of glorification in "the hour" of the passion, death, resurrection, and ascension.

Miguens, pp. 13–16, and Ford, *art. cit.*, suggest another factor that may explain why John emphasizes that blood flowed *immediately* from the lance wound in Jesus' side (and indeed mentions the blood before the water). We have already seen that John seems to think of Jesus going to his death as a sacrificial victim (pp. 917–18 above). One of the strict requirements of Jewish sacrificial law was that the blood of the victim should not be congealed but should flow forth at the moment of death so that it could be sprinkled (Mishnah *Pesaḥim* 5:3, 5). Miguens, pp. 17–20, also points to the similarity between the idea that the soldier cut open Jesus' side with a lance and the insistence of Jewish law that the priest should slit the heart of the victim and make the blood come forth (Mishnah *Tamid* 4:2). Thus, the final episode on the cross may have been meant to emphasize the theme that Jesus died as a sacrificial victim.

We have discussed thus far the primary theological significance of the flow of blood and water. Is there also a secondary sacramental symbolism here? (See S. Tromp, *Gregorianum* 13 [1932], 523–27, for a short history of the exegesis of this verse.) Tertullian (*De Baptismo* xvi 2; SC 35:89), followed by Cyril of Alexandria and Thomas Aquinas, saw a reference in John to the two different types of Baptism, Baptism by water and Baptism by blood (i.e., martyrdom for the faith). Another ancient interpretation, reaching back into the 2nd century, has a better chance of being within the intent of the evangelist, namely, that the two sacraments most closely related to the death of the Lord, Baptism and the Eucharist, are prefigured by the water and the blood. Cullmann adopts this interpretation in ECW, pp. 114–16; and Bultmann, p. 525, states that the flow of blood and water is a miracle that "can scarcely have any meaning other than that in the death of Jesus on the cross the Sacraments of Baptism and of the Lord's Supper have their origin." Yet it is not easy to prove from internal evidence that John intended a reference to the two sacraments. There is not much difficulty about a secondary reference to Baptism, as our whole discussion of water and Spirit above indicates (see vol. 29, pp. 142, 179–80). But in the "blood" is there a reference to the Eucharist? It is true that the only other mention of Jesus' blood in John is in vi 53–56, the Eucharistic passage. *If* there is a secondary reference to the Eucharist at Cana (vol. 29, pp. 109–10), then the presence of the mother of Jesus at the foot of the cross may contribute to the sacramental interpretation by recalling the Cana scene to the reader's attention. I John i 7 says that the blood of Jesus cleanses us from all sin (see also Rev vii 14); but this conception is more in terms of Jewish sacrificial ritual than in terms of Eucharistic sacramentalism. (It is noteworthy, however, that if we invoke I John i 7, then both blood and water can signify the cleansing power of Jesus' death. In a fragment dubiously attributed to the time of Claudius Apollinaris of Hierapolis [ca. A.D. 170; see Bernard, II, 648], we read that "from his side came the twofold cleansing [*katharsia*], water and blood, word and spirit.") Thus, at most we can give a probability to the double sacramental reference of xix 34b (on a secondary level), with better proof for the baptismal than for the Eucharistic reference (see Costa, *art. cit.*).

We now pass on briefly to another problem in this episode: the relation between the flow of blood and water in 34b and *the appeal to testimony in 35*. It is interesting that I John v 6–8, which, as we have seen, mentions water and blood, also stresses testimony; but there it is the Spirit who testifies, while in John xix 35 it is the Beloved Disciple. But for John the witness of the Spirit and the witness of a disciple of Jesus are two facets of the same reality. In xv 26–27 the testimony of the Paraclete and the testimony of the disciples are juxtaposed because it is through the disciples that the Paraclete speaks. Thus, there may be an intimate connection between the flow of blood and water and the giving of testimony. If we are right in maintaining that this flow symbolizes proleptically the pouring out of the Spirit by the dead and glorified Jesus, then it is the Spirit that makes it possible both for the Beloved Disciple to testify and for those who listen to him to have faith.

By way of additional symbolism, some have proposed that, if the Beloved Disciple is John the son of Zebedee, there is an inclusion with the beginning of the Gospel. In i 19 we heard of testimony given to Jesus by *John* the Baptist; in xix 35 we hear of testimony given by *John* the Beloved Disciple. Medieval painters have not missed this possibility, for in triptychs the two Johns are often depicted on either side of the cross. However, the fact that the Beloved Disciple is unnamed makes an inclusion with John the Baptist too subtle. If there is any inclusion with John the Baptist in 34–35, it is more likely in terms of a comparison between his baptism with water and Christian Baptism symbolized by water accompanied by blood.

Our last problem in Episode 5 concerns *the Scripture citations in vss. 36 and 37*, which offer a clearer inclusion with the beginning of the Gospel than the proposals just mentioned. In the NOTE on vs. 36 we discussed two possible OT identifications for the citation, "Not a bone is to be broken." A reference to the provisions for the paschal lamb is the more likely of the two because of other echoes of the lamb motif in the Passion Narrative (the date is Passover Eve; Jesus is sentenced by Pilate at the noon hour when the slaughter of the paschal lambs begins; the mention of hyssop in xix 29). As for the OT passages mentioned in the NOTES, Miss Guilding, p. 170, points out that Exod xii 46 was read in the synagogue lectionaries at Passover in the second year of the three-year cycle, and Num ix 12 in the third year (see vol. 29, pp. 278–80). Thus, any association that John might make between Jesus and the paschal lamb would not be too foreign to Christian readers of Jewish background. We are uncertain whether the paschal lamb motif is also echoed in a secondary way in the haste to have Jesus' body removed before the next day (Passover, the 15th of Nisan) which would begin at sunset; for while, as we have stated, this attitude was dictated by the law of Deut xxi 22–23, there is also the provision in Exod xii 10 that, when the next day comes, nothing must remain of the lamb that has been killed "between the two evenings" (i.e., on the evening that ends the 14th of Nisan and begins the 15th). In any case, the evocation of the paschal lamb motif in John xix 36 forms an excellent inclusion with the Baptist's testimony given at the beginning of Jesus' ministry (i 29): "Here is the Lamb of God who takes away the world's sin." For this is the hour when, in the words of I John i 7, "The blood of Jesus, His Son, cleanses us from all sin." Some scholars have further suggested that in picturing Jesus as the paschal lamb John is attributing sacrificial character to Jesus' death. Certainly this is possible, for we pointed out above (p. 917) that in having Jesus carry his own cross, John may have been introducing the typology of Isaac and in ancient Jewish thought a relation had been established between the sacrifice of Isaac and the paschal lamb. Moreover, we saw the theme of Jesus as priest in the symbolism of the tunic in Episode 2. In addition to evoking the theme of sacrifice, the paschal lamb symbolism may also evoke the idea of covenant, of which we have found traces in the Last Discourse (pp. 614, 643–44, 653, 753, 781 above).

Thus far we have been taking the citation, "Not a bone is to be broken," as an allusion to the provisions for the paschal lamb. But we cannot rule out the possibility that it is *also* an allusion to Ps xxxiv 21(20), a psalm that deals with the innocent suffering servants of God. In the psalm this verse is a promise that God will not allow their bones to be broken; and thus according to (later?) Jewish thought, they will avoid a mutilation that will prevent resurrection. Dodd, *Interpretation*, p. 234[1], associates these psalms of the righteous sufferer with the poems of the Suffering Servant in Deutero-Isaiah. And so in John xix 36 we may well have a double inclusion with the reference to the Lamb of God at the beginning of the Gospel (i 29); for in vol. 29, pp. 60–61, we saw that the Lamb of God referred not only to the paschal lamb but also to the Suffering Servant. Jesus is the suffering innocent one who takes on himself the sins of others; and even if he is brought to the slaughter like a lamb (Isa liii 7), God does not allow his bones to be broken and thus does not deprive him of the victory of resurrection.

The second citation that John sees fulfilled in this episode on the cross

is found in vs. 37: "They shall look on him whom they have pierced."
This is a variant of Zech xii 10, and chs. ix–xiv of Zechariah are an important OT source for citations about Jesus. In John vii 37 the rain and water motif plays a role in what Jesus says at the feast of Tabernacles, and this is related to Zechariah's vision of what shall happen on the feast of Tabernacles in the messianic days (ch. xiv; see vol. 29, pp. 322–23, 326). The theme of the shepherd in John x is found also in Zech xi. John xii 15 cites Zech ix 9 about the coming of the king seated on a donkey (vol. 29, pp. 457–58, 460). In the Passion Narrative Matt xxvi 15 takes the idea of thirty pieces of silver from Zech xi 12, while Mark xiv 27, "I will strike the shepherd and the sheep will be scattered" (and seemingly John xvi 32), echoes Zech xiii 7. The passage we are now considering, Zech xii 10, is also cited in Rev i 7 in relation to the parousia: "Behold he is coming with the clouds, and every eye will see him, everyone who pierced him; and all the tribes of the earth will wail on account of him." (The passage is used in a similar way by Justin, *Apology* i 52.)

How does John interpret Zech xii 10? In the OT context the sight of the one who is pierced is associated with a spirit of compassion, so that the onlookers "mourn for him, as one mourns for an only child, and weep bitterly over him." In the episode at the cross does John think of the onlookers as "the Jews" of vs. 31 (and perhaps the Roman soldiers of 32–34) who, looking upon Jesus pierced with a lance at their instigation, repent and mourn for him? Although this would agree with the OT context and with the theme of Luke xxiii 48, there is nothing in John's description to suggest repentance; "the Jews" remain hostile afterwards (xix 38, xx 19). Another possible interpretation is that by using a future verb, "They shall look," John alludes to the parousia, even as does the author of Revelation. Among those who think that, while the citation in 36 refers to what has already happened, the citation of Zechariah in 37 will not be realized until the parousia, we may list Lagrange, Loisy (hesitantly), Wikenhauser, and Schlatter. The verse then becomes a threat of judgment upon those who pierced Jesus. However, in light of the Gospel's emphasis on realized eschatology, the author is probably thinking not of a future parousia but of a type of judgment that has already taken place. With some hesitation we suggest that the "they" who look upon Jesus as pierced consists of two groups. First, "the Jews," who are his enemies, are defeated by the very act they instigated; for as they look upon the Jesus who died on the cross, there flows forth, along with his life blood, a stream of life-giving water. The Pharisees had decided to put Jesus to death because the whole world was running after him (xii 19); but, ironically, by having him crucified they have fulfilled his prophecy that, when he would be lifted up from the earth, he would draw all men to himself (xii 32). They have caused him to be lifted up on the cross; by their request to Pilate they have been the occasion of the lance thrust that opened the fount of living water. Now the Spirit that will beget men (iii 5) as followers of Jesus is being given, the same Spirit/Paraclete who will vindicate Jesus against those who thought they had destroyed him (xvi 8–11). However, a second group also looks upon the pierced Jesus, since in the person of the Beloved Disciple those who have faith in Jesus (xix 35) behold the scene. For them the confrontation is not an occasion of condemnation but of the gift of life (iii 18, v 24). For them Jesus hangs upon the cross in fulfillment of his words in iii 14–15: "And just as Moses lifted up the serpent in the desert, so must the Son of Man be lifted up, that everyone who believes may have eternal life in him." Thus, the dead Jesus remains the focal point of judgment even as did the living Jesus: at the foot of the cross there stand those who reject the light as well as those who are attracted to it (iii 18–21). The former look upon the pierced Jesus to be condemned; the latter look upon him to be saved.

It will be noted that we have connected intimately the citation from Zech xii 10 with the whole of John xix 34: not only with the lance thrust but also with the flow of blood and water. This was one of the reasons why we rejected Bultmann's thesis that 34b is an addition because it is not cited in 37. We find justification for our procedure in the immediate context of the Zechariah citation—here as elsewhere the NT author is citing a verse as evocative of a whole context (see also vol. 29, p. 124). In Zech xii 10, just before the words cited by John, Yahweh says: "I shall *pour out* on the house of David and the inhabitants of Jerusalem *a spirit* of compassion." A few verses later (xiii 1) Zechariah tells us of God's promise to *open a fountain* for the house of David and for Jerusalem *to cleanse them of their sins*. All the italicized themes have figured in our interpretation of John xix 34b as the fulfillment of John vii 38–39. (Perhaps we may add that further on Zech xiv 8 pictures living waters flowing out from Jerusalem, probably a development of Ezek xlvii 1–12 where the Temple is the source of the water that flows out from Jerusalem. Need we recall that for John Jesus' body replaces the Jerusalem Temple [ii 21]. Another Johannine work, Rev xxii, was influenced both by Zech xiii 1 and xiv.) And so John's citation in vs. 37 reflects a whole soteriology and christology, even as does the citation in vs. 36. That is why the two are closely joined.

In the NOTE on 37 we pointed out that the MT of Zech xii 10 differs from the citation given in John, for it seems to speak of the piercing of Yahweh himself. To avoid this difficulty there sprang up a messianic interpretation, namely, that the Messiah would be pierced and men would look to Yahweh. In particular, the Messiah from the tribe of Joseph was featured in some Jewish speculations on this text (TalBab *Sukkah* 52a; StB, II, 584; S. Mowinckel, *He That Cometh* [New York: Abingdon, 1954], p. 291). If this tradition was known in John's time, it is not unthinkable that John found in the fulfillment of Zech xii 10 a confirmation that Jesus was the Messiah (cf. John xx 31). Some would relate the anonymous pierced figure of Zech xii 10 to the Suffering Servant of Isa liii 5, 10, who was bruised and whipped. Again, if this connection was made in John's time, John may have been confirming that Jesus was the Servant, a theme we suggested as possible in the citation of vs. 36. On the other hand, we reject the suggestion of O'Rourke, ScEccl 19 (1967), 441, that, because in the MT Yahweh himself is pierced, possibly John is referring the text to Jesus to imply the divinity of Jesus. The fact that John does not cite the text according to the MT shows that he is not thinking in this way.

Conclusion: The Burial of Jesus by Joseph and Nicodemus (xix 38–42)

Although the deposition from the cross is not explicitly mentioned in these verses, it is implicit in the story of the care expended upon Jesus' body; and so the Conclusion of the crucifixion scene is counterposed to the Introduction where we were told that Jesus was put on the cross. See also the common theme of the place where he was crucified in xix 17–18 and 41. By way of comparing the Conclusion with the various episodes of the crucifixion, Hoskyns, p. 536, notices an interesting progression in Pilate's responses to the requests he receives concerning the crucified Jesus: in Episode 1 he refuses the first request of "the Jews" to change the title (xix 22); in Episode 5 he tacitly grants the second request of "the Jews" to hasten the removal of the bodies (the "accordingly" of xix 32); here he explicitly grants the request of Jesus' clandestine disciple to remove the body (vs. 38). And so Pilate's last appearance in the Gospel is a positive one.

We pointed out that, except for the opening phrase, Episode 5 had no Synoptic parallels. In the Conclusion, as in the rest of the crucifixion narrative with the exclusion of Episode 5, there is a partial Synoptic parallel (although characteristically the Johannine symbolism is not built upon the details that have Synoptic parallels). John shares with the Synoptics the request made of Pilate by Joseph of Arimathea, and the taking of the body for burial to a hitherto unused tomb because it was the Day of Preparation before a holy day which was rapidly approaching. A comparison of Episode 5 and the Conclusion raises a difficulty: in each a request is presented to Pilate to have the body taken away; Pilate tacitly grants the first request to "the Jews" and explicitly grants the second request to Joseph; but there is nothing said to resolve the obvious duplication. (Scholars like Baldensperger have relied on this to construct a theory of a twofold burial of Jesus: first by the Jews [see Acts xiii 39], and then a reburial by Joseph. Such a theory has been used to explain away the empty tomb, namely the first tomb.) Of course, with imagination one can harmonize, for example, by claiming that the first request brought forth an order to the soldiers to hasten death and get the bodies down from the cross, while the second request led to a permission to dispose of the body once it was down. So critical a scholar as Bultmann, p. 516, holds that both scenes stood side by side in John's source and consequently neither represents an addition by the evangelist (who was responsible only for vs.

39a: the appearance of Nicodemus). Many, however, doubt that the two scenes were consecutive in the tradition and think that the writer joined variant, but partially overlapping, versions of how Pilate made disposition of Jesus' body—the first version (Episode 5) being an entirely Johannine account, the second (the Conclusion) representing a borrowing from the Synoptic tradition. A refinement of this approach is Loisy's thesis (p. 496) that vss. 40a, 41–42 were once the conclusion of the first version, and that this version was broken up by the addition of 38 from the Synoptic tradition, and then further broken up by the addition of 39 and 40b (the story of Nicodemus and the burial preparations).

No simple solution is possible. If there are clear Synoptic parallels in the Conclusion, no one can seriously maintain that the whole narrative of the Conclusion can be traced to the Synoptics. The story of Nicodemus and the preparation of the body with myrrh and aloes is a major problem in the discussion. (If the "aromatic oils" of vs. 40b [see NOTE] are not the same as the myrrh and aloes of 39, then the reference to Nicodemus may be thought to consist of only one verse, namely 39, inserted in the burial narrative and accompanied by 40a which serves as a connective to what follows. The "in accordance" of 40b would continue the narrative from 38.) Obviously the story of Nicodemus is independent of the Synoptic tradition, for it is scarcely reconcilable with the statement of Mark xvi 1 and Luke xxiv 1 that the women came to the tomb on Sunday morning with aromatic oils (to anoint Jesus, according to Mark). One must reject the harmonization theory that the preparations on Friday described in John were provisional and the women came to complete the task on Sunday. John gives no indication that there were to be further burial procedures; and certainly the staggering amount of spices and oils used on Friday would make otiose the bringing of oils on Sunday. In particular, Luke's independent tradition (xxiii 55–56) that the women watched the burial of the body on Friday and then immediately went and bought aromatic oils and perfumes is an implicit contradiction of John's tradition that the body was prepared with aromatic oils before burial. Lagrange's suggestion (p. 504) that the women saw only the tomb and not the burial process and consequently did not know what Joseph and Nicodemus had done is an even more desperate harmonization. A more subtle harmonization between John and the Synoptics is possible if one postulates that the Marcan/Lucan tradition conflates two independent and somewhat contradictory narratives: *a burial narrative*, which by its silence on the subject implied that the customary burial procedures were followed (and thus was in agreement with John's tradition), and an *"empty tomb"* narrative, which supposed that the customary burial procedures were not followed and Jesus' body was not anointed. One would have to presume that Mark did not see the contradiction in combining such divergent narratives. Such a solution is so speculative that it is probably better to face the problem of disagreement between John and the Synoptics.

It is not easy to settle the question as to which of the two descriptions of the burial rites is more plausible, the Sunday (Marcan/Lucan) presentation, or the Friday (Johannine) presentation. Because of the enormous amount of myrrh and aloes in John xix 39, many scholars favor the Sunday presentation; for instance, Bultmann, p. 516, characterizes John's account as an edifying legendary construction. Yet Benoit, *Passion*, p. 225, favors the Friday presentation. Since the Sunday presentation is intimately connected with the historicity of the narrative of the finding of the empty tomb, we shall leave its difficulties until we discuss John xx 1. John's account of the burial preparation on Friday has no relation to the resurrection narrative; indeed, such an elaborate burial shows no anticipation of imminent resurrection. If we leave aside the amount of the spices, the greatest difficulty in the Johannine presentation is the seeming contradiction between the elaborate burial rites and the haste dictated by the approach of the feast day. However, we should not underestimate the Jewish insistence that a body be properly prepared for burial. The Mishnah *Sanhedrin* 6:5 says that a dead body may even be allowed to remain overnight without burial if that time is required to get a shroud or a coffin for it.

If we move on from the story of Nicodemus and the spices, which is peculiarly Johannine material, we still encounter a problem in analyzing the origins of the Johannine account of Joseph of Arimathea and the tomb. Even though this has Synoptic parallels, it is far from clear that John has drawn upon the Synoptic Gospels or their sources; in the NOTES on vss. 38, 41–42 we pointed out numerous differences of vocabulary and detail. Dodd, *Tradition*, pp. 138–39, is probably right in insisting once more that John is drawing upon an independent tradition similar to those behind the Synoptic Gospels rather than on the Synoptic Gospels or pre-Gospel traditions themselves.

By way of summary, then, the Johannine account of what happened after the death of Jesus combines material of two types: first, material that has no Synoptic parallel in vss. 31b–37 (Episode 5), and 39–40; second, material that is closer to the Synoptic tradition in vss. 31a, 38, and 41–42. This division is similar to but not as neat as that of Benoit, *art. cit.*, whereby a Johannine account without Synoptic parallels (31–37) is joined to another original account with Synoptic parallels (39–42) by a connecting verse (38) borrowed from the Synoptic tradition. (In reality, vs. 38 is no closer to the Synoptic tradition than are 41–42; and there is no good reason to posit different origins for these verses.) The signs that two types of material were combined are rather clear: not only, as mentioned, does the request to Pilate in 38 duplicate that in 31b, but also the taking of Jesus' body in 38 is duplicated in 40. Yet there is not sufficient evidence to enable us to work out an exact theory about how or why such a combination occurred.

What is the purpose or theme of the Conclusion, especially of the peculiarly Johannine parts? Some of the details of the narrative may have had their origins in apologetic interplay (whether or not the Johannine writer used them apologetically). Bultmann, p. 527[10], thinks that the stress on the hitherto unused character of the tomb ("new"; "in which no one had ever been buried") is meant to underline its holiness—the tomb had never been subjected to secular use. It seems more likely to us that it reflects apologetics—there was no confusion in the report of the empty tomb, for Jesus was not buried in a common tomb where his body might have been mixed with others, and the tomb was in an easily identifiable place near the well-known site of public execution.

Is there any theological symbolism here? We hesitated about whether to classify xix 38–42 as Episode 6 in the crucifixion narrative or as the Conclusion. Our decision not to treat it as another Episode was based on the fact that we could see no major theological emphasis or symbolism that would place the description of burial on a plane with Episodes 1–5. In the NOTES we rejected what we regarded as far-fetched attempts to read symbolism into these verses: for example, further references to the paschal lamb or Suffering Servant; a play on the Garden of Eden; and the theme of a sweet-smelling sacrifice. Frankly we are uncertain if any theological motif underlies a possible connection between the preparations for burial in 39–40 and John's insistence in xii 3, 7 that Mary of Bethany had already anointed Jesus' body for burial (vol. 29, p. 454—one would have expected that after such insistence the Fourth Gospel would not narrate any further preparation for burial, and yet it is the only Gospel to do so). We are also quite dubious about the thesis of R. Mercurio, CBQ 21 (1959), 50–54, that John's description of the burial has a special baptismal motif, for example, the use of spices is reminiscent of Baptism as anointing by the Holy Spirit, and the presence of Nicodemus recalls the baptismal theme of the dialogue in ch. iii (vol. 29, pp. 141–44).

But there remain two proposals for finding minor theological symbolism that are worthy of consideration. The first is a continuation of the theme that once Jesus has been lifted up, he draws all men to himself (xii 32). We saw this theme at work in Episode 5 in the testimony that the Beloved Disciple gives about the flow of blood and water, for that testimony was directed to all those who have faith in Jesus. But perhaps in the Conclusion John is turning his attention to another type of believer, exemplified in Joseph and Nicodemus. In the Introduction to the Gospel (vol. 29, pp. LXXIII and LXXVII) we proposed that John had in mind at least a twofold audience: those who were already fully Christian believers, and those still in the Synagogue who believed in Jesus but did not have the courage to profess this belief publicly and be excommunicated. If Episode 5 envisages the first group, represented by the Beloved Disciple, the Conclusion may envisage the second. Joseph was a secret disciple who now had the courage to show his adherence by burying Jesus' body. Nicodemus came secretly to Jesus at night, but now he brings an enormous amount of spices to prepare Jesus' body for burial. (More tenuously one may theorize that, since Jesus had spoken to Nicodemus about the necessity of being begotten of water and spirit [iii 5], he now reappears because of the giving of the Spirit prefigured in the flow of water from Jesus' side.) John may be hinting that crypto-believers in the Synagogue of his own time should follow the example of Joseph and Nicodemus.

The second possible symbolism is a continuation of the theme that Jesus is king. The large outlay of spices may be meant to suggest that Jesus was given a royal burial, for we know of such an outlay on behalf of kings. Josephus, *Ant.* XVII.viii.3;※199, tells us that at the burial of Herod the Great five hundred servants carried the aromatic oils or spices (*arōma*). There is a tradition preserved in a "minor tractate" of the Talmud (TalBab, *Ebel Rabbathi* or *Semaḥoth*, 8:6—a medieval work but containing older materials) that at the death of Rabbi Gamaliel the Elder (probably ca. A.D. 50) the proselyte Onkelos burned more than eighty pounds of spices. When asked why, he cited Jer xxxiv 5 as an instance where spices were burned at the death of kings and affirmed that Gamaliel was better than one hundred kings. The mention of a garden may point in the same direction, for the OT references to burial in a garden concern the entombment of the kings of Judah (II Kings xxi 18, 26). From the LXX of Neh iii 16 we learn that the popular tomb of David (see Acts ii 29) was in a garden. Obviously the evidence is far from probative, and we confess uncertainty about its value; but the theme that Jesus was buried as a king would fittingly conclude a Passion Narrative wherein Jesus is crowned and hailed as king during his trial and enthroned and publicly proclaimed as king on the cross. Such an insight would accord with Bultmann's observation that in John the burial is not properly a transition or prelude to the resurrection, as it is in the Synoptics where the women carefully observe the tomb so that they can come back to anoint Jesus after the Sabbath. John does not mention the closing of the tomb with a stone, as Mark/Matthew do by way of preparing for the Easter scene where the stone will be rolled back. For John the burial is the end of the crucifixion: those who are present are not women who will bear witness to the risen Lord on Easter, but men who partially accepted Jesus during his ministry but have been brought by his death to show their love for him. Thus, if there is a theological theme hidden symbolically in the narrative, it should be the terminal stage of a theme, such as kingship, that played a prominent part in the crucifixion.

BIBLIOGRAPHY
(xix 16b–42)

See the general bibliography on the Passion Narrative at the end of §60.

Bampfylde, G., "John XIX 28, a Case for a Different Translation," NovT 11 (1969), 247–60.

Barbet, P., *A Doctor at Calvary* (New York: Kenedy, 1953), pp. 113–27 on xix 34.

Barton, G. A., "'A Bone of Him Shall Not Be Broken,' John 19:36," JBL 49 (1930), 12–18.

Benoit, P., "Marie-Madeleine et les disciples au tombeau selon Joh 20, 1–18," in *Judentum, Urchristentum, Kirche* (J. Jeremias Festschrift; Berlin: Töpelmann, 1960), pp. 146–48 on xix 31–42.

Braun, F.-M., "Quatre 'signes' johanniques de l'unité chrétienne," NTS 9 (1962–63), 150–52 on xix 23–24.

——— *Mother of God's People* (Staten Island, N.Y.: Alba, 1968—translation of the book cited in vol. 29, p. 110), pp. 74–124 on xix 26–27.

——— "L'eau et l'Esprit," RThom 49 (1949), 5–30, especially 15–20 on xix 34.

Ceroke, C. P., "Mary's Maternal Role in John 19, 25–27," *Marian Studies* 11 (1960), 123–51.

Costa, M., "Simbolismo battesimale in Giovanni," RivBib 13 (1965), 347–83, especially 359–69 on xix 31–37.

Dauer, A., "Das Wort des Gekreuzigten an seine Mutter und den 'Jünger den er liebte,'" BZ 11 (1967), 222–39; 12 (1968), 80–93.

de Goedt, M., "Un schème de révélation dans le Quatrième Évangile," NTS 8 (1961–62), 142–50, especially 145 ff. on xix 26–27.

de Tuya, M., "Valor mariológico del texto evangélico: 'Mulier, ecce filius tuus,'" *Ciencia Tomista* 255 (1955), 189–223.

Feuillet, A., "L'heure de la femme (Jn 16, 21) et l'heure de la Mère de Jésus (Jn 19, 25–27)," *Biblica* 47 (1966), 169–84, 361–80, 557–73.

——— "Les adieux du Christ à sa Mère (Jn 19, 25–27) et la maternité spirituelle de Marie," NRT 86 (1964), 469–89. Condensed in English in TD 15 (1967), 37–40.

——— "Le Nouveau Testament et le coeur du Christ," *L'Ami du Clergé* 74 (May 21, 1964), 321–33, especially 327–33 on xix 31–37.

Ford, J. M., "'Mingled Blood' from the Side of Christ (John xix. 34)," NTS 15 (1968–69), 337–38.

Gaechter, P., *Maria im Erdenleben* (Innsbruck: Tyrol, 1953), pp. 201–26 on xix 26–27.

——— "Zum Begräbnis Jesu," ZKT 75 (1953), 220–25.

Hultkvist, G., *What Does the Expression "Blood and Water" Mean in the Gospel of John 19, 34?* (Vrigstad, Sweden, 1947).

Kerrigan, A., "Jn. 19, 25–27 in the Light of Johannine Theology and the Old Testament," *Antonianum* 35 (1960), 369–416.

Koehler, Th., "Les principales interprétations traditionnelles de Jn. 19, 25–27, pendant les douzes premiers siècles," *Études Mariales* 16 (1959), 119–55.

Langkammer, H., "Christ's 'Last Will and Testament' (Jn 19, 26.27) in the

Interpretation of the Fathers of the Church and the Scholastics," *Antonianum* 43 (1968), 99–109.

Meyer, E., "Sinn und Tendenz der Schlussszene am Kreuz im Johannesevangelium," *Sitzungsberichte der Preussischen Akademie der Wissenschaften* (1924), pp. 157–62.

Michaels, J. R., "The Centurion's Confession and the Spear Thrust," CBQ 29 (1967), 102–9.

Miguens, M., " 'Salio sangre y agua' (Jn. 19, 34)," *Studii Biblici Franciscani Liber Annuus* 14 (1963–64), 5–31.

Moretto, G., "Giov. 19, 28: La sete di Cristo in croce," RivBib 15 (1967), 249–74.

Sava, A. F., "The Wound in the Side of Christ," CBQ 19 (1957), 343–46.

Schwank, B., "Der erhöhte König (19, 16b–22)," SeinSend 29 (1964), 244–54.

———— "Die ersten Gaben des erhöhten Königs (19, 23–30)," SeinSend 29 (1964), 292–309.

———— " 'Sie werden schauen auf ihn, den sie durchbohrt haben' (19, 31–42)," SeinSend 29 (1964), 340–53.

Spurrell, J. M., "An Interpretation of 'I Thirst,' " ChQR 167 (1966), 12–18.

Thurian, M., *Mary, Mother of All Christians* (New York: Herder & Herder, 1963), pp. 144–75 on xix 26–27.

Unger, D., "The Meaning of John 19, 26–27 in the Light of Papal Documents," *Marianum* 21 (1959), 186–221.

Zerwick, M., "The Hour of the Mother—John 19:25–27," BiTod 1, no. 18 (1965), 1187–94.

THE BOOK OF GLORY

Part Three: The Risen Jesus

OUTLINE

PART THREE: THE RISEN JESUS
(XX 1–29)

A.   XX 1–18:   *Scene One:* AT THE TOMB. (§68)

     (1–10)   *Episode 1:* Visits to the empty tomb.

         1–2:   *Setting:* Early on Sunday morning Magdalene finds the tomb opened and reports to the disciples.

         3–10:   *Main Action:* Peter and the other disciple run to the tomb and see the burial clothes; the other disciple believes.

     (11–18)   *Episode 2:* Jesus appears to Magdalene.

         11–13:   *Transition:* Magdalene looks into the tomb and sees angels.

         14–18:   *Main Action:* Jesus appears to Magdalene and is recognized with difficulty; Magdalene proclaims the Lord to the disciples.

B.   XX 19–29:   *Scene Two:* WHERE THE DISCIPLES ARE GATHERED. (§69)

     (19–23)   *Episode 1:* Jesus appears to the disciples.

         Setting: On Sunday evening Jesus appears to and greets the disciples who rejoice at seeing the Lord.

         Message: Jesus sends the disciples as he is sent; breathes the Holy Spirit on them; gives them power to forgive sins.

     (24–29)   *Episode 2:* Jesus appears to Thomas.

         24–25:   *Transition:* Thomas who was absent refuses to believe that the others have seen the Lord.

         26–29:   *Main Action:* On the following Sunday Jesus appears to the disciples with Thomas present and invites Thomas to touch him. Thomas proclaims Jesus as Lord and God. The beatitude of those who have not seen but have believed.

67. THE RESURRECTION:
GENERAL REMARKS

A critical analysis of the NT shows that Christian faith in Jesus' victory over death has been expressed in various ways. In Heb ix we have a picture of Jesus as a high priest entering the heavenly holy of holies with his own blood that was shed in sacrifice—thus, seemingly, a direct progression from crucifixion to ascension without an intervening act of resurrection (also iv 14, vi 19–20). Nevertheless, resurrection is by far the commonest way in which Jesus' victory is described. While the resurrection itself is never pictured in the NT (but see the *Gospel of Peter*, 39–42, which describes Jesus' emergence from the tomb), there are two types of material most pertinent to the resurrection. First, there are short formulae, often confessional in nature, springing from the preaching, the catechesis, and the liturgy of the primitive Church. These formulae vary in style; below we shall discuss the formulae in Acts and in I Cor xv 3–7, but the reader should also consult such diverse examples as Rom i 4 and Mark viii 31. Second, in the Gospels and Acts there are developed narratives of the finding of the empty tomb and of the appearances of the risen Jesus. Scholars generally affirm that the formulae provide us with our earliest information about the resurrection.

Although many begin their discussion of these formulae with I Cor xv 3–7, P. Seidensticker, TGl 57 (1967), 286–323, especially 289–90, makes a good case for the thesis that one can distill from the sermons in Acts (ii 23–24, iv 10, v 30–31, x 39–40) an earlier formulation consisting of two members. The first member proclaims Jesus' death ("You crucified him"; "Jesus whom you killed by hanging him on a tree"); the second proclaims that God raised him up from the dead. In the Pauline kerygma reflected in I Cor xv 3–7 (written ca. A.D. 57, but stemming from a primitive tradition of the mid-thirties—Jeremias, EWJ, pp. 101–3), the formulation has been expanded to four members or two groups of two: Christ died and was buried; he was raised and appeared (see below p. 976). A list of appearances is also included. Some argue that the "appearances" were originally revelations by God rather than manifestations of the body of Jesus. While a discussion of the nature of the appearances lies beyond the scope of this commentary, we should point out that Paul, who presents himself as a witness of an appearance of Jesus, distinguishes between this appearance and all the subsequent revelations and visions that were granted him. In any case, the formulae do not mention the empty tomb and make no attempt to localize the appearances of Jesus. These aspects appear only in the subsequent narratives pertaining to the resurrection.

The fact that there is a development within the formulae and also from formulae to narratives raises an obvious question about the historicity of the narratives. In discussing the narratives in general and later in discussing the Johannine narratives in particular, we shall be concerned with isolating the earliest material in these narratives; but we do not think it our task in a commentary to go further and to speculate about whether or not bodily resurrection is possible. Objections to the *possibility* of resurrection take their origin in philosophy and science and not in exegesis, which is our task. (We note, however, that such objections have their force against a crassly physical understanding of the resurrection whereby it is looked on as resuscitation; they are less forceful against the type of sophisticated understanding enunciated by Paul in I Cor xv 42 ff.: "It is sown a physical body; it is raised a spiritual body.") There can be no question that the evangelists themselves thought that Jesus' body did not remain in the grave but was raised to glory. Yet, even if by comparative exegesis we trace this idea back to the earliest days, we cannot prove that this Christian understanding corresponded to what really happened. That is a matter of faith.

Before we can deal with the Gospel narratives about the resurrection and their divergencies, we should clarify for the reader three suppositions of biblical criticism that affect our procedure. *First,* the verses that conclude the Gospel of Mark in most bibles (Mark xvi 9–20, called the Marcan Appendix or the Longer Ending of Mark) were not the original ending of the Gospel but were added because of the abrupt termination in xvi 8. (Scholars are divided on whether Mark originally terminated with xvi 8 or whether there was a further narrative that was lost; the latter is probably the majority opinion, although the present writer inclines toward the former.) The Marcan Appendix is missing in Codices Vaticanus and Sinaiticus; in fact, minor textual witnesses of Mark preserve for us other attempts at completing the Gospel. The date of the Appendix is difficult to determine precisely, but it is later than the other Gospel accounts. Some scholars attribute no importance to its evidence about the resurrection, for they think of it as a secondary reshuffling of material already found in the canonical Gospels (it is closest to Luke and Matthew). But a close vocabulary comparison suggests that, at least in part, the writer of the Appendix may have drawn on sources similar to the canonical Gospels rather than on the Gospels themselves; and so we think it worth while in our comparisons to include information taken from the Appendix. (Thus, in what follows "Mark" refers to Mark xvi 1–8, and we shall refer to the remaining verses as the Marcan Appendix.)

Second, the Resurrection Narrative in Luke xxiv contains verses (3, 6, 12, 36, 40, 51, and 52) that are textually dubious. These verses are found in the majority of important textual witnesses but are regularly

THE VARIANT GOSPEL NARRATIVES OF THE POST-RESURRECTIONAL APPEARANCES

	Mark xvi 1–8	Matt xxviii	Luke xxiv	Mark xvi 9–20	John xx	John xxi
Tomb Area		To women returning from tomb / They clasped his feet / He repeated message about Galilee		First to Mary Magdalene	At tomb to Mary Magdalene / "Don't cling to me" / He spoke of ascending	
			To Simon (vs. 34)			
Country Road			To two disciples on road to Emmaus	To two of them walking in the country		
Jerusalem			To Eleven / At meal / Easter night	To Eleven / At table / Afterwords	To disciples minus Thomas, one of the Twelve / At meal / Easter night // To disciples with Thomas / Week later	
Galilee	See promise in xvi 7	To Eleven / On a mountain				To seven disciples / At Sea of Tiberias

absent from Codex Bezae and from the Itala form of the OL—two Western witnesses that are usually characterized by interpolations or additions rather than by omissions. The absence of these verses in the very type of Western witnesses that one would have expected to contain them has earned for them the peculiarly negative designation of "Western Noninterpolations." Although it was fashionable in the early part of this century to dismiss these verses as scribal additions, their presence in the recently discovered P[75] (vol. 29, p. cxxxi) has made many rethink this position. For instance, it is possible that these verses were added to Luke by a redactor of the Gospel, but were omitted by the Western scribes precisely on the grounds that they seemed to be an addition. In any case, we shall consider the verses in collecting evidence about the resurrection but keep reminding the reader of the textual problem.

Third, we shall have to anticipate our conclusions on pp. 1077–80 below by assuming that ch. xxi of John was written by someone other than the evangelist who was responsible for the body of the Gospel. It represents Johannine tradition added to the Gospel by the redactor, and its witness to the post-resurrectional appearances is different from and independent of the witness preserved in ch. xx. As a result of these critical suppositions we may speak of six Gospel accounts as sources for our knowledge of the resurrection: Mark, Matthew, Luke, John xx, John xxi, and the Marcan Appendix. In accompanying charts we summarize the evidence from these accounts in reference to the two types of narratives we shall discuss: the narratives of the post-resurrectional appearances and the narratives of the empty tomb.

The Narratives of the Post-Resurrectional Appearances

It is quite obvious that the Gospels do not agree as to where and to whom Jesus appeared after his resurrection. Mark mentions no appearance of Jesus, although xvi 7 indicates that Peter and the disciples will see him in Galilee. Matthew mentions an appearance to the women in Jerusalem (xxviii 9–10) that seemingly contradicts the instruction to go to Galilee where Jesus will be seen (xxviii 7). The main appearance for Matthew is in Galilee when Jesus is seen by the Eleven disciples on a mountain (xxviii 16–20). Luke narrates several appearances in the Jerusalem area: to the two disciples on the road to Emmaus (xxiv 13–32), to Simon (34), and to the Eleven and others gathered together in Jerusalem (36–53). All of these are described by Luke as having taken place on the same day, Easter itself; and Jesus is pictured as finally departing from his disciples (to heaven—Western Noninterpolation of 51) on Easter night (yet see Acts i 3). In John xx, as in Luke, we find appearances in the Jerusalem area: to Mary Magdalene (xx 14–18), to the disciples without Thomas (19–23), and to Thomas a week later (26–29). Finally, in the Marcan Appendix there is a set of appearances, all seemingly in the Jerusalem area: to

Mary Magdalene (xvi 9), to two disciples in the country (12–13), and to
the Eleven at table (14–19). At the end of these Jesus is taken up to
heaven. We may summarize this as follows:

Appearances in Jerusalem area (principally Luke, John xx, Marcan Appendix):
- to Mary Magdalene: John xx, Matthew (several women), Marcan Appendix
- to Peter: Luke, Paul (I Cor xv 5—place not specified)
- to two disciples on road: Luke, Marcan Appendix
- to the Eleven gathered together: Luke, John xx, Marcan Appendix

Appearances in Galilee (Mark? Matthew, John xxi)
- to the Eleven on a mountain (Matthew)
- to seven disciples at the Sea of Tiberias (John xxi)

We may well wonder how such diverse traditions, each seemingly
ignorant of the other, came into existence. Let us compare this information
to what we find in the earlier testimony of I Cor xv 5–8:

He appeared	(1)	to Cephas;
	(2)	then to the Twelve;
	(3)	then he appeared to more than five hundred brethren. . . .
Then he appeared	(4)	to James;
	(5)	then to all the apostles;
	(6)	last of all he appeared to me [Paul]. . . .

E. Bammel, TZ 11 (1955), 401–19, argues that the Pauline formula represents in part a combination of two reports of the same appearances:
one report was that he appeared to Cephas and to the Twelve; the other
was that he appeared to James and to all the apostles. However, Paul was
well informed about the main characters of the Jerusalem church and
certainly was in a position to know whether there was a tradition that
Jesus had appeared both to Peter and to James. An appearance to Peter
has independent support in the NT, and one must probably postulate an
appearance to James to account for the fact that a disbelieving "brother"
of the Lord (disbelief in John vii 5; Mark iii 21 combined with 31) became
a follower of Jesus. Yet, if we doubt that we are dealing with two reports
of the *same* appearances, Bammel and others may well be right in thinking
that Paul's formula represents a combination of two different reports.
This possibility cautions us against too easily accepting the idea that the
Pauline list is chronological (Von Campenhausen, p. 45[6]). Moreover, it
suggests that various communities preserved reminiscences of different sets
of appearances, so that the primitive Church may never have had a
universally accepted sequential list of all the appearances of Jesus. Thus
we question Von Campenhausen's assumption (p. 51) that Paul's list

automatically excludes the historicity of an appearance to Magdalene. Paul recalls the tradition of the appearances of Jesus to show that, even if he came out of time and last of all, he did see the risen Jesus, just as did the other well-known apostles. There is no reason why such a tradition should have included an appearance to a woman who could scarcely be presented as either an official witness to the resurrection or as an apostle. We note also that the Pauline list contains no indications as to where the appearances took place, again because geographical considerations were not pertinent to the purpose for which the list was composed or recalled.

The difficulties in the Pauline list may help to explain the variations between the Gospel narratives, for in the Gospels we have preserved independent reminiscences of individual communities. V. Taylor, *The Formation of the Gospel Tradition* (London: Macmillan, 1953), pp. 59–62, has pointed out why the story of the resurrection would take form differently from the story of the passion and would not necessarily emerge in uniform sequence. The details of the passion would be meaningless unless from the start they were fitted into a sequence leading from arrest to crucifixion. One could scarcely tell of the arrest of Jesus without telling of the outcome; the sentencing had to precede the execution, etc. But the resurrection appearances were first reported to root Christian faith in the risen Jesus and to justify the apostolic preaching. To do this it would be enough to report one or two appearances of Jesus and not necessary to supply a chain of these appearances. And obviously the appearances that were reported would be those made to the more important figures known by Christians, for example, Peter, the Twelve, and James; appearances to women and to minor disciples would be put into the background and would not form part of the kerygma. The important Palestinian communities of Jerusalem and of Galilee might retain the memory of appearances with local associations. If at the stage of preaching recalled by Paul the geographical location of an appearance was not a matter of import, this factor would become important when the evangelists tried to fit appearances into a continuous narrative beginning with the empty tomb in Jerusalem. At times the story that came to an evangelist may have had a fixed locale that he preserved; at other times he may have adapted the story and made it fit into a locale dictated by his purpose in writing. It is no accident that Luke and John xx favor the tradition of appearances at Jerusalem. John has stressed Jerusalem in describing the public ministry of Jesus; and Luke (ix 51, xiii 33) made Jerusalem the goal of Jesus' life and the place from which the Christian message was to spread to the world (xxiv 47; Acts i 8).

Thus the divergency as to locale and sequence found in the Gospel narratives of the post-resurrectional appearances of Jesus is not necessarily a refutation of the historicity of those appearances but may be the product of the way in which and the purpose for which the stories were told and preserved. Today can we get behind the divergencies and construct a sequence of appearances, and thus settle the problem of whether originally Jesus was thought to have appeared *to the disciples* first in Galilee or in Jerusalem? The fact that a redactor appended a chapter of Galilean appearances (John xxi) to a chapter of Jerusalem appearances (John xx) has naturally guided harmonistic approaches. It has become customary to think that Jesus first appeared to the Twelve (Eleven) in Jerusalem, that they subsequently went to Galilee where Jesus appeared to them again, and that finally they returned to Jerusalem where Jesus appeared to them once more before ascending (Acts i). Such a sequence does too much violence to the Gospel evidence. *If* one must venture beyond the evidence to establish a sequence of appearances to the disciples, then one should probably place the appearances in Galilee before the appearances in Jerusalem. The Marcan/Matthean view, expressed in the words of the angel to the women at the tomb, is that the disciples were to go to Galilee that they might see Jesus (Mark xvi 7; Matt xxviii 7). Such a directive leaves no room for immediate Jerusalem appearances. Moreover, if Jesus did appear immediately to the disciples in Jerusalem and commissioned them, why would they then have returned to Galilee and resumed their normal occupations (John xxi 3)? On the other hand, if one recognizes that the Lucan and Johannine dating of the Jerusalem appearances on Easter Sunday was probably dictated by theological interests, there is nothing in the appearances themselves that would militate against placing these appearances after the Galilee appearances. If Jesus first commissioned the disciples in Galilee, they might very well have returned to Jerusalem to begin their ministry of preaching, and there Jesus could have appeared to them a final time. But such reconstruction is highly speculative and represents an interest not shared by the evangelists themselves in any marked way.

A more biblical approach is to suppose that one basic appearance underlies all the main Gospel accounts of appearances to the Twelve (Eleven), no matter at what time or place the appearances are placed by the evangelists (A. Descamps, *Biblica* 40 [1959], 726–41). Dodd, "Appearances," has made a form-critical study of the narratives of the appearances of Jesus and noted the common patterns. He distinguishes two general types, namely the Concise Narratives and the Circumstantial Narratives, along with narratives that contain features of both. (Benoit prefers another designation for the two types: narratives that contain a mission and narratives that contain a recognition.)

(A) Concise Narratives. Their pattern may be broken down into five features:

1. A situation is described in which Jesus' followers are bereft of him.
2. The appearance of Jesus.
3. His greeting to his followers.
4. Their recognition of him.
5. His word of command or mission.

As pure examples of this type Dodd classifies the accounts of the appearance to the women as they left the tomb (Matt xxviii 8–10), the appearance to the Eleven on a mountain in Galilee (Matt xxviii 16–20), and the appearance to the disciples in Jerusalem on Easter evening (John xx 19–21).

(B) Circumstantial Narratives. These are carefully composed and dramatic tales that serve as a vehicle for reflections upon the meaning of the resurrection. The recognition of Jesus is the central point of the narrative, and often there is no clear command. As pure examples of this type Dodd classifies the accounts of the appearance to the disciples on the road to Emmaus (Luke xxiv 13–35) and the appearance to the disciples by the shore of the Sea of Tiberias (John xxi 1–14).

(C) Mixed Narratives. These are basically Concise Narratives with some developments evocative of the Circumstantial Narratives. Dodd classifies here the appearance to the Eleven described in the Marcan Appendix (xvi 14–15), the appearance to the Eleven and others in Jerusalem (Luke xxiv 36–49), and the appearance to Thomas (John xx 26–29). Dodd finds the appearance to Mary Magdalene in John xx 11–17 quite unique and difficult to classify.

If we concentrate on the appearances to the Twelve (Eleven; disciples as a group), they are all found in the Concise or Mixed Narratives with the exception of John xxi 1–14. This means that Matthew, Luke, John xx, and the Marcan Appendix all follow a basic pattern in describing this appearance of Jesus to the Twelve. When the disciples are gathered together, not without fear, Jesus appears and is recognized (sometimes after an initial greeting). He then gives them a solemn missionary command. This appearance does far more than assure the disciples of Jesus' victory over death; it commissions them to preach, to baptize, to forgive sins—in short to carry to men the news of Jesus and the salvation wrought by him. (The idea that the sight of the risen Jesus is an essential part of what constitutes a man an apostle is very similar to the OT idea that a vision of the heavenly court constituted a man a prophet, enabling him to speak God's word: Isa vi 1–13; Jer i 4 ff.; I Kings xxii 19–22; Ezek i–ii.) Thus it makes little sense to construct a series of such appearances to the Twelve; each Gospel witness is reporting a slightly different version of an appearance that was constitutive of the Christian community.

Turning from the appearance to the Twelve, which is basically a Concise Narrative in type, we may consider for a moment the conversation and details that appear in the Mixed and Circumstantial Narratives and ask what prompted the addition or preservation of such material. Some of the additional material stems from the compositional efforts of the evangelist who has made an appearance serve as a vehicle for theological emphases. Thus, the conversation of Jesus with the two disciples on the road to Emmaus (Luke xxiv 13–35) and with the Eleven on the same evening (especially 44–49) is almost a compendium of the kerygma that

THE VARIANT GOSPEL NARRATIVES OF THE VISIT OF THE WOMEN TO THE TOMB

	Mark xvi 1-8	Matt xxviii	Luke xxiv	John xx
Time	Very early First day of week Sun risen	First day of week Growing light	First day of week At first dawn	Early First day of the week Still dark
Women	Mary Magdalene Mary, mother of James Salome	Mary Magdalene Other Mary	Mary Magdalene Mary, mother of James Joanna Others	Mary Magdalene (Note "we" in vs. 2)
Purpose	Bought aromatic oils Came to anoint	Came to see tomb	Had aromatic oils from Friday Took aromatic oils along	
Visual Phenomena	Stone already rolled back Youth sitting inside on right	Earthquake Angel descended He rolled back the stone He sat on stone (outside)	Stone already rolled back Two men standing (inside)	Stone already moved away (Later) two angels sitting inside
Conversation	Youth said: Not to fear Jesus not here He is raised Tell disciples that he is going to Galilee There you will see him	Angel said: Not to fear Jesus not here He is raised Tell disciples that he is going to Galilee There you will see him	Men asked: Why seek living among dead? Jesus not here He is raised As he told you while still in Galilee	(Later) angels asked: Why do you weep? (Later) Mary answered: They took my Lord away (Later Jesus gives Mary a message for disciples)
Reaction	Women fled trembling, astonished Told no one	Women went away quickly with fear, great joy To tell disciples	Women left Told Eleven and rest	Mary ran to Peter and to Beloved Disciple Told them that body had been taken

Luke gives in greater detail in Acts. John xx 17 uses Jesus' words to Magdalene to expound the thesis that the resurrection of Jesus is part of his return to the Father who will now beget the disciples as His own children by giving the Spirit through Jesus. The statement of Jesus to Thomas in John xx 29 reflects Johannine interest in the relation of sight to faith. If we may trace such expansions to the editorial work of the evangelist himself, there are other developments, often apologetic in purpose, that may have been part of the narratives as they came down to the evangelists. The Jerusalem tradition of appearances seems to have stressed the reality of Jesus' body, and this appears in different ways in the different accounts: for example, the risen Jesus could eat (Luke xxiv 41–43; Acts x 41) and his wounds could be seen (Luke xxiv 39; John xx 20—developed at length in 25 and 27). Perhaps, too, some of the drama of the recognition in the Circumstantial Narratives is more the product of long recitation than of the evangelist's individual genius. Although these additional details and conversations have occasionally entered the narrative of the appearance to the Twelve (especially in Luke), they were naturally given greater play in descriptions of appearances that had less constitutive force for the Christian community.

The Narratives of the Finding of the Empty Tomb

There are also some observations about this type of narrative that are important before we turn to our commentary on John. The tomb narrative is found in the four Gospels, but obviously not in the Marcan Appendix and John xxi which have been added to accounts that already tell of the empty tomb. There is more uniformity in narratives of the finding of the empty tomb than there is in the narratives of the appearances of Jesus. Nevertheless, most critics assign the narratives of the empty tomb to a later stratum of tradition than that from which the main narratives of the appearances come, and some scholars regard them as purely apologetic creations. In part, this attitude stems from the fact that there is no specific mention of the empty tomb in the primitive formulae, for example, in Acts or in I Cor xv. Moreover, the tomb narratives as they now stand contain features, such as angelic appearances, that may reflect popular storytelling. Bultmann, HST, pp. 287–90, reduces all the stories to one, namely, the basic story of Mark xvi 1–8; and he characterizes this as an apologetic legend told to prove the reality of the resurrection. He contends that only secondarily was the story of the tomb related to the future appearances of Jesus (in Galilee).

In the judgment of other scholars more caution is required. It is interesting that in a recent collection of articles on the resurrection (SMRFJC), three of the five writers, C. F. D. Moule, U. Wilckens, and G. Delling, are not at all ready to dismiss the story of the empty tomb either as very late or purely apologetic. See also the articles of W. Nauck and H. von Campenhausen for detailed criticism favoring the historicity of the story. We must make two important distinctions in considering the evidence. First, we must recognize that it is one thing to judge that the story of the empty tomb was not a part of the primitive preaching about the resurrection and it is another thing to claim that the fact of the empty tomb was not presupposed by this preaching. Second, we must distinguish in the story itself between the basic narrative and later accretions designed to explain the narrative.

Our first question, then, is whether or not the early preaching presupposed the fact that Jesus' body was no longer in the tomb. The most frequently cited argument still has force: How did the preaching that Jesus was victorious over death ever gain credence if his corpse or skeleton lay in a tomb known to all? His enemies would certainly have brought this forward as an objection; yet in all the anti-resurrection argumentation reflected indirectly in the Gospels or in the 2nd-century Christian apologists we never find an affirmation that the body was in the tomb. There are Christian arguments to show that the body was not stolen or confused in a common burial, but the opponents seem to accept the basic fact that the body can no longer be found. Even in the Jewish legend that a gardener named Judas took the body only to bring it back, there is a recognition that the tomb was empty. Moreover, the Christian memory of Joseph of Arimathea, which can only with great difficulty be explained as a fabrication, would be rather pointless unless the tomb he supplied had special significance.

Besides this practical consideration, one may question whether the story of the empty tomb was purely apologetic in origin, as many have claimed. R. H. Fuller, BiRes 4 (1960), 11–13, suggests that there was a close relationship between the story of the empty tomb and the primitive kerygma. The Pauline formula in I Cor xv 3–5 consists of two sets of two members:

> He died for our sins according to the Scriptures,
> and he was buried.
> And he was raised on the third day according to the Scriptures,
> and he appeared (to Cephas, etc.).

Fuller makes inquiry about the third member which is antecedent to the appearance of Jesus, just as his death is antecedent to burial. Jesus' appearances to his disciples gave rise to the confession that he had been seen, but what gave rise to the confession that he was raised? Since in the Gospels it is the story of the empty tomb that is related to this (angelic) proclamation, Fuller proposes that this story did not take its origin in apologetics but as background for the kerygmatic formulation, "He was raised." (We may add in passing that the contention that the story was fashioned for purely apologetic purposes is difficult to believe, for then why would one choose to make the witnesses to the empty tomb *women* whose testimony in contemporary estimation would be of less value than that of men?) Many argue that the Pauline references to *burial* and to being raised *on the third day* also suppose the fact of the empty tomb. The earliest evidence gives no precise time for the resurrection itself (which is not described); the first fixed time is Sunday morning when the women come to the tomb. It was the discovery of the empty tomb on the third day that probably gave rise to the Christian stress on three days, a stress that was deemed important because it could be related to some OT passages. (Some scholars find in the OT the origin of the idea of three days, but the passages are too vague to have served as more than confirmation once the idea arose from the Easter events themselves.) As for the relation between Paul's mention of burial and the fact of the empty tomb, this has some force because the Pauline understanding of resurrection in I Cor xv 20 ff. supposes the transformation of a body that has gone into the earth and not merely a non-corporeal victory over death. There is also the imagery of Jesus as the first-born of the dead in Rom viii 29. (See J. Mánek, "The Apostle Paul and the Empty Tomb," NovT 2 [1957], 276–80.) Several other references in the apostolic preaching of the resurrection that mention burial have also been interpreted as supposing the empty tomb (Rom vi 4; Acts ii 29–32; xiii 36–37). These arguments are not without flaw, but they do make it clear that the problem of how the idea of an empty tomb originated is not easily dismissed.

The second distinction that we made concerned the substance of the tomb story and its legendary accretions. The chart we have given shows a considerable variation in the details of what the women saw at the tomb, and one can plausibly argue that the varied angelic appearances and angelic conversations represent a dramatization of the import of the empty tomb. There are also secondary apologetic features, for instance, in Matthew's attempt to make the women witnesses of the opening of the tomb and also in Matthew's whole story about the guard at the tomb. But behind these variations there is a basic tradition that some women followers of Jesus came to the tomb on Easter morning and found it empty—a tradition that is older than any of the preserved accounts.

The question of antiquity might be settled if we could decide whether the story of the empty tomb was originally part of the primitive passion account (Marcan A source on p. 788). Both Bultmann and Taylor doubt that Mark xvi 1–8, in its present form, was part of A; but Taylor, p. 659, contends that the story of burial and some reference to the resurrection did belong to the A source. Bultmann, HST, p. 274, acknowledges that the burial account is for the most part historical and without legendary traits; yet he is not certain at what stage it became part of the primitive passion account (p. 279). He denies that the narrative of the empty tomb was ever part of this primitive account (p. 284). Dodd, *Tradition*, p. 143, thinks that the traditional passion account would have ended in the pattern found in I Cor xv 3–5: death, burial, finding of empty tomb from which Jesus had been raised, and appearances (with the last detail showing much variance). Wilckens, SMRFJC, pp. 72–73, argues that the primitive passion account concluded with the story of the empty tomb but had no story of appearances. W. Knox, *Sources of the Synoptic Gospels* (Cambridge University, 1953), I, 149, reconstructs a primitive "Twelve-source," somewhat resembling the A account, which contained the story that the women found the tomb empty and told the Eleven (the Pauline phrase "he was raised on the third day" is a summary of this). The diversity of views shows the difficulty of the question, and perhaps there is no way to settle it, although it is hard to conceive of a basic Christian narrative that ended with the death and burial without an explicit assurance of Jesus' victory over death. The fact that the evangelists differ in their narratives of the appearances is sufficient proof that no localized appearance was part of the primitive passion account. Correspondingly the fact that they agree in telling us that the women followers of Jesus found the tomb empty on Sunday morning suggests that in the primitive passion account the story of the burial of Jesus was followed by this indication that the grave was not the end for him. One could then theorize that in subsequent Gospel development the basic story of the finding of the tomb was expanded by the addition of interpretive material serving to clarify the significance of the empty tomb (this would have been done somewhat differently in the Marcan/Matthean tradition, in the Lucan, and in the Johannine). Finally, narratives of the appearances of Jesus would have been added, with corresponding adaptation of the tomb story. In such a theory, one might propose that Mark xvi 1–8, if it never had the lost ending, represents (without vs. 7) the stage before the addition of the appearance narratives, and thus, though expanded, is quite faithful to the outline of the primitive passion account.

In summary, the Christian claim that the women found the tomb empty has not really been proved to be of late origin; rather such a claim may have been presupposed as far back as we can trace the tradition of the proclamation that Jesus had been raised. Moule, SMRFJC, p. 10, may well be right in insisting that the idea that Jesus' body is no longer in the tomb is not just an interesting detail about his victory over death but is essential to understanding a major aspect in Christian theology, namely, that what God creates is not destroyed but is re-created and transformed.

[The Bibliography for this section is included in the Bibliography for the whole of ch. xx, at the end of §69.]

68. THE RISEN JESUS:
—SCENE ONE
(xx 1–18)

At the Tomb

XX 1 Early on the first day of the week, while it was still dark, Mary Magdalene came to the tomb. She saw that the stone had been moved away from the tomb; 2 so she went running to Simon Peter and to the other disciple (the one whom Jesus loved) and told them, "They took the Lord from the tomb, and we do not know where they put him!"

3 Peter and the other disciple started out on their way to the tomb. 4 The two of them were running side by side; but the other disciple, being faster, outran Peter and reached the tomb first. 5 He bent down to peer in and saw the cloth wrappings lying there, but he did not go in. 6 Presently, Simon Peter came along behind him and went straight into the tomb. He observed the wrappings lying there, 7 and the piece of cloth that had covered the head, not lying with the wrappings, but rolled up in a place by itself. 8 Then, in turn, the other disciple who had reached the tomb first also entered. He saw and believed. (9 Remember that as yet they did not understand the Scripture that Jesus had to rise from the dead.) 10 With this the disciples went back home.

11 Meanwhile, Mary was standing [outside] by the tomb, weeping. Even as she wept, she bent down to peer into the tomb, 12 and observed two angels in white, one seated at the head and the other at the foot of the place where Jesus' body had lain. 13 "Woman," they asked her, "why are you weeping?" She told them, "Because they took my Lord away and I do not know where they put him."

14 She had just said this when she turned around and caught sight of Jesus standing there. She did not realize, however, that it was Jesus. 15 "Woman," he asked her, "why are you weeping? Who is it you are looking for?" Thinking that he was the gardener, she said to him, "Sir,

1: *came, saw;* 2: *went running, told;* 5: *saw;* 6: *came along, observed;* 12: *observed;* 13: *asked, told;* 14: *caught sight;* 15: *asked, said.* In the historical present tense.

if you are the one who carried him off, tell me where you have put him, and I will take him away." 16 Jesus said to her, "Mary!" She turned to him and said [in Hebrew], "Rabbuni!" (which means "Teacher"). 17 "Don't cling to me," Jesus told her, "for I have not yet ascended to the Father. But go to my brothers and tell them, 'I am ascending to my Father and your Father, to my God and your God!' " 18 Mary Magdalene went to the disciples. "I have seen the Lord!" she announced, reporting what he had said to her.

16: *said, said;* 17: *told;* 18: *went.* In the historical present tense.

NOTES

xx 1. *Early.* The adverb *prōi,* omitted in some minor textual witnesses, is also found in Mark xvi 2 ("very early") and the Marcan Appendix (xvi 9). For the possible range of time, namely 3–6 A.M., see NOTE on xviii 28. To speak of these hours as early in the day implies the Roman calculation of hours from midnight, for by Jewish reckoning the day had begun Saturday evening after sunset.

on the first day of the week. This expression (also vs. 19 below), *mia sabbatōn,* employing a cardinal numeral for an ordinal (a Semitism? BDF, §247[1]; MTGS, p. 187), occurs with slight variation in the four Gospels: Luke xxiv 1 and John have identical expressions. The Marcan Appendix (xvi 9) uses an ordinal numeral; the *Gospel of Peter,* 50, speaks of "the Lord's day." Note that here the Gospels do not employ the kerygmatic expression "on the third day" or "after three days," perhaps because the basic time indication of the finding of the tomb was fixed in Christian memory before the possible symbolism in the three-day reckoning had yet been perceived. The Gospel phrase is possible in Greek because in that language *sabbaton* means both "week" and "Sabbath"; in the Hebrew of the OT *šabbāt* does not mean "week" (E. Vogt, *Biblica* 40 [1959], 1008–11), although it has that meaning in later Hebrew.

while it was still dark. If the expression "early" leads us to think of the period between 3 and 6 A.M., the evangelists do not agree as to when in that span of time the women came to the tomb. In general, the Synoptic Gospels favor an hour when it was already light. Luke xxiv 1 speaks of "first dawn" (*orthrou batheōs*—the *Gospel of Peter,* 50, uses just *orthrou*). Mark xvi 1–2 reports that the women bought spices on Saturday night after the Sabbath was over and then came to the tomb Sunday morning "very early . . . when the sun had risen," the latter phrase being almost a direct contradiction of John's report. (Taylor, pp. 604–5, considers this Marcan phrase to be a corruption of the original time indication, but really "when the sun had risen" need be no more than a specification of "very early.") Matt xxviii 1 has the difficult expression: "After the Sabbath [*opse sabbatōn*] at the first rays of light on the first day of the week [*sabbatōn* again!]." (*Opse sabbatōn* is probably not to be translated "late on the Sabbath"; cf. BDF, §164[4].) Drawing on Mishnaic Hebrew, J. M. Grintz, JBL 79 (1960), 37–38, interprets Matthew to mean that the women came to the tomb at night right after the Sabbath ended, but most exegetes understand Matthew to be referring to dawn on Sunday morning.

Some try to harmonize the Synoptic-Johannine discrepancy by maintaining that Mary Magdalene, the only woman mentioned by John, went ahead of the other women and reached the tomb while it was still dark (so John), but that by the time the other women got there it had lightened. Another interpretation would see a theological motif behind the respective chronologies. In the Synoptic tradition "light" is appropriate, for the women find an angel (or angels) at the tomb who gives them the good news that Jesus has been raised, and thus light has triumphed over the darkness of the tomb (G. Hebert, ScotJT 15 [1962], 66–73). On the other hand, "darkness" is appropriate for John, for all that the empty tomb means to Mary is that the body of Jesus has been stolen.

Mary Magdalene. John names only her (cf. Marcan Appendix); Matthew names two women; Mark names three; and Luke (xxiv 10) names three along with "the other women." The *Gospel of Peter,* 51, records that Mary Magdalene took women friends with her to the tomb. We note that, although the Synoptics name other women, Magdalene is always mentioned first. Bernard, II, 656, finds the Synoptic tradition more plausible, for a woman would not be likely to go alone in the dark to a place of execution outside the city walls. Except for Luke viii 2, which places Magdalene in the Galilean ministry as a woman from whom seven devils were cast out, she is mentioned only in relation to the crucifixion and the empty tomb. The *Gospel of Peter,* 50, calls her "a disciple [*mathētria*] of the Lord." Her surname indicates that she probably came from Magdala (Taricheae) on the northwest shore of the Lake of Galilee, about seven miles southwest of Capernaum. Bernard, II, 657, is one of the few modern authors to continue to identify her with Mary of Bethany near Jerusalem, and he suggests that she had been keeping perfume for the day of Jesus' embalming (xii 3–7; see vol. 29, pp. 449–52). The OS[sin] omits "Magdalene" both here and in 18, leaving the ambiguous "Mary." From the time of Tatian's *Diatessaron* (2nd century) there are elements of a tradition among the Church Fathers, especially those writing in Syriac, that it was Mary the mother of Jesus who came to the tomb. For instance, Ephraem, *On the Diatessaron* xxi 27; CSCO 145 (Armenian 2):235–36, clearly applies John's account in xx 1–18 to Mary the mother of Jesus. Loisy, p. 504, thinks that such a reference may be original and that the account may have been conformed to the Magdalene tradition of the Synoptics. But John never speaks of Jesus' mother as "Mary"; and, as Loisy admits, xix 25–27 seems to represent the final appearance of Jesus' mother in the Gospel.

came to the tomb. John does not specify why. Mark and Luke indicate that the women had bought aromatic oils and were coming to anoint Jesus' body. Matthew says only that they came to see the tomb—probably a modification dictated by the logic of Matthew's narrative; for Matthew (alone) has reported that the tomb was guarded, and thus the women would not have been allowed to enter the tomb to anoint the corpse. The *Gospel of Peter,* 50, says that Mary came because hitherto she had not done what women customarily did for their beloved departed, seemingly to wail and to lament (52–54). Whether or not one accepts the reason offered by Mark and Luke will depend on whether one regards as probable the Johannine tradition that Jesus' body had been amply prepared for burial on Friday. If one does follow John, one may suppose that the *Gospel of Peter* divined correctly. The custom of mourning at the grave site is mentioned in John xi 31. The Midrash Rabbah c 7 on Gen 1 10 reports a dispute about whether intense mourning could be cut down to two days and gives the opinion of Rabbi Bar Kappara (ca. A.D. 200) that mourning was at its height on the third day. The minor tractate of TalBab, *Semaḥoth* or *Ebel Rabbathi* 8:1, says that one may go out to the tomb and examine the body within a three-day period after death without being suspected of superstition. If one follows the Synoptic tradition that the women were coming to anoint the body, then John's omission of that detail was probably deliberate, following from the (inaccurate) introduction of an anointing before burial. Little credence should be given to the objection that in a hot country no one would come to anoint a body that would have begun to rot. Actually, it can be quite cool in mountainous Jerusalem in early spring; moreover, those who recounted the story presumably knew local weather and customs and would scarcely have invented a patently silly explanation.

the stone. John writes as if the reader would have known of this stone; yet in describing the burial John, along with Luke, did not mention the sealing of the tomb with a stone. Contrast Mark xv 46 and Matt xxvii 60 where we are told that Joseph rolled a large stone against the opening of the tomb. Here the Fourth Gospel may be preserving the wording of an earlier tradition.

had been moved away. The Synoptics speak of its being "rolled away." In Mark and Luke this had been done before the women arrived, presumably by the angels who were there to greet the women; Matt xxviii 2 is more specific: "An angel of the Lord descended from heaven and came and rolled back the stone." The *Gospel of Peter*, 37, reports that the stone rolled by itself and went off to the side. John gives no hint of how he thinks the stone was moved.

from the tomb. John uses *ek*, "from"; Luke xxiv 2 has the same phrase with *apo*; Mark xvi 3 has "from [*ek*] the door of the tomb"; a few textual witnesses of John have the Marcan expression with *apo*. We are probably to think of a horizontal cave tomb rather than a vertical shaft tomb (see NOTE on xi 38). Palestinian archaeology shows us that the entrance to such tombs was on ground level through a small doorway, usually less than a yard high, so that adults had to crawl in (notice "bent down to peer in" in vs. 5). The tomb could be sealed by a boulder rolled against the entrance; but the more elaborate tombs had a wheel-shaped slab of stone that rolled in a track across the entrance, having the effect of a sliding door. (Matt xxviii 2 apparently supposes a boulder rather than a wheel-stone; for the angel is said to roll away the stone and sit upon it, and a wheel-stone would have been rolled back into a rock recess.) On the inside some of the larger tombs had an antechamber, leading off from which there were burial chambers. We find several basic types of burial accommodations. There were *kōkīm* or tunnels, cut in a "pigeon-hole" arrangement, about six or seven feet deep into the rock, approximately two feet wide and two feet high. The body was inserted headfirst, filling up the tunnel. Secondly, there were *arcosolia* or semicircular niches, formed by cutting away the side walls of the cave for a depth of about two or three feet, beginning about two and a half feet up from ground level. The niche was so cut as to leave either a flat shelf or a trough on which or into which a body could be placed. Thirdly, there were also "bench tombs," where the body was laid on a bench that ran around three sides of the burial chamber. Sometimes a sarcophagus was used. It is interesting that in the Church of the Holy Sepulcher (NOTE on xix 17, "he went out") Jewish graves within sixty feet of the traditional tomb of Jesus are of the *kōkīm* type; but in a nearby area a family tomb of Jesus' era consisted of a chamber with *arcosolia* shelf graves on either side. John probably thinks of

Jesus' tomb as belonging to the *arcosolium* type, for in vs. 12 he describes angels seated at the head and the foot of the place where Jesus' body had lain. The sitting may also imply a shelf rather than a trough, but the early pilgrims to Jesus' tomb in the Church of the Holy Sepulcher saw a trough (Kopp, HPG, p. 393). The possibility that John's description reflects a genuine Palestinian tradition is increased by the observations of G. Schille and J. Jeremias, as developed by Nauck, pp. 261–62. He proposes that the Jerusalem Christian community may have come to the grave of Jesus to celebrate the memory of the resurrection, so that the empty tomb became a type of *weli* or shrine. Thus its description could have been known in later generations.

2. *so.* In the logic of the present sequence are we meant to think that Mary looked into the tomb or that she surmised the absence of the body from the fact that the tomb was no longer sealed? While the former is often assumed on the basis of common sense, the latter is suggested by John's indication that it was still dark and by the report in vs. 11 that she did peer in at a later time. Many solve the difficulty by literary criticism, supposing that at one time vs. 1 was followed by 11.

to Simon Peter. We may compare to this the angelic message to the women at the tomb in Mark xvi 7: "Go tell his disciples *and Peter.*" It is often suggested that Mary went to Peter because he was the leader of Jesus' followers; but more simply it must be remembered that he did not flee with the others and is recorded as being near at hand during Jesus' interrogation by the Jewish authorities (John xviii 27).

and to the other disciple (the one whom Jesus loved). He, too, is recorded as having been present during the passion (xix 26–27). The repetition of the preposition "to" has been noted by commentators. Those who think that the Beloved Disciple was not mentioned in the original form of the story find here the sign of an addition. Others theorize that Peter and the Beloved Disciple were not at the same place (yet see vs. 19 where the disciples are huddled together); if so, this separate housing is scarcely to be related to xvi 32 which speaks of the disciples being scattered, "each on his own." Grass, p. 55, thinks that the two were together; perhaps the other disciples were there as well, but only these two wanted or dared to go. In any case, they are pictured as setting out for the tomb from the same place, running side by side.

Although we have previously heard of the disciple whom Jesus loved (xiii 23–26, xix 26–27), this is the first time we find him identified with "the other disciple" (see vol. 29, pp. xciii–xciv; also NOTE on "another disciple" in xviii 15). The textual witnesses show variation in the clause "the one whom Jesus loved"; it is almost certainly a parenthetical editorial insertion, for in vss. 4 and 8 this man is called only "the other disciple," the more original designation. (We agree, therefore, with Boismard, RB 69 [1962], 202, footnote, that "the other disciple" and "the Beloved Disciple" represent the terminology of two different stages of composition; but we do not find any real evidence for Boismard's contention that "the Beloved Disciple" appears only in scenes of John that were edited by Luke.) Bultmann, p. 530[3], does not agree that these are two titles; he would read "to another, namely, the disciple whom Jesus loved."

told them. If the two men are pictured as being at different places, this must be understood in terms of successive telling.

They took. It is useless to speculate about the identity of the "they," for the indefinite third person plural, used thus, may simply be equivalent to the English passive: "The Lord has been taken" (cf. NOTE on "they collect" in xv 6). Tomb robbery was a troublesome crime at this time, as witnessed in an imperial edict against it. This edict, first published by F. Cumont, has been carefully translated and studied by F. de Zulueta, *Journal of Roman Studies* 22 (1932), 184–97. (For just a translation see C. K. Barrett, *The New Testament Background: Selected Documents* [London: SPCK, 1956], p. 15.) It dates from the early 1st century A.D.; the "Caesar" who issued it may have been Augustus, Tiberius, or Claudius. Although it was acquired among antiquities at Nazareth, we are not certain that the marble slab on which it was inscribed actually stood in that town. Therefore, any connection with Christians or "Nazarenes" and the burial of Jesus is highly tenuous.

the Lord. Tatian and the Palestinian Syriac read "my Lord," probably under the influence of vs. 13. In his account of the ministry John has avoided use of "the Lord" as a title (see NOTES on iv 1, vi 23, xi 2), a common Lucan usage. Perhaps, now that he is describing the post-resurrectional period, the evangelist becomes more free, acknowledging that this title became common as an expression of the faith of the Christian community. One may object that Mary does not yet believe in Jesus as the Lord, but this objection also applies to the use of "my Lord" in 13. Hartmann, p. 199, argues that the use of "the Lord" in 2 is a sign that this verse came down to the evangelist from tradition (so also vss. 18, 20, and 25).

we do not know. Is the "we" an implicit reminiscence that others were involved in the visit to the tomb, as in the Synoptic tradition? (Tatian and some versions read a singular here, again probably in imitation of vs. 13 which has "I do not know.") Wellhausen and Spitta think of the "we" as a redactional attempt to harmonize John and the Synoptics; but it is strange that, when so many differences were left in John, such a minor and subtle harmonization should have been attempted. Bultmann, p. 529[4], 530[3], who thinks that vs. 2 is an editorial connective, judges that the "we" is a Semitic way of speaking with Greek analogues. Support for this can be found in G. Dalman, *Grammatik des jüdisch-palästinischen Aramäisch* (Darmstadt, 1960 reprint), p. 265: "In Galilean Aramaic the first person plural was frequently used for the first person singular." One wonders, then, why the singular appears in vs. 13.

they put him. The verb is *tithenai*, translated as "buried" in xix 41–42.

3. *started out on their way.* Literally "Peter went out . . . and they were coming." The singular verb is pointed out by Hartmann, p. 200, as a sign that in the original form of the story Peter was the only one who accompanied Mary back to the tomb, so that we should understand that Peter went out and he and Mary were coming to the tomb. If Mary were Peter's companion, her presence at the tomb in vs. 11 would offer no difficulty.

to the tomb. Literally "into [*eis*] the tomb." If vss. 4–6a have been added in the process of later editing (see COMMENT), then the literal meaning may have been intended—they came into the tomb. But as the narrative now stands, a modification is required, for in vss. 4–5 the two disciples are still not within the tomb. Some have posited a tomb with an antechamber which the disciples would have entered in vs. 3. This is dubious, since in vss. 11–12 Magdalene can see the burial place from her position outside the tomb—at most this would allow a small, open anteroom. (Schwank, "Leere Grab," p. 394, observes that the chapter is composite and proposes that possibly two different conceptions of the tomb may be found in 3–8 and in 11b–14a, with the latter less accurate.) More simply *eis*, "into," is used confusedly for *pros*, "to, toward," in koine Greek (ZGB, §97). We note that *eis* is used in vs. 1 ("came to the tomb") as well; and there it is patent that Mary is outside, for she sees that the stone has been moved from the entrance.

4. *The two of them were running.* Luke xxiv 12a, a Western Noninterpolation, offers the only Synoptic parallel, with a slight difference of vocabulary: "Peter rose and ran to the tomb."

being faster, outran. John's expression is tautological (BDF, §484), a fact that has produced some scribal variants. The greater speed of this disciple has contributed to the depicting of John as a young man and Peter as older. Ishodad of Merv traces John's greater speed to the fact that he was unmarried!

reached the tomb. Literally "came into the tomb"; the preposition is *eis* (see vs. 3 above) as contrasted with *epi* in Luke xxiv 12a.

5. *He bent down to peer in and saw the cloth wrappings lying there.* The author evidently imagines that by now there was sufficient daylight to allow a small, low opening to serve as the source of illumination for the burial chamber. We have mentioned the parallel to vs. 3 in Luke xxiv 12a; the second part of the Lucan verse reads: "[Peter] bent down to peer in and saw the cloth wrappings lying alone." Some textual witnesses of Luke drop the "alone," while some witnesses of John contain it. The "cloth wrappings" are the *othonia* of John xix 40 (see NOTE there); the mention of *othonia* in Luke xxiv 12 indicates that this verse is an addition, for the Lucan burial narrative referred only to a *sindōn*, "shroud."

The expression "lying there" translates a form of the verb *keisthai* which, while it means "to lie, recline," can indicate mere presence without any stress on position (thus, "there," instead of "lying there"). In any case, presumably the "there" is where the body had been, either on the shelf or in the trough of the *arcosolium*, although the fact that the wrappings can be seen from the entrance suggests that the evangelist is thinking of a shelf. Many English translations render the Greek as "lying on the ground," but this gives a wrong image of where the corpse would have lain. Balagué, pp. 185–86, discusses *keisthai* and argues that it means that the wrappings were lying flat or smoothed out, having collapsed once the body was no longer contained in them. By contrast, he would argue that in vs. 7 the head cloth, which was "not lying with the wrappings" (our translation), was not flat but rolled up, maintaining a certain consistency that made it stand out (under the *sindōn* that Balagué assumes to have covered the whole). Auer, *op. cit.*, traces the history of the Latin translation of the Greek, maintaining that the OL *posita*, "placed there," was a poor translation and opting for *jacentia*, "lying there"—all this in support of his theory that the wrappings preserved the form of Jesus' body.

he did not go in. We shall discuss in the COMMENT the possible theological import of Peter's entering before the Beloved Disciple. Many interpreters offer practical explanations: the Beloved Disciple did not go in because he was surprised, or afraid, or wished to avoid the ritual contamination that came from touching a corpse. Such explanations are not in harmony with the idealized portrait of this disciple in the Gospel.

6. *behind him.* Literally "following him." Since "to follow" is Johannine terminology for discipleship (vol. 29, p. 78), Barrett, p. 468, thinks that the author may be trying to subordinate Peter to the Beloved Disciple (see COMMENT).

went straight into the tomb. In Mark (xvi 5—same vocabulary) and Luke the women enter the tomb; in John only Peter and the Beloved Disciple enter.

observed. While in 5 John uses *blepein* to describe the Beloved Disciple's seeing the wrappings (also Luke xxiv 12), he uses *theōrein* here for Peter's sight. No progression of meaning is verifiable, as if Peter's look was more leisurely or penetrating. *Theōrein* will be used of Mary's seeing the angels in 12 (a sight that did not enable her to understand why they were there) and of her seeing Jesus in 14 (whom she mistakes as the gardener). The verb *idein* will be used in 8 where sight is accompanied by faith. See vol. 29, pp. 501–2.

7. *the piece of cloth that had covered the head.* Soudarion, a loanword in Greek, is from the Latin *sudarium,* a cloth used to wipe off perspiration (*sudor*), something akin to our handkerchief. As conceived here, it was probably the size of a small towel or large napkin. In Luke xix 20 the third servant puts his money in a *soudarion* (see also Acts xix 12—yet the word itself does not specify the size, and Auer, pp. 30–32, identifies the *soudarion* with the *sindōn* of the Synoptics). While this cloth was not mentioned in John's description of Jesus' burial, it was part of Lazarus' burial garb: "his face wrapped in *a cloth*" (xi 44). Probably it passed under the chin and was tied on the top of the head, to prevent the dead man's mouth from falling open.

not lying with the wrappings, but rolled up in a place by itself. The translation of this description is greatly disputed, e.g., Balagué renders it: "not flattened like the wrappings, but on the contrary rolled up in the same place." Almost each word must be considered. First, to what does the negative apply? The negative does not immediately precede *keisthai* (see NOTE on vs. 5), as Balagué's translation implies, but the phrase "with [*meta*] the wrappings." In other words, the *soudarion* may have been "lying," but it was not with the other burial clothes. Balagué, p. 187, contends that here *meta* does not mean "with" but "like" (as occasionally its Hebrew counterpart *'im*), so that the comparison concerns the condition of the cloths rather than their position. Auer, pp. 37–38, proposes that *meta* means "between, among": the *soudarion* (which, for him, covered the whole body) was no longer bound up among the bandages. The words that follow are *alla chōris,* which mean "but separately." However, Balagué and Lavergne suggest that here the expression resembles the Heb. *lᵉbad min* ("apart from, besides") and that *chōris* serves only to emphasize the adversative, whence the translation "but on the contrary." The words *eis hena topon* mean "into one place"; but Balagué, p. 189, sees here a Hebraism for "in the same place." This is a possible translation (see I Cor xii 11; LXX of Eccles iii 20), but then why would the author specially mention the place of the *soudarion* if it was where the other clothes were? We think that the phrase must be rendered in light of the preceding *chōris,* and so a separate place is meant. We are not impressed by Balagué's attempted *reductio ad absurdum,* namely, his argument that this implies the *soudarion* was outside the tomb—it was simply in another part of the burial chamber. (Evidently ancient scribes felt some of the same difficulties encountered by modern scholars, for minor textual witnesses omit one or the other word or phrase in this description.) Last of all we must note the verbal expression "rolled up." Lavergne contends that this meaning for *entylissein* is not attested before the 4th century A.D. (it is reflected in the Vulgate *involutum*). In Luke xxiii 53 and Matt xxvii 59 the verb constitutes part of the description of how Joseph wrapped up the body of Jesus in a shroud, and Lavergne understands John as meaning that the *soudarion* was "wrapped up" in the other burial clothes. However, John may simply mean that the *soudarion* was rolled up in an oval loop, i.e., the shape it had when it was around the head of the corpse.

8. *Then, in turn.* For this use of *tote oun* see BDF, §459².

He saw and believed. This is difficult on two scores. First, the "he" does not agree with the explanatory remark, *"they* did not understand," in vs. 9. Second, the Beloved Disciple, if he came to faith, does not seem to have shared this faith with Magdalene or the other disciples, for no echo of his faith is found in vss. 11–13 or in 19. These difficulties have left their mark in both textual variants and different interpretations. Codex Bezae (suppletor) has the erratic reading "he did *not* believe"; OS^sin and a few Greek mss. read *"they* saw and believed." Since the verb *pisteuein*, "to believe," can have the more profane meaning of "accept as true, be convinced," Augustine, followed by such moderns as Oepke, Von Dobschütz, and Nauck, contends that the Disciple did not come to faith in the resurrection but was convinced that Magdalene spoke the truth when she said that the body was no longer there. However, the evangelist certainly did not introduce the Beloved Disciple into the scene only to have him reach such a trite conclusion. Rather he is the first to believe in the risen Jesus (compare the combination of seeing and believing in vs. 29). For the use of *pisteuein* in an absolute sense without an object, see vol. 29, p. 513; also Dodd, *Interpretation,* pp. 185–86.

9. A few minor textual witnesses place this parenthetical comment after vs. 11, probably so that the "they" who did not understand can include Mary Magdalene along with Peter and thus not apply to the Beloved Disciple. Parenthetical explanations about the effect that the resurrection/glorification of Jesus had on his followers are not infrequent in the Fourth Gospel (ii 22, vii 39, xii 16).

as yet they did not understand the Scripture. In order to reconcile this with the statement in vs. 8 that the Beloved Disciple believed, some OL witnesses read "he" (i.e., Peter) instead of "they." Some interpreters seek to alleviate the difficulty by maintaining that the Gospel is not offering an explanation of why the two disciples failed to believe in the resurrection but of why they ran to the tomb in bewilderment when they heard that Jesus' body was gone. If that is what was meant, the explanation has been inserted in a very awkward place. Hartmann, *art. cit.,* thinks that the "they" originally referred to Peter and to Magdalene, for Hartmann holds that in the original form of the story she was Peter's companion. A second problem concerns "the Scripture" that is referred to. (A few witnesses omit "the Scripture," and thus avoid the problem.) John's implication that only after the appearances of Jesus was the import of the OT prophecies understood agrees with Luke xxiv 25–27. It runs contrary to the thesis of the Synoptic Gospels that Jesus made three detailed predictions of his resurrection (vol. 29, p. 146). Is John's "Scripture" a general reference similar to I Cor xv 4: "He was raised on the third day according to the Scriptures"? Does John mean a number of passages (see p. 929 above in reference to xix 28)? Or does he mean a specific passage, for example, Ps xvi 10 (so Bernard, Hoskyns), or Hos vi 2, or Jon i 17, ii 1? We cannot be sure of the answer; but we do not find plausible a third proposal made by Freed, OTQ, pp. 57–58, that "Scripture" refers to Jesus' own words as written in another Gospel (Luke xxiv 46). We have no evidence that the

Johannine author or editor knew the written Gospel of Luke, nor that he would classify Jesus' words as Scripture. Bultmann, p. 530, regards vs. 9 as an addition by the Ecclesiastical Redactor, in part because interest in a prediction of the resurrection is reflective of community theology. But we cannot assume that the earlier stages of the Gospel were devoid of the influence of community theology. The verse resembles closely xii 14–16, which Bultmann takes to be original (see Smith, p. 224).

had to rise from the dead. The necessity stems from the fact that the resurrection was willed by God, for the Scripture is a guide to God's plan. The verb "to rise" is *anistanai*. Bultmann, pp. 530 and 491, characterizes this as an unJohannine expression, since John more typically speaks of Jesus' ascending or going away. See, however, ii 22: "after his resurrection [=being raised: *ēgerthē*] from the dead"; but Bultmann attributes this also to the redactor.

10. *the disciples went back home.* John says nothing of their cast of mind. The last part of the parallel in Luke xxiv 12 tells us that Peter "went home, wondering at what had happened." Luke xxiv 24 reports that the disciples who went to the tomb found the body gone, as the women had said, but they did not see Jesus. "Home" here is not Galilee, but to wherever they had been in Jerusalem when Magdalene called them. The real purpose of this verse is to get the disciples off the scene and to give the stage to Magdalene.

11. *Mary was standing.* The pluperfect verb suggests to Lagrange, p. 509, that Mary had come back with the two disciples and had waited outside the tomb until they withdrew. If so, why had the Beloved Disciple not communicated to her his insight and faith? Moreover, why is it that when she looks into the tomb, she sees angels and not the burial clothes? This awkwardness is a sign that we have here an editorial joining of once independent episodes.

[outside] by the tomb. The best witnesses have *pros* with the dative, meaning "near, at, by" (BDF, §240²). Sinaiticus reads *en*, "in the tomb," probably a result of the scribe's imagining that the tomb had an antechamber (see NOTE on "to the tomb" in vs. 3). *Exō*, "outside," appears in most witnesses but in different positions; it is omitted by Sinaiticus*, Alexandrinus, OL, OS^sin, the Peshitta, and some witnesses of the Diatessaron. It may well be a scribal clarification. But even without *exō*, quite clearly Mary was outside in the garden. In the Synoptic tradition (Mark xvi 5; Luke xxiv 3) Mary entered the tomb.

weeping. This was not the ordinary lamentation expected from a female relative or friend of the deceased; she wept because she thought that Jesus' body was stolen.

12. *observed.* See NOTE on this verb in 6. In John the angelic apparition inspires in Mary none of the fear, amazement, and prostration that we hear of in the Synoptic accounts of the women at the tomb.

two angels. The "two" is omitted by Sinaiticus* and one OL ms. See the chart on p. 974 for the variation in the number and designation of the angels. The fact that Mark xvi 5 and Luke xxiv 4 speak of men rather than angels led earlier rationalistic critics to assume that originally human beings rather than angels were involved, but a heavenly apparition is in the mind of all the evangelists. The development was not from men to angels; rather heavenly spokesmen were introduced to clarify the meaning of the empty tomb. The *Gospel of Peter* has the most complicated picture. The heavens opened and two men, resplendent in light, came down and entered the tomb which opened for them. The soldiers at the tomb saw these two emerge, supporting another (Jesus) whose head went above the sky (36–40). While the soldiers discussed this, still another man came down from heaven and entered the tomb (44). Presumably he was the one whom the women found when they came to the tomb (55). As for John's *pair* of angels, this was not an unusual concept (II Macc iii 26; Acts i 10).

in white. In Mark xvi 5 the young man (angel) is clothed in a white robe; in Matt xxviii 3 the angel of the Lord has an appearance like lightning and a garment white as snow; in Luke xxiv 4 the two men (angels according to xxiv 23) are in dazzling apparel; in the *Gospel of Peter*, 55, the charming young man the women see in the tomb is clothed in a shining robe. In general, heavenly visitors are dressed in something white or bright, frequently in linen (Ezek ix 2; Dan x 5; Enoch lxxxvii 2; II Macc iii 26; Acts i 10)—also the transfigured Jesus in Mark ix 3.

one seated at the head and the other at the foot. For the tomb arrangement implied here see NOTE on vs. 1, "from the tomb." John may mean simply that there was an angel at either end of the burial shelf; but sometimes the rock was so cut as to provide a headrest for the corpse, so that the place of the head could be distinguished. The chart on p. 974 shows the Gospel variations in describing the position of the angels; the *Gospel of Peter*, 55, has the heavenly young man seated in the middle of the tomb. The detail in John is the most elaborate. Bernard, II, 664, recalls Wetstein's thesis that the two angels guarding the burial place were the counterpart of the two bandits who hung on either side of the crucified Jesus. Another proposed symbolism recalls the two cherubs on either side of the Ark of the Covenant in the Holy of Holies.

13. *"Woman."* For this form of address see NOTE on ii 4.

why are you weeping? A few Western textual witnesses add "Who is it you are looking for?" taken from vs. 15. While the angelic conversation in John is quite different from that in the Synoptics, both in Luke and in John the two angels ask a question.

they took . . . him. Mary's statement reproduces that of vs. 2, with "my Lord" instead of "the Lord," and "I" instead of "we."

14. *caught sight of Jesus.* For the verb *theōrein* see NOTE on "observed" in 6. Bernard, II, 665, points out that this verb was used in the promise of xiv 19: "The world will not see me any more, but *you will see me.*" However, since Mary thought the man she saw was the gardener, this sight is hardly the vision Jesus promised.

She did not realize, however, that it was Jesus. Some commentators have traced the lack of recognition to the possibility that Magdalene was not looking directly at him (an inference from the statement in 16 that she turned to him) or that it was still too dark to see clearly (yet it has been bright enough to look into the tomb). Others see a theological symbolism; for instance, Lightfoot, p. 334, is reminded of the Baptist's not recognizing Jesus in i 26, 31 (but that incident involved the special theme of the hidden Messiah—see vol. 29, p. 53). John's report should be joined to the other Gospel instances of failure to recognize the risen Jesus because he has been transformed (see COMMENT).

15. *Woman . . . why are you weeping?* Jesus repeats the angel's words (13). Similarly, when Jesus appears to the women in Matt xxviii 9–10, he repeats the angel's message from xxviii 5, 7.

Who is it you are looking for? This question is a rare parallel in John to the Synoptic tradition of the conversation between the angels and the women: "You are looking for Jesus" (Mark/Matthew); "Why are you looking for the living among the dead?" (Luke).

Thinking that he was the gardener. Evidently there was nothing startling about his appearance, and so we may reject the thesis of Kastner, *art. cit.*, that the risen Jesus appeared naked, having left his burial garments in the tomb. Bernard, II, 666, romantically muses, "The eye of love clothes the vision in familiar garments"—a weak solution to a pseudo-problem. This is the only biblical instance of *kēpouros*, "gardener," a not uncommon word in the secular papyri. John's story is consonant with the information, peculiar to him, that Jesus' tomb was in a garden. Presumably the gardener's task would have been to care for the trees and fruit or crops; there is no reason to make of him a custodian whose very presence would render self-contradictory the visits to the tomb mentioned by John. Von Campenhausen, pp. 66–67, thinks that John is writing apologetically to refute the Jewish claim that a gardener took the body of Jesus. Tertullian, *De spectaculis* xxx; PL 1:662A, gives us our first trace of this legend: the gardener so acted because he was afraid that the crowds coming to see the tomb would trample his cabbages. Later forms of the story identify the gardener as Judas (confusion with Iscariot?) and tell us that he subsequently brought back the body which was then dragged through the streets of Jerusalem. Other scholars find an equally tenuous theological explanation for John's mention of the gardener: the garden is the Garden of Eden (NOTE on xix 41) where God Himself is the gardener (Hoskyns, Lightfoot).

Sir. Kyrie (NOTE on iv 11).

16. *"Mary!"* The best textual witnesses have *Mariam* here instead of *Maria*, which seems to be the normal form for Mary Magdalene. Since *Mariam* is closer to Masoretic Heb. *Miryam*, some have proposed that John portrays Jesus as speaking to Mary "in Hebrew," even as John portrays Magdalene as answering Jesus "in Hebrew." More precisely, Schwank, "Leere Grab," p. 398, specifies that *Mariam* renders Aramaic rather than Hebrew, just as *Rabbuni* reflects Aramaic. The whole theory is dubious on a number of scores. *First,* the textual witnesses fluctuate greatly on whether to read *Maria* or *Mariam* in the five instances of Magdalene's name in this Gospel. The form *Mariam* is probably to be read also in vs. 18 where there is no special reason for John to be rendering the Semitic form of the name. We summarize the textual evidence below: italics indicate the reading preferred in the critical Greek NT of Nestle (23rd ed.), Merk (7th ed.), Tasker (NEB), and Aland (Synopsis); the codices are abbreviated thus: B=Vaticanus; S=Sinaiticus; A=Alexandrinus.

xix 25	*Maria*	B, A	Mariam	S
xx 1	*Maria*	B	Mariam	S, A
xx 11	*Maria*	B, A, P66*	Mariam	S, P66c
xx 16	Maria	A	*Mariam*	S, B
xx 18	Maria	A	*Mariam*	S, B, P66

Second, the problem of the 1st-century A.D. Hebrew original underlying the name "Mary" is complex. It is true that *Mrym* is the consonantal form found in the MT as the name of Moses' sister; but in Jesus' time *Mryh* also appears in inscriptions, so that it is no longer correct to claim that *Maria* is necessarily a Hellenized form (BDF, §53³). "Maria" may have been an informal designation for women named "Mariam." *Third,* the claim that *Mariam* represents *Maryam,* an Aramaic form, rather than *Miryam,* a Hebrew form, is highly dubious. In the case of biblical names, Hebrew forms were frequently retained in Jewish Aramaic; thus the Targum Onkelos renders Moses' sister's name as *Miryam,* the Masoretic vocalization. But more pertinent, the Masoretic vocalization is late and is the result of a dissimilation (technically called the *qatqat* to *qitqat* dissimilation). This dissimilation in the pronunciation of Hebrew did not take place until after NT times, so that in Jesus' time Heb. *Mrym* was pronounced *Maryam* (as attested in the LXX transliteration).

She turned to him. The use of Mary's name draws her attention because obviously the gardener knows her personally. Yet Mary had already turned toward this man (same verb) in vs. 14. Those who try to deal with the duplication without resorting to literary criticism (i.e., the joining of once independent accounts) usually suppose that Mary had turned away in the meantime. In conformity with his thesis that Jesus stood there naked (the new Adam), Kastner, *art. cit.,* offers modesty as the reason why Mary had turned away! A more common explanation is that John means that Mary now turned her full attention to Jesus (so Lagrange) and grasps him (Bultmann, on the basis of "Don't cling to me"). Others propose that the Greek renders poorly an Aramaic original. The OS^sin and Tatian have "recognized" (representing the ithpeel of *skl*) instead of "turned"; and Black, pp. 189–90, supposes that the standard Greek rendition misread Aram. *skl* as *shr* under the influence of vs. 14 where a form of *shr* occurred. Boismard, ÉvJean, p. 47, adds evidence from Ambrose and from the Georgian version supporting this theory. However, the reading "recognized," which eliminates the difficulty, may well represent a scribal improvement.

[*in Hebrew*]. Actually the expression referred to, namely *Rabbuni,* is Aramaic. This phrase is missing in an interesting combination of textual witnesses: some of the Western versions, the Byzantine tradition, the Vulgate, and the Lake family of Greek mss. It is found in reference to Aramaic place names in v 2, xix 13, 17; and a scribe may have imitated the usage.

"Rabbuni!" The Greek form is *rabbouni,* with *rabbōni* as a Western variant; the word also appears in Mark x 51. The later rabbinic literature (e.g., the Targum of Onkelos) has the vocalized form *ribbōni,* used chiefly in addressing God. In a copy of the earlier Palestinian Targum to the Pentateuch, Black, p. 21, finds the vocalized Aramaic form *rabbūnī* (a form that can be used in addressing a human lord). Although John's usage of a transliteration of *rabbūnī* rather than of *ribbōni* has been cited as a proof that John knew 1st-century Palestinian usage, J. A. Fitzmyer CBQ 30 (1968), 421, shows the fallacy in such an argument. The early targumic form would have been written without vocalization as *rbwny,* which could be either *rabbūnī* or *ribbōnī;* and if we argue from the vocalized form of the Targum, we are drawing upon considerably later evidence.

The *Rabbuni* form has been described as a caritative (W. F. Albright, BNTE, p. 158), i.e., a diminutive form of endearment: "My dear Rabbi [master]." Many have thought that its use expresses Mary's affection for Jesus, an affection implicit throughout the whole scene. (A 19th-century romanticizer like Renan pictured Jesus as the love of Magdalene's life, leaving open the way to interpreting the "Don't cling to [touch] me" of vs. 17 as an indication that the previous relationship between them must cease—perhaps on the analogy of Mark xii 25!) It is claimed that *Rabbuni* must be especially meaningful, for eight other times John uses the simple *Rabbi*. However, John translates *Rabbuni* into Greek as "Teacher," the same translation given for Rabbi (i 38), so that the writer gives his Greek readers no indication of the caritative. There is even less basis for supposing that the writer is deliberately using a form primarily addressed to God, so that Magdalene is making a declaration of faith comparable to Thomas' "My Lord and My God" (Hoskyns, p. 543).

(*which means "Teacher"*). Perhaps precisely because of the simplicity of the address, some Western witnesses add "Lord" or substitute it for "Teacher." In fact, however, "lord, master" is a more literal rendering of *rabbi* than "teacher" (see NOTE on i 38). After "Teacher," some lesser witnesses add "and she ran forward to touch him." This is a scribal attempt to make an easier transition to 17. The idea may have been to portray an action similar to that of Matt xxviii 9 where the women come forward, take hold of Jesus' feet, and worship him.

17. "*Don't cling to me.*" The use of the present imperative (*mē mou aptou*), literally "Stop touching me," probably implies that she is already touching him and is to desist; however, it can mean that she is trying to touch him and he is telling her that she should not (cf. BDF, §336[3]). We have translated the continuing aspect of this imperative by "cling," so that Jesus is asking her not to hold on to him (see BAG, p. 102, col. 1; ZGB, §247—perhaps the same meaning should be given to the verb *aptesthai* in Luke vii 14). Dodd, *Interpretation*, p. 443[2], argues that it is the aorist of this verb that means "to touch," while the present means "to hold, grasp, cling." B. Violet, ZNW 24 (1925), 78–80, shows that twice in LXX *aptesthai* translates forms of the Heb. *dābaq* (*dābēq*) which means "to cling to." (One may accept this observation without embracing Violet's theory that the original meaning, mistranslated in John, was "Don't follow me"; cf. F. Perles, ZNW 25 [1926], 287.) We remember that in the parallel scene in Matt xxviii 9 the women seize (*kratein*) Jesus' feet; and sometimes *aptesthai* is interchangeable with *kratein*, for example, compare Matt viii 15 with Mark i 31.

Those who argue for the meaning "to touch" and who think that John's concept of the ascension was the same as Luke's, namely, something that would occur in about forty days after a series of appearances, have encountered extraordinary difficulty in explaining Jesus' command to Magdalene. They cannot understand why Jesus should forbid her to touch him, when a week later (and still before his ascension) he will invite Thomas to probe his wounds. M. Miguens, "Nota," discusses both patristic and modern approaches to this problem; and J. Maiworm, TGl 30 (1938), 540–46, lists twelve different types of explanations. One wonders which is worse: the utterly banal explanation that Jesus does not want to be touched because his wounds are still sore, or Belser's fanciful thesis that, having heard of the eucharistic meal on Thursday evening, Magdalene sees Jesus risen and is holding onto him, pleading that he give her holy communion! H. Kraft, TLZ 76 (1951), 570, thinks that Jesus was cautioning Magdalene against the ritual defilement that she would incur in touching a dead body; for, though risen, Jesus is in a state of abasement until he ascends to the Father. Chrysostom and Theophylact are among the many who think that Jesus is asking Mary to show more respect for his glorified body. If the objection is raised that a similar respect was not demanded of Thomas, some would solve the difficulty by claiming that a man and especially one of the Twelve might be permitted what would be unseemly for a woman, especially a woman with a sinful past. C. Spicq, RSPT 32 (1948), 226–27, drawing upon Heb vii 26, proposes that when Jesus has ascended, he will be a high priest, holy, unstained, separated from sinners; and so he is telling Magdalene not to sully him with ordinary contact. Kastner, *art. cit.*, ever faithful to his thesis that the risen Jesus was naked, thinks he has the obvious explanation why Mary's ministrations were inappropriate, until she too would have ascended to heaven and no longer be in danger of temptation! Still others think that Magdalene is being told not to test the physical reality of Jesus' body.

An even more frequent approach is to emend the text or to translate the Greek in an unusual way, thus avoiding the difficulty. Bernard, II, 670–71, and W. E. P. Cotter, ET 43 (1931–32), 46, champion the proposal that the original read *mē ptoou*, "Don't fear." The theme of fear is found in the Synoptic narratives of Jesus' appearances, and the verb *ptoein* occurs in Luke xxiv 37 where the disciples are frightened. However, this verb is not used in the Synoptic tomb scene where the women show fear; in particular, the Matthean parallel (xxviii 10) to this scene in John has the command not to fear in the words *mē phobeisthe*. Other emendations (without textual support) eliminate the negative and read *mou aptou* or *sy aptou*, "Touch me." Among the unusual translations, we may note that of F. X. Pölzl and J. Sickenberger, proposed independently by Cotter, *art. cit.*, namely, that the phrase means: "No need to cling to me, for I am not leaving immediately, but will be around a short time [forty days] before I ascend." W. D. Morris, ET 40 (1928–29), 527–28, proposes that the Greek means: "Don't (fear to) touch me," since the idea of fear is implicit in seeing a dead man who has come back to life. Lagrange, p. 512, and Barrett, p. 470, seek to avoid the difficulty thus: "Do not insist on touching me; it is true that I have not yet ascended to the Father, but I am about to do so." X. Léon-Dufour, *Études d'Évangile* (Paris: Seuil, 1965), p. 74, defends this concessive use of *gar*, meaning "true." By different reasoning but with the same practical result, Loisy, p. 505, regards the words "for I have not yet ascended to the Father" as a gloss, so that the original import was: "Don't touch me, but go to my brothers; for my part I am ascending. . . ." Similarly, ZGB, §476, defends the grammatical possibility that the "for" that follows "Don't touch me" should be interpreted, not with "I have not yet ascended" but with "go to my brothers." In the COMMENT we shall try to deal with the text without emendation or extraordinary syntax.

ascended to the Father. P[66], OL, OS[sin], and Vulg. read "my Father"— an interesting combination of witnesses. Yet the reading has probably been influenced by "I am ascending to my Father" at the end of the verse.

go to my brothers. A few important witnesses omit "my." Dodd, *Tradition*, p. 147, suggests that the brothers may be the physical relatives of Jesus, for in I Cor xv 7 there is recorded an appearance of Jesus to James, one of the "brothers" (see also Acts i 14). We remember too that in John vii 8 it was to his "brothers" or relatives that Jesus said, *"I am not going up [anabainein]* to this festival because the time is not yet ripe for me"; and one could argue that now he is telling Magdalene to inform them that he is ascending (*anabainein*). While this possibility cannot be ruled out for the pre-Gospel tradition, the evangelist certainly was referring to the disciples, as we see in 18. The use of the term "brothers" for the disciples is related to the idea expressed later in the sentence that now Jesus' Father is their Father. There is a similar use of "brothers" in xxi 23; also cf. the Matthean parallel (xxviii 9–10) where Jesus says to the women who hold his feet, "Don't be afraid; be on your way and tell *my brothers* [Matt xxviii 7 refers to the disciples] to go to Galilee."

I am ascending to my Father. All attempts to make this refer to an ascension occurring much later so that the appearance in xx 19 ff. can be pre-ascensional go against the obvious meaning of the text. The present tense here means that Jesus is already in the process of ascending but has not yet reached his destination (BDF, §323³). Jesus has frequently spoken about going to his Father (*hypagein* in vii 33, xvi 5, 10; *poreuesthai* in xiv 12, 28, xvi 28). The verb *anabainein* is one of the several used in the NT to describe the ascension, but in the later era of the creeds it became the term par excellence.

my Father . . . my God. This almost corresponds to the Pauline description "the God and Father of our Lord Jesus Christ" (Rom xv 6; II Cor i 3, etc.). In vs. 28 Thomas will call Jesus "God" (vol. 29, p. 24); yet John has Jesus refer to the Father as his God. Perhaps we have here the echoes of various stages in the development of christology.

18. In the Greek of this verse there is an awkward combination of direct and indirect discourse, and the various textual witnesses bear traces of scribal attempts to standardize. Lagrange, p. 513, comments that Mary's haste carries over into the writer's style. Others have sought a literary explanation: John is combining the end of the christophany ("'I have seen the Lord!' she announced") with the original ending of the scene involving the angels at the tomb ("reporting what he [they, originally] had said to her"). Loisy, p. 506, contends that vs. 18 is a rewriting of the angelophany in Matt xxviii 8.

went to the disciples. The Marcan Appendix (xvi 10) also has Magdalene go to the disciples after the christophany, but uses *poreuesthai* in contrast to John's *erchesthai* for the verb "to go" and calls the disciples "those who had been with him." John tells us nothing of the reaction of the disciples. In the Marcan Appendix they are mourning and weeping as Mary comes; and "when they heard that he was alive and had been seen by her [*theasthai*—a verb John does not use for seeing the risen Jesus], they would not believe it." John does not say where the disciples were, but presumably it was where we find them in vs. 19.

"I have seen the Lord!" The verb is *horan*, comparable to the *idein* used in 9 (see vol. 29, p. 502). For the post-resurrectional use of "the Lord," see NOTE on 2. As in 2 where Magdalene reports on the empty tomb, John is the only Gospel to give a direct quotation as part of her report.

she announced. Angellein; a derivative, *apangellein,* is used in Matt xxviii 8, 10 and Luke xxiv 9 for the message that the women bring to the disciples after visiting the empty tomb (cf. also Marcan Appendix xvi 10).

COMMENT: GENERAL

The Structure of xx 1–18

On p. 965 we have given an outline that shows the careful balance in this chapter dealing with the post-resurrectional period. We note that the story of the risen Jesus is divided into two scenes both of which begin with a time setting (vss. 1 and 19). Each scene consists of two episodes. The first episode in each scene involves disciples and their coming to faith. (Although we recognize the possibility of subdividing each of these first episodes, the setting in vss. 1–2 is more distinct from the main action in 3–10 than is the setting in 19–20 from the message of Jesus in 21–23.) The second episode in each scene has as its main point Jesus' appearance to an individual, respectively Magdalene and Thomas. And in these second episodes there is considerable attention to how this individual came to know that Jesus was really there (the recognition). In turn, the individual's coming to faith is related to a larger audience: Magdalene goes off to tell the disciples; Jesus turns from Thomas to the mass of those who have not seen but have believed.

Moving on from the balanced structure of the chapter, we must concern ourselves in particular with xx 1–18 where, despite the organization just detected, there are an extraordinary number of inconsistencies that betray the hand of an editor who has achieved organization by combining disparate material. We notice the following difficulties (for details see NOTES):

- Magdalene comes to the tomb alone in vs. 1, but speaks as "we" in 2.
- She concludes that the body has been stolen in 2, but apparently does not look into the tomb until 11.
- There is duplication in the description of Peter and the Beloved Disciple:
    —two "to" phrases in 2;
    —literally "Peter went out . . . and they were coming" in 3;
    —the repetition in what was seen in 5 and 6;
    —the contrast between "he saw and believed" in 8 and "they did not understand" in 9.
- The belief of the Beloved Disciple has no effect on Magdalene nor on the disciples in general (19).
- It is not clear when or how Magdalene got back to the tomb in 11.
- Why in 12 does she see angels in the tomb instead of the burial clothes that Peter and the Beloved Disciple saw?
- Her conversation with the angels in 13 does not advance the action at all.
- Twice she is said to have turned to Jesus (14 and 16).

The possibility of detecting the hand of an editor is increased when we compare the material in xx 1–18 with what we find in the Synoptic accounts (Lindars, *art. cit.,* supplies tables of vocabulary comparison). We may distinguish three types of material:

(1) Material with close parallels to all three Synoptic Gospels:

vss. 1–2a: Magdalene goes to the tomb, finds the stone rolled back, and reports to Peter.

vss. 11–12:   Magdalene sees two angels in the tomb. The fact but not the substance of the conversation in 13 also has parallels.

(2) Material that resembles a much briefer notice in one of the Synoptics:

part of vss. 3–10, especially 3, 6–7, 10: Peter goes to the tomb, enters, sees Jesus' burial wrappings, and returns home, seemingly not having come to faith. This is similar to the Western Noninterpolation in Luke xxiv 12 and to Luke xxiv 24.

parts of vss. 14b–18: Jesus appears to Magdalene; she clings to him; he gives her a message for the disciples; she subsequently reports to them. This is similar to Matt xxviii 9–10.

(3) Material that is peculiarly Johannine:

vs. 2b: The words of Magdalene's report to Peter.

part of vss. 3–10: The role of the Beloved Disciple who accompanies Peter to the tomb, sees the burial clothes, and comes to belief.

vs. 13:   The contents of the conversation between Magdalene and the angels.

part of vss. 14b–18: Jesus speaks to Magdalene about his ascension to his Father and its theological effects.

One may theorize that the editor has put together different types of material that have come down to him and has added some theological insights of his own. As a curiosity, however, we note that, despite the variety of material isolated on the basis of Synoptic parallels, the remarkably high number of verbs in the historical present tense seems to be distributed throughout (with somewhat less frequency in type 2 material). Bernard, II, 665, comments on the lack of connectives (otherwise frequent in John) in vss. 14–18.

Theories of Composition

Scholars are not at all in agreement on how the composition or editing of the material took place. A survey of the older views hints at the difficulties: vss. 2–10 are an interpolation for Wellhausen and A. Schweitzer; vss. 2–11 are the interpolation for Hirsch, vss. 11b–13 for Spitta, and vss. 5b, 6, 8, and 9 for Delafosse. We shall report briefly on some modern analyses that we have found of profit in forming our own theory.

Lindars, *art. cit.*, while not proposing a whole theory of composition, sees in ch. xx a pattern of Synoptic relationships that we found especially helpful in reconstructing xx 19–29. *Adapting* his observations, we can distinguish in the Synoptic accounts of what happened at the tomb the following sequence: (a) the women come to the tomb and find the stone rolled away; (b) they see angels who tell them that Jesus is risen; (c) the women go to tell the disciples. It would seem that in John the (*b*) member has been moved to the end of the sequence (xx 11–18), expanded, and combined with a christophany. Its former position has been filled in by another story (Peter and the Beloved Disciple going to the tomb). Lindars detects a similar sequence in the Synoptic accounts of Jesus' appearance to the disciples: (a) Jesus appears to the assembled group; (b) they disbelieve and he upbraids them; (c) he gives them their apostolic commission, describing some of the effects of their mission. Once again in John the (*b*) member has been moved to the end of the sequence (xx 24–29) where it is individualized in the story of Thomas' disbelief. Its former position has been filled by the giving of the Spirit in xx 22. Lindars concludes that part of John's material comes from the traditions that lie behind the Synoptic Gospels; the rest is composed by John, rather than drawn from a pre-Johannine source, for its vocabulary is entirely Johannine.

Other scholars think of one basic underlying narrative that has been added to. Bultmann (see Smith, p. 50) posits a short original story behind xx 1–18, consisting of the whole or part of vss. 1, 6, 7, 11, 12, and 13. Magdalene goes to the tomb, finds the stone moved away (and perhaps sees the burial clothes). As she weeps by the tomb, she looks in and sees two angels and converses with them, wondering who has taken the body of the Lord. Thus Bultmann reduces the original story virtually to the material in our type (*1*). A difficulty in this approach is that some of the other material supposedly added by the evangelist is scarcely the result of his free composition. For instance, the narrative of the visit to the tomb by Peter and the Beloved Disciple is itself composite (see the inconsistencies we pointed out in vss. 3–10), and so we should posit that part of it came down to the evangelist from the pre-Gospel tradition.

Hartmann, *art. cit.*, posits a considerably longer original story behind xx 1–18 (continued in 19–29), consisting of the whole or part of vss. 1–3, 5, 7–11, 14–18. Magdalene goes to the tomb, finds the stone moved away, and reports to Peter who accompanies her to the tomb and sees the burial clothes. Peter returns home, not explicitly believing, for neither he nor Magdalene has understood the Scripture. Magdalene stays by the tomb and encounters Jesus who speaks to her. She recognizes him, falls at his feet, and receives the mission to tell his brothers. She reports to the disciples that she has seen the Lord. Hartmann's reconstruction, which carefully removes almost all the inconsistencies we noted, really consists of a smooth combination of much of the material in our types (*1*) and (*2*). The editing, then, would have consisted chiefly in adding material of type (*3*). The only exception would be that, for Hartmann, the vision of the angels in 11b–13 was not part of the original story.

Another approach is to posit that the Johannine editor/evangelist combined two different narratives that came down to him, a "Synoptic-like" narrative and a non-Synoptic narrative. For instance, two stories about visits to the empty tomb may have been joined, one featuring the women (Magdalene), the other featuring the disciples (Peter, Beloved Disciple). An important variation of this theory has been offered by Benoit, "Marie-Madeleine," who thinks of two stories, one Synoptic-like, the other non-Synoptic, cemented together by verses borrowed directly from the Synoptic tradition. For Benoit, xx 1–10 is a Johannine story without parallel in the Synoptic tradition (the parallel in Luke xxiv 12 is thought to have been borrowed from an earlier form of the Johannine tradition). A second story is found in xx 11a, 14b–18 (the christophany to Magdalene), and this has some parallels in the Synoptic tradition (Matt xxviii 9–10). They have been cemented together by vss. 11b–14a, borrowed from the Synoptic accounts of the angelic vision at the tomb. We remember (p. 958 above) that Benoit had a similar theory about the construction of xix 31–42; and while we found some truth in it, we judged that the theory glossed over some difficulties. We make the same judgment here. For instance, vss. 11b–14a have direct similarity to the Synoptic tradition only in the fact that angels are present. It is in vs. 1 that one has vocabulary parallels to the Synoptic tradition.

It is difficult to evaluate all these approaches. The one basic story supposed by Hartmann (Bultmann is too simplified) is attractive; but may not this one story itself be the result of combining material, so that one could ultimately trace several stories behind it? We are inclined to find behind xx 1–18 the traces of three narratives: two narratives of visits to the empty tomb, and the narrative of an appearance of Jesus to Magdalene. Whether these were combined by the evangelist himself (so Benoit) or came to him in whole or partial combination (so Hartmann) we are unable to say. However, the evangelist made his own contribution in any case, for he adapted these stories to serve as a vehicle for his theology about faith and about the meaning of the resurrection.

Analysis of the Three Basic Narratives Combined in John

(A) A story that several of the women followers of Jesus came to the tomb on Sunday morning, found it opened, and returned to the disciples with the disturbing news. In itself the fact of the empty tomb did not originally convey the idea of resurrection; the subsequent appearances of Jesus clarified the meaning of the empty tomb. This is probably why the finding of the empty tomb was not a part of the earliest preaching of the resurrection but only implicit background (see pp. 975–78 above), in the sense that the absence of the body helped the Christians understand something about the Jesus who had appeared. When the empty tomb entered explicitly into the story of the resurrection as an independent narrative, the meaning given to it by the subsequent appearances of Jesus was anticipated and made part of the story itself. This was accomplished by the insertion of an angel interpreter who proclaimed that Jesus had been raised and was no longer there. A further development occurred when the narrative of the women's visit to the empty tomb was joined to or at least made to prepare for the narrative(s) of the appearance(s) of Jesus—the angel spokesman now gave a promise that Jesus would be seen (e.g., Mark xvi 7, probably an addition to the earlier form of the Marcan story).

The story of the women's visit to the tomb is preserved in John in vss. 1–2 and 11–13. There are two possible ways to explain this separation of verses. *First,* one may propose that John gives us two forms of the story, vss. 1–2 being an early form, and vss. 11–13 being a truncated later form where the actual coming to the tomb has been dropped because of the sequence into which the story has been placed. (It is gratuitous to assume, as does Loisy, p. 502, that 11–13 presents a form of the story in which the tomb was found unopened.) If one accepts this proposal, vss. 1–2 would preserve the earliest form of the empty tomb story found in any Gospel. Its only non-primitive feature would be that the original group of women has been reduced to Magdalene—this editorial reduction is an instance of the Johannine tendency to individualize for dramatic purposes, and is also designed to prepare the way for the christophany in 14–18. In vss. 11–13 the editor has changed the purpose for which the angelic spokesman was introduced into the empty tomb story (in this case, two angels, a duplication that itself may be a secondary development). The angels do not interpret the meaning of the empty tomb— that is done by the christophany that follows—and the conversation between Mary and the angels is merely a repetition of vs. 2. Perhaps Grass, p. 55, is correct in seeing an apologetic feature in the persistent emphasis on Mary's thinking that the body was stolen: when this suggestion was made by the opponents of the resurrection, Christians could claim that they had thought of this possibility themselves, but it was not true. By allowing the following christophany to interpret the empty tomb, John begins a process that culminates in the 2nd-century *Epistula Apostolorum,* 10, where the angelophany in the tomb is replaced entirely by a christophany.

Second, one may propose that John contains only one form of the story of the women's visit to the tomb, since vss. 1 and 11–13 were originally continuous. Verse 2 would then be a connective created to allow the insertion of the narrative of Peter's visit to the tomb (3–10). Hartmann, p. 197, objects to this theory on the grounds that 11 does not give a good sequence after 1; he contends that the mere sight of the opened tomb would not cause Magdalene to weep. But this objection has little force since in the present sequence of 1 and 2 the mere sight of the opened tomb causes Magdalene to conclude that the body has been taken away, so that one is dealing with equally hazardous logic whether 2 or 11 follows 1. A greater difficulty concerns the rationale behind the supposed splitting up of 1 and 11–13 in order to insert 3–10. Would the pattern of the chapter be less logical if 3–10 had followed 1, 11–13? But one can always guess that the editor did not want Magdalene's visit to the tomb too far removed from the story of Jesus' appearance to her in 14–18. The most serious objection to this whole thesis is centered on vs. 2. If this is a free composition of the editor, created for transitional purposes, why the awkward "we" in vs. 2 (see NOTE). That is more easily explained as a reminiscence of an original story that mentioned several women.

In conclusion, while the first proposal that two forms of the story have been preserved seems more complicated, it is less open to objection than the second proposal whereby one form of the story has been divided up.

(B) A story that several disciples (Peter, in particular) visited the tomb after they heard the women's report and, finding the tomb empty, went away puzzled. As we have noted, there are traces of this story in Luke xxiv 12 and 24. The Western Noninterpolation (p. 969 above) in xxiv 12 is obviously an addition to the narrative, but in our opinion a redactor's addition, not a later scribe's (Jeremias, EWJ, pp. 149–51, defends it as "the original text of Luke"). Although some have presumed that John xx 3–10 expanded the information in Luke xxiv 12, Benoit, "Marie-Madeleine," p. 143, argues convincingly that the dependence is in the opposite direction. Much of the language of Luke xxiv 12 is non-Lucan in style, and the redactor may have borrowed it from an earlier form of the Johannine tradition (where Peter but not the Beloved Disciple was mentioned). If this is true, Luke xxiv 12 does not constitute an independent witness to the story of the disciples' visit to the tomb. The other verse, Luke xxiv 24, is more important; for although it appears in the context of the Emmaus narrative, it is part of a summary of post-resurrectional happenings that may have come to Luke partially formed. Certainly what it says, "Some of those who were with us went to the tomb and found it just as the women had said, but they did not see Jesus," is independent of the material in vs. 12, "Peter rose and ran to the tomb; he bent down to peer in and saw the cloth wrappings lying there; and he went home wondering at what had happened." Indeed, 24 must have been part of Luke xxiv before 12 was added; for the original composer of ch. xxiv did not know that the "some of those who were with us" included Simon Peter—he says that these disciples who came to the tomb did not see Jesus, yet in 34 he says that the Lord appeared to Simon. Since there is nothing in vs 24 to suggest that it was borrowed from John, this verse constitutes an independent witness to the story of a visit to the empty tomb by the disciples. We note that wherever such a story occurs, it always follows a reference to the women's visit to the tomb. Therefore, if we speak of two stories of visits to the empty tomb, we are not thinking of rival or substitute accounts; in Christian tradition, as far back as we can trace it, the primacy in the discovery of the empty tomb belongs to the women followers of Jesus. As for the historicity of a visit to the tomb by the disciples, even though we may have independent witnesses in John xx 3–10 and Luke xxiv 24, both are relatively late. Yet, if one accepts the fact that the women found the tomb empty, quite logically their report of this should have produced a desire among the disciples to see for themselves.

The Johannine form of the story has undergone considerable development. In the earlier form of the story did Peter alone figure? This would be the obvious implication of Benoit's thesis that Luke xxiv 12, which mentions only Peter, was borrowed from an earlier form of the Johannine tradition. Yet the redactor who supplied Luke xxiv 12 may have simplified, and even in the early stage of the story Peter may have been accompanied by another nameless disciple. The presence of several disciples would agree with Luke xxiv 24 which speaks of "some of those who were with us." Moreover, the parenthetical observation in John xx 9 seems to suppose that there were several disciples who saw and yet did not understand the import of the empty tomb (as we shall see, the "they" of 9 scarcely included the Beloved Disciple). In any case, the hypothetical companion of Peter in the original form of the Johannine story was unimportant (and so could be neglected by Luke xxiv 12). But John has changed the story by identifying him as the Beloved Disciple and giving him a major role: he runs with Peter to the tomb; he reaches it first and looks in; ultimately the sight of the burial clothes leads him to believe. (We do not mean to foreclose the possibility that the Johannine writer correctly identified Peter's nameless companion; a late addition need not be legendary.) It is this introduction of the Beloved Disciple that has caused the inconsistencies listed above on p. 995. As we pointed out in the NOTE, we find the traces of insertion in vs. 2: "the other disciple (the one whom Jesus loved)"; and we suggest that the modest designation, "the other disciple," described Peter's inconspicuous companion in the earlier form of the story. (In xix 35 there is a somewhat parallel instance of the introduction of the Beloved Disciple into a narrative where he did not originally appear.) The Beloved Disciple's role in the story of the disciples' visit to the tomb is functionally the same as the role of the angel interpreter in the story of the women's visit to the tomb, namely, he is the one who indicates what the empty tomb means, for he sees the burial clothes and believes in the risen Jesus. In the original form of the story Peter and his companion did not come to faith because they did not understand the Scripture that he had to rise from the dead. (Whether or not the parenthetical explanation in 9 was part of the original story, it correctly interprets the import of that story and was seemingly added before the figure of the Beloved Disciple was introduced.)

And so, if we are correct in positing the existence of two Christian stories about visits to the tomb, one by women and one by disciples, it would seem that in its earliest form neither story claimed that a visit to the tomb produced faith in the risen Jesus. Incidentally, this makes it unlikely that either was invented purely for apologetic purposes. The strong apologetic element appears in the later insertions (the angel interpreter and the Beloved Disciple, respectively).

(C) A story of an appearance of Jesus to Mary Magdalene. Traces of this story are found only in relatively late Gospel witnesses: John xx 14–18; Matt xxviii 9–10; and the Marcan Appendix (xvi 9–11). This fact casts doubt on whether the story represents an early tradition. However, before we treat the three accounts, it may be worth recalling that in the last century a skeptic like Renan gave importance and priority to this story. Renan claimed that the hallucinatory vision that Magdalene had while she wept longingly for her beloved by the tomb was the real spark to Christian faith in the resurrection. Her love did what logical argument never could do: it raised up Jesus. And so it was the passion of a deranged woman (Luke viii 2) that gave the world a risen Lord! Truly an explanation worthy of 19th-century French romanticism.

First, the narrative in Matthew xxviii 9–10. As the women are hurrying from the tomb to announce to the disciples what they have heard and seen, Jesus meets them and says, "Rejoice." They come forward, grasp his feet, and worship him. Then Jesus says to them, "Don't be afraid. Go and announce to my brothers that they should go to Galilee, and there they will see me." (The reference to "brothers" is the only significant vocabulary parallel between Matthew and John.) There is a problem about the context in which Matthew places the story. After the angel's directive to the women in vs. 7 that they should tell the disciples to go to Galilee where they would see Jesus, one would not have expected an immediate appearance of Jesus. And what the risen Jesus says to the women simply repeats what the angel had already told them. When we add to these difficulties the fact that vs. 8 in Matthew could easily be connected directly to vs. 11, it becomes reasonable to assume that the christophany in 9–10 is a later insertion into the narrative. Although such commentators on Matthew as W. C. Allen and A. Plummer think that there may have been an appearance to the women in the lost ending of Mark, most exegetes would judge that Matthew is not drawing upon Mark here. That the core of the Matthean insertion had its origin in independent tradition rather than in the evangelist's imagination is suggested by the awkwardness of the present sequence (*pace* Neirynck, pp. 182–84, who maintains that Matthew created the story to prepare for the appearance to the disciples in Galilee).

Second, the narrative in the Marcan Appendix (xvi 9–11). The account is brief: "Now when he rose *early* on the first day *of the week,* he appeared first to *Mary Magdalene,* from whom he had cast out seven devils. She went and told those who had been with him, as they mourned and wept. But when they heard that he was alive and had been seen by her, they would not believe it." Although the author of the Appendix sometimes draws upon the canonical Gospels for his material, here he does not seem to be dependent upon either Matthew or John. The only thing he has in common with John xx are the few words we have italicized, and he has even less in common with Matthew's account of the appearance to the women. (If anything, the Marcan Appendix in these three verses is evocative of Luke viii 2 and xxiv 11.) Dodd, "Appearances," p. 33, is almost certainly correct in concluding that here the Marcan Appendix is dependent on a tradition not preserved in the canonical Gospels.

Finally, the narrative in John xx 14–18. If our observations above are correct, this longest and most meaningful account constitutes a third independent form of the story of a christophany to Mary Magdalene. Therefore, despite the lateness of the witnesses, we are inclined to believe that the tradition of the appearance to Magdalene may be ancient. The absence of her name in the lists of appearances cited by the early preachers is not really surprising (see p. 971 above). An argument in favor of antiquity is the primacy all the Gospels give her among the women followers of Jesus, whenever they are listed; this may well be because she was the first one to see the risen Jesus. We think then that John and the Marcan Appendix are more correct than Matthew in making her the sole witness of the christophany. If John simplified the story of the women coming to the tomb by mentioning only Magdalene, Matthew complicated the christophany by relating it too closely to the visit of the women to the tomb and thus making "the other Mary" as well as Magdalene (Matt xxviii 1) witnesses. In our judgment, Neirynck's thesis (*art. cit.*) that John borrowed the story from Matthew (who invented it) does not do justice to the differences of vocabulary and detail between the two accounts or to the apparent independence of the reference to this appearance in the Marcan Appendix.

As the story is now related in John xx 14–18, it has undergone development. The necessity of relating the christophany to what precedes it accounts for vs. 14a: "She had just said this when she turned around." The turning around toward Jesus is borrowed from 16 where it belongs (see NOTE on 16). If one follows the pattern that Dodd has detected in the Concise Narratives of appearances (pp. 972–73 above), we may plausibly isolate in John's narrative these original elements: Magdalene was disconsolate because she thought the body had been taken away; Jesus appeared to her, and as he spoke she recognized him; he directed her to go tell his brothers, and she did. Such a pattern can be confirmed to a large extent from the other forms of the story in Matthew and in the Marcan Appendix. Her seizing his feet (cf. Matt xxviii 9), hinted at in John's "Don't cling to me," may also have been part of the original story. Both the time and the locale of the appearance may have been mentioned: early on Easter, in proximity to the tomb. In any case, we regard John's localizing the appearance at the tomb and Matthew's localizing it after the women had left the tomb as a meaningless variant (compare the variations in the miracle story that mentioned Capernaum, pointed out in vol. 29, p. 192). In Matthew's shorter form of the story, Jesus' words to Magdalene have been supplied by repeating the words of the angel; but the Johannine Jesus has an important comment to make on the meaning of the resurrection and its implications for the disciples (see below, p. 1011–17). Perhaps the original story contained no significant words of Jesus, a fact that forced each evangelist to fill in as he thought best. It is difficult to judge the provenance of the information that Magdalene mistook Jesus for the gardener (see NOTE). We are inclined to regard it as Johannine dramatization; but we do not wish to discount too summarily Dodd's contention ("Appearances," p. 20) that there is "something indefinably first-hand" about the Johannine narrative of the appearance and that it may have come down from an original source through some highly individual channel. It is interesting that Dodd, *Tradition*, p. 149, judges the Johannine form of the story better preserved than the shorter Matthean form.

In summary, then, a qualified judgment about the antiquity of the substance of John xx 14–18 is to be preferred to Bultmann's thesis that the awkward angelophany of 11–13 came to John from his source, but 14–18 is the evangelist's free creation. We think of 11–13 as a late form of the story of the women's visit to the empty tomb, a form that is awkward precisely because it has been heavily edited to serve as a connective between the once independent stories underlying 3–10 and 14–18.

contra Bultmann

COMMENT: DETAILED

Having already treated the structure and development of the main passages in xx 1–18, we shall confine ourselves here to the special significance that John has given to some details in the narratives.

The Role of the Beloved Disciple in xx 3–10 in Relation to Peter

We have suggested that the story of the disciples' visit to the tomb originally terminated in their bewilderment at the absence of Jesus' body and that John has introduced the Beloved Disciple so that his coming to faith might interpret the significance of the empty tomb. This introduction has the secondary effect of contrasting the Beloved Disciple with Peter who sees the same evidence but does not come to belief. This is not because of Peter's hardness of heart; rather faith is possible for the Beloved Disciple because he has become very sensitive to Jesus through love. (While, to be precise, the Gospel stresses Jesus' love for the Disciple, we are meant to assume that this love was reciprocated—otherwise the Disciple would scarcely rank as a hero in Johannine thought where love must be mutual.)

Many commentators do not see any contrast at all, for they think that the Johannine writer meant that Peter believed along with the Beloved Disciple. Bultmann, p. 530, for instance, argues that otherwise the evangelist would have said specifically that Peter did not believe (so also Willam, art. cit.). However, such a specification would have been necessary only if the writer wanted the contrast to denigrate Peter. The writer's purpose is not to detract from Peter but to exalt the status of the Beloved Disciple. As we have constructed the original story above, Peter (and his companion) did not come to faith. If the writer wished to change the story so that Peter would come to faith, he would have had no reason to introduce the Beloved Disciple. "He saw and believed" refers only to the Beloved Disciple. We find a close parallel in xxi 4, 7: when Jesus stands on the shore of the Sea of Tiberias, the Beloved Disciple is the first to recognize him, and it is he who informs Peter, "It is the Lord." The lesson for the reader is that love for Jesus gives one the insight to detect his presence. The Beloved Disciple, here as elsewhere the ideal follower of Jesus, sets an example for all others who would follow.

Almost parenthetically we must comment on the type of faith exhibited by the Beloved Disciple at the tomb. It has become fashionable (e.g., Bernard, II, 661) to see in his faith a dramatic anticipation of what Jesus will say to Thomas in xx 29b: "Happy those who have not seen and yet have believed"—the Beloved Disciple believed in the risen Jesus without having seen him. W. J. Moulton, ET 12 (1900–01), 382, even goes so far as to suggest that Jesus looked at the Beloved Disciple when he spoke those words. And some fit this praise of the Beloved Disciple into their thesis that the real purpose of the Johannine writer was to deemphasize the appearances of Jesus and to devalue faith that stemmed from such appearances. We question this entire line of exegesis. In discussing xx 29 (pp. 1049–51 below) we shall attempt to show that the praise of those who believe without having seen Jesus by no means implies a lesser beatitude on those who have seen and have believed. More crucial here, we deny that the Beloved Disciple comes under the macarism of 29b. True, he believed without having seen the risen Jesus; but he believed on the basis of what he saw in the tomb, not on the basis of hearing, as would those envisaged in 29b. The fact that vs. 8 states clearly "He saw and believed" should make it obvious that he is not one of "those who have not seen and yet have believed." (In fact, O. Cullmann, Salvation in History [New York: Harper, 1967], p. 273, calls upon this incident as a proof that in John faith is intimately related to seeing but that seeing alone does not produce faith: "Both aspects, the eyewitness and the interpretation of faith, are emphasized in their necessary *connection* and *distinction*.") The lesson here is one of the power of love and has nothing to do with the relative value of the appearances of Jesus.

Returning to the implicit contrast with Peter, we must ask whether this contrast runs throughout the narrative, for example, in the fact that he outruns Peter and yet Peter enters first. The question of this contrast will also enter our commentary on ch. xxi. Unfortunately much of what has been written on the subject bears the imprint of the debate between Roman Catholics and the rest of Christianity about the primacy of Peter and of his successors in the Roman See. For instance, Catholic scholars have often argued that in waiting and allowing Peter to enter the tomb first, the Beloved Disciple was showing deference to the leader of the Twelve (and thus tacitly acknowledging papal supremacy). On the other hand, some anti-Romans have found in the Johannine writer a kindred soul, since they think that he is exalting the Beloved Disciple as part of an early protest against Petrine claims, for example, in making the Beloved Disciple the first believer while Peter remains in ignorance. (Sometimes, inconsistently, this contention is accompanied by the argument that, in any case, Peter had no special position among the Twelve, as if the Johannine writer would spend his time conducting a polemic against a man or a symbol that had no importance.) Other interpreters do not see the rivalry in terms of the papal question (which would be anachronistic) but in terms of an internal question within the Johannine community. Loisy, p. 500, claims that Peter entered the tomb first as the representative of Jewish Christianity, while the Beloved Disciple entered later as a representative of the more perceptive Gentile Christianity (so also, with modifications, Bultmann, p. 531). Still others think of Peter as a representative of fleshly Christianity (whatever that may be) and the Beloved Disciple as a representative of spiritual Christianity. In our judgment, all these interpretations sharpen the contrast beyond what the writer intended. We remember that Peter was in the original form of the story; and so, while the introduction of the Beloved Disciple inevitably created a contrast, to an extent that contrast is accidental and is scarcely a major aspect of Johannine polemic. Moreover, to be precise, the Beloved Disciple is placed in Peter's company and is not set over against him. Indeed, throughout the Gospel Peter and the Beloved Disciple are portrayed as friends and not as rivals (vol. 29, p. XCVII). At the Last Supper the Beloved Disciple receives Peter's signals and conveys Peter's question to Jesus (xiii 23–25). If the Beloved Disciple is the anonymous figure in xviii 15–16, he goes to the trouble of gaining admittance for Peter into the high priest's palace. And we shall find the two men together fishing in xxi 7. We detect, then, no attitude deprecatory of Peter in the Johannine writings; in fact xxi 15–17 pays the great tribute of making him shepherd of the sheep, a role that ch. x gives to Jesus himself. But Peter is not the special hero of the

Johannine writer. The Beloved Disciple has that role; and the writer takes special interest in showing the Beloved Disciple's "primacy of love," a superiority that does not exclude Peter's possessing another type of primacy (so M. Goguel, HTR 25 [1932], 11). As for the incidents in xx 3–10, the two disciples' running to the tomb is expressive of their concern upon hearing Magdalene's report; such concern touches upon love, so naturally the Beloved Disciple outdistances Peter—he loves Jesus more. We cannot exclude the possibility that there was some deference to the memory of Peter (presumably dead when the Gospel was written) in allowing him to enter the tomb first; but more likely the writer wanted to arrange the scene dramatically by delaying the entrance of the Beloved Disciple so that his seeing and believing would come as a climax. We see no basis for all the polemic and symbolic interpretations; the writer is simply telling us that the disciple who was bound closest to Jesus in love was the quickest to look for him and the first to believe in him.

What the Beloved Disciple Saw: the Burial Clothes (xx 5–7)

The Beloved Disciple was led to belief by seeing Jesus' burial wrappings lying where the corpse had been and the piece of cloth that had covered the head (*soudarion*), not lying with the wrappings, but rolled up in a place by itself. Why? Two types of solutions have been proposed. *First,* most scholars think that the very presence of the burial clothes in the tomb led the Beloved Disciple to conclude that the body had not been stolen. Grave robbers would not have taken the time to unwrap the body, thus giving themselves the burden of carrying a stiff, naked corpse around. This is an ancient explanation. Grass, p. 55, cites a Coptic apocryphal fragment wherein Pilate is called by the Jewish authorities to see the tomb from which the body has been stolen; but when he sees the burial clothes, he observes that if the body had been taken away, the wrappings would also have been taken. Chrysostom, *In Jo. Hom.* LXXXV 4; PG 59:465, phrases the argument well: "If anyone had removed the body, he would not have stripped it first; nor would he have taken the trouble to remove and roll up the *soudarion* and put it in a place by itself."

Second, a smaller group of scholars think that it was the position or form of the clothes and not their mere presence that brought the Beloved Disciple to faith. The holders of this view translate the key words of the Johannine description in different ways (NOTES on 5 and 7), but all of their translations suggest that Jesus so emerged from his burial wrappings that it was obvious that the clothes had not merely been taken off him. (The view that Jesus' risen body passed through his burial clothes in a volatile manner goes back at least as far as the 5th-century writer Ammonius of Alexandria.) Balagué thinks that the burial wrappings (*othonia*) were collapsed flat, the *soudarion* was coiled where the head had been, and the whole was covered by the *sindōn* mentioned in the Synoptic accounts, so that the garments preserved the rough outline of the former position of the corpse. This led the Beloved Disciple to perceive that Jesus had simply passed through his clothes leaving them behind. Auer, *op. cit.*, devotes a whole book, illustrated by sketches, to propound the thesis that the bindings (*othonia*), impregnated with the aromatic oil of xix 40, had remained stiffly erect after the body had passed through them, almost as if somehow one were to slide a corpse out of its mummy wrappings and have the wrappings preserve the form. Moreover, the *soudarion* (=*sindōn*), a large cloth that had been around the whole body *inside* the bindings, was now carefully folded in the corner on the left-hand side of the tomb. For further variations of this thesis see the articles of Willam and Lavergne; also W. McClellan, CBQ 1 (1939), 253–55. All these approaches are based on what is, at most, implied in John xx 19, namely, that the risen body of Jesus had the power to pass through solid objects. If the Johannine writer described the position of the burial clothes in such a way as to imply that Jesus' body had passed through them and left them undisturbed, would he have waited until later to hint subtly at such an unexpected power? Moreover, a translation, such as ours, whereby the *soudarion* is not with the other wrappings, militates against such a theory—Jesus would have passed through all the burial clothes at the same time, leaving them in the one place. Finally, such a theory demands that Peter also should have come to believe; for if the position of the clothes miraculously preserved the image or location of the body, Peter could scarcely have missed the import. Yet Luke xxiv 12 reports that Peter "saw the cloth wrappings lying there, and he went home wondering at what had happened."

Because of these difficulties it seems better to accept the first theory and not to attribute any special importance to the position or shape of the burial clothes. If these garments figured in the early pre-Gospel form of the story, their presence could only have been incidental, as in Luke xxiv 12 —part of the detail to be expected in what purports to be a factual account. But when the Beloved Disciple was introduced into the story, the Johannine writer capitalized on the presence of the burial garments as the explanation of what led the Disciple to believe. We are not certain whether the writer also had a theological purpose in mentioning them, namely, the fact that they were left behind symbolized that Jesus would not use them again. "Christ being raised from the dead will never die again" (Rom vi 9). We remember the suggestion that Lazarus emerged from the tomb still wrapped in his burial clothes to symbolize that he was to die again (NOTE on xi 44).

Mary Magdalene's Recognition of Jesus (xx 15–16)

John devotes much of the christophany narrative to Magdalene's failure to know Jesus immediately and her sudden recognition as he calls her name. Some have found here an adaptation of the recognition scene that appears in stories of the Greco-Roman gods as they walk among men

(M. Dibelius, BZAW 33 [1918], 137). However, Dodd is correct in insisting that a prolonged recognition is common in the Circumstantial Narratives of Jesus' appearances (p. 973 above). The two disciples on the road to Emmaus walked and talked with Jesus for a while before they recognized him in the breaking of the bread (Luke xxiv 31, 35). In John xxi we shall find Jesus standing on the shore of the Sea of Tiberias and talking with the disciples about fishing, before finally the Beloved Disciple recognizes him. Such difficult recognitions may have had an apologetic purpose: they show that the disciples were not credulously expecting to see the risen Jesus. But they also have a theological dimension, and that is what concerns us here.

One important motif may have been to stress that the risen Jesus had undergone a change from the Jesus of the ministry. The Marcan Appendix (xvi 12) summarizes the (Lucan) story of the appearance of Jesus to the two disciples on the country road by saying that he appeared to them "in another form [morphē]." Perhaps such a change is hinted at in the Concise Narratives by the insistence that, although the disciples see Jesus, they cannot believe that it is really he (Matt xxviii 17; Luke xxiv 37). In his discussion of resurrection in I Cor xv 42 ff. Paul brings out a twofold aspect of continuity and transformation: he clearly speaks of the resurrection of a body that has died and been buried; yet that body is changed so that it is no longer physical but spiritual. Seemingly the Gospel accounts preserve the same twofold aspect: the stories of the empty tomb emphasize continuity, but the recognition scenes emphasize transformation.

Still another theological motif may be present in John's recognition scene in the fact that Magdalene knows Jesus *after he calls her by name*. She has searched earnestly for Jesus; she has consulted the disciples, the angels, and the supposed gardener about the removal of his body (vss. 2, 13, 15). Yet when she sees Jesus, she does not recognize him. The wrong identification of Jesus as the gardener may be an acted-out form of Johannine misunderstanding (Barrett, p. 469) to illustrate that mere sight of the risen Jesus does not necessarily lead to understanding or faith. Perhaps the same lesson is found in the Lucan narrative of the disciples on the road to Emmaus who recognize Jesus only in the breaking of the bread. (As regards their respective contextual sequences this appearance in Luke and that to Magdalene in John have much in common: both follow visits to the tomb by the women and by Peter; both precede and introduce the appearance of Jesus to the body of disciples.) Luke may be telling his Christian readers that in the eucharistic breaking of the bread they have the means of recognizing Jesus' presence in their midst. Likewise John may be telling his readers that in the spoken word of Jesus they have the means of recognizing his presence. Magdalene, by recognizing Jesus when he calls her "Mary," plays out a role delineated in John x 3: "The sheep hear his voice as he calls by name those that belong to him." The episode illustrates the claim of the Good Shepherd, "I know my sheep and mine know me" (x 14, also 27). Mary Magdalene could serve as an example to Christians of the Johannine community at the end of the 1st century whose contact with the risen Jesus is through the Paraclete who declares to them what he has received from Jesus (xvi 14).

Feuillet, "La recherche," pp. 103–7, raises the possibility that the story of Magdalene's search for Jesus echoes Song of Sol iii 1–4. In that passage the woman searches for the man whom her soul loves. She rises early and goes asking watchmen whether they have seen him. When she finds him, she seizes him and will not let him go. (See also M. Cambe, "L'influence du Cantique des Cantiques sur le Nouveau Testament," RThom 62 [1962], 5–26.) Since in Feuillet's interpretation the woman of the Song is symbolic of Israel looking for Yahweh, this background would suggest that the Johannine Magdalene is representative of the Christian or messianic community searching for Jesus. Feuillet would see in Jesus' answer to Magdalene an implicit promise of post-resurrectional presence, and the Eucharist is one form of this presence. Thus he gives to the scene possible ecclesiastical and sacramental dimensions. We are dubious about the ecclesiastical dimension (Magdalene more probably exemplifies the individual's quest for Jesus), and we find no support whatsoever for the eucharistic interpretation—the analogy with the Lucan Emmaus scene cannot be stretched that far. As for possible OT background, Isa xliii 1 is also cited: "Fear not, for I have redeemed you; I have called you by name; you are mine."

A final remark concerns Mary's response to Jesus whereby she calls him, "Rabbuni," or "my (dear) Rabbi" (see NOTE). The vocabulary in this episode is strangely reminiscent of the scene in i 38 where Jesus asks the disciples of the Baptist, "What are you looking for?" and they address him as "Rabbi." So here too Mary addresses him as a rabbi after he has asked her, "Who is it you are looking for?" (xx 15). The parallel brings out forcefully the modesty of the title that Magdalene gives to the risen Jesus, a title that is characteristic of the beginning of faith rather than of its culmination. Certainly, it falls far short of Thomas' "My Lord and my God" in 28. One is tempted to theorize that by using this "old" title the Johannine Magdalene is showing her misunderstanding of the resurrection by thinking that she can now resume following Jesus in the same manner as she had followed him during the ministry. (Below we shall see that such a concept may lie behind her grasping him and seeking to hold his presence.) Also one may wonder if her use of an inadequate title does not imply that only when the Spirit is given (vs. 22) is full faith in the risen Jesus possible. However, such reasoning is made less plausible by the fact that in 18 Magdalene announces to the disciples, "I have seen *the Lord*"; and so she knows that it was her Lord and not merely her teacher who stood before her.

The Imminent Ascension of Jesus (xx 17)

We have already devoted a long NOTE to the many ways in which commentators have tried to explain the logic of the statement of Jesus, "Don't cling to me, for I have not yet ascended to the Father." It is unfortunate that so much attention has had to be paid to the meaning of "Don't cling to me," when the real stress should be on the latter part of the verse where it is made clear that Jesus is going to his Father *with a salvific purpose*. He is not going to be content to prepare heavenly dwelling places to which one day he will take his disciples (xiv 2–3); rather he will return from his Father to the disciples to establish them in a new relationship to God by giving them the Spirit.

The basis of much of the difficulty lies in the comparison that many commentators have made between Jesus' instruction to Magdalene (often translated, "Don't touch me") and his later invitation to Thomas to touch him. It is our conviction that the two attitudes of Jesus have nothing to do with one another and that the evangelist intended no comparison between them, as if Thomas were being invited to do what had been refused to Magdalene. It is the commentators who have created the contrast by speaking as if Thomas was invited to "touch" Jesus; the verb "to touch" used in the instruction to Magdalene does not appear in the Thomas episode. Jesus told Magdalene not to cling to him; he invited Thomas to probe his wounds—what is there in common between the two actions? And so we reject Hoskyns' comment (p. 543) quoted with favor by many: "So intimate will be the new relationship with Jesus that, though Mary must for the time being cease from touching him, because he must ascend and she must deliver his message, yet, after the Ascension, both she and the disciples will be concretely united with him in a manner which can actually be described as 'touching,' and of this the eating of the Lord's Body and the drinking of his Blood is the most poignant illustration." Not only is there no evidence for a eucharistic allusion; but, more important, there is no reason to speak of the new relationship as "touching." We also reject Bultmann's contention (p. 533) that the "Don't touch me" is an indirect way of telling us that the appearances of the risen Jesus are not tangible, so that here John contradicts the impression created by Luke xxiv 38–43 and Matt xxviii 9 (and by John xx 27!), passages indicating that the risen Jesus could be grasped and felt. (We think that John was no more "sophisticated" than the other evangelists who accepted the tangibility of the risen Jesus—it is another question whether or not they were correct in this view.) Grass, pp. 61–65, is right in judging that here Bultmann is reading his own demythologization into the mind of the Johannine writer. If we are accurate in proposing that Jesus was telling Magdalene that she should not try to hold onto him, his words had no reference either to immediate or to future tangibility.

Why would Magdalene try to hold on to Jesus, and why would he tell her not to do so on the grounds that he had *not yet* ascended? (Notice that he said, "for I have not yet ascended"; he did not say, "for I am going to ascend," as many explanations would imply.) Magdalene's attitude may be interpreted in light of Jesus' promise at the Last Supper: "I am coming back to you. In just a little while the world will not see me any more, but you will see me" (xiv 18–19). When Magdalene sees Jesus, she thinks that he has returned as he promised and now he will stay with her and his other followers, resuming former relationships. He had said, "I shall see you again, and your hearts will rejoice with a joy that no one can take from you" (xvi 22). Magdalene is trying to hold on to the source of her joy, since she mistakes an appearance of the risen Jesus for his permanent presence with his disciples. In telling her not to hold on to him, Jesus indicates that his permanent presence is not by way of appearance, but by way of the gift of the Spirit that can come only after he has ascended to the Father. (We shall see below that this gift is implied both in the concept of ascension and in the reference to "my brothers" in vs. 17b.) Bultmann, p. 533, has made the penetrating observation that the "not yet" of Jesus' "I have not yet ascended" is really applicable to Magdalene's desire—she cannot yet have Jesus' enduring presence. Instead of trying to hold on to Jesus (not, of course, that she could actually have prevented his ascension), she is commanded to go and prepare his disciples for that coming of Jesus when the Spirit will be given.

Our interpretation of vs. 17 assumes that John's understanding of Jesus' ascension must be differentiated from the concept of an ascension after forty days found in the Book of Acts. P. Benoit, "L'Ascension," RB 56 (1949), 161–203 (English summary in TD 8 [1960], 105–10), has made a useful distinction between the ascension understood as the glorification of Jesus in the Father's presence, and the ascension understood as a levitation symbolizing the terminus of the appearances of the risen Jesus. Acts i 3 remarks that Jesus appeared during forty days, and then was visibly taken up from his followers by a cloud. Critics have been severe in their judgment of this scene, but a more nuanced appraisal is found in P.-H. Menoud's "La Pentecôte lucanienne et l'histoire," RHPR 42 (1962), 141–47. Luke is not giving us a date for the glorification of Jesus; the very mention of "forty days" is incidental, as part of the Lucan preparation for the Pentecost feast which is the important date. (When Luke is not concerned with Pentecost, he is perfectly capable of describing an ascension on Easter evening, as in Luke xxiv 51, especially if the whole verse is accepted.) In traditional imagery Luke is dramatizing the end of the earthly appearances of Jesus; and he is not alone among the NT writers in maintaining that there was a series of post-resurrectional appearances over a period of time and that this series came to an end (that is implied in I Cor xv 5–9). Now John is not concerned with the ascension as a terminus of Jesus' appearances, but rather with the terminus of "the hour" in which Jesus passed from this world to the Father (xiii 1). Wellhausen claimed that the appearances of Jesus in John xx 19–28 must be secondary in the Johannine plan, for there can be no appearances after the ascension mentioned in xx 17; but this is an example of the failure to make the distinction between the two concepts of ascension.

It is a basic NT understanding that the risen Jesus is not restored to the normal life that he possessed before death; he possesses eternal life and is in God's presence. The time and place that characterize earthly existence no longer apply to him in his eschatological state; and so we cannot imagine his dwelling some place on earth for forty days while he is making appearances and before he departs for heaven. From the moment that God raises Jesus up, he is in heaven or with God. If he makes appearances, he appears from heaven. "Ascension" is merely the use of spatial language to describe exaltation and glorification. Many of the early NT statements acknowledge the identity of the resurrection and the ascension (=glorification), as has been shown both by Benoit and by Archbishop A. M. Ramsey, "What was the Ascension?" in *History and Chronology in the New Testament* (Theological Collections 6; London, SPCK, 1965). Acts ii 32–33 reports, "God raised up Jesus. . . . Being therefore exalted at the right hand of God . . ." (see also Acts v 30–31). In Rom viii 34 we hear of Christ Jesus "who was raised from the dead, who is at the right hand of God" (see also Eph i 20). In Phil ii 8–9 the humbling of Jesus unto death is contrasted with the high exalting of him by God. Peter speaks of "the resurrection of Jesus Christ who has gone into heaven and is at the right hand of God" (I Pet iii 21–22). Luke xxiv 26 has Jesus explain that it was "necessary that the Messiah should suffer these things and enter into his glory." The Jesus of Matt xxviii 16–20 who appears after the resurrection is a Jesus to whom all power in heaven and on earth has been given. See also the *Gospel of Peter*, 56, and the *Epistle of Barnabas* xv 9 (cited in our NOTE on xx 26, "a week later").

This NT concept whereby resurrection from the dead involves ascension to God's presence and exaltation at His right hand enables us to understand John's dramatization in xx 17. On the cross the Johannine Jesus had already entered into the process of exaltation and glorification, for crucifixion is a step upwards in the course of being lifted up to the Father (xii 32–33). Perhaps it would have been more logical if John had joined the author of the Epistle to the Hebrews in having Jesus go directly to the Father from the cross, for the resurrection does not fit easily into John's theology of the crucifixion. We remember that while the Synoptic Jesus three times predicts his resurrection, the Johannine Jesus has preferred to speak of being lifted up (vol. 29, p. 146). And in the Last Discourse Jesus has not described his victory in terms of his being raised up from the dead but in terms of his going to the Father (xiv 12, 28, xvi 5, 10, 28). Nevertheless, the Fourth Gospel could not dispense with the resurrection which was too firm a part of Christian tradition. Consequently the evangelist had to make the effort to fit the resurrection into the process of Jesus' passing from this world to the Father. If John reinterprets the crucifixion so that it becomes part of Jesus' glorification, he dramatizes the resurrection so that it is obviously part of the ascension. Jesus is lifted up on the cross; he is raised up from the dead; and he goes up to the Father—all as part of one action and one "hour."

The vehicle for this reinterpretative dramatization of the resurrection is the appearance to Magdalene, a story that came down from early times but was not part of the official preaching. As we have explained, by clinging to Jesus Mary acts out the misapprehension that the Jesus who has come forth from the tomb has fulfilled God's plan and is ready to resume the closeness of earthly relationship to his followers. Jesus answers by explaining that resurrection is part of ascension, and his enduring presence in the Spirit can be given only when he has ascended to the Father. And so, when in the next scene he appears to the disciples, he is the glorified Jesus who gives the Spirit (xx 22—a glorification is implied, for vii 39 stated that there could be no gift of the Spirit until Jesus had been glorified).

This use of the Magdalene appearance as a vehicle for Johannine theological reinterpretation accidentally creates a problem. Does John mean literally that the appearance to Magdalene took place before the ascension, while the other appearances took place later? Taken at face value, such an interpretation would paradoxically deny that the resurrection is the same as the ascension, for an interval would separate the two. Moreover, it would mean that it was not the glorified Lord who appeared to Magdalene and thus she was granted only an inferior-grade appearance. Many authors accept such a premise. For Schwank, "Leere Grab," p. 398, the Jesus of the Magdalene appearance is earthbound—the Word who became flesh. For Kraft, TLZ 76 (1951), 570, the Jesus of this appearance is not yet in the process of being lifted up but is in the depth of his abasement, for he still has his dead body. We may also ask whether, by placing the ascension before the appearance to the disciples, John does not dispense with a terminus to the earthly appearances; for no other ascension or departure is described in the Fourth Gospel after the appearances to the disciples and to Thomas.

In our judgment, all such conclusions fail to make allowance for John's technique. He is fitting a theology of resurrection/ascension that by definition has no dimensions of time and space into a narrative that is necessarily sequential. If John's purpose is forgotten, the attempt to dramatize in temporal scenes what is *sub specie aeternitatis* creates confusion. When the risen Jesus has to explain to Magdalene that he is about to ascend, the emphasis is on the identification of the resurrection and the ascension, not on the accidental time lag. In Johannine thought there is only one risen Jesus, and he appears in glory in all his appearances. Magdalene who sees him apparently before the ascension announces, "I have seen the Lord" (xx 18), while the disciples who see him after the ascension make exactly the same proclamation (xx 25). Thus, in our opinion, the statement "I am ascending to my Father" in 17b is not an exact determination of time and has no implication for the state of the risen Jesus previous to that statement. It is a theological statement contrasting the passing nature of Jesus' presence in his post-resurrectional appearances and the permanent nature of his presence in the Spirit. In the parallel appearance of Jesus to the women in Matt xxviii 10, he instructs Magdalene and her companion to go and tell the disciples that he will appear to them in Galilee. Instead of such a statement concerning the fact of the resurrection and the sequence and locus of appearances, John has Jesus make a statement to Magdalene about the meaning of the resurrection. A willingness to neglect temporal implications for theological significance is not unusual in John. We pointed out that, in having the dying Jesus *hand over* his Spirit (xix 30), the evangelist was probably making a symbolic reference to the giving of the Spirit, even though the evangelist did not mean to imply that this was the actual moment of the gift (a moment described in xx 22). Similarly, in the next section we shall find out that Thomas was not present at the moment when the apostles were commissioned, and when the Spirit was given, and the power to forgive sins conferred. This has bothered theologians who have speculated whether later Jesus favored Thomas privately with these graces. Such a consideration probably never entered the evangelist's mind. He had withdrawn Thomas from the general appearance so that Thomas could exemplify apostolic doubt; he was not concerned with the accidental inequity of apostolic position thus created. Finally, we take the same general approach to the thesis that, by placing appearances after the ascension, John has no terminus for the earthly appearances of Jesus. The word "after" has no strict temporal meaning here. John is concerned about showing that the disciples were given the Spirit by the risen Jesus, and there is no terminus to the Spirit's presence. Obviously the evangelist could not have foreseen that a later generation, having read Acts, might start wondering when in that period of the dispensation of the Spirit Jesus stopped appearing to the disciples.

Turning back now from what we consider a false problem, we would like to point out how meaningful this interpretation of vs. 17 is when Jesus' words are placed in the context of his previous statements and in the context of Johannine theology as a whole. In vi 62, when his disciples seemed to doubt his words, Jesus said, "If, then, you behold the Son of Man ascending to where he was before . . . ? It is the Spirit that gives life." He was making an intimate connection between the ascension of the Son of Man and the giving of the Spirit. Words that Jesus spoke at the Last Supper also become clearer. In xvi 7 he said, "If I do not go away, the Paraclete will never come to you; whereas, if I do go, I shall send him to you." This seems to mean that the coming of the Paraclete/Spirit would immediately follow his death—a meaning that is verified in xx 17 and 22 which associate the resurrection, the ascension, and the giving of the

Spirit. By speaking of his ascension in xx 17, Jesus is not drawing attention primarily to his own glorification—that process has been going on throughout "the hour"—but to what his glorification will mean to men, namely, the giving of the Spirit that makes them God's children. Dodd, *Interpretation*, p. 442, is correct when he observes, "It is not the resurrection as Christ's resumption of heavenly glory that needs to be emphasized, but the resurrection as the renewal of personal relations with the disciples."

These relations are in mind when Jesus speaks of the disciples as "my brothers" and describes the goal of his ascension as "my Father and your Father, my God and your God." The traditional exegesis, repeated even by such penetrating scholars as Loisy, Bernard, Hoskyns, and Lightfoot, is that Jesus says "your Father" and "my Father," rather than "our Father," because he wants to keep distinct his special relationship to the Father (he is the natural Son) from that of his followers (adopted sons). Catharinet, *art. cit.*, has proved just the opposite. To understand the "my Father and your Father, my God and your God" pattern, one should recall Ruth i 16. Urged by Naomi to stay behind in Moab, Ruth insists that, even though not an Israelite, she will come to Israel with Naomi; for from this moment, "Your people shall be my people, and your God my God." Similarly the statement of the Johannine Jesus is one of identification and not of disjunction. Jesus is ascending to his Father *who will now become the Father of his disciples*. In Johannine thought they alone are children of God who believe in Jesus (i 12) and are begotten by the Spirit (iii 5). Jesus' ascension will make possible the giving of the Spirit who will beget the believing disciples as God's children—that is why, in anticipation, Jesus now refers to them as "my brothers." As God's children, they will be sent as the Son is sent (xx 21) and they will have the power over sin (xx 23) that he had (see Bouttier, "La notion de frères chez saint Jean," RHPR 44 [1964], 179–90, especially 187). This idea that the resurrection/ascension/Spirit-giving constitutes men the brothers of Jesus is found elsewhere in the NT, for example, in Rom viii 29, which characterizes the risen Jesus as "the firstborn among many brothers." After speaking of the death of Jesus, Heb ii 9–10 says that "he brought many sons to glory." On the cross Jesus made his earthly mother symbolically the mother of the Beloved Disciple, that is, of the representative of those disciples whom he would have on this earth. His ascension will make it possible for his heavenly Father to be their father. In Gnostic thought the redeeming figure would lead his followers away from earth to heaven; after his ascension to the Father the Johannine Jesus will return to sanctify his followers while they remain on earth, and in his Spirit Jesus will be a continuing presence among them. In an excellent article, Grundmann shows that the reference to the Father in xx 17 and the implicit promise that a new relationship will be established for the disciples by the resurrection/ascension is in harmony not only with other NT passages (especially those reflecting Hellenistic Christian thought, e.g., Eph ii 18, "Through Jesus we have access in one Spirit to the Father"), but especially with the thought of I John which shows us how the promise works out. "Look at what love the Father has bestowed on us in letting us be called God's children; yet that is what we really are" (I John iii 1); "Our communion [koinōnia] is with the Father and with His Son, Jesus Christ" (i 3).

We note that Jesus says both that his Father will become the Father of the disciples and that his God will become their God. As Feuillet, "La recherche," pp. 101–2, has pointed out, the latter phraseology is covenantal. The Father will beget new children, and God will make a new covenant with a new people, namely, those who believe in Jesus. In describing the renewed covenant Jer xxxi 33 repeats the Pentateuchal formula: "I will be their God and they shall be my people" (Lev xxvi 12; see also Ezek xxxvi 28).

The christophany to Magdalene ends with her going off to Jesus' new brothers (the disciples) and announcing, "I have seen the Lord." Many interpreters have proposed that here John has in mind a verse from the greatest of the "Passion psalms" (Ps xxii 23[22]): "I will proclaim your name to my brothers; in front of the congregation I will praise you." The possibility becomes more interesting when we reflect that "Lord" (kyrios) is truly the name of the risen Jesus, and that in LXX kyrios renders the tetragrammaton, YHWH, which is the proper name of God.

"The hour" announced in xiii 1 for Jesus to pass from this world to the Father is now complete; Jesus' prayer in xvii 5 for glory with the Father is now answered; all that remains is for him to return to share his glory with his disciples. The first half of what he said in xiv 28, "I am going away," is fulfilled; we now turn to the second half of his promise, "I am coming back to you."

[The Bibliography for this section is included in the Bibliography for the whole of ch. xx, at the end of §69.]

69. THE RISEN JESUS:
—SCENE TWO
(xx 19–29)

Where the Disciples Are Gathered

XX 19 Now on the evening of that first day of the week, when, for fear of the Jews, the disciples had locked the doors of the place where they were, Jesus came and stood in front of them. "Peace to you," he said. 20 And when he had said this, he showed them his hands and side. At the sight of the Lord the disciples rejoiced. 21 "Peace to you," he said to them again:

> "As the Father has sent me,
> so do I send you."

22 And when he had said this, he breathed on them, with the words:

> "Receive a holy Spirit.
> 23 If you forgive men's sins,
> their sins are forgiven;
> if you hold them,
> they are held fast."

24 It happened that one of the Twelve, Thomas (this name means "Twin"), was absent when Jesus came. 25 So the other disciples kept telling him: "We have seen the Lord!" But he answered them, "I'll never believe it without first examining the mark of the nails on his hands, and putting my finger right into the place of the nails and my hand into his side."

26 Now, a week later, Jesus' disciples were once more in the house; this time Thomas was with them. Even though the doors were locked, Jesus came and stood in front of them. "Peace to you," he said. 27 Then he told Thomas, "Reach out your finger and examine my hands; reach out your hand and put it into my side. And do not persist in your

19: *said;* 22: *with the words (=and said);* 26: *came;* 27: *told.* In the historical present tense.

disbelief, but become a believer." 28 Thomas answered with the words,
"My Lord and my God!" 29 Jesus told him,

"You have believed because you have seen me.
Happy those who have not seen and yet have believed."

29: *told*. In the historical present tense.

NOTES

xx 19. *Now*. Oun represents the writer's attempt to connect this narrative
to what has preceded. Magdalene has told the disciples that she has seen the
Lord; now they are to see him.

on the evening of that first day of the week. This time indication may
also be an editorial connective, associating the appearance with Jerusalem and
Easter Day. (Dodd, *Tradition*, p. 197, points to the editorial annotation in Mark
iv 35: "When evening had come on that day. . . .") The parallel appearance
to the Eleven in Luke xxiv 33–49 is also pictured as taking place late in
the day; for it was already near evening when Jesus dined with the two
disciples in Emmaus, and these disciples made their way back to Jerusalem before
Jesus appeared. The Marcan Appendix (xvi 14) lists an appearance to the Eleven
at table after an appearance to the two disciples on a country road, without
any time indications. "*That* first day of the week" means the same first day
mentioned in vs. 1. Some would see here, however, an evocation of the OT
concept of the day of the Lord, sometimes called "that day," for example,
"My people shall know my name; on that day they shall know it is I who
speak" (Isa lii 6). It would not be at all unlikely that John would regard
as the eschatological day this Sunday on which, through the gift of the Spirit,
Jesus makes possible his permanent presence among his followers; see John xiv
20: "*On that day* you will recognize that I am in my Father, and you are in
me, and I in you" (also xvi 23, 26). However, we cannot agree with the
Archimandrite Cassien, pp. 267, 276, that John's usage is purely eschatological
and not chronological, so that he is not referring to the Sunday of the finding
of the empty tomb but to Pentecost, fifty days later! (Cassien thus harmonizes
John and Acts on the giving of the Spirit and also explains why Christians
celebrate Pentecost on a Sunday.)

The fact that John mentions the first day of the week at the beginning of
both scenes in this chapter and that he places the appearance to Thomas
exactly a week later (vs. 26) suggests that his presentation may have been
influenced by the Christian custom of celebrating the Eucharist on "the first
day of the week" (Acts xx 7; cf. I Cor xvi 2). That Sunday had a significance
in the Johannine community may be seen from the dating of the seer's
vision in Rev i 10 to "the Lord's day," presumably Sunday. Loisy, p. 510,
proposes that John has painted his portrait of Jesus' presence among the
assembled disciples in order to anticipate Jesus' eucharistic presence in the
Christian assemblies on Sunday. Barrett, p. 477, sees traces of a liturgy in xx
19–29: "The disciples assemble on the Lord's Day. The blessing is given:
'Peace to you.' The Holy Spirit descends upon the worshippers and the word of
absolution (cf. vs. 23) is pronounced. Christ himself is present (this may

suggest the Eucharist and the spoken Word of God) bearing the marks of his passion; he is confessed as Lord and God." Indeed, this passage in John has been cited as the first evidence that the Christian observance of Sunday arose from an association of that day with the resurrection—an idea that shortly later Ignatius gave voice to: "No longer living for the Sabbath, but for the Lord's Day on which life dawned for us through him and his death" (*Magnesians* ix 1). However, H. Riesenfeld is probably right in claiming that the association of Sunday and the resurrection was a secondary development ("Sabbat et Jour du Seigneur," in NTEM, pp. 210–17). Originally, on Saturday evening after the close of the Sabbath (ca. 6 P.M.) and thus, by Jewish reckoning, on what was already Sunday, Jewish Christians who had observed the Sabbath now met at their homes to break the eucharistic bread (cf. Acts ii 46), as a prolongation of the Sabbath. Thus it would seem that the earliest Christian celebrations on "the first day of the week" were not on the day of Sunday but late in the evening on the vigil of Sunday.

for fear of the Jews. In the other Gospels fear marks the guards and the women as they see the angelic vision at the tomb (Mark xvi 8; Matt xxviii 4, 5, 8; Luke xxiv 5), and the women and the disciples as they see Jesus (Matt xxviii 10; Luke xxiv 37). In John it is "the Jews" who cause the fear (also vii 13), not the supernatural visions. Both Bultmann and Hartmann regard this reference to "the Jews" as the Johannine writer's addition to the narrative that came down to him. Does he mean that the disciples are afraid that they will now be persecuted by the Jewish authorities as Jesus was? Or is it that, in the wake of rumors of the resurrection, they will be accused by Jewish authorities of complicity in stealing the body (Matt xxviii 13)? The apocryphal *Gospel of Peter*, 26, reports a search for the disciples on the ground that they were evildoers and had tried to burn the Temple.

had locked the doors. Does the evangelist want us to think that the locked doors were to serve as a barrier to the possible entrance of police sent by the Jewish authorities to arrest the disciples? Or is it a question of the concealment of the disciples' whereabouts and an attempt to avoid public notice? Despite the explicit reason that John gives for the locking of the doors (i.e., the fear of the Jews), many scholars see another motive behind this description, namely, that John wants us to think that Jesus' body could pass through closed doors (see COMMENT). Such an interpretation receives more support if we give adversative force to the preceding participial construction: "Even though the doors were locked, Jesus came." That is the meaning in vs. 26 where no "fear of the Jews" is mentioned; but we do not think it is the meaning here. Some would find a parallel for such a spiritual attribute of Jesus' risen body in Luke's description of his sudden disappearance from the sight of the disciples at Emmaus and his sudden appearance in front of the Eleven in Jerusalem (Luke xxiv 31, 36), although Luke does not mention that the disciples were closed in. The story of the empty tomb may reflect an earlier attitude toward the properties of Jesus' body; for the insistence that the stone was rolled or moved away seems to imply that Jesus' body emerged through an open entrance.

the place where they were. Some late textual witnesses add "gathered together" (in imitation of Matt xviii 20?). John probably thinks of a house *in Jerusalem* (where "the Jews" would pose a threat), presumably the same place where the disciples were when Magdalene came to them in vs. 18.

Luke xxiv 33 makes it clear that the appearance was at Jerusalem. The popular view that this took place in "the upper room" arises from the identification of this unspecified place with the upper room (*hyperōon*) of Acts i 13, where the Eleven were staying after Jesus' departure for heaven forty days later, and the further identification of this composite with the large upper room (*anagaion mega*) where the Last Supper was eaten (Luke xxii 12). The Marcan Appendix specifies that the Eleven were reclining at table, and a meal is also at hand in the Lucan account of the appearance.

Jesus came and stood in front of them. Luke xxiv 36 has almost the same expression without the "came." John's use of "came" may be accidental, but many commentators see here a specific fulfillment of the promise to come back in xiv 18, 28 (same verb).

"Peace to you," he said. In the Western Noninterpolation (p. 969 above) of Luke xxiv 36 we find exactly the same words. The Vulgate and the Peshitta add to the Lucan passage: "It is I; do not be afraid," an expression found in the account of Jesus walking on the water (John vi 20; Mark vi 50; Matt xiv 27). In rabbinic Hebrew "Peace [be] to you" became a standard greeting: in the plural it is *šālōm 'ălēkem*, less frequently *šālōm lᵉkem*. In biblical Hebrew only the form with *lᵉ* appears and then often in more solemn moments, so that the Koehler Hebrew dictionary (p. 974, col. 2) calls some instances of *šālōm lᵉ* a "formula of revelation." For instance, in Judg vi 23, when Gideon is frightened by seeing the angel of the Lord, the Lord says to him, "Peace to you; do not be afraid; you shall not die." Gideon responds by building an altar there, entitled "The Lord is peace." Similarly, an angelic apparition reassures the frightened Daniel (x 19) with the words, "Peace to you." Obviously in John xx 19 we are also dealing with a solemn context and should not assume that "Peace to you" is an ordinary greeting. Perhaps with that assumption many translations have "Peace *be* to [or with] you," a rendering implying the wish that peace be restored or granted. In this eschatological moment, however, Jesus' words are not a wish but a statement of fact. W. C. van Unnik has made a minute study of the similar liturgical formula, "The Lord with you" or *Dominus vobiscum* (in NTEM, pp. 270–305); and he points out (p. 283) that (a) in the instances when a verb is supplied, the note of certainty is stronger than the subjunctive note of wish or possibility, and (b) when a verb is not found (as here), the phrase is practically always a declaration and thus one should not use the subjunctive "be." The idea that the risen Jesus has brought peace is probably echoed in the initial greeting of the Pauline letters where the habitual use of "peace" is more than a formality or a simple translation of the *šālōm* of Jewish secular letters (see J. A. Fitzmyer, *The Jerome Biblical Commentary*, ed. by R. E. Brown et al. [Englewood Cliffs, N.J.: Prentice-Hall, 1968], art. 47, §8A).

20. *he showed them his hands and side.* The place of "them" varies in the textual witnesses. The Western Noninterpolation of Luke xxiv 40 has an almost identical reading, with "hands and feet" instead of John's "hands and side"; Luke xxiv 39 has: "See my hands and my feet." In vs. 25 John will make it clear that he means the nail marks in the hands and the lance wound in the side; Luke never specifies, but presumably he means nail marks both in the hands and in the feet. The Lucan and Johannine pictures have been combined in Christian piety to produce a devotion to Jesus' "five wounds" (two hands, two feet, side) and the belief that either four nails (earlier conven-

tion in art) or three nails were used. (The latter computation comes from supposing that the legs were crossed and one nail held the feet, a depiction that is related to the idea that there was a *suppedaneum* or footrest on the cross.) It is difficult to decide which is more original, John's "hands and side" or Luke's "hands and feet." Many proposed that John changed "feet" to "side" in order to harmonize with his description of a lance wound in xix 34; yet Benoit, *Passion*, p. 284, argues in favor of John against Luke. We are inclined to agree with Hartmann, p. 213, that both Luke and John present us with a development and that the original statement mentioned only hands—a development that is not necessarily fictional.

Parenthetically we may discuss the contention that Luke's evidence is suspect because hitherto we have had little reliable support from antiquity for the custom of nailing the feet to the cross. While in the 2nd century it is clearly indicated that Jesus' feet were nailed to the cross (Justin *Trypho* xcvii 3; PG 6:705A; and Tertullian *Adv. Judaeos* xiii; PL 2:635A), the patristic statements specifically relate this detail to the fulfillment of Ps xxii 17(16): "They have pierced [LXX] my hands and feet." And so it is thought that Luke too may have been adapting the memory of the crucifixion to the psalm. This solution remains possible; but Luke's description of nail marks in Jesus' feet has gained verisimilitude from the 1968 discovery in Palestine of a 1st-century ossuary containing the remains of a crucified man, both of whose feet had been pierced through the ankle bones by a nail. (Reference to this find was made by V. Tzaferis in a paper [with an English abstract] given at the 1969 World Congress of Jewish Studies in Jerusalem.)

If the original pre-Gospel account of the appearance of Jesus mentioned only his hands, we encounter a minor problem: normally either the arms were tied to the crossbar, or the *wrists* were nailed, the latter method being adopted when it was desirable to hasten death, as in Jesus' case. The mention of nail marks in the hands would then be a slight inaccuracy (influence of the psalm?), for nails put through the palms of the hands would not have carried the weight of the body on the cross. (See J. W. Hewitt, "The Use of Nails in Crucifixion," HTR 25 [1932], 29–45.) It is not impossible that the difficulty is created by a too literal translation, since both the Hebrew and Greek words for "hand" (*yād, cheir*) sometimes include the arm.

At the sight of the Lord. Literally "having seen" (BDF, §415). Now the Johannine writer himself begins to use "the Lord," the post-resurrectional title of Jesus (see NOTE on vs. 2).

21. *"Peace to you."* The repetition (see end of 19) is probably the result of editorial additions, although some commentators have supposed that the disciples needed more assurance because of (unmentioned) fear and doubt.

sent . . . send. The verbs, respectively *apostellein* (perfect tense) and *pempein* (present), stand in parallelism here with no visible sign of distinction. In the closely parallel xvii 18, "As you sent me into the world, so I sent them," *apostellein* is used in the aorist in both parts. Although this verse probably does reflect the commissioning of apostles, it cannot be used to argue that only the Eleven were present, for an earlier understanding of "apostle" did not confine that term to the Twelve.

22. *he breathed on them.* For this action as evocative of God's creative breath in Gen ii 7, see COMMENT. The MT and LXX of that verse have God *breathing* into Adam the *breath* (*pnoē*) of life, and some have wondered

whether John was dependent on a form of the passage that read "spirit" (*pneuma*) instead of "breath." For instance, Philo, *Quod deterius* xxii;≯80, seems to read *pneuma* in Gen ii 7; yet in *Legum allegoria* I xiii;≯42 Philo reads *pnoē* in this verse and even comments on the use of this word rather than *pneuma* (see also *De opificio mundi* xLvi;≯134–35 where *pnoē* is read but is interpreted as *pneuma*). A few commentators have interpreted the Johannine passage in light of the popular Near Eastern belief that the breath of a holy man has supernatural power, for example, the ability to heal or to immobilize a person. Because in John this breathing is connected with the power to forgive sins, which is a sacramental power in much of Christianity (Eastern churches and Roman Catholicism), some have thought that here John reflects an early Christian ordination rite (cf. Grass, p. 67). Others have claimed the Johannine passage as the point of origin for a later practice of ordination by insufflation. The most famous example of this was the custom of filling a skin bag with the holy breath of the Coptic Patriarch of Alexandria, tying it up, and transporting it up river to Ethiopia where it was let loose on the one designated to be the Abuna or head of the Ethiopian church. Lootfy Levonian, *The Expositor*, 8th Series, 22 (1921), 149–54, discussing such beliefs and practices in relation to John xx 22, says (with confidence!) of the latter custom: "No one can doubt apostolic succession when it comes in this form." Finally, we may mention that a later generation of Western theologians called upon vs. 22 as proof that within the Trinity the Holy Spirit proceeded by spiration and that the Son had a role not only in the mission but also in the procession of the Spirit (Augustine *De Trinitate* iv 29; PL 42:908). The controversy is not dead; the modern Russian Orthodox writer Cassien, pp. 264–65, finds evidence in John that the procession of the Spirit is from the Father alone.

Receive a holy Spirit. Although our translation preserves the fact that there is no definite article in the Greek, we would point out that the article is missing in other biblical texts that clearly refer to the Holy Spirit in the full NT understanding of that term (Acts ii 4). In trying to harmonize John xx 22 with the Lucan account of Pentecost, some have tried to show from John's omission of the article that here no more than an impersonal gift of the Spirit was meant while Luke was talking of the personal Spirit (Swete, pp. 166, 396). Cassien, pp. 156–59, wisely rejects such an approach both on philological and theological grounds.

23. *If you forgive men's sins.* The verb is *aphienai*, "let go, release." Those who suppose a Semitic background generally suggest that it reflects Heb. *naśa'* (the Greek verb has a legal connotation, while the Hebrew verb is more cultic). The initial Greek particle *an*, which we translate by an "if" clause, can, without real difference in meaning (BDF, §107; Moule, IBNTG, p. 152), also be translated: "When you forgive . . ."; "Whose ever sins you forgive. . . ." More important is the fact that an aorist subjunctive is used in this clause, while the parallel clause, "if you hold them," has a present subjunctive. The aorist implies an act that in a moment brings forgiveness, whereas the present implies that the state of holding or refusing forgiveness continues (ZGB, §249). "Men's sins" is literally "the sins of some [plural]"; yet there is substantial textual support for reading a singular "of someone."

their sins are forgiven. The textual witnesses differ notably in the form of the verb to be read here. The best witnesses have the perfect passive, but the future and present passives also have support. In an article professedly written to refute the sacramental interpretation of this verse, J. R. Mantey, JBL 58 (1939), 243–49, insists that the perfect tense implies past action and that the present and future readings are attempts to make the verse fit a sacramental theology. Therefore, he would translate it as "their sins *have been* forgiven," with the theological implication that no more is involved than declaring the forgiveness of sins that has already taken place. Mantey has been answered by H. J. Cadbury, JBL 58 (1939), 251–54, who, although he professes no interest in defending the sacramental interpretation of the verse, shows that Mantey's understanding of the perfect tense does not apply to conditional sentences. A perfect tense used in the apodosis of a general condition does not necessarily refer to an action that is prior to the protasis; rather such a perfect can have a future reference (BDF, §344). Thus the textual variants of 23 with the present and future tenses (see BDF, §323[1]) have exactly the same meaning as the reading with the perfect tense, except that the perfect tense draws more attention to the continuous character of the action: the sins are forgiven and stay so. The passive is a circumlocution for describing God's action, and one may paraphrase the first part of 23 thus: When you forgive men's sins, at that moment God forgives those sins and they remain forgiven. J. Jeremias, TWNTE, III, 753, finds here the idea that on the Last Day God will confirm the remission, and that conversely the unremitted sins will be held fast till Judgment Day.

if you hold them. The verb is *kratein*, "hold fast, hold on to, retain." In place of "them" a singular is read by some textual witnesses. It is not absolutely clear whether the object held is the men who committed the sins (so OS[sin]) or their sins. The latter is more likely by reason of parallelism with the first part of the verse. The phrasing "to hold sins" is strange in Greek even as it is in English; it probably was introduced as a counterpart to the imagery of releasing them or letting them go (*aphienai*). Mark vii 8 contrasts the two verbs: "You *leave* (unobserved) the commandment of God, but you *hold on to* the tradition of men." A possible parallel to the idea involved in John's idiom is found in the Greek of Sir xxviii 1: "He that takes vengeance will receive vengeance from the Lord who will surely keep [*diatērein*] his sins."

24. *one of the Twelve.* Without Judas there are now only the Eleven, but the more traditional designation of the group is maintained. Because the Twelve have little role in John's Gospel, Bultmann, p. 537, holds that the evangelist must have found this phrase in the pre-Gospel tradition. However, certainly the evangelist knew and could have imitated such a standard designation, for example, Judas is "one of the Twelve" in vi 71. The pattern is quite similar to "one of the disciples" (vi 8, xii 4, xiii 23).

Thomas (this name means "Twin"). The explanation of this designation can be found in the NOTE on xi 16—it is romantic to maintain that the name is explained here in order to prepare for Thomas' "two-minded" or doubting role. In both xi 16 and xiv 5 Thomas exhibits a skeptical attitude, but there is no evidence for Bernard's surmise (II, 681) that Thomas' pessimism kept him away for the gathering of the disciples on Easter evening. In apocryphal tradition Thomas became the recipient of marvelous revelations. The *Gospel of Thomas*, saying 13, has Thomas profess to Jesus, "My mouth is not capable of saying whom you are like." In return Jesus praises Thomas for having drunk from Jesus' bubbling spring and speaks three ineffable words to Thomas.

25. *the other disciples.* "Other" is omitted by a small but important combination of witnesses.

kept telling. Perhaps the imperfect is conative (BDF, §326): they tried to tell him.

I'll never believe it. In the Greek word order this refusal to believe comes at the end of the sentence; the pattern is: "If I do not examine [literally: see] . . . , I'll never believe." The negative is the strong *ou mē* with the future indicative (BDF, §365).

mark of the nails . . . place of the nails. "Mark" is *typos;* "place" is *topos;* and the textual witnesses exhibit a confusion of the two words (and even of singular and plural forms). Although many would read *typos* as original in both phrases (so SB, American Bible Society Greek NT), the variant readings are more easily explained if the original had two different words.

putting my finger right into. The translation tries to catch the sense of motion in the verb *ballein,* "to throw."

26. *a week later.* Literally "after eight days"; as the OS^sin makes explicit, John means us to understand this as the second Sunday (see NOTE on vs. 19, "that first day of the week"). Some would find here an instance of the early Christian theology of the eighth day (vol. 29, p. 106). The *Epistle of Barnabas* xv 9 seems to echo the Johannine sequence of the happenings on Easter Sunday when it says, "We celebrate with gladness *the eighth day* in which Jesus also rose from the dead and appeared and ascended into heaven." Another possible symbolism is that at the end of the Gospel John has placed a week to match the week at the beginning of the Gospel (vol. 29, pp. 105–6). The two weeks would share the theme of creation (exemplified in xx 22 in the creative breathing forth of the Spirit). Such imaginative interpretations are difficult to substantiate.

The sequence would indicate that John supposes a continued presence of the disciples in Jerusalem. This is hard to reconcile with the Marcan/Matthean outlook wherein the angelic message instructs the disciples to go to Galilee where they will see Jesus (see pp. 971–72). Consequently some harmonizers, for example, Zahn, want to locate this scene in Galilee where the disciples are thought to have gone in the intervening week; the argument is advanced that they are in Galilee in xxi 1, and one must account for the move. Lagrange, p. 517, assumes that the disciples stayed in Jerusalem for the week-long celebration of Passover/Unleavened Bread (Deut xvi 3), and now they have gathered together ready to depart for Galilee.

once more. The impression is given that there were no gatherings and hence no appearances during the elapsed week.

in the house. Literally "inside," without a specific mention of a house; but see the Greek of Ezek ix 6: "inside, in the house."

Jesus came. The use of the historical present here (as contrasted with the aorist in the similar expression in 19) suggests to Bernard, II, 682, an implication that Jesus was expected. Would Jesus have been any less expected in 19, after the words to Magdalene in 17? There is no apparent reason beyond the aesthetic for such variations of tense.

27. *he told Thomas.* Jesus knows what Thomas said in his absence; but we are not sure that such knowledge is a special privilege of the *risen* Jesus, for even during the ministry the Johannine Jesus has been extraordinarily perceptive (see i 48).

Reach out your finger and examine my hands. Literally "Bring your finger here and see my hands." The invitation in Luke xxiv 39, "See my hands and my feet," is similar to the second part of John's invitation.

reach out your hand and put it into my side. The fact that Jesus' side could be touched is used by Kastner, *art. cit.*, as proof for his contention that the risen Jesus was naked; but from the fact that Jesus does not say "see" or "examine" my side, as was the case with his hands, others judge that his side was covered with a loose garment beneath which one could reach (Loisy, p. 510). The evangelist scarcely intended to supply information on the haberdashery appropriate for a risen body. Loisy qualifies as naïve the idea that there was still a gaping wound in the side of the body, but one wonders if he would not have also judged it naïve had the risen body appeared with the wounds healed.

And do not persist in your disbelief, but become a believer. Literally "And do not become [*ginou*] unbelieving but believing." Wenz, p. 18, argues that Bultmann's translation of the initial "and" is inaccurate, for Bultmann makes this a purpose clause: "so that you are no longer disbelieving." Wenz rejects the implication that Thomas' touching and seeing are not part of faith. But, while we do not accept Bultmann's general interpretation of this verse (see COMMENT), we agree that the demand of Thomas in 25 is certainly not representative of faith, and if Thomas had accepted Jesus' invitation to examine and touch him, Thomas would not have been a believer, in the Johannine sense. The present imperative used here is durative; its use in a prohibition implies that something already existing is to stop (BDF, §§335, 336³); and so Thomas is being asked to change his attitude. Thus, we cannot agree with Barrett, p. 476, who suggests that possibly Thomas is being asked to show himself as a believer rather than a non-believer, without the necessary implication that he has been an unbeliever. Nor do we agree with Loisy, p. 511, who stresses that the verb is "become" and holds that Thomas, who is barely oriented to incredulity, is being urged toward belief. Here *ginesthai* means "to be, show oneself" (as implied in the variant reading found in Codex Bezae: *mē isthi*, "do not be"). Thomas had manifested incredulity and is being challenged to change. This is the only instance in John of the adjectives *apistos* and *pistos*—John prefers the verb *pisteuein* (vol. 29, pp. 512–14)—but they are found in Revelation. Elsewhere the adjectives occur in Acts and in Paul; and Dodd, *Tradition,* p. 354, points out that they are contrasted in a slightly different sense in the parable of the faithful and unfaithful steward (Luke xii 42–48).

28. *"My Lord and my God!"* Against the theory of Theodore of Mopsuestia, the Second Council of Constantinople (fifth ecumenical council, A.D. 553) insisted that these words were a reference to Jesus and not merely an exclamation in honor of the Father (DB, §434). There is no tendency among modern scholars to follow Theodore. The expression, as used in John, is a cross between a vocative and a proclamation of faith ("You are my Lord and my God"). Dodd, *Interpretation,* p. 430², suggests that "my Lord" refers to the Jesus of history and "my God" is a theological evaluation of his person; he cites with favor F. C. Burkitt's paraphrase: "Yes, it is Jesus—and he is divine." But Bultmann, p. 538⁷, is correct in insisting that in combination with "God," "Lord" must also be a cultic title (see COMMENT). The article is used before "God"; it was not used, we recall, in the Greek of i 1 (vol. 29, p. 5).

However, the difference of meaning should not be pressed too sharply, as if i 1 were a markedly less exalted statement (Moule, IBNTG, p. 116).

29. *You have believed.* Some Syriac witnesses preface this with a "Now." The sentence is taken as a question in many minuscule mss. and by many modern scholars (Westcott-Hort, Bernard, Loisy, Tillmann, Lagrange; see MTGS, p. 345): "Have you believed because you have seen me?" For other examples where the first part of such two-member comparisons is a question, see i 50, iv 35, xvi 31–32. We have hesitatingly accepted it as an affirmation, since that is the more difficult reading.

because you have seen me. Some take this to mean: "because you have been content with seeing me rather than touching me as I challenged"; but that is not the obvious meaning.

Happy. For the nature of a beatitude or macarism, see NOTE on xiii 17. The only other beatitude in the NT concerning believing is Luke i 45 where Elizabeth speaks of Mary: "Happy is she who believed that there would be a fulfillment of the words spoken to her from the Lord." A reference to John xx 29 as the ninth beatitude, while clever, has the unfortunate implication that Matthew's assemblage of eight (Matt v 3–11) is a complete collection.

and yet have believed. Many treat this as a gnomic or timeless aorist, equivalent to a present ("and yet believe"). But the past tense is not inappropriate, for the evangelist is probably thinking of his own era when for many years there has been a group that has not seen but has believed.

COMMENT: GENERAL

On p. 965 we have given the outline of this scene, and on p. 995 we have compared it with Scene One (xx 1–18) and noted the similarities of organization. Yet the history of the composition of Scene Two seems to have been different from that of Scene One. If Scene One was put together by combining three once independent narratives, Scene Two is an expansion and rearrangement of one basic narrative concerning the first appearance of Jesus to the Eleven. We recall (p. 970 above) that two Gospel witnesses besides John xx place this appearance in the Jerusalem area (Luke; Marcan Appendix), while two other witnesses place it in the Galilee area (Matthew; John xxi). John xx is closest in detail to the accounts of the Jerusalem group, especially to Luke, but we shall find an occasional similarity to the accounts of the Galilee group.

An Analysis of the Narrative of the Appearance to the Disciples (xx 19–23)

We maintained above (p. 978) that the narratives of appearances were not originally united to the narratives of visits to the tomb, and so we are not surprised to find signs that John xx 19–23 was once independent of the material in xx 1–18. Despite the attempt in 19 ("now"; *"that* first day") to sew the two accounts together, the narrative of the appearance to the disciples could directly follow the Passion Narrative. If the Beloved Disciple believed on the basis of what he saw in the empty tomb (vs. 8), there is no trace of his belief as the disciples huddle together behind locked doors in 19. Nor has the faith of Magdalene detectably penetrated this group, despite her message in 18.

The episode in vss. 19–23 has the five characteristics attributed by Dodd to the Concise Narratives of post-resurrectional appearances (p. 972 above), although one or the other characteristic is slightly blurred. The *bereft situation* of Jesus' followers is described in expanded form in 19; the explanation that the disciples had locked the doors of the place where they were for fear of "the Jews" is probably a Johannine development of the motif of surprise in an earlier form of the narrative. The *appearance* and the *greeting* in 19 are concise; nevertheless, "Peace to you" reflects a Johannine theological motif, as we shall see. The consequent *recognition* of Jesus by his disciples in 20 is a bit awkward, for we are not told how the disciples reacted to the greeting nor is a reason given why Jesus should have felt compelled to show his hands and side. (In analyzing the appearance to Thomas we shall suggest that the expression of doubt that is now dramatized in the Thomas story once preceded vs. 20 and provided the occasion for Jesus' action, as also in Luke xxiv 37–39.) The element of *command* appears explicitly in 21, but is accompanied by two somewhat related sayings in 22 and 23.

Just as there were two types of Lucan parallels to the Johannine account of the visit of the disciples to the tomb (pp. 1000–1 above), so there are two types of Lucan parallels to the present narrative. A direct parallel to John xx is found in the Western Noninterpolations (p. 969 above) of Luke xxiv 36 and 40, namely, " 'Peace to you,' he said" and "And when he had said this, he showed them his hands and his feet." Except for the Lucan reference to the feet (see NOTE on vs. 20), this is verbatim the same as the end of vs. 19 and the beginning of vs. 20 in John xx. Since these verses are essential to John's account but are not really essential to Luke, we may suppose that at a late stage in the editing of Luke someone added these words taken from an early form of the Johannine tradition. If we set aside these Western Noninterpolations, there remains a similarity between the basic Lucan account of the appearance (xxiv 36, 39, 41, 47, 49) and the basic Johannine account; they are probably independent developments of the original Jerusalem narrative of the appearance of Jesus to his disciples. They both describe the appearance as occurring on Easter Sunday evening. In each Jesus comes with a certain suddenness, and we are told he "stood in front of them" (John xx 19; Luke xxiv 36). There is a similar emphasis on the reality or tangibility of Jesus' body, for in each account attention is drawn to his hands. The joy of the disciples is a common motif; and in each account there is a type of pause or transition before the risen Jesus gives his message (cf. John xx 21 and Luke xxiv 44). Both Gospels mention the forgiveness of sins (John xx 23; Luke xxiv 47). John specifically refers to the sending of the disciples (vs. 21) and the giving of the Holy Spirit (22), while the Lucan references are subtler: "forgiveness of sins *should be preached in his name* to all nations" (xxiv 47) and the "promise of my Father" (49). This comparison with Luke xxiv 33–53 does not work to John's disfavor, for John xx 19–23 has better preserved the original outline of the scene. John does not have the apologetic development about Jesus' ability to eat found in Luke xxiv 41–42 (cf. Acts x 41), nor the long instruction of Luke xxiv 44–47, much of which parallels the kerygmatic sermons in Acts. In fact, John's account is only a little less concise than that of the Galilean appearance in Matt xxviii 16–20.

When we consider the message of Jesus in John xx 21–23, it is very difficult to decide which elements are the oldest. The repetition of "Peace to you" (21 duplicating the end of 19) and of "And when he had said this" (22 duplicating the beginning of 20) suggests that an earlier form of the message may have been expanded by adding other traditional sayings of Jesus. The simplest approach to the problem would be to suppose that the original narrative ended with the command in vs. 21, and that 22 and 23 are additions (so Dodd, *Tradition,* p. 144; also Loisy, p. 508, with some hesitancy about 23). However, because the words in 21 are Johannine in style (compare the "[just] as . . . , so" pattern in vi 57, xv 9, xvii 18, 22), while the words of 23 are not, many think that it is vs. 21 (Hartmann) or 21–22 (Bultmann) that represents the expansion and that 23 is original. We are reluctant to pass judgment simply on the basis of whether a verse has Johannine style or vocabulary; for when that becomes the sole criterion for identifying the evangelist's expansion of a more original tradition, then one is making the assumption that the tradition that came down to the evangelist was strange to his own thought and expression pattern. We have worked with the supposition that, while a tradition came to the evangelist which he did not create (vol. 29, p. xxxiv, Stage 1), this tradition came from his master whose thought patterns and style influenced the evangelist. Moreover, we have contended that the evangelist himself may have had an important role in the oral, pre-Gospel shaping of this material (*ibid.,* Stage 2). Such an evaluation of the origins of the Fourth Gospel vitiates any too mechanical application of canons of style. In addition to the criterion of style, we insist here on comparing vss. 21–23 to the words of Jesus found in the other Gospel accounts of his appearance to the disciples in order to isolate the common elements that have the best chance of belonging to the earliest form of the narrative. Let us take the verses individually.

First, the mission or sending of the disciples in 21: "As the Father has sent me, so do I send you." In Matt xxviii 19 there is the command, "Go therefore and make disciples of all nations, baptizing them"; and similarly in the Marcan Appendix xvi 15 the command is, "Go into all the world and preach the Gospel to the whole creation." In Luke xxiv 47 we hear that "Repentance and the forgiveness of sins should be preached in his [Christ's] name to all nations." Paul relates the concept of the existence of apostles to a mission given by the risen Christ in his appearances to men (I Cor xv 8–9; Gal i 16). Therefore, there is no reason to think that the account of the appearance that came down to the Fourth Evangelist lacked a missionary command to the disciples. In fact, in John xx 21 the significant command of the Lord is at its briefest. Yet the formulation of it has been recast, for the paradigm of the mission is now the Son's relation to the Father, a Johannine theological theme. We may compare it to xvii 18: "As you sent me into the world, so I sent them into the world."

Second, the insufflation in 22 with the words: "Receive a holy Spirit." A mention of the Spirit is found also in other accounts of Jesus' appearance to his disciples. In Matt xxviii 19 it is incorporated in the words of what must have been a relatively late baptismal formula: "Baptizing them in the name of the Father and of the Son and of the Holy Spirit." Luke xxiv 49 has Jesus say, "I am sending the promise of my Father upon you" (=the Holy Spirit; cf. Acts i 4–5), but this is by way of preparation for the Pentecostal scene in Acts. The most one may argue from these late references to the Holy Spirit is that the early tradition of the appearance may have contained a reference to an outpouring of the Spirit (see Bultmann, p. 537[2]), a reference that the various Gospels adapted in different ways. Yet, of the three sayings of Jesus in John xx 21–23, the mention of the giving of the Spirit is the one most intimately related to the Johannine theological dialogue about the purpose of the ascension in 17, and so vs. 22 may very well represent the evangelist's expansion of the primitive appearance narrative. We do not find persuasive Dodd's contention (*Interpretation*, p. 430) that the insufflation of the Spirit is an image so strange to Johannine thought that it must have come to the evangelist from his source. This imagery is similar to the idea of the Spirit as wind in iii 8 (Dodd, *Tradition*, p. 144, modifying his view).

Third, the power of forgiving sins in 23. In the other Gospel accounts of Jesus' appearance to the disciples we find a tendency to specify the general mission of the disciples: in Luke the specification is to preach the forgiveness of sins; in Matthew it is to baptize; in the Marcan Appendix it is to preach the Gospel and baptize. In the Fourth Gospel vs. 23 supplies this element of specification. The Johannine formulation is elaborate; and from the viewpoint of form alone we may say that John xx 23 is to Luke xxiv 47 as the Marcan Appendix xvi 16 is to Matt xxviii 19:

Matt xxviii 19: "Make disciples of all nations, baptizing them"—the simple command to baptize.

Marcan Appendix xvi 16: "He who believes and is baptized will be saved; but he who does not believe will be condemned"—a prognostication of the ways in which Baptism will divide men.

Luke xxiv 47: "Repentance and the forgiveness of sins should be preached in his name to all nations"—the simple proclamation of forgiveness.

John xx 23: "If you forgive men's sins, their sins are forgiven; if you hold them, they are held fast"—a prognostication of the ways in which the power of forgiveness will divide men.

Yet the non-Johannine vocabulary and the parallelism of vs. 23 warn us against assuming that the elaborate formulation is the creation of the evangelist. We shall discuss below the relation of this verse to the two similar Matthean sayings about binding and loosing, and this comparison leads us to think that John preserves a modified form of a very old saying of Jesus, a saying that can be plausibly related to the risen Jesus' provision for the community he left behind.

In summary, then, we are inclined to think that the pre-Gospel narrative of the appearance contained the subject matter of at least two of the three sayings of Jesus in vss. 21–23 (namely, the sayings in 21 and 23). Yet the present form of 21 represents an adaptation to the general theology of the Gospel. If vs. 22 is the evangelist's addition to the episode, then some of the awkwardness of the present sequence in 21–23 can be accounted for, as well as the fact that the beginning of 22 repeats the beginning of 20. These conclusions are tentative.

An Analysis of the Narrative of the Appearance to Thomas (xx 24–29)

There is virtual scholarly unanimity that this was never an independent narrative and so is not comparable, for instance, to the narrative of an appearance to Peter. The substance of the Thomas story is intimately related to the earlier appearance to the disciples and would make little sense without the preceding narrative. Yet, when one first reads vss. 19–23, one would not expect a follow-up about one of the disciples who was absent; and the writer has to insert vs. 24 to tie the two stories together. How can one reconcile these facts in speculating about the origin of the Thomas story?

With some hesitation Bultmann proposes that the substance of the Thomas story was in the tradition that came down to the evangelist. We find more plausible the suggestion of Lindars (p. 997 above) that the Thomas story (which has no Synoptic parallels) has been created by the evangelist who has taken and dramatized a theme of doubt that originally appeared in the narrative of the appearance to the disciples. No other Gospel account of a post-resurrectional appearance pays so much attention as does the Thomas story to an individual's attitude toward the risen Jesus. This is because Thomas has become here the personification of an attitude. (See vol. 29, p. 429, for our suggestion that the present localization and use of the Lazarus miracle represents a somewhat similar individualization and dramatization.) If we return for a moment to the Lucan narrative of the appearance to the Eleven, we find that when Jesus suddenly stood in front of them (Luke xxiv 36=John xx 19), they were startled, frightened, and supposed that they saw a spirit. Jesus' reference to seeing his hands and feet (Luke xxiv 39) was in response to this. The theme of disbelief continues in Luke xxiv 41 and is found also in the Marcan Appendix xvi 14 and in Matt xxviii 17. John alone has no reference to doubt in the narrative of the appearance to the disciples, and that is why the statement, "He showed them his hands and side," in xx 20 seems illogical. We propose that this statement was originally preceded by an expression of doubt, as in Luke xxiv 37–39, but that the evangelist has transferred this doubt to a separate episode and personified it in Thomas. (Hartmann has a similar theory, but he supposes that the doubt was in response to Magdalene's report rather than in response to Jesus' appearance—thus after vs. 18 rather than after vs. 19.) The doubt now expressed by Thomas is used by the evangelist as an apologetic means of emphasizing the tangible character of Jesus' body, just as Luke xxiv 41–43 has Jesus answer the continuing doubt of the disciples by eating. Thomas' doubt is an acted-out misunderstanding, even as Magdalene's failure to recognize Jesus was an acted-out misunderstanding.

There is a patently secondary character to much of the setting that the evangelist has had to create so that Thomas can dramatize apostolic doubt. Verse 25 draws on 20, and vs. 26 paraphrases 19. The three new elements are the command: "And do not persist in your disbelief, but become a believer" (27); the confession by Thomas, "My Lord and my God" (28); and the macarism or beatitude concerning "Those who have not seen and yet have believed" (29). All three reflect distinctive Johannine theological themes and have no parallel in the other Gospel accounts of post-resurrectional appearances. Perhaps the command in 27 is a concise form of a saying originally associated with the ministry of Jesus. As parallels, Dodd, *Tradition*, p. 355, points out Mark iv 40 ("Why are you afraid? Have you no faith?"), and Matt xiv 31 ("O man of little faith, why did you doubt?"). The confession in 28 serves a clear-cut theological purpose: if Thomas has become the spokesman of apostolic doubt, the evangelist does not leave him in that unenviable role but so arranges it that the last word spoken by a disciple in the Gospel is an expression of full Christian faith. The highly developed christology of this confession belongs to the latest, not to the earliest, stratum of NT thought. The saying in 29 also reflects a theological problem of the latter part of the 1st century, when apostolic eyewitnesses were dying out; it may contain a rewritten older macarism (pp. 1049–50 below). Thus there is not much likelihood that John xx 24–29 preserves elements of an early narrative of an appearance of Jesus. The one basic fact that may lie behind the whole dramatization is that Thomas was one of those who initially disbelieved when Jesus appeared to the disciples. (Presumably he was one of the disciples mentioned in xx 19, even as he is one of the disciples to whom Jesus appears in xxi

2.) The choice of Thomas as the subject to personify doubt is consistent with the characterization of him in xi 16 and xiv 5, and one hesitates to affirm that such a picture was totally the work of the writer's skill.

Finally, we should mention the theory of M.-E. Boismard that John xx 24–31 represents a redactional addition to the Fourth Gospel *by Luke*. He associates this theory closely with the contention that Luke was the redactor who added iv 48–49, 51–53 (a contention rejected in vol. 29, p. 196), for (rightly) he sees a similarity between iv 48–49 and xx 29. His other arguments touch on the large number of macarisms in Luke (John xx 29b is a macarism) and on the Lucan verbal peculiarities he detects in this section of John (see last Note on vs. 27, concerning *apistos* and *pistos*). None of these arguments is particulary convincing in our estimation; for a detailed attempt to refute Boismard, see Erdozáin, pp. 39–42.

COMMENT: DETAILED

The Appearance to the Disciples (xx 19–20)

On the one hand, John seems to envision that the body of Jesus had marvelous, non-physical powers (the ability to pass through closed doors); on the other hand, he implies its tangibility and corporality ("he showed them his hands and side"). However, it is difficult to be certain that in these first verses John is *stressing* either aspect of Jesus' body. The possibility of Jesus' passing through closed doors is by inference here (see Note on "had locked the doors" in 19); only in the wording of vs. 26 is that inference clarified. Likewise, in 20 there is an implication that Jesus can be touched; but this implication is made unambiguous in vs. 27, where even the differing size of the two wounds is crudely underscored (a finger can probe the nail wound, but the side wound is large enough for a whole hand). Thus, in the Thomas story there is a more explicit concentration on the nature of Jesus' body than there is in the narrative of the appearance to the disciples. This fact fits our thesis that the Thomas story is a secondary elaboration.

Perhaps the primary significance of the stress on the wounds of Jesus in vs. 20 is that they establish a continuity between the resurrection and the crucifixion. The risen Jesus who stands before his disciples is the Jesus who died on the cross, and now they are to receive the fruits of his having been lifted up. This interpretation would explain the joy with which the disciples greet his offer to show them his hands and side.

Those to whom Jesus appears in this scene are called "the disciples" by John. Exactly whom does he mean? This question is of more than incidental interest, for it colors the discussion of those to whom the power to forgive sins (vs. 23) has been granted. There can be little doubt that what came to the evangelist from his pre-Gospel source was the story of an appearance to *the Eleven* (the Twelve minus Judas). This is a common factor in the various Gospel accounts of the appearance (Luke xxiv 33; Matt xxviii 16; Marcan Appendix xvi 14). There may have been some others present beside the Eleven, as in Luke xxiv 33 ("the Eleven gathered together, and those who were with them," plus the disciples from Emmaus); but in the tradition of the appearance only the Eleven had importance, and the words that Jesus spoke were addressed to them. These accounts are all elaborating what Paul recalls tersely in I Cor xv 5: "He appeared to Cephas and *then to the Twelve*."

John does not mention the Eleven in the present form of the appearance narrative, although his reference to Thomas as "one of the Twelve" *may* recall the original situation. Some scholars have argued that John deliberately avoided mentioning the Twelve/Eleven because he wanted to play down their importance or was against a theory of apostolic succession. Yet John mentions the Twelve in vi 67 and 70 without any sign of disapproval, and really there is no particular reason to think that the evangelist did not take for granted the importance of the Twelve and the respect due to them. Another work of the Johannine school, Rev xxi 14, names the foundations of the wall of the heavenly Jerusalem after the Twelve. The characteristically Johannine outlook does not demote the Twelve, but rather turns these chosen disciples into representatives of all the Christians who would believe in Jesus on their word. And so, sometimes it is very difficult to know when John is speaking of the disciples in their historical role as the intimate companions of Jesus and when he is speaking of them in their symbolic role. For instance, in vi 66–67 the Twelve are distinguished from the rest of the disciples and a special attachment to Jesus is expected of them. Seemingly in the Last Supper scene the disciples who are addressed are chiefly the Twelve (NOTE on "disciples" in xiii 5); yet through most of the Last Discourse Jesus is not speaking only to those envisaged as present but also to the much wider audience whom they represent. Only in xvii 20 is there a clear attempt in the Last Discourse to separate the present and future audiences.

Thus, our real problem here concerns the intention of the evangelist. While the pre-Gospel narrative referred to the Eleven, does the evangelist now intend these disciples to represent a wider audience who would also be recipients of the mission in vs. 21, of the Spirit in 22, and of the power to forgive sins in 23? Some would argue from 21 that the disciples cannot represent all Christians, for this verse refers to an apostolic mission; and even if historically the apostolic mission was entrusted to a larger group than the Twelve, nevertheless all Christians were not apostles (see I Cor xii 28–29). Yet in 21 John has modified the apostolic mission by making it dependent on the model of the Father's having sent the Son, and usually for John the Father-Son relationship is held up for all Christians to imitate. Can we be certain that John means "As the Father has sent me, so do I send you" in a more restricted sense than he means "As the Father has loved me, so have I loved you" (xv 9)? Nevertheless, even if 21 does give some support to the idea that only the Twelve/Eleven are in direct view, vs. 22 points in the opposite direction. As we shall see, this verse recalls Gen ii 7 and is meant to symbolize Jesus' new creation of men as God's children by the gift of the Spirit. Certainly this re-creation, this new begetting, this gift of the Spirit is meant for all Christians. We have suggested (p. 1030 above) that vs. 22 represents the evangelist's addition to the original narrative of the appearance; and so one may theorize that by the addition of this verse and by the theological modification introduced into 21 (modeling the mission on the Father-Son relationship), the evangelist is widening the horizon of the original appearance scene to include not only the Twelve but also those whom they represent. Nevertheless, it would be risky to assume that this same widened horizon is in mind in vs. 23, which is a modified form of an ancient saying of Jesus. It will require further discussion below to decide that question.

Before we leave vss. 19–20 we must give some attention to the peace and joy that Jesus' appearance brings to his disciples. We pointed out in the NOTE on 19 that "Peace to you" is not to be mistaken for an ordinary greeting. As in the appearances of "the angel of the Lord" in the OT, this formula reassures the audience that they have nothing to fear from the divine manifestation that they are witnessing. Beyond this, in the context of Johannine theology, the risen Jesus' gift of peace is the fulfillment of the words spoken in the Last Discourse (xiv 27–28): " 'Peace' is my farewell to you. My 'peace' is my gift to you, and I do not give it to you as the world gives it. Do not let your hearts be troubled, and do not be fearful. You have heard me tell you, 'I am going away,' and 'I am coming back to you.' " In other words, when the disciples were fearful at the Last Supper, Jesus assured them that his parting gift of peace would not be ephemeral; and he related this peace to the promise that he was coming back to them. Now that he has come back to them, he grants this peace, for in the Holy Spirit (vs. 22) they have the enduring presence of Jesus and the gift of divine sonship that is the basis of Christian peace. (Note that the "Peace" farewell of xiv 27 is immediately preceded by a reference to the Paraclete to be sent in Jesus' name.)

The rejoicing of the disciples mentioned in vs. 20 is also to be understood as the fulfillment of a promise uttered at the Last Discourse. In xvi 21–22 Jesus compared the situation of the disciples to that of a woman in labor who suffers intense pain but is rewarded with joy at the birth of her child. "You are sad now; but I shall see you again, and your hearts will rejoice with a joy that no one can take from you." In Jewish thought peace and joy were marks of the eschatological period when God's intervention would have brought about harmony in human life and in the world. John sees this period realized as Jesus returns to pour forth his Spirit upon men. Another Johannine work, Rev xix 7 and xxi 1–4, associates the eschatological joy, peace, and sense of divine presence with the second coming—a good example of two types of eschatological outlook (vol. 29, pp. cxvi–cxxi) in the same general school of thought.

The Apostolic Mission and the Gift of the Spirit (xx 21–22)

Throughout the account of Jesus' ministry John has avoided designating the disciples as apostles (those sent) and he has not described an occasion on which they were sent out (cf. Mark vi 7 and par.; yet see vol. 29, p. 183, in reference to John iv 38). But in vs. 21 John joins the common Gospel tradition that the risen Jesus constituted apostles by entrusting a salvific mission to those to whom he appeared. The special Johannine contribution to the theology of this mission is that the Father's sending of the Son serves both as the model and the ground for the Son's sending of the disciples. Their mission is to continue the Son's mission; and this requires that the Son must be present to them during this mission, just as the Father had to be present to the Son during his mission. Jesus said, "Whoever sees me is seeing Him who sent me" (xii 45); similarly the disciples must now show forth the presence of Jesus so that whoever sees the disciples is seeing Jesus who sent them. As it is phrased in xiii 20, "Whoever welcomes anyone that I shall send welcomes me; and whoever welcomes me, welcomes Him who sent me." This becomes possible only through the gift of the Holy Spirit (vs. 22), whom the Father sends in Jesus' name (xiv 26) and whom Jesus himself sends (xv 26).

Like the themes of peace and joy in vss. 19 and 20, the theme of the sending of the disciples in 21 picks up a motif that has already been heard in the Last Discourse. In xvii 17–19 Jesus prayed for his own who were to remain behind in the world: "Consecrate them in the truth— 'Your word is truth'; for as you sent me into the world, so I sent them into the world. And it is for them that I consecrate myself, in order that they too may be consecrated in truth." When we discussed that passage in the prayer of Jesus (pp. 763–65 above), we saw that there was a relationship between the consecrating or making holy of the disciples and their being sent. Before they can be sent, they must be remade through the truth, that is, through the revealing word of Jesus and also, of course, through the Spirit of Truth who is also the *Holy* Spirit. Thus, once again there is a close relation between the mission of the disciples (21) and the giving of the Spirit (22), for it is the Spirit who consecrates them or makes them holy so that, consecrated as Jesus was consecrated, they can be sent as Jesus was sent.

Reflection on the Paraclete passages of the Last Discourse carries the relationship between mission and the Spirit even further. (In App. V we acknowledge that the Paraclete concept had an origin somewhat different from that of the more general Christian concept of the Holy Spirit and has its own special connotation. Nevertheless, the Fourth Gospel ultimately identifies the Paraclete with the Holy Spirit, and so we cannot dissociate the promise of "the Paraclete, the Holy Spirit," in xiv 26 from the words "Receive a holy Spirit" in xx 22.) Jesus said that his going away would make it possible for the Paraclete to be *sent* to the disciples (xvi 7; also xiv 26, xv 26). This sending of the Paraclete/Spirit is accomplished now in conjunction with the post-resurrectional sending of the disciples. If they are to go and bear witness, it is because the Paraclete/Spirit whom they receive will bear witness (xv 26–27). In xiv 17 we heard that the Paraclete is the Spirit of Truth whom the world cannot receive; but now Jesus says to the disciples, "Receive a holy Spirit," and sends them out to the world. Their mission, even as Jesus' mission, brings an offer of life and salvation to those who believe (vi 39–40, 57) because they have received the Spirit that begets life (iii 5–6) and in turn can give this Spirit to others who wish to become disciples of Jesus.

As we turn to a direct discussion of vs. 22 and the breathing forth of the Spirit, we recognize that for John this is the high point of the post-resurrectional activity of Jesus and that already in several ways the earlier part of this chapter has prepared us for this dramatic moment. The association of the resurrection with the ascension in 17 and the implication that through Jesus' return to the Father men would become God's children pointed to the work of the Spirit. Perhaps even the reference to Jesus' side in 20 was meant secondarily to remind the reader of the blood and water that flowed from that side and symbolized the Spirit (pp. 949–51 above).

Before Jesus says, "Receive a holy Spirit," he breathes on his disciples. The Greek verb *emphysan*, "to breathe," echoes LXX of Gen ii 7, the creation scene, where we are told: "The Lord God formed man out of the dust of the earth and breathed into his nostrils the breath of life." The verb is used again in Wis xv 11, which rephrases the creation account: "The One who fashioned him and . . . breathed into him a living spirit." Symbolically, then, John is proclaiming that, just as in the first creation God breathed a living spirit into man, so now in the moment of the new creation Jesus breathes his own Holy Spirit into the disciples, giving them eternal life. (The Gospel opened with the theme of creation in the Prologue i 1–5—see also vol. 29, p. 106—and the theme of creation returns at the end.) In the impressive vision of the valley of the bones, Ezekiel (xxxvii 3–5), addressed by God as "son of man," was told to prophesy to the dry bones: "Hear the word of the Lord . . . I will cause breath [spirit] to enter you, and you shall live." Now, another Son of Man, himself fresh from the tomb, speaks as the risen Lord and causes the breath of eternal life to enter those who hear his word. In the secondary, baptismal symbolism of John iii 5 the readers of the Gospel are told that by water and Spirit they are begotten as God's children; the present scene serves as the Baptism of Jesus' immediate disciples and a pledge of divine begetting to all believers of a future period represented by the disciples. (Small wonder that the custom of breathing upon the subject to be baptized found its way into the baptismal ceremonial.) Now they are truly Jesus' brothers and can call his Father their Father (xx 17). The gift of the Spirit is the "ultimate climax of the personal relations between Jesus and his disciples" (Dodd, *Interpretation*, p. 227).

We have commented on the giving of the Spirit in the light of Johannine thought, but many exegetes have been disturbed by the problem of reconciling John's dating of this event on Easter night with the picture in Acts ii of the outpouring of the Spirit on Pentecost fifty days later. In antiquity we see this problem reflected in the action of the Second Council of Constantinople (fifth ecumenical council, A.D. 553) which condemned the view of Theodore of Mopsuestia that Jesus did not really give the Spirit on Easter but acted only figuratively and by way of promise (DB, §434). In a survey of conservative views on the question Scholte, *op. cit.*, finds few scholars in recent centuries (chiefly Grotius and Tholuck) who follow in Theodore's steps by reducing John's scene to the pure symbolism of a future giving of the Spirit. Most think that the Spirit was truly given on Easter but in a way different from the Pentecostal giving. Some make a qualitative distinction. One form of such a distinction is already found in John Chrysostom (*In Jo. Hom.* LXXXVI 3; PG 59:471) who relates the gift of the Spirit in John xx 22 to the forgiveness of sins, and the gift of the Spirit in Acts ii to the power to work miracles and raise the dead. Often the Easter gift of the Spirit is said to be concerned only with the individual and his relation to the Father, while the Pentecostal gift is characterized as ecclesiastical or missionary. A few propose that the Easter gift had the limited immediate function of enabling the disciples to recognize and confess the risen Lord (a view based on I Cor xii 3: No one can say "Jesus is Lord" except by the Holy Spirit). See also the NOTE on "Receive a holy Spirit" in vs. 22 for the distinction between an impersonal gift of the Spirit on Easter and a personal gift on Pentecost. Another group of scholars make a quantitative distinction. The gift of the Spirit on Easter is transitional or anticipatory (Bengel speaks of an *arrha* or earnest), while the gift on Pentecost is complete and definitive. Swete, p. 167, calls one potential and the other actual.

Many critical scholars approach the problem differently. They point out that there is nothing in John's Gospel that would cause us to characterize the gift of the Spirit in xx 22 as provisional or partial; rather it is the total fulfillment of earlier Gospel passages that promised the giving of the Spirit or the coming of the Paraclete. Nor is the gift in xx 22 purely personal or individual; it is closely related to the sending of the disciples into the world in vs. 21. It is bad methodology to harmonize John and Acts by assuming that one treats of an earlier giving of the Spirit and the other of a later giving. There is no evidence that the author of either work was aware of or making allowance for the other's approach to the question. And so we may hold that functionally each is describing the same event; the one gift of the Spirit to his followers by the risen and ascended Lord. The descriptions are different, reflecting the diverse theological interests of the respective authors; but do we not have the same phenomenon of variance among the Gospel descriptions of the same event in Jesus' ministry? In particular, there is no insurmountable obstacle in the fact that John and Acts assign a different date to the gift of the Spirit. As we have acknowledged, John's dating of Jesus' first appearance to his disciples is artificial, for Galilee has a better claim than Jerusalem to be the original site of this appearance, and that would obviously rule out Easter Sunday as the date of the appearance (p. 972 above). But there is also much that is symbolic in Acts' choice of Pentecost, for Luke is using the background of the Sinai covenant motif associated with that feast in his description of the coming of the Spirit (see vol. 29, p. 206). Yet we do not discount the possibility that Luke preserves an authentic Christian memory of the first charismatic manifestation of the Spirit in the community on Pentecost. What is interesting is that both authors place the giving of the Spirit after Jesus has ascended to his Father, even if they have different views of the ascension. For both of them the Spirit's task is to take the place of Jesus, to carry on his work, and to constitute his presence in the world. Thus, with a certain justification we may join the Archimandrite Cassien, *art. cit.*, in speaking of John xx 22 as "the Johannine Pentecost," even though we do not try to date this event to the feast of Pentecost, as he does.

The Power over Sin (xx 23)

The last saying of Jesus in the post-resurrectional appearance to his disciples is often regarded as a variant form of the saying recorded in Matt xvi 19 and xviii 18 (see Dodd, *Tradition*, pp. 347–49):

Matthew	John
"Whatever you bind (*dein*) on earth	"If you forgive (*aphienai*) men's sins,
will be bound in heaven;	their sins are forgiven;
whatever you loose (*lyein*) on earth	if you hold (*kratein*) them,
will be loosed in heaven."	they are held fast."

The comparison is more obvious when we realize that John's passive tenses ("are forgiven"; "are held fast") and Matthew's reference to heaven are two circumlocutions for describing God's action. It is generally conceded that in speaking of binding and loosing Matthew is translating a Hebrew/Aramaic formula well attested in later rabbinical writings with the verbs *'āsar* and *nātar* or *šᵉrāh*. John's expression "to forgive sins" offers no problem, but we are not certain about the precise Hebrew equivalent for the awkward expression "to hold [sins]" (*šāmar* or *nātar?*). J. A. Emerton, JTS 13 (1962), 325–31, has made an interesting suggestion. He points out that the reference to binding and loosing in Matt xvi 19 is in the context of Jesus' giving the keys to Peter and that this whole scene echoes the thought of Isa xxii 22 where the symbol of royal authority, the key of the palace, is promised to Eliakim, thus constituting him the king's prime minister: "The key of the house of David—he will open and none will shut; and he will shut and none will open." Emerton wonders if Jesus' original saying was not modeled on the Isaian imagery: "Whatever you shut will be shut; and whatever you open will be opened." In such a hypothesis the Matthean tradition would have conformed Jesus' saying to a well-known Jewish legal formula ("open" becoming "loosen"; "shut" becoming "bind"), while the Johannine tradition would have reshaped the saying to apply to sin ("open" becoming "release, forgive"; "shut" becoming "hold in"). In any case John emerged with a formula that to Greek ears was more intelligible than the Matthean formula.

The setting of the saying varies in the two Gospels. In John it is post-resurrectional. Matt xviii 18 is directed to the disciples as a group (see xviii 1) and is in a context of how authorities should handle disputes within the Christian community. The whole chapter represents a Matthean collection of material that could be adapted for application to life in well-established Christian communities, and so we do not have here the original context for the binding-loosing saying. Matt xvi 19 is part of a special Matthean addition (vss. 16b–19) to the Caesarea Philippi scene, an addition consisting of a collection of material pertaining to Peter, some of it post-resurrectional (see vol. 29, pp. 301–2; also pp. 1088–89 below). Thus Matthew's localization of the saying has no authoritative claim, and indeed it is not impossible that the saying was originally post-resurrectional as in John.

As a possible guide for the meaning of John's saying, we may ask what Matthew's saying means. The rabbinic formula of binding and loosing that Matthew reflects refers most often to the imposition or removal of an obligation by an authoritative doctrinal decision. Another, less frequent, meaning of bind/loose is to impose or remove a ban of excommunication. This second meaning of the formula affects people directly; the first meaning affects them indirectly through their actions. Scholars argue about which of the two meanings best fits the Matthean passages. F. Büchsel, "*deō (lyō)*," TWNTE, II, 60–61, opts for excommunication. K. Stendahl, *The School of St. Matthew* (Philadephia: Fortress, 1968), p. 28, argues that promulgation of an obligation best fits xvi 19 (Peter is given the authority of chief rabbi), while excommunication best fits xviii 18. The fact that the Matthean saying can have different meanings in different contexts warns us of the possibility that the variant form of the saying in John xx 22 may have still another meaning. Only indirectly can John's forgiving and holding of sins be understood as related to the power of welcoming back into the congregation or expelling from it, for example, if the person whose sin is forgiven is at that moment out of community fellowship (so Dodd, *Tradition*, p. 348). Furthermore, to forgive sins seems to be a step beyond simply declaring that there is no moral obligation affecting a certain action. In many ways the Johannine formula is more kerygmatic and perhaps preserves more of the original import of the saying than does the juridic formula used in Matthew.

The problem of the meaning, extent, and exercise of the power to forgive sins granted in xx 23 has been divisive in Christianity. For instance, in reaction to the Protestant reformers the Council of Trent condemned the proposal that this power to forgive sins was offered to each of Christ's faithful; rather this verse should be understood of the power exercised by the ordained priest in the Sacrament of Penance and not simply applied to the Church's power to preach the Gospel (DB, §§1703, 1710). Many modern Roman Catholic scholars do not think that this declaration of their Church necessarily concerns or defines the meaning that *the evangelist* attached to the verse when he wrote it; the import of the declaration is to insist against critics that the Sacrament of Penance is a legitimate (even if later) exercise and specification of the power of forgiveness conferred in this verse. Nevertheless, the Roman Catholic position reflects an interpretation whereby the power mentioned in xx 23 concerns the forgiveness of sins committed *after* Baptism and is given to a specified group, the Eleven, who pass it on through ordination to others. This interpretation has been rejected by other Christians who maintain that the power is given to a larger group symbolized by the disciples and that it is a power of preaching God's forgiveness of sins in Christ and/or of admitting sinners to Baptism.

It is probably impossible to settle this dispute on purely exegetical grounds, for some of the presuppositions on both sides reflect post-biblical concerns. We have already stressed (p. 1034 above) that while in the Johannine pre-Gospel tradition "the disciples" to whom the risen Jesus speaks were the Eleven, we cannot be certain whether the evangelist is thinking of them as a historical group or as symbols of all Christian disciples. As for the power to forgive/hold sins, there is nothing in the text itself that associates the forgiveness with either preaching the Gospel or admission to Baptism. These ideas come from a harmonization with other Gospel accounts of the appearance of the risen Jesus to the Eleven. For instance, Luke xxiv 47 has Jesus instruct the Eleven (and those who were with them) that "repentance and the forgiveness of sins should be preached [*kēryssein*, "proclaim"] in his name to all nations"; and Marcan Appendix xvi 15 has the instruction to preach the Gospel. The relation of the forgiveness to Baptism is drawn in part from an analogy with Matt xxviii 19 where Jesus tells his disciples to baptize all nations and from Marcan Appendix xvi 16 where the twofold effect of the mission to baptize is specified: "He who believes and is baptized will be saved, but he who does not believe will be condemned." But harmonization is a poor way to solve the problem of the Johannine meaning of the power to forgive just as it is a poor way to solve what John means by "the disciples." (Curiously many who harmonize to decide the first problem are not willing to harmonize to solve the second.) There is little internal support in Johannine theology for interpreting vs. 23 as a power to preach the forgiveness of sins. That emphasis is logical in Luke, for Acts shows how this preaching was done; but for that very reason such an emphasis may well be attributable to Luke himself rather than to a pre-Gospel tradition. There is better internal Johannine support for relating the forgiveness of sins to admission to Baptism, for some of the Johannine passages that have a secondary baptismal symbolism touch on the question of sin. It was the Baptist who proclaimed Jesus as "the Lamb of God who takes away the world's sin" (i 29). In ch. ix the opening of the blind man's eyes (baptismally symbolic; vol. 29, p. 381) is contrasted with having the Pharisees' sins remain (ix 41). It is important that the Church Fathers of the first three centuries understood John xx 23 in reference to the baptismal forgiveness of sins; see also the creedal formula "one Baptism for the forgiveness of sins." The failure of these early writers to relate the verse to the problem of sins committed after Baptism is all the more significant because the question of whether or not such sins could be forgiven was heavily disputed at the period (T. Worden, "The Remission of Sins," *Scripture* 9 [1957], 65–67).

Nevertheless, we doubt that there is enough evidence in John to say that the evangelist meant to refer exclusively to the power of admitting or not admitting applicants to Baptism. In the immediate context the only thing that is remotely evocative of Baptism is the idea that the giving of the Spirit to the disciples is in a way their Baptism. Rather than trying to interpret vs. 23 in the light of parallels in the other Gospel accounts and of tenuous relations to secondary baptismal symbolism, let us see what emerges if we interpret it in the light of the immediate context and of the major themes of Johannine theology.

Verse 23 should be related to vs. 21. The disciples can forgive and hold men's sins because now the risen Jesus has sent them as the Father sent him. Thus the forgiveness and holding of sins should be interpreted in the light of Jesus' own action toward sin. In ix 39–41 Jesus says that he came into the world for judgment: to enable some to see and to cause blindness for others. Deliberate blindness means remaining in sin; and, implicitly, willingness to see results in being delivered from sin. John iii 17–21 describes a separation of those whose lives are good from those whose lives are evil, and this discriminatory process is related to the purpose for which God *sent* the Son into the world. And so if the disciples are sent just as the Son was sent, they must continue the discriminatory judgment between good and evil. We have mentioned that xx 21 echoes xvii 18 which also treats of the disciples' being sent into the world, and the context of this latter passage shows that the presence of the disciples causes hate on the part of some ("the world," xvii 14) but leads others to believe (xvii 20). We see, then, that Johannine realized eschatology and dualism offer background for understanding the forgiveness and holding of sin in xx 23. The disciples both by deed and word cause men to judge themselves: some come to the light and receive forgiveness; some turn away and are hardened in their sins.

Verse 23 should be related to vs. 22. The disciples can forgive and hold men's sins because Jesus has breathed the Holy Spirit upon them. In his ministry Jesus forgave sin, but how does this power continue to work after his departure? One Christian answer is found in I John ii 1–2: Jesus Christ, our intercessor with the Father, "is an expiation for our sins, and not only for our sins but also for the whole world." However, the Gospel is more concerned with the application of forgiveness on earth, and this is accomplished in and through the Spirit that Jesus has sent. If we call upon the Johannine Paraclete passages, then the giving of the Paraclete/Spirit reinforces the idea that the disciples are the organ of discriminatory judgment in the world (see Beare, p. 98). Working through the disciples, the Paraclete, like Jesus before him, divides men into two groups: those who believe and can recognize and receive him, and the world which does not recognize or see him and which he will prove wrong (xiv 17, xvi 8). If we turn from the Paraclete passages to more general Johannine ideas about the Spirit, we may relate the forgiveness of sins to the eschatological outpouring of the Spirit that cleanses men and begets them to new life (see COMMENT on i 33 and iii 5). In xx 22 the primary symbolism of the giving of the Spirit concerns the new creation, a creation that wipes out evil, for the *Holy* Spirit consecrates men and gives them the power to make others holy in turn. In a very important article, J. Schmitt has shown how John xx 22–23 (the juxtaposition of the giving of the Spirit and the forgiveness of sins) may be related to the Qumran idea that God has poured forth his holy spirit on anyone who is admitted into the community: "He shall be cleansed from all sins by the spirit of holiness" (1QS iii 7–8). This initial eschatological cleansing from sin, confirmed and publicized by the waters of Qumran purification, does not obviate the necessity for continued forgiveness in community life. The supervisor (*mᵉbaqqēr*—etymologically the equivalent of the Christian *episkopos* or bishop) of CD xiii 9–10 is to take pity on those under his care just as a father takes pity upon his sons, and he is to bring back all that have strayed: "He shall *loosen* all the fetters that *bind* them so that no one should be oppressed or broken in his congregation." A. Dupont-Sommer, *The Essene Writings from Qumran* (Cleveland: Meridian, 1962), p. 157[4], thinks that this is a reference to the bonds of sin, and that the supervisor is being told to loosen these bonds in order that all members of the congregation, formerly oppressed by Belial and weighed down by their consciousness of sin, may know liberty and spiritual joy. É. Cothenet, in *Les Textes de Qumran*, ed. by J. Carmignac (Paris:

Letouzey, 1963), II, 201, denies that absolution is involved in the Qumran passage. Rather the supervisor, by the paternal exercise of authority and by establishing a climate of justice and fraternity, permits the members to receive pardon from God. If we interpret John xx 22–23 in light of this Qumran background, we can see how the power to forgive sins, related to the outpouring of the creative Spirit, may involve both an initial forgiveness by admission to Baptism and a continuing exercise of forgiveness within the bonds of Christian community life. Thus we join Hoskyns, Barrett, and Dodd (*Tradition*, p. 348²) in finding no convincing reason to confine the forgiveness to sins committed before Baptism. If Jesus is "the one whom God has sent" and "truly boundless is his gift of the Spirit" (iii 34), then presumably the same boundless character marks the gift of the Spirit on the part of those whom Jesus has sent. Grass, pp. 67–68, is right in insisting that here John does not envisage a purely missionary situation but rather an established ecclesiastical community. Such a community would need forgiveness not only at the time of admission but also afterwards.

Verse 23 should be related to what follows in John xx, especially to xx 29. The Thomas story supplies a transition from the eyewitness disciples to the many Christians who believe without having seen. Just as the Holy Spirit, breathed upon the disciples by Jesus, is given in turn through Baptism to all believers, so the power to forgive sins is meant to affect all believers. This role of forgiveness in the life of the Christians of a later period is attested in I John i 7–9 where the author tells his companions in the community that when they honestly acknowledge that they continue to sin, "He forgives us our sins and cleanses us from all that is wrong" (see also ii 12). Now obviously this refers to direct forgiveness of sins by God; but the possibility that Christians have a role in the forgiveness of one another's sins, at least by prayer, is seen in I John v 16–17, where there is encouragement to pray for the forgiveness of sins that are not deadly, but not for sins that are deadly. One may wonder whether some within the Johannine community were vested with power over sin (see Grass, p. 68), but it is difficult to be certain of this.

In summary, we doubt that there is sufficient evidence to confine the power of forgiving and holding of sin, granted in John xx 23, to a specific exercise of power in the Christian community, whether that be admission to Baptism or forgiveness in Penance. These are but partial manifestations of a much larger power, namely, the power to isolate, repel, and negate evil and sin, a power given to Jesus in his mission by the Father and given in turn by Jesus through the Spirit to those whom he commissions. It is an effective, not merely a declaratory, power against sin, a power that touches new and old followers of Christ, a power that challenges those who refuse to believe. John does not tell us how or by whom this power was exercised in the community for whom he wrote, but the very fact that he mentions it shows that it was exercised. (In

Matthew's community the power over sin, expressed in the binding/loosing saying, must have been exercised in formal decisions about what was sinful and/or in excommunication.) In the course of time this power has had many different manifestations, as the various Christian communities legitimately specified both the manner and agency of its exercise. Perhaps John's failure to specify may serve as a Christian guideline: exegetically, one can call upon John xx 23 for assurance that the power of forgiveness has been granted; but one cannot call upon this text as proof that the way in which a particular community exercises this power is not true to Scripture.

Thomas Passes from Disbelief to Belief (xx 24–27)

As indicated in the outline (p. 965 above), vss. 24–25 are transitional between the two episodes of Scene Two: 24 relates to the first episode, explaining Thomas' absence; 25 prepares for the second episode, explaining Thomas' refusal to believe without physically examining Jesus' body.

The other disciples have seen and have believed in the risen Lord, but Thomas does not accept their word. His obstinacy is reminiscent of his attitude in the Lazarus story (xi 14–16): after telling the disciples of Lazarus' death, Jesus says, "And I am happy for your sake that I was not there so that you may come to have faith"; yet Thomas is not in the least impressed by Jesus' manifestation of knowledge at a distance. He agrees to go up to Judea with Jesus, but he insists that they are going up to be put to death.

In demanding that he be able to examine Jesus' body with finger and hand, Thomas is asking more than was offered to the other disciples. Jesus showed them his hands and side (20), and they rejoiced at this sight of the Lord. But Thomas wants both to see and to feel. Literally he says, "If I do not see . . . and put my finger . . . , I'll never believe" (25). We can tell that the Johannine writer disapproves of Thomas' demand, for he phrases 25 in almost the same terms used for the attitude that Jesus condemned in iv 48: "Unless you people can see signs and wonders, you never believe." Wenz, *art. cit.*, has argued that there is nothing reprehensible in Thomas' request to examine Jesus' wounds with his hand for, in fact, the evangelist thought that the body of Jesus was tangible. However, while the evangelist also thought that Jesus' miracles were visible, he found reprehensible a concentration on seeing the miraculous (ii 23–25). Two different attitudes toward the appearance of Jesus are represented by the disciples and by Thomas. When they see Jesus, the disciples are led to confess him as Lord (vs. 25); but Thomas is interested in probing the miraculous as such.

And so it seems that Thomas is to be reprimanded on two counts: for refusing to accept the word of the other disciples, and for being taken up with establishing the marvelous or miraculous aspect of Jesus' appearance. Scholars such as B. Weiss, Lagrange, and Wendt think that it was on the first score that Jesus accused him of being a disbeliever. However, Jesus' words in 27 challenge Thomas only on the second count. As also in the instance of the royal official to whom iv 48 was addressed, Thomas, despite his tendencies, is capable of being led to real faith; vss. 26–28 describe this progression in belief. When Jesus appears and somewhat sarcastically offers Thomas the crass demonstration of the miraculous that he demanded, Thomas comes to belief without probing Jesus' wounds. Certainly that is the obvious implication of John's account; for the evangelist would not have considered Thomas' faith adequate if the disciple had taken up Jesus' invitation and would never have put on Thomas' lips the tremendous confession of vs. 28. In the words of 27 Thomas did not persist in his disbelief but became a believer, eligible to be included among the others who had seen and believed (29a). While the evangelist was satisfied with making it clear that Jesus' body *could be* touched, a later generation of Christian writing lost sight of the fineness of John's distinction between what was good and what was bad in seeing the miraculous. Consequently there developed a tradition that Thomas or the disciples actually touched Jesus. Ignatius, *Smyrnaeans* iii 2, says that Jesus came to those who were with Peter and invited them to handle him and see that he was not a phantom: "And they immediately touched him and believed." In the 2nd-century *Epistula Apostolorum*, 11–12, Peter is said to have touched the nail marks in the hands, Thomas to have touched the lance wound in the side, and Andrew to have looked at the footprints that Jesus left. Incidentally, we may observe that there is no support for this misinterpretation of John in the words of I John i 1 which speaks of "what we looked at and felt with our own hands." There the reference is to the reality of incarnate eternal life or what the Gospel Prologue would call the Word become flesh; the passage has nothing to do with touching the risen Jesus.

Whether or not he intended to do so, the evangelist has given us in the four episodes of ch. xx four slightly different examples of faith in the risen Jesus. The Beloved Disciple comes to faith after having seen the burial wrappings but without having seen Jesus himself. Magdalene sees Jesus but does not recognize him until he calls her by name. The disciples see him and believe. Thomas also sees him and believes, but only after having been overinsistent on the marvelous aspect of the appearance. All four are examples of those who saw and believed; the evangelist will close the Gospel in 29b by turning his attention to those who have believed without seeing.

The Confession of Thomas' Faith (xx 28)

When finally he does believe, Thomas gives voice to his faith in the ultimate confession, "My Lord and my God." The Jesus who has appeared to Thomas is a Jesus who has been lifted up in crucifixion, resurrection,

and ascension to his Father and has received from the Father the glory
that he had with Him before the world existed (xvii 5); and now Thomas has
the faith to acknowledge this. Thomas has penetrated beyond the miraculous
aspect of the appearance and has seen what the resurrection-ascension
reveals about Jesus. Jesus' response in 29a accepts as valid Thomas' understanding of what has happened: "You have believed."

The combination of the titles "Lord" and "God" appears in pagan
religious literature and is represented in the *"Dominus et Deus noster"*
affected by the Emperor Domitian (A.D. 81–96; see Suetonius, *Domitian,*
13), who was probably the reigning emperor when the Gospel was being
written and against whose pretensions the Book of Revelation was directed.
Nevertheless, there is scholarly agreement that John's source for the titles
is biblical, combining the terms used by LXX to translate YHWH (=
kyrios) and Elohim (=*theos*). Actually in LXX the usual translation of
the combination *YHWH Elohāy* is "Lord, my God" (*Kyrie, ho theos mou*
—Bultmann, p. 538[8]); the closest we come to the Johannine formula is
Ps xxxv 23: "My God and my Lord."

This, then, is the supreme christological pronouncement of the Fourth
Gospel. In ch. i the first disciples gave many titles to Jesus (vol. 29, pp.
77–78), and we have heard still others throughout the ministry: Rabbi,
Messiah, Prophet, King of Israel, Son of God. In the post-resurrectional
appearances Jesus has been hailed as the Lord by Magdalene and by
the disciples as a group. But it is Thomas who makes clear that one may
address Jesus in the same language in which Israel addressed Yahweh. Now
is fulfilled the will of the Father ". . . that all men may honor the Son
just as they honor the Father" (John v 23). What Jesus predicted has come
to pass: "When you lift up the Son of Man, then you will realize that I
AM" (viii 28). We note, however, that it is in *a confession of faith* that
Jesus is honored as God. We have insisted (vol. 29, p. 24) that the NT
use of "God" for Jesus is not yet truly a dogmatic formulation, but
appears in a liturgical or cultic context. It is a response of praise to the
God who has revealed Himself in Jesus. Thus, Thomas' "My Lord and
my God" is closely parallel to "The Word was God" in the opening line
of the hymn that has been prefixed to the Fourth Gospel. If Barrett
is right in thinking that the appearance of Jesus in xx 19 ff. is evocative
of an early Christian liturgy (see NOTE on "that first day of the week"
in 19), Thomas speaks the doxology on behalf of the Christian community.
We find a reflection of such a community acclamation in the scene depicted
by the author of Rev iv 11, when the elders fall before the throne of
God singing, "Worthy are you, *our Lord and God,* to receive glory
and honor and power." In Revelation the acclamation is for the Father;
in John it is for the Son; but then the Father and the Son are one (John
x 30). It is no wonder that Thomas' confession constitutes the last
words spoken by a disciple in the Fourth Gospel (as it was originally

conceived, before the addition of ch. xxi)—nothing more profound could be said about Jesus.

Having treated Thomas in vs. 28 as a spokesman for the faith of the Christian community responding to the kerygma proclaimed in the Gospel, we are now in a position to understand the covenantal aspect of his confession. As we pointed out (p. 1016 above), xx 17 promised that after Jesus' ascension God would become *a Father to the disciples* who would be begotten by the Spirit, and also would in a special way become *the God of a people* bound to him by a new covenant. The words that Thomas speaks to Jesus are the voice of this people ratifying the covenant that the Father has made in Jesus. As Hos ii 25(23) promised, a people that was formerly not a people has now said, "You are my God." This confession has been combined with the baptismal profession "Jesus is Lord," a profession that can be made only when the Spirit has been poured out (I Cor xii 3).

The Beatitude of Those Who Have Not Seen But Have Believed (xx 29)

The theme of a new covenant can lead us into the discussion of Jesus' last words in the Gospel. The basic OT covenant at Sinai was with the people that Moses had led out of Egypt. How did that covenant encompass the succeeding generations of Israel who had not witnessed the Sinai event? According to the Midrash Tanhuma (a late homiletic work, cited in StB, II, 586) Rabbi Simeon ben Lakish (ca. A.D. 250) made the following observation: "The proselyte is dearer to God than all the Israelites who were at Sinai. For if those people had not witnessed thunder, flames, lightning, the quaking mountain, and the trumpet blasts, they would not have accepted the rule of God. Yet the proselyte who has seen none of these things comes and gives himself to God and accepts the rule of God. Is there anyone who is dearer than this man?" So also now the Johannine Jesus praises the majority of the people of the new covenant who, though they have not seen him, through the Spirit proclaim him as Lord and God. He assures these followers of all times and places that he foresees their situation and counts them as sharing in the joy heralded by his resurrection.

The statement in 29 comes fittingly at the end of the Gospel. Only when he has recounted what has been seen by the disciples (especially by the Beloved Disciple) does the writer turn to an era when Jesus can no longer be seen but can be heard. Up to this point in the Gospel narrative only one type of true belief has been possible, a belief that has arisen in the visible presence of Jesus; but with the inauguration of the invisible presence of Jesus in the Spirit, a new type of faith emerges. What is important, as both lines of vs. 29 attest, is that one must believe, whether that faith comes from seeing or not. Throughout the Gospel and more particularly in the Last Discourse, in what the evangelist has been describing on the stage of early 1st-century Palestine, he has had in mind an audience seated in the darkened theater of the future, silently viewing what Jesus was saying and doing. True to the limitations and logic of the stage drama imposed by the Gospel form, the Johannine Jesus could address that audience only indirectly through the disciples who shared the stage and gave voice to sentiments and reactions that were shared by the audience as well. But now, as the curtain is about to fall on the stage drama, the lights in the theater are suddenly turned on. Jesus shifts his attention from the disciples on the stage to the audience that has become visible and makes clear that his ultimate concern is for them—those who have come to believe in him through the word of his disciples (xvii 20). A few verses before (xx 21) we have heard of the mission of the disciples; now those who are the fruit of that mission are brought into view.

The two lines of vs. 29, then, are a contrast between two situations: the situation of seeing Jesus and that of not seeing Jesus. (Note that, despite the supposition of some commentators, no contrast is drawn in this verse between seeing and touching, or between seeing with touching and seeing without touching.) In this contrast Thomas is no longer the doubter of vs. 25 but the believer of 28; like his fellow disciples he is one who has seen and has believed and, therefore, is one of those blessed with the joy of the resurrection. Although 29a has no formal beatitude and does not call "happy" those who see and believe, their joy is presumed from 20. They are those whom Jesus has come back after death to *see* again, bringing a joy that no one can take from them (xvi 22). And so we interpret the contrast in 29 as existing between two types of blessedness, not between blessedness (29b) and an inferior state (29a). Whatever there is of the adversative in 29b is by way of contradicting the idea that the eyewitnesses alone or in a markedly higher way possessed the joy and blessings of the risen Jesus. The evangelist wants to emphasize that, despite what one might imagine, those who do not see are equal in God's estimation with those who did see and are even, in a certain way, nobler. (Luke seems to have a similar emphasis in the Emmaus scene: the two disciples see Jesus but recognize him only in the breaking of the bread—Luke's community has a similar opportunity to recognize the risen Jesus' presence in the breaking of the bread [xxiv 30–31, 35].) If one asks what life situation in his community caused the fourth evangelist to stress this, we may well imagine that it was a milder form of the same difficulty reflected in ch. xxi, namely, the death of the eyewitnesses and the passing of the apostolic generation. (For the Johannine esteem for eyewitnesses, see I John i 1–3.) As regrettable as this moment is, the evangelist may be saying to his readers, it is not a moment when the surety of the continued presence of the risen Jesus is lost, for God has blessed those who have not seen just as much as He blessed those who did see. Dodd, *Tradition*, pp. 354–55, suggests that John's macarism or beatitude in 29b is a rewriting of an earlier beatitude reflected in the

Synoptic tradition: "Happy are that eyes that see what you see" (Luke x 23; Matt xiii 16). The Synoptic form would have been appropriate during the ministry as Jesus proclaimed the eschatological presence of the kingdom; John's form would represent an adaptation of the proclamation of eschatological blessing to the situation of the post-resurrectional Church. We see the latter situation in I Pet i 8, a statement that closely resembles John xx 29b in thought and expression: "Without having seen him, you love him; though you do not now see him, you believe in him and rejoice with unutterable and exalted joy."

We have emphasized our understanding of 29 as a contrast between seeing and non-seeing (so also Prete, Erdozáin, Wenz) precisely as a rejection of the attempt to find in this verse a contrast between seeing and believing. Both groups in 29 truly believe; and we find no evidence for Bultmann's contention (p. 539) that the faith spoken of in 29a, despite the fact that it gave expression to the confession "My Lord and my God," is not praiseworthy because seeing is sensible perception and thus radically opposed to faith. This is another instance of Bultmann's thesis that John has presented the appearances of the risen Jesus only to show their unimportance. (Bultmann does not think the appearances really took place; they are symbolic pictures in which the Father is brought together with his own.) In this approach the appearances of Jesus are like his signs, concessions to the weakness of men; the word of Jesus should suffice, and in true faith there is no recourse to signs. In our judgment, this exegesis of John reflects Bultmann's personal theology rather than the evangelist's thought. In John there is no dichotomy between sign and word; both are revelatory and word helps to interpret sign. We pointed out in vol. 29, App. III, that the Johannine attitude toward the value of signs and their relation to faith is complex. There are two different reactions to seeing signs and both are called belief. One type of belief is inadequate, for the "believer" is superficially impressed by the marvelous. As regards the appearances of the risen Jesus, Thomas represented this attitude in 25—he would believe if he could see tangible proofs of the miracle involved. The other type of belief is adequate, for it sees a heavenly reality behind the miraculous, namely, what Jesus reveals about God and himself. Thomas was brought to this stage of faith in 28. This second type of belief does not discard the sign or the appearance of the risen Jesus, for the use of the visible is an indispensable condition of the Word's having become flesh. As long as Jesus stood among men, one had to come to faith through the visible. Now, at the end of the Gospel, another attitude becomes possible and necessary. This is the era of the Spirit or the invisible presence of Jesus (xiv 17), and the era of signs or appearances is passing away. The transition from 29a to 29b is not merely that one era precedes the other, but that one leads to the other. "But for the fact that Thomas and the other apostles saw the incarnate Christ there would have been no Christian faith at all" (Barrett, p. 477). Or as the evangelist himself phrases it in xx 30–31, he has narrated signs so that people may believe—certainly not a rejection of the value of signs for faith.

Parenthetically we may mention the strange echo of this Johannine passage in the recently published 2nd-century (?) Gnostic or semi-Gnostic work from Chenoboskion (see vol. 29, p. LIII), *The Apocryphal Letter of James:* "You have seen the Son of Man and have spoken with him and have heard him. Woe to those who have (only) seen the Son of Man. Happy [*makarios*] shall they be who have not seen the man, have not had contact with him, have not spoken with him, and have not heard anything from him" (3:13–24). "Happy shall they be who came to know me. Woe to those who heard and did not believe. Happy shall they be who did not see but [believed]" (12:38 – 13:1).

It is fitting that the last words in the original Johannine Gospel are words of Jesus—who is not said to have departed. (Here John differs from the tradition found in the other Gospel accounts of Jerusalem appearances: Luke xxiv 51; Acts i 9; and Marcan Appendix xvi 19 specifically mention Jesus' departure from his disciples.) He *remains present* in the Paraclete/ Spirit who is to be with the disciples forever (John xvi 19). His last words bear the mark of the timeless Word who was spoken before the world was created.

BIBLIOGRAPHY
(xx 1–29)

(In reference to the Spirit in xx 22 see also the Bibliography for App. V.)

Auer, E. G., *Die Urkunde der Auferstehung Jesu* (Wuppertal: Brockhaus, 1959). A study of xx 5–7.

Balagué, M., "La prueba de la Resurrección (Jn 20, 6–7)," EstBíb 25 (1966), 169–92.

Beare, F. W., "The Risen Jesus Bestows the Spirit: A Study of John 20:19–23," *Canadian Journal of Theology* 4 (1958), 95–100.

Benoit, P., "Marie-Madeleine et les Disciples au Tombeau selon Joh 20, 1–18," in *Judentum, Urchristentum, Kirche* (J. Jeremias Festschrift; Berlin: Töpelmann, 1960), pp. 141–52.

——— *The Passion and Resurrection of Jesus Christ* (New York: Herder & Herder, 1969), pp. 231–87.

Boismard, M.-E., "Saint Luc et la rédaction du Quatrième Évangile," RB 69 (1962), 200–3 on xx 24–31.

Cassien (Serge Besobrasoff), "La Pentecôte Johannique," *Études Théologiques et Religieuses* 13 (1938), 151–76, 254–77, 327–43; 14 (1939), 32–62, 98–106. Subsequently published as a book.

Catharinet, F.-M., "Note sur un verset de l'évangile de Jean (20, 17)," in *Mémorial J. Chaine* (Lyon, 1950), pp. 51–59.

Dodd, C. H., "Some Johannine 'Herrnworte' with Parallels in the Synoptic

Gospels," NTS 2 (1955–56), 85–86. A discussion of xx 23, reprinted in *Tradition*, pp. 347–49.

—— "The Appearances of the Risen Christ: An Essay in Form-Criticism of the Gospels," in *Studies in the Gospel* (R. H. Lightfoot Volume; Oxford: Blackwell, 1957), pp. 9–35.

Erdozáin, L., *La función del signo en la fe según el cuarto evangelio* (Analecta biblica 30; Rome: Pontifical Biblical Institute, 1968), especially 36–48 on xx 24–29.

Feuillet, A., "La recherche du Christ dans la Nouvelle Alliance d'après la Christophanie de Jo 20, 11–18," in *L'homme devant Dieu* (Mélanges H. de Lubac; Paris: Aubier, 1963), I, 93–112.

Grass, H., *Ostergeschehen und Osterberichte* (3rd ed.; Göttingen: Vandenhoeck, 1964), especially pp. 51–73.

Grundmann, W., "Zur Rede Jesu vom Vater im Johannesevangelium," ZNW 52 (1961), 213–30. A study of xx 17.

Hartmann, G., "Die Vorlage der Osterberichte in Joh 20," ZNW 55 (1964), 197–220.

Kastner, K., "Noli me tangere," BZ 13 (1915), 344–53. Notable as a curiosity.

Lavergne, C., "Le sudarium et la position des linges après la résurrection," part of an article in *Sindon* 3, nos. 5/6 (1961), 1–58.

Leaney, A. R. C., "The Resurrection Narratives in Luke (xxiv. 12–53)," NTS 2 (1955–56), 110–14. A comparison with John xx.

Lindars, B., "The Composition of John xx," NTS 7 (1960–61), 142–47.

Michel, O., "Ein johanneischer Osterbericht," in *Studien zum Neuen Testament und zur Patristik* (E. Klostermann Festschrift; Texte und Untersuchungen 77; Berlin: Akademie Verlag, 1961), pp. 35–42.

Miguens, M., "Nota esegética a Juan 20, 17," *Studii Biblici Franciscani Liber Annuus* 7 (1956–57), 221–31.

Nauck, W., "Die Bedeutung des leeren Grabes für den Glauben an den Auferstandenen," ZNW 47 (1956), 243–67.

Neirynck, F., "Les femmes au Tombeau: Étude de la rédaction Matthéenne," NTS 15 (1968–69), 168–90, especially 184–90 on xx 11–18.

Prete, B., " 'Beati coloro che non vedono e credono' (Giov. 20, 29)," BibOr 9 (1967), 97–114.

Schmitt, J., "Simples remarques sur le fragment Jo., xx, 22–23," in *Mélanges en l'honneur de Monseigneur Michel Andrieu* (Strasbourg University, 1956), pp. 415–23.

Scholte, F. E., "An Investigation and an Interpretation of John 20:22," (Dallas Theological Seminary Dissertation, 1953).

Schwank, B., "Das leere Grab (20, 1–18)," SeinSend 29 (1964), 388–400.

—— " 'Selig, die nicht sehen und doch glauben' (20, 19–31)," SeinSend 29 (1964), 435–50.

—— "Die Ostererscheinungen des Johannesevangeliums und die Post-mortem-Erscheinungen der Parapsychologie," *Erbe und Auftrag* 44 (1968), 36–53.

von Campenhausen, H., "The Events of Easter and the Empty Tomb," in *Tradition and Life in the Church* (Philadelphia: Fortress, 1968), pp. 42–89.

Wenz, H., "Sehen und Glauben bei Johannes," TZ 17 (1961), 17–25. A study of xx 29.

Willam, F. M., "Johannes am Grabe des Auferstandenen (Jo 20, 2–10)," ZKT 71 (1949), 204–13.

THE BOOK OF GLORY

Conclusion: A Statement of the Author's Purpose

(xx 30–31)

70. A STATEMENT OF THE AUTHOR'S PURPOSE
(xx 30–31)

XX 30 Of course, Jesus also performed many other signs in the presence of his disciples, signs not recorded in this book. 31 But these have been recorded so that you may have faith that Jesus is the Messiah, the Son of God, and that through this faith you may have life in his name.

NOTES

xx 30. *Of course. Men oun* is found elsewhere in John only in xix 24. It occurs twenty-six times in Acts and is cited by Boismard as an example of Lucan style, as part of his contention that the last part of John xx was written by Luke (p. 1033 above). It is difficult to translate these particles well; Westcott, p. 297, paraphrases: *"So then,* as naturally might be expected by any reader who has followed the course of my narrative. . . ."

many other signs. The use of *kai* after *polla* to introduce a second adjective is more characteristic of Lucan than of Johannine style (Luke iii 18; Acts xxv 7).

in the presence of. Enōpion occurs only here in the Gospel; *emprosthen* is found in the parallel passage in xii 37. *Enōpion* is common in Luke/Acts but is very frequent too in Revelation (also I John iii 22); it may represent Septuagintal influence on the NT.

his disciples. The textual witnesses are about evenly divided on whether or not to read "his."

signs not recorded. Literally "written." To what other "signs" does John refer? Hoskyns, p. 549, suggests that he means other post-resurrectional appearances. Bultmann thinks that this statement was once a part of the Sign Source he posits for the Gospel (vol. 29, p. XXIX) and that the original import was that the evangelist had made a selection from the source. He agrees with Faure that the original context of the verse was after xii 37: "Even though Jesus had performed so many of his signs before them, they refused to believe in him." (Perhaps then there would be a distinction between signs performed before Jesus' enemies, some of which John recorded, and signs before the disciples, most of which he did not record.) More general is Dodd's suggestion, *Tradition,* p. 216[1], that John is referring to a broader primitive tradition about the ministry of Jesus from which he has drawn; on p. 429 Dodd reconstructs the lines of this tradition. One might theorize, in particular, that if the evangelist chose from a larger body of "sign" (and other?) material current in Johannine circles, perhaps some of what he did not include in the original Gospel was what the redactor later added (vol. 29, p. XXXVI, Stage 5). Finally, Loisy and Barrett are among those who think that in whole or in part the reference may be to Synoptic material.

31. *these*. The neuter plural *tauta* can refer to "signs" or more generally to all "the things" in the Gospel. Schwank thinks that the latter is meant, but the contrast between signs not written down and signs that have been written down is too obvious to overlook.

that you may have faith. Both the textual witnesses and the critical editions of the Greek NT are divided as to whether one should read an aorist subjunctive (so Bezae, Alexandrinus, Byzantine tradition; Von Soden, Vogels, American Bible Society Greek NT) or a present subjunctive (so Vaticanus, Sinaiticus*, probably P⁶⁶; Westcott, Bover, Nestle, Merk, Tasker NEB, Aland Synopsis). Some contend that the present has been introduced by way of conformity with the present subjunctive in the second part of the sentence ("may have life"); yet the present appears as the best attested reading in a similar statement in xix 35. Moreover, Riesenfeld, ST 19 (1965), 213–20, argues that the normal usage in Johannine *hina* purpose clauses is the present tense. Since here the present would mean "keep believing," it would imply that the readers of the Gospel are already Christian believers. Riesenfeld thinks that John is not dealing primarily with a missionary situation but is demanding perseverance; and he cites as a parallel I John v 13: "I have written this to you to make you realize that you possess eternal life—you who believe in the name of God." The aorist could be translated "may come to faith," implying that the readers are not yet Christians; however, the aorist is also used in the sense of having one's faith corroborated (John xiii 15).

Jesus is the Messiah, the Son of God. There is a similar juxtaposition in xi 27; Matt xvi 16, xxvi 63. The textual variants include: "Jesus [Christ] is the Son of God." There is probably no special emphasis on "Jesus," as if the writer were indicating that these titles should not be given to John the Baptist (vol. 29, p. LXVIII).

that through this faith you may have life in his name. Literally "believing." A large number of witnesses read "eternal life," but this may be under the influence of I John v 13. This sequence of "believing" and "life in [*en*] his name" does not occur elsewhere in John; and Bernard, II, 686, would change this to harmonize with the theme in i 12 and elsewhere that belief in (*eis*, not *en*, as here) the name of Jesus gives one life. Yet a similar variation of the idea modified by the "in" phrase occurs in iii 15–16: ". . . that everyone who believes may have eternal life *in* [*en*] *him*," and ". . . that everyone who believes *in* [*eis*] *him* . . . may have eternal life." "In his name" can modify the sphere of salvation as well as the sphere of belief, as we see from xvii 11–12, "Keep them safe with your name"; also Acts x 43, ". . . forgiveness of sins through his name"; and I Cor vi 11, ". . . washed . . . sanctified . . . justified in the name of the Lord Jesus Christ." In promising life in the name of Jesus, John is echoing the idea of xvi 23: "If you ask anything of the Father, He will give it to you in my name."

COMMENT

The air of finality in these two verses justifies their being called a conclusion despite the fact that in the present form of the Gospel a whole chapter follows. This has been recognized even by some who do not regard ch. xxi as an appendix; for instance, Lagrange, p. 520, and L. Vaganay, RB 45 (1936), 512–28, argue that, since xx 30–31 constitute a conclusion, these verses once stood at the end of ch. xxi (after xxi 23 according to Lagrange; after xxi 24 according to Vaganay) and were moved here when the extant conclusion of xxi was added. There is no textual evidence to support this thesis. Vaganay, p. 515, would construct an argument from the fact that, although Tertullian knew of ch. xxi, he speaks of xx 30–31 as the close (clausula) of the Gospel; but this need mean no more than that Tertullian anticipated the modern belief that ch. xxi was added after the Gospel had apparently concluded. Hoskyns, p. 550, is one of the few modern critical writers who refuses to interpret xx 30–31 as a conclusion. He draws support from the fact that a similar verse in I John (v 13) is not the end of the letter; but one can account more easily for a few post-conclusion remarks by a letter writer than for a whole chapter that follows a Gospel writer's explanation of why he has not included more. For the literary and historical difficulties that are persuasive of the secondary character of ch. xxi, see pp. 1077–80 below.

If we accept xx 30–31 as the conclusion of the original form of the Gospel, we note that among the Gospels only John gives a conclusion which evaluates what has been written and its purpose. That the supplying of such a conclusion was not haphazard is indicated by the presence of a similar conclusion in xxi 24–25 and in I John v 13. There are good parallels in secular literature (Bultmann, p. 540[3]) and in the late, deuterocanonical biblical books. After describing the creative and preservative work of God in the universe, Sir xliii 28(27) has a conclusion to a section of the book: "More than this we need not add; let the last word be: He is all in all." As in John, this conclusion reports that all has not been said and implicitly gives the purpose for what has been said. The wording of I Macc ix 22 is somewhat closer to John's wording: "Now the rest of the deeds of Judas have not been recorded . . . for they were many." In analyzing special reasons why John added vs. 30 as a conclusion, some have thought that the evangelist wanted to make it clear that he was not giving a historically complete or biographical account; others have thought that he was trying to protect himself from criticism by those who knew the Synoptic tradition. But Bultmann is surely right in insisting that the primary purpose was to draw attention to the inexhaustible riches of what Jesus had done (see also xxi 25). In any case, we are not true to the evangelist's intention if we concentrate on his statement that he has not recorded all;

the main emphasis in the conclusion is on the purpose of what he has recorded. Verse 30 is subordinate in importance to vs. 31.

What does John mean when he speaks of the signs that he has recorded? This is an important question because it affects one's outlook on the Johannine understanding of "sign." Lagrange and Bultmann are among those who think that John means the whole content of the Gospel, sign and word. (Part of Bultmann's motive in extending the meaning beyond signs is that he does not want to interpret John to mean that miraculous signs can lead people to faith—miracles are crutches for the infirm, and one should believe on the word of Jesus.) While we do not think that John means deliberately to exclude word or discourse and while we agree that the whole Gospel would have the same purpose as that enunciated for the signs, we think that John mentions "signs" alone because of the context in which this conclusion appears and that one should not try to change the statement by including discourses. This conclusion at the end of The Book of Glory is meant to match the conclusion at the end of The Book of Signs (xii 37—or perhaps the matching process was in the other direction if chs. xi–xii were a later addition to the Gospel). There the writer was concerned with the fact that Jesus had performed so many signs before "the Jews," and yet they refused to believe in him. Here he is concerned with the signs performed before his disciples which lead to faith in Jesus as the Messiah, the Son of God. K. H. Rengstorf, TWNT, VII, 253–54, has tried to argue that in xx 30–31 the evangelist is referring to the signs performed in chs. i–xii and not to the post-resurrectional appearances that constituted ch. xx. But why then would the evangelist put this conclusion here and speak of signs performed "in the presence of his disciples"? The conclusion in xii 37 is far more appropriate than xx 30–31 to serve as a description of both the audience and the result of the signs narrated in the first half of the Gospel.

In xx 30–31 John probably does not mean to exclude the signs described in chs. i–xii (especially a sign such as the first Cana miracle which was performed before his disciples that they might believe in him [ii 11]), but he must mean also to include the appearances to the disciples in xx 1–28 that led them to confess Jesus as Lord. The similarity between xx 25 and iv 48 (p. 1045 above) indicates that John thinks of the appearances as signs. This is not because he considers them as merely symbolic and unreal (rather he goes out of his way to present them as real), but because they are miraculous and are capable of revealing the heavenly truth about Jesus. In our judgment the fact that they are miraculous is important; for, despite the many scholars who argue to the contrary, there is really no evidence that John calls anything that is not miraculous, or at least extraordinary, a sign (vol. 29, p. 528). As miracles, the appearances present the would-be believer with a choice, as dramatized in the story of Thomas, namely, the choice of settling for the marvelous or of penetrating beyond it to see what it reveals. The disciples who saw the risen Jesus, including the Thomas of xx 28, chose the second course: they penetrated beyond the startling appearance to believe that Jesus is Lord and God. John has recorded these appearances so that the reader who believes without seeing the risen Jesus may also come to this high point of faith. After all, the disciples mentioned in vs. 30 were commissioned in vs. 21 to bring the challenge to believe to those who were not eyewitnesses. Thus, in moving in vss. 30–31 from the signs worked before the disciples to the faith of the reader, John is carrying on the chain of thought we found in 29a and 29b. The signs Jesus performed during his ministry revealed in an anticipatory manner his glory and his power to give eternal life. The signs of the post-resurrectional period reveal that the work of the hour has been completed, that Jesus is glorified and now gives eternal life. Both those who saw these signs and those who read of them must believe in order to receive this life.

A word of clarification is called for. If we think that the evangelist thought of the post-resurrectional appearances as signs, there is no evidence that he thought of the resurrection itself as a sign, or that the main events of The Book of Glory, the passion and death of Jesus, were on the level of signs. We question the affirmation of Lightfoot, p. 336, "The crucifixion was to St. John doubtless the greatest sign of all," and that of Barrett, p. 65, "The death and resurrection are the supreme *sēmeion*." Barrett is on much solider ground when he maintains that the death and resurrection are not called signs because they are not merely a token of something other than themselves but are the thing they signify. We maintain that in "the hour" of his return to his Father Jesus is no longer pointing symbolically to his glory but is actually being glorified. He has passed from the realm of sign to that of truth in his passion, death, resurrection, and ascension. At most we would allow the possibility that incidents in the description of this return of Jesus to the Father were signs; for example, possibly the surprising flow of blood and water from the side of the dead Jesus was meant by John as a sign: it is something extraordinary, witnessed by a disciple, which was symbolic of the giving of the Spirit.

In the NOTE on "that you may have faith" in 31, we mentioned the problem about the audience of readers envisioned by the writer: those who already believe or those who do not yet believe. A somewhat similar problem is reflected in the discussion of the two titles given to Jesus: "the Messiah, the Son of God." Those who think of the Gospel as primarily a missionary writing addressed to Jewish non-believers often argue that here "Son of God" is entirely synonymous with "Messiah," and that John is simply trying to show the Jews that Jesus is their promised Messiah. On the other hand, those who hold that the Gospel is also or even primarily addressed to Gentiles or to already believing Christians tend to give a more profound meaning to "Son of God," treating it either as a separate title from "Messiah," or as a special interpretation of "Messiah." In their mind John is stressing not only that Jesus is the (Davidic) Messiah of Jewish expectation but also the unique Son of God and thus a divine Messiah. (Some of the difficulty in this question may arise precisely from equating Messiah with Davidic Messiah, as has been traditional; recently Meeks, *The Prophet-King*, has shown persuasively that John reflects some aspects of the expectation of a rather mystical Moses-Messiah that lends itself more easily to "divine" categories.)

The best way to solve this dispute is by considering the over-all Gospel picture of Jesus, and certainly the evangelist has not been satisfied with presenting Jesus as the Messiah in any minimalist sense. If in xi 27 Martha confessed Jesus as "the Messiah, the Son of God" in what might approach a customary Jewish understanding of Messiahship, the whole purpose of the subsequent Lazarus miracle was to show that such an understanding was not adequate, for Jesus had divine power to give eternal life (vol. 29, pp. 434–35). Throughout the Gospel John demands not only belief that Jesus is the Messiah predicted by the prophets (that is, as the prophets were understood in NT times), but also belief that Jesus came forth from the Father as His special representative in the world (xi 42, xvi 27, 30, xvii 8), that Jesus and the Father share a special presence to one another (xiv 11), and that Jesus bears the divine name "I AM" (viii 24, xiii 19). Having had Thomas confess Jesus as Lord and God by way of a climactic Christian response to the presence of the risen Jesus through the Spirit, the evangelist can scarcely have stated in xx 31 that he wrote his Gospel to bring about faith in Jesus simply as the Messiah. (Parenthetically we note that a proper understanding of the uniqueness of "Son of God" in 31 nullifies the argument that the title "God" given to Jesus in 28 has no literal significance because John wrote only to prove that Jesus was the Messiah. Probably because the title "God" for Jesus was relatively recent, John preferred in his statement of purpose to use the more traditional "Son of God"; but his approval of the "Lord and God" profession shows how he understood "Son of God.")

In conclusion then, we admit that there may well be an apologetic motif in xx 31, as John seeks through the signs to prove that Jesus is the expected Jewish Messiah—note that we say apologetic rather than purely missionary, for we have insisted in vol. 29, pp. LXX–LXXV, that John's main interest as regards the Jews was to prove them wrong and that he had no real hope of converting them. Nevertheless, the major thrust of the statement in xx 31 reflects the evangelist's desire to deepen the faith of those who were already Christians so that they would appreciate Jesus' unique relation to the Father. As W. H. G. Thomas, "The Purpose of the Fourth Gospel," BS 125 (1968), 256–57, has pointed out, we must evaluate the evangelist's statement of purpose in light of the fact that he relates the content of the gospel to signs performed in the presence of *disciples*.

Loisy's paraphrase of John's mind (p. 513) is quite accurate: "The earthly existence of . . . Christ has served as a sign or as a series of signs, for which the Gospel discourses have supplied a commentary—the Johannine Christ revealing himself as light and life in his teaching and in his action. Once one has seen in Jesus the unique revealer of God, the only one who has an absolute right to the title 'Son of God,' and once one has recognized the Father in Jesus, then one understands just what the name and quality of Son are and, in this understanding that constitutes faith, one possesses eternal life."

It is interesting that John's statement of purpose in 31 ends on a salvific note. Although the evangelist demands what amounts to a dogmatic stance from his readers who must profess Jesus as the Messiah, the Son of God, he does not do this simply as a test of intellectual orthodoxy. He does this "that through this faith you may have life in his name." Unless Jesus is the true Son of God, Jesus has no divine life to give. Unless he bears God's name, he cannot fulfill toward men the divine function of giving life (vol. 29, p. 217). Nor does the Johannine insistence on a right understanding of and belief in Jesus degenerate into a Gnosticism, for always there is the supposition that only the man who acts in truth will come to the light (iii 21).

IV. THE EPILOGUE

An added account of a post-resurrectional appearance of Jesus in Galilee, which is used to show how Jesus provided for the needs of the Church.

OUTLINE
(ch. XXI)

A.   xxi 1–14:   THE RISEN JESUS APPEARS TO THE DISCIPLES AT THE SEA OF TIBERIAS. (§71)

         (1–8)   The fishing scene.

         (9–13)   The meal on land.

         (14)   A parenthetical observation: this was the third time that Jesus revealed himself to the disciples.

B.   xxi 15–23:   THE RISEN JESUS SPEAKS TO PETER. (§72)

         (15–17)   Jesus rehabilitates Peter in love and commissions him to shepherd the sheep.

         (18–23)   Jesus speaks of the fates of Peter and the Beloved Disciple.

               18–19: Peter will follow Jesus to a martyr's death.

               20–22: The Beloved Disciple will perhaps remain until Jesus comes.

               23: A comment by the writer on Jesus' real meaning.

C.   xxi 24–25:   THE (SECOND) CONCLUSION. (§73)

         (24)   The true witness of the Beloved Disciple.

         (25)   The many other deeds of Jesus.

71. THE RISEN JESUS APPEARS TO THE DISCIPLES
AT THE SEA OF TIBERIAS
(xxi 1–14)

XXI 1 Later on Jesus [again] revealed himself to the disciples at the Sea of Tiberias, and this is how it took place. 2 Gathered together were Simon Peter, Thomas (this name means "Twin"), Nathanael (the one from Cana in Galilee), the sons of Zebedee, and two other disciples. 3 Simon Peter said to the others, "I am going fishing." "We will come along with you," they replied; and so they all went off and got into the boat. However, that night they caught nothing. 4 Now, just after daybreak, Jesus stood on the shore, but none of the disciples knew that it was Jesus. 5 "Lads," he called to them, "you haven't caught anything to eat, have you?" "No," they answered. 6 "Cast your net to the right of the boat," he directed, "and you'll find something." So they cast the net, and the number of fish was so great that they were not able to haul it in. 7 Then that disciple whom Jesus loved exclaimed to Peter, "It is the Lord!" Once he heard it was the Lord, Simon Peter tucked in his outer garment (for he was otherwise naked) and jumped into the sea. 8 Meanwhile the other disciples came in by boat, towing the net full of fish. Actually they were not far from land—only about a hundred yards.

9 When they landed, they saw there a charcoal fire, with a fish laid on it, and bread. 10 "Bring some of the fish you caught just now," Jesus told them. 11 [So] Simon Peter went aboard and hauled ashore the net loaded with large fish—one hundred and fifty-three of them! Yet, in spite of the great number, the net was not torn.

12 "Come and eat your breakfast," Jesus told them. Not one of the disciples dared to inquire, "Who are you?", for they knew it was the Lord. 13 Jesus came over, took the bread and gave it to them, and did the same with the fish.

(14 Now this was the third time that Jesus revealed himself to the disciples after his resurrection from the dead.)

3: *said;* 5: *called;* 7: *exclaimed;* 9: *saw;* 10: *told;* 12: *told;* 13: *came over, took, gave.* In the historical present tense.

NOTES*

xxi 1. *Later on.* The vague *meta tauta* (see NOTE on ii 12) is a stereotyped connective conveniently used to attach extraneous matter. After the conclusion in xx 30–31 its temporal value is very weak; contrast xx 26 with its more precise "a week later," relating two post-resurrectional appearances.

[again]. This frequently used Johannine word (forty-three times) is attested in all the best Greek witnesses, but in three different positions in the sentence. It is missing in OS^sin, the Sahidic, and some minor Greek witnesses.

revealed himself. The verb *phanēroun*, which is used nine times in the Gospel, occurs twice in this verse and once in vs. 14. It has the general connotation of emergence from obscurity, and for John involves a concrete revelation of the heavenly upon earth. The only other example of this verb used to describe a post-resurrectional appearance is in the Marcan Appendix (xvi 12, 14).

to the disciples. The term "disciples" also described those who witnessed the post-resurrectional appearance in xx 19; and there we suggested that, at least in the primitive form of the story, it meant the Eleven. The writer of ch. xxi implies that the same group mentioned in xx is involved here, but we do not know that he thought of the disciples of ch. xx as the Eleven. Seven (or five) disciples will be listed in vs. 2; and one of them, Nathanael, was probably not a member of the Eleven (NOTES on i 45 and vi 60).

at the Sea of Tiberias. The preposition is *epi* which in the Johannine writings governs both the accusative and the genitive without apparent difference of meaning (BDF, §233¹); see NOTE on vi 19 for this phrase used in the sense of "upon the sea." In vi 1 the body of water was designated "the Sea of Galilee . . . of Tiberias" (see NOTE there); the name "Tiberias" would have been more acceptable to a Greek-speaking audience than "Gennesaret," and perhaps its use is a mark of the redactor. We are not told when the disciples returned to Galilee from Jerusalem. The *Gospel of Peter*, 58–60, which gives an incomplete account of an appearance by the sea, says that the disciples left Jerusalem for home on the last day of the eight-day Passover feast. Medieval pilgrim accounts associated the site of this appearance with the site of the multiplication of the loaves, the only other scene in the Fourth Gospel placed by the sea (also see p. 1099 below).

this is how. Usually in John *houtōs* refers to what precedes; here it refers to what follows.

it took place. Literally "he revealed (himself)"; Loisy, p. 515, rightly complains about the awkwardness of this introductory sentence.

2. *Simon Peter.* The double name is typically Johannine (NOTE on i 40). Five of the seven disciples will be named here; three are named in the account of the post-resurrectional appearance by the sea in the *Gospel of Peter*, 60, to wit, Simon Peter, Andrew, and Levi of Alphaeus (sic!)—only Simon Peter is common to both lists.

---

* We shall pay unusually close attention to grammatical peculiarities in discussing this chapter because of their importance in determining whether it was written by the evangelist or by a redactor. Boismard, *art. cit.*, is very helpful for this aspect.

Thomas (*this name means "Twin"*). For the name see NOTE on xi 16. Here he is one of the general group of disciples; we suggested that originally he was also one of the group in xx 19 who witnessed the appearance, before he was taken out and made the subject of a second appearance in xx 26 (pp. 1031–32 above).

Nathanael (*the one from Cana in Galilee*). Although Nathanael's call was described in i 45–50, we were not told there that he was from Cana. It is difficult to be certain whether this information represents traditional knowledge or is a deduction from Nathanael's knowledge of the local Galilean situation in i 46, combined with ii 1, 2. Dibelius has suggested that this narrative came from a cycle in which Nathanael-stories were circulated; yet Nathanael's role here is minimal.

the sons of Zebedee. The word "sons" is omitted in the Greek, while it regularly appears in the other NT references to Zebedee's offspring (MTGS, p. 207, regards the frequent use of *huios*, "son," as a product of Semitic influence). Although prominent in the Synoptic Gospels, James and John, the sons of Zebedee, are not mentioned by name elsewhere in the Fourth Gospel. Lagrange, p. 523, proposes that the original text of John mentioned only five disciples and that this phrase was a very ancient marginal gloss identifying the "two other disciples," a gloss that found its way into the body of the text. This would harmonize with the theory that John is the Beloved Disciple and that he and his relatives are always anonymous in the Gospel. In the Synoptic tradition (Mark i 16–20 and par.) the fishing foursome among the Twelve consists of Peter, Andrew, James, and John. In the account of the miraculous catch of fish in Luke v 1–11, Peter, James, and John are mentioned.

two other disciples. The partitive *ek* is typically Johannine, as is the word order (see Greek of i 35). Unnamed disciples are also a Johannine feature: the Beloved Disciple is alluded to as "the other disciple" in xx 2, 4, and 8; and there is an unnamed disciple in i 35, as well as "another disciple," known to the high priest, in xviii 15. If one does not accept Lagrange's thesis that these two disciples are "the sons of Zebedee," the next best candidates are Philip and Andrew, from the fishing village of Bethsaida, who appear together in vi 7–8 and xii 22. (This would mean that disciples who figured importantly in the Johannine account of the ministry are explicitly or implicitly mentioned in the Epilogue but in a peculiar order: Thomas and Nathanael preceding the sons of Zebedee, and Andrew and Philip following. In the Synoptic lists of the Twelve, the first four are always Peter and Andrew, James and John, although within the foursome the order of names varies.) Since in its account of the appearance by the sea, the *Gospel of Peter*, 60, mentions Andrew and Levi, these two names have also been proposed as candidates for the "two other disciples," but the *Gospel of Peter* shows no dependence on John xxi. Nonnus of Panopolis, in his rhyming paraphrase of the Fourth Gospel (ca. A.D. 450), also mentions Andrew, but not as one of the two unnamed disciples (Peter, Andrew, Nathanael, and two other men).

3. *Simon Peter said . . . , "I am going fishing."* The initiative is also his in the *Gospel of Peter*, 60: "And I, Simon Peter, and Andrew my brother, we took our fishing nets and went off to the sea. . . ." The verb "to fish" has the form of an infinitive of purpose which is rare in John (iv 7, xiv 2) and more frequent in Matthew and Luke; MTGS, pp. 134–35, reports that this construction was becoming increasingly popular in Greek from ca. 150 B.C. on. McDowell, pp.

430 ff., argues that the present tense of the verb "to go" expresses more than momentary intention: Peter is going back to his earlier way of life and will stay with it. The point of the story, then, is that Jesus caused Peter to change his mind, especially in vs. 15: "Do you love me more than these [nets, boats, etc.]?" This is dubious.

"We will come along with you." The preposition is *syn* which occurs only twice elsewhere in John (*meta* is frequent) but some seventy-five times in Luke/Acts. Loisy, p. 515, finds the dialogue banal and thinks it illustrates the writer's awkward attempt to create a framework for the story he is going to tell. Some scholars have found an inconsistency in the fact that the redactor thinks of these disciples as fishermen, something that the evangelist never mentions. However, it is rash to assume that the evangelist did not know this; he sometimes assumes a general Christian knowledge of details, as when he speaks about John without first calling him the Baptist or Baptizer. Others have found an inconsistency in having Nathanael join in the fishing, since he was a man from the hill country. While none of these are insuperable objections, in the COMMENT we shall propose that the names of Peter's companions did not originally belong to the fishing narrative.

went off. Although Westcott, Lagrange, and Bernard are among those who discover in the verb *exerchesthai* the implication that the disciples went out of the house where they were in Capernaum (Peter's?) or Bethsaida, more likely the verb is pleonastic and has no special meaning, as often in Semitic style. The *Gospel of Peter*, 60, cited above, uses *aperchesthai* in the same way.

the boat. The article, which implies that this is the boat habitually used for fishing (see NOTE on vi 17), is not necessarily a sign that the writer is dependent on the Synoptic tradition about the disciples' boat (Mark iv 1, 36); again he may be drawing on general Christian knowledge. *Ploion* is used here and in 6, but the diminutive *ploiarion* occurs in 8—we saw a similar variation in ch. vi: *ploion* was used in vss. 17, 19, 21, 22, 23(?); and *ploiarion* in 22, 23(?), 24 (see NOTE on vi 22). Although some of the older commentators took the diminutive seriously, from it we can tell nothing of the size of the boat (for the difficulty of "faded diminutives" in NT Greek, see D. C. Swanson, JBL 77 [1958], 134–51). Certainly the use of the two words is no proof that John agrees with the Lucan account of the miraculous catch of fish where two boats are specifically mentioned (Luke v 1–11; both are called *ploion*, although a textual variant has *ploiarion*).

that night they caught nothing. The Greek verb *piazein* (here and vs. 10), which appears in John six times in reference to arresting Jesus, is not often used for catching animals or fish (yet see Rev xix 20). Luke v 5 says, "Although we worked all night, we took nothing." Those knowledgeable in Palestinian customs assert that on the Lake of Galilee night fishing is usually better than day fishing; and fish caught at night could be sold fresh in the morning.

4. just after daybreak. Literally "when dawn was already breaking"; in some important witnesses of the Western textual tradition "already" is missing; Codices Sinaiticus and Bezae and the Byzantine tradition have "had already broken." *Prōia*, "dawn," never occurs in the body of the Gospel which has *prōi* two or three times.

Jesus stood on the shore. The textual witnesses are divided on whether to read *epi* ("on") or *eis* ("into, toward"). The latter probably should be favored as the more difficult reading and as having been changed by scribes who forgot that the verb "to stand" was a verb of motion in classical Greek and so could be coupled with *eis* (ZGB, §103). It is used with *eis* in xx 19 and 26 where Jesus "stood in front of" (in the midst of) the disciples. In the narrative we are to imagine that, after catching nothing, the disciples are coming back to shore and so are close enough to hear and see someone standing there. Jesus' sudden appearance on the shore is probably meant to be mysterious, for in several of the post-resurrectional narratives he materializes suddenly. There is no warrant for the imaginative contrast that Westcott, p. 300, suggests between Jesus on firm ground and the disciples on the restless water.

none . . . knew that it was Jesus. Scholars who do not think of ch. xxi as appended but rather as a continuation of ch. xx are hard pressed to explain the disciples' failure to recognize Jesus after they had seen him twice before. The distance and the dimness of the early morning light are offered as possible explanations; yet there is still hesitation in vs. 12 even though there the disciples see him close at hand and by the fire. Almost certainly we are dealing with Jesus' first appearance to his disciples in an account independent of ch. xx, and this is another instance of the transformed appearance of the risen Jesus (p. 1009 above).

5. *"Lads."* This is the plural of *paidion* (a diminutive noun from *pais,* "boy"; see NOTES on iv 49, 51). Only here in the Gospel is it employed as an address to the disciples; yet see the NOTE on xiii 33 where there is a similar use of *teknion* (a diminutive noun from *teknon,* "child"). Sometimes *teknion* is considered a more tender term than *paidion;* but the two words are seemingly interchangeable in I John ii 12 and 14, where both are kept distinct from *neaniskos,* "young man." Lagrange, p. 524, assumes that *teknion* was more habitual when Jesus addressed the disciples and that he used the unfamiliar *paidion* here so that he would not be recognized. However, to support such a distinction one would have to find exact Aramaic counterparts; moreover, *teknion* is used as an address in the Fourth Gospel but once and then in the stylized context of a farewell speech where the mention of children is customary (p. 598 above); and so one can scarcely be certain about the Johannine Jesus' custom. As for *paidion* the diminutive force may be completely faded—a double diminutive *paidarion* is used for a little boy in vi 9; yet *paidion* is used for a baby in xvi 21. The fatherly atmosphere implied in the use of *paidion* in I John ii 18 and iii 7 is not appropriate here because one who is presumably a stranger is addressing the disciples. Thus, we have settled for Bernard's contention (II, 696) that *paidion* has a colloquial touch in the present scene. As Bernard inimitably phrases it, ". . . we might say 'My boys,' or 'lads,' if calling to a knot of strangers of a lower social class."

"you haven't caught . . . have you?" "Caught" translates the Greek verb "to have"; but Bernard, II, 696, cites a scholium on Aristophanes to show that this is the way one would idiomatically ask a fisherman or hunter whether he had had success. The question is prefixed by *mē* and so by classical rules anticipates a negative answer. Yet many commentators avoid such a sharp connotation; for instance, Bultmann thinks that the question has been formulated from the viewpoint of those addressed who knew they had been unsuccessful; Barrett finds merely a hint of doubt; the note in BDF, §427[2], if we understand it correctly, sees an implicit "by chance" and follows Chrysostom in supposing an implied offer to buy if they had caught fish. While these less derogatory interpretations are plausible, especially the last, the writer may well have intended

an ironical hint that Jesus knew the helplessness of the disciples when left on their own. It is notable that never in the Gospels do the disciples catch a fish without Jesus' help.

anything to eat. It is generally held that *prosphagion,* a Hellenistic Greek word, originally referred to a side dish that was eaten with bread to give taste to it and that, since fish often constituted this dish, the word came to mean "fish." (A similar history is proposed for *opsarion,* used in vss. 9, 10, and 13; see NOTE on vi 9.) However, J. H. Moulton and G. Milligan, *The Vocabulary of the Greek Testament* (Grand Rapids: Eerdmans, 1949), p. 551, assert: "To judge from the papyrus evidence *prosphagion* is best understood of some staple article of food of the *genus* fish, rather than of mere 'relish.'" In the Lucan account of the miraculous catch of fish, Jesus does not direct a question to the disciples about their success. Yet, in the appearance of the risen Jesus in Luke xxiv 41-43, he asks them, "Have you any food here?" They respond by giving him a piece of cooked fish (*ichthys*).

6. *Cast your net.* In Luke v 4 Jesus says, "Put out into the deep and let down your nets for a catch." John's verb "to cast" (*ballein*) appears in the Matthean account (iv 18) of how Peter and Andrew were fishing when Jesus came along and called them. John uses *diktyon* for "net"; the post-resurrectional account in the *Gospel of Peter,* 60, uses *linon.*

to the right of the boat. An awkward phrase in Greek, this specification does not appear in the parallel Lucan story of the catch of fish. The right side was the auspicious side (see Matt xxv 33; also instances in StB, I, 980); in fact, Barrett, p. 482, points out that a secondary meaning of *dexios,* "right," was "fortunate." Yet the writer certainly did not think of this as an instance of luck; nor is Bernard's suggestion (II, 696) acceptable whereby Jesus may have seen a shoal of fish and was directing the disciples to it. John implies a more than natural knowledge on Jesus' part and the corresponding moral duty to obey him exactly if one is his disciple.

find something. After these words an addition is found in a group of textual witnesses (P66, Codex Sinaiticus corrector, the Ethiopic, some Latin texts of Irish descent, and Cyril of Alexandria): "But they said, '[Master,] we worked all night and took nothing; but in your name [word] we shall cast.'" This is a scribal borrowing from Luke v 5.

So. The use of *oun* in this chapter is typically Johannine.

the number of fish was so great. The Greek of this verse involves a causative use of *apo* not found elsewhere in John (who prefers *dia*—twenty-six times) but found nine times in Luke/Acts and frequently in LXX. Luke v 6-7 has a similar picture but couched in different words: "They enclosed a great quantity of fish, and their nets were breaking, so they signaled to their partners in the other boat to come and help them."

not able. This is the only time in the Gospel *ischyein* is used in the sense "to be able"; John prefers *dynasthai* (thirty-six times).

to haul it in. This verb, used here, in vs. 11, and three times in the body of the Gospel, is always in the late form *helkyein,* rather than *helkein.*

7. *that disciple whom Jesus loved.* Even if his presence belongs to the latest stratum of the story, it is clear that for the redactor he must have been one of the six companions of Peter mentioned in vs. 2 and, more specifically, one of the two sons of Zebedee or one of the "two other disciples." The verb *agapan* is used here and in vs. 20, as in xiii 23 and xix 26 (*philein* is used in xx 2).

"That disciple" may be compared to the use of *ekeinos* in xix 35 (see NOTE there; also xiii 25).

"It is the Lord!" A few Western witnesses read "our Lord." This title has served as a confession to the risen Jesus in xx 18, 25, and 28. Barrett, p. 483, notes that "It is" coincides with the "I am" formula (see vol. 29, p. 534).

Once he heard. Seemingly he still could not recognize Jesus visually; see also vs. 12.

tucked in his outer garment (for he was otherwise naked). The passage is usually translated in this manner: "Peter threw on some clothes, for he was naked." The idea then would be that Peter was working in a loin cloth (total nudity would offend against Jewish sensibilities and would not fit the picture of his working throughout the cool night), but for the sake of modesty and reverence he put on his outer garment before he swam to land to meet Jesus. Barrett, p. 483, points out that the giving of greetings was a religious act and could not be performed without clothing. Still it seems incredible that someone should put on a garment before jumping into the water and thus impede swimming. Recognizing this difficulty, Loisy, p. 518, finds here another instance of the redactor's awkwardness. Yet Lagrange and Marrow suggest a more plausible meaning for the Greek, a meaning that removes much of the difficulty. The verb *diazōnnynai,* which means "to tie (clothes) around oneself," is found in the NT only in John (Luke uses the LXX form *perizōnnynai*). It can mean to put on clothes, but more properly it means to tuck them up and tie them in with a cincture so that one can have freedom of movement to do something. In xiii 4–5 the verb is used for Jesus' tying a towel around himself that he might use it while he washed the disciples' feet. The item of clothing involved in the present scene is an *ependytēs,* a garment put on over underclothes. The word can be used to describe a workingman's overalls, and in this case it was probably a fisherman's smock that Peter was wearing in the chill of the morning. The adjective *gymnos,* "naked," can mean lightly clad, and Marrow thinks that because Peter was wearing the *ependytēs,* he could be described as lightly clad. Here we prefer Lagrange's suggestion: the writer means that Peter was naked underneath the *ependytēs* and that is why he could not take it off before he jumped into the water. Thus we get a more logical picture: clad only in his fisherman's smock, Peter tucks it into his cincture so that he can swim more easily and dives into the water. Bernard, II, 697–98, seems to give a double meaning to *diazōnnynai,* namely, "put on and tucked up," but then one is still faced with the absurdity of adding clothes before swimming.

jumped into the sea. Literally "threw himself." OS[sin] adds: "and came in swimming, for they were not far from dry land"; the latter part anticipates the information about distance found at the end of vs. 8. It is more likely that we are to think of his swimming rather than wading, for the shoreline drops off rapidly in most parts of the lake.

8. *came in by boat.* We are taking the dative of *ploiarion* (see NOTE on "the boat" in vs. 3) instrumentally. Lagrange translates it as a dative of place ("on the boat"), but BDF, §199, denies the existence of such a dative in the NT.

towing the net. In Luke v 7 apparently the nets are taken aboard, for the two boats are almost sinking from the weight of the fish in the net.

a hundred yards. Literally "two hundred cubits." The Hellenistic use of *apo* with the genitive in place of an accusative of distance is quite Johannine (xi 18;

Rev xiv 20; see BDF, §161¹; ZGB, §71). This information about distance would have come more naturally at the end of vs. 7, as OS^sin recognized.

9. *landed.* In place of *apobainein,* a few textual witnesses read *anabainein,* "went aboard," but this is probably by confusion with vs. 11.

there a charcoal fire. For *keimenēn,* "placed there," some OL witnesses seem to have read *kaiomenēn,* "burning." John evinces a partiality for charcoal fires; the only other NT incidence is at Peter's denial in John xviii 18.

a fish . . . and bread. As in vi 9, *opsarion* normally refers to dried or preserved fish; but in the next verse it is used to describe freshly caught fish and thus, for the Johannine redactor, at least, is interchangeable with the *ichthys* of vs. 11 (*pace* BDF, §111³, which tries to make a sharp distinction). It is possible that, in part, the variety of the Johannine vocabulary for "fish" in vss. 5–13 (*prosphagion, ichthys, opsarion*) reflects the combination of two stories (see COMMENT), with *ichthys* being original in the story of the catch of fish, and *opsarion* in the story of the meal of bread and fish. As for the mention of bread, it is not clear whether the bread was also on the charcoal fire. The fact that the singular is used for both fish and bread, as contrasted, for instance, with the plural for fish in vs. 11, has seemed significant to some: the author wished to illustrate the theme of unity at a sacral meal by referring to one fish and one loaf—but in fact the author does not say "one." This has led further to the assumption that Jesus miraculously multiplied the one fish and the one loaf to feed the seven disciples (so Lagrange, p. 526). We cannot believe that so important a miracle would have only been hinted at obliquely. We leave open the possibility that, in fact, there was only one fish on the fire, since Jesus asks for more, but the bread is probably meant collectively.

10. *Bring.* This aorist imperative is a curiosity, for elsewhere in the NT the present imperative of *pherein* is universal (BDF, §336³); in fact, the present occurs in a post-resurrectional context in xx 27.

some of the fish. The partitive use of *apo* is found only here in John, as contrasted with fifty-one uses of partitive *ek.* At the same time, the noun governed by the preposition, *opsarion,* is peculiarly Johannine in the NT. This one phrase, then, is a practical example of how difficult it is to decide whether or not the style of the chapter is Johannine.

11. *[So].* This is missing in both Western and Byzantine textual witnesses.

went aboard. Literally "went up" or "came up." Zahn and Loisy are among those who raise the possibility that Peter was only now coming up on the shore from his swim and that the other disciples got there first by rowing. However, since the writer tells us that Peter started out first, he would certainly have had to mention that Peter did not arrive first, if that were what he intended. Rather we are to think that Peter has been ashore, even if he has been strangely unobtrusive, and that he springs into action at Jesus' request. The idea that he has been prostrate at Jesus' feet and now *gets up* is unwarranted. (As we shall see in the COMMENT, the awkwardness about what Peter has been doing ashore is caused by the fact that two different incidents are combined here and that Peter's coming to Jesus was originally the occasion for the dialogue in vss. 15–17.) Bultmann, p. 544, thinks that the verb refers to Peter's *getting up* on the bank to pull the net in. However, it is more likely that Peter is pictured as going aboard the boat. The verb *anabainein* can mean "to go up" in the sense of boarding, although the other NT instances of this (Mark vi 51=Matt xiv 32) are accompanied in Greek by the clarifying phrase "into the boat." The scribal tradition behind the Codex Sinaiticus understood the writer's mind in this way; for there the verb *embainein* is used, and this clearly means that he got into the boat. Bultmann says that Peter cannot have boarded the boat, for the net full of fish was not in the boat. Yet it was towed behind the boat, and Peter may have had to go to the back of the beached boat to get hold of the net. Lightfoot, p. 342, sees in Peter's action a manifestation of his leadership among the disciples; this symbolism is possible, but more simply one may think with Loisy that the logic of the scene is that Peter acted so peremptorily because he owned the boat (cf. Luke v 3).

hauled ashore. Despite the size and number of the fish, no miraculous feat of strength is implied; such a miracle would have been specified and stressed (Bultmann, p. 548[11]).

large fish. The suggestion that there were other, smaller fish besides the 153 large ones is unlikely. In the catch directed by Jesus all is superlative.

one hundred and fifty-three. Although John frequently qualifies his numerals with "about" (i 39, vi 10, xxi 8, etc.), the more convenient "about 150" is not employed here. The idea that the writer may have had a hidden, symbolic purpose in citing the exact numeral 153 has led to an enormous amount of speculation—"everything from gematria to geometrical progression" (Marrow), but nothing dispelling Augustine's contention that the number is "a great mystery." For a survey, see Kruse, *art. cit.* Let us mention some of the more significant theories. (a) In his commentary on Ezek xlvii 6–12 (PL 25:474C), Jerome tells us that the Greek zoologists had recorded 153 different kinds of fish; and so by mentioning this number John may have been symbolizing the totality and range of the disciples' catch and symbolically anticipating that the Christian mission would bring in all men or at least all types of men. One could find a parallel in the parable of the kingdom in Matt xiii 47 where the net thrown into the sea gathers fish "of every kind." Nevertheless, Jerome's interpretation supposes that the Johannine writer would have known the conclusions of the Greek zoologists. Moreover, Jerome cites as his authority "the most learned poet" among the zoologists Oppian of Cilicia (ca. A.D. 180); and as R. Grant, HTR 42 (1949), 273–75, has shown, the form of Oppian's *Halieutica* that has reached us does not support Jerome's contention. Oppian states that there are countless types of fish and actually lists 157. Pliny (*Natural History* IX 43) knew of 104 varieties of fish and crustacea. Grant suspects that Jerome was interpreting Greek zoology by way of John. (b) Augustine, *In Jo.* CXXII 8; PL 35:1963–64, gives us the first instance of a mathematical approach to 153, wherein the number is seen as the sum of all numbers from 1 to 17. The symbolism that one may find in 17 varies, and much of what is proposed by Church writers is anachronistic for the Gospel (10 commandments and 7 gifts of the Spirit; 9 choirs of angels and 8 beatitudes). Hoskyns, pp. 553–54, takes the idea in a different direction: 153 dots can be arranged into an equilateral triangle with 17 dots on each side. Triangular numbers were of interest both to Greek mathematicians and to the biblical authors (see F. H. Colson, JTS 16 [1914–15], 67–76). Thus, one may theorize that 153 is a numerical symbol for perfection, a symbolism helped by the fact that 17, the basic constituent, is made up by two numbers symbolic of completion, namely, 7 and 10—numbers important in contemporary Jewish thought (*Pirqe Aboth* v 1–11). Barrett, p. 484, backs up this suggestion by pointing out that a total of 7 disciples were mentioned in vs. 2 (although the writer calls no attention to this total) and that in the Book of Revelation 7 is a symbolic number (see vol. 29, p. CXLII). The conclusion of all this would be that for John the perfect number 153 anticipated the fullness of the Church. (c) An allegorical approach is proposed by Cyril of Alexandria (*In Jo.* XII; PG 74:745) who breaks the number down into 100 and 50 and 3. The 100 represents the fullness of the Gentiles; the 50 represents the remnant of Israel; the 3 represents the Holy Trinity. For Rupert of Deutz, the 100 represents the married; the 50 represents the widows; and the 3 represents the virgins. These allegories reflect the theological interests of a later period; for example, the Johannine writer scarcely thought of the Holy Trinity as such. (d) Gematria finds some modern exponents. Kruse, *art. cit.*, stresses that 153 represents the sum of the numerical value of the letters in the Hebrew expression for "the Church of love," *qhl h'hbh*. One cannot deny that gematria was known to the Johannine school of writers (e.g., the 666 of Rev xiii 18, where, however, the reader's attention is called to the gematria), but it is the sheerest speculation to base the gematria on an expression that never occurs in the Johannine writings. R. Eisler (cited by Bultmann, p. 549[1]) ingeniously points out that the numerical value of *Simōn* is 76 and that of *ichthys*, "fish," is 77. Of more interest is the gematria proposed by J. A. Emerton, JTS 9 (1958), 86–89, based on the passage in Ezek xlvii mentioned as the subject of Jerome's remarks in theory (*a*) above, namely, the description of the stream of water that flows from the Temple toward the Jordan valley, ultimately to water the whole land of Palestine. This passage was known in Johannine circles, for it forms the background for Rev xxii 1–2 (the river of life flowing from the throne of the Lamb) and perhaps for John vii 37 (the river of living water flowing from within Jesus—vol. 29, p. 323). Now, in Ezek xlvii 10 we hear that, after the stream has watered the land and is teeming with fish of every kind, fishermen will stand by the sea from En-gedi to En-eglaim, spreading their nets. Emerton observes that the numerical value of the Hebrew consonants of (En-)gedi is 17, and that of (En-)eglaim is 153! (Subsequently P. R. Ackroyd, JTS 10 [1959], 153–55, working with variant spellings in LXX mss., proposed that by gematria based on the Greek the names En-gedi and En-eglaim can yield a total value of 153. This was countered by Emerton, JTS 11 [1960], 335–36, who objected that the two spellings of the names on which Ackroyd made his calculations never occur together in any one Greek ms.) By way of interesting support for Emerton's contention that the secret of the number 153 may lie in Ezek xlvii, we refer to J. Daniélou, *Études d'exégèse judéo-chrétienne* (Paris: Beauchesne, 1966), p. 136. He remarks that in early Christian art Peter and John (the two prominent disciples in John xxi) were portrayed next to a stream of water flowing from the Temple (which in turn may be connected with the rock of Jesus' sepulcher).

One cannot deny that some of these interpretations (they are not mutually exclusive) are possible, but they all encounter the same objection: we have no evidence that any such complicated understanding of 153 would have been intelligible to John's readers. We know of no speculation or established symbolism related to the number 153 in early thought. On the principle that where there is smoke there is fire, we would concede to the above-mentioned interpretations the likelihood that the number may be meant to symbolize the breadth or even the universality of the Christian mission. But we are inclined to think that because this symbolism is not immediately evident, it did not prompt the invention of the number; for certainly the writer, were he choosing freely, could have come up with a more obviously symbolic number, for example, 144. The origin of the number probably lies in the direction of an emphasis on the authentic eyewitness character of what has been recorded (xxi 24). The Beloved Disciple is present. In xix 35 he was seemingly the one who transmitted the fact that blood and water flowed from the side of Jesus; in xx 7 he was the source for the exact description of the position of the burial wrappings; so here perhaps we are to think of his reporting the exact number of fish that the disciples caught. The number would have been retained in the story because it was so large; and when the account received a symbolic interpretation, the number would have been interpreted as a figurative indication of the magnitude of the results from the disciples' mission. Large numbers indicative of abundance are not strange to the Johannine writings, for instance, the 15 to 25 gallons of water to be made into wine at Cana (ii 6) and the 144,000 of Rev vii 4. By way of caution we should note in conclusion that the explanation we have offered of the number's origin is not a solution to the problem of historicity.

the great number. Literally "being so many." Luke v 6 reports that after they let down the nets, "they enclosed a great multitude of fish"; and v 7 says that there were enough to fill both boats to the point of sinking. Those who know Palestine state that there are very dense shoals of fish in the Lake of Galilee.

the net was not torn. Luke v 6 reports: "Their nets were breaking," using the verb *diarēssein* while John uses *schizein.* Writers like Lagrange, Hoskyns, and Barrett think that in the Lucan picture the nets broke, filling the boats with fish; but ZGB, §273, interprets this as an instance of the use of the imperfect tense to indicate an attempt that was not carried into effect—the nets almost broke.

12. *eat your breakfast.* The classical use of *aristan* is for the morning meal that ends the night's fast; yet in Luke xi 37, the only other NT instance of the verb, it refers to eating the main meal of the day (Luke uses the noun *ariston* similarly). Does the meal consist only of the fish (singular or collective?) and of the bread that were mentioned in vs. 9; or are we to think that Peter has brought some of the freshly caught fish, as he was instructed to do in vs. 10, and has added them? The latter solution is easier, but most interpreters choose the former and point to the seemingly senseless command of vs. 10 as a sign that two narratives have been illogically joined: one where Jesus supplies the meal (miraculously?), and another where the catch made by the disciples constitutes the meal. Lagrange, p. 527, explains that, since the freshly caught fish symbolize the converts resulting from the Christian mission, they cannot be eaten—it would be a type of spiritual cannibalism!

Not one. There is considerable textual support for the addition of an adversative conjunction.

dared to inquire, "Who are you?". Because Jesus' appearance is strange (vs. 4), they recognize him but they are puzzled and unsure. The Jesus they knew has undergone transformation in becoming the risen Lord. Bernard, II, 700, remarks that the familiarity of the old days has passed, but actually a similar hesitation about questioning Jesus was encountered in iv 27. Barrett, p. 484, says, now that Jesus had manifested himself to his own, such questions are needless (xvi 23); but why then the disciples' hesitancy? In the COMMENT we shall propose that this was originally a recognition scene in one of the two post-resurrectional appearance stories that have been blended in ch. xxi (the recognition scene in vs. 7 belonged to the other story). The infrequent verb *exetazein*, "to inquire" (sometimes "to cross-examine"), occurs nowhere else in John. The question "Who are you?" was put to Jesus by "the Jews" in viii 25.

it was the Lord. As in vs. 7 this title expresses the post-resurrectional acknowledgment of Jesus.

13. *came over.* All the verbs in this verse are in the historical present tense, as contrasted with the aorist tenses in the very similar vi 11. The picture is confused, for up to now one would have naturally assumed that Jesus was standing by the fire he had ignited. Perhaps, however, the verb is pleonastic and does not really indicate motion.

gave. Codex Bezae, OS^sin, and two OL mss. make the resemblance to vi 11 even closer by adding "gave thanks" (*eucharistein*). Since, as we shall point out in the COMMENT, the present verse has eucharistic symbolism, the lack of the verb *eucharistein* is notable. Bultmann, p. 550[2], explains that the risen Lord does not give thanks as did the Jesus of the ministry.

14. *Now this was the third time.* Pace Bernard, II, 701, this is scarcely an attempt to correct the Marcan tradition that Jesus would appear first in Galilee. It is the redactor's attempt to sew chs. xx and xxi together by making this appearance sequential to the two in xx 19 and 26. Note that the redactor evinces the primitive outlook, attested in I Cor xv 5–8, whereby the appearances to apostolic witnesses have special rank; he counts only the appearances to the disciples and ignores Mary Magdalene. As for style, compare "This was the second sign" in iv 54. Goguel, p. 25, finds the analogy between the two verses so close that he theorizes that the story of the miraculous catch of fish was originally not post-resurrectional (it is not post-resurrectional in Luke v 1–11) and was the third sign in John's Sign Source after the two Cana miracles. Many scholars have thought it possible that this story once belonged to a collection of signs, but scarcely in the sequence imagined by Goguel (Bultmann, p. 546[1]). Agourides, p. 129, thinks that the *third* time is emphasized because in vss. 15–17 there will be a threefold question rehabilitating Peter after his three denials.

after his resurrection. Literally "after his being raised"; the use of the passive of *egeirein* for the resurrection of Jesus here and in ii 22 (see NOTE there) may be contrasted with the sole use of *anistanai* in xx 9.

COMMENT

The Nature and Purpose of Chapter xxi

From textual evidence, including that of such early witnesses as P[66] and Tertullian, the Gospel was never circulated without ch. xxi. (A 5th- or 6th-century Syriac ms. [British Museum cat. add. no. 14453] that ends with John xx 25 has apparently lost the final folios.) This still leaves us with two basic questions. First, was ch. xxi part of the original plan of the Gospel? Second, if not, was it added before "publication" by the evangelist or by a redactor? With Lagrange and Hoskyns as notable exceptions, few modern scholars give an affirmative answer to the first question. The principal reasons are these: (a) The clear termination in xx 30–31, explaining the author's reason for what he has chosen to narrate, seems to preclude any further narrative. It is in recognition of this difficulty that Lagrange attempts to move xx 30–31 to a position following xxi 23. (b) In ch. xx, after describing the appearances of Jesus to his disciples, the author records a beatitude for those who have not seen (xx 29). Thus, it is highly unlikely that he intended to narrate more appearances to those who did see. (c) The story in xxi stands in awkward sequence after that of xx, so that it is hard to believe that the events of the two chapters are in their original order. (Parenthetically, we find it noteworthy that, despite the many theories of rearrangements in the Fourth Gospel [vol. 29, pp. XXVI–XXVIII], there has not been a concerted attempt to relocate the post-resurrectional appearance of ch. xxi before the appearances of ch. xx.) After having seen the risen Jesus in Jerusalem and having been commissioned as apostles, why would the disciples return to Galilee and aimlessly resume their ordinary occupations? After having seen Jesus twice face to face, why would the disciples fail to recognize him when he appeared again?

In defense of the idea that the author planned to include ch. xxi, Hoskyns, p. 550, argues that a Gospel's closing should include not only an appearance of the risen Lord but also a mission of the disciples to the world for its salvation. He points to Mark xvi 20; to Matt xxviii 20; and to the Book of Acts which he regards as the real close of Luke's Gospel; and he rightly finds a reference to such a mission in the fishing symbolism of John xxi. However, his argument for the inclusion of xxi is weakened by the fact that there is a reference to a mission in xx 21: "As the Father has sent me, so do I send you." The universality of the mission is not explicit in xx, but its wide success is postulated by the beatitude concerning those who have not seen but have believed (xx 29). If ch. xxi had never been composed, we may safely guess that Hoskyns would not have judged as inadequate the closing of the Gospel in ch. xx. And so we consider it certain that ch. xxi is an addition to the Gospel, consisting of a once independent narrative of Jesus' appearance to his disciples.

By way of transition to the second question, we raise the problem of the name to be given to ch. xxi. Shall we call it an appendix, a supplement, or an epilogue? If, as often defined, an appendix is something not related to the completeness of a work, it is not the exact term for ch. xxi. Certainly this chapter is more closely integrated into Johannine thought than the "Marcan Appendix" is integrated into Marcan thought. We shall see, for instance, that ch. xxi takes up some of the themes of the Gospel (Peter's denial; the shepherd's care for the sheep; the role of the Beloved Disciple) and shows their consequences for the Church. Neither is "supplement" a good designation for xxi. A supplement often supplies information acquired later, and we shall see that some of the information in John xxi may antedate information in ch. xx, at least in origin. In any case, it is a difference of ecclesiastical focus that sets off ch. xxi and not simply a difference of time. As indicated in vol. 29, p. cxxxviii, we prefer "epilogue" (so also Marrow, pp. 43–44) as the term that has the most exact English nuance for the relationship of xxi to the Gospel. A good parallel is offered by the form of literary epilogue where a speech or narrative is added after the conclusion of a drama to complete some of the lines of thought left unfinished in the play itself. Moreover, having an epilogue at the end of the Gospel gives balance to the presence of a prologue at the beginning. This is more than a nicety of our classification, for, as indicated in vol. 29, p. xxxviii, both were added by the same hand.

Thus we are led to the second question: Who composed the Epilogue? Was it added by the evangelist himself in a second edition of his Gospel, or was it added by a redactor who exhibited or imitated some of the peculiarly Johannine stylistic features? From the start it should be clear that in thought and expression ch. xxi belongs to the Johannine group of writings; and had it been preserved separately in the NT, all would have recognized its close affinities to the Gospel. (Thus, not only in textual attestation, but also in style, ch. xxi presents an entirely different problem from that presented by the story of the adulteress in vii 53 – viii 11—see vol. 29, pp. 335–36.) If a study of style is the ultimate criterion of whether the Epilogue was composed by the evangelist or by a redactor, the results of that study are not going to be unambiguous; and both answers command impressive support among scholars. The question is so debatable that exegetes like Bauer (in the 3rd edition of his commentary) and Howard have changed their opinions in the course of their careers, ultimately accepting the evangelist's authorship.

It is customary to list the stylistic features wherein ch. xxi agrees with the body of the Gospel (features favoring the evangelist's authorship) and those wherein it does not agree (features favoring a redactor's authorship) —see Bultmann, p. 542; Barrett, p. 479; and exhaustively, Boismard, *art. cit.* All admit that some of the differences of style are meaningless. For instance, twenty-eight words used in ch. xxi do not appear elsewhere in the Gospel; yet since this is the only fishing scene in the Gospel, we expect a percentage of appropriate vocabulary. Other proposed differences between ch. xxi and the Gospel are based on somewhat tendentious hypotheses about the Gospel; for instance, Bultmann, p. 543, observes that the Beloved Disciple is a real person in this chapter, while in the body of the Gospel he is only a symbol (many disagree with the latter position); or, again, Dodd, *Interpretation,* p. 431, claims that xxi 22 evinces a naïve expectation of the second coming not found in the Gospel (many would find the latter contention overstated).

In the NOTES we made an effort to point out Johannine and non-

Johannine features in the chapter, and we shall list here the more significant. Noticeably Johannine features include: the designation "Sea of Tiberias" in vs. 1; the names Simon Peter, Thomas the Twin, and Nathanael from Cana in 2; the word *opsarion* for fish in 6, 9, 11; the Beloved Disciple and the interplay with Peter in 7; the charcoal fire in 9; the hesitant question in 12; the echoes of vi 11 in 13; the numbering of appearances in 14; the name of Simon's father in 15; some of the vocabulary variations and the sheep imagery of 15–17; the double "Amen" and the obscure symbolism in 18; the explanatory parenthesis in 19; the Beloved Disciple in 20–23; the theme of true witness in 24; the reference to other deeds in 25. Ruckstuhl, pp. 141–49, a specialist in Johannine style (see vol. 29, pp. XXXI, XL), finds the presence of so many Johannine features adequate proof for the evangelist's authorship; so also Cassian, *art. cit.* Among scholars who share this view one can list Westcott, Plummer, Schlatter, Lagrange, Bernard, Kragerud, and Wilkens. (Some would exclude vss. 24–25 from the evangelist's authorship.) Features that noticeably do not match the style of the Johannine Gospel include: mention of the sons of Zebedee in 2; the preposition *syn*, "with," in 3; the word for "daybreak" in 4; the causative *apo* and the verb *ischyein*, "to be able," in 6; the partitive *apo* in 10; the verb *epistrephein*, "to turn," in 20. Boismard, *art. cit.*, who has given us the most detailed stylistic study of the chapter, has concluded from such differences that the evangelist did not write the Epilogue. (At first, tentatively, and later more certainly, Boismard has argued for Lucan authorship; but he has had little following in identifying the redactor as Luke.) Among scholars who share this view one can list Michaelis, Wikenhauser, Kümmel, Bultmann, Barrett, Goguel, Dibelius, Lightfoot, Dodd, Strathmann, Schnackenburg, and Käsemann.

In this commentary we shall work on the hypothesis of authorship by a redactor, a conclusion reached for reasons other than the uncertain criterion supplied by style. Appeal to a redactor better explains why the Galilean appearance(s) of xxi was (were) artificially tacked onto the narrative of Jerusalem appearances in xx and made sequential to them ("Later on" in vs. 1; "third time" in 14). We have maintained that the Galilean appearances of Jesus to the disciples once preceded the Jerusalem appearances. In re-editing the Gospel, the evangelist would have been able to smoothly intercalate (if he knew the sequence); a redactor would be more likely to add on. Moreover, even if the evangelist himself added on a new set of appearances, he would have felt free to move or modify his previous conclusion in xx 30–31, whereas a redactor might not wish to tamper with the Gospel that had come down to him.

Yet, if we agree that a redactor wrote ch. xxi, we remind the reader that scholars have very different conceptions of this redactor. In fact, it is ch. xxi that supplies the main evidence for fashioning a view of this redactor; it is "the key and cornerstone for any redactional theory" (Smith,

p. 234). We think of him as a Johannine disciple who shared the same general world of thought as the evangelist and who desired more to complete the Gospel than to change its impact. As we mentioned in vol. 29, p. xxx, we do not agree with Bultmann who thinks of the redactor as adding in ch. xxi and elsewhere an ecclesiastical and sacramental outlook that was foreign and even contrary to the mind of the evangelist. Rather, we believe that the redactor has incorporated here some ancient material that was not included in the first edition of the Gospel, including the story of Jesus' first post-resurrectional appearance to Peter. (Few today would agree with Loisy's contention that the Epilogue is a pastiche of elements drawn from the Synoptic Gospels—a theory reflecting his thesis that the redactor wanted to harmonize John with the Synoptics.) The fact that this material comes from the same general reservoir of Johannine tradition from which the evangelist drew, plus the fact that the evangelist and the redactor were disciples in the same school of thought, explain the similarities of style between the Gospel and ch. xxi. The fact that the material in ch. xxi was formulated into its final shape by a writer other than the evangelist explains the dissimilarities of style.

An important motive, then, for adding ch. xxi was the redactor's desire not to lose such important material. The evangelist concluded the Gospel by saying that there were many other signs that he had not included; now the redactor gives one of those signs, namely, the appearance of Jesus on the occasion of a miraculous catch of fish. (We discussed above, p. 1058, the applicability of the designation "sign" to a post-resurrectional appearance; "sign" is even more applicable here because a miracle forms the context of the appearance.) Beyond the motive of preserving material, most commentators theorize that ch. xxi was added to the Gospel in order to emphasize specific theological themes. For instance, in the catch of 153 fish and in the command to Peter to care for the sheep there comes to the fore the theme of an apostolic mission that would bring many men to Jesus and would keep them together as a community. Since Peter plays a dominant role in the fishing scene and also in the dialogue that follows the meal (xxi 15–18), some have thought that the redactor was interested in calling attention to Peter's rehabilitation after his denial of Jesus and to his subsequent prominence in the Church. The interplay between Peter and the Beloved Disciple in vss. 7 and 20–23 has caught the eye of other commentators who propose that the chapter was meant to clarify the respective positions in the Church of these two men. Drumwright, p. 134, observes that while the Fourth Gospel is an interpretation of Jesus, the Epilogue is more an interpretation of the significance of two disciples, so that the final explanation of the Epilogue lies in the personal value of the material it contains. More particularly, Agourides, p. 127, contends that the main point of ch. xxi is to answer a question that has arisen from a comparison of the deaths of Peter and of the Beloved Disciple. Certainly, in xxi 23 the redactor is at pains to correct a misinterpretation about the relation of the death of the Beloved Disciple to the second coming of Jesus. Finally, some scholars think that the real goal of the Epilogue is expressed in vs. 24 which establishes that the Beloved Disciple through eyewitness testimony supports and verifies what the evangelist has written and the redactor has added. Thus, there are a variety of themes to which the Epilogue seems to address itself, themes to be discussed in detail later. It is probably a wasted effort to try to determine the relative importance of these themes in the mind of the redactor. What is significant to note, as Marrow and others have done, is that these themes have a common motif, for they all reflect on Church life. The themes of Peter's rehabilitation, his role as shepherd of the sheep, his death as martyr, the role of the Beloved Disciple, his death, its relation to the second coming—these are questions that affected the relation of the Johannine community to the Church at large. The analogy whereby ch. xxi is to the Johannine Gospel as the Book of Acts is to the Lucan Gospel is too strong by far, but certainly this is an ecclesiastical chapter. It reflects on themes pertinent to the period between the appearances of the risen Jesus (vss. 1, 14) and his second coming (vss. 22–23)—the time of the Church. If the concentration on the Church is stronger than elsewhere in the Gospel, this represents a development of what is at least hinted at in the Gospel (vol. 29, pp. cv–cxi), rather than the introduction of a theme that is foreign and even contrary to the Gospel.

The Structure of Chapter xxi

Unlike ch. xx (p. 995 above), the Epilogue has no series of appearances that can be arranged in carefully balanced episodes. All the action of ch. xxi is localized in the course of one encounter with the risen Jesus on the shore of the Sea of Tiberias. However, the writer himself indicates stages in the action, so that we may distinguish three subdivisions within the chapter, as indicated on p. 1065 above. Leaving aside the third subdivision (xxi 24–25), which is the redactor's conclusion, we find that the chapter consists of two main parts, namely, the first subdivision (xxi 1–14) describing an appearance of Jesus on the occasion of a miraculous catch of fish—a peculiar appearance not accompanied by any significant statement or prolonged theological dialogue—and a second subdivision (xxi 15–23) consisting entirely of sayings of the risen Jesus. It is generally held that the sayings in 15–23 interpret the appearance in 1–14 and supply the missing element of command or directive, but the relation of the dialogue to the appearance is more tenuous than in any other post-resurrectional narrative. Our discussion of the relationship between the two subdivisions is complicated by the fact that both the subdivisions are themselves probably composite. In order to proceed effectively let us leave until the next section (§72) the problem of the internal unity of 15–23 and discuss here only two points of structure: first, the unity between the narrative in 1-14 and the dialogue in 15-17; second, the internal unity of 1-14.

First, then, was the threefold interchange between Peter and Jesus in 15-17 originally a part of the story of the catch of fish in 1-14? The redactor himself has given some cause to doubt this by inserting the parenthetical comment in vs. 14 which suggests that the narrative of the appearance of Jesus in 1-13 was once a unit in itself. (Note the inclusion that exists between vss. 1 and 14 in stating that Jesus revealed himself.) This impression is reinforced by the fact that Luke v 1-11, which is closely parallel to John xxi 1-14, contains nothing similar to 15-17. If seven disciples figure in the fishing episode of 1-14, only Peter and the Beloved Disciple seem to be present in 15-23. Yet, these arguments against unity are not totally persuasive. Despite the redactor's insertion of vs. 14, he clearly thought of the two subdivisions as belonging to the same scene, for he introduced the dialogue in vs. 15 by a reference to the meal mentioned in vs. 12 ("When they had eaten breakfast"). The parallel in Luke must be treated cautiously as a guide to the original contents of the Johannine scene, since in moving the story to a new context, as we shall see below, Luke had to make modifications. The absence of Peter's fishing companions in 15 ff. is not overly significant, for they have no important role in 1-14. Rather, Peter is the unifying element between the two subdivisions, with the Beloved Disciple as his only important companion in each. There is a certain parallelism between Simon Peter's starting the action in the first subdivision by addressing the disciples in vs. 3, and Jesus' starting the dialogue in the second subdivision by addressing Simon Peter in vs. 15.

Indeed, the role of Peter in 1-14 seems incomplete without some terminating dialogue such as that found in 15-17 (Grass, p. 82, recognizes this but proposes that the original termination of 1-14, which involved a commission for Peter, has been replaced by what is now found in 15-17). In vs. 7 Peter jumps overboard to hasten ashore to Jesus, and in 11 he responds to Jesus' request for more fish by hauling the catch ashore, but in these verses there is no real confrontation between Peter and Jesus, no meeting and meaningful dialogue. Many scholars associate Peter's importance in the early Church with Jesus' appearance to him (Cullmann, *Peter,* p. 64), and one can scarcely imagine that a post-resurrectional story in which Peter is the center of activity came to an abrupt end without Jesus' having spoken to Peter and given him a commission. Such a commission is supplied by xxi 15-17. Moreover, since these verses seem to contain ancient material, on what other occasion would they have been spoken, if they are not in their original context? Most commentators interpret the threefold question about Peter's love for Jesus in 15-17 as a rehabilitation of Peter after his threefold denial, and such a rehabilitation would logically have taken place on the occasion of the first post-resurrectional appearance of Jesus to Peter, which is what we seem to have in xxi 1-14 (see below).

Perhaps the strongest argument against the unity of 1–14 and 15–17 is that the symbolism of the two is quite different: one speaks symbolically of fish, the other of sheep. However, the fish symbolism, while well suited to the theme of a Christian mission in 1–14, could scarcely have been adapted to the theme of the care of the faithful, which is the central idea in the threefold command of 15–17. (Note that there is no redundancy in the role assigned to Peter in the two subdivisions: in 1–14 he and the other disciples are implicitly and symbolically made missionary fishers of men; in 15–17 he is given pastoral care.) One can catch fish, but fishermen do not take care of fish the way shepherds take care of sheep. Also, it is noteworthy that I Pet v 1–5 has Peter speaking of himself as one of the elders who must take care of the flock, so that the association of Peter and shepherd symbolism is not peculiar to John and may plausibly have originated in connection with the first appearance of Jesus to Peter. In summary, then, one cannot establish with certainty the original unity of 1–14 and 15–17, but the arguments in favor of it seem more persuasive than the arguments against it.

This leads us to the *second* question about structure: Is 1–14 a composite of different scenes? Although some exegetes have more trouble than others in following the logic of the action in these verses (see NOTE on "went aboard" in 11), everyone recognizes difficulties. In vs. 5 Jesus seems to have no fish; yet when the disciples come ashore and before they haul in their large catch, Jesus has a fire prepared with a fish laid on it (9). Jesus asks that some of the freshly caught fish be brought to him (10), but it is not clear that they become part of the meal (12–13). The large catch of fish causes the Beloved Disciple and then Peter to recognize Jesus (7), but later on the other disciples seem still to be puzzled over Jesus' identity (12). Not surprisingly, then, scholars have posited a history of composition behind 1–14. Loisy, p. 519, phrases the alternatives well when he says that either the author combined several traditions or he was working out an allegorical symbolism to which he has sacrificed the logical development of the narrative—or perhaps he was doing both. Wellhausen and Bauer are among those who posit that two accounts have been sewn together, namely, 1–8, which is the story of the catch of fish, and 9–13, which is the story of a meal that in some details is a variant of the story of the multiplication of the loaves and fish (John vi 1–13). Yet, vss. 10–11 offer a difficulty to such an analysis since they refer to the catch of fish, and so most scholars favor a more complicated history of composition. For instance, Loisy, p. 521, maintains that originally vs. 5 led directly into 9 and then into 12–13: when the disciples had caught nothing, Jesus provided the meal, and thus they recognized him. Schwartz, p. 216, finds traces of an original story in 1–3, 4a, 9, 12–13, 15–17: a post-resurrectional meal story without a miraculous catch of fish. Bultmann, pp. 544–45, finds the original story in 2–3, 4a, 5–6, 8b–9a, 10–11a, 12: a more complicated narrative than that of Schwartz; for, while it incorporates the catch of fish, it eliminates not only the ready prepared meal but also in part the special role of Peter (e.g., his coming ashore first). For Bultmann, it was the redactor who introduced the Beloved Disciple and emphasized Peter's role in order to prepare for the addition of vss. 15–23 where these two disciples would figure prominently.

In our judgment these analyses are correct in postulating a combination of two strands of narrative, one concerned primarily with a catch of fish, and the other with a meal. However, we are dubious about how well the original narratives can be reconstructed by pure literary criticism, which here is largely a process of weeding out inconsistencies and making a consecutive story. If two narratives have been put together, the joining was not necessarily done by the redactor, who then would be guilty of leaving the obvious inconsistencies. The two narratives may have come to the redactor already joined and he himself may not have been able to solve the inconsistencies. Perhaps all that we can hope to discern behind the composite narrative are blurred outlines of the original narratives which were more complicated than we can reconstruct. Let us try to supplement the results of literary criticism and correct some of its weaknesses by approaching the problem from another direction, namely, that of NT parallels to material found in 1–14 and 15–17. We shall treat the parallels to the narrative of the catch of fish by discussing the tradition that Jesus appeared first to Peter, and we shall discuss the parallels to the narrative of the meal by discussing what we know of Jesus' first Galilean appearance to the Twelve.

The Catch of Fish in John xxi and the Tradition of an Appearance to Peter

A. The Direct Evidence about the Appearance. Our primary information comes from the tradition that Paul cites in I Cor xv 5 (see p. 970 above): the first of the post-resurrectional appearances of Jesus (i.e., appearances to those who had some claim to be considered commissioned witnesses or apostles) was to Cephas. Paul does not localize the appearance, but most scholars assume that it took place either in Jerusalem or in Galilee. (K. Lake located it at Bethany, while Burkitt placed it on the road from Jerusalem to Galilee—so also Fuller, p. 314, who suggests that it may underlie the *Quo vadis?* legend.) Support for a Jerusalem localization comes from Luke xxiv 34: "The Lord has been raised and has appeared to Simon." Since this announcement greets the two disciples who have just returned from Emmaus to Jerusalem, the implication is that the appearance was in the Jerusalem area on Easter day. (We shall not consider the possibility that Simon was one of the two disciples who went to Emmaus; see J. H. Crehan, CBQ 15 [1953], 418–26.) The assumption that Luke and Paul are talking about the same appearance is reasonable since their description is quite similar and in some other instances, for example, the eucharistic formula, they depend on the same tradition. Nevertheless, although the Lucan localization is accepted by scholars like Lohmeyer and Benoit, it is suspect precisely because the whole Lucan sequence of post-resurrectional appearances with the priority given to Jerusalem is dubious (see pp. 971–72 above). The mention of the appearance to Peter is particularly awkward in the Lucan narrative since in xxiv 12 (a Western Noninterpolation) Luke has told us that Peter went to the empty tomb and returned puzzled, obviously without having seen Jesus. Thus, it is plausible that Luke did not know under what circumstances the appearance to Simon had taken place and that he mentioned it where he did in deference to the memory that it was the first of Jesus' post-resurrectional appearances to his disciples.

An appearance to Peter in the Jerusalem area is virtually precluded by Mark xvi 7 where the angel instructs the women to tell the disciples *and Peter* that Jesus is going before them to Galilee and they will see him there. Many have suggested that the reason for singling out Peter was that he would receive a special appearance in Galilee. The *Gospel of Peter,* 58–60, though incomplete, retains the tradition that the first appearance of the risen Jesus to Peter took place near the Lake of Galilee considerably after Easter. (It does not seem worth while to enter into the speculation that this apocryphal gospel and John xxi draw on what stood originally in the lost ending of Mark—it would be guesswork, and the very existence of a lost ending of Mark is uncertain.) In summary of the evidence, while no firm conclusion can be reached, there is nothing emerging from a critical Gospel evaluation that would exclude the Sea of Tiberias as the site of the first appearance of the risen Jesus to Peter. For a more detailed discussion of localization, see Gils, pp. 28–32.

Another argument that has been advanced against the identification of the scene in John xxi with the first appearance to Peter is that both Paul and Luke indicate *prima facie* that Jesus appeared to Peter alone, while in John xxi Peter has companions. Yet the Pauline information is far from decisive. In I Cor xv 8 Paul speaks of Christ's appearance to himself: "Last of all, as to one born out of time, he appeared also to me." One would not suppose from that description that Paul had been accompanied by companions, as Luke three times indicates (Acts ix 7, xxii 9, xxvi 13). Thus, the presence of similar "silent" companions in the appearance to Peter cannot be excluded. In John xxi, if we leave aside the Beloved Disciple who is clearly a Johannine addition to the narrative, and if we separate the story of the catch of fish from that of the meal, Peter's fishing companions have no important role in the appearance of Jesus in vs. 7 and disappear entirely in the dialogue of 15 ff. It is true that those named are disciples of the Lord (Thomas, Nathanael, the sons of Zebedee), but we suspect that this is a contamination arising from combining the fishing story which concerned an appearance to Peter and the meal story which originally concerned an appearance to the body of disciples. Klein,

p. 29, is probably right in arguing that originally the companions of Peter were anonymous fishermen as they still are in Luke v 7, 9, so that Peter was the only disciple identified in the narrative (Grass, p. 76, leaves open the possibility that the sons of Zebedee were also involved). If one objects that this suggestion of anonymous companions is too tenuous, there is still no insurmountable obstacle in Peter's being accompanied by known disciples on the occasion of the first appearance of the risen Lord—the *Gospel of Peter*, 60, surrounds Peter with Andrew and Levi of Alphaeus on this occasion.

We may add that in the Johannine narrative there are certain features that are best explained if this is the *first* appearance of Jesus to Peter. In vs. 3 Peter goes back to his trade as if he is unaware of a higher calling—certainly one would not suspect that Jesus had previously appeared to him and sent him on the apostolic mission. The failure to recognize Jesus in 4–7 implies that the risen Jesus had not been seen before. Furthermore, as we have mentioned, the rehabilitation scene in 15–17, made to correspond to Peter's denials, is more intelligible in the context of Jesus' first appearance to Peter.

B. **The Indirect Evidence about the Appearance.** If the direct evidence supplied by Paul, Luke, Mark, and the *Gospel of Peter* does nothing to disprove the thesis that John xxi contains a version of the first appearance of Jesus to Peter, confirmatory evidence comes from an analysis of scattered Synoptic material concerning Peter. The Synoptics do not describe that first appearance, but it has been suggested that elements from the story of the appearance have been preserved in fragments of the Synoptic description of Jesus' ministry. We shall discuss three scenes.

(1) *Peter's walking on the water* (*Matt xiv 28–33*). After describing the multiplication of the loaves, Matthew, Mark, and John present a night scene where the disciples are out at sea in a boat and Jesus comes to them walking on the water (vol. 29, pp. 253–54). Matthew alone attributes to Peter a special role in this scene. Peter addresses Jesus from the boat, "Lord, if it is you, bid me come to you on the water." At Jesus' bidding Peter gets out of the boat and walks on the water toward him; but then he becomes afraid and begins to sink. At Peter's plaintive cry, "Lord, save me," Jesus reaches out his hand to catch Peter, saying, "O man of little faith, why did you doubt?" Then all in the boat worship Jesus as the Son of God. As we judge this peculiarly Matthean material, it seems more likely that Matthew has added it than that Mark and John have independently preserved a shortened form of the scene. Dodd, "Appearances," pp. 23–24, acknowledges that in the part of the scene that is common to the three Gospels there are many of the features appropriate to the literary form of a post-resurrectional narrative (p. 972 above), and that the story may have originally concerned an appearance of the risen Jesus. Some hesitation about this suggestion is caused by the fact that in all three

Gospels Jesus' walking on the water is firmly welded into the context of the multiplication of the loaves, and this localization goes back to a pre-Gospel period (vol. 29, pp. 238–39). Yet, even if the general story is not easily made post-resurrectional, the incident that Matthew added about Peter may have been post-resurrectional. We note some interesting similarities between the Matthean material and John xxi: Peter sees Jesus at a distance from the boat and hesitatingly recognizes him; Peter addresses Jesus as Lord and gets out of the boat to come to him; Jesus saves Peter, after chiding him for a lack of faith. (The last incident is capable of being interpreted as a dramatization of Peter's rehabilitation after his denials of Jesus and thus may be parallel in theme to John xxi 15–17.) Of course, in John there is no miracle of Peter's walking on the water, but that element in Matthew may stem from the story's having been placed in the context of Jesus' walking on the water—here probably John is more primitive than Matthew. We admit that the comparison between Matt xiv 28–32 and John xxi is far from perfect; but it does have some force, particularly in the light of the next passage to be discussed, which gives further evidence that the Petrine material peculiar to Matthew may have been post-resurrectional in origin.

(2) *Peter as the foundation rock of the Church* (*Matt xvi 16b–19*). While Mark, Luke, and Matthew have a scene during the ministry where Simon Peter confesses Jesus as the Messiah (Mark viii 27–29 and par.), only in Matthew does that confession include the title Son of God, the same title that Matthew has in the Petrine scene just discussed. Moreover, only in Matthew does Jesus praise Simon for possessing an insight that must have been revealed to him by the Father. Then Jesus goes on to change Simon's name to Peter, to make him the rock on which the Church will be built, and to give him the keys of the kingdom with power to bind and to loose. Today there is wide agreement among scholars, including such Roman Catholics as Cardinal Alfrink, Benoit, Stanley, Sutcliffe, and J. Schmid, that Matthew has added this material to the original scene (for exegetical reasons, see W. Marxsen, *Der Frühkatholizismus in Neuen Testament* [Neukirchen, 1959], pp. 40–47). There remains disagreement about the unity of the material and about its original localization. Cullmann, *Peter*, pp. 187–90, thinks that the Petrine material may have originally been set in the context of the Last Supper where Luke xxii 31–32 has a saying about Peter, but a wider group of scholars opt for a post-resurrectional setting (see Fuller, *art. cit.*). In our opinion there is a good chance that the Matthean material is composite; for, as pointed out in vol. 29, p. 302, parallels to Matt xvi 16b–19 are found scattered throughout John. Yet it is quite probable that the post-resurrectional period was the original setting for some of the words of Jesus in this Matthean passage; for instance, see pp. 1039–41 above, where we compared the binding and loosing saying of Matt xvi 19b with John xx 23. Our particular concern here is Matt xvi 18–19a where Peter is made the rock on which the Church

will be built, a Church against which death will not prevail, and where Peter is given the keys of the kingdom of heaven. The latter metaphor echoes Isa xxii 22 (p. 1040 above) and certainly involves authority. There is a parallel of thought between these words addressed to Peter and the words of John xxi 15–17 where Jesus constitutes Peter as shepherd over the flock by commissioning him to tend the sheep (for the implication of ruling authority in these words, see NOTE on 15, "Feed my lambs"). The two sayings are not close enough to be doublets, but they may represent fragments of a longer original narrative of a post-resurrectional appearance to Peter wherein he was given authority in the early Church. (One should probably also consider Luke xxii 31–32 which, we note, places Peter's role of strengthening his brethren *after* he has turned again, i.e., seemingly after he has repented his denial.)

(3) *The call of Peter and the miraculous catch of fish* (*Luke v 1–11*). In Mark i 16–20 and Matt iv 18–22 the call of the first disciples is narrated without much ado. Jesus sees two sets of brothers who are fishermen, Peter and Andrew, James and John; he urges them, "Follow me, and I will make you fishers of men"; they leave their boats and nets and follow him. The story in Luke v 1–11 is more complicated. As Jesus is preaching by the Lake of Gennesaret, the fishermen from two boats are washing their nets. Jesus gets into Simon's boat, puts out from the land, and teaches the people from the boat (parallel in Mark iv 1–2; Matt xiii 1–2). When Jesus finishes, he tells Simon to put out into the deep and lower the nets for a catch. Simon protests that they have toiled all night and caught nothing; but he lowers the net, and they catch so much that the nets are breaking. When the fishermen in the other boat come to help, both boats are so filled that they begin to sink. Peter falls at Jesus' knees and says, "Depart from me, for I am a sinful man, O Lord"; in reply Jesus says, "Do not be afraid; henceforth you will catch men." Finally the boats are brought to land, and the fishermen leave everything and follow him. Does Luke have a fuller form of the call of the first disciples than is found in Mark/Matthew, or has Luke added to the call of the disciples another narrative about Peter and a miraculous catch of fish? In a certain way the Lucan story is more logical: the miracle offers a reason why the fishermen would leave everything and follow Jesus. Yet there are real inconsistencies in the Lucan story. The details of the fishermen on shore and of Jesus' teaching from a boat are found in different places in Mark/Matthew (Mark i 16–20 and iv 1–2) and are probably artificially joined in Luke. Since Jesus asks Simon to put out to sea, we would presume that the others stayed on shore; but when the catch of fish takes place, the other boat is apparently at sea. Simon's action in falling down at Jesus' knees would be more appropriate on land than in a boat, as would his words, "Depart from me." Finally the transition from Simon's reaction to the call of the disciples is awkward. And so, while the evidence that the catch of fish is a Lucan addition is not so strong as was the

evidence for the two Matthean Petrine scenes we have just discussed, from internal reasons alone the theory of addition remains a good possibility.

The thesis of a Lucan addition becomes more persuasive when we compare the Lucan story of the catch of fish with John xxi. The following details are shared by both:

- The disciples have fished all night and have caught nothing.
- Jesus tells them to put out the net(s) for a catch.
- His directions are followed and an extraordinarily large catch of fish is made.
- The effect on the nets is mentioned (see NOTE on 11).
- Peter is the one who reacts to the catch (John xxi mentions the Beloved Disciple, but that is clearly a Johannine addition).
- Jesus is called Lord.
- The other fishermen take part in the catch but say nothing.
- The theme of following Jesus occurs at the end (cf. John xxi 19, 22).
- The catch of fish symbolizes a successful Christian missionary endeavor (explicitly in Luke; implicitly in John).
- The same words are used for getting aboard, landing, net, etc., some of which may be coincidental. The mutual use of the name "Simon Peter" when he responds to the catch (Luke v 8; John xxi 7) is significant, for this is the only instance of the double name in Luke.

There are two other points of resemblance but these are dubious. First, John xxi 2 mentions the presence of the sons of Zebedee, as does Luke v 10a. However, this half-verse in Luke, which is parenthetical and breaks up the sequence, may not have been an original part of the story of the catch of fish and may belong to the context of the call of the disciples into which the story of the catch was inserted. The mention of James and John in 10a seems to be a duplication of the more anonymous reference to "all who were with him" in 9. Second, Peter's statement in Luke v 8, "Depart from me, for I am a sinful man, O Lord," is capable of being interpreted as a reference to Peter's denials and thus as a parallel in thought to the rehabilitation of Peter in John xxi 15–17. In fact, many commentators use this verse to show that the Lucan story is not in its original context, for at his first meeting with Jesus Peter had no reason to confess himself a sinner. Yet Peter's exclamation may be no more than the expression of an ordinary mortal's sense of unworthiness in the presence of one who has worked a stupendous miracle.

The similarities listed above make it reasonable to conclude that independently Luke and John have preserved variant forms of the same miracle story—we say independently because there are many differences of vocabulary and detail. (That the event happened twice is not a serious possibility, pace Plummer, Lagrange, and others; for, if one would accept the historical view behind such a harmonization, one would still have to explain how in John xxi Peter could go through the same situation and much of the same dialogue a second time without recognizing Jesus!) Which Gospel has the more original version of the story, and which has the more original setting? We are concerned here only with the earliest traceable form of the story, not with its historicity which cannot be scientifically determined. (Attempts to explain it away include: Goguel's thesis, pp. 23–24, that there was a lucky catch of fish superstitiously interpreted as a miracle; Grass's confident assertion, p. 81, that a miraculous catch of fish never occurred; Bultmann's suggestion [HST, p. 304] that the idea may have been borrowed from pagan Hellenism, or that a miracle story may have developed out of a saying [HST, p. 230].) That the answer to these questions of originality is not simple may be seen from Bultmann's vacillation: in HST, pp. 217–18, he concludes that John has a later version that in some way derives from Luke; but in his commentary on John, pp. 545–46, he finds John more original in some features and in localization. B. Weiss, Von Harnack, and Grass favor Johannine originality, while Wellhausen, Goguel, Macgregor favor Lucan originality. Probably no unqualified answer can be given to the question about the original form of the story: in certain details Luke seems to have undergone development (nets almost breaking; two boats almost sinking); in others John has undergone development (perhaps the mention of 153 fish).

The question of localization is more important. One argument for the Lucan localization is that the disciples would more likely have been engaged in fishing before they began to follow Jesus than after the resurrection. However, if we treat John xxi as the first appearance of the risen Jesus, then, after finding the tomb empty, Peter could have gone back to Galilee puzzled and discouraged and have resumed his occupation. The most persuasive argument in favor of Johannine localization is that there is no apparent reason why an early Christian preacher would have taken a story from the ministry and made it post-resurrectional. As Klein, p. 35, points out, all our examples are in the other direction, namely, retrojection of post-resurrectional material into the ministry. And indeed, if the story of the catch of fish involved an appearance of the risen Jesus on the Lake of Galilee, Lucan tradition could scarcely have preserved it as post-resurrectional; for Luke xxiv has constructed a sequence where all the appearances of Jesus take place in Jerusalem and Jesus ascends into heaven on Easter night. One may theorize that in having to transfer the story of the catch of fish and Peter's rehabilitation back into the ministry, Luke thought it most appropriate to attach it to the common Synoptic story of the call of the first disciples and thus to associate the call with the apostolate into which it ultimately developed. We think it plausible, then, that Luke v 4–9, 10b, 11a was once part of a post-resurrectional story of the first appearance of Jesus to Peter (with his fellow fishermen serving as silent companions, even as in John xxi). It is true that Dodd, "Appearances," p. 23, has examined the whole pericope Luke v 1–11 and found it wanting in the form-critical features of a post-resurrectional appearance (p. 972 above). But, as he hints, form-criticism is not an entirely satisfactory tool here; for, in relocating the incident in the ministry, Luke would have had to suppress some of the characteristic post-resurrectional features, for example, the sorrow of the disciples because of Jesus' absence, and the appearance of Jesus. A trace of the original recognition may be preserved in the "O Lord" of Luke v 8, while the equivalent of an apostolic mission is found in v 10, "Henceforth you will catch men." (Because a similar statement, "I will make you fishers of men," appears in the Marcan/ Matthean call of the disciples, most scholars hold that this commission belongs to the calling rather than to the catch of fish, but Klein, p. 34, argues that it was part of the catch and originally addressed only to Peter. One can accept this without accepting Klein's conclusion that there was no call of Peter during the ministry.) Also the "Do not be afraid" of Luke v 10 may be an echo of the original post-resurrectional setting where fear greets the risen Jesus (cf. Matt xxviii 10; Luke xxiv 37–38).

By way of conclusion from our study of John xxi in the light of the direct and indirect evidence pertaining to the first appearance of Jesus to Peter, we suggest that in the tradition this appearance took place while Peter was fishing, that it involved a miraculous catch of fish at the command of one whom Peter came to recognize as the risen Lord, that Peter jumped from the boat to greet him, that in the ensuing dialogue Peter acknowledged his sin and was restored to Jesus' favor, and that Peter received a commission that gave him eminent authority in the community. John xxi has preserved a reasonably faithful form of this story, with some admixtures of another scene, as we shall see below. (Since one of these confusing admixtures involves a meal of bread and fish, it is difficult to ascertain whether originally the appearance to Peter also contained, as an incident, a meal consisting of the freshly caught fish. Klein, p. 32, is probably right in denying this, for there is no trace of a meal in any of our other evidence about the appearance to Peter. The catch of fish did not have as its theme the supplying of food; rather it offered the possibility of the recognition of Jesus by Peter.) In the details of how Peter acknowledged his sin and was restored to Jesus' favor, there is considerable variance in the material we have studied (Luke v 8; Matt xiv 30–31); and what we now find in John xxi 15–17 with its elaborate threefold question about love may have undergone considerable dramatization, even though it was part of the Johannine story as far back as we can trace. As to the authoritative commission of Peter, we have mentioned the possibility that the shepherd imagery of John xxi 15–17 and the rock-foundation imagery of Matt xvi 18 are fragments of what was once a longer dialogue and that both represent a development of simple metaphors.

The Meal in John xxi and the Tradition of the Galilean Appearance to the Twelve

In I Cor xv 5 Paul reports that after Jesus appeared to Cephas, he appeared to the Twelve. We have seen that one group of NT writers place this appearance in Jerusalem (pp. 970–72 above) and that the Johannine form of the Jerusalem tradition is found in xx 19 ff. The more original tradition, recorded by Mark (implicitly) and by Matthew, locates this first appearance in Galilee, and the Johannine form of the Galilean tradition is found in ch. xxi. Now, Matt xxviii 16–20 has the appearance take place on "the mountain to which Jesus had directed them." Many NT events are associated with "the mountain" (the Sermon on the Mount, the Transfiguration, the multiplication of the loaves); and whether or not historically some of these events did take place on a mountain, for the Gospel writers "the mountain" seems to have taken on the symbolic value of a Christian Sinai. This raises a question about the likelihood of Matthew's localization of the Galilean appearance to the Twelve. There is no logical reason why the disciples should have gone to a mountain, and that is why Matthew has to add the explanatory clause "to which Jesus had directed them"—a direction for which there is no other Gospel evidence, not even in Matthew. On the other hand, if the disciples left Jerusalem without having seen the risen Jesus and still puzzled by the empty tomb, naturally they would have returned to their homes, and for many this would mean the neighborhood of the Lake of Galilee. That at least one of them did come into this neighborhood is implied in our reconstruction of the appearance to Peter while he was fishing. Thus, it is at least possible that the Galilean appearance to the Twelve took place near the Lake rather than on a mountain, and such a localization would help to explain why the narrative of this appearance got confused with that of an appearance to Peter at the lake shore.

What were the circumstances and details of the Galilean appearance to the Twelve? Matthew gives virtually no information, and so it is worth while to raise the question of whether John xxi may retain traces of this appearance. We are inclined to attribute to the appearance to Peter such details from ch. xxi as the fishing expedition by Peter and unnamed companions, the miraculous catch of fish and the subsequent recognition of Jesus as the man on the shore, the bringing of the catch to land, and the dialogue in 15–17. What remains is the naming of the disciples (vs. 2) and the story of the meal at which these disciples recognized Jesus (9b, 12–13). Some scholars would also relate 5a to the meal story: since the disciples had caught nothing to eat, Jesus offered them a meal; but this supposes that the meal took place on the lake shore—that it did is not certain. While the evidence is insufficient, we are tempted to reconstruct the pre-Gospel narrative thus: somewhere in the lake region a man invited the hungry disciples to a meal of fish and bread which he had prepared over a fire; although he looked familiar, they were hesitant and yet they did not dare to inquire; finally they knew that it was the Lord when he gave them bread and fish in the same manner as he had distributed bread and fish after the multiplication in this same region (see below on the resemblance between xxi 13 and vi 11). Such a narrative would have four of the five features that Dodd finds characteristic of post-resurrectional appearances (p. 972 above), but does not have the apostolic commission, perhaps because in the final sequence it was replaced by the commission that belonged to the story of the appearance to Peter (xxi 15–17).

Is there any NT support for such a post-resurrectional narrative? In the Lucan traditions of Jerusalem appearances, meals figure prominently. In Luke xxiv 41–43 Jesus appears to the Twelve at a meal at which fish is served (see also Acts x 41; Marcan Appendix xvi 14). However, this detail is used apologetically by Luke to show that Jesus could eat food and so was not a ghost. More apropos for comparison to John xxi is the role of the meal in the appearance of Jesus to the two disciples on the road to Emmaus (Luke xxiv 30–31): "When he was at table with them, he took the bread, blessed and broke it, and gave it to them. Their eyes were opened, and they recognized him." It is interesting that in a fragment of the *Gospel according to the Hebrews* (Jerome *De viris illustribus* II; PL 23:613) we are told that Jesus appeared to James (I Cor xv 7) at a meal: "He took the bread, blessed it, and gave it to James the Just, and said to him, 'My brother, eat your bread, for the Son of Man is risen from among those who sleep.'" Almost every detail of the narrative we have distilled from John xxi appears in one or the other of these Lucan and apocryphal post-resurrectional stories.

We may summarize our remarks about the origin of the material in John xxi 1–14 plus 15–17 by offering a rather speculative hypothesis. This part of the chapter may consist of a combination of the story of the first appearance to Peter in a fishing scene and the story of the first Galilean appearance of Jesus to the Twelve at a meal of bread and fish. Although added to the Gospel at its last stage, John xxi apparently draws on very old material from the Galilean tradition of post-resurrectional appearances. Despite the development that the material has undergone and the awkwardness produced by the combination, these two Galilean stories seem to have survived in John xxi in a more consecutive form than anywhere else in the NT, for the appearance to Peter has otherwise been fragmented and scattered through the Synoptic accounts of the ministry, and the appearance to the Twelve at a meal is known only through its parallels in the Lucan Jerusalem tradition. (These parallels in Luke are important, for we have found many close similarities between John and Luke in the post-resurrectional narratives.) Of the two stories, that of the catch of fish is much better preserved in John xxi than that of the meal. These stories had already been combined long before they came to the redactor responsible for ch.

xxi. In the course of the transmission of the combined narrative, this composite acquired an ecclesiastical and a sacramental symbolism (to be discussed below), similar to the symbolism acquired by material in the Gospel proper, but with a slightly different orientation. The redactor who added the narrative to the Gospel may have been responsible for introducing the figure of the Beloved Disciple into vs. 7 (and also for appending the words of Jesus pertinent to the fates of Peter and of the Beloved Disciple in vss. 18–23—see §72 below). In regarding the Beloved Disciple as a late addition we do not prejudice the possibility that he may have figured anonymously in the original stories as one of Peter's silent companions or as one of the Twelve and that therefore his appearance is not pure fiction.

The Import and Ecclesiastical Symbolism of the Narrative in xxi 1–14

Thus far we have analyzed these verses by detecting the original stories that underlie them. However, the redactor has not given us the original stories but a combined narrative with its own sequence and theological import. It is to this end product that we now turn. Before we reflect on its import, we should say a word about the format. Dodd, "Appearances," pp. 14–15, lists John xxi 1–14 as an obvious example of the Circumstantial Post-resurrectional Narratives (p. 973 above), with an abundance of detail, drama, and lively dialogue. "The centre of interest is the recognition of the risen Lord, but here the recognition is not immediate but spread over an appreciable period." Although it does not embody didactic passages within itself, as does the Circumstantial Narrative in Luke xxiv 13–35, it is made to lead up to significant dialogue in vss. 15–17. Nevertheless, while Dodd may be right in this classification, Marrow, pp. 13–14 of his dissertation, is correct in pointing out that the five features of Concise Narratives appear in John xxi, so that it may be more of a hybrid form than Dodd would have us think.

Turning now to the import of these verses, we may begin with the expression "Jesus revealed himself" in vss. 1 (see NOTE) and 14, which creates a bond between the activity of the risen Jesus and the Jesus of the ministry. The verb is employed twice in I John i 2, which summarizes the earthly activity of Jesus in terms of the visible *revelation* of life: "We proclaim to you this eternal life such as it was in the Father's presence and has been revealed to us." In the Gospel in i 31 John the Baptist stated that his whole purpose in coming and baptizing was that the one to come might be *revealed* to Israel. After the Baptist pointed out Jesus to the disciples as the Lamb of God, the initial process of revelation was completed for these disciples at Cana when Jesus worked the first of his signs and *revealed* his glory to them (ii 11). In ix 3 we were told that Jesus' healing of the blind man was for the purpose of letting God's glory be revealed in him. As Jesus revealed himself to men through his works, he was revealing God to men: "I revealed your name to the men whom you gave me" (xvii 6). The resurrection is the final revelation, for it enables men to see Jesus as Lord. "For us God's love was *revealed* in this way: in His having sent His only Son into the world that we should have life through him" (I John iv 9), and it is the risen Jesus who gives the Spirit that is the source of life. And so the task of the Baptist proclaimed in the first chapter of the Gospel has been brought to completion in the last: Jesus has been fully revealed to Israel, that is, to the community of believers represented by the disciples. It may have been with the intention of echoing the first chapter that the redactor has given us here a group of disciples somewhat like the five disciples who figured in John i. Among them is Nathanael, that genuine Israelite (i 47), who now may be thought to be seeing the greater things that were promised him (i 50). If the verb "revealed" connects the appearance of the risen Jesus with what he has done during the ministry, it also anticipates the future, for in I John ii 28 the final coming is spoken of in terms of his revealing himself (see also I John iii 2; I Pet v 4; Col iii 4).

A fishing scene provides the occasion for Jesus' revelation of himself. After Jesus' death Peter has returned to the occupation he knows best; as prophesied in John xvi 32, he and his companions have been scattered on their own. Hoskyns, p. 552, describes the scene as one of complete apostasy, but it is rather one of aimless activity undertaken in desperation. The fishing expedition is unsuccessful, for without Jesus, they can do nothing (xv 5). It is at this nadir that Jesus comes to reveal himself. The marvelous catch of fish causes recognition—who else but Jesus could work such a sign? The import of the catch may have been more obvious than we suspect, for *Testament of Zebulun* vi 6 implies that an abundant catch of fish was known as a sign of God's favor. In the original story of the appearance to Peter, it was probably Peter who recognized Jesus, but this honor now belongs to the Beloved Disciple, who, because he is closely bound to Jesus by love, is best attuned to recognize him. (He was more perceptive than Peter also in the story of the empty tomb—pp. 1004-6 above.) In the course of time, as we shall see below, the catch of fish, once primarily the occasion for recognition, became the vehicle of symbolism; but it is less certain that a symbolic meaning is to be attached to the vigorous action of Peter's swimming ashore. The obvious meaning is that the impetuous Peter cannot wait to greet his master; and so he hastens ashore, even as he hastened to the tomb at the news that it was empty (xx 3-4). However, Agourides, p. 128, and others see a deeper meaning: Peter's nakedness in the boat symbolizes his spiritual state after his denial of Jesus; his putting on clothes has been interpreted as his conversion, and his plunging into the water as his purification. Agourides asks, "Does not the plunging into the water hint at the exchange between Jesus and Peter concerning washing and purity in 13:9-11?" We are skeptical. Certainly Agourides goes too far when he tries to find in the 200 cubits (100 yards; vs. 8) a symbolism related to Peter's repentance. It is true that Philo (*Quaestiones et solutiones in Gen.* i #83) treats the number 200 symbolically; however, John does not attach that number to Peter's swim but to the disciples' rowing.

The symbolic meaning that developed around the catch of fish in John xxi is the same as in Luke v 10: it symbolizes the apostolic mission that will "catch men." Since this symbolism is fairly obvious, it could have developed independently in the two traditions; in any case we suspect that Klein, p. 34, is right in maintaining that Luke found it already present when he first came across the story. Bultmann, pp. 544–45, thinks of the allegorization of the story as the work of the final redactor, but Klein, pp. 30–31, correctly argues that it antedates the redactor and certainly antedates the introduction of sacramental symbolism (see below), for the two do not agree. Be that as it may, the symbolism of mission is carried further in John than in Luke. They agree on the great numbers to be brought in by the apostolic mission, but only John (xxi 11) mentions 153 fish and stresses the fact that the net was not broken. The number 153 (see NOTE) may, by way of minimal interpretation, be meant to symbolize the all-embracing character of the mission. The unbroken state of the net means that the Christian community is not rent by schism, despite the great numbers and different kinds of men brought into it. The verb we translate in 11 as "torn" is *schizein*, related to the *schisma* or division over Jesus prominent in vii 43, ix 16, x 19. It was also used in xix 24 when the soldiers decided not to tear the tunic of Jesus, woven in one piece from top to bottom—seemingly another symbol of unity (p. 921 above). Some would carry the Johannine quest for unity so far as to think that the Johannine tradition suppressed the two boats found in the Lucan story of the catch of fish in favor of *one* boat, but this borders on fantasy. More plausible is the suggestion that we should relate the use of the verb *helkein* (*helkyein*), "to haul," in 6 and 11 to the instances in the Gospel where it is used for the drawing of men to Jesus (for the OT background see NOTE on vi 44). Particularly pertinent is xii 32: "When I am lifted up from the earth, I shall *draw* all men to myself." In Johannine thought the resurrection belongs to the process of lifting up Jesus to his Father, and the risen Jesus accomplishes his prophecy of drawing all men to himself through the apostolic ministry symbolized by the catch of fish and the hauling ashore. Some authors would find in *helkein* a hint that the mission encounters resistance that must be overcome by dragging the fish in, but we may be assured that in a mission guided by Jesus the disciples will overcome any natural resistance. We note that it is Peter who takes the lead in hauling the net ashore. If the Johannine writer has given the Beloved Disciple a primacy of love and of sensitivity in recognizing Jesus, he has left Peter the first place in the apostolic ministry.

The basic symbolism of the catch of fish thus far discussed is widely accepted by scholars, but there are other proposed symbolic interpretations that are less certain. Hoskyns, p. 552, points out that the catch takes place in Galilee of the Gentiles (Isa ix 1), a setting appropriate for the symbolism of a wide-ranging mission. J. Mánek, "Fishers of Men," NovT 2 (1957), 138–41, thinks that the background for the idea of fishers of men is to be sought in Jer xvi 16 (where the symbolism, however, refers to hostile pursuit). Moreover, he thinks that the water from which the fish are drawn represents the place of sin and death, an imagery frequent in the ancient Semitic cosmogonies; consequently, the fisher of men is one who rescues men from sin. In almost an opposing interpretation, some have thought of the fish as those who are saved by the waters of Baptism, so that the water has sacramental significance. This imagery is somewhat similar to Tertullian's thought (*De Baptismo* I 3; SC 35:65): "But we little fish, who are so named in the image of our *ichthys*, Jesus Christ, are born in water and only by staying in water are we saved."

We have noted that there are no words of apostolic mission in xxi 1–14 (an essential feature of a post-resurrectional appearance to the disciples) and that this lack is only partially filled by the commission to Peter in 15–17. Nevertheless, the symbolism that has developed around the catch of fish now supplies the element of mission. It is not too great an exaggeration to say that the catch of fish is the dramatic equivalent of the command given in the Matthean account of the Galilean appearance: "Go therefore and make disciples of all nations" (Matt xxviii 19). Thus, although the composite scene that comes to us in John xxi 1–14 represents a later development of the format of post-resurrectional appearances, in its own way it has preserved the basic import common to the other appearance narratives: Jesus is truly risen and has been seen by witnesses who in turn have been sent forth to proclaim him to other men. Whether we should carry the idea of apostolic mission over to the meal of 9b, 12–13 is not certain. There are interpreters who think of the invitation to the meal as an implicit act of forgiveness made necessary by the fact that the disciples had deserted Jesus (xvi 32), but this emphasis is not clear in the account.

The Eucharistic Symbolism of the Meal in xxi 9b, 12–13

Originally, in one of the stories that lies behind xxi 1–14, the meal of bread and fish that Jesus offered his disciples led them to recognize him as the risen Jesus. An element of this is still found in vs. 12, but attenuated by the fact that a recognition of Jesus by the Beloved Disciple and Peter is recorded in 7. In the present sequence the second hesitating recognition reflects the awe that the disciples have for the risen Jesus and hints at the mystery of his transformed appearance. But many think that the meal has also taken on a sacramental symbolism and become evocative of the Eucharist. It should be stressed that here we are not raising the question of whether or not the meal was an actual Eucharist, for there is no way to solve that. Nor is there any way to verify the contention of Gray, pp. 696–97, that the Johannine writer is describing an agape meal, with fish substituted for the meat of the Pauline agape. C. Vogel, *Revue des Sciences Religieuses* 40 (1966), 1–26, has carefully studied the evidence pertaining to early Christian sacral meals with fish; and he concludes that they were not directly related to the Eucharist but to Jewish fish meals that had an eschatological import, sometimes involving the imagery of conquering Leviathan, the primeval sea monster. Such questions as whether there were Eucharists that had fish instead of wine lie beyond our interest here, as does also the symbolism first proposed by Augustine in reference to John xxi (*In Joh.* CXXIII; PL 35:1966): "The cooked fish is Christ who suffered, and he is the bread who has come down from heaven." Our question is a modest one: To what extent was the description of this meal meant to remind the reader of the Eucharist and to cause him to associate the Eucharist with the presence of the risen Christ in the Christian community? In a brief study of the eucharistic symbolism of meals eaten with the risen Jesus, J. Potin, *Bible et Terre Sainte* 13 (March 1961), 12–13, points out that such meals could have been used pedagogically to show that Jesus wished to share the intimacy of his messianic banquet table with all believers during the whole post-resurrectional era until he would come again to invite them to the heavenly banquet. The accounts of these post-resurrectional meals are almost dramatizations of the rubric attached to the eucharistic institution in I Cor xi 25 and Luke xxii 19: "Do this in memory of me."

The eucharistic symbolism in John xxi is complicated by the history of composition we have posited for the chapter. The symbolism that developed in the narrative of the catch of fish whereby the fish represent converts has seemed to some scholars to rule out the possibility of a eucharistic symbolism for the meal of bread and fish (see NOTE on "eat your breakfast" in 12). Most likely, however, the fish at the meal is a detail from another story different from that of the catch of fish, and the sacramental symbolism attached to it came into the combined narrative at a later period than the missionary symbolism attached to the catch of fish.

There are good arguments for finding eucharistic symbolism in the meal of John xxi. The description of this meal in vs. 13, wherein Jesus "took the bread and gave it to them, and did the same with the fish," echoes the description of the meal eaten after the multiplication of the loaves and the fish in vi 11: "Jesus then took the loaves of bread, gave thanks, and passed them around to those sitting there; and he did the same with the fish." (The similarity is so close that Wellhausen considered the meal in John xxi to be a variant of the multiplication meal.) The fact that the scenes in vi and xxi are the only ones in the Fourth Gospel to occur by the Sea of Tiberias naturally helps the reader to make a connection between the two meals. We pointed out in vol. 29, pp. 247–48, and the chart on p. 243, that in all the Gospels the account of the multiplication meal has been conformed to the account of the actions of Jesus at the Last Supper, with the result that a connection was made between the multiplication meal and the Eucharist. In particular, in John's account of the multiplication meal there were several peculiar details evocative of the Eucharist. We doubt, then, that a meal so similar to the multiplication meal could be described in John xxi without reminding the Johannine community of the Eucharist. Moreover, we have already called attention to the resemblance between the meal in John xxi and the meal that Luke xxiv 30–31, 35 describes in the account of the appearance of Jesus to the two disciples on the road to Emmaus. Luke's insistence that the disciples recognized Jesus in the breaking of the bread is often taken as eucharistic teaching meant to instruct the community that they too could find the risen Jesus in their eucharistic breaking of the bread.

Some external support for the eucharistic interpretation of John xxi is found in Cullmann's contention, ECW, pp. 15–17, that the early communities made a direct connection between their eucharistic meals and the meals eaten by the risen Jesus with his disciples. Certainly in primitive iconography, meals of bread and fish (rather than of bread and wine) were the standard pictorial symbols of the Eucharist. Of course, it is often impossible to be sure whether the artist had the multiplication meal or John xxi in mind. Gray, p. 699, points out an interesting artistic pattern where in the meals of bread and fish *seven* men are participants, often seated at a table. It is tempting to find here a reminiscence of the seven disciples mentioned in John xxi 2, but other historians of art claim that the use of seven participants was a convention in Roman iconography. Gray mentions one early painting of a eucharistic meal where Jesus and Mary and five men are gathered, seemingly a blending of the bread and fish meal and the Cana scene (five disciples are called in the days preceding the Cana feast). We suggested in vol. 29, pp. 109–10, the possibility of a secondary eucharistic symbolism in the Cana story. Some have sought to lend liturgical support to the eucharistic interpretation of ch. xxi by pointing out that this scene, which is set in the early morning, would make ideal reading at the vigil celebration of the Eucharist, but we know of no ancient evidence supporting the custom of so using ch. xxi.

If we accept the plausibility of the proposed eucharistic symbolism, then the risen Jesus in xxi plays somewhat the same role he played in ch. xx. In xx 19–23 he was the dispenser of gifts, especially of the Spirit, the source of eternal life. Here too the risen Jesus dispenses life: "The bread that I shall give is my own flesh for the life of the world" (vi 51).

[The Bibliography for this section is included in the Bibliography for the whole of ch. xxi, at the end of §73.]

72. THE RISEN JESUS SPEAKS TO PETER
(xxi 15–23)

XXI 15 When they had eaten breakfast, Jesus addressed Simon Peter, "Simon, son of John, do you love me more than these?" "Yes, Lord," he said, "you know that I love you." "Then feed my lambs," Jesus told him.

16 A second time Jesus repeated the question, "Simon, son of John, do you love me?" "Yes, Lord," he said, "you know that I love you." "Then tend my sheep," Jesus told him.

17 For the third time Jesus asked, "Simon, son of John, do you love me?" Peter was hurt because Jesus had asked for the third time, "Do you love me?" So he said to him, "Lord, you know everything; you know well that I love you." "Then feed my little sheep," Jesus told him.

18 "Truly, I assure you,
    when you were a young man,
    you used to fasten your own belt
    and set off for wherever you wished.
    But when you grow old,
    you will stretch out your hands,
    and another will fasten a belt around you
    and take you where you do not wish to go."

(19 What he said indicated the sort of death by which Peter was to glorify God.) After these words, Jesus told him, "Follow me."

20 Then Peter turned around and noticed that the disciple whom Jesus loved was following (the one who had leaned back against Jesus' chest during the supper and said, "Lord, who is the one who will betray you?"). 21 Seeing him, Peter was prompted to ask Jesus, "But Lord, what about him?" 22 "Suppose I would like him to remain until I come," Jesus replied, "how does that concern you? Your concern is to

15: *addressed, said, told;* 16: *repeated, said, told;* 17: *asked, said* (in many witnesses), *told;* 19: *told;* 20: *noticed;* 21: *was prompted to ask;* 22: *replied.* In the historical present tense.

follow me." 23 This is how the word got around among all the brothers that this disciple was not going to die. As a matter of fact, Jesus never told him that he was not going to die; all he said was: "Suppose I would like him to remain until I come [how does that concern you]?"

NOTES

xxi 15. *When they had eaten breakfast.* Many scholars do not take this as a real time indication but as an artificial attempt to make a connection between 15–17 and 12–13; they note that the disciples ("they") play no further role in the scene. Nevertheless, when the Johannine writers wish to make a vague connection, they usually employ "Later on," as in vs. 1.

Simon, son of John. Here the Greek word for "son" is not used as it was in i 42 (see NOTE there). Only in the Fourth Gospel is Peter's father's name given as John. (Schwank, "Christi," p. 532, suggests that the writer may be playing on the idea that Peter is a disciple and hence a spiritual son of *John* the Baptist; this is highly unlikely.) Some scholars, for example, Lightfoot, p. 340, have thought that Jesus' failure to address the apostle as "Simon *Peter*" is indicative of the fact that Peter is in disfavor after his denial of Jesus; however, except for Luke xxii 34 and for the instance where Jesus changes Simon's name, Jesus does not address Simon as either "Peter" or as "Simon Peter" in any of the Gospels. More plausible is the thesis that by addressing Peter with the patronymic used when they first met (John i 42), Jesus is treating him less familiarly and thus challenging his friendship.

do you love me? . . . I love you. An extraordinary variation in the Greek vocabulary appears in the three repetitive verses, 15, 16, and 17. Respectively, there are two different verbs for "to love," for "to know," and for "to feed or tend," and two or three different nouns for sheep. With the partial exception of Origen, the great Greek commentators of old, like Chrysostom and Cyril of Alexandria, and the scholars of the Reformation period, like Erasmus and Grotius, saw no real difference of meaning in this variation of vocabulary; but British scholars of the last century, like Trench, Westcott, and Plummer, found therein subtle shades of meaning. We shall discuss their thesis, but we note that most modern scholars have reverted to the older idea that the variations are a meaningless stylistic peculiarity (see Moule, IBNTG, p. 198; E. D. Freed, "Variations in the Language and Thought of John," ZNW 55 [1964], especially 192–93). Why the variation is not consistently introduced elsewhere remains a puzzle; for instance, in ch. x John uses the same word for sheep fifteen times, and in xiii 34 and xiv 21 John uses the same verb "to love" (*agapan*) three and four times respectively.

For the verb "to love" in the questions and answers of xxi 15–17, the variations are these:

> 15: *agapas me . . . philo se*
> 16: *agapas me . . . philo se*
> 17: *phileis me . . . philo se*

As pointed out in vol. 29, p. 498, this is the proof text for those who wish to distinguish between *agapan* and *philein*, a distinction that goes back to

Origen's time. Yet, as we saw from our report of the interpretations of 15–17 offered by Trench, Westcott, and Evans, the advocates of distinction between the verbs are not in agreement about the shades of meaning. Is Jesus asking Peter for a more noble form of love (*agapan*) and then settling for the lower form of friendship (*philein*), which is all that Peter can give? Is Jesus asking for a reverential love (*agapan*) and then conceding to Peter's expression of passionate personal affection (*philein*)? Or even vice versa? McDowell, pp. 425–38, insists on a distinction flowing from the classic use of *agapan* ("to esteem, prize, prefer"): Jesus first asks Peter if he prefers him (Jesus) to these (boats, fishing)—is he willing to leave them to become a fisher of men? Peter's answer is not only in terms of esteem or preference but of real passion (*philein*). In his work *Agape in the New Testament*, III, 95, C. Spicq writes with confidence: "Commentators are divided about the respective value of the two verbs, but those who make them synonymous either ignore the semantics of *agape* or minimize the importance of the scene."

Despite the danger of being guilty of one of those two crimes, the present writer is forced to align himself with scholars ancient (the OL translators, Augustine) and modern (Lagrange, Bernard, Moffatt, Strachan, Bonsirven, Bultmann, Barrett, etc.) who find no clear distinction of meaning in the alternation of *agapan* and *philein* in vss. 15–17. The reasons for this are: (a) There seems to be a general interchangeability of the two verbs in John; see vol. 29, p. 498; also Bernard, II, 702–4. (b) In Hebrew and Aramaic there is one basic verb for expressing the various types of love, so that all the subtlety of distinction that commentators find in the use of the two verbs in 15–17 scarcely echoes the putative Semitic original. We note that LXX uses both verbs to translate Heb. *'āhēb*, although *agapan* is twenty times more frequent than *philein*. In the Syriac translations of 15–17 only one verb is used. (c) Peter answers "Yes" to the questions phrased with the verb *agapan* even though he expresses his love in terms of *philein* and thus shows no awareness that he is answering a request for a higher or more spiritual or more rational type of love (*agapan*) with an offer of a lower or more affectionate form of love (*philein*).

more than these. For the comparative "more," *pleon* is used here, while in four other instances in John the alternative form *pleiōn* appears. This inconsistency is not too important for it occurs also in Luke and in Acts; there is one instance of *pleon* in each as contrasted with eight and eighteen uses of *pleiōn* respectively. Here and in John vii 31 a genitive follows the comparative; in iv 1 the particle *ē* follows (BDF, §185[1]). It is noteworthy that this comparative clause appears in only the first of the three questions about Peter's love. The exact reference of the "these" is not certain. Bernard and McDowell are among those who treat "these" as the equivalent of an English neuter object of the verb: "Do you love me more than you love these things (i.e., boats, fishing)?" As a support for such a translation we recall that in the aftermath of the miraculous catch of fish in Luke v 1–11, Peter was among the disciples who left all things to follow Jesus. However, it would be normal to repeat the verb in such a construction as posited above (see viii 31); and, besides, by Johannine standards the choice thus offered to Peter between material things and the risen Jesus would be rather ridiculous, however real and difficult such a choice may have been historically. Another interpretation is given by A. Fridrichsen, *Svensk Exegetisk Årsbok* (1940), pp. 152–62, who understands "these" as the masculine object of the verb: "Do you love me more than you love these other disciples?" Again it is difficult to think that the Johannine writer would present seriously the offer of a choice between the other disciples and the risen Jesus. Most scholars take the "these" as the masculine subject of an implied verb: "Do you love me more than these other disciples do?" (Compare the Greek of iv 1.) This translation too is not without grammatical difficulty, for normally one would have expected the emphatic Greek "you" by way of contrast with the "these." It has been proposed that there is irony here: Jesus is testing Peter who boasted at the Last Supper of a love greater than that of the other disciples. However, this boast was not made in John but in the Synoptic accounts (Mark xiv 29; Matt xxvi 33: "Even though they all fall away, I will not"), unless the fact that only Peter protested his loyalty in John xiii 37 is tantamount to a boast of greater love. The real difficulty is that such a question might seem to encourage a rivalry among the disciples, something that Jesus elsewhere rejects (Mark ix 34–35, x 42–44). This objection is usually answered by claiming that greater love would be expected from Peter than from the others because he was being forgiven a more serious denial (Luke vii 42–47) or because he was being offered a leadership as shepherd that would call for a pre-eminence in love. Yet, in the Fourth Gospel it is inconceivable that Peter could be held up as the example of greater love—that is the prerogative of the Beloved Disciple. Perhaps the best solution is the one offered by Bultmann, p. 551[1], namely, that the implications of the clause should not be considered too seriously, for it is only an editorial attempt to bring the other disciples into the picture and thus to bind 15–17 to 1–13.

In OS[sin] this clause is missing in the first question (also in some minor Greek and some OL witnesses). Basing himself on this, J. A. Bewer, *Biblical World* 17 (1901), 32–34, made an interesting attempt to rearrange the questions (and the answers) so that there is a progression: Do you love me? Do you love me much? Do you love me more than these? However, any progression in the dialogue is not in the wording but in the repetition.

"*Yes, Lord, . . . you know that I love you.*" Peter's answer does not allude to the "more than these" of the question—perhaps a confirmation that the comparative clause is not too important. The same basic answer will be given again in 16 and, with some elaboration, in 17; the first two times the verb "to know" is *eidenai (oida)*, while the last time it is *ginōskein*, which we translated "to know well," although *oida* also appears in 17 in the "you know everything" clause. Seemingly there is no distinction of meaning (vol. 29, p. 514). In all three answers the Greek pronoun "you" is expressed, and this is a sign of emphasis.

"*feed my lambs.*" In the three instances of Jesus' command to Peter there is a considerable variety of vocabulary:

15: "Feed my lambs"	=	*boskein arnion*
16: "Tend my sheep"	=	*poimainein probaton*
17: "Feed my little sheep"	=	*boskein probation*

As for the verb, in LXX both *boskein* and *poimainein* translate Heb. *rā'āh*, and so we can be dubious about attempts to find a sharp distinction between them (the Vulgate of 15–17 uses *pascere* to translate both). Yet, if they are largely synonymous, *poimainein* covers a somewhat broader field of meaning. *Boskein* is used both literally and figuratively (Ezek xxxiv 2) for feeding animals. *Poimainein* includes such duties toward the flock as guiding, guarding, and feeding, whether literally (Luke xvii 7) or figuratively (Ezek xxxiv 10; Acts xx 28; I Pet v 2; Rev ii 27, vii 17); equivalently it may mean "to rule, govern" (II Sam vii 7; Ps ii 9; Matt ii 6). A sentence from Philo, *Quod deterius* VIII ✻25, catches the nuance of the two verbs: "Those who feed [*boskein*] supply nourishment . . . but those who tend [*poimainein*] have the power of rulers and governors." Combined, the two verbs express the fullness of the pastoral task assigned to Peter.

As for the noun, *arnion* (only here in John; twenty-nine times in Rev) is clearly the best reading in 15, but there is uncertainty about what should be read in 16 and 17:

16: *probation;* 17: *probation:* Codex Vaticanus, Nestle, Aland Synopsis, Barrett, Bultmann.

16: *probaton;* 17: *probaton:* Codex Sinaiticus, Merk, Bible Societies' NT, Lagrange.

16: *probation;* 17: *probaton:* Loisy, Burkitt, Bernard.

16: *probaton;* 17: *probation:* Codex Alexandrinus, Zahn.

It seems that in one verse *probation* should be read; the word occurs nowhere else in the NT, and a scribe would not have introduced it to replace the more common *probaton* (fifteen times in John x alone). It is possible that *probation* occurred in both verses, and the instances of *probaton* are scribal attempts to introduce a more common word. Yet, while it is understandable that a scribe would replace *probation* by *probaton* in both verses, we find it more difficult to see why he would have done this in only one verse. We have followed Alexandrinus, and suggest that the readings in Vaticanus and in Sinaiticus are scribal attempts to bring conformity into the two verses. The versions show much variety, and we cannot be certain how literally they followed the variations of the Greek. Some Latin witnesses have one word in all three verses, corresponding to Codex Bezae which has *probaton* throughout. Other Latin witnesses and the Vulgate employ two nouns but not necessarily in the same pattern. The Syriac, Arabic, and Armenian witnesses tend to have three different nouns, with the last two using a word for "ram" (F. Macler, *Revue de l'Histoire des Religions* 98 [1928], 17–19). In any case, here too we are inclined to treat the variant Greek nouns as synonyms and the variation as stylistic, serving at most to emphasize that the flock includes all the faithful (Loisy, p. 524). Some have tried to interpret the three nouns as references to three different groups in the Church, for example, the three groups mentioned in I John ii 12–14, or (patristic interpretation) the laity, priests, and bishops. But the fact that there are possibly three words for sheep in 15–17 is no more significant than that there are three different words for fish in vss. 5–13 (*prosphagion, ichthys, opsarion*). Nor is there much plausibility in the thesis that the diminutives should be taken literally and thus there is a progression in the size of the sheep, for example, *arnion, probation, probaton* (Bernard), with the symbolic import that the flock includes the younger as well as the older, or those of newer and more tender faith as well as those of mature faith. The difficulty of evaluating the diminutives of NT Greek is notorious, and certainly there is nothing tender about *arnion*, if we may judge from Rev vi 16, xvii 14. Whatever diminutive force there may be is scarcely significant in reference either to the constitution of the flock or to the gentleness to be expected of the shepherd (*pace* Spicq, III, 236).

16. *A second time Jesus repeated.* Literally "he said to him again a second time." The somewhat tautological *palin deuteron* occurs also in iv 54 (see NOTE there); both it and its less awkward alternative *ek deuterou* (ix 24) occur in LXX. We find implausible the suggestion that *palin* refers to the asking again, while *deuteron* emphasizes that the request is in terms of *agapan* a second time. Such a thesis implies that the choice of the verb is important.

17. *For the third time Jesus asked.* While there was no article used with *deuteron*, "a second time," the definite article appears before *triton*, "the third time," indicating emphasis. Spicq, III, 234[4], wants to translate it "this third time," and to find the offense of the third request in the fact that this time Jesus has asked in terms of *philein*, even though Peter has already twice stated his love in terms of *philein*. Similarly Westcott, p. 303, comments that Jesus seems to be doubting Peter's human affection (*philein*) for him. The idea that the sadness is related to the change of verb goes as far back as Origen (*In Proverb.* VIII 17; PG 17:184CD). However, Gaechter, p. 329, insists more plausibly that the real stress is not on the use of *philein* but on the *to triton*: "Still a third time Jesus asked"—a translation that implies the synonymous character of the questions.

Peter was hurt. It is notable that after Peter is hurt, Jesus does not ask again—the scene is well constructed dramatically. Although the hurt is based on having been asked three times, some interpreters would trace Peter's sorrow also to the fact that by his denials he had given Jesus cause to doubt him. An interesting parallel appears in Mark xiv 72 and par. where, after the cockcrow that marks Peter's third denial, we are told that Peter wept (bitterly).

you know everything. The verb is *oida*, while *ginōskein* appears in the next clause: "you know well" (see NOTE on "you know that I love you" in 15). The "you" may be emphatic. What type of knowledge is attributed to the risen Jesus here? Even during the ministry John insists on Jesus' superhuman knowledge (ii 25), and in xvi 30 this is expressed in much the same language as here: "Now we know that you know everything." In the context of this scene as the rehabilitation of Peter after his denials of Jesus, some have thought that by these words Peter was acknowledging that Jesus knew prophetically that Peter would deny him three times before cockcrow (xiii 38). Or is Peter simply appealing to Jesus' thorough familiarity with him? He can say no more for himself: if Jesus does not know that Peter loves him, what can Peter say to assure him? As Lagrange, p. 530, remarks, such a protestation is mild for so ardent a character.

18. *Truly, I assure you.* Chapter xxi preserves the most Johannine of expressions, the double "Amen" (NOTE on i 51); of course, it is a stylistic trait that could easily be imitated. It was addressed to Peter in xiii 38 when Jesus predicted Peter's denials. Its use here has been cited as an argument for the close relationship between 15–17 and 18–23; yet there are instances in the Gospel of its being employed as a loose connective (NOTE on x 1).

were a young man . . . when you grow old. The same age contrast is found in Ps xxxvii 25. The comparative *neōteros*, "younger," is used; but because of both the traditional nature of the comparison and the looseness of koine Greek comparatives (ZGB, §150), we cannot determine from it much about Peter's age, other than that he is between early youth and old age. It is too much to conclude with Loisy, p. 525, that from the writer's point of view Peter was already old, but that the writer is trying to make allowance for the fictional setting of the saying when Peter was younger.

fasten your own belt. The verb *zōnnynai* or *zōnnyein* (BDF, §92), used twice in this verse, is literally "to gird," that is, to tie a belt or cincture around one's freeflowing clothes, so that one can move and act without encumbrance. Often it has the sense of getting dressed, but here a more literal rendition is desirable in order that the same verb can be applicable to the binding of an old man in line 6.

you will stretch out your hands, and another will fasten a belt around you and take you where you do not wish to go. A plural subject ("others") for the second and third clauses is found in a few witnesses. As Marrow points out, there are four items in the comparison: (a) Young—old; (b) Fastening your own belt—having it fastened by another; (c) Going—being taken; (d) Wherever you wish—to where you do not wish to go. For the stretching out of the old man's hands there is no contrasting action on the part of the youth. The language is very vague, for example, Schlatter, p. 371, holds that the outstretched arms refers to the position assumed in prayer; and many think that a more general statement about Peter's future has subsequently and *post eventum* been applied to Peter's death (vs. 19). In itself the comparison need imply no more than that, unlike a youth, an old man is helpless and needs to be dressed and led about by another (although the "where you do not wish to go" is awkward). Several scholars have raised the possibility that a well-known proverb or maxim underlies the Johannine comparison, e.g., "The young go where they choose; the old must permit themselves to be carried" (Cullmann, *Peter,* pp. 88–89). But what significance would such a contrast have had for Peter's future? Schwartz, p. 217, thinks that some type of emendation is necessary to get at the original meaning. He proposes this comparison: When you were young, you girded yourself and walked where you wished, but now I gird you and I will take you where I wish. The idea is that having been called to the apostolate in 15–17, Peter is no longer his own master and is to serve Jesus. Unwilling to resort to such a rewording, others think that the comparison predicts that when he is old Peter will follow Jesus in suffering and imprisonment (an ideal found, fittingly, in I Pet ii 21–23). The imagery of being fastened with a belt would be appropriate; for, when Jesus was arrested, he was bound (xviii 12, 24); and Agabus acted out the drama of binding his hands and feet with Paul's belt in order to predict Paul's arrest (Acts xxi 11–12).

It is clear that vs. 19 applies the comparison in 18 to Peter's death; and the phraseology "the sort of death by which Peter was to glorify God" refers, in particular, to death by martyrdom (see next NOTE). In John it is not unusual to find vague, obscure predictions by Jesus that could not be understood until after the event (ii 19, iii 14, xi 50). There is no good Synoptic parallel for a prediction about Peter's death, unless Luke xxii 33 be interpreted ironically as an unconscious prediction: "Lord, I am ready to go with you to prison and death." Many interpreters have proposed that, even more specifically, the Johannine comparison in 18 refers to death *by crucifixion.* The key clause for this interpretation is "You will stretch out your hands"; for OT passages referring to an extension of hands were interpreted by early Christian writers as prefiguring crucifixion (the *Epistle of Barnabas* xii 4, and the writings of Justin, Irenaeus, and Cyprian, as cited in Bernard, II, 709). That this symbolism was common outside Christian circles is suggested by Epictetus (*Discourses* III xxvi 22): "You have stretched yourself in the manner of those crucified." Unfortunately the idiomatic use of "being girded or fastened with a belt" as an allusion to the binding of a criminal is not attested, even though those who support the crucifixion interpretation have assumed that "another will fasten a belt around you and take you where you do not wish to go" is a reference to binding the criminal and taking him off to the place of execution. If this is so, the normal sequence of the execution procedure has been reversed in 18, since the crucifixion (stretching out of hands) is mentioned before the binding (fastening a belt). Bauer has tried to solve the problem by proposing that the stretching out of hands is not the actual crucifixion but the prisoner's extending his hands to be tied to the crossbeam that had to be carried to the place of execution. However, this explanation destroys the only part of the crucifixion symbolism for which we have some clear evidence. It is better to suggest that by a type of hysteron proteron the Johannine writer placed the stretching out of the hands first in order to call attention to it, precisely because it was the key to the whole interpretation. If vs. 18 does refer to Peter's crucifixion, it constitutes our earliest evidence for that incident. A reference to Peter's martyrdom is found in *I Clement* v 4, but the manner is not specified. The tradition of Peter's crucifixion next appears ca. A.D. 211 in Tertullian's *Scorpiace* xv; PL 2:151B, who says in obvious reference to John xxi 18: "Another fastened Peter with a belt when Peter was bound to the cross" (see also Eusebius *Hist.* II 25:5; GCS 9^1:176). The detail that Peter was crucified upside down, which Eusebius, *Hist.* III 1:2–3; GCS 9^1:188, seemingly attributes to Origen, is a later elaboration.

19. *indicated the sort of death by which Peter was to glorify God.* The last words echo Christian terminology for martyrdom or a death suffered for Christ's sake (see I Pet iv 16; *Martyrdom of Polycarp* xiv 3, xix 2); and many scholars, for example, Westcott, Loisy, think that nothing more specific is meant. The idea that 19 refers to crucifixion comes from the parallelism of this verse with xii 33 and xviii 32 where a similar expression ("indicated the sort of death he was to die") interprets the symbolism of Jesus' being lifted up from the earth as an allusion to his crucifixion.

"Follow me." Since the next verse seems to picture Jesus as walking along with Peter and the Beloved Disciple, the literal meaning of "follow" need not be excluded. However, the figurative dimensions of the Christian following are also meant, namely, following in discipleship and to death. See COMMENT.

20. *Then.* While the textual witnesses are about evenly divided about whether or not to read *de,* a "then" is implied by the flow of thought.

turned around. Four times elsewhere John employs the simple verb *strephein* (see i 38); here the compound *epistrephein* is used. Both verbs occur in Matthew and in Luke with about equal frequency.

was following. This is omitted in some textual witnesses. It is probably Jesus rather than Peter whom the Beloved Disciple is following; but we doubt that the writer means to imply that the Beloved Disciple is already doing spontaneously what Peter has to be told to do. A fortiori we see here no innuendo that the Beloved Disciple is also following Jesus to death (Barrett,

p. 488). Bultmann, p. 553[5], is right in his contention that too much force should not be given to "following," for it has been inserted chiefly to supply an antecedent for the relative clause. There is no play on the idea that both Peter and the Beloved Disciple were following; the contrast is that Peter is to follow Jesus while the Beloved Disciple is to remain. In picturing the scene, we are to imagine that, while Jesus has told Peter to follow, here is the Beloved Disciple coming along as well; and so naturally Peter asks about him. Loisy, p. 525, comments that both Luke and John think of the risen Jesus as acting in the same way as he did during the ministry, walking along with his disciples.

(*the one who had leaned back against Jesus' chest during the supper and said, "Lord, who is the one who will betray you?"*). This reference is a mosaic from xiii 2 ("during supper"); xiii 21 ("Jesus declared, 'One of you will betray me' "); and especially xiii 25 (the disciple whom Jesus loved "leaned back against Jesus' chest and said to him, 'Lord, who is it?' "). Parenthetical reminders are very Johannine (see NOTE on xix 39); yet it is curious that the identification is supplied with the *second* mention of the Beloved Disciple instead of in xxi 7. Is this a sign that the redactor had a freer hand in 20–23 than he had in 1–13?

21. *Seeing.* The verb here is *eidein;* in 20 ("noticed") it was *blepein.* We find no particular distinction (vol. 29, pp. 501–2).

"*But . . . what about him?*" The Greek *houtos de tí* is elliptical (BDF, §299[2]); commentators supply various verbs, for example, "is to become of him" (*ginetai*—Lagrange).

22. *Suppose.* Literally "If"; BDF, §373[1], points out that such a conditional clause could point to something that is expected to happen in the future, but the writer rejects that interpretaion in vs. 23.

would like. It is difficult to be certain whether *thelein* here has the simple connotation of "desire" (so our translation) or the more sovereign implication of "purpose, will," for it is the verb used to express God's will.

to remain. The verb *menein* can mean "to stay alive," as in I Cor xv 6, and that is the idea here; but it is uncertain whether some of the Johannine theological meaning of *menein* (vol. 29, pp. 510–12) is applicable—"stay alive united to me in love." E. Schwartz, ZNW 11 (1910), 97, proposed the adventurous thesis that *menein* means "to remain in the grave," that the saying originally had nothing to do with the Disciple's not dying, and that vs. 23 is a complete misinterpretation.

until I come. Even without the evidence of vs. 23, this is scarcely a reference to Jesus' coming in death, for every Christian must remain until Jesus visits him in death. Though Marrow suggests the possibility of hyperbole ("Suppose I want this disciple to live forever"), most commentators find in this saying an expectation that Jesus' second coming would happen within a short time after the resurrection. The word *heōs*, translated "until," can also mean "while" (so J. Huby, *Revue apologétique* 39 [1924–25], 688–89; but see BDF, §383[1]); and so some would translate "while I go" (all the time of my departure) or "while I am coming" (Westcott, p. 305: the coming is a slow and continuous realization). Such translations may be motivated by a desire to avoid imputing any mistake about the second coming.

how does that concern you? Literally "what to you?"; this expression, *tí pros* with a pronoun is classical (BDF, §127[3]) and is akin to the expression used in ii 4 (which lacked the *pros*). It is also used in Matt xxvii 4 where, after Judas accuses himself of guilt in betraying Jesus, the high priests respond, "What is that to us?"

Your concern is to follow me. Literally "You follow me." In the similar command in 19 the Greek pronoun "you" is not used, so that its appearance here is emphatic, by way of contrasting Peter with the Beloved Disciple who will not follow Jesus to death in the same way that Peter will follow.

23. *This is how the word got around.* Literally "So this word went out"; there is a similar phrasing in Mark i 28 ("The report [*akoē*] went out"), and some think of it as an Aramaism. *Logos*, "word," is often used for a saying of Jesus in John (ii 22, iv 50, etc.). In line with the thesis explained in the NOTE on "to remain" in 22, Schwartz thinks that this quasi-parenthetical explanation is a late addition to the Gospel. There is no textual evidence to support his contention, and the verse was already known to Tertullian (*De anima* L; PL 2:735B).

the brothers. In xx 17 we saw this term applied to the immediate disciples of Jesus, because they would be begotten as God's children through the gift of the Spirit and thus become Jesus' brothers. Here it is applied to the Christians of the Johannine community (probably with the same theological understanding), a usage attested also in III John 5, and widely in the NT (some fifty-seven times in Acts; Matt v 22–24, xviii 15, etc.).

was not going to die. Imaginative traditions grew up about John, identified as the Beloved Disciple, for instance, that he has been wandering through the world throughout the centuries, or that he sleeps in his grave at Ephesus and the movement of the earth's surface above it attests to his breathing (Augustine *In Jo.* cxxiv 2; PL 35:1970).

As a matter of fact. The *de* (well attested but not certain) has an unusual position for Johannine Greek (Abbott, JG, §2075), and we have given it force. The Byzantine tradition and some OL mss. read *kai* instead. Reflective comments are not unusual in John (ii 22, xii 16).

[*how does that concern you*]. This is found in the best textual witnesses but perhaps by scribal imitation of 22.

COMMENT

"Do you love me?"—Peter's Rehabilitation (vss. 15–17)

In §71 we proposed the thesis that one of the two narratives that were combined to compose vss. 1–14 concerned the first appearance of the risen Jesus to Peter and that this narrative concluded with the rehabilitation of Peter and his being accorded a place of authority in the Christian community (pp. 1083–84 above). The Johannine form of this rehabilitation and commission is found in a dramatic form in vss. 15–17 —a form that may represent a considerable development of the dialogue original to the scene, especially in the adoption of a threefold pattern of question, answer, and response, a pattern that may reflect liturgical influence. It is interesting to note that while for different reasons neither

Bultmann nor Grass thinks that the connection of 15–17 to 1–14 is original, both agree that 15–17 reproduces traditional material and is not the creation of the redactor. (Bultmann thinks that the attachment of 15–17 caused the artificial emphasis on Peter in the narrative of 1–14; Grass thinks that the original presence of Peter in 1–14 caused the addition of 15–17 at the end.) The association of shepherd imagery with Peter is found independently in I Pet v 1–4.

Most commentators have found in Jesus' thrice-repeated question "Do you love me?" and in Peter's threefold "You know that I love you" a symbolic undoing of Peter's threefold denial of Jesus. Consequently, they have seen in 15–17 Peter's rehabilitation to discipleship after his fall. (It is better to speak of rehabilitation to discipleship than to apostleship: he was a disciple before; now he is rehabilitated as a disciple and becomes an apostle—see NOTE on ii 2.) Jesus' question would be meant to establish that Peter has the devoted love that is of the essence of discipleship. Peter's repentance would be implicit in his pathetic insistence on his love and in the anguish that the thrice-repeated question causes him (vs. 17). Instead of boasting that he loves Jesus more than others (15), a chastened Peter rests his case on Jesus' knowledge of what is in his heart (17).

Spitta, Goguel, and Bultmann are among those who do not interpret the scene as a rehabilitation. Bultmann, p. 551[8], points to the fact that there is no other real trace in the NT of the idea that Peter underwent rehabilitation. However, this is scarcely probative precisely because, outside of John xxi, the story of the first appearance of Jesus to Peter has been preserved only partially and in scattered fragments. Moreover, if we are right in contending that Luke v 1–11 is one of these fragments, then Peter's "Depart from me, for I am a sinful man, O Lord" (v 8) and Jesus' "Do not be afraid; henceforth you will catch men" (v 10) *may* be interpreted as a scene of repentance, forgiveness, and rehabilitation. The same may be said of Peter's cry, "Lord, save me," and Jesus' response, "O man of little faith, why did you doubt?", as Jesus saves Peter in Matt xiv 30–31. A rehabilitation may also be hinted at in Luke xxii 31–34 where, in the context of a reference to Peter's denials, Jesus predicts that when Peter has *turned again,* he will strengthen his brethren. In addition, there is some internal evidence in xxi that supports the idea of a rehabilitation after Peter's fall. The reference to a charcoal fire in xxi 9 recalls the fact that there was a charcoal fire in the courtyard scene where Peter denied Jesus (xviii 18). We do not rely too strongly on the argument that there were three denials in xviii and there are three questions and answers in xxi, but in fact these are the only groups of three related to Peter in the Fourth Gospel. In xxi 19, 22 Peter is twice commanded to follow Jesus in the context of a saying referring to Peter's death (18–19). This is almost a counterpart of the dialogue associated with Jesus' prediction of Peter's threefold denial in xiii 36–38. There, in reference to his own death, Jesus had said, "Where I am going, you cannot follow me now; but you will follow me later." Peter had protested, "Why can't I follow you now? I will lay down my life for you." To this Jesus had replied that, instead of dying for him, Peter would thrice deny him. In ch. xxi, if we look on 15–17 as rehabilitating Peter, then Jesus predicts Peter's death and urges Peter to follow him even to the point of this death (crucifixion?). At last Peter's words in xiii 37 will come true: he will lay down his life for Jesus.

Perhaps we should mention Glombitza's theory, art. cit., that when Jesus invited Peter along with the other disciples to the meal in xxi 12, he offered a gesture of friendship that supposes or involves forgiveness. While there may be some truth in the idea that the question about Peter's love should not be divorced from the background of the meal as a gesture of friendship, we are hesitant about associating forgiveness with the meal; it seems too subtle an allusion. Moreover, in the history of the composition of the chapter the meal originally belonged to another story different from that of the appearance to Peter, and Peter's role in the meal remains too insignificant to constitute a rehabilitation corresponding to Peter's open denial of Jesus.

Some who interpret Gospel scenes psychologically find it petty and even harsh that Jesus would challenge Peter's love three times in order to remind him that he had denied Jesus three times. If one accepts this dubious approach, one would have to be consistent by pointing out that Peter's denials are not presented as occurring by surprise or in a moment of weakness, but as foretold and spread out over a period of time, and thus reflective of radical weakness. Moreover, Jesus shows himself merciful: despite Peter's betrayal, once Peter professes his love, Jesus grants him a position of trust and authority. But certainly a better approach is to eschew psychological speculation and to settle for the emphasis of the text itself. Only indirectly does 15–17 refer to Peter's denials and rehabilitation; the direct import of the threefold question and answer is not so much that Jesus doubts Peter but that Peter's love for Jesus is earnest.

"Feed my lambs"—Peter's Commission (vss. 15–17)

The three questions and answers about love are accompanied by a thrice-repeated command that Peter should feed or tend the sheep. It is usually assumed that the command is given three times by way of artistic style to match the three questions and answers, the number of which was determined by the three denials. However, Gaechter, art. cit., makes an interesting case for considering the threefold character of the command separately. He gives examples, ancient and modern, of the Near Eastern custom of saying something three times before witnesses in order to solemnize it, especially in the instance of contracts that confer rights and of legal dispositions. On this juridical and cultural analogy Gaechter proposes that the threefold character of Jesus' command lends a special authoritativeness and emphasis to Peter's role as shepherd (so also Bultmann, p. 551[5]).

Is this command to be interpreted as the equivalent of the apostolic mission conferred on the other disciples in the post-resurrectional appearances of the various Gospels, or are we dealing here with an authoritative commission peculiar to Peter? In the past the answer to this question has been colored by the dispute between Roman Catholics and Protestants or Orthodox over the authority of the Pope which presupposes Peter's special authority in the early Church. Today there is greater tendency to try to interpret Scripture independently of later doctrinal disputes, and it is no longer a peculiarly Roman Catholic thesis that Peter had a special role in NT times. Two Protestant scholars of such different persuasion as Cullmann and Bultmann are quite firm in interpreting the command of 15–17 in terms of an authoritative commission for Peter, a view already espoused by Von Harnack, W. Bauer, Loisy, and others. In fact, Bultmann, p. 552, argues that the commission to Peter represents an earlier stratum of Johannine thought than that represented by the larger mission to the disciples in xx 21.

Personally, we do not think that the line between apostolic mission and special authoritative commission need be drawn so exclusively. Cullmann, *Peter*, p. 65, is perceptive: "The command to feed the sheep includes two activities which we have shown to be the successive expressions of Peter's apostolate: leadership of the Primitive Church in Jerusalem and missionary preaching." In other words, there is both general apostolic mission or discipleship and special authoritative commission in the command to Peter. For instance, there is a strong emphasis on *apostolic mission* in the context that precedes (the symbolism of the catch of fish), while, in the context that follows, the twice-repeated instruction "Follow me" (19 and 22) is the language of discipleship (John i 37, 43, x 27, xii 26; Rev xiv 4; Mark i 18, ii 14; etc.). If we are right in thinking that much of Luke v 1–11 is a parallel of John xxi and was originally part of a post-resurrectional appearance to Peter, it is interesting to observe that the scene ends on the note of Peter and his companions following Jesus. This note may have belonged to the call of the first disciples, but it can serve double duty in expressing the theme of apostolic mission. In particular, N. Arvedson, as reported in NTA 3 (1958–59), #77, detects a parallelism between John xxi 15 ff. and the prescription for discipleship in Mark viii 34 and par.: "If anyone wishes to come after me, let him deny himself, take up his cross, and follow me" (see also vol. 29, p. 475). Arvedson suggests that the love of Jesus demanded of Peter in xxi 15–17 is equivalent to denial of self; the carrying of the cross is hinted at in the prophecy of Peter's death in 18–19; and the command to follow is made explicit in 19 and 22. We may add in conclusion that the wide expanse that is often a part of the apostolic mission in post-resurrectional appearances may be implicit in the command to Peter because of the Johannine notion that the sheep herd contains sheep of more than one fold (x 16).

If there is an element of apostolic mission or discipleship in the command to Peter to feed or tend the sheep, there is also and even more clearly an *authoritative commission*. The imagery of the shepherd from Babylonian times (Hammurabi) down through the OT period involves authority. Sheehan, *art. cit.*, illustrates the theme of authoritatively tending the flock of the people in the case of the Judges (I Chron xvii 6) and of David and Saul (II Sam v 2). Tending the flock means ruling over it (see remarks on *poimainein* in NOTE on "feed my lambs" in 15); and since God Himself is the shepherd of Israel (Gen xlix 24; Hos iv 16; Jer xxxi 10; Isa xl 11; Ps lxxx 2[1]), this rule over the flock of Israel is a divinely delegated authority. Sheehan, p. 27, sums up the situation thus: "The figure [of the shepherd] is used in situations which emphasize that Israel's leaders share in divine authority and act as God's delegates in the use of that authority." Besides the OT use of shepherd imagery we may now call upon background contemporary with the NT, namely, the Qumran use of this imagery to describe the task of the authoritative $m^e baqq\bar{e}r$ or overseer (CD xiii 9–10) who had the power to examine, teach, and correct the members of the community. In the light of all this, it is quite understandable that John xxi 15–17 has been interpreted as the granting to Peter of some of both the responsibility for the flock and the authority over it that Jesus himself possessed as the model shepherd (ch. x). In the post-resurrectional appearance of xx 21 we found Jesus, the one sent by the Father, sending the disciples even as he himself was sent; similarly in this appearance we find Jesus, the model shepherd, making Peter a shepherd to tend Jesus' flock. It is true that a few scholars, for example, Loisy, p. 523, have questioned the relationship of xxi 15–17 to the shepherd imagery of ch. x and have claimed that the redactor was more dependent on the Synoptic imagery of the shepherd; but Cassian, *art. cit.*, shows the close relationship of the two Johannine passages, which are the only instances of shepherd imagery in the Fourth Gospel. It is particularly significant that a reference to Peter's death (xxi 18–19) immediately follows the command to tend the sheep; for among all the NT uses of shepherd imagery, only John x specifies that one of the functions of the model shepherd is to lay down his life for his sheep (vol. 29, p. 398).

Further support for interpreting xxi 15–17 in terms of Peter's authority is found in the fact that it is often regarded as a parallel to Matt xvi 16b–19, which, as we saw above (pp. 1088–89), may have come from the same first post-resurrectional appearance to Peter, an appearance that was possibly the cause of Peter's being listed first among the apostles. In Matt xvi 19 the imagery is that of a gift of keys that makes Peter the prime minister of the kingdom; this is not too far ideologically from the imagery of being made shepherd of the flock.

What type of authority does Peter possess as shepherd? Many commentators, for example, Spicq, III, 233–36, propose that Jesus first questioned Peter's love because Peter's task as shepherd would have to be exercised in love for the flock. Ambrose, *In Luc.* x 175; PL 15:1848B, remarks: "He was leaving Peter to us as the vicar of his love." Spicq observes that Jesus entrusts those whom he loves to one who loves him, and Peter's pastoral care is the demonstration of Peter's love. However, while no one questions that pastoral care involves love, we are not certain that this can be derived from the connection in 15–17 between the question about Peter's love and the command to tend the sheep. The love demanded from Peter is for Jesus and not explicitly for the flock; it is a love of total attachment and exclusive service (cf. Deut vi 5, x 12–13). The logical connection with the command given to Peter is that, if Peter is so devoted to Jesus, then Jesus can entrust his flock to Peter with the assurance that Peter will comply with Jesus' will (cf. Isa xliv 28). The threefold command to tend the sheep puts less emphasis on the prerogatives accruing to Peter than on his duties: it stresses his obligation to care for the sheep. In the description of the shepherd in ch. x there is no emphasis on the shepherd's superior position but rather on his familiarity with the sheep and his total dedication to the flock even to the point of death. And certainly this would be in harmony with the OT prophetic attitude toward the shepherd-rulers of Israel: there is bitter condemnation of those shepherds who make the flock serve them, and there is a yearning for shepherds after God's own heart who spend themselves with wisdom and devotion for the flock (Ezek xxxiv; Jer iii 15). Whether I Peter was written by the apostle or some unknown Petrine disciple, the Peter who speaks therein of shepherding is not disloyal to the Johannine ideal. He exhorts his fellow elders: "Tend the flock of God that is in your care, exercising your role of overseer [*episkopein*] not by constraint but willingly, as God would have it, not for base gain but eagerly, not as domineering over those in your charge but by being examples to the flock" (I Pet v 2–3). Furthermore, we note that in John xxi 15–17 the fact that the command to tend the sheep follows the rehabilitation of Peter makes it clear that Peter's being made shepherd is not because of a special worthiness on his part. The choice of Peter is a demonstration of God's working through the weak things of this world. (The other two Gospel passages that have reference to Peter's special position, Matt xvi 16b–19 and Luke xxii 31–32, are in the context of a rebuke to Peter for his faults.)

As shepherd, Peter's authority is not absolute. Jesus is the model shepherd to whom the Father has given the sheep and no one can take them from him. They remain his even when he entrusts their care to Peter: "Feed *my* sheep." Augustine, *In Joh.* cxxiii 5; PL 35:1967, paraphrases: "Tend my sheep as mine, not as yours." Thus, one cannot think of Peter's replacing Jesus as the shepherd of the sheep. Once again I Peter (v 2–4) is harmonious with Johannine thought about shepherding: the flock of God has been given into the charge of Christian elders who are shepherds over it, but Jesus remains the chief shepherd (see also I Pet ii 25).

Is Peter the only shepherd whom Jesus appoints? Clearly elsewhere in the NT the shepherd imagery is applied to various types of Christian leaders (Matt xviii 12–14; Acts xx 28–29; I Pet v 1–5), but we are concerned with the import of John xxi 15–17. Some writers have claimed that Peter is the representative of all the disciples and that the command to tend the sheep, addressed to him, is meant for them as well. We doubt this because of our reconstruction of the history of the chapter where 15–17 serves as the conclusion of an appearance to Peter, accompanied only by some anonymous fishermen, an appearance that is distinct from the appearance to the Twelve. Even in the mixture of appearances that now exists in ch. xxi, while the other disciples figure to some extent in the fishing scene and symbolically become fishers of men, only Peter is addressed in the language of shepherding. The disciples have faded into the background and are mentioned only *by contrast* to Peter: "Do you love me *more than these?*" In fact, there is no suggestion even that the Beloved Disciple is a shepherd. It would seem that the ideal of x 16 is carried over into xxi: one sheep herd, one shepherd.

Yet, if we think that only Peter is given the command to tend the flock, we do not agree with those who go to the other extreme by interpreting 15–17 to mean that Peter is explicitly made shepherd over the other disciples or over the other members of the Twelve. The sheep mentioned in 15–17 are undoubtedly the Christian believers brought into the fold by the missionary efforts symbolized by the catch of fish. It is very doubtful that John meant to include the missionaries in the image of the flock. Like Matt xvi 16b–19, this passage concerns the relation of Peter to the Church at large, not interrelationships between Peter and the other disciples in matters of authority. The comparative phrase in "Do you love me more than these?" cannot be used to establish that because Peter loved more (which is uncertain in itself), he had more authority. The First Vatican Council in 1870 cited John xxi 15–17 along with Matt xvi 16–19 in relation to its dogmatic definition that "Peter the apostle was constituted by Christ the Lord as *chief of all the apostles* and as visible head of the Church on earth" (DB, §§3053–55; italics ours). This is often cited as one of the few examples where the Roman Catholic Church has solemnly committed itself about the literal meaning of a biblical text, that is, about what the author meant when he wrote it. However, this evaluation has been challenged by V. Betti, *La costituzione dommatica 'Pastor aeternus' del Concilio Vaticano I* (Rome, 1961), p. 592: "The interpretation of these two texts as proof of the two dogmas mentioned [Petrine primacy; Roman succession to that primacy] does not fall *per se* under dogmatic definition—not only because no mention is made of them in the canon [the exact formulation of the dogma, distilled from the discussion], but also because there is no trace of a desire in the

Council to give an authentic interpretation of them in this sense." If Betti
is right, Vatican I was not necessarily defining for Catholics the limited
meaning the biblical passage had for its author at the moment it was
written, but rather the broader meaning it had and has for the Church in
the light of a living tradition and ecclesiastical history. In our judgment,
exegetes who think that Peter had authority over the other disciples
cannot conclude this from John xxi 15–17 *taken alone* but must bring
into the discussion the larger NT background of Peter's activities.

How enduring was Peter's role as shepherd of the flock? Cullmann,
Peter, p. 214, argues from the mention of Peter's death in 18–19 that this
role must, at maximum, have been limited to Peter's lifetime. Benoit,
Passion, p. 307, argues that if Jesus felt the role of shepherd to be so
important that he appointed Peter as a vicar-shepherd, by analogy Peter
at death would, in turn, have had to pass on the role to another. Obviously
these opinions are shaped by disputes over the Roman claim to succession,
a question that goes beyond the limited horizon of the biblical text.
A logical argument based on the implications of figurative language is
always problematic. A more fruitful area of discussion, into which we
have no plans to enter, would be the question of why it was important
for the Johannine redactor (and, respectively, for Matthew and Luke)
to remind the community that the role of pastoral authority was given
to Peter, when presumably Peter had already been dead for twenty
or thirty years. Was this just an interesting fact, or did Peter's pastoral
authority have some continuing importance?

Predictions of the Fate of Peter and of the Beloved Disciple (vss. 18–23)

Were vss. 18–23 also part of the appearance of Jesus to Peter, or have
they been subsequently added? Some scholars would regard at least
19b ("After these words, Jesus told him, 'Follow me'") as originally belonging to 15–17 and thus to the appearance narrative. But Bultmann, p. 552[4],
is representative of a wider view when he classifies the whole of 18–23 as
an addition. Our other Gospel evidence pertinent to the appearance of
Jesus to Peter has no mention of the death of Peter, such as now found
in John xxi 18–19 (unless it be the idea in Matt xvi 18 that Hades [death]
will not prevail over the Church of which Peter is the foundation).
Probably, the fact that 15–17 deals with Peter's future made appropriate
the addition of an independent saying concerning Peter's death. We have
pointed out above (p. 1112) that a connection can also be made between
the theme of Peter's rehabilitation after the three denials and that of his
following Jesus to death. Peter's death is the proof of the sincerity of his
threefold profession of love for Jesus, for "No man can have greater love
than this: to lay down his life for those he loves" (xv 13).

Is the connection between 18–19 and 20–23 original? The little
drama in vs. 20 sews together two sayings about the fate of Peter and

that of the Beloved Disciple; but the suture seems artificial, for the sudden appearance of the Beloved Disciple in Jesus' following is awkward. (Perhaps the chain of thought we have just mentioned is still at work: it was seemingly the Beloved Disciple ["another disciple" in xviii 15] who introduced Peter into the high priest's palace where Peter denied Jesus three times.) Since the Johannine writer is primarily interested in the problem of the death of the Beloved Disciple, the saying about Peter's death may have been inserted as a convenient transition to the more important saying about the Beloved Disciple. It is true that in the same scene Jesus could have discussed both deaths (in a type of "last testament" dealing with the fate of his followers—p. 600 above), but more likely two independent sayings transmitted in the Johannine tradition have been joined to each other and added to the post-resurrectional narrative.

Bultmann contends that the material in 18–23 was composed by the redactor. In our judgment, while the redactor may be responsible for the joining of the sayings, the sayings themselves are old, for neither lends itself easily to the interpretation that has been given to it. In a NOTE on 18 we showed the difficulty of finding in the vague language of that verse the prediction of a martyr's death (or even crucifixion), as has been done in 19. Certainly, if the statement had been fashioned in the light of Peter's death, the wording would not have been so ambiguous. Similarly, in the case of vs. 22, the very fact that the writer claims the saying has been misunderstood makes it incredible that the saying had been recently invented, for then it would simply have been denied. Both of these sayings were well known and traditional and could not be reworded to favor the desired interpretations. The saying about the Beloved Disciple may represent a specification of a type of general saying found in the Synoptic Gospels, predicting that the coming of the Son of Man would take place before the generation of Jesus' disciples had died out; for example, Matt xvi 28: "There are some standing here who will not taste death before they see the Son of Man coming in his kingdom" (also Matt x 23; Mark xiii 30, xiv 62; I Thess iv 15). In App. V we shall stress that the death of the apostolic generation caused a crisis in the parousiac expectations of the Church, and for the Johannine community the Beloved Disciple seems to have been the last of the apostolic generation.

If the basic sayings in 18 and 22 are old, by the time the redactor was writing probably both Peter and the Beloved Disciple were dead, and this fact colors the interpretations given to the sayings. In 19 it is clear that the redactor knows that Peter has died a martyr's death and perhaps even that Peter was crucified on Vatican hill (for the evidence for the latter detail, see Cullmann, *Peter*, p. 156; D. W. O'Connor, *Peter in Rome* [New York: Columbia University, 1969]). It is more difficult to be certain that the wording of 23 shows that the Beloved Disciple was dead. Since the redactor is so firm in denying that Jesus meant that the Beloved Disciple would not die before the second coming, it is reasonable to assume that this interpretation has been rendered impossible by the Disciple's death. But Westcott, Zahn, Tillmann, Bernard, Hoskyns, and Schwank are among the many scholars who do not agree. A variety of other explanations are offered. Goguel, p. 17[16], theorizes that the Beloved Disciple may have left the place where he was living and gone away; then when nothing was heard from him, speculation could have arisen that he was hidden away until the second coming. Many have suggested that the Disciple was on the point of death. Others have doubted even this and thought that as the Beloved Disciple was getting old, he wanted to stop a rumor that was spreading and to clarify a saying of Jesus. In our opinion, these theories do not do justice to the sense of crisis in 23. It is hard to believe that the writer would go to such trouble, even to employing a type of casuistry, if there was still a possibility that the Beloved Disciple would live to the parousia. Moreover, the suggestion that the Beloved Disciple was not dead is often part of the thesis that the Beloved Disciple was the evangelist or the author of the Gospel, including ch. xxi—a thesis that we regard as indefensible on other grounds (vol. 29, p. c).

G. M. Lee, JTS N.S. 1 (1950), 62–63, has shown that the application of common sense to vss. 20–23 greatly enhances what we know about the Beloved Disciple. In the mind of the redactor and of the community for whom he wrote the Beloved Disciple was a real person; he may have been idealized but he was not an abstract ideal or a pure symbol, for one does not fret about the death of an idea. Bultmann, p. 554, admits that this was the mentality of the redactor but thinks that the redactor was mistaken in identifying some long-lived figure of importance as the Beloved Disciple. Such a thesis is tenable only if we suppose that the redactor knew little about the Gospel, that he had no association with the evangelist or with other Johannine disciples, that he was writing for a community unfamiliar with the real thought of the evangelist, and that he was artificially creating a crisis about the death of a man who was not important to the Johannine community (unless one wants to suppose that there really was no Johannine community or that the redactor was a deliberate falsifier). It is far less demanding on one's credibility to think that the redactor reports a historical datum when he implies that the community was disturbed by the death of their great master since they had expected him not to die. The fact that the community thought there was a statement of Jesus applicable to the Beloved Disciple means that he had to be a man of whom Jesus could have made such a statement and, therefore, one of Jesus' companions. If he had lived to an advanced age when all the other well-known disciples of Jesus were dead, the idea that he was not to die could have gained verisimilitude. We have mentioned in vol. 29, p. xcv, the thesis that Lazarus was the Beloved Disciple, and Drumwright, p. 132, points out that it might very well have been expected that Lazarus would not die again. However, by putting the Beloved Disciple in the boat with Peter in xxi 7, the redactor indicates that he identifies the Disciple with one of the six companions of Peter mentioned in vs. 2, and, more specifically, with one of the sons of Zebedee or one of the "two other disciples," unless these two groups are the same (NOTE on 2). Loisy, Schwartz, and others are wrong, however, when they claim that it was a major purpose of the redactor to identify the Beloved Disciple with John, son of Zebedee, for obviously no well-defined identification is made. Our own tendency is to assume that the information about the Beloved Disciple given us by the redactor is true, since we think of the redactor as a Johannine disciple (see also pp. 1127–29 below); and so we cannot escape the implication that a venerable apostolic figure has stood in intimate relationship to the community for whom the Fourth Gospel was written.

We must now turn to vss. 20–21, the connecting verses between the sayings about Peter and about the Beloved Disciple. We have already indicated that we think of this as an artificial connection. Nevertheless, because of the question that Peter asks about the Beloved Disciple in 21 and the implicit rebuff that he receives from Jesus in 22, many scholars have detected here a rivalry about the importance of the two men. Sometimes the rivalry is seen in terms of the deaths they died. Bacon, p. 72, contends that Peter would have been honored as a martyr who gave "red" witness to Christ, and that the Johannine writer may have wanted to insist that the Disciple, who did not die a martyr's death, was a witness too (the theme of his witness appears in 24). To do this the redactor records that even as Jesus prophesied Peter's death as a martyr, so he made a prediction about the Disciple's destiny. Accordingly, the Disciple's death was just as much a part of Jesus' plan as was Peter's death; both gave glory to God but in a different way.

Other commentators carry the rivalry beyond a comparison of the type of death the two men died and think that the role of the Beloved Disciple in 20–23 must be compared not only with 18–19 but also with 15–17 and Peter's role as shepherd. For instance, Bultmann, p. 555, proposes that the main theme of 15–23 is to show that the ecclesiastical authority of Peter was passed on after his death to the Beloved Disciple. Agourides, p. 132 (also "Peter and John in the Fourth Gospel," StEv IV, 3–7), thinks that the figure of the Beloved Disciple counteracts an exaggerated honor or authority being attributed to Peter within certain Christian circles in the Province of Asia. This is a popular thesis, almost to the point where the Beloved Disciple becomes the ancestral hero of all subsequent protests against the encroachments of the Roman See. On the other hand, but with the same underlying resentment, Loisy, p. 524, argues that the redactor, unlike the evangelist, has come into contact with Roman propaganda and pressure and accordingly has presented the Beloved Disciple as subordinate to Peter. Many Roman Catholic scholars think that ch. xxi was written by a disciple who had to admit honestly that his master, the Beloved Disciple, was not the dominating figure in the Church.

Schwank, "Christi," p. 540, proposes that the passage was written while the Disciple was still alive in order to teach the Johannine community that their affection for their master should not blind them to the fact that it is to Peter and to his successors that the authority of the shepherd has been given. Schwank wonders whether the action of Clement of Rome (counted as the third Pope) in writing to the church at Corinth ca. A.D. 95 had not provoked a discussion requiring this clarification.

We are dubious about any extension of the shepherd question into 18–23. Cullmann, *Peter*, p. 31, is right when he claims that in John uniquely important roles have been assigned both to Peter and to the Beloved Disciple, but that the respective roles are different and it is Peter who is the shepherd. To make Peter's question about why the Beloved Disciple was following Jesus (vs. 21) the basis of a whole theory of conflicting authority is extravagant. We have already rejected a similarly exaggerated theory of conflict in relation to xx 3–10 (pp. 1006–7 above). There may be an echo here of the proud desire of the Johannine community to show that the natural death of their special apostle was no less a witness to Jesus than Peter's martyrdom. The constant association of the Beloved Disciple with Peter here and elsewhere may well be meant to emphasize that in his own way the Disciple was no less important than Peter, the best known of the original companions of Jesus. At most we may hear an echo of the not unfriendly rivalry of primitive Christian communities, associating their history with prominent figures of the early days about whom they boasted. But there is not a single incident in this Gospel where the Beloved Disciple is presented as a figure with ruling authority over the Church or over a church; his authority is as a witness. In our opinion, all attempts to interpret the presence of the Beloved Disciple alongside Peter in this scene as part of an apologetic *against or for* the claims of Petrine or Roman primacy are eisegesis.

Before we pass on to the conclusion of the Epilogue, there are a few scattered observations to be made about points in 18–23. The statement in 19 about "the sort of death by which Peter was to glorify God" is, as mentioned, standard Christian language for martyrdom. Nevertheless, it has a certain kinship with Johannine thought about the death of Jesus which glorified Jesus himself and showed God's glory to men (vii 39, xii 23, xvii 4–5). By imitating Jesus in following him to death (even to the death of the cross), Peter acknowledges God's glory. There has been considerable speculation about Peter's motivation in 21 when he asks about the Beloved Disciple. Schwank, "Christi," pp. 538–39, thinks of Peter as showing concern for his friend and wanting Jesus to include the Disciple in his plans for the future. But in the light of the seeming rebuke in 22, most scholars have thought that Peter was jealous or imprudently inquisitive. B. Weiss interprets Jesus' answer to Peter as an indication that Peter's question was unwarranted or meddlesome, but not blameworthy or culpable. P. N. Bushill, ET 47 (1935–36), 523–24, thinks of Peter's question merely as an attempt to shift a conversation that has become too personal in its reference to death (compare the Samaritan woman's maneuver in iv 19–20 after Jesus has spoken about her "husband"). Perhaps we should not take such psychological speculations too seriously if the whole pattern of question and answer is a secondary suture between independent sayings about Peter and the Beloved Disciple. It is interesting that Smith, pp. 236–37, following E. Schweizer, interprets vs. 22 as directed to the Christian at large: You are not to be concerned that you may die or suffer martyrdom while another lives until the parousia; your one calling is to follow me no matter where that following may lead you. It has been noted by Bernard, II, 711, that the risen Jesus' last words (vs. 22) are those of his directive to Peter: "Your concern is to follow me"; and after all, that is the essential precept of the Christian life. By way of inclusion between chs. xxi and i, we may observe that the disciples began their contact with Jesus on the note of following him (i 37), and their contact with him is closed on the same note.

Dodd, *Interpretation*, p. 431, remarks, "The naïve conception of Christ's second Advent in xxi 22 is unlike anything else in the Fourth Gospel." But is this conception so radically different from what is said in v 27–29 and xiv 3? Hoskyns, p. 559, thinks that despite the redactor's disclaimer in vs. 23, there may still be a valid aspect of the deathlessness of the Beloved Disciple: "Perhaps the opinion may be hazarded that the reader is meant to understand that the perfect discipleship of which the Beloved Disciple is the type and origin will never fail the Church." While Hoskyns' interpretation is not really warranted by the text, we shall stress in App. V that the Johannine answer to the void left by the death of the Beloved Disciple, the witness par excellence, is that the Paraclete who bore witness through and in him remains with all believers (xiv 17, xv 26–27).

[The Bibliography for this section is included in the Bibliography for the whole of ch. xxi, at the end of §73.]

73. THE (SECOND) CONCLUSION
(xxi 24–25)

XXI   24 It is this same disciple who is the witness for these things; it is he who wrote these things; and his testimony, we know, is true. 25 Still, there are many other things that Jesus did. Yet, were they ever to be written down in detail, I doubt that there would be room enough in the whole world for the books to record them.

NOTES

xxi 24. *who is the witness . . . it is he who wrote.* The best Greek textual witnesses coordinate a present and an aorist participle, literally, "who bears witness . . . and who wrote." The aorist "wrote" implies that the task has been completed; and perhaps in making the first verbal form past ("bore witness") the OS^{sin} may mean no more than that—yet the past tense could reflect the idea that the witness is dead (see pp. 1118–19 above). On the other hand, the present tense need not mean that he is still alive, but only that his witness is enshrined as a present reality in the Gospel he wrote.

Scholars are divided on how to interpret "wrote." F. R. Montgomery Hitchcock, JTS 31 (1930), 271–75, has argued strongly that the ancient evidence favors the implication that he wrote by his own hand. Bernard, II, 713, is one of the many who understand the verb in what we may call a moderate causative sense: "he had these things written," inasmuch as he dictated them to a scribe or, at least, carefully directed the writing. (The standard example for such a causative meaning is John xix 19, where it does not seem that Pilate wrote the charge against Jesus with his own hand—but even that is hard to prove.) Still others think that "wrote" can include authorship in a much more remote sense. G. Schrenk, *"graphō,"* TWNTE, I, 743, asks whether this verse of John "might not simply mean that the Beloved Disciple and his recollections stand behind this Gospel and are the occasion of its writing. This is a very possible view so long as we do not weaken unduly the second aspect. Indeed, it would be difficult to press the formula to imply more than an assertion of spiritual responsibility for what is contained in the book." Following the last interpretation, in our theory of the composition of the Gospel (vol. 29, pp. XXXIV–XXXIX) we have attributed only the first of five stages to the Beloved Disciple, namely, that he was the source of the historical tradition that has come into the Gospel.

these things. Dodd, "Note," suggests that this phrase refers to the words of Jesus in 20–23 and their correct interpretation, so that the writer is marshaling support for his contention that an inaccurate report has been spread among the brothers. However, Dodd allows the possibility that the whole of ch. xxi is included under the phrase, a view held by many of those who hold that the chapter was appended as a unit. A more widely held view is that vs. 24 is a type of colophon indicating the writer's outlook upon the authorship (in the broad sense) of the entire Gospel. Verse 25 would imply that the "these things" of 24 included all the recorded deeds performed by Jesus.

his testimony, we know, is true. Who is represented by the "we" in this affirmation? Dodd, "Note," is inclined to interpret it indefinitely, reducing "we know" to "as is well known" or "it is a matter of common knowledge." (By way of illustration he contrasts the similarly indefinite oidamen of John ix 31 with the definite hēmeis oidamen of ix 29, but we do not consider ix 31 a real parallel to the present passage.) However, most commentators attribute to "we" a definite reference. A common view in times past was that the Beloved Disciple himself (still alive) used the editorial "we." (Interestingly, Chrysostom read "I know"—probably taking oidamen as oida men, or else reading by harmonization with the use of "I" in the next verse.) Such a theory faces the serious objection that the Beloved Disciple would be referring to himself in the same short clause both in the third person singular ("his") and in the first person plural ("we"). Chapman, art. cit., has gathered impressive proof that the Johannine writers frequently employed the first person plural, especially in reference to witness or testimony; but he gives no example of its combination with a third person singular, as here. If the Beloved Disciple were speaking of himself in such a circumstance, we would expect something closer to what we find in xix 35: "He is telling what he knows to be true." An attempt to circumvent this objection has been to propose that the Beloved Disciple used the third person singular to express his personal witness, that is, what he saw or heard himself, but that he used the first person plural when he associated himself with others and became the spokesman for a collective witness. In the present instance it has been suggested that the Beloved Disciple was associating with himself either the Johannine community or the apostles of the Lord. The latter view (Hoskyns, pp. 559–60) echoes the tradition, found in the Muratorian fragment and Clement of Alexandria, that John the Beloved Disciple undertook to write on behalf of the other apostles who approved his work. Some would even specify that two apostles were involved with John in the "we" of this verse, namely, Andrew and Philip who appear several times in the Fourth Gospel. This tradition of apostolic approval, however, while it may indirectly contain an element of truth, namely, that several men were involved in the production of the Fourth Gospel, is too simplified and probably represents an imaginative attempt to apply to the Gospel the ideal of apostolic authorship.

We think it more realistic to exclude the Beloved Disciple from the "we" and to let him stand as the (deceased) object of the affirmation made by the "we." Among the possibilities for the "we" are the leaders of the Johannine community (sometimes called the Ephesian elders), the Johannine writers and preachers, and even the Johannine community itself which has heard the Gospel message many times. In evaluating these suggestions, we are hesitant about the concept that the "we" represents an authoritative group that did not take part in the writing but is now adding a seal of approval. We know of no early attestation of the practice of adding such colophons in Christian writing, at least before the 5th century. More likely the writer is part of the "we." It is notable that in III John 12, the Elder, who elsewhere writes as "I," says to Gaius whom he is addressing: "You know that *our* testimony is true"— seemingly because in this instance he speaks in a more representative capacity. According to our theory of Gospel composition (vol. 29, p. XXXVI) the "we" represents the Johannine writer responsible for the addition of ch. xxi and his fellow Johannine disciples. We do not find convincing the argument of Goguel and Bultmann that the "we" cannot represent a fixed group, since if they were unknown to the reader, it would do no good to mention them, and if they were known, there would be no need to mention them. Precisely because one of the Johannine writers had taken it upon himself to add material to an already written Gospel, it may have been quite appropriate for him and his fellow disciples to assure the readers that the new work was no less authoritative than the old and that the whole stemmed from the Beloved Disciple whose witness was true. Moreover, since the witness of the Beloved Disciple, taken alone, was not legally sufficient (see NOTE on v 31), the additional witness of the Johannine disciples gives status to the work.

The emphasis both on testimony (witness) and on its truth is characteristically Johannine. The word for "true" in the present verse is *alēthēs*, whereas in the parallel in xix 35 it was *alēthinos*. While there is a shade of distinction between the two words (vol. 29, pp. 499–501), it is not always preserved. Indeed, G. Kilpatrick, JTS 12 (1961), 272–73, sees the difference as grammatical: *alēthēs* is used predicatively, and *alēthinos* attributively. After vs. 24 a small group of cursive mss. of the Lake Family place the Story of the Adulteress (vol. 29, pp. 335–36).

25. The conjecture of some early scholars that this verse is an addition is noted in scholia preserved in a Greek commentary written before the 8th century (Chapman, pp. 386–87). Tischendorf thought that this verse was omitted by the original scribe of Codex Sinaiticus. However, ultra-violet examination of this codex after it was acquired by the British Museum in 1934 has clarified the situation (H. J. M. Milne and T. C. Skeat, *Scribes and Correctors of the Codex Sinaiticus* [London: British Museum, 1938], p. 12). At first the original scribe brought the Gospel to a close with vs. 24, as signified by a coronis (flourish of penmanship) and a subscription. But later the same scribe washed the vellum clean and added vs. 25, repeating the coronis and subscription in a lower position on the page. Was the omission in the first instance an act of carelessness or was the scribe copying from a ms. that did not have vs. 25 (which he subsequently got from another ms.)? Even if the latter is the case, the textual evidence for treating vs. 25 as a scribal gloss is very slim.

Still. The particle *de* is used here, whereas the parallel in xx 30 has *men oun*.

there are. This phrase is missing in some Western witnesses and Chrysostom.

many other things. Alla polla is awkward Greek; the expression in xx 30 is more graceful: *polla kai alla sēmeia*, "many other signs." Presumably, the conclusion in xx 30–31 (drawn from the Signs Source?) was the work of the evangelist, while this conclusion is the work of the redactor.

were they ever. Literally "which things if they were ever"; this construction involving the indefinite relative in the plural is not Johannine style, and the relation of the relative to the conditional clause that follows it is awkward (BDF, §294[5]).

in detail. Literally "one by one" (cf. BDF, §305); this distributive *kata* is not found elsewhere in John, except in the (non-Johannine) Story of the Adulteress.

I doubt. Literally "I do not think"; we understand the negative *oude* to modify the main verb rather than the infinitive of indirect discourse, "there would be room enough" (an infinitive would normally be negated by *mē*; BDF, §429). The verb *oimai* is used only here in John. If vss. 24 and 25 are by the same hand, the "I" of 25 may reflect a more personal comment than the "we" of 24, whether that "we" is editorial, collective, or general. Some remark that this is the only personal reflection of a Johannine writer in the Gospel, but the whole clause is primarily oratorical.

would be room enough. Seemingly *chōrēsein* is an instance of a future infinitive, extremely rare in the NT (BDF, §350); yet it could be an aorist infinitive with a present ending. Many of the Byzantine witnesses (followed by the Bible Societies' *Greek New Testament*) have corrected it to a regular aorist infinitive.

the whole world. Here simply the universe, rather than, as often in John (vol. 29, pp. 508–10), a sphere hostile to Jesus.

to record them. At the end of the verse the Byzantine textual tradition and the Vulgate have the liturgical addition "Amen."

COMMENT

Some scholars (Howard, Ruckstuhl, Wilkens) who attribute ch. xxi to the evangelist rather than to a redactor admit that vss. 24–25 were written by the redactor, in part because of the difficulty of the "we" in 24 (see NOTE). Generally these verses are considered as a secondary conclusion on the model of xx 30–31, the original conclusion of the Gospel; yet this understanding must be qualified. The two verses that end ch. xx belong together; they give two aspects of a general picture. There is no such close connection between xxi 24 and 25. Verse 24 resembles xix 35, and only vs. 25a has a similarity of theme to xx 30–31 (and indeed may be a poor imitation of it). There is slight textual evidence for the omission of 25, but the very possibility of omission shows that the connection to 24 is loose. An ingenious but implausible hypothesis is that of L. S. K. Ford, *Theology* 20 (1930), 229, who thinks that 25 once preceded 24, because 25 is the Beloved Disciple's reflection after the Gospel had been read back to him, while 24 is the real conclusion supplied by the Ephesian elders. We recall that Lagrange thought that xx 30–31 originally stood where xxi 24–25 now is, and that only when xx 30–31 was moved to its 'present situation was xxi 24–25 added. Vaganay, *art. cit.,* modifies Lagrange's thesis by suggesting that 24 was originally part of xxi 1–23 and that the original position of xx 30–31 was after 24, so that only 25 is an addition. Vaganay has had few followers, but his proposal again illustrates the loose connection between 24 and 25 and also the fact that 24 is closely related to xxi 1–23 (more closely, in our opinion, than xx 30–31 is to its immediately preceding context).

The True Witness of the Beloved Disciple (vs. 24)

The Beloved Disciple, whose death was discussed in xxi 20–23, is now identified by the redactor as the witness who stands behind the Johannine tradition—this is the minimal evaluation of the statement that he is the witness for "these things" and "wrote" them (see NOTES). Before we discuss views about why 24 places this emphasis on the Beloved Disciple, let us recall the similar passage in xix 35: literally, "He who has seen has borne witness, and his testimony is true, and that one [ekeinos] knows that he tells the truth." We argued that the disciple-witness mentioned in that verse was the Beloved Disciple; and we agree with Smith, p. 223, against Bultmann, that the differences between xix 35 and xxi 24 are such that both verses were not written by the redactor (the former does not mention the Beloved Disciple and has the grammatically awkward "that one knows"). Rather xxi 24 is probably the redactor's attempt to rewrite more clearly the message of xix 35. If we are right about xix 35, then the thesis that the Beloved Disciple stands behind the Gospel as its authority is not peculiar to the redactor but was shared by the evangelist as well. True, only the redactor has attributed writing to the Beloved Disciple; but, as we have interpreted "wrote" (see NOTE), this attribution means no more than the claim that the Beloved Disciple is the one who has borne the witness echoed in the written Gospel.

In an interesting study, D. E. Nineham, "Eye-Witness Testimony and the Gospel Tradition, III," JTS 11 (1960), 254–64, points out that, while dependence on eyewitness testimony for the appearance of the risen Jesus is attested early in NT writings (I Cor xv 5–8), the claim to have eyewitness backing for an account of the ministry of Jesus appears only in later works, like Luke, Acts, John, and II Peter. A question naturally arises, then, as to what extent the claim to eyewitness testimony has been exaggerated at this later period in order to bolster apologetics. In particular, the claim in John xxi 24 has been challenged, often on the assumption that only the redactor, and not the evangelist, made it. E. Meyer, art. cit. (above on p. 962), p. 161, thinks that the author of the Gospel, followed by the redactor, was trying to introduce a new conception of Christ, one that rejected the Synoptic tradition. In order to gain acceptance he pretended that the Gospel was based on the eyewitness of the Beloved Disciple, namely, John son of Zebedee. (As support for this, one must admit that 2nd-century Christian communities did make fictional or exaggerated claims of apostolic origin or patronage for their works, e.g., Jewish Christian works associated with James.) Meyer contends that the Johannine writer himself was the witness; but since he felt that his witness was guided by the Paraclete, he thought he had the right to affirm that the Gospel contained true witness. Bacon, pp. 75–80, also contends that the writer is trying to gain credence for a new tradition that he is introducing: "It is the addition of the Appendix [Epilogue] which made for John all the difference between neglect and highest honor." There are many variations of this approach; but we question the basic thesis, first, because in fact the Fourth Gospel preserves some truly ancient tradition about Jesus, and second, because we doubt whether the evangelist and the redactor, who were both involved and who wrote at different times in the 1st century, could successfully have made such a totally fictional claim. It must be remembered that in this instance we are dealing with a claim about an eyewitness who has only recently died and who, presumably, was alive when the first edition of the Gospel was completed by the evangelist. We find particularly weak the contention that because the Beloved Disciple is left anonymous in the Fourth Gospel he is not likely to have been a historical figure and even less likely to have been persuasive as a witness, since anonymous testimony is rarely acceptable. Comparing the Beloved Disciple to the Qumran Teacher of Righteousness, J. Roloff, NTS 15 (1968–69), 129–51, points out that for the community the latter figure, despite his anonymity in the sectarian writings, is a major interpreter of God's deeds and his witness is highly revered. The fact that he is known by a title rather than by a personal name gives emphasis to the fact that he had an appointed role in God's plan. The consequent symbolic value that the Teacher assumes in the community's thought, especially after his death, casts no real doubt on the historicity of the part he played in building up that community. There is every reason to presume that both for the Qumran and Johannine communities the anonymity of their respective heroes is only literary and symbolic—the people within the two communities knew perfectly well the identity of their heroes.

If a fictional apologetic is not the reason for an appeal to an eyewitness in 24, what other reasons suggest themselves? F. W. Grosheide, in a brief note in *Gereformeerd Theologisch Tijdschrift* 53 (1953), 117–18, points out that John xxi may well represent the threshold of the period of canon formation. With the passing of the apostolic generation, of which the Beloved Disciple may have been one of the last prominent members, there seems to have arisen in the Church a desire to preserve a witness that would never again be given; and it was this desire that led to the collection of writings associated (rightly or wrongly) with the apostolic generation. The redactor's purpose in adding miscellaneous Johannine material to the Gospel reflects a similar preservative intent, and his insistence that the work reflects the testimony of an eyewitness of Jesus' ministry exemplifies the mentality behind canon formation. C. Masson, "Le témoinage de Jean," *Revue de Théologie et de Philosophie* 38 (1950), 120–27, reminds us that throughout the Gospel John prefers the language of witness or testimony (*martyrein*) to that of proclamation (*kēryssein;* see Mark i 4; Matt iii 1; Luke iii 3) or of evangelizing (*euangelizesthai;* Luke iii 18) in order to describe what Jesus was doing. We have seen that this usage was part of a larger usage of legal terminology (vol. 29, p. 45); and Masson comments that such a preference is in accord with the Christian situation in the Johannine era. The early missionary times were over; it was no longer sufficient to proclaim the Gospel; for now the Gospel was challenged systematically by the Synagogue and others, and one had to defend it. If the Fourth Gospel really had a basis in historical tradition, that basis would now be expressed in terms of witness. Moreover, as we suggested in vol. 29, p. xcvii, only the witness of a really important figure in the early Church (the Beloved Disciple=John son of Zebedee?) would carry much weight and find wide acceptance, especially if it challenged another form of the tradition already well established, namely, the tradition underlying the Synoptic Gospels.

Even if the claim of vs. 24 is taken seriously, we should not let modern historical preoccupations distract us from the Johannine theological understanding of true witness. The witness is *true* not only because it ultimately stems from an eyewitness but also because it concerns Jesus who is the truth (xiv 6) and whose own witness was true (v 31–32). It is *witness* not only because it comes from one who was there but also because the Paraclete has expressed himself in the memories and in the theological reflections that are found in the Gospel (xv 26; see App. V). The Johannine notion of true witness goes beyond an eyewitness report of exactly what happened; it includes the adaptation of what happened so that its truth can be seen by and be significant for subsequent generations. The Paraclete is the witness to Jesus par excellence since he is the presence of Jesus and has been active not only in Stage 1 of the Gospel (the historical tradition for which the Beloved Disciple was responsible) but also in Stages 2 to 5 (the work of the evangelist and the redactor—vol. 29, pp. XXXIV–XXXVI).

The Many Other Deeds of Jesus (vs. 25)

We pointed out above that there is no close connection between xxi 24 and 25. Indeed, some have wondered if 25 might not have been added by someone other than the redactor because of the many stylistic peculiarities of the verse (see NOTES) and because of the shift from "we" in 24 to "I." Accumulated endings of biblical books are no rarity (Dan xii 11 and 12). However, the "I" of 25 is probably explicable as a rhetorical device in a literary hyperbole; and we are reluctant without real proof to posit besides the redactor still another Johannine writer who could have added the verse (there is inadequate evidence for thinking of a scribal addition by a later manuscript copier). It seems best, then, to look on 25 as the redactor's last thought and, perhaps, afterthought.

The first part of 25, "Still, there are many other things Jesus did," repeats somewhat awkwardly xx 30: "Of course, Jesus also performed many other signs in the presence of his disciples, signs not written down in this book." Why such a repetition? Perhaps the redactor felt that the repetition of a conclusion would make it clear that he was now bringing his own addition to a conclusion. Or perhaps he meant the words of 25a as a self-defense—what he had done was to add a section from the many things not included in the Gospel.

The second part of 25 is a hyperbole to explain why no attempt has been made to include all the other things that Jesus did. Some commentators have been troubled by the obvious exaggeration about the world's inability to contain the library that would be produced in recording all Jesus' deeds. Most likely it was a feeling that this statement was not true and therefore did not belong in Scripture that explains the minor textual evidence for the failure of scribes to include the verse. Today, however, it is widely recognized that such flamboyant hyperbole was a well-accepted literary convention of the times, both in Gentile and Jewish literature. The Book of Ecclesiastes (xii 9–12) ends on the note that there were many more teachings of the Preacher, but that, while it was useful to have a collection of the sayings of one shepherd, "of the making of many books there is no end." In the minor talmudic tractate *Sopherim* 16:8, Rabbi Johanan ben Zakkai (ca. A.D. 80) is reported to have said: "If all the heavens were sheets of paper, and all the trees were pens for writing, and all the seas were ink, that would not suffice to write down the wisdom I have received from my teachers; and yet I have taken no more from the wisdom of the sages than a fly does when it dips into the sea and bears away a tiny drop." In speaking of God's communications to men, Philo, *De posteritate Caini* XLIII ✳144, remarks: "Were He to choose to display His riches, even the entire earth, with the sea turned into dry land, would not contain them" (also *De ebrietate* IX ✳32; *De vita Moysis* I 38;✳213).

While what the Johannine writer says is technically inexact, perhaps Origen (*Peri archōn* II VI 1; PG 11:210A) was not far from interpreting the writer's true purpose by applying the saying not to a record of the deeds of Jesus but to a written attempt to explain the significance of Jesus: "It is impossible to commit to writing all those particulars that belong to the glory of the Saviour." John xxi 25 would then be expressing figuratively the same message found in Col ii 3: Christ is the one "in whom are hidden all the treasures of wisdom and knowledge."

In any case, having added another long commentary to the already ample bibliography on the Fourth Gospel, and still feeling that much has been left unsaid, the present writer is not in the least inclined to cavil about the accuracy of the Johannine redactor's plaint that no number of books will exhaust the subject.

BIBLIOGRAPHY
(ch. xxi)

Agourides, S., "The Purpose of John 21," *Studies in the History and Text of the New Testament—in Honor of K. W. Clark*, ed. by B. L. Daniels and M. J. Suggs (Salt Lake City: University of Utah, 1967), pp. 127–32.

Bacon, B. W., "The Motivation of John 21. 15–25," JBL 50 (1931), 71–80.

Benoit, P., *The Passion and Resurrection of Jesus Christ* (New York: Herder & Herder, 1969), pp. 289–312.

Boismard, M.-E., "Le chapitre xxi de saint Jean: essai de critique littéraire," RB 54 (1947), 473–501.

Braun, F.-M., "Quatre 'signes' johanniques de l'unité chrétienne," NTS 9 (1962–63), 153–55 on xxi 1–11.

Cassian, Bishop (Archimandrite Cassien or Serge Besobrasoff), "John xxi," NTS 3 (1956–57), 132–36.

Chapman, J., " 'We Know That His Testimony Is True,' " JTS 31 (1930), 379–87 on xxi 24–25.

Cullmann, O., *Peter: Disciple, Apostle, Martyr* (2nd ed.; Philadelphia: Westminster, 1962).

Dodd, C. H., "Note on John 21, 24," JTS n.s. 4 (1953), 212–13.

Drumwright, H. L., Jr., "The Appendix to the Fourth Gospel," *The Teacher's Yoke*, ed. by E. J. Vardaman et al. (H. Trantham volume; Waco, Texas: Baylor Press, 1964), pp. 129–34.

Fuller, R. H., "The 'Thou Art Peter' Pericope and the Easter Appearances," *McCormick Quarterly* 20 (1967), 309–15.

Gaechter, P., "Das dreifache 'Weide meine Lämmer,' " ZKT 69 (1947), 328–44.

Gils, F., "Pierre et la foi au Christ ressuscité," ETL 38 (1962), 5–43.

Glombitza, O., "Petrus, der Freund Jesu. Überlegungen zu Joh. xxi 15 ff.," NovT 6 (1963), 277–85.

Goguel, M., "Did Peter Deny His Lord? A Conjecture," HTR 25 (1932), 1–27, especially 15–25.

Grass, H., *Ostergeschehen und Osterberichte* (3rd ed.; Göttingen: Vandenhoeck, 1964), especially pp. 74–85.

Gray, A., "The Last Chapter of St. John's Gospel as Interpreted by Early Christian Art," *Hibbert Journal* 20 (1921–22), 690–700.

Klein, G., "Die Berufung des Petrus," ZNW 58 (1967), 1–44, especially 24–34.

Kruse, H., " 'Magni pisces centum quinquaginta tres' (Jo 21, 11)," VD 38 (1960), 129–48.

McDowell, E. A., Jr., " 'Lovest Thou Me?' A Study of John 21:15–17," RExp 32 (1935), 422–41.

Marrow, S. B., *John 21—An Essay in Johannine Ecclesiology* (Rome: Gregorian University, 1968). This is an excerpt from a longer unpublished dissertation which the author kindly permitted the writer to use.

Schwank, B., "Der geheimnisvolle Fischfang (21, 1–14)," SeinSend 29 (1964), 484–98.

———— "Christi Stellvertreter (21, 15–25)," SeinSend 29 (1964), 531–42.

Schwartz, E., "Johannes und Kerinthos," ZNW 15 (1914), 210–19, especially 216–17.

Sheehan, J. F. X., " 'Feed My Lambs,' " Scripture 16 (1964), 21–27.

Spicq, C., Agapè (Paris: Gabalda, 1959), III, 230–37 on xxi 15–17. An abbreviated form of this appears in Agape in the New Testament (St. Louis: B. Herder, 1966), III, 94–99. References to French unless otherwise indicated.

Vaganay, L., "La finale du Quatrième Évangile," RB 45 (1936), 512–28.

APPENDIXES

APPENDIX V: THE PARACLETE

The word *paraklētos* is peculiar in the NT to the Johannine literature. In I John ii 1 Jesus is a *paraklētos* (not a title), serving as a heavenly intercessor with the Father. In five passages in John (xiv 15–17, 26; xv 26–27; xvi 7–11, 12–14) the title *paraklētos* is given to someone who is not Jesus, nor an intercessor, nor in heaven. Christian tradition has identified this figure as the Holy Spirit, but scholars like Spitta, Delafosse, Windisch, Sasse, Bultmann, and Betz have doubted whether this identification is true to the original picture and have suggested that the Paraclete was once an independent salvific figure, later confused with the Holy Spirit. To test this claim we shall begin by isolating under four headings the information that John gives in the Paraclete passages, keeping the resultant picture distinct from what is said in the NT about the Holy Spirit.

(a) The coming of the Paraclete and the Paraclete's relation to the Father and the Son:
- The Paraclete will *come* (but only if Jesus departs): xv 26, xvi 7, 8, 13.
- The Paraclete *comes forth* from the Father: xv 26.
- The Father will *give* the Paraclete at Jesus' request: xiv 16.
- The Father will *send* the Paraclete in Jesus' name: xiv 26.
- Jesus, when he goes away, will *send* the Paraclete from the Father: xv 26, xvi 7.

(b) The identification of the Paraclete:
- He is called "another Paraclete": xiv 16 (see NOTE there).
- He is the Spirit of Truth: xiv 17, xv 26, xvi 13.
- He is the Holy Spirit: xiv 26 (see NOTE there).

(c) The role the Paraclete plays in relation to the disciples:
- The disciples recognize him: xiv 17.
- He will be within the disciples and remain with them: xiv 17.
- He will teach the disciples everything: xiv 26.
- He will guide the disciples along the way of all truth: xvi 13.
- He will take what belongs to Jesus to declare to the disciples: xvi 14.
- He will glorify Jesus: xvi 14.
- He will bear witness on Jesus' behalf, and the disciples too must bear witness: xv 26–27.
- He will remind the disciples of all that Jesus told them: xiv 26.
- He will speak only what he hears and nothing on his own: xvi 13.

(d) The role the Paraclete plays in relation to the world:
- The world cannot accept the Paraclete: xiv 17.
- The world neither sees nor recognizes the Paraclete: xiv 17.
- He will bear witness to Jesus against the background of the world's hatred for and persecution of the disciples: xv 26 (cf. xv 18–25).
- He will prove the world wrong about sin, justice, and judgment: xvi 8–11.

Thus the basic functions of the Paraclete are twofold: he comes to the disciples and dwells within them, guiding and teaching them about Jesus; but he is hostile to the world and puts the world on trial.

We should supplement the information given above with material taken from the general context of the five Paraclete passages in the Last Discourse. The very fact that they appear as part of Jesus' farewell to his disciples reinforces the connection between Jesus' departure and the coming of the Paraclete.

Analysis of the title Paraklētos

What does the name given to this salvific figure tell us about him? The closest study has not yet produced a Hebrew or Aramaic title for which paraklētos is clearly a translation. (Mēlîṣ, "interpreter," is a frequent suggestion in Hebrew, e.g., Johnston, p. 32.) Indeed the quest may be in vain, for prqlyt appears as a loanword in Jewish writings of the 2nd century A.D. (Pirqe Aboth iv 11); and thus the paraklētos of John may have been simply the retroversion of a loanword into Greek rather than the translation of a true Hebrew title. At any rate our analysis of the meaning of the term must be based on the Greek word.

We may distinguish two interpretations of paraklētos that have forensic coloring and two non-forensic interpretations.

(a) Paraklētos as a passive form from para/kalein in its elementary sense ("to call alongside"), meaning "one called alongside to help," thus an advocate (OL advocatus) or defense attorney. Some point to the role of the Holy Spirit as a defender of the disciples when they are put on trial (Matt x 20; Acts vi 10); but this is not the Johannine picture. If anything, the role of the Paraclete is that of a prosecuting attorney proving the world guilty. Moreover, in Jewish court procedure the role of a defense attorney is out of place since the judge did much of the interrogation and at most there were witnesses for the defense. If the Paraclete has a forensic function, it must be that of witness (xv 26).

(b) Paraklētos in an active sense, reflecting parakalein in its meaning "to intercede, entreat, appeal to," thus an intercessor, a mediator, a spokesman. This is clearly the meaning in I John ii 1, but in the Gospel the Paraclete does not intercede for the disciples or for Jesus. Nor is he a spokesman in defense of the disciples as in Matt x 20; rather he speaks through the disciples (xv 26–27) in defense of the absent Jesus. Related to this interpretation is the suggested meaning of paraklētos as "helper, friend." In part this understanding of the term is related to the theory of proto-Mandean origins mentioned below. It is true that the Paraclete helps the disciples, but this is too general to be of much value. Moreover, "helper" does not do justice to the Paraclete's role in relation to the world. We may also mention the thesis of H. F. Woodhouse, Biblical Theology 18 (1968), 51–53, that paraklētos should be rendered as "interpreter."

(c) Paraklētos in an active sense, reflecting parakalein in the meaning "to comfort," thus a comforter or consoler (OL consolator; Luther's Tröster). Although

Davies has argued for this translation on the basis of the LXX usage of *parakalein* (a verb John does not use), no Paraclete passage speaks of the Paraclete in the role of consoling the disciples. The element of consolation is confined to the context, for example, xvi 6–7 which prefaces a Paraclete passage.

(d) *Paraklētos* as related to *paraklēsis*, the noun used to describe the exhortation and encouragement found in the preaching of the apostolic witnesses (I Thess iii 2; Rom xii 8; Heb xiii 22; Acts xiii 15—see Lemmonyer, *art. cit.*). Acts ix 31 refers to the Church as walking in the *paraklēsis* of the Holy Spirit. The argument is weakened by the fact that John does not use *paraklēsis*, but this interpretation agrees with John xv 26–27 where the Paraclete bears witness through the disciples. (In Acts ii 40 "bearing witness" and "exhorting" are combined.) Mussner, *art. cit.*, shows how the various functions attributed to the Paraclete are worked out in the ministry of the apostles. Barrett, *art. cit.*, has said that the Paraclete is the Spirit who spoke in the apostolic *paraklēsis*, and this is certainly one of the functions of the Paraclete.

By way of summary we find that no one translation of *paraklētos* captures the complexity of the functions, forensic and otherwise, that this figure has. The Paraclete is a *witness* in defense of Jesus and a *spokesman* for him in the context of his trial by his enemies; the Paraclete is a *consoler* of the disciples for he takes Jesus' place among them; the Paraclete is a teacher and guide of the disciples and thus their *helper*. In rendering the Greek word into Latin for the Vulgate, Jerome had a choice among such OL renderings as *advocatus* and *consolator* and the custom of simply transliterating the term as *paracletus*. In the Gospel he took the latter expedient (*advocatus* appears in I John), a course also followed in the Syriac and Coptic traditions. We would probably be wise also in modern times to settle for "Paraclete," a near-transliteration that preserves the uniqueness of the title and does not emphasize one of the functions to the detriment of others.

Background of the concept

Earlier in this century the attempt of the History of Religions School, especially W. Bauer, Windisch, and Bultmann, to find the origins of the Paraclete in proto-Mandean Gnosticism enjoyed a certain vogue. Bultmann's thesis is that the Paraclete is an adaptation of the Mandean Yawar (which he translates as "Helper"), one of a number of heavenly revealers in Mandean thought. Michaelis and Behm have subjected this theory to penetrating criticism, and it has few followers today. (For a summary of arguments, see Brown, "Paraclete," pp. 119–20.) A Jewish background is more generally postulated. Mowinckel and Johansson were strong advocates of this even before the Qumran discoveries, and F. M. Cross (*The Ancient Library of Qumran* [New York: Doubleday Anchor ed., 1961], pp. 213–15) has pointed out the very important confirming evidence from Qumran. Betz, *op. cit.*, has developed the Qumran background. We may cull from the evidence of the OT, the Apocrypha, and the Qumran scrolls the following four points that contribute to an understanding of the Paraclete.

(a) In the OT we find examples of a tandem relationship wherein a principal figure dies and leaves another to take his place, carry on his work, and interpret his message, for example, Moses/Joshua and Elijah/Elisha (Bornkamm, *art. cit.*, adds the Baptist/Jesus). The second figure is usually closely patterned on the first. The concept of the spirit enters this relationship: Deut xxxiv 9 describes Joshua as filled with the spirit of wisdom when Moses lays hands upon him; Elisha receives a double share of Elijah's spirit (II Kings ii 9, 15); John the Baptist is instrumental in the coming of the Spirit upon Jesus.

(b) In the OT *the spirit of God* comes upon the prophets that they may speak the words of God to men; in the Lucan picture of Pentecost in Acts ii the coming of the Spirit of God makes preachers of the apostles. This concept of the prophetic spirit may offer background for the Paraclete as the teacher of the disciples who moves them to bear witness.

(c) Late Jewish angelology offers the best parallel for the forensic character of the Johannine Paraclete. (In the apocalyptic books the angels also have teaching functions, for they guide the visionaries to truth. The verb *anangellein* used of the Paraclete in John xvi 13–14 is used in these books to describe the unveiling of the truth of a vision; NOTE on xvi 13, "declare.") We remember that the angels are frequently called "spirits." From the ancient picture of the angels of the heavenly court there emerged the figure of a particular angel or spirit who zealously protected God's interests on earth, rooting out evil (the satan of Job i 6–12 and of Zech iii 1–5). Later, under the impact of dualism, there was a bifurcation in this figure: the satan became the evil tempter, while a "good" angel took over the task of protecting God's interests and people, for example, Michael in Dan x 13. Even in the Book of Job, besides the satan who tests Job, there is scattered and somewhat obscure reference to an angelic spokesman (*mal'ak mēlīṣ*) who takes the part of the just (xxxiii 23), a heavenly witness (xvi 19) who after Job's death will prove the justice of Job's case (xix 25–27). The medieval targum or Aramaic translation of Job reads *prqlyṭ* in several of these passages. We note that the Johannine Paraclete exercises a similar role in relation to Jesus. At Qumran the angelic dualism is fully worked out, and the *Spirit of Truth* leads the sectarians in their struggle against the forces of evil who are under the Spirit of Falsehood. The Qumran literature (cf. also the *Testament of Judah* xx 1–5) supplies the only pre-Christian instances of the title "Spirit of Truth" which John uses synonymously with "Paraclete." If the Spirit of Truth is an angel, one gets the impression that "spirit of truth" can also refer to a way of life or something that penetrates man's very being. For example, in 1QS iv 23–24 we hear: "Until now the spirits of truth and falsehood struggle in the hearts of men, and they walk in both wisdom and folly." So also does the Johannine Paraclete dwell within man. Undoubtedly the concept of the angelic spirit (the angel spokesman and prosecutor, the Spirit of Truth) was originally a different concept from that of the spirit of God given to the prophets, as discussed in (b) above. But this distinction may have begun to disappear in later thought. In Wis i 7–9 the spirit of the Lord has almost the forensic function of the heavenly satan, for it hunts down wickedness in the world and condemns it. In *Jubilees* i 24 the evil Belial is opposed not by an angel but by God's holy spirit within men. If the Qumran sectarians were men who walked in the way of the Spirit of Truth, they were also men who had been cleansed by God's holy spirit which united them to God's truth (1QS iii 6–7).

(d) The figure of personified Wisdom, which offers a very important background for the Johannine Jesus, also offers background for the Paraclete (who is very similar to Jesus, as we shall see). Wisdom comes from God to dwell within the chosen people of the Lord (Sir xxiv 12) and brings them the gift of understanding (26–27). Wisdom says (33): "I will pour out teaching like prophecy and leave it to all future generations"—a role not unlike that of the Johannine Paraclete who "will declare to you the things to come" (John xvi 13). Enoch xlii 2 mentions the rejection of Wisdom by men, and this may be compared to John's contention (xiv 17) that the world cannot accept the Paraclete. In the commentary we have seen a partial relationship between the role of the Paraclete in John xv 26–27 and that of the Spirit in Matt x 19–20, the Spirit of the Father given to the disciples that they may speak before hostile tribunals. In the parallel passage in Luke xxi 14–15 it is *wisdom* (not personified) that is given to them. (The present writer is indebted for several of these suggestions to R. L. Jeske.)

In summation, we find scattered in Jewish thought the basic elements that appear in the Johannine picture of the Paraclete: a tandem relationship whereby a second figure, patterned on the first, continues the work of the first; the passing on of his spirit by the main salvific figure; God's granting a spirit that would enable the recipient to understand and interpret divine deed and word authoritatively; a personal (angelic) spirit who would lead the chosen ones against the forces of evil; personal (angelic) spirits who teach men and guide them to truth; Wisdom that comes to men from God, dwells within them, and teaches them, but is rejected by other men. And in the passages describing these various relationships and spirits there is much of the vocabulary of witnessing, teaching, guiding, and accusing that appears in the Johannine Paraclete passages, including the title "Spirit of Truth."

The Johannine understanding of the Paraclete

The combination of these diverse features into a consistent picture and the reshaping of the concept of the Holy Spirit according to that picture are what have given us the Johannine presentation of the Paraclete. We must examine this presentation in more detail. It is our contention that John presents the Paraclete as the Holy Spirit in a special role, namely, as the personal presence of Jesus in the Christian while Jesus is with the Father.

This means, first of all, that the Johannine picture of the Paraclete is not inconsistent with what is said in the Gospel itself and in the other NT books about the Holy Spirit. It is true that the Paraclete is more clearly personal than is the Holy Spirit in many NT passages, for often the Holy Spirit, like the spirit of God in the OT, is described as a force. Yet there are certainly other passages that attribute quasi-personal features to the Holy Spirit, for example, the triadic passages in Paul where the Spirit is set alongside the Father and the Son, and the Spirit performs voluntary actions (I Cor xii 11; Rom viii 16). If the Father gives the Paraclete at Jesus' request, the Father gives the Holy Spirit to those who ask Him (Luke xi 13; also I John iii 24, iv 13). In Titus iii 6 we hear that God has poured out the Spirit through Jesus Christ. If both the Father and Jesus are said to send the Paraclete, the Holy Spirit is variously called the Spirit of God (I Cor ii 11; Rom viii 11, 14) and the Spirit of Jesus (II Cor iii 17; Gal iv 6; Philip i 19). John iv 24 says "God is Spirit," meaning that God reveals Himself to men in the Spirit, and John xx 22 has Jesus giving the Spirit to men. Thus there is nothing said about the coming of the Paraclete or about the Paraclete's relation to the Father and the Son that is totally strange to the NT picture of the Holy Spirit.

If the Paraclete is called the "Spirit of Truth" and is said to bear witness on Jesus' behalf, in I John v 6(7) we are told, "It is the Spirit that bears witness to this, for the Spirit is truth." If the witness of the Paraclete is borne through the disciples, so in Acts the coming of the Holy Spirit is what moves the disciples to bear witness to Jesus' resurrection. Conceptually there is a very close parallel to John xv 26–27 in Acts v 32: "We are witnesses to these things, and so is the Holy Spirit whom God has given to those who obey Him" (see Lofthouse, art. cit.). If the Paraclete is to teach the disciples, Luke xii 12 says that the Holy Spirit will teach them (see also discussion of I John ii 27 in vol. 30). If the Paraclete has a forensic function in proving the world wrong, the Spirit in Matt x 20 and Acts vi 10 also has a forensic function, namely, that of defending the disciples on trial.

This does not mean that the Paraclete is simply the same as the Holy Spirit. Some of the basic functions of the Holy Spirit, such as baptismal regeneration, re-creation, forgiving sins (John iii 5, xx 22–23), are never predicated of the Paraclete. Indeed by emphasizing only certain features of the work of the Spirit and by placing them in the context of the Last Discourse and of Jesus' departure, the Johannine writer has conceived of the Spirit in a highly distinctive manner, so distinctive that he rightly gave the resultant portrait a special title, "the Paraclete." Nevertheless, we would stress that the identification of the Paraclete as the Holy Spirit in xiv 26 is not an editorial mistake, for the similarities between the Paraclete and the Spirit are found in all the Paraclete passages.

The peculiarity of the Johannine portrait of the Paraclete/Spirit, and this is our second point, centers around the resemblance of the Spirit to Jesus. Virtually everything that has been said about the Paraclete has been said elsewhere in the Gospel about Jesus. Let us compare the Paraclete and Jesus under the four headings we used for classification at the beginning of the Appendix:

(a) The coming of the Paraclete. The Paraclete will *come;* so also has Jesus come into the world (v 43, xvi 28, xviii 37). The Paraclete comes forth (*ekporeuesthai*) from the Father; so also did Jesus come forth (*exerchesthai*) from the Father. The Father will *give* the Paraclete at Jesus' request; so also the Father gave the Son (iii 16). The Father will *send* the Paraclete; so also Jesus was sent by the Father (iii 17 and *passim*). The Paraclete will be sent in *Jesus' name;* so also Jesus came in the Father's name (v 43— in many ways the Paraclete is to Jesus as Jesus is to the Father).

(b) The identification of the Paraclete. If the Paraclete is "another Paraclete," this implies that Jesus was the first Paraclete (but in his earthly ministry, not in heaven as in I John ii 1). If the Paraclete is the Spirit of Truth, Jesus is the truth (xiv 6). If the Paraclete is the Holy Spirit, Jesus is the Holy One of God (vi 69).

(c) The role the Paraclete plays in relation to the disciples. The disciples will be granted the privilege to know or recognize the Paraclete; so also it is a special privilege to know or recognize Jesus (xiv 7, 9). The Paraclete is to be within the disciples and remain with them; so also Jesus is to remain in and with the disciples (xiv 20, 23, xv 4, 5, xvii 23, 26). If the Paraclete is to guide the disciples along the way of all truth, Jesus is both the way and the truth (xiv 6). If the Paraclete is to teach the disciples, Jesus also teaches those who will listen (vi 59, vii 14, 18, viii 20). If the Paraclete declares to the disciples the things to come, Jesus identifies himself as the Messiah to come who announces or declares all things (iv 25–26). If the Paraclete will bear witness, so also Jesus bears witness (viii 14). We note, moreover, that John stresses that all the witness and teaching of the Paraclete is about Jesus, so that the Paraclete glorifies Jesus. (Jesus has the same role in relation to the Father: viii 28, xii 27–28, xiv 13, xvii 4.)

(d) The role the Paraclete plays in relation to the world. The world cannot accept the Paraclete; so also evil men do not accept Jesus (v 43, xii 48). The world does not see the Paraclete; so also men are told they will soon lose sight of Jesus (xvi 16). The world does not know or recognize the Paraclete; so also men do not know Jesus (xvi 3; cf. vii 28, viii 14, 19, xiv 7). The Paraclete will bear witness in a setting of the world's hate; so also Jesus bears witness against the world (vii 7). The Paraclete will prove the world wrong concerning the trial of Jesus, a trial that colors John's whole portrait of the ministry of Jesus.

Thus, the one whom John calls "another Paraclete" is another Jesus. Since the Paraclete can come only when Jesus departs, the Paraclete is the presence of Jesus when Jesus is absent. Jesus' promises to dwell within his disciples are fulfilled in the Paraclete. It is no accident that the first passage containing Jesus' promise of the Paraclete (xiv 16–17) is followed immediately by the verse which says, "I am coming back to you." We need not follow E. F. Scott and Ian Simpson in maintaining that John is correcting the mistaken view that the Holy Spirit is distinct from Jesus. John insists that Jesus will be in heaven with the Father while the Paraclete is on earth in the disciples; and so the two have different roles. On the other hand, John's interest is not that of later Trinitarian theology where the main problem will be to show the distinction between Jesus and the Spirit; John is interested in the similarity between the two.

The "Sitz im Leben" for the Johannine concept of the Paraclete

What brought the Johannine tradition to put emphasis in the Last Discourse on the Spirit as the Paraclete, that is, as the continued post-resurrectional presence of Jesus with his disciples, teaching them and proving to them that Jesus was victorious and the world was wrong? We suggest that the portrait of the Paraclete/Spirit answered two problems prominent at the time of the final composition of the Fourth Gospel. (In the commentary, pp. 699–700, we have noted that there may have been promises of the Spirit in the primitive forms of the Last Discourse, but that the transformation of these into Paraclete passages was catalyzed by the introduction into the Last Discourse of the material that now appears in xv 18–xvi 4a. This material, dealing with the persecution of the disciples by the world, has parallels with Matt x 17–25 where [x 20] the Spirit has a forensic function. Reflection on this forensic function may have led to the emergence of the Paraclete/Spirit concept, a concept which then would be proper to the last stages of editing of the Last Discourse.)

The first problem was the confusion caused by the death of the apostolic eyewitnesses who were the living chain between the Church and Jesus of Nazareth. It is the thesis of many scholars that one of the purposes of the Fourth Gospel was to show the true connection between the church life of the late 1st century and the already distant Jesus of Nazareth (vol. 29, p. LXXVIII). For such a mentality the death of the apostolic eyewitnesses was a tragedy, since a visible link between the Church and Jesus was being severed. Previously these men had been able to interpret the mind of Jesus in face of the new situations in which the Church found itself. Undoubtedly the impact of the loss of the eyewitnesses was felt acutely in the period after 70, but for the Johannine community the full impact did not come until the death of the Beloved Disciple, the eyewitness *par excellence* (xix 35, xxi 24), a death which occurred seemingly just before the Gospel was put in final form. Either this death or its obvious imminence must have presented to the Johannine community the agonizing problem of survival without the principal living link to Jesus.

The concept of the Paraclete/Spirit is an answer to this problem. If the eyewitnesses had guided the Church and if the Beloved Disciple had borne witness to Jesus in the Johannine community, it was not primarily because of their own recollection of Jesus. After all, they had seen Jesus but not understood (xiv 9). Only the post-resurrectional gift of the Spirit taught them the meaning of what they had seen (ii 22, xii 16). Their witness was the witness of the Paraclete speaking through them; the profound reinterpretation of the ministry and words of Jesus effected under the guidance of the Beloved Disciple and now found in the Fourth Gospel was the work of the Paraclete. (Here we agree, at least in principle, with the many scholars, like Loisy, Sasse, Kragerud, and Hoeferkamp, who see in the Beloved Disciple the "incarnation" of the Paraclete.) And the Paraclete does not cease to function when these eyewitnesses have gone, for he dwells within all Christians who love Jesus and keep his commandments (xiv 17). (Mussner, pp. 67–70, is scarcely correct in suggesting that the indwelling of the Paraclete is the privilege of the Twelve and is passed along with the apostolic office.) The later Christian is no further removed from the ministry of Jesus than was the earlier Christian, for the Paraclete dwells within him as he dwelt within the eyewitnesses. And by recalling and giving new meaning to what Jesus said, the Paraclete guides every generation in facing new situations; he declares the things to come (xvi 13).

The second problem was the anguish caused by the delay of the second coming. In the period after A.D. 70 the expectation of the return of Jesus began to pale. His return had been associated with God's wrathful judgment upon Jerusalem (Mark xiii), but now Jerusalem had been destroyed by Roman armies and Jesus had not yet returned. In particular, Jesus' return had been expected within the lifetime of some of those who had been his companions (Mark xiii 30; Matt x 23). Certainly the Johannine community had expected his return before the death of the Beloved Disciple (John xxi 23); yet this was now imminent or even a reality, and yet Jesus had not returned. That this delay caused skepticism is seen in II Pet iii 3–8 where the rather naïve answer is given that no matter how long the interval is, the coming will occur soon, for with the Lord one day is as a thousand years. The Johannine answer is more profound. The evangelist does not lose faith in the second coming but emphasizes that many of the features associated with the second coming are already realities of Christian life (judgment, divine sonship, eternal life—vol. 29, p. cxx). And in a very real way Jesus has come back during the lifetime of his companions, for he has come in and through the Paraclete. (Bornkamm, p. 26, points out that the concept of the Paraclete demythologizes several apocalyptic motifs, including world judgment, e.g., xvi 11.) The Christian need not live with his eyes constantly straining toward the heavens from which the Son of Man is to come; for, as the Paraclete, Jesus is present within all believers.

BIBLIOGRAPHY

Barrett, C. K., "The Holy Spirit in the Fourth Gospel," JTS N.S. 1 (1950), 1–15.

Behm, J., "paraklētos," TWNTE, V, 800–14.

Berrouard, M.-F., "Le Paraclet, défenseur du Christ devant la conscience du croyant (Jean xvi 8–11)," RSPT 33 (1949), 361–89.

Betz, O., Der Paraklet (Leiden: Brill, 1963).

Bornkamm, G., "Der Paraklet im Johannesevangelium," Festschrift für R. Bultmann (Stuttgart: Kohlhammer, 1949), pp. 12–35. Updated in Geschichte und Glaube I (Gesammelte Aufsätze III; Munich: Kaiser, 1968), pp. 68–89.

Brown, R. E., "The Paraclete in the Fourth Gospel," NTS 13 (1966–67), 113–32. A shorter form is "The 'Paraclete' in the Light of Modern Research," StEv, IV, 157–65.

Davies, J. G., "The Primary Meaning of PARAKLETOS," JTS N.S. 4 (1953), 35–38.

de Haes, P., "Doctrina S. Joannis de Spiritu Sancto," ColctMech 29 (1959), 521–26.

de la Potterie, I., "Le Paraclet," Assemblées du Seigneur 47 (1963), 37–55. Reprinted in De la Potterie, I., and Lyonnet, S., La vie selon l'Esprit (Paris: Cerf, 1965), pp. 85–105.

Giblet, J., "De missione Spiritus Paracliti secundum Joa. xvi 5–15," ColctMech 22 (1952), 253–54.

Hoeferkamp, R., "The Holy Spirit in the Fourth Gospel from the Viewpoint of Christ's Glorification," ConcTM 33 (1962), 517–29.

Holwerda, D. E., The Holy Spirit and Eschatology in the Gospel of John (Kampen: Kok, 1959).

Johannson, N., Parakletoi (Lund: Gleerup, 1940).

Johnston, G., "The Spirit-Paraclete in the Gospel of John," Perspective 9 (1968), 29–37.

Lemmonyer, A., "L'Esprit-Saint Paraclet," RSPT 16 (1927), 293–307.

Locher, G. W., "Der Geist als Paraklet," EvTh 26 (1966), 565–79.

Lofthouse, W. F., "The Holy Spirit in the Acts and in the Fourth Gospel," ET 52 (1940–41), 334–36.

Michaelis, W., "Zur Herkunft des johanneischen Paraklet-Titels," *Coniectanea Neotestamentica* 11 (1947: Fridrichsen Festschrift), 147–62.

Miguens, M., *El Paráclito* (Jerusalem: Studii Biblici Franciscani Analecta, 1963).

Mowinckel, S., "Die Vorstellungen des Spätjudentums vom heiligen Geist als Fürsprecher und der johanneische Paraklet," ZNW 32 (1933), 97–130.

Mussner, F., "Die johanneischen Parakletsprüche und die apostolische Tradition," BZ 5 (1961), 56–70.

Sasse, H., "Der Paraklet im Johannesevangelium," ZNW 24 (1925), 260–77.

Schlier, H., "Zum Begriff des Geistes nach dem Johannesevangelium," *Besinnung auf das Neue Testament* (Freiburg: Herder, 1964), pp. 264–71.

Schulz, S., "Die Paraklet-Thematradition," *Untersuchungen zur Menschensohn-Christologie im Johannesevangelium* (Göttingen: Vandenhoeck, 1957), pp. 142–58.

Simpson, I., "The Holy Spirit in the Fourth Gospel," *The Expositor,* 9th series, 4 (1925), 292–99.

Stockton, E., "The Paraclete," *Australasian Catholic Record* 16 (1962), 255–62.

Swete, H. B., *The Holy Spirit in the New Testament* (London: Macmillan, 1931 reprint). Especially pp. 147–68.

Windisch, H., *The Spirit-Paraclete in the Fourth Gospel* (Philadelphia: Fortress, 1968). Translation of two German articles "Die fünf johanneischen Paraklet-sprüche" (1927) and "Jesus und der Geist im Johannesevangelium" (1933).

APPENDIX VI: THE ENGLISH TEXT OF THE GOSPEL
(chs. i–xii)

(For the convenience of the reader we reproduce here the translation of the first twelve chapters of the Gospel as given in vol. 29 of The Anchor Bible.)

The Prologue

I 1 In the beginning was the Word;
    the Word was in God's presence,
    and the Word was God.
2 He was present with God in the beginning.

3 Through him all things came into being,
    and apart from him not a thing came to be.
4 That which had come to be in him was life,
    and this life was the light of men.
5 The light shines on in the darkness,
    for the darkness did not overcome it.

(6 There was sent by God a man named John 7 who came as a witness to testify to the light so that through him all men might believe—8 but only to testify to the light, for he himself was not the light. 9 The real light which gives light to every man was coming into the world!)

10 He was in the world,
    and the world was made by him;
    yet the world did not recognize him.
11 To his own he came;
    yet his own people did not accept him.
12 But all those who did accept him
    he empowered to become God's children.

That is, those who believe in his name—13 those who were begotten, not by blood, nor by carnal desire, nor by man's desire, but by God.

14 And the Word became flesh
and made his dwelling among us.
And we have seen his glory,
the glory of an only Son coming from the Father,
filled with enduring love.

(15 John testified to him by proclaiming: "This is he of whom I said, 'The one who comes after me ranks ahead of me, for he existed before me.'")

16 And of his fullness
we have all had a share—
love in place of love.

17 For while the Law was a gift through Moses, this enduring love came through Jesus Christ. 18 No one has ever seen God; it is God the only Son, ever at the Father's side, who has revealed Him.

The Book of Signs

I   19 Now this is the testimony John gave when the Jews sent priests and Levites from Jerusalem to ask him who he was.
20 He declared without any qualification, avowing, "I am not the Messiah."
21 They questioned him further, "Well, who are you? Elijah?" "I am not," he answered.
"Are you the prophet?" "No!" he replied.
22 Then they said to him, "Just who are you?—so that we can give some answer to those who sent us. What have you to say for yourself?"
23 He said, quoting the prophet Isaiah, "I am—

'a voice in the desert crying out,
"Make the Lord's road straight!"'"

24 But the emissaries of the Pharisees 25 questioned him further, "If you are not the Messiah, nor Elijah, nor the Prophet, then what are you doing baptizing?" 26 John answered them, "I am only baptizing with water; but there is one among you whom you do not recognize—27 the one who is to come after me, and I am not even worthy to unfasten the straps of his sandal." 28 It was in Bethany that this happened, across the Jordan where John used to baptize.

29 The next day, when he caught sight of Jesus coming toward him, he exclaimed,

"Look! Here is the Lamb of God
who takes away the world's sin.

30 "It is he about whom I said,

> 'After me is to come a man
> who ranks ahead of me,
> for he existed before me.'

31 "I myself never recognized him, though the very reason why I came and baptized with water was that he might be revealed to Israel."

32 John gave this testimony also,

> "I have seen the Spirit descend
> like a dove from the sky,
> and it came to rest upon him.

33 "And I myself never recognized him; but the One who sent me to baptize with water told me, 'When you see the Spirit descend and rest on someone, he is the one who is to baptize with a holy Spirit.' 34 Now I myself have seen and have testified, 'This is God's chosen one.'"

35 The next day John was there again with two disciples; 36 and watching Jesus walk by, he exclaimed, "Look! Here is the Lamb of God." 37 The two disciples heard what he said and followed Jesus. 38 When Jesus turned around and noticed them following him, he asked them, "What are you looking for?" They said to him, "Rabbi, where are you staying?" ("Rabbi," translated, means "Teacher.") 39 "Come and see," he answered. So they went to see where he was staying and stayed on with him that day (it was about four in the afternoon).

40 One of the two who had followed him, after hearing John, was Andrew, Simon Peter's brother. 41 The first thing he did was to find his brother Simon and tell him, "We have found the Messiah!" ("Messiah," translated, is "Anointed.") 42 He brought him to Jesus who looked at him and said, "You are Simon, son of John; your name shall be Cephas" (which is rendered as "Peter").

43 The next day he wanted to set out for Galilee, so he found Philip. "Follow me," Jesus said to him. 44 Now Philip was from Bethsaida, the same town as Andrew and Peter. 45 Philip found Nathanael and told him, "We have found the very one described in the Mosaic Law and the prophets—Jesus, son of Joseph, from Nazareth." 46 But Nathanael retorted, "Nazareth! Can anything good come from there?" So Philip told him, "Come and see for yourself." 47 When Jesus saw Nathanael coming toward him, he exclaimed, "Look! Here is a genuine Israelite; there is no guile in him." 48 "How do you know me?" Nathanael asked. "Before Philip called you," Jesus answered, "I saw you under the fig tree." 49 Nathanael replied, "Rabbi, you are the Son of God; you are the King of Israel." 50 Jesus

answered, "You believe, do you, just because I told you that I saw you under the fig tree? You will see far greater things than that."

51 And he told him, "Truly, I assure all of you, you will see the sky opened and the angels of God ascending and descending upon the Son of Man."

II 1 Now on the third day there was a wedding at Cana in Galilee. The mother of Jesus was there, 2 and Jesus himself and his disciples had also been invited to the celebration. 3 When the wine ran short, Jesus' mother told him, "They have no wine." 4 But Jesus answered her, "Woman, what has this concern of yours to do with me? My hour has not yet come." 5 His mother instructed the waiters, "Do whatever he tells you." 6 As prescribed for Jewish purifications, there were at hand six stone water jars, each one holding fifteen to twenty-five gallons. 7 "Fill those jars with water," Jesus ordered, and they filled them to the brim. 8 "Now," he said to them, "draw some out and take it to the headwaiter." And they did so. 9 But as soon as the headwaiter tasted the water made wine (actually he had no idea where it came from; only the waiters knew since they had drawn the water), the headwaiter called the bridegroom, 10 and pointed out to him, "Everyone serves choice wine first; then, when the guests have been drinking awhile, the inferior wine. But you have kept the choice wine until now." 11 What Jesus did at Cana in Galilee marked the beginning of his signs; thus he revealed his glory and his disciples believed in him.

12 After this he went down to Capernaum, along with his mother and brothers [and his disciples], and they stayed there only a few days.

13 Since the Jewish Passover was near, Jesus went up to Jerusalem. 14 In the temple precincts he came upon people engaged in selling oxen, sheep, and doves, and others seated, changing coins. 15 So he made a [kind of] whip out of cords and drove the whole pack of them out of the temple area with their sheep and oxen, and he knocked over the money-changers' tables, spilling their coins. 16 He told those who were selling doves, "Get them out of here! Stop turning my Father's house into a market place!" 17 His disciples recalled the words of Scripture: "Zeal for your house will consume me."

18 At this the Jews responded, "What sign can you show us, authorizing you to do these things?" 19 "Destroy this Temple," was Jesus' answer, "and in three days I will raise it up." 20 Then the Jews retorted, "The building of this Temple has taken forty-six years, and you are going to raise it up in three days?" 21 Actually he was talking about the temple of his body. 22 Now after his resurrection from the dead his disciples recalled that he had said this, and so they believed the Scripture and the word he had spoken.

23 While he was in Jerusalem during the Passover festival, many believed in his name, for they could see the signs he was performing. 24 For his part, Jesus would not trust himself to them because he knew them all. 25 He needed no one to testify about human nature, for he was aware of what was in man's heart.

III   1 Now there was a Pharisee named Nicodemus, a member of the Jewish Sanhedrin, 2 who came to him at night. "Rabbi," he said to Jesus, "we know you are a teacher who has come from God; for, unless God is with him, no one can perform the signs that you perform." 3 Jesus gave him this answer:

> "I solemnly assure you,
> no one can see the kingdom of God
> without being begotten from above."

4 "How can a man be born again once he is old?" retorted Nicodemus. "Can he re-enter his mother's womb and be born all over again?" 5 Jesus replied:

> "I solemnly assure you,
> no one can enter the kingdom of God
> without being begotten of water and Spirit.
> 6 Flesh begets flesh,
> and Spirit begets spirit.
> 7 Do not be surprised that I told you:
> you must all be begotten from above.
> 8 The wind blows about at will;
> you hear the sound it makes
> but do not know where it comes from or where it goes.
> So it is with everyone begotten of the Spirit."

9 Nicodemus replied, "How can things like this happen?" 10 Jesus answered, "You hold the office of teacher of Israel, and still you don't understand these things?

> 11 I solemnly assure you,
> we are talking about what we know,
> and we are testifying to what we have seen;
> but you people do not accept our testimony.
> 12 If you do not believe
> when I tell you about earthly things,
> how are you going to believe
> when I tell you about heavenly things?
> 13 Now, no one has gone up into heaven

except the one who came down from heaven—
the Son of Man [who is in heaven].

14 And just as Moses lifted up the serpent in the desert,
so must the Son of Man be lifted up,
15 that everyone who believes
may have eternal life in him.
16 Yes, God loved the world so much
that He gave the only Son,
that everyone who believes in him may not perish
but may have eternal life.
17 For God did not send the Son into the world
to condemn the world,
but that the world might be saved through him.
18 Whoever believes in him is not condemned,
but whoever does not believe has already been condemned
for refusing to believe in the name of God's only Son.
19 Now the judgment is this:
the light has come into the world,
but men have preferred darkness to light
because their deeds were evil.
20 For everyone who practices wickedness
hates the light,
and does not come near the light
for fear his deeds will be exposed.
21 But he who acts in truth
comes into the light,
so that it may be shown
that his deeds are done in God."

22 Later on Jesus and his disciples came into Judean territory, and he spent some time there with them, baptizing. 23 Now John too was baptizing, at Aenon near Salim where water was plentiful; and people kept coming to be baptized. (24 John, of course, had not yet been thrown into prison.) 25 This led to a controversy about purification between John's disciples and a certain Jew. 26 So they came to John saying, "Rabbi, the man who was with you across the Jordan—the one about whom you have been testifying—well, now he is baptizing and everybody is flocking to him." 27 John answered,

"No one can take anything
unless heaven gives it to him.

28 You yourselves are my witnesses that I said, 'I am not the Messiah, but am sent before him.'

29 It is the bridegroom who gets the bride.
The bridegroom's best man,
who waits there listening for him,
is overjoyed just to hear the bridegroom's voice.
That is my joy, and it is complete.
30 He must increase
while I must decrease."

31 "The one who comes from above is above all;
the one who is of the earth is earthly,
and he speaks on an earthly plane.

The one who comes from heaven [(who) is above all]
32 testifies to what he has seen and heard,
but no one accepts his testimony.
33 Whoever does accept his testimony
has certified that God is truthful.

34 For the one whom God has sent
speaks the words of God;
truly boundless is his gift of the Spirit.
35 The Father loves the Son
and has handed over all things to him.

36 Whoever believes in the Son
has eternal life.
Whoever disobeys the Son
will not see life,
but must endure God's wrath."

IV 1 Now when Jesus learned that the Pharisees had heard that he was winning and baptizing more disciples than John (2 in fact, however, it was not Jesus himself who baptized, but his disciples), 3 he left Judea and once more started back to Galilee.

4 He had to pass through Samaria; 5 and his travels brought him to a Samaritan town called Shechem, near the plot of land which Jacob had given to his son Joseph. 6 This was the site of Jacob's well; and so Jesus, tired from the journey, sat down at the well.

It was about noon; 7 and when a Samaritan woman came to draw water, Jesus said to her, "Give me a drink." (8 His disciples had gone off into town to buy supplies.) 9 But the Samaritan woman said to him, "You are a Jew—how can you ask me, a Samaritan woman, for a drink?"

(Jews, remember, use nothing in common with Samaritans.) 10 Jesus replied:

> "If only you recognized God's gift
> and who it is that is asking you for a drink,
> you would have asked him instead,
> and he would have given you living water."

11 "Sir," she addressed him, "you haven't even a bucket, and this well is deep. Where, then, are you going to get this flowing water? 12 Surely, you don't pretend to be greater than our ancestor Jacob who gave us this well and drank from it with his sons and flocks?" 13 Jesus replied:

> "Everyone who drinks this water
> will be thirsty again.
> 14 But whoever drinks the water I shall give him
> shall never be thirsty.
> Rather, the water I shall give him
> will become within him a fountain of water
> leaping up unto eternal life."

15 The woman said to him, "Give me this water, sir, so that I won't get thirsty and have to keep coming here to draw water."

16 He told her, "Go, call your husband and come back here." 17 "I have no husband," the woman replied. Jesus exclaimed, "Right you are in claiming to have no husband. 18 In fact, you have had five husbands, and the man you have now is not your husband. There you've told the truth!"

19 "Lord," the woman answered, "I can see that you are a prophet. 20 Our ancestors worshiped on this mountain, but you people claim that the place where men ought to worship God is in Jerusalem." 21 Jesus told her:

> "Believe me, woman,
> an hour is coming
> when you will worship the Father
> neither on this mountain
> nor in Jerusalem.
> 22 You people worship what you do not understand,
> while we understand what we worship;
> after all, salvation is from the Jews.
> 23 Yet an hour is coming and is now here
> when the real worshipers
> will worship the Father in Spirit and truth.
> And indeed, it is just such worshipers
> that the Father seeks.

24 God is Spirit,
and those who worship Him
must worship in Spirit and truth."

25 The woman said to him, "I know there is a Messiah coming. Whenever he comes, he will announce all things to us." (This term "Messiah" means "Anointed.") 26 Jesus declared to her, "I who speak to you—I am he."

27 Now just then his disciples came along. They were shocked that he was holding a conversation with a woman; however, no one asked, "What do you want?" or "Why are you talking to her?" 28 Then, leaving her water jar, the woman went off into the town. She said to the people, 29 "Come and see someone who has told me everything that I have ever done! Could this possibly be the Messiah?" 30 [So] they set out from the town to meet him.

31 Meanwhile the disciples were urging him, "Rabbi, eat something." 32 But he told them,

"I have food to eat
that you know nothing about."

33 At this the disciples said to one another, "You don't suppose that someone has brought him something to eat?" 34 Jesus explained to them:

"Doing the will of Him who sent me
and bringing His work to completion—
that is my food.
35 Do you not have a saying:
'Four [more] months
and the harvest will be here'?
Why, I tell you,
open your eyes
and look at the fields;
they are ripe for the harvest!
36 The reaper is already collecting his wages
and gathering fruit for eternal life,
so that both sower and reaper can rejoice together.
37 For here we have the saying verified:
'One man sows; another reaps.'
38 What I sent you to reap
was not something you worked for.
Others have done the hard work,
and you have come in for the fruit of their work."

39 Now many Samaritans from that town believed in him on the strength of the woman's word. "He told me everything that I have

ever done," she testified. 40 Consequently, when these Samaritans came to him, they begged him to stay with them. So he stayed there two days, 41 and through his own word many more came to faith. 42 As they told the woman, "No longer is our faith dependent on your story. For we have heard for ourselves, and we know that this is really the Saviour of the world."

43 When the two days were up, he departed from there for Galilee. (44 For Jesus himself had testified that it is in his own country that a prophet has no honor.) 45 And when he arrived in Galilee, the Galileans welcomed him because, having gone to the feast themselves, they had seen all that he had done in Jerusalem on that occasion.

46 And so he arrived again at Cana in Galilee where he had made the water wine. Now at Capernaum there was a royal official whose son was ill. 47 When he heard that Jesus had come back from Judea to Galilee, he went to him and begged him to come down and restore health to his son who was near death. 48 Jesus replied, "Unless you people can see signs and wonders, you never believe." 49 "Sir," the royal official pleaded with him, "come down before my little boy dies." 50 Jesus told him, "Return home; your son is going to live." The man put his trust in the word Jesus had spoken to him and started for home.

51 And as he was on his way down, his servants met him with the news that his boy was going to live. 52 When he asked [them] at what time he had shown improvement, they told him, "The fever left him yesterday afternoon about one." 53 Now it was at that very hour, the father realized, that Jesus had told him, "Your son is going to live." And he and his whole household became believers. 54 This was the second sign that Jesus performed on returning again from Judea to Galilee.

V 1 Later, on the occasion of a Jewish feast, Jesus went up to Jerusalem. 2 Now in Jerusalem, by the Sheep Pool, there is a place with the Hebrew name Bethesda. Its five porticoes 3 were crowded with sick people who were lying there, blind, lame, and disabled [, waiting for the movement of the waters].   [4]   5 In fact, one man there had been sick thirty-eight years. 6 Jesus knew that he had been sick a long time; so when he saw him lying there, he said to him, "Do you want to be cured?" 7 "Sir," the sick man answered, "I haven't anybody to plunge me into the pool once the water has been stirred up. By the time I get there, someone else has gone in ahead of me." 8 Jesus said to him, "Stand up; pick up your mat, and walk around." 9 The man was immediately cured, and he picked up his mat and began to walk.

Now that day was a Sabbath. 10 Therefore, the Jews kept telling the man who had been healed, "It's the Sabbath, and you are not allowed to be carrying that mat around." 11 He explained, "It was the man who cured me who told me, 'Pick up your mat and walk.'" 12 "This person who told you to pick it up and walk," they asked, "who is he?" 13 But the man who had been restored to health had no idea who it was, for, thanks to the crowd in that place, Jesus had slipped away.

14 Later on Jesus found him in the temple precincts and said to him, 'Remember now, you have been cured. Sin no more, for fear that something worse will happen to you." 15 The man went off and informed the Jews that Jesus was the one who had cured him.

16 And so, because he did this sort of thing on the Sabbath, the Jews began to persecute Jesus. 17 But he had an answer for them:

> "My Father is at work even till now,
> and so I am at work too."

18 For this reason the Jews sought all the more to kill him—not only was he breaking the Sabbath; worse still, he was speaking of God as his own Father, thus making himself God's equal. 19 This was Jesus' answer:

> "I solemnly assure you,
> the Son cannot do a thing by himself—
> only what he sees the Father doing.
> For whatever He does,
> the Son does likewise.
> 20 For the Father loves the Son,
> and everything that He does, He shows him.
> Yes, much to your surprise,
> He will show him even greater works than these.
> 21 Indeed, just as the Father raises the dead and grants life,
> so also the Son grants life to those whom he wishes.
> 22 In fact, it is not the Father who judges anyone;
> no, He has turned all judgment over to the Son,
> 23 so that all men may honor the Son
> just as they honor the Father.
> He who refuses to honor the Son,
> refuses to honor the Father who sent him.
> 24 I solemnly asssure you,
> the man who hears my word
> and has faith in Him who sent me
> possesses eternal life.
> He does not come under condemnation;
> no, he has passed from death to life.

25 I solemnly assure you,
   an hour is coming and is now here
   when the dead shall hear the voice of God's Son,
   and those who have listened shall live.

26 Indeed, just as the Father possesses life in Himself,
   so has He granted that the Son also possess life in himself.
27 And He has turned over to him power to pass judgment
   because he is Son of Man—
28 no need for you to be surprised at this—
   for an hour is coming
   in which all those in the tombs will hear his voice
29 and will come forth.
   Those who have done what is right will rise to live;
   those who have practiced what is wicked will rise to be damned.
30 I cannot do anything by myself.
   I judge as I hear;
   and my judgment is honest
   because I am not seeking my own will
   but the will of Him who sent me.

31 If I am my own witness,
   my testimony cannot be verified.
32 But there is Another who is testifying on my behalf,
   and the testimony that He gives for me
   I know can be verified.

33 You have sent to John,
   and he has testified to the truth.
(34 Not that I myself accept such human testimony—
   I simply mention these things for your salvation.)
35 He was the lamp, set aflame and burning bright,
   and for a while you yourselves willingly exulted in his light.

36 Yet I have testimony even greater than John's,
   namely, the works the Father has given me to complete.
   These very works that I am doing
   testify on my behalf
   that the Father has sent me.

37 And the Father who sent me
   has Himself given testimony on my behalf.
   His voice you have never heard;
   nor have you seen what He looks like;
38 and His word you do not have abiding in your hearts,
   because you do not believe
   the one He sent.

39 You search the Scriptures
in which you think you have eternal life—
they also testify on my behalf.
40 Yet you are not willing to come to me
to have that life.

41 Not that I accept human praise—
42 it is simply that I know you people
and in your hearts you do not possess the love of God.
43 I have come in my Father's name;
yet you do not accept me.
But let someone else come in his own name,
and you will accept him.
44 How can people like you believe,
when you accept praise from one another,
but do not seek that glory which is from the One [God]?
45 Do not think that I shall be your accuser before the Father;
the one to accuse you is Moses
on whom you have set your hopes.
46 For if you believed Moses,
you would believe me,
since it is about me that he wrote.
47 But if you do not believe what he wrote,
how can you believe what I say?"

VI 1 Later on Jesus crossed the Sea of Galilee [to the shore] of Tiberias,
2 but a large crowd kept following him because they saw the signs he
was performing on the sick. 3 So Jesus went up the mountain and sat
down there with his disciples. 4 The Jewish feast of Passover was near.

5 When Jesus looked up, he caught sight of a large crowd coming
toward him; so he said to Philip, "Where shall we ever buy bread for
these people to eat?" (6 Actually, of course, he was perfectly aware of
what he was going to do, but he asked this to test Philip's reaction.)
7 He replied, "Not even with two hundred days' wages could we buy
enough loaves to give each of them a mouthful."

8 One of Jesus' disciples, Andrew, Simon Peter's brother, remarked to
him, 9 "There is a lad here who has five barley loaves and a couple of
dried fish, but what good is that for so many?" 10 Jesus said, "Get the
people to sit down." Now the men numbered about five thousand, but
there was plenty of grass there for them to find a seat. 11 Jesus then took
the loaves of bread, gave thanks, and passed them around to those sitting there; and he did the same with the dried fish—just as much as
they wanted. 12 When they had enough, he told his disciples, "Gather
up the fragments that are left over so that nothing will perish." 13 And

so they gathered twelve baskets full of fragments left over by those who had been fed with the five barley loaves.

14 Now when the people saw the sign[s] he had performed, they began to say, "This is undoubtedly the Prophet who is to come into the world." 15 With that Jesus realized that they would come and carry him off to make him king, so he fled back to the mountain alone.

16 As evening drew on, his disciples came down to the sea. 17 Having embarked, they were trying to cross the sea to Capernaum. By this time it was dark, and still Jesus had not joined them; 18 moreover, with a strong wind blowing, the sea was becoming rough. 19 When they had rowed about three or four miles, they sighted Jesus walking upon the sea, approaching the boat. They were frightened, 20 but he told them, "It is I; do not be afraid." 21 So they wanted to take him into the boat, and suddenly the boat reached the shore toward which they had been going.

22 The next day the crowd which had remained on the other side of the sea observed that there had only been one boat there and that Jesus had not gone along with his disciples in that boat, for his disciples had departed alone. 23 Then some boats came out from Tiberias near the place where they had eaten the bread [after the Lord had given thanks]. 24 So, once the crowd saw that neither Jesus nor his disciples were there, they too embarked and went to Capernaum looking for Jesus.

25 And when they found him on the other side of the sea, they said to him, "Rabbi, when did you come here?" 26 Jesus answered,

"Truly, I assure you,
   you are not looking for me because you have seen signs,
   but because you have eaten your fill of the loaves.
27 You should not be working for perishable food
   but for food that lasts for eternal life,
   food which the Son of Man will give you;
   for it is on him that God the Father has set His seal."

28 At this they said to him, "What must we do, then, to 'work' the works of God?"
29 Jesus replied,

"This is the work of God:
   have faith in him whom He sent."

30 "So that we can put faith in you," they asked him, "what sign are you going to perform for us to see? What is the 'work' you do? 31 Our an-

cestors had manna to eat in the desert; according to Scripture, 'He gave them bread from heaven to eat.' " 32 Jesus said to them:

> "Truly, I assure you,
> it is not Moses who gave you the bread from heaven,
> but it is my Father who gives you the real bread from heaven.
> 33 For God's bread comes down from heaven
> and gives life to the world."

34 "Sir," they begged, "give us this bread all the time."

35 Jesus explained to them:

> "I myself am the bread of life.
> No one who comes to me shall ever be hungry,
> and no one who believes in me shall ever again be thirsty.
> 36 But, as I have told you,
> though you have seen [me], still you do not believe.
> 37 Whatever the Father gives me will come to me;
> and anyone who comes to me I will never drive out,
> 38 because it is not to do my own will
> that I have come down from heaven,
> but to do the will of Him who sent me.
> 39 And it is the will of Him who sent me
> that I should lose nothing of what He has given me;
> rather, I should raise it up on the last day.
> 40 Indeed, this is the will of my Father,
> that everyone who looks upon the Son
> and believes in him
> should have eternal life.
> And I shall raise him up on the last day."

41 At this the Jews started to murmur in protest because he claimed: "I am the bread that came down from heaven." 42 And they kept saying, "Isn't this Jesus, the son of Joseph? Don't we know his father and mother? How can he claim to have come down from heaven?" 43 "Stop your murmuring," Jesus told them.

> 44 "No one can come to me
> unless the Father who sent me draws him.
> And I shall raise him up on the last day.
> 45 It is written in the prophets:
> 'And they shall all be taught by God.'
> Everyone who has heard the Father
> and learned from Him
> comes to me.
> 46 Not that anyone has seen the Father—

only the one who is from God
has seen the Father.

47 Let me firmly assure you,
the believer possesses eternal life.

48 I am the bread of life.

49 Your ancestors ate manna in the desert, but they died.

50 This is the bread that comes down from heaven,
that a man may eat it and never die."

51 "I myself am the living bread
that came down from heaven.
If anyone eats this bread,
he will live forever.
And the bread that I shall give
is my own flesh for the life of the world."

52 At this the Jews started to quarrel among themselves, saying, "How can he give us [his] flesh to eat?" 53 Therefore Jesus told them,

"Let me firmly assure you,
if you do not eat the flesh of the Son of Man
and drink his blood,
you have no life in you.

54 He who feeds on my flesh
and drinks my blood
has eternal life.
And I shall raise him up on the last day.

55 For my flesh is real food,
and my blood, real drink.

56 The man who feeds on my flesh
and drinks my blood
remains in me and I in him.

57 Just as the Father who has life sent me
and I have life because of the Father,
so the man who feeds on me
will have life because of me.

58 This is the bread that came down from heaven.
Unlike those ancestors who ate and yet died,
the man who feeds on this bread will live forever."

59 He said this in a synagogue instruction at Capernaum.

60 Now, after hearing this, many of his disciples remarked, "This sort of talk is hard to take. How can anyone pay attention to it?" 61 Jesus was quite conscious that his disciples were murmuring in protest at this. "Does it shake your faith?" he said to them.

62 "If, then, you behold the Son of Man
   ascending to where he was before . . . ?
63 It is the Spirit that gives life;
   the flesh is useless.
   The words that I have spoken to you
   are both Spirit and life.
64 But among you there are some who do not believe."

(In fact, Jesus knew from the start those who refused to believe, as well as the one who would hand him over.) 65 So he went on to say:

"This is why I have told you
that no one can come to me
unless it is granted to him by the Father."

66 At this many of his disciples broke away and would not accompany him any more. 67 And so Jesus said to the Twelve, "Do you also want to go away?" 68 Simon Peter answered, "Lord, to whom shall we go? It is you who have the words of eternal life; 69 and we have come to believe and are convinced that you are God's Holy One." 70 Jesus replied to them, "Did I not choose the Twelve of you myself? And yet one of you is a devil." (71 He was talking about Judas, son of Simon the Iscariot; for, though one of the Twelve, he was going to hand Jesus over.)

VII 1 [Now,] after this, Jesus moved about within Galilee because, with the Jews looking for a chance to kill him, he decided not to travel in Judea. 2 However, since the Jewish feast of Tabernacles was near, 3 his brothers advised him, "Leave here and go to Judea so that your disciples too may get a look at the works you are performing. 4 For no one keeps his actions hidden and still expects to be in the public eye. If you are going to perform such things, display yourself to the world." (5 In reality, not even his brothers believed in him.) 6 So Jesus answered them:

"It is not yet time for me,
but the time is always suitable for you.
7 The world cannot possibly hate you,
but it does hate me
because of the evidence I bring against it
that what it does is evil.

8 Go up to the festival yourselves. I am not going up to this festival because the time is not yet ripe for me." 9 After this conversation he stayed on in Galilee. 10 However, once his brothers had gone up to the festival, then he too went up, but [as it were] in secret, not for all to see.

11 Of course, the Jews were looking for him during the festival, asking, "Where is that man?" 12 And among the crowds there was much guarded

debate about him. Some maintained, "He is good," while others insisted, "Not at all—he is only deceiving the crowd." 13 However, no one would talk openly about him for fear of the Jews.

14 The feast was already half over when Jesus went up into the temple precincts and began to teach. 15 The Jews were surprised at this, saying, "How did this fellow get his education when he had no teacher?" 16 So Jesus answered them:

> "My doctrine is not my own
> but comes from Him who sent me.
> 17 If anyone chooses to do His will,
> he will know about this doctrine—
> whether it comes from God,
> or whether I am speaking on my own.
> 18 Whoever speaks on his own
> seeks his own glory.
> But whoever seeks the glory of the one who sent him—
> he is truthful
> and there is no dishonesty in his heart.
> 19 Has not Moses given you the Law?
> Yet not one of you keeps the Law.
> Why are you looking for a chance to kill me?"

20 "You're demented," the crowd retorted. "Who wants to kill you?" 21 Jesus gave them this answer:

> "I have performed just one work,
> and all of you are shocked 22 on that account.
> Moses has given you circumcision
> (really, it did not originate with Moses but with the Patriarchs);
> and so even on a Sabbath you circumcise a man.
> 23 If a man can receive circumcision on a Sabbath
> to prevent violation of the Mosaic Law,
> are you angry at me
> because I cured the whole man on a Sabbath?
> 24 Do not judge by appearances,
> but give an honest judgment."

25 This led some of the people of Jerusalem to remark, "Isn't this the man they want to kill? 26 But here he is, speaking in public, and they don't say a word to him! Have even the authorities recognized that this is truly the Messiah? 27 Yet we know where this man is from. When the Messiah comes, no one is to know where he is from." 28 At that, Jesus, who was teaching in the temple area, cried out,

"So you know me
and you know where I am from?
Yet I have not come on my own.
No, there is truly One who sent me,
and Him you do *not* know.
29 I know Him
because it is from Him that I come
and He sent me."

30 Then they tried to arrest him, but no one laid a finger on him because his hour had not yet come. 31 In fact, many in the crowd came to believe in him. They kept saying, "When the Messiah comes, can he be expected to perform more signs than this man has performed? 32 The Pharisees overheard this debate about him among the crowd, so they [namely, the chief priests and the Pharisees,] sent temple police to arrest him. 33 Accordingly, Jesus said,

"I am to be with you only a little while longer;
then I am going away to Him who sent me.
34 You will look for me and not find me,
and where I am, you cannot come."

35 That caused the Jews to exclaim to one another, "Where does this fellow intend to go that we won't find him? Surely he isn't going off to the Diaspora among the Greeks to teach the Greeks? 36 What is this he is talking about: 'You will look for me and not find me,' and 'Where I am, you cannot come'?"

37 On the last and greatest day of the festival Jesus stood up and cried out,

"If anyone thirst, let him come [to me];
and let him drink 38 who believes in me.
As the Scripture says,
'From within him shall flow rivers of living water.' "

(39 Here he was referring to the Spirit which those who came to believe in him were to receive. For there was as yet no Spirit, since Jesus had not been glorified.)
40 Some of the crowd who heard [these words] began to say, "This is undoubtedly the Prophet." 41 Others were claiming, "This is the Messiah." But an objection was raised: "Surely the Messiah isn't to come from Galilee? 42 Doesn't Scripture say that the Messiah, being of David's family, is to come from Bethlehem, the village where David lived?" 43 Thus, the crowd was sharply divided because of him. 44 Some of them even wanted to arrest him; yet no one laid hands on him.
45 And so, when the temple police came back, the chief priests and

Pharisees asked them, "Why didn't you bring him in?" 46 "Never has a man spoken like this," replied the police. 47 "Don't tell us you have been fooled too!" the Pharisees retorted. 48 "You don't see any of the Sanhedrin believing in him, do you? Or any of the Pharisees? 49 No, it's just this mob which knows nothing of the Law—and they are damned!" 50 One of their own number, Nicodemus (the man who had come to him), spoke up, 51 "Since when does our Law condemn any man without first hearing him and knowing the facts?" 52 "Don't tell us that you are a Galilean too," they taunted him. "Look it up and you won't find the Prophet arising in Galilee."

[53 Then each went off to his own house, **VIII** 1while Jesus went out to the Mount of Olives. 2 But at daybreak he again made his appearance in the temple precincts; and when all the people started coming to him, he sat down and began to teach them. 3 Then the scribes and the Pharisees led forward a woman who had been caught in adultery, and made her stand there in front of everybody. 4 "Teacher," they said to him, "this woman has been caught in the very act of adultery. 5 Now, in the Law Moses ordered such women to be stoned. But you—what do you have to say about it?" (6 They were posing this question to trap him so that they could have something to accuse him of.) But Jesus simply bent down and started drawing on the ground with his finger. 7 When they persisted in their questioning, he straightened up and said to them, "The man among you who has no sin—let him be the first to cast a stone at her." 8 And he bent down again and started to write on the ground. 9 But the audience went away one by one, starting with the elders; and he was left alone with the woman still there before him. 10 So Jesus, straightening up, said to her, "Woman, where are they all? Hasn't anyone condemned you?" 11 "No one, sir," she answered. Jesus said, "Nor do I condemn you. You may go. But from now on, avoid this sin."]

VIII   12 Then Jesus spoke to them again,

> "I am the light of the world.
> No follower of mine shall ever walk in darkness;
> no, he will possess the light of life."

13 This caused the Pharisees to object, "You are your own witness, and your testimony cannot be verified." 14 Jesus answered,

> "Even if I am my own witness,
> my testimony *can* be verified
> because I know where I came from and where I am going.
> But you know neither where I come from nor where I am going.
> 15 You pass judgment according to human standards,
> but I pass judgment on no one.

16 Yet even if I do judge,
    that judgment of mine is valid
    because I am not alone—
    I have at my side the One who sent me [the Father].
17 Why, in your own Law it is stated
    that testimony given by two persons is verified.
18 I am one who gives testimony on my behalf,
    and the Father who sent me gives testimony for me."

19 Then they asked him, "Where is this 'father' of yours?" Jesus replied,

"You do not recognize me or my Father.
If you recognized me, you would recognize my Father too."

20 He spoke these words while teaching at the temple treasury. Still, no one arrested him because his hour had not yet come.

21 Then he said to them again,

"I am going away and you will look for me,
    but you will die in your sin.
Where I am going, you cannot come."

22 At this the Jews began to say, "Surely he is not going to kill himself, is he?—because he claims, 'Where I am going, you cannot come.'" 23 But he went on to say,

"You belong to what is below;
    I belong to what is above.
You belong to this world—
    this world to which I do not belong.
24 That is why I told you that you would die in your sins.
    Unless you come to believe that I AM,
    you will surely die in your sins."

25 "Well then, who are you?" they asked him. Jesus answered,

"What I have been telling you from the beginning.
26 Many are the things that I could say about you and condemn;
    but the only things I say to this world
    are what I have heard from Him,
    the One who sent me, who is truthful."

27 They did not understand that he was talking to them about the Father.
28 So Jesus continued,

"When you lift up the Son of Man,
    then you will realize that I AM,
    and that I do nothing by myself.

No, I say only those things
that the Father taught me.
29 And the One who sent me is with me.
He has not left me alone
since I always do what pleases Him."

30 While he was speaking in this way, many came to believe in him.

31 Then Jesus went on to say to those Jews who had believed him,

"If you abide in my word,
you are truly my disciples;
32 and you will know the truth,
and truth will set you free."

33 "We are descendant from Abraham," they retorted, "and never have we
been slaves to anyone. What do you mean by saying, 'You will be free'?"
34 Jesus answered them,

"Truly, I assure you,
everyone who acts sinfully
is a slave [of sin].
(35 While no slave has a permanent place in the family,
the son has a place there forever.)
36 Consequently, if the Son sets you free,
you will really be free.
37 I know that you are descendant from Abraham.
Yet you look for a chance to kill me
because my word makes no headway among you.
38 I tell what I have seen in the Father's presence;
therefore, you should do what you heard from the Father."

39 "Our father is Abraham," they answered him. Jesus replied,

"If you are really Abraham's children,
you would be doing works worthy of Abraham.
40 But actually you are looking to kill me,
just because I am a man who told you the truth
which I heard from God.
Abraham did not do that.
41 You are indeed doing your father's works!"

They protested, "We were not born illegitimate. We have but one father,
God Himself." 42 Jesus told them,

"If God were your father,
you would love me,
for from God I came forth and am here.

> Not on my own have I come,
> but He sent me.
>
> 43 Why do you not understand what I say?—
> because you are incapable of hearing my word.
> 44 The devil is the father you belong to,
> and you willingly carry out your father's wishes.
> He was a murderer from the beginning
> and never based himself on truth,
> for there is no truth in him.
> When he tells a lie,
> he speaks his native language,
> for he is a liar and the father of lying.
> 45 But since I, for my part, tell the truth,
> you do not believe me.
> 46 Can any one of you convict me of sin?
> If I am telling the truth,
> why do you not believe me?
> 47 The man who belongs to God
> hears the words of God.
> The reason why you do not hear
> is that you do not belong to God."

48 The Jews answered, "Aren't we right, after all, in saying that you are a Samaritan and demented?" 49 Jesus replied,

> "I am not demented,
> but I do honor my Father,
> while you fail to honor me.
> 50 I do not seek glory for myself;
> there is One who does seek it and He passes judgment.
> 51 I solemnly assure you,
> if a man keeps my word,
> he shall never see death."

52 "Now we are sure you are demented," the Jews retorted. "Abraham died; so did the prophets. Yet, you claim, 'A man shall never experience death if he keeps my word.' 53 Surely, you don't pretend to be greater than our father Abraham who is dead?—or the prophets who are dead? Just who do you pretend to be?" 54 Jesus answered,

> "If I glorify myself,
> my glory amounts to nothing.
> The One who glorifies me is the Father
> whom you claim as 'our God,'
> 55 even though you do not know Him.
> But I do know Him:
> and if I say I do not know Him,

> I will be just like you—a liar!
> Yes, I do know Him
> and I keep His word.
> 56 Your father Abraham rejoiced
> at the prospect of seeing my day.
> When he saw it, he was glad."

57 This caused the Jews to object, "You're not even fifty years old. How can you have seen Abraham?" 58 Jesus answered,

> "I solemnly assure you,
> before Abraham even came into existence, I AM."

59 Then they picked up rocks to throw at Jesus, but he hid himself and slipped out of the temple precincts.

IX 1 Now, as he walked along, he saw a man who had been blind from birth. 2 His disciples asked him, "Rabbi, who committed the sin that caused him to be born blind, he or his parents?" 3 "Neither," answered Jesus.

> "It was no sin on this man's part,
> nor on his parents' part.
> Rather, it was to let God's work be revealed in him.
> 4 We must work the works of Him who sent me
> while it is day.
> Night is coming
> when no one can work.
> 5 As long as I am in the world,
> I am the light of the world."

6 With that he spat on the ground, made mud with his saliva, and smeared the man's eyes with the mud. 7 Then Jesus told him, "Go, wash in the pool of Siloam." (This name means "one who has been sent.") And so he went off and washed, and he came back able to see.

8 Now his neighbors and the people who had been accustomed to see him begging began to ask, "Isn't this the fellow who used to sit and beg?" 9 Some were claiming that it was he; others maintained that it was not, but just someone who looked like him. He himself said, "I'm the one, all right." 10 So they said to him, "How were your eyes opened?" 11 He answered, "That man they call Jesus made mud and smeared it on my eyes, telling me to go to Siloam and wash. When I did go and wash, I got my sight." 12 "Where is he?" they asked. "I have no idea," he replied.

13 They took the man who had been born blind to the Pharisees. (14 Note that it was on a Sabbath day that Jesus had made the mud and opened his eyes.) 15 In their turn, the Pharisees too began to inquire how he had got

his sight. He told them, "He put mud on my eyes and I washed and now I can see." 16 This prompted some of the Pharisees to assert, "This man is not from God because he does not keep the Sabbath." Others objected "How can a man perform such signs and still be a sinner?" And they were sharply divided. 17 Then they addressed the blind man again, "Since it was your eyes he opened, what have you to say about him?" "He is a prophet," he replied.

18 But the Jews refused to believe that he really had been born blind and had subsequently gained his sight until they summoned the parents of the man [who had gained his sight]. 19 "Is this your son?" they asked. "Do you confirm that he was born blind? If so, how can he see now?" 20 The parents gave this answer: "We know that this is our son and that he was born blind. 21 But we do not know how he can see now, nor do we know who opened his eyes. [Ask him.] He is old enough to speak for himself." (22 His parents answered this way because they were afraid of the Jews, for the Jews had already agreed that anybody who acknowledged Jesus as Messiah would be put out of the Synagogue. 23 That was why his parents said, "He is old enough. Ask him.")

24 And so, for the second time, they summoned the man who had been born blind and said to him, "Give glory to God. We know that this man is a sinner." 25 "Whether he's a sinner or not, I do not know," he replied. "One thing I do know: I was blind before, now I can see." 26 They persisted, "Just what did he do to you? How did he open your eyes?" 27 "I told you once and you didn't pay attention," he answered them. "Why do you want to hear it all over again? Don't tell me that you too want to become his disciples?" 28 Scornfully they retorted, "You are the one who is that fellow's disciple; we are disciples of Moses. 29 We know that God has spoken to Moses, but we don't even know where this fellow comes from." 30 The man objected, "Now that's strange! Here you don't even know where he comes from; yet he opened my eyes. 31 We know that God pays no attention to sinners, but He does listen to someone who is devout and obeys His will. 32 It is absolutely unheard of that anyone ever opened the eyes of a man born blind. 33 If this man were not from God, he could have done nothing." 34 "What!" they exclaimed. "You were born steeped in sin, and now you are lecturing us?" Then they threw him out.

35 When Jesus heard about his expulsion, he found him and said, "Do you believe in the Son of Man?" 36 He answered, "Who is he, sir, that I may believe in him?" 37 "You have seen him," Jesus replied, "for it is he who is speaking with you." [38 "I do believe, Lord," he said and bowed down to worship him. 39 Then Jesus said,]

> "I came into this world for judgment:
>   that those who do not see may be able to see,
>   and those who do see may become blind."

40 Some of the Pharisees who were there with him overheard this and said to him, "Surely we are not to be considered blind too?" 41 Jesus told them,

> "If only you *were* blind,
> then you would not be guilty of sin.
> But now that you claim to see,
> your sin remains."

X   1 "Truly I assure you,
> anyone who does not enter the sheepfold through the gate,
> but climbs in some other way,
> is a thief and a bandit.
> 2 The one who enters through the gate
> is shepherd of the sheep;
> 3 for him the keeper opens the gate.
>
> And the sheep hear his voice
> as he calls by name those that belong to him
> and leads them out.
> 4 When he has brought out [all] his own,
> he walks in front of them;
> and the sheep follow him
> because they recognize his voice.
> 5 But they will not follow a stranger;
> they will run away from him
> because they do not recognize the voice of strangers."

6 Although Jesus drew this picture for them, they did not understand what he was trying to tell them. 7 So Jesus said [to them again],

> "Truly I assure you,
> I am the sheepgate.
> 8 All who came [before me]
> are thieves and bandits,
> but the sheep did not heed them.
>
> 9 I am the gate.
> Whoever enters through me
> will be saved;
> and he will go in and out
> and find pasture.
> 10 A thief comes
> only to steal, slaughter, and destroy.
> I came

that they may have life
and have it to the full.

11 I am the model shepherd:
the model shepherd lays down his life for the sheep.
12 The hired hand, who is not the shepherd
and does not own the sheep,
catches sight of the wolf coming,
and runs away, leaving the sheep
to be snatched and scattered by the wolf.
13 And this is because he works for pay
and has no concern for the sheep.

14 I am the model shepherd:
I know my sheep
and mine know me,
15 just as the Father knows me
and I know the Father.
And for these sheep I lay down my life.
16 I have other sheep, too,
that do not belong to this fold.
These also must I lead,
and they will listen to my voice.
Then there will be one sheep herd, one shepherd.
17 This is why the Father loves me:
because I lay down my life
in order to take it up again.
18 No one has taken it away from me;
rather, I lay it down of my own accord.
I have power to lay it down,
and I have power to take it up again.
This command I received from my Father."

19 Because of these words the Jews were again sharply divided. 20 Many
of them were claiming, "He is possessed by a devil—out of his mind! Why
pay any attention to him?" 21 Others maintained, "These are not the words
of a demented person. Surely a devil cannot open the eyes of the blind!"

22 It was winter, and the time came for the feast of Dedication at Jerusalem. 23 Jesus was walking in the temple precincts, in Solomon's Portico,
24 when the Jews gathered around him and demanded, "How long are you
going to keep us in suspense? If you are really the Messiah, tell us so in
plain words." 25 Jesus answered,

"I did tell you, but you do not believe.
The works that I am doing in my Father's name
give testimony for me,

26 but you refuse to believe
    because you are not my sheep.
27 My sheep hear my voice;
    and I know them,
    and they follow me.
28 I give them eternal life,
    and they shall never perish.
    No one will snatch them from my hand.
29 My Father, as to what He has given me, is greater than all,
    and from the Father's hand no one can snatch away.
30 The Father and I are one."

31 When the Jews [again] got rocks to stone him, 32 Jesus protested to them, "Many a noble work have I shown you from the Father. For just which of these works are you going to stone me?" 33 "It is not for any 'noble work' that we are stoning you," the Jews retorted, "but for blaspheming, because you who are only a man make yourself God." 34 Jesus answered,

    "Is it not written in your Law,
     'I have said, "You are gods" '?
35 If it calls those men gods
    to whom God's word was addressed—
    and the Scripture cannot lose its force—
36 do you claim that I blasphemed
    when, as the one whom the Father consecrated and sent into the
    I said, 'I am God's Son'? |world,
37 If I do not perform my Father's works,
    put no faith in me.
38 But if I do perform them,
    even though you still put no faith in me,
    put your faith in these works
    so that you may come to know [and understand]
    that the Father is in me
    and I am in the Father."

39 Then they tried [again] to arrest him, but he slipped out of their clutches.

40 Then he went back across the Jordan to the place where John had been baptizing earlier; and while he stayed there, 41 many people came to him. "John may never have performed a sign," they commented, "but whatever John said about this man is true." 42 And there many came to believe in him.

XI 1 Now there was a man named Lazarus who was sick; he was from Bethany, the village of Mary and her sister Martha. (2 This Mary whose brother Lazarus was sick was the one who anointed the Lord with perfume and dried his feet with her hair.) 3 So the sisters sent to inform Jesus, "Lord, the one whom you love is sick." 4 But when Jesus heard it, he said,

> "This sickness is not to end in death;
> rather it is for God's glory,
> that the Son [of God] may be glorified through it."

(5 Yet Jesus really loved Martha and her sister and Lazarus.) 6 And so, even when he heard that Lazarus was sick, he stayed on where he was two days longer.

7 Then, at last, Jesus said to the disciples, "Let us go back to Judea." 8 "Rabbi," protested the disciples, "the Jews were just now trying to stone you, and you are going back up there again?" 9 Jesus answered,

> "Are there not twelve hours of daylight?
> If a man goes walking by day, he does not stumble
> because he can see the light of this world.
> 10 But if he goes walking at night, he will stumble
> because he has no light in him."

11 He made this remark, and then, later, he told them, "Our beloved Lazarus has fallen asleep, but I am going there to wake him up." 12 At this the disciples objected, "If he has fallen asleep, Lord, his life will be saved." (13 Jesus had really been talking about Lazarus' death, but they thought he was talking about sleep in the sense of slumber.) 14 So finally Jesus told them plainly, "Lazarus is dead. 15 And I am happy for your sake that I was not there so that you may come to have faith. In any event, let us go to him." 16 Then Thomas (this name means "Twin") said to his fellow disciples, "Let us go too that we may die with him."

17 When Jesus arrived, he found that Lararus had [already] been four days in the tomb. 18 Now Bethany was not far from Jerusalem, just under two miles; 19 and many of the Jews had come out to offer sympathy to Martha and Mary because of their brother. 20 When Martha heard that Jesus was coming, she went to meet him, while Mary sat quietly at home. 21 Martha said to Jesus, "Lord, if you had been here, my brother would never have died. 22 Even now, I am sure that whatever you ask of God, God will give you." 23 "Your brother will rise again," Jesus assured her. 24 "I know he will rise again," Martha replied, "in the resurrection on the last day." 25 Jesus told her,

> "I am the resurrection [and the life]:
> he who believes in me,
> even if he dies, will come to life.
> 26 And everyone who is alive and believes in me
> shall never die at all.—

Do you believe this?" 27 "Yes, Lord," she replied. "I have come to believe that you are the Messiah, the Son of God, he who is to come into the world."

28 Now when she had said this, she went off and called her sister Mary. "The Teacher is here and calls for you," she whispered. 29 As soon as Mary heard this, she got up quickly and started out toward him. (30 Actually Jesus had not yet come into the village but was [still] at the spot where Martha had met him.) 31 The Jews who were in the house with Mary, consoling her, saw her get up quickly and go out; and so they followed her, thinking that she was going to the tomb to weep there. 32 When Mary came to the place where Jesus was and saw him, she fell at his feet and said to him, "Lord, if you had been here, my brother would never have died." 33 Now when Jesus saw her weeping, and the Jews who had accompanied her also weeping, he shuddered, moved with the deepest emotions.

34 "Where have you laid him?" he asked. "Lord, come and see," they told him. 35 Jesus began to cry, 36 and this caused the Jews to remark, "See how much he loved him!" 37 But some of them said, "He opened the eyes of that blind man. Couldn't he also have done something to stop this man from dying?" 38 With this again arousing his emotions, Jesus came to the tomb.

It was a cave with a stone laid across it. 39 "Take away the stone," Jesus ordered. Martha, the dead man's sister, said to him, "Lord, it is four days; by now there must be a stench." 40 Jesus replied, "Didn't I assure you that if you believed, you would see the glory of God?" 41 So they took away the stone. Then Jesus looked upward and said,

"Father, I thank you because you heard me.
42 Of course, I knew that you always hear me,
    but I say it because of the crowd standing around,
    that they may believe that you sent me."

43 Having said this, he shouted in a loud voice, "Lazarus, come out!" 44 The dead man came out, bound hand and foot with linen strips and his face wrapped in a cloth. "Untie him," Jesus told them, "and let him go."

45 This caused many of the Jews who had come to visit Mary and had seen what Jesus did, to put their faith in him. 46 But some of them went to the Pharisees and reported what he had done. 47 So the chief priests and the Pharisees gathered together the Sanhedrin. "What are we going to do," they said, "now that this man is performing many signs? 48 If we let him go on like this, everybody will believe in him; and the Romans will come and take away our holy place and our nation."

49 Then one of their number who was high priest that year, a certain Caiaphas, addressed them: "You have no sense at all! 50 Don't you realize that it is more to your advantage to have one man die [for the people] than

to have the whole nation destroyed?" (51 It was not on his own that he said this; but, as high priest that year, he could prophesy that Jesus was to die for the nation—52 and not for the nation alone, but to gather together even the dispersed children of God and make them one.) 53 So from that day on they planned to kill him.

54 For this reason Jesus no longer moved about openly among the Jews, but withdrew to a town called Ephraim in the region near the desert, where he stayed with his disciples.

55 Now the Jewish Passover was near; so many people from the country went up to Jerusalem to purify themselves for Passover. 56 They were on the lookout for Jesus; and people around the Temple were saying to one another, "What do you think? Is there really a chance that he'll come for the feast?" 57 The chief priests and the Pharisees had given orders that anyone who knew where Jesus was should report it so that they could arrest him.

XII 1 Six days before Passover Jesus came to Bethany, the village of Lazarus whom Jesus had raised from the dead. 2 There they gave him a dinner at which Martha served and Lazarus was one of those at table with him. 3 Mary brought in a pound of expensive perfume made from real nard and anointed Jesus' feet. Then she dried his feet with her hair, while the fragrance of the perfume filled the house. 4 Judas Iscariot, one of his disciples (the one who was going to hand him over), protested, 5 "Why wasn't this perfume sold? It was worth three hundred silver pieces, and the money might have been given to the poor." (6 It was not because he was concerned for the poor that he said this, but because he was a thief. He held the money box and could help himself to what was put in.) 7 To this Jesus replied, "Leave her alone. The purpose was that she might keep it for the day of my embalming. [8 The poor you will always have with you, but you will not always have me.]"

9 Now the large crowd of the Jews found out that he was there and came out, not only because of Jesus, but also to see Lazarus whom he had raised from the dead. 10 The chief priests, however, planned to kill Lazarus too, 11 because on his account many of the Jews were going over to Jesus and believing in him.

12 The next day the large crowd that had come for the feast, having heard that Jesus was to enter Jerusalem, 13 got palm fronds and came out to meet him. They kept on shouting:

> "Hosanna!
> Blessed is he who comes in the Lord's name!
> Blessed is the King of Israel!"

14 But Jesus found a young donkey and sat on it. As the Scripture has it:

> 15 "Do not be afraid, O daughter of Zion!
> See, your king comes to you
> seated on a donkey's colt."

(16 At first, the disciples did not understand this; but when Jesus had been glorified, then they recalled that it was precisely what had been written about him that they had done to him.)

17 And so the crowd which had been present when Jesus called Lazarus out of the tomb and raised him from the dead kept testifying to it. 18 This was [also] why the crowd came out to meet him: because they heard that he had performed this sign. 19 At that the Pharisees remarked to one another, "You see, you are getting nowhere. Look, the world has run off after him."

20 Now among those who had come up to worship at the feast there were some Greeks. 21 They approached Philip, who was from Bethsaida in Galilee, and made a request of him. "Sir," they said, "we would like to see Jesus." 22 Philip went and told Andrew; then both Philip and Andrew came and told Jesus. 23 Jesus answered them:

> "The hour has come
> for the Son of Man to be glorified.
> 24 I solemnly assure you,
> unless the grain of wheat falls to the earth and dies,
> it remains just a grain of wheat.
> But if it dies,
> it bears much fruit.
> 25 The man who loves his life
> destroys it;
> while the man who hates his life in this world,
> preserves it to live eternally.
> 26 If anyone would serve me,
> let him follow me;
> and where I am,
> my servant will also be.
> The Father will honor
> anyone who serves me.
> 27 Now my soul is troubled.
> Yet, what should I say—
> 'Father, save me from this hour'?
> No, this is just the reason why I came to this hour.
> 28 'Father, glorify your name!' "

Then a voice came from the sky:

> "I have glorified it
> and will glorify it again."

29 When the crowd that was there heard it, they said that it was thunder; but others maintained, "It was an angel speaking to him." 30 Jesus answered, "That voice did not come for my sake, but for yours.

31 Now is the judgment of this world.
Now will the Prince of this world be driven out.
32 And when I am lifted up from the earth,
I shall draw all men to myself."

(33 This statement of his indicated what sort of death he was going to die.) 34 To this the crowd objected, "We have heard from the Law that the Messiah is to remain forever. How can you claim that the Son of Man must be lifted up? Just who is this Son of Man?" 35 So Jesus told them:

"The light is among you only a little while longer.
Walk while you have the light,
or the darkness will come over you.
The man who walks in the dark
does not know where he is going.
36 While you have the light,
keep your faith in the light,
and so become sons of light."

After this speech Jesus left them and went into hiding.

37 Even though Jesus had performed so many of his signs before them, they refused to believe in him. 38 This was to fulfill the word of Isaiah the prophet:

"Lord, who has believed what we have heard?
To whom has the might of the Lord been revealed?"

39 The reason they could not believe was that, as Isaiah said elsewhere,

40 "He has blinded their eyes
and numbed their minds,
for fear they might see with their eyes
and perceive with their minds
and so be converted,
and I shall heal them."

41 Isaiah uttered these words because he had seen his glory, and it was of him that he spoke.

42 Nevertheless, there were many, even among the Sanhedrin, who believed in him. Yet, because of the Pharisees they refused to admit it, or they would have been put out of the synagogue. 43 They preferred by far the praise of men to the glory of God.

44 Jesus proclaimed aloud:

"Whoever believes in me
is actually believing, not in me,
but in Him who sent me.
45 And whoever sees me
is seeing Him who sent me.
46 As light have I come into the world
so that no one who believes in me
need remain in darkness.
47 And if anyone listens to my words without keeping them,
it is not I who condemn him;
for I did not come to condemn the world
but to save the world.
48 Whoever rejects me and does not accept my words
already has his judge,
namely, the word that I have spoken—
that is what will condemn him on the last day,
49 because it was not on my own that I spoke.
No, the Father who sent me
has Himself commanded me
what to say and how to speak,
50 and I know that His commandment means eternal life.
So when I speak,
I speak just as the Father told me."

INDEXES

BIBLIOGRAPHICAL INDEX OF AUTHORS

(This is primarily an index that lists the first occurrence of an author's book or article. In a few instances reference is made to a longer treatment of a particular author's ideas.)

INDEX OF SUBJECTS